Lazuli Finch
JOHN J. AUDUBON

MICROECONOMICS
THEORY AND APPLICATIONS

Fred R. Glahe
University of Colorado, Boulder

Dwight R. Lee
Virginia Polytechnic Institute
and State University, Blacksburg

Harcourt Brace Jovanovich, Inc.
New York • San Diego • Chicago • San Francisco • Atlanta
London • Sydney • Toronto

Illustrations by Carol Schwartzback

Cover photograph © by Charles Merkle 1980/Free Lance Photographers Guild, Inc.

Copyright © 1981 by Harcourt Brace Jovanovich, Inc.

Printed in the United States of America
Library of Congress Catalog Card Number: 80-84392
ISBN: 0-15-558623-8

To Charles, Jeff, and Jennifer

PREFACE

Our goal in writing this book has been to present in a clear, precise, and non-mathematical manner the essential core of microeconomics so that the student can acquire a solid understanding of the theory. To assist in the attainment of this goal, a large number of examples and applications that are relevant to the theory are discussed. These examples and applications are designed to shorten the lag that students encounter between the mastery of a theory and the illumination and satisfaction that result from applying it. Although they require no knowledge of statistical or econometric techniques, the examples and applications are often based on research that employs those methods.

The examples show how the theory that has just been examined is useful in understanding important and topical issues. The applications tend to be longer and to use, rather than simply illustrate, the theory developed in the chapter. Both the examples and the applications reinforce the theory that has been developed and further an appreciation for it. It is our belief that this presentation will appeal to students and will make their course in intermediate microeconomics an intellectually satisfying experience.

The book is also useful from the perspective of the professor. Although the chapters can be assigned out of sequence to parallel classroom lectures, there is a logical flow to the existing order that provides a useful continuity to the presentation. In many respects, this order should complement the organization of most microeconomics courses as they are conventionally taught.

There is one significant departure from the conventional sequence of topics. The chapter on welfare economics and general equilibrium is not the final chapter of the book. All too often, the last thing that the student learns from a microeconomics textbook is that some rather heroic assumptions must be satisfied if the market economy is to perform properly. The assumptions behind the perfectly competitive general equilibrium model and the efficiency conditions that flow from those assumptions are important and are carefully developed in Chapter 12. But the theoretical and practical significance of this model needs to be put into a reasonable perspective—a perspective we strive for in the two remaining chapters. In Chapter 13, market failure is treated in detail in conjunction with the development of the theory of public goods and externalities, and an in-depth application dealing with the problem of pollution is provided. Chapter 13 also examines the importance of property rights and contains examples of how market arrangements develop spontaneously through the extension of property rights and then internalize previous externalities. This chapter provides both a justification of the political process and the means to take a realistic look at how this process works—a topic that is developed in the concluding chapter. By applying many of the tools that have served so well in analyzing private markets and by drawing on the increasingly important literature of public choice, useful insights into the political process are developed in Chapter 14. At this point, it should be clear to the student that the public sector does not provide a perfect substitute for imperfect markets.

A *Student Workbook* and an *Instructor's Manual* are available for use in conjunction with the text. The main feature of the *Student Workbook* is an extensive program review of each chapter. The workbook also contains a self-quiz for each chapter and problems that focus on the graphical and mathematical analyses. The *Instructor's Manual* contains a summary of the highlights of each chapter, comments on the problems in the text, and additional questions and problems for quizzes and examinations.

Many people have played an important role in the preparation of this book. We would especially like to acknowledge the assistance of our colleagues at the University of Colorado, particularly Philip Graves, Charles W. Howe, Larry Singell, Bernard Udis, Frank Vorhies, and Wesley Yordon. In addition, we are indebted to the critical reviewers of our manuscript: George Babilot, San Diego State University; Paul Barkley, Washington State University; Ralph Bradburd, State Universtiy of New York at Albany; Charles R. Chittle, Bowling Green University; Robert Cooter, University of California—Berkeley; James Moore, Purdue University; James Ramsey, Michigan State University; Eugene Silberberg, University of Washington; and Norman J. Simler, University of Minnesota. Lastly, we are indebted to Colene Priebe for her speedy and accurate typing of the manuscript.

Fred R. Glahe
Dwight R. Lee

CONTENTS

Chapter Three

**Price Elasticity:
Measuring Response to Price   61**

Chapter Four

Consumer Behavior   93

Appendix:
The Optimal Consumption Pattern Over Time

Chapter Five   The Theory Behind the Demand Curve   139

Chapter Six   Production   177

Chapter Seven   **Production Cost Theory**   **207**

Appendix:
Linear Programming

Chapter Eight   **Perfect Competition**   **251**

CHAPTER ONE

INTRODUCTION TO MICROECONOMICS

Introduction   1–1

This textbook is about basic economic theory and how it is used to analyze economic problems. The theory is somewhat conceptual and abstract, but the economic problems we will consider are unfortunately quite real and concrete. The feeling is sometimes expressed that a practical–rather than a theoretical–approach must be employed to address and understand real problems. What this view overlooks is that we are unable to formulate a practical approach if we do not understand the problem being considered–and all of our understanding is ultimately rooted in some theoretical structure. This opening chapter is intended to convey the concept of why theory is so important to our understanding of the real world and to provide an introduction to the ways in which economists theorize. The importance of theory will become increasingly evident as we progress through this book. We will develop theories and then apply them to practical problems that concern all of us, providing insights and understanding that will never be available to those who reject economic theory as impractical. As good theorists, however, we must first spend a little time defining our topic and looking at the types of questions that our definitions will lead us to consider.

What Is Economics?   1–2

Economics existed as a social science for many years before attempts were made to define it precisely. Once economists did begin to attempt to define the scope and nature of economics, they were often at odds with each other. In fact, the controversy over what economics is all about once reached such proportions that the Canadian economist Jacob Viner was prompted to quip, "Economics is what economists do." Although this may be an entertaining anecdote, it is not very satisfying to you as an economics student.

1

The English economist Alfred Marshall defined economics as the "study of mankind in the ordinary business of life." This was perhaps the most popular and widely used definition 60 years ago, but it fails to shed much light on the precise scope and nature of economics. Acknowledging the limitations of his definition, Marshall also remarked: "Every short statement about economics is misleading (with the possible exception of my present one)."

Recent definitions of economics have centered around aspects of the human condition, such as unlimited human wants versus the scarcity of resources available to satisfy these wants. The economist chiefly responsible for this approach to the problem of defining economics, Lord Lionel Robbins, states in his path-breaking book *The Nature and Significance of Economic Science*:[1]

> Economics is the science which studies human behavior as a relationship between ends and scarce means which have alternative uses.

Most contemporary definitions of the scope and nature of economics are merely elaborations and extensions of Lord Robbins' basic thought. For example, consider today's most widely read definition of economics, written by Nobel Laureate Paul A. Samuelson:

> Economics is the study of how men and society end up *choosing*, with or without the use of money, to employ *scarce* productive resources that could have alternative uses, to produce various commodities and distribute them for consumption, now or in the future, among various people and groups in society. It analyzes the costs and benefits of improving patterns of resource allocation.[2]

Throughout this book, we will demonstrate that Samuelson's (and our) definition of **economics** is applicable to all forms of conscious human action, ranging from such common, everyday problems as deciding how to allocate our time to the very important questions concerning the protection and quality of the environment in which we live.

The Fundamental Economic Problem

As more specific definitions of economics evolved, it became increasingly clear that one fundamental problem lies at the heart of all economic problems—the problem of **scarcity.** We are simply unable to convert our limited resources into all the goods and services we wish to consume. No matter how productive we become, or how many new resources we discover, we will still want more than what is available.

Economics has often been called the "dismal science"—a description first

---

[1]Lionel Robbins, *The Nature and Significance of Economic Science,* 2nd ed. (London: Macmillan and Co., 1935), p. 16.
[2]Paul A. Samuelson, *Economics,* 9th ed. (New York: McGraw-Hill Book Co., 1973), p. 3.

applied by the Scottish historian Thomas Carlyle in the early nineteenth century. There is an element of truth in Carlyle's remark, but this is not because economics is dull and uninteresting. Far from it. Any subject that deals with such a range of interesting problems could hardly be called dull. Economics is dismal only in the sense that the conclusions economists ultimately reach are often gloomy. Economic theory can guide us in the more efficient use of our resources, create more productive employment opportunities, and produce more wealth, but the end result will always be the same. Because resources are scarce, we will always be denied many things we would dearly enjoy having. So in some respects, economics is like the messenger who brings bad news, and many people resist the conclusions of economic analysis for the same reason that the king killed the messenger. Unfortunately, neither tactic changes the message.

An immediate implication of scarcity is that choices must be made and that each choice will be a costly one. Every time we choose to have more of one good, we are choosing to consume less of some other desirable commodity, and the value of this *sacrificed consumption* is the **opportunity cost** of every choice that is made. The economists' message is that every decision involves a cost—a message captured in the statement, popular among economists, that "there is no such thing as a free lunch." When someone begins talking about the benefits that will be realized from the expansion of a program or project, the economist is trained to point out that the resulting benefits can only be acquired by diverting resources from the production of other desirable goods and services. This does not make economists universally popular, of course; people often do not care to be reminded that their pet projects have disadvantages as well as advantages.

But if we are to make intelligent economic decisions, it is essential to consider opportunity cost. A rather obvious objective of any economy is to put available resources to use in the most valuable ways possible. The problem of scarcity can then be translated into the problem of directing limited resources into activities where they will be most valuably used. To do this, we must determine the value of a resource in each of its many possible employments, so that we can calculate the opportunity cost of each resource decision. A desirable resource decision directs that a resource be used where it will provide the most value—that is, where its value will exceed its cost.

Microeconomics

The branch of economics concerned with how individuals deal with the problem of scarcity is **microeconomics.** The analysis in this textbook will focus on individual decision makers and how they attempt to achieve their goals in their roles as consumers and producers. Understanding how consumers and producers behave and how their behaviors interact will help us understand how the economic process determines what goods will be produced, who will produce them, how they will be produced, and where they will be distributed. These are the basic questions that are answered by microeconomic analysis.

Although microeconomic analysis is based on the behavior of individual decision makers, many important questions would go unanswered if we studied individual consumers and producers in isolation from one another. Almost all economic activities require interaction and coordination between many individuals. For example, the coordinated efforts of literally thousands of individuals provided you with the clothes you are wearing. Untold numbers of people in oil fields, agricultural fields, garment shops, trucking companies, and clothing stores coordinated their efforts to produce the fiber, cloth, workmanship, transportation, and merchandising to make it possible for you to acquire the shirt you have on. The successful implementation of your decision to buy a shirt, a pair of shoes, a television set, a car, or any of the other thousands of items you routinely enjoy depends on countless other people making decisions compatible with your plans. Similarly, the decisions that each supplier makes, if they are to be carried out successfully, must be coordinated with the plans of thousands (often millions) of consumers and other suppliers. Somehow the economic decisions made by millions of individuals, each guided by relatively limited information and motivated by rather narrow interests, are consistent and compatible with each other. What maintains this coordination? The answer is that markets and prices serve as a system of social control, directing seemingly unrelated economic activities into a coordinated, consistent behavior pattern. An important aspect of the study of microeconomics is an understanding of how this market or price system coordinates economic activity.

Of course, the economic system should do more than simply coordinate economic activity; it should direct resources to their most valuable employments. To analyze how successfully an economic system accomplishes this objective, criteria for desirable resource allocation must be established. Microeconomic analysis can be used to establish the conditions that must be met if resources are to be allocated desirably and then to determine how closely these conditions are satisfied in a market economy. Under certain conditions, a market economy will lead to a desirable allocation of resources. Economists refer to this as an **efficient allocation of resources**—a situation in which it is impossible to improve anyone's position as a consumer or producer without making someone else's position worse. This efficiency is based on the ability of market prices to convey information to resource owners about the opportunity costs of resource uses. But the market process is often inefficient, and reallocations can be made to improve the well-being of some at no cost to anyone else. The tools of microeconomics allow us to understand the reasons for these market imperfections and to suggest policy prescriptions for moderating the inefficiencies they cause.

This suggests that government policy will often have a significant influence on the performance of the economy. All economies operate under the influence of a mix of market and political institutions, but this mix varies from economy to economy. Some economies allocate resources largely through political channels; others are organized predominantly around markets. But even the most complete market economy operates in an environment that is shaped to a great degree by the political structure. Although microeconomics is the study of how individual decision makers respond to scarcity, it explains why individuals often find it advantageous to make collective decisions through political organizations. Microeconomics is also useful in analyzing how efficiently the political process allocates scarce resources among consumers and producers.

Normative and Positive Economics   1–3

Economic knowledge can be systematically arranged and classified as *positive* or *normative*. **Positive economics** explains *what is, was,* or *will be;* **normative economics** prescribes what *ought to be.* When economists disagree over the validity of a positive statement, they rely on their interpretation of facts to settle the argument. But normative statements are based on ethical or moral principles and by their very nature cannot be supported by scientific fact. Disagreements over normative statements such as "the price charged for gasoline should be the fair price" therefore cannot be resolved by scientific methods. Of course, we can measure the price of gasoline, but we cannot deduce whether or not this price is "fair" from positive measurement.

Even though positive and normative economics are dissimilar, they are necessarily related. Since positive economics can be an objective science, it is independent, in principle, of any ethical or moral goals—it is value free. However, normative economics is concerned with what ought to be and is dependent on positive economics to achieve its goals. Suppose you take the normative position that every worker should receive a "living wage" and that you advocate minimum-wage legislation to achieve this end. Your advocacy of this policy is dependent on a positive statement of what will be—on a prediction that workers who are paid less than the minimum wage prior to enactment of the legislation will receive the higher wage after the law is passed. But suppose your prediction is wrong, and workers who are receiving less than a "living wage" are fired because their labor services are now valued by their employers at less than the legal minimum wage. Then you would not have achieved your normative goal; instead, you would have made the situation you sought to improve even worse.

This example clearly illustrates that the policy goals derived from normative economics must rely on positive economic predictions if they are to be attained. Individuals who wish to attain normative economic goals must first achieve an in-depth understanding of positive economics. Conversely, economists who are chiefly concerned with the construction of positive economic theories can devote their intellectual efforts to only a few of the multitude of economic issues. Choosing and ordering economic issues on the basis of the value of their importance is a normative decision. Thus, normative and positive economics are interdependent.

1-4 Economic Theories

Economic theories, or interchangeably, **economic models,** are categorized in several different ways. As the title of this book suggests, we will be primarily concerned with **microeconomic models,** which are based on assumptions about the behavior of individual persons and are used to predict how these economic decision makers will respond to different economic conditions.

One common means of categorizing microeconomic models is to divide them into models of *general* or *partial equilibrium.* Before we can discuss the differences between these two categories, however, it will be useful to define what we mean by *equilibrium.* **Equilibrium** *is a state in which opposing forces are balanced.* To borrow an analogy from physics, the ball at the bottom of the trough in Figure 1–1(a) is in equilibrium, because the opposing forces are equal; unless some outside force acts on this ball, it will remain at rest at the bottom of the trough. The ball in Figure 1–1(b) is in **disequilibrium;** since it is not at the bottom of the trough, the forces acting on it are *unequal.* This ball will move toward equilibrium unless some outside force prevents it from doing so. In addition to the concepts of equilibrium and disequilibrium, economists are also concerned with whether or not an equilibrium is *stable* or *unstable.* A **stable equilibrium** is characterized by the property that if the equilibrium is disturbed, the original forces that created the equilibrium will act in such a way to restore the original equilibrium. The physical analogy of this property is illustrated in Figure 1–1(a). If we displace the ball to the right or the left of its position of rest, the original forces will restore the initial equilibrium of the ball after the displacing force is removed. On the other hand, Figure 1–1(c) illustrates an **unstable equilibrium,** because if the ball on top of the hill is displaced even slightly to the right or the left, the resulting unequal forces will permanently displace the ball from its initial equilibrium.

In economic terms, **market equilibrium** is achieved when all participants

**Example
1-1**

The Just Price

Given the distinction that positive economics is concerned with *what is* and normative economics is concerned with *what ought to be,* it should not surprise you to learn that the group of scholars who first tried to resolve the problem of the "fair price"—or, as they called it, the "just price"—were theologians. The Scholastics began writing in the thirteenth century and reached their peak in the sixteenth century at the University of Salamanca in Spain.* A minority of the Scholastics, including John Duns Scotus, held "that the just price is the cost of production plus a reasonable profit."**

*Murray N. Rothbard, "New Light on the Prehistory of the Austrian School," in Edwin G. Dolan (ed.), *The Foundations of Modern Austrian Economics* (Mission, KA: Sheed Andrews and McMeel, Inc., 1976), pp. 52–74.
**Ibid., p. 59.

Figure 1–1
(a) A Physical Equilibrium That Is Stable   (b) A Physical Disequilibrium
(c) A Physical Equilibrium That Is Unstable

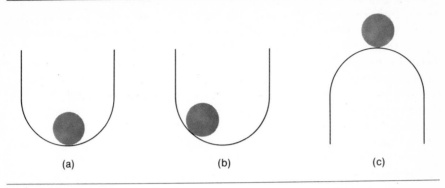

(a)   (b)   (c)

in the market (producers, workers, wholesalers, retailers, customers, and so on) make exactly the same decisions in each economic period in terms of what will be produced, how it will be produced, the payments that will be made to factors of production, and the quantities that will be purchased. This idea is fundamental to a large body of economic analysis, and this book will elaborate on and further extend the concept of market equilibrium.

In a **general-equilibrium model,** everything depends on everything else. In other words, the price of gasoline not only affects the quantity of gasoline consumed; it influences everything from the price and quantity of automobiles produced to the price and quantity of popcorn. These effects are the result of the general interdependence of all markets. It is not hard to see that an increase in gasoline prices will induce firms and households to economize on gasoline. A

However, the great majority of the Scholastics—men such as the Dominican theologian Domingo de Soto and the Portuguese Jesuit Luis de Molina—held views similar to that of Thomas Aquinas, who argued that the just price is "the one which at a given time can be gotten from the buyers, assuming common knowledge and the absence of all fraud and coercion."† In other words, the **just price** is the price that is determined by the interaction of the forces of demand and supply in the marketplace. In Chapter 2, we will discuss this market-determined price. There, we will see that the market price has many advantages—but positive economic analysis cannot establish that justice is or is not one of them.

†Raymond de Roover, "The Concept of the Just Price: Theory and Economic Policy," *Journal of Economic History* (December 1958), p. 423.

direct solution is to purchase automobiles that weigh less, because they provide more miles per gallon in general. Automobiles that weigh less also usually require smaller inputs of labor and raw materials and therefore cost less to produce and purchase. Changes in the desired characteristics of automobiles will not only affect automobile producers but will also affect their suppliers, their suppliers' suppliers, and so on. As we move further and further away from the markets that are directly affected by the increase in gasoline prices, it becomes more and more difficult to predict what will happen. In terms of the popcorn market, people will react to an increase in gasoline prices by going to movies, baseball games, circuses, and similar forms of entertainment less often, thereby reducing popcorn sales at these activities. On the other hand, if people spend more evenings at home watching television, they will probably consume more popcorn at home. Without measurement, it is difficult to say which factor will be dominant, so that we cannot be certain whether the price of popcorn will go up or down. We know only that higher gasoline prices will have some effect on the prices of popcorn.

General-equilibrium analysis provides economists with insights into the overall working of a market economy. Economists have used general-equilibrium analysis to probe the questions of whether or not a free-market economy has an equilibrium and, if it does, whether this equilibrium is stable or unstable. In Chapter 12 we will examine one approach to general-equilibrium analysis and apply it to some real-world problems.

In contrast to general-equilibrium analysis, economists use **partial-equilibrium analysis** to examine one or more individuals, firms, or markets in isolation from the rest of the economy. A **partial-equilibrium model** is based on the implicit assumption that all other things remain constant (in Latin, *ceteris paribus*). A slightly different interpretation is that the individual, firm, or market under analysis is unaffected by any change in the rest of the economy, and *vice versa*. We know from our previous discussion of general-equilibrium analysis that this is never true, strictly speaking. In many situations, however, the *ceteris paribus* assumption will introduce only a negligible error into our predictions.

If in exploring the impact on automobile purchases of a rise in the price of petroleum sold by the Organization of Petroleum Exporting Countries (OPEC), for example, we neglect the interaction between the automobile and popcorn markets, the effect on the accuracy of our predictions will probably be negligible. However, this will not always be the case. Higher OPEC oil prices, *ceteris paribus,* would increase gasoline prices, which could lead us to predict that (1) the sales of large, gas-guzzling cars will decline and the value of used cars of this type will depreciate, and (2) the sales of small, gas-efficient compact cars will increase and their value as used cars will appreciate. These predictions are based on the implicit assumption that OPEC producers control the bulk of the world's oil production. The *ceteris paribus* assumption is that petroleum production in the rest of the world remains constant. Although this assumption may be reasonable in the short run, in the long run it is possible that the incentives provided by higher petroleum prices will increase oil exploration and production in non-OPEC regions of the world and possibly reverse the escalation in oil prices. This, in turn, could reverse the production mix between large and compact cars.

Therefore, if economists are to make accurate predictions, they must know which factors are assumed to be constant, why they are assumed to be constant, and the time span over which *ceteris paribus* is assumed to prevail. The alternative, general-equilibrium approach usually produces much more complex economic models and much less accurate predictions than partial-equilibrium analysis. For this reason, most economic analysis is conducted within a *partial-equilibrium framework*. Therefore, although much of the economic theory developed in this book is based on general-equilibrium as well as partial-equilibrium analysis, most of our applications will be examined within the framework of partial-equilibrium analysis.

Microeconomic models can also be categorized as *static* or *dynamic*. A **static microeconomic model** considers a state of equilibrium—that is, the situation that will prevail when all forces being examined are balanced. **Comparative statics** is the comparison of an initial static equilibrium with a static equilibrium that results when one of the factors that established the initial equilibrium is altered. In comparative static analysis, we do not explicitly consider what occurs during the process of moving from one equilibrium to another. A **dynamic microeconomic model** is used to examine the path of adjustment from one equilibrium to another. Most of the economic models we will construct in later chapters will be static-equilibrium models, and we will use the concept of comparative statics to analyze change. These relatively simple economic models will enable us to analyze a large number of economic problems.

Methodology   1-5

Like any other science, economics is concerned with the methods that are employed to construct theories and to ascertain their validity. Economic methodology is an issue that well-known economists frequently view from different perspectives. In this section, we will consider methodologies that reflect the predominant approaches used by economists today.

Deductive reasoning is based on a given set of assumptions or axioms that are believed to be self-evident and that cannot be logically proved or disproved within a theoretical framework. Theories are then deduced by applying the rules of logic to these axioms.

Advocates of this methodology argue that if initial axiom A is true, then "all the propositions that can be logically deduced from this axiom must also be true. For if A implies B, and A is true, then B must also be true."[3] The foremost

---

[3] Murray N. Rothbard, "Praxeology: The Methodology of Austrian Economics," in Edwin G. Dolan (ed.), *The Foundations of Modern Austrian Economics* (Mission, KA: Sheed Andrews & McMeel, Inc., 1976), p. 20.

advocate of deductive reasoning in the twentieth century has been the Austrian-school economist Ludwig von Mises, who based an entire body of systematic economic thought on the fundamental axiom that human beings engage in conscious actions to achieve chosen goals.[4] Mises also argued that the problems associated with the empirical testing of any economic theory are so great that, for all practical purposes, proper testing is impossible. Thus, from this methodological point of view, the acceptance or rejection of all economic theory must rest entirely on deductive reasoning.

Theories formulated by **inductive reasoning** are based on real-world observations. Defenders of this methodology argue that deductions based on "some 'Fundamental Assumption' or 'principle' concerning economic conduct are more or less useless, because no relevant 'Fundamental Assumption' can, on our present knowledge, be made."[5] Only slightly less extreme is the view of Nobel Laureate Herbert Simon, who argues that constructing economic theories to explain real-world decisions "requires a basic shift in economic style, from an emphasis on deductive reasoning within a tight system of axioms to an emphasis on detailed empirical exploration...."[6]

The methodology of **logical positivism** incorporates both deductive and inductive reasoning. Perhaps the most widely accepted logical positivist approach is Nobel Laureate Milton Friedman's methodology of *positive economics*,[7] which seeks to construct *theories, hypotheses,* or *models* that will enable economists to make predictions about events that have occurred in the past or that will occur in the future. Because an infinite number of theories can be applied to explain an event, we must be able to employ some method to select the best theory. The methodology of **positive economics** is based on the idea that the only relevant way to determine the validity of a given theory is to empirically compare the accuracy of its predictions with alternative theories. Of course, this criterion does not ensure that a single theory will prove to be a better predictor than any other theory. Two or more theories of equal predictive ability may exist for any set of finite facts. Economists employ the criteria of *simplicity* and *fruitfulness* whenever they must choose between theories of equal predictive ability. A theory is said to be simpler than another theory if less information is required to use the theory to predict the outcome of an event. The fruitfulness of a theory is measured by how applicable it is to a wider range of phenomena than those at issue and the extent to which the theory suggests further avenues of research. In the methodology of positive economics, simplicity is preferred to complexity and fruitfulness is preferred to narrowness.

---

[4]Ludwig von Mises, *Human Action: A Treatise on Economics,* 3rd rev. ed. (Chicago: Henry Regnery Co., 1966).
[5]T.W. Hutchison, "Expectation and Rational Conduct," *Zeitschrift für Nationalökonomie,* Band VIII, Heft 5 (1937), p. 652.
[6]Herbert Simon, "From Substantive to Procedural Rationality," in S. Latsis (ed.), *Method and Appraisal in Economics* (Cambridge: Cambridge University Press, 1976), p. 147.
[7]Milton Friedman, "The Methodology of Positive Economics," in Milton Friedman (ed.), *Essays in Positive Economics* (Chicago: University of Chicago Press, 1958), pp. 3–43.

Assumptions and Limitations of Economic Theory

By their very nature, theories are abstractions from reality. In other words, theories are designed to focus only on the factors that the economist considers to be of primary importance in explaining the causal relationship between sets of observations. For example, in the course of constructing a theory of consumer demand for hamburgers, the economist starts with a set of definitions, such as "the price of a hamburger is the dollar value at which one hamburger can be exchanged for money" and "a hamburger is a substitute good if it can take the place of another good" (for example, hot dogs). Next, the economist adopts a set of assumptions—for example, "an individual always prefers having more hamburgers to having less" and "the prices of all other goods *except* hamburgers will remain constant." Logical deductions are then drawn from this theory. In our example, a logical deduction would be "as the price of hamburgers declines, more hamburgers and less hot dogs will be purchased."

In our example, we have assumed that the prices of all goods—with the exception of the good in question—are constant, even though we know that this never happens in the real world. Students who are encountering economic theory for the first time usually object to the conflict between the theoretical assumptions and reality. But if we tried to construct a model that took the changes in all other prices into consideration, we would have so much information that it would be extremely difficult, if not impossible, to determine which factors were causing the quantity of hamburgers consumed to increase. By ignoring these other price changes, we are saying, in effect, that they are not important for our purposes. Assumptions of this type can be considered equivalent to the variables that we hold constant in a controlled experiment, so that we can focus our attention on the effect of those variables in which we are most interested. According to the methodology of positive economics, the extent to which these rationalizations of our assumptions can be justified ultimately depends on the accuracy of the predictions that result from a theory constructed in this manner.

The acceptance or rejection of economic theories according to the methodology of deductive reasoning rests on whether or not the fundamental assumptions are realistic, provided there are no errors in logic. Logical positivists argue that the fallacy in this approach lies in the fact that the assumptions of *any* theory are "unrealistic." As we will learn in subsequent chapters, the most important and significant economic theories are based on highly inaccurate descriptive representations of reality. To be important and significant, a theory must explain a wide and varied class of phenomena, but as the theoretical assumptions become more and more "realistic," the constraints imposed by these assumptions limit the range of phenomena over which the theory can accurately predict. Of course, it does not follow that theories with "unrealistic" assumptions will automatically be significant theories.

When we say that a theory should be rejected because its assumptions are unrealistic, what we mean is that in our opinion the assumptions should be "more realistic." Suppose that another critic tells us that the same theory should be rejected because its assumptions are "too restrictive" or "too realistic." Obviously, we cannot resort to an examination of the assumptions to determine which opinion is correct. In the final analysis, we can only base our rejection or acceptance of any theory on the predictive ability of the theory compared with that of another theory.

Since this methodology is the essence of positive economics, it is absolutely essential that the theories yield predictions that can be empirically falsified, at least in principle. A theory that cannot be falsified can never be refuted—and therefore can never be rejected.

In economics, it is difficult to determine whether a theory has been falsified, because economists are seldom able to test their theories under "controlled experimental conditions," where all variables, except those under study, are held constant. If an experiment yields a false prediction, this may not mean that the theory is a poor one; a factor that the theory assumed to be constant may simply not have remained constant. Of course, the lack of controlled experiments does impose some special constraints and their accompanying problems on empirical economic research, which the specialized field of *econometrics* attempts to overcome.

1-6   A Look Ahead

The concepts of demand and supply are among the most important and useful in the economist's tool kit. We will begin our formal study of microeconomics by examining the fundamental ideas embodied in demand and supply analysis and by employing the theory in several real-world applications (Chapters 2 and 3). We will then consider the foundations on which the demand curve is based in greater detail (Chapters 4 and 5). As we will see, the supply of commodities by firms is dependent on the state of technology, the cost of the inputs used in production, and the way in which the firms are organized within markets.

Next, we will examine the theory of production in terms of the constraints imposed on the firm by the available technology and the cost of the productive inputs (Chapters 6 and 7). Given these common constraints, we will then explore the theory of the supply of commodities by firms that are organized into various market structures (Chapters 8, 9, and 10). Next, we will examine the demand and supply of the inputs of production and the determinants of the distribution of the firm's revenue among various inputs (Chapter 11).

The problem of economic efficiency will then be addressed within the context of general-equilibrium analysis (Chapter 12). We will learn that the market economy does not always produce conditions that result in maximum economic efficiency, and we will consider some theoretical and real-world examples of market failure and present some solutions for alleviating these problems (Chapter 13). Lastly, we will illustrate the fruitfulness of microeconomic analysis by examining the economic theory underlying political decision making (Chapter 14).

Summary 1–7

In Chapter 1, we have learned that *economics* is the social science concerned with how people choose to allocate limited resources to provide for unlimited individual wants. We have also been introduced to *microeconomics,* which focuses on the decision-making processes of individual consumers or producers as they attempt to achieve given goals. Whenever decisions or choices are made, costs are involved. We have seen that the *opportunity cost* of making one choice is the alternative choice that the decision maker must forgo.

We have defined *positive economics* as the study of what was, is, or will be, and *normative economics* as the study of what ought to be. We must depend on positive economics to achieve the goals of normative economics, because no matter how pure or noble our intentions are, we cannot attain our objectives if we base our policy recommendations on false concepts of reality.

In their attempt to understand reality, economists construct theories. We have examined the methodologies economists use to construct and evaluate *economic theories* or *economic models,* which can be based on *deductive reasoning, inductive reasoning,* or *logical positivism.* The methodology of *positive economics* is a form of logical positivism that is based on the idea that the validity of economic theories should be determined by their predictive ability vis-à-vis other theories and that questioning the realism of economic assumptions only produces fruitless argument.

We have also defined the concepts of *equilibrium* and *stability* in very general terms. And we have seen how *microeconomic models* can be categorized as general-equilibrium or partial-equilibrium models or as static or dynamic models. In a *general-equilibrium model,* every factor depends on every other factor; in a *partial-equilibrium model,* the *ceteris paribus* assumption is invoked. *Static models* provide equilibrium solutions. *Comparative static analysis* is the comparison of an initial static equilibrium with a static equilibrium that results when one of the factors that established the initial equilibrium is altered. *Dynamic models* explain how the process of movement from one equilibrium to another is achieved.

In Chapter 2, we will examine the concept of *market equilibrium* in greater detail and apply comparative static analysis to some real-world economic problems.

References

Dolan, Edwin G. (ed.). *The Foundations of Modern Austrian Economics.* Mission, KA: Sheed Andrews & McMeel, Inc., 1976.

Friedman, Milton. "The Methodology of Positive Economics." In Milton Friedman (ed.). *Essays in Positive Economics.* Chicago: University of Chicago Press, 1958.

Hutchison, T.W. "Expectations and Rational Conduct." *Zeitschrift für Nationalökonomie,* Band VIII, Heft 5 (1937).

Latsis, S. (ed.). *Method and Appraisal in Economics*. Cambridge: Cambridge University Press, 1976.

Mises, Ludwig von. *Human Action: A Treatise on Economics*, 3rd rev. ed. Chicago: Henry Regnery Co., 1966.

Robbins, Lionel. *The Nature and Significance of Economic Science*, 2nd ed. London: Macmillan, 1935.

Roover, Raymond de. "The Concept of the Just Price: Theory and Economic Policy." *Journal of Economic History* (December 1958).

Samuelson, Paul A. *Economics*, 9th ed. New York: McGraw-Hill, 1973.

Problems

1. Suppose that you have to take three final exams next week. Why is the decision you must make regarding how much time you will spend preparing for each exam an economic problem?

2. To be scientific, a theory must yield predictions that can be empirically refuted. Suppose you have been asked to evaluate a 200-year-old theory that has yet to yield an accurate prediction of the population growth rate in England. Advocates of this theory claim that enough time has not elapsed yet to validate the theory. Is this theory a scientific theory? Explain your answer.

3. Why is it a necessary evil to make unrealistic assumptions when constructing economic theories?

4. When U.S. gasoline prices first began to escalate in 1974, some economists predicted that this would not affect the driving habits of Americans. Explain why this was a correct prediction in the short run but not in the long run.

5. Assume that you own a house on which you make a mortgage payment of $200 per month. You rent this house for $250 per month and live in an apartment, where you pay $220 per month in rent. Would it be cheaper for you to move back into your house? Explain. If your monthly mortgage payment were increased to $220, how would this affect the cost of moving back into your house? What would the effect be if your mortgage rate were increased to $240 per month?

6. Consider how many people cooperated with one another to provide you with the watch you own, and attempt to explain how your simple decision to purchase a watch was sufficient to prompt this cooperation. Now assume that you are in charge of an economy that does not allow individuals to engage freely in any economic activity. Nothing is produced without an order from you. You are ready to send out manufacturing orders in accordance with an overall production plan you have devised. With all this power and control, do you think you will have more or less ability to generate the production of a watch than you have now? Explain.

7. In Chapter 2, we will develop and apply analytical tools of demand and sup-

ply. There, we will make extensive use of the *ceteris paribus* assumption to argue that price controls can increase rather than reduce the cost of goods. A natural tendency is to criticize this analysis because it is based on the *ceteris paribus* assumption. But those who support price controls are also making some *ceteris paribus* assumptions. Think about the potential advantages of price controls, and then attempt to identify the *ceteris paribus* assumption you are making.

8. The following theory is designed to explain and predict the tennis-playing behavior of Jimmy Connors: Jimmy understands the laws of theoretical physics that determine the trajectory of a tennis ball in flight, and he can also instantly solve the mathematical equations required to determine the proper stroke to use on each shot. Comment on this theory from the perspective of each of the three methodologies discussed in this chapter.

9. If you won $10 million playing blackjack in Las Vegas, would you be free from the constraint of economic scarcity?

APPENDIX

MATHEMATICAL AND GRAPHIC ANALYSIS

1A-1 Introduction

Economists today widely employ the tools of mathematical and graphic analysis to derive and explain their economic theories. These tools have become generally accepted and employed because they usually provide more precise derivations of logical conclusions from an underlying set of initial assumptions. In addition, an economist's theoretical results can usually be transmitted more quickly and clearly to other economists if mathematics and graphs are used.

1A-2 Functions

As we have previously stated, an economic theory is an attempt to explain the relationships among variables with the objective of predicting what will happen to one variable when one or more other variables are altered. For example, suppose that Y is the dependent variable and X is the independent variable. The value of Y is therefore dependent on the value of X. In mathematical terms, we would say that Y is a **function** of X, and we would express this *functional relationship* symbolically as

$$Y = f(X) \tag{1A-1}$$

where f stands for "a function of."[1] This notation does not tell us the exact relationship between X and Y or whether X and Y are directly related (when X increases, Y increases) or inversely related (when X increases, Y

---

[1]We are not restricted to using the symbol f. The alternative notations g, h, and j are frequently used. In economics, functional notation in the form $Y = Y(X)$ is often used. In this notational form, the dependent variable serves as the function notation.

16

decreases). These relationships can be expressed notationally as

$$\frac{\Delta Y}{\Delta X} > 0 \tag{1A–2}$$

or

$$\frac{\Delta Y}{\Delta X} < 0 \tag{1A–3}$$

Here, ΔX represents the amount of increase in the variable X and is calculated by subtracting the initial value of X from the final value (a positive value, by definition); ΔY represents the change in the dependent variable calculated in the same manner. If Y increases as X increases, then the final value of Y will be greater than the initial value of Y; ΔY will therefore be positive and $\Delta Y/\Delta X$ will be greater than 0. Hence, the inequality in (1A–2) symbolizes a **direct relationship** between X and Y. If Y decreases as X increases, then ΔY will be negative and $\Delta Y/\Delta X$ will be less than 0. Thus, the inequality in (1A–3) symbolizes an **inverse relationship** between X and Y.

Suppose that we know that the exact functional relationship between X and Y is given by

$$Y = 2 + 3X \tag{1A–4}$$

We can use this information to construct the tabular sequence of Y values for *specific* values of X that appears in Table 1A–1.

Although such schedules are useful and can convey a great deal of information, they do not tell us what value Y will assume if X lies somewhere in between two of the values given in the table. We do not have this limitation with a graph, however, as we can see from the graph of Equation (1A–4) shown in Figure 1A–1. Figure 1A–1 is a two-dimensional graph with four quadrants labeled I, II, III, and IV. Quadrant I contains the plotted values of X and Y when both variables are positive. The plotted values of X and Y when X is negative and Y is positive appear in quadrant II. Both X and Y are negative in quadrant III, and X

**Table 1A–1
Schedule of Y Values for
Specific Values of X**

X	Y
−3	−7
−2	−4
−1	−1
0	2
1	5
2	8
3	11

is positive and Y is negative in quadrant IV. Since Equation (1A–4) never yields negative values of Y when X is positive, no plotted points appear in quadrant IV in the figure. In economic analysis, we normally deal only with variables that have positive values. For this reason, all graphic representations of functions in this book will be restricted to the first quadrant.

Although graphs convey more information than schedules, graphs still have inherent limitations. If the dependent variable is a function of two independent variables X and Y, this relationship can be expressed symbolically as

$$Z = Z(X,Y) \qquad\qquad (1A–5)$$

Since three variables are involved, the graphic representation of this function is a three-dimensional figure. It is difficult to draw three-dimensional figures on a two-dimensional surface and even more difficult to interpret them. Fortunately, almost all basic economic concepts can be reduced to two-dimensional analysis.

Figure 1A–1
Graph of Y = 2 + 3X

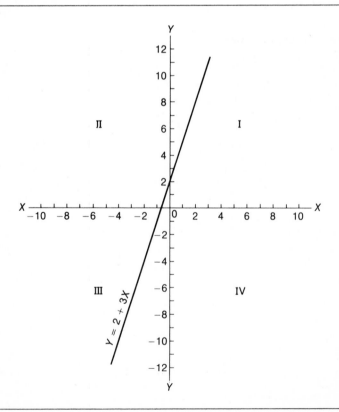

One method that economists use to reduce three-dimensional functions so that they can be graphically represented on a two-dimensional surface is borrowed from cartography. To indicate elevation, cartographers draw lines of constant elevation, called *contour lines*, on a map. An example of this technique is illustrated in Figure 1A–2.

Figure 1A–3 illustrates how a three-variable function, such as equation (1A–5), can be drawn on a two-dimensional surface. The dependent variable Z is measured in the vertical direction; the independent variables X and Y are both measured horizontally. Although all axes originate at the origin 0, for reasons of clarity, the Z axis has been shifted to point A at the back of the surface. The solid curved line BB drawn on the surface of the figure represents various combinations of X and Y for which $Z = Z_3$. Since Z measures the height above the horizontal surface, the projection of this line on the horizontal floor (line $B'B'$) is equivalent to a map contour line for a constant elevation of $Z = Z_3$. Similarly, surface lines CC (for $Z = Z_2$) and DD (for $Z = Z_1$) are drawn in Figure 1A–3. Their projections $C'C'$ and $D'D'$ are the contour lines of $Z = Z_2$ and $Z = Z_1$, respectively.

The information contained in Figure 1A–3 is presented in much simpler two-dimensional form in Figure 1A–4. The three curves in Figure 1A–4 are the three

---

Figure 1A–2
A Map with Contour Lines

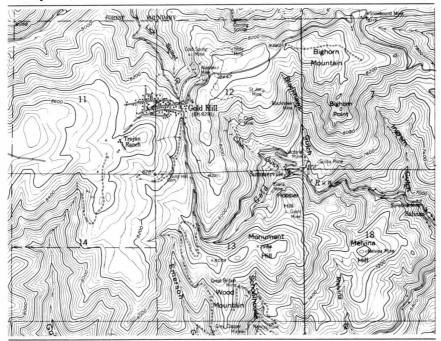

SOURCE: U.S. Geological Survey. Reprinted by permission.

Figure 1A–3
Derivation of Contour Lines
from a Three-Dimensional Surface

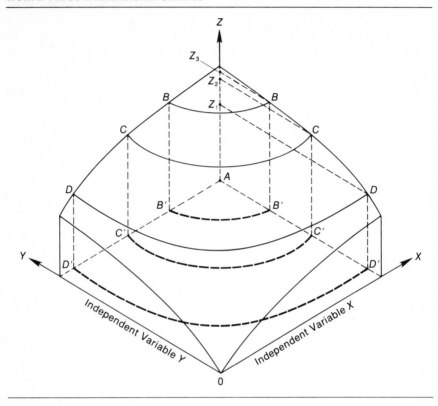

contour lines in Figure 1A–3. The curve furthermost from the origin in Figure 1A–4 (curve $B'B'$ in Figure 1A–3) gives the various combinations of X and Y values such that $Z = Z_3$. The Z_2 and Z_3 curves in Figure 1A–4 correspond to curves $C'C'$ and $D'D'$, respectively, in Figure 1A–3. Although we have constructed curves for only three constant values of Z here, we could actually construct as many of these curves as we wished. Thus, any amount of information described by a three-dimensional function can be presented in a two-dimensional graph.

1A–3   The Concept of Slope

Slope is a property of plotted points on the graph of a function. This is an extremely useful concept that we will apply extensively in our graphic analyses. Consider the following functional relationship

$$Y = 1 + 1.5X \qquad\qquad\qquad (1A-6)$$

Figure 1A–4
Two-Dimensional Graph
of a Three-Variable Function Z = Z(X,Y)

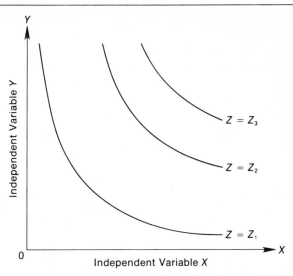

This function when X and Y are both positive is graphed in Figure 1A–5. To determine the slope at point A on this line, we construct a right triangle whose hypotenuse is formed by the graph of the function and whose horizontal side originates at point A. The **slope** of this *linear* (straight-line) *function* at point A is defined to be *equal to the ratio of the height of the vertical side of the triangle to the length of the horizontal side.* Since we are dealing with the ratio of the sides of a right triangle, we can conveniently draw the horizontal distance so that it is unity, as in Figure 1A–5. Thus, the slope of the line at point A can easily be read as the height of the vertical side of the triangle. In this example, the slope is 1.5.

If we were to choose any other point on the line drawn in Figure 1A–5 and construct a right triangle originating from that point, we would obtain exactly the same measurement for the slope at this point as we did at point A. In general, we ascribe to a straight line the slope that exists at every point along the line. In this example, we would say that the slope of the line is 1.5. The value of the slope of this line is *positive,* because the relationship between X and Y is direct, so that when X increases, Y also increases. Graphically, this produces a straight line that slopes upward and to the right, as shown in Figure 1A–5. Suppose, however, that an *inverse functional relationship* exists, such as that given by

$$Y = 4 - .75X \qquad\qquad (1A\text{–}7)$$

Here, Y decreases as X increases, as illustrated in Figure 1A–6. The slope at point *B* in Figure 1A–6 is computed in exactly the same manner as the slope at point *A* in Figure 1A–5, except that the right triangle is now facing in the opposite direction. Since *Y* decreases as *X* increases, we affix a minus sign to the value of the vertical síde of the triangle. Thus, the slope at point *B* (and of the line in general) is −.75. Due to this sign convention, we say that a line that slopes downward and to the right has a *negative* slope.

Until this point, we have limited our discussion of slope to *linear functions*—that is, functions that can be graphed as straight lines. Since straight lines have the same slope at all points, we are able to say not only that the slope of the line is positive or negative but also that it has a specific value. When we consider the slope of a *nonlinear function*, however, the process becomes more complicated.

Suppose that we are given the nonlinear function

$$Y = \frac{2}{X} \qquad (1A-8)$$

which is graphed in Figure 1A–7. To determine the slope at point *C* on the curved line, we draw a straight line tangent to the curve at point *C*. The slope of this tangent line is the slope of the curve at point *C*, which is determined simply by defining it as the hypotenuse of a right triangle whose horizontal side is unity. The vertical side of this triangle is the slope of the tangent and therefore the slope of the curved line at point *C*. Such a triangle has been constructed at point *C* in Figure 1A–7, and from it we can see that the slope at the point on the curve

---

Figure 1A–5
A Linear Function with Positive Slope

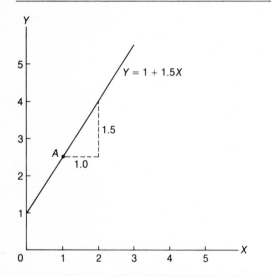

Figure 1A–6
A Linear Function with Negative Slope

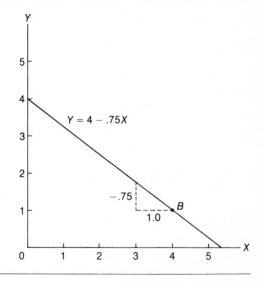

Figure 1A–7
Determination of Slope at Points
on a Nonlinear Function

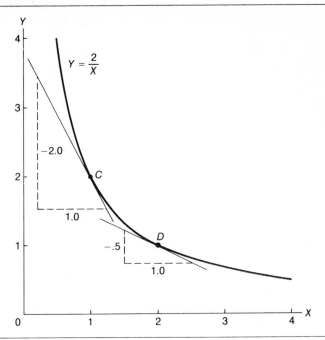

is -2.0. The value of the slope is negative because the slope of the tangency line drawn at point C is negative. Therefore, we say that nonlinear lines that slope downward and to the right have a negative slope. However, that is *all* that we can say about the slope of the line in Figure 1A–7, because even though the slope at any point on the line is less than 0, its precise value depends on the value of X. For example, at point D where $X = 2$, the slope is equal to $-.5$.

As we move down the graph in Figure 1A–7, lines drawn tangent to the curve become less and less steep. Since the graph is negatively sloped, the values of the slope at points along the curve increase *algebraically;* that is, they approach 0 from the negative side as X increases. In some cases, we are concerned with the *absolute value*[2] of the slope rather than its algebraic value. Then we say that the slope at points along the curve diminishes as we move downward along the curve.

If we wish to determine the slope at a point on a nonlinear curve that slopes upward and to the right, we apply almost the same technique that we do for a curved line with a negative slope. The only difference is that the vertical side of the triangle would then be a positive value, so that the slope of the line would be positive.

---

[2]The absolute value of a negative slope is obtained by simply ignoring the minus sign.

Problems

1. Given the equation

$$Y = 10 - 2X$$

   (a.) Construct a table similar to Table A1–1 and calculate the values of Y when $X = 0, 1, 2, 4$, and 6.
   (b.) Use the values you calculate in (a) to graph the equation.
   (c.) What is the slope of the graph when $X = 2$? When $X = 4$?

2. Given the equation

$$Z = 100 - X^2 - Y^2$$

   (a.) For values of $Z = 0$ and $Z = 75$, calculate five pairs of positive values of X and Y.
   (b.) Graph the contour lines for $Z = 0$ and $Z = 75$.

3. Given the equation

$$Y = 1 + X^2$$

   (a.) Calculate values of Y for $X = 2, 1.5, 1.0, .5, 0, -.5, -1.0, -1.5$, and -2.0.
   (b.) Graph the equation.
   (c.) What is the value of the slope when $X = 1.0$? When $X = -1.0$?

4. Given the equations

$$Y = 10 - .5X$$
$$Y = 1 + 2X$$

   (a.) Graph each equation.
   (b.) What are the values of X and Y at the point of intersection of the two graphs?

CHAPTER TWO

DEMAND AND SUPPLY

In this chapter, we will examine two of the most important concepts in micro-economic theory—demand and supply. Although these concepts are quite simple in theory, their proper application can give us many important insights into major social issues. There is much to be gained by learning how to enlist the aid of these two valuable tools of economic analysis.

Yet, like any set of tools, demand and supply analysis can be incorrectly used and can lead us to erroneous conclusions. In fact, if misused, demand and supply analysis—like a little knowledge—can be a dangerous thing. Few people reach college without hearing something about the law of demand and supply. For example, most of us recognize that this law should enable us to predict that a decrease in supply will raise prices or that a decrease in demand will lower prices. But this premise can be misleading in that it allows people to conclude that something is amiss when consumers are reducing their purchases of, say, automobiles or petroleum products and the prices of these goods are going up, not down. Common conclusions are that automobile and oil companies are so large and powerful that the law of demand and supply does not apply to them, or that the old concepts of demand and supply are simply no longer relevant to our modern economy.

Such conclusions are wrong and are based on an incomplete understanding of the implications of demand and supply. Accurate application of these tools requires a thorough understanding of the concepts on which they are based and the ways in which economists use them to give meaning to the ideas of equilibrium price and quantity. The purpose of this chapter is to develop such an understanding, so that the reader will be able to apply these concepts to the analysis of interesting and relevant problems with justified confidence.

2-2 Demand

Individual Demand Curves

Many things determine the quantity of a commodity that an individual will desire to consume over some specified period of time. For example, if we were interested in compiling a list of all the things that affect an individual's demand for, say, pork, we would have to include such things as his or her religious background, geographical location, exercise habits, income, the prices of all other goods, and, of course, the price of pork. This is obviously only a partial list, and little ingenuity would be required to expand it indefinitely. But such an exercise is of little value if our goal is to predict and explain how consumers will respond to changes in what are considered to be important variables. If this is our objective, it is much more sensible to restrict our interest to those variables that we feel are most important for our purposes and to consider everything else as fixed.

The choice of which variables to focus on depends on the type of questions we wish to address. A cultural anthropologist, for example, would be interested in how an individual's religious beliefs, class status, and general cultural background affect his or her consumption patterns. Not surprisingly, economists are much more concerned with how such economic variables as prices and income can be used to explain consumer demand. Economists simply group under the heading of "preferences" most of the things that are of primary interest to anthropologists and psychologists, and assume that these preferences are constant for purposes of analysis. This does not mean that economists consider these preferences and the things that determine them unimportant. Rather, they are simplifying the problem under investigation by concentrating on those variables that are of primary interest, so that they can make meaningful statements about the effects of economic variables on consumer demand. As pointed out in Chapter 1, the usefulness of this approach is not determined by whether or not consumer preferences are always constant; of course, they are not. Rather the utility of the approach should be judged on the basis of how well the implications of our analysis explain and predict the particular behavior in which we are interested.

What we are interested in here is the effect a consumer's income and the prices of the goods he or she purchases will have on his or her consumption of a particular good. Initially, it is convenient to construct the consumer's demand curve for the good being considered. To be specific here, we will talk about the demand for coffee—although any good would serve just as well.

Because demand curves are drawn in two dimensions, we will confine our attention to two variables when constructing these curves. Customarily, the two variables represented on a **demand curve** are the price of the good and the quantity of the good that is consumed over some interval of time. It is important to emphasize that the demand curve always relates price to a *rate of consumption*—the amount of a good that is consumed over some specified interval of time. To know only that an individual will consume 4 pounds of coffee at $3 per pound is to know nothing. Will the 4 pounds be consumed in the next 5 minutes or over the remainder of the consumer's life? (If 4 pounds of coffee were to be consumed in 5 minutes, there probably would not be any difference between these two time intervals!)

In Figure 2-1, we have constructed a hypothetical demand curve for coffee. The vertical axis measures the price of coffee in dollars per pound, and the horizontal axis measures the rate at which the individual consumes coffee in pounds per year. The demand curve DD in Figure 2-1 tells us the rate at which an individual will wish to consume coffee at different prices for coffee. It is natural to assume that the lower the price, the greater the desired consumption will be. This is known as the **law of demand** and is reflected by the downward slope of the demand curve.[1] For any given demand curve such as DD, the prices of other goods, the individual's income, and the consumer's preferences are assumed to be constant and are not shown in the graph. Demand curve DD tells us that as the price of coffee decreases, the rate at which the individual wishes to purchase coffee will increase, assuming the prices of other goods and the individual's income and preferences do not change.

This means that it is the price of coffee *relative to other prices* that is important in determining the individual's consumption rate for coffee. This is an important point and worth emphasizing. The *price* of coffee by itself tells us very little about the cost of *consuming* coffee. The cost of consuming an additional pound of coffee is determined by the value of the consumption that has to be given up to consume that pound. Only by knowing the prices of the other goods that could be purchased instead of coffee, as well as the prices of coffee, can this cost be determined. So in Figure 2-1, the importance of a drop in the price of coffee from P_1 to P_2 is that the *relative price* of coffee has declined. This means that less alternative consumption has to be forgone to consume another pound of coffee, and, in response, desired coffee consumption increases from Q_1 to Q_2. Thus, a more accurate statement of the law of demand is that the lower the relative price of a good, the greater will be the desired rate of consumption.

Although the prices of all other goods are assumed to be constant when we construct an individual demand curve, we do not want to ignore the effect of these prices. We will often be interested in the effect the price of one good has on the demand for another. To determine this, however, we must construct more than one demand curve. The demand curve DD in Figure 2-1 is based on a given set of prices for all other goods except coffee and a given income for our consumer. If any of these factors change, we no longer have the same demand curve. For instance, if the price of tea increases, we can expect the entire demand curve for coffee to shift. A different desired rate of coffee consumption would be associated with each coffee price. The direction of this shift would depend on the relationship we observe between coffee and tea. In this example, the

---

[1] In Chapter 5, we will see that it is theoretically possible for the law of demand not to hold. Under some unlikely conditions, an increase in the price of a commodity will cause the consumption rate to increase. In terms of practical applications, however, we are on solid ground with the law of demand.

relationship is clear. People do not tend to consume coffee and tea jointly; rather, they substitute one for the other. Therefore, if the price of tea increases, we can expect the typical consumer to reduce consumption of tea and increase consumption of coffee as a substitute. Coffee and tea are referred to as **substitute goods.** With every price of coffee now lower relative to the price of tea, we will find that at each price more coffee is desired than it was before the increase in the price of tea.

This shift in the demand curve is shown in Figure 2–2. The demand curve for coffee has already been determined to be *DD* at the original price of tea. But when a higher price is charged for tea, the demand curve for coffee shifts out to *D'D'*.

A similar analysis applies when we consider the effect on the demand for coffee of an increase in the price of a good like sugar, which is used as a complement to coffee. Goods such as coffee and sugar are referred to as **complementary goods.** An increase in the price of sugar can be expected to reduce the rate of an individual's sugar consumption. If our individual likes sugar with his coffee, this will also result in less coffee than before being consumed at every coffee price. The increase in the price of sugar will therefore shift the entire demand curve for coffee, as shown in Figure 2–2. There *DD* again represents the initial demand curve for coffee. After the price of sugar increases, the demand curve shifts to *D"D"*.

In many cases we really do not know what effect a change in the price of one good will have on the demand for another. Goods like coffee and tea or coffee and sugar are obviously substitutes and complements, respectively, which makes the results easy to predict. But what effect do you think a change in the price of razor blades would have on the demand for coffee? Coffee and razor blades are

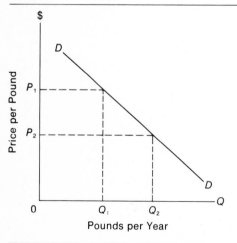

Figure 2–1
Demand for Coffee

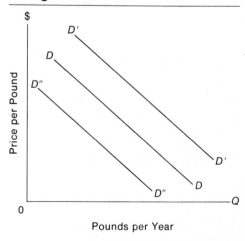

Figure 2–2
Changes in Demand for Coffee

not normally considered substitutes or complements. For most purposes, it would be completely acceptable to assume that a change in razor-blade prices would have no effect at all on the demand for coffee. This does not mean that there will not be an effect; it simply means that the effect will probably be so small that it can be safely ignored. Obviously, if the price of one good that our individual consumes increases and everything else remains constant, the consumer's real income will decline because he can no longer purchase the same quantity of all goods. A smaller real income will affect the demand curve for all goods. Of course, because expenditures on a good like razor blades are normally only a tiny fraction of total consumer expenditures, a change in the price of razor blades is not likely to have any noticeable effect on real income. But this is not true of a good like housing, for example. A change in the price of housing could have a noticeable impact on the demand curve for coffee—not because coffee and housing are substitute or complementary goods, but because housing prices can have a significant effect on real income.

The demand curves shown in Figure 2-2 can also be used to describe the effect of a change in the consumer's income on his or her demand curve. It seems reasonable to expect that an increase in a consumer's income will increase his or her demand for a commodity and thereby increase the desired rate of consumption at each price of the commodity. If this were true, then our consumer's demand curve for coffee would shift from DD and $D'D'$ in Figure 2-2 as his income increased, but this is not necessarily true. Although there is evidence that the demand for goods like air travel, tailored suits, lobster tails, and university educations increases as income rises, the demand for other goods and services, such as pork and beans, home haircutting kits, and coin-operated laundries, decreases as income rises. Economists categorize the former type of goods as **normal goods** and the latter type of goods as **inferior goods.** As a consumer's income increases, his or her demand curve for an inferior good will decrease, shifting down and to the left, as shown by the move from demand curve DD to $D''D''$ in Figure 2-2.

It should be noted that any time we refer to a *change in demand,* we refer to a *shift in the entire demand curve.* A change in the demand for a good always means that the rate at which the consumer desires to consume the good will change for every price.[2] This is to be distinguished from a *change in the rate of demand,* or quantity demanded, which can result from a change in the price of the good. This would not be a change in demand but a *movement along a given demand curve.* This distinction is made graphically in Figure 2-3, where the vertical axis measures the price of some commodity (say, oranges) and the horizontal axis measures the desired rate of orange consumption. If the demand curve is given by DD and the price is P_1, the desired rate of consumption is Q_1. As shown in Figure 2-3, the desired consumption rate can increase to Q_2 for

---

[2]To be perfectly accurate, every price should refer only to those prices at which a positive quantity of the good was being consumed before the change in demand. For example, an individual who did not purchase any thumbtacks at a price of $100 per tack would probably continue to do without them at this price, even if his or her demand for thumbtacks were to increase.

Figure 2-3
Change in Demand Versus Change in Amount Demanded

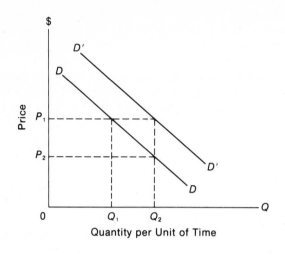

Quantity per Unit of Time

Example
2-1

Mass Transit Versus Wealth

Most people who worked in cities used to commute to and from their jobs using some form of mass transit. This is no longer the case. Despite the fact that most mass-transit systems are increasingly subsidized, so that users now pay only a fraction of the cost of their ride, the number of people using mass-transit systems has declined consistently until quite recently. For example, ridership declined 18% in New York City between 1950 and 1962 and 35% in Philadelphia over the same period. When we consider the rapid population growth during these years, it is obvious that this represents a large per-capita decrease in the demand for mass transit. Chicago's small increase in ridership (a little more than 3%) between 1950 and 1962 still represents a decline in demand on a per-capita basis.

Some insight into the reason for the frustration that mass-transit promoters have experienced is gained by noting the large increase in per capita income since 1950 and then observing how an increase in income affects the demand for automobiles. It has been estimated that for every 1% increase in income, the demand for new cars shifts enough to cause a 3% increase in new-car purchases. As people become wealthier, they choose to purchase more convenient transportation–private automobiles–and thus their demand for buses, trolleys, and subways two quite separate reasons. The price can remain at P_1 but demand can increase, shifting the demand curve to $D'D'$. In this case, an increase in demand is the sole reason for the increase in the desired rate of consumption to Q_2. On the other hand, the demand can remain the same at DD, but the price can decline to P_2. In this situation, the consumer will move along the demand curve in response to the lower price until the desired rate of orange consumption is Q_2, but there will be no change in demand.

Although we may appear to be overemphasizing the difference between a change in demand and a change in the rate of demand, this distinction is important. As we will see in later discussions, serious mistakes in applying demand and supply analysis can be made if this distinction is not kept clearly in mind.

Market Demand

Thus far, we have been talking about an individual consumer's demand curve. For most purposes of economic analysis, however, we are not particularly interested in how any one individual responds to changes in prices and incomes. Normally, economists are concerned with the aggregate response of large numbers of consumers. For example, in determining how coffee consumption will change in response to an increase in the price of coffee relative to the price of,

decreases. The automobile is a normal good, and mass transit is an inferior good. So an important explanation for the problems confronting mass-transit supporters is that they have been fighting a losing battle with increasing wealth.

Unfortunately or fortunately—depending on your perspective—mass transit may be making a comeback, precipitated by an important change in relative prices. The sharp increase in the price of gasoline in recent years has increased the price of operating an automobile relative to the price of mass-transit services. The fact that mass transit is a substitute for the gas-guzzling automobile will increase the demand for mass transit. However, it should be pointed out that economy cars are also substitutes for the gas guzzlers. It seems likely that increased gasoline prices will stimulate the demand for small cars more than the demand for mass transit.

The figures on the decline in mass-transit ridership are from J.R. Meyer, J. Kain, and M. Wohl, *The Urban Transportation Problem* (Cambridge: Harvard University Press, 1965).

The figure on the response of automobile demand to income is from G.C. Chow, *Demand for Automobiles in the U.S.* (Amsterdam: North-Holland Publishing Co., 1957). Daniel McFadden has presented evidence that both bus transit and rapid-rail transit are inferior goods. See Daniel McFadden, "The Measurement of Urban Travel Demand," *Journal of Public Economics* (November 1974), pp. 303–28.

say, tea, we really cannot be sure how any particular individual will behave. We may be dealing with an individual who hates tea and whose greatest pleasure in life is preparing and drinking espresso. Faced with anything less than a mammoth increase in the relative price of coffee, this individual's coffee consumption would probably remain unchanged.

This does not invalidate our previous discussion of the demand curve for coffee. Many people do reduce their consumption of coffee relative to its price increases, and few, if any, coffee drinkers will increase their consumption. Therefore, if we are interested in how the total demand for coffee will be affected by higher coffee prices, we will not be misled with a downward-sloping demand curve, even though we may be ignoring the idiosyncracies of individual consumers.

Obtaining the total or market demand curve from individual demand curves is conceptually easy. At any given price, the **market demand curve** for a good indicates the total amount of the good that all consumers collectively desire at a given time. For example, let's assume that there are only three consumers of coffee and that at $1 per pound the first wishes to consume 5 pounds of coffee per year, the second wishes to consume 4 pounds per year, and the third wishes to consume 3 pounds per year. In this case, the market demand curve would indicate a desired rate of coffee consumption of 12 pounds per year when the price is $1 per pound. Of course, to obtain points on the market demand curve for other prices, the desired consumption rates for our three consumers would have to be totaled at these prices.

Graphically, this means that the market demand curve for a product is obtained by horizontally summing the individual demand curves. This is illustrated in Figure 2–4, where demand curve D_1D_1 represents the demand for cof-

Figure 2–4
Market Demand as Horizontal Summation
of Individual Demands

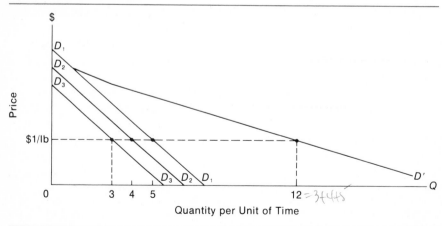

fee of the consumer who desires 5 pounds per year when the price is $1 per pound, D_2D_2 represents the demand of the consumer who desires 4 pounds per year at that price, and D_3D_3 represents the demand of the consumer who desires only 3 pounds per year at $1 per pound. The market demand in this case is given by demand curve D_1D', which is obtained by totaling the individually desired yearly coffee consumptions at each price. As we can see in Figure 2–4, market demand will be 12 pounds of coffee per year when the price is $1 per pound.

Supply   2–3

We now turn our attention to the other component of demand and supply analysis and discuss the considerations that are necessary to determine the rate at which goods will be supplied. As is true of demand, many variables are important here.

Obviously, the price of a good is an important consideration. A firm, in trying to operate as profitably as possible, will base supply decisions on comparisons between production costs and sales revenues. Normally, the cost of producing an additional unit of a good will increase as the firm attempts to produce at a faster and faster rate.[3] If this is the case, we can expect firms to be willing to supply commodities at slower rates at lower prices than at higher prices.

Such factors as the prices of other goods, the prices of productive inputs, and the available technology also influence a firm's supply decisions. However, since supply curves, like demand curves, are drawn in two dimensions, only two variables are graphed. Traditionally, the two variables represented on a **supply curve** are the price of the good and the rate at which it is supplied. For a given supply curve, all other relevant considerations are held constant. Thus, a firm's supply curve for a good shows the rate at which the firm will supply the good at each price, assuming everything else remains constant.

A supply curve, denoted by SS, is drawn in Figure 2–5. The vertical axis measures the price per unit of the good, and the horizontal axis measures the quantity of the good the firm supplies per unit of time. The upward slope of the curve reflects the fact that greater quantities will be produced at higher prices. An increase in the price from P_1 to P_2, for example, will result in an increase in the rate of supply from Q_1 to Q_2 per unit of time. This change in the rate of supply is the result of a move along a given supply curve; it is *not* a change in supply. It is just as important to make this distinction when dealing with supply curves as it is with demand curves. A change in supply is the result of a shift in the *entire* supply curve. Such a shift is caused by a change in something other than the good's price that has an impact on the supply decision.

---

[3]Actually, this is true only beyond some critical rate of production. Before this rate is reached, the cost of an additional unit of production may decline as the production rate increases. But as we will see in Chapter 8, only that range of production rates where this cost is increasing is relevant to the firm's supply.

As we mentioned earlier, the prices of other goods can also affect the supply of a particular good. For example, if we want to know the rate at which beef liver will be supplied to the market, it will be helpful to know the price of T-bone steaks. Why? Because if there is a strong consumer demand for T-bone steaks and their price is high, the rate at which beef liver is supplied will increase. The reason is that the higher price of T-bones will encourage meat suppliers to increase their production of cattle. And this cannot be done without increasing the production of beef liver at the same time. By similar reasoning, the prices of hamburger, New York steaks, and cowhide will have an impact on the supply of beef liver.

Curve *SS* in Figure 2–6 represents the supply of beef liver when all factors affecting supply other than the price of beef liver are assumed to be constant. Now if we consider an increase in the price of T-bone steaks, there will be a change in supply, which is shown in Figure 2–6 as a shift in the supply curve from *SS* to *S'S'*. We can see that the rate at which beef liver will be supplied is now greater at all beef-liver prices. Note that an increase in T-bone prices causes an *increase* in the supply of its *production complements*, one of which is beef liver.

We might also want to consider goods that are *production substitutes*. For a farmer with only so much acreage, wheat and barley are production substitutes. The more land he devotes to wheat, the less land he will have available for barley, and *vice versa*. For an oil refinery, gasoline and heating oil are production substitutes. Crude oil that is refined into gasoline cannot be refined into heating oil, and *vice versa*. For obvious reasons, an increase in the price of a good with production substitutes will reduce the supply of those substitute goods.

Supply curves also will shift in response to changes in the price of productive inputs and in the state of technology. If the price of productive inputs

Figure 2–5
Supply Curve

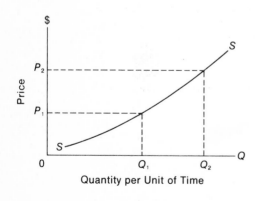

Figure 2–6
Change in Supply of Beef Liver

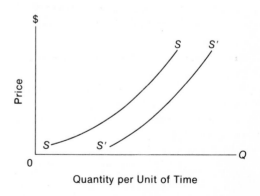

increases, the supply curve for goods whose production requires these inputs will shift to the left. The higher the input prices and therefore the cost of production, the higher the product's price must be to entice a firm to supply it at a given rate. Improvements in production technology also have an impact on the supply curve of a product. Since improvements reduce the cost of producing a product, they increase the supply of that product. We could cite many examples. Technological improvements in recent years have increased the supply of color TVs, electronic computers, self-processing cameras, pocket calculators, and digital wristwatches. In the case of these and many other goods, technological advances have increased the rate at which firms will supply them at all relevant price levels.

Most of our comments on supply apply whether we are talking about the supply of an individual firm or the market supply curve. The **market supply curve** for a good indicates the total amount of the good that all firms collectively will be willing to provide at a given price. However, obtaining the market supply curve for a good from the supply curve of an individual firm is not always a straightforward procedure. Our first impulse is to simply sum the individual supply curves horizontally to obtain the market supply curve—an analogous procedure to the one used to derive the market demand curve from individual demand curves. However, this may not lead to the correct result.

We must always remember that the supply curve for an individual firm shows how it will increase its rate of supply in response to a price increase if all other factors remain constant. So in dealing with only one firm, it is reasonable to look at the firm's supply response to a change in its product price, assuming all other things to be constant. The actions of *one* firm are not likely to have much impact on these other factors, but when we consider the market supply curve, the actions of *all* firms in an industry must be taken into account. And when an entire industry is moving in the same direction in response to a change in its product price, we cannot expect all other things to remain constant.

For example, if one soybean farmer decides to increase production in response to higher soybean prices by acquiring more land and using fertilizer more intensively, this will not have any measurable effect on the price of farm land or fertilizer. The farmer's individual supply response alone will leave everything else unchanged. However, if all soybean farmers expand their output and increase their demand for land and fertilizer in reaction to higher soybean prices, the prices of these productive inputs may rise. And when these prices do not remain constant, the supply curves of individual farmers shift from their original position. In this case, we would obtain misleading results if we determined the market supply curve by horizontally summing the individual supply curves that were appropriate only for lower land and fertilizer prices.

This discussion can be easily clarified with the aid of a graph. The supply curve SS in Figure 2-7 represents the production of a single soybean farmer when fertilizer and land prices are at their initial levels. This supply curve shows the different quantities the farmer will supply per unit of time at different soybean prices at these initial prices for fertilizer and land. With soybean prices at P_1, the farmer will supply Q_1 soybeans per unit of time. If the price of soybeans

Figure 2–7
Market Supply from Individual Supply Curves

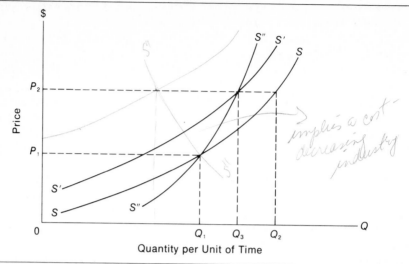

increases to P_2 and all other prices remain constant, our farmer will expand output to Q_2 soybeans per unit of time. Now if all farmers expand their production and therefore their use of inputs, input prices will rise and cause our farmer's supply curve to shift up and to the left. Curve $S'S'$ represents the farmer's supply curve at the higher input prices that will prevail after all farmers have adjusted to the new price P_2 of soybeans. With this supply curve, a price of P_2 will entice our farmer to supply a quantity of Q_3 soybeans per unit of time. Taking into consideration the response of all suppliers to a price change, we see that a price increase from P_1 to P_2 will cause the farmer's output to expand from Q_1 to Q_3 per unit of time, and the appropriate supply curve is shown as $S''S''$. If we could obtain a supply curve like $S''S''$ for all suppliers, we would sum these curves horizontally to obtain the market supply curve.[4]

When an entire industry expands its output, it is possible for certain economies from larger production to be realized. And these savings can shift the supply curve of individual firms down and to the right (increase supply). In this case, the graphic analysis is quite similar to that in Figure 2–7. However, with individual supply curves shifting out as industry output expands, the supply curve that accounts for this expansion will be less steeply sloped than the supply curves that assume all else is constant.

---

[4]Supply curve $S'S'$ could have been drawn far enough above supply curve SS in Figure 2–7 to make $S''S''$ backward bending (negatively sloped). This was not done for a very good reason, however. The reader should be able to explain why such a construction would be contradictory. Chapter 8 contains additional discussion of the difference between a firm's individual supply curve and the market supply curve. The difference between short-run supply curves (the type we are discussing now) and long-run supply curves will also be analyzed in Chapter 8.

Equilibrium   2–4

The demand curve for a good tells us the rate at which consumers are willing to consume that good at different prices. The lower the price, the greater the desired rate of consumption. The supply curve for a good provides us with information about the rate at which producers are willing to supply the good at different prices. The higher the price, the greater the desired rate of supply.

The market for a good is said to be in **equilibrium** when all consumers are able to purchase the good at their desired rate and all suppliers are able to sell the good at their desired rate. Only under these conditions are all participants in the market able to behave in accordance with their plans; no one has any motivation to alter their market behavior.

Price and Quantity Equilibrium

To obtain a market equilibrium, a particular price must exist for the good. Only when the price of the good is such that the desired rate of consumption is equal to the desired rate of supply can the market for that good be in equilibrium. This is illustrated in Figure 2–8, which shows both the demand curve DD and the supply curve SS on the same graph. Only at price $\bar{P}$ will the rate at which consumers wish to consume the good $\bar{Q}$ be equal to the rate at which suppliers are willing to sell the good, also $\bar{Q}$. Price $\bar{P}$ and quantity rate $\bar{Q}$ are referred to as the **equilibrium price** and the **equilibrium quantity,** respectively, and are determined by the point of intersection of the demand and supply curves.[5]

It is very important to recognize that the equilibrium price accomplishes something truly remarkable by providing all the information that millions of people need to make individual consumption and production decisions that are mutually compatible. When any one individual decides how much of a particular product to consume, this decision can be successfully implemented only if it is consistent with the consumption and supply decisions that are being made by countless other individuals. These people live in different countries, speak different languages, and have no contact or communication with most of the consumers with whom they must coordinate their decisions, yet they successfully carry out their economic plans regarding thousands of products every day. The explanation for this amazing accomplishment is that equilibrium prices communicate all the information people need to enable them to coordinate their decisions with one another, and actual market prices are generally close to equilibrium prices.

If the price of a product is not equal to the equilibrium price, forces will come into play to restore equilibrium. If, for example, the price of a good is less than $\bar{P}$ in Figure 2–8 (say, P_1), the rate at which consumers wish to consume the

---

[5]Letting $D(P)$ represent demand as a downward-sloping function of price P and $S(P)$ represent supply as an upward-sloping function of price, the mathematical condition for equilibrium is given by $D(P) = S(P)$. Given the slopes of these two functions, there is only one P that will satisfy this condition.

Figure 2–8
Equilibrium Price and Quantity

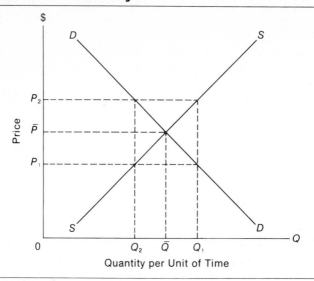

Quantity per Unit of Time

good Q_1 will exceed the rate at which suppliers are willing to provide the good Q_2. Consumers will be frustrated in their attempts to act on their consumption plans because they will have to consume at a rate $Q_1 - Q_2$ less than they had planned. On the other hand, if the price is greater than $\bar{P}$ (say, P_2 in Figure 2–8), the rate at which suppliers are willing to provide the good Q_1 will exceed the desired consumption rate Q_2. In this case, the suppliers will be frustrated because they will want to sell at a rate $Q_1 - Q_2$ greater than they will be able to. In both of these situations, we say that the market is in **disequilibrium.**

When a market is in disequilibrium, the frustrations of consumers or suppliers lead to reactions that usually push price and quantity back toward their equilibrium values. At price P_1 in Figure 2–8, for example, consumers will only be able to obtain the good at rate Q_2, even though they would like to consume the good at rate Q_1. The height of the demand curve at Q_2 shows how much some consumers would be willing to pay to increase their consumption rate by one unit when only Q_2 is available. Clearly, some consumers would be willing to pay more than P_1 to achieve additional consumption rather than to forgo that consumption. These consumers will offer suppliers more than P_1, hoping to receive a greater allocation of the good. Suppliers will respond to the higher price some consumers are willing to pay by increasing the rate at which the good is supplied. As this occurs, consumers will be able to consume more of the good, but as long as the price remains below $\bar{P}$, consumers will be frustrated in their efforts to consume at their desired rate and will be willing to pay more than the prevailing price to increase their consumption. This willingness will continue to push the price up until it reaches $\bar{P}$, the point at which the desired consumption rate is matched by the desired supply rate.

When the price of the good is above the equilibrium price, we can also expect market responses to push the price back toward equilibrium. Assume that the price is P_2 in Figure 2–8. At that price, suppliers will want to sell at the rate Q_1 but will find that sales are only at the rate Q_2. The supply curve indicates that at this rate of supply, producers will be willing to increase the supply rate another unit for any price greater than P_1. Therefore, producers will be willing to lower their price below P_2 in an effort to increase the rate of sales. This tendency for suppliers to lower their price will continue as long as the price is above the equilibrium price $\bar{P}$ and suppliers cannot sell as much of the good as they would like.

Changes in Equilibrium

Although forces may be at work to push market prices toward their equilibrium values, this does not necessarily mean that a price will ever reach equilibrium. For a given demand or supply curve, the only relevant variable that is not held constant is the price of the good. At least some of the many variables that influence demand and supply decisions and that are held constant along any given curve will surely change over any interval of time. When these variables do change, the effect is to shift demand and supply curves. This means that a change in the economic environment causes the desired consumption and the desired supply to change at every price. So while at any moment in time market forces are exerting pressure on price to move toward one equilibrium position, shifts in the demand or supply curves can create a new equilibrium position. It is quite possible that the market price will be chasing a moving target—an equilibrium position that does not stay in one place long enough to be realized.

Despite the fact that market equilibriums may only rarely be reached and maintained for any length of time, it will be useful in our analysis to consider equilibrium positions as important bench marks toward which economic forces tend to move. This is not unlike the value of a concept like sea level—a position that the sea achieves only occasionally and briefly, but toward which it tends to gravitate. In fact, many economic analyses are concerned with comparing equilibrium positions before and after changes in economic conditions, with little emphasis on the path of adjustment from one equilibrium position to the next. As pointed out in Chapter 1, this is known as *comparative static analysis.* The word "static" indicates a concern with stationary equilibrium points rather than the dynamic adjustments between these points.

A simple example of comparative static analysis is provided if we examine what happens to the price–quantity equilibrium we have been discussing when changes occur that shift the demand and supply curves. In Figure 2–9, the demand curve DD and the supply curve SS establish the price–quantity market equilibrium $(\bar{P}, \bar{Q})$. If either of these curves shifts for any reason, a new equilibrium position is established. For example, let's assume that due to increasing input costs the supply curve for the good shifts to the new supply curve $S'S'$. The new equilibrium shows a higher price P_1 and a lower rate of demand and supply Q_1, compared with the initial equilibrium position.

Despite the fact that this is a straightforward analysis, it can easily be misinterpreted as contradictory to demand and supply analysis. To the casual observer, we may seem to have described a situation in which the price of a good increases at a time when consumers are purchasing less of the good. This may appear strange to people who have been told that when there is a decrease in demand, price also declines, and too often they conclude that demand and supply analysis is not applicable to the particular situation being observed. The problem, however, is the failure to distinguish between *a decrease in the amount demanded* (a movement along the demand curve) and *a decrease in demand* (a shift in the demand curve). There *has not been a decrease in demand* in the situation we described; the demand curve has *not* shifted. Instead, supply has decreased, causing a disequilibrium at the original price, $\bar{P}$; given the lower supply curve, the desired rate of demand exceeds the desired rate of supply. The response to this is an increase in price from $\bar{P}$ to P_1, which reduces the desired consumption rate from $\bar{Q}$ to Q_1 due to a movement along the demand curve DD.

If there is an increase in demand and the supply curve remains constant, there will be an increase in the rate of supply. This is demonstrated in Figure 2–10, where the initial demand curve DD and the supply curve SS establish the equilibrium $(\bar{P}, \bar{Q})$. If the demand curve for the good shifts to the right due to changing consumer preferences, increased income, or a change in the prices of related goods, then a new equilibrium will be established. With the increased demand given by demand curve $D'D'$ in Figure 2–10, this new equilibrium results in both an increased price P_1 and an increased demand and supply rate Q_1. Here, the increase in demand has caused a disequilibrium at the initial price $\bar{P}$. As before, the desired consumption rate is greater than the desired supply rate, and the price tends upward as consumers offer to pay

Figure 2–9
Equilibrium with a Change in Supply

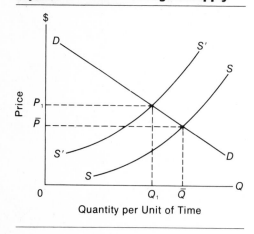

Figure 2–10
Equilibrium with a Change in Demand

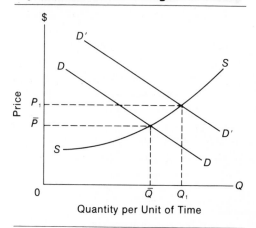

more for the good to increase their rate of consumption. The increasing price causes a movement up the supply curve until the new equilibrium is established.

Notice that this situation can also appear confusing to the casual observer who does not distinguish between a change in supply and a change in the rate of supply. We know that an increase in supply should reduce price, but in this case price may appear to be increasing as supply increases. Of course, what Figure 2–10 shows is not an increase in supply, but an increase in the rate of supply in response to an increase in demand.

The effect on equilibrium of an increase in supply or a decrease in demand can also easily be determined by using demand and supply diagrams, although we will not cite specific cases to demonstrate these effects here.

Application: Outlawing High Prices

We have seen that market prices tend to move toward equilibrium positions that equate the quantity producers are willing to supply with the quantity consumers are willing to purchase. When market prices are in equilibrium, consumers are able to purchase as much of each good as they want and suppliers are able to sell as much of each good as they want. However, this does not mean that there will be great bursts of public enthusiasm in support of market prices. Most people feel that the prices of the goods they buy are too high and that the prices of the goods they sell are too low. In response to public pressure, the political process may determine that the market price for a particular good is becoming too high and may establish a legal price ceiling for the good. In other cases, public opinion may be that a particular good will probably be priced too low by market forces, and some legal price floor for the good may be established. In this application, we will look at the implications of imposing a legal ceiling on a price that is below the market equilibrium price.[6]

Price Ceilings: Shortages, Frustration, and Waste

Figure 2–11 depicts the demand and supply curves for a good. To be specific, let's assume that the product is electronic calculators. For demand curve DD and supply curve SS, the equilibrium price and quantity are P_1 and Q_1, respectively. Now suppose that a **price ceiling** is imposed at $\bar{P}$, making it illegal to buy or sell electronic calculators for more than this price. Consumers can be expected to prefer this controlled price to the higher equilibrium price P_1, because they will now have to sacrifice lesser amounts of other desirable goods to obtain a calculator. Thus, more people will want to purchase calculators now

---

[6]We will not discuss the case of a floor below which a price cannot legally fall. The reader is encouraged to consider this case independently, using the analysis presented in this section as a guide. The effects of a minimum wage—which is a legal **price floor** below which a price cannot fall—will be discussed in Chapter 11.

Figure 2–11
Price Ceiling and a Shortage of Calculators

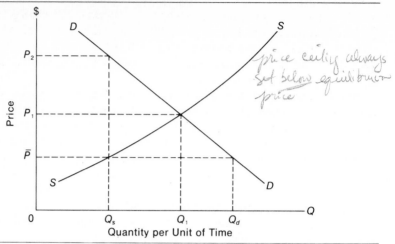

(handwritten note on figure: price ceiling always set below equilibrium price)

than they did before the price was controlled. This situation is represented in Figure 2–11, which shows consumers desiring to purchase Q_d calculators at price $\bar{P}$.

While consumers are planning to expand their consumption of calculators, producers will be reassessing their production plans in response to the price ceiling. At the lower price $\bar{P}$, producers will find that the return from the use of their limited resources in calculator production is declining relative to the return these resources would generate if employed elsewhere. Not surprisingly, they will reallocate some of their resources in calculator production to other areas where they will be of greater value. This motivation lies behind the positive slope of supply curves and explains why the quantity of calculators that producers are willing to supply declines from Q_1 to Q_s as the price of calculators decreases from P_1 to $\bar{P}$, as shown in Figure 2–11.

Obviously, consumer and producer responses to the price ceiling are incompatible: Consumers now wish to purchase more calculators than producers are willing to supply. The result is a **shortage** of calculators, and the magnitude of this shortage is given by the difference Q_d–Q_s in Figure 2–11. A shortage results in two related phenomena – frustrated consumers and an inappropriate response to resource scarcity.[7] The reason for consumer frustration is obvious. Because more calculators are being demanded than supplied,

---

[7]Although the terms "shortage" and "scarcity" are commonly viewed as synonymous, they have two distinct meanings in the lexicon of the economist. By *scarcity* we mean that resource availability and technological knowledge are insufficient to allow us to produce all we are capable of enjoying. As we discussed in Chapter 1, scarcity is an inevitable problem that all economies must face. Scarcity dictates that any increase in the consumption of one good must cause a decrease in the consumption of other goods. Obviously, the quantity of a good that we are willing to consume depends on how much

many consumers will not be able to purchase as many calculators as they would like to have.

But to understand why this represents an inappropriate response to resource scarcity, we need to refer back to Figure 2–11. Notice that when Q_s calculators are being supplied, as is the case when the price ceiling is in effect, the demand curve DD indicates that some consumers will be willing to pay P_2 for an additional calculator rather than be denied. The amount P_2 then represents the value of an additional calculator. On the other hand, at Q_s, the cost of producing an additional calculator in terms of the value of sacrificed alternatives is represented by $\bar{P}$, the height of the supply curve SS at Q_s. This explains why the price $\bar{P}$ motivates calculator production to move up to Q_s, but no further. Below Q_s, the supply curve indicates that producing another calculator would require an alternative sacrifice worth less than $\bar{P}$. Obviously, the fact that producers can sell calculators for $\bar{P}$ will motivate them to expand calculator production rather than to produce alternative goods. Manufacturers will not expand calculator production beyond Q_s, however, because the supply curve indicates that producing an additional calculator beyond Q_s would require the sacrifice of the production of alternatives worth more than $\bar{P}$. In Chapter 8, we will devote more attention to the relationship between cost and supply.

Comparing the value of an additional calculator with the cost of producing one clearly suggests that it is desirable to expand production beyond Q_s. Producing more calculators and fewer alternative goods will reallocate productive resources from lower-valued employments to a higher-valued employment—the type of reallocation that is desirable in our world of scarcity. Failure to make this reallocation is a waste of our scarce resources. The price ceiling, by transmitting the erroneous information to suppliers that an additional electronic calculator is only valued at $\bar{P}$, discourages a desirable shift in resource use and is therefore wasteful.

In the absence of a price ceiling, consumer frustration will be moderated and desirable resource allocation will be encouraged as the rising price of calculators motivates additional production and this production is rationed to the consumers who are willing to pay the highest price. This procedure is known as **price rationing.**

"Legal" Responses to Price Ceilings

However, we are interested in adjustments to the shortage that must be made when the ceiling does not permit buyers and sellers to legally agree to transactions at a higher price than $\bar{P}$. In the absence of price rationing, some other means of rationing must be employed. There are several forms of nonprice rationing.

---

our consumption costs in terms of forgone alternative consumption, or the price of the good relative to other prices. If the price of a good causes desired consumption to exceed available quantity, there will be a shortage of the good. But note that this shortage is not inevitable; it depends entirely on the good's relative price. By increasing this relative price sufficiently, the shortage can quickly be transformed into a *surplus*, where the available quantity exceeds the quantity consumers are willing to purchase.

A common method of nonprice rationing is to allocate goods on a **first-come, first-served basis.** This means that the consumers who are willing to get up the earliest or wait in line the longest will be able to purchase the product at the controlled price. Long lines and long waits are quite common when price controls are instituted. In the Soviet Union, where most prices are controlled by the State, the average shopper spends about 14 hours a week waiting in line.[8] In the United States, the most dramatic recent examples of this type of rationing occurred during 1973–1974 and the summer of 1979 when the price rationing of gasoline was outlawed by price controls, and it was not uncommon for motorists to wait in line for hours for the privilege of buying ten gallons of gas.

The cost of obtaining a product under these circumstances is obviously higher than the controlled price would indicate. The cost also must be measured in terms of the alternative activities that consumers sacrificed to wait in line. The nonprice cost can be significant, because consumers will be willing to wait in line long enough to raise the total cost of obtaining the good up to the price they would have been willing to pay for the good without the controls (P_2 in Figure 2–11). It is worth noting that this price is higher than the price they would have had to pay without the controls (P_1 in Figure 2–11).

When a price ceiling is enforced, another substitute for price rationing is rationing on the basis of **favoritism** and **discrimination.** In general, the suppliers of a price-controlled good will find that more consumers wish to purchase the good than can be satisfied. Since none of these consumers can pay more than the price ceiling, it will not cost suppliers anything to ensure that the people they favor or find more acceptable obtain as much of the good as they like, while those they consider less desirable do without. Obviously, people who are in a position to return favors, who are attractive and person-

Example 2–2

The High Cost of Price-Controlled Gas

The gas shortages experienced during the summer of 1979 in the United States provide an example of the high nonprice cost of acquiring price-controlled goods. On the basis of Washington, D.C.'s experience during the 1979 gas shortage, economists at the U.S. Department of Energy estimated that nationwide gas lines during that summer cost consumers about $200 million per month in lost time.

The nonprice cost of gasoline when its price is controlled is not only paid in the form of lost time. Department of Energy economists also estimated that a nationwide extension of the shortage would result in the monthly waste of 100 million gallons of gas from idling and moving forward in gas lines.

Note: These figures were reported in the *Roanoke Times and World News* (July 5, 1979), p. A12.

---

[8]This figure is obtained from Hedrick Smith, *The Russians* (New York: Ballantine Books, 1977), p. 83.

able, who have specific ethnic or religious backgrounds, and so on, will be in a better position to compete for the price-controlled good than those who are viewed less favorably by suppliers. Not that this type of favoritism and discrimination does not occur with price rationing. There is no doubt that it does. But under price rationing, the supplier can only discriminate against some consumers by reducing sales and passing up some opportunities to sell to those who are willing to pay the most. In other words, there is a cost associated with discrimination under price rationing. But imposing a price ceiling eliminates this cost, since consumers who are discriminated against cannot pay any more for a good than those who are not. Therefore, our analysis indicates that imposing a price ceiling at less than the equilibrium price may lead to an increase in discriminatory behavior. Again, gasoline price-controls provide an example. There was ample evidence during the periods of shortage that gas station operators were filling the tanks of their friends and family after normal hours without making them wait. This became so blatant during the 1973–1974 shortage that the Federal Energy Administration issued an order prohibiting this type of discrimination, but it was soon rescinded because it could not be enforced.

Our analysis also indicates that a price ceiling may lead to reduced product quality. Although suppliers will not be able to benefit from the excess demand for their product by increasing their prices, they can cut costs by producing lower-quality goods. Suppliers will be motivated to reduce quality as long as they can sell all they desire at the controlled price.

This situation can be illustrated graphically if we recognize that a decrease in quality will *increase supply* by making the product cheaper to produce and will *decrease demand* by making the product less attractive to consumers. In Figure 2–12, the original demand and supply curves are given by DD and SS, and P_1 and Q_1 are the price and quantity equilibrium. If a pricing ceiling $\bar{P}$ is imposed, a shortage equal to the excess demand $Q_d - Q_s$ will be created. To illustrate, let's assume that the only rationing response to this excess demand is a reduction in product quality. Quality will be reduced as long as the quantity demanded at price $\bar{P}$ exceeds the amount suppliers are willing to produce. In Figure 2–12, the end result of this quality reduction is represented as an increase in supply from SS to S'S' and a reduction in demand from DD to D'D'. Now $\bar{P}$ is the equilibrium price, and the equilibrium quantity remains unchanged at Q_1. Although this process will always establish the equilibrium price at $\bar{P}$, the equilibrium quantity may increase or decrease, depending on the relative magnitudes of the shifts in demand and supply that result from the quality reduction.

Again, the U.S. gas shortage during 1979 provides a good example of quality reduction in response to a price control. As gas lines started forming in the spring and summer of 1979, there was an increase in the incidence of watered gasoline. Water in gasoline not only impairs automotive performance but eventually damages the engine and rusts the gas tank. Garages did a booming business during this period repairing rusted gas tanks and damaged engines. During the shortage, it was also reported that fuel oil was being sold as diesel fuel.[9]

---

[9]Reported in *The Wall Street Journal* (August 8, 1979), pp. 1, 37.

Figure 2-12
Diminishing Quality Induced by Price Ceiling

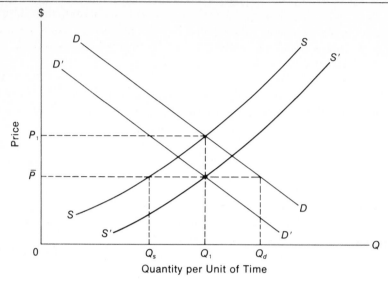

Quantity per Unit of Time

Another common response to a price ceiling is an increase in **tie-in sales,** which permit suppliers to take advantage of the excess demand caused by the ceiling. A tie-in sale ties the purchase of the price-controlled good to the sale of another good that is invariably overpriced. Unable to charge anxious buyers of the price-controlled product a high price, suppliers find it profitable to ration the product to those who will pay the most for another product. An interesting example of this response to price controls occurred during the 1971–1973 price-control program in the United States. At one point during this period, toilets were in short supply, and manufacturers were not able to increase the price of toilets legally–although many contractors would have been happy to pay more than the ceiling price to meet completion dates on houses. As a result of this excess demand, one supplier of bathroom fixtures was able to unload his entire inventory of rubber bathtubs–a product for which he previously had found lit-tle demand–by requiring contractors who wanted to buy toilets to purchase a rubber bathtub as well.

Price Ceilings and the Black Market

So far, we have considered responses to a legal price ceiling that operate within the letter, if not the spirit, of the law. Not all responses to price controls are lim-ited by legalities, however. Inevitably, price controls are accompanied by wide-spread violations of the law, as buyers and sellers agree on illegally high prices and secret exchanges, which are referred to as **black-market transactions.** These transactions are widespread, because they benefit both buyers and sellers. During a shortage caused by a price ceiling, consumers would rather pay an illegally high price for a good than do without it, and sympathetic sellers can always be found to accommodate them. Both parties to the "crime" realize a mutual advantage, which explains why attempts to enforce price controls have always been frustrating.

Even during World War II when the wartime price-control program received widespread patriotic support, countless violations occurred, despite the fact that the government used approximately 400,000 paid and volunteer price watchers.

Rent Controls

In general, when a price ceiling is imposed, some of the price-controlled product will be allocated on a first-come, first-served basis, some will be distributed according to favoritism, some will be rationed through reduced quality or tie-in sales, and some will be sold on the black market. Experiences with **rent**

Example 2-3

Gasoline and the Black Market

The Office of Price Administration (OPA), which was responsible for administering price controls during World War II, estimated that 2,500,000 gallons of gasoline per day were sold on the black market throughout that war. This was accomplished by diverting gas-rationing coupons, which were required to acquire gas legally, into the black market. The OPA had issued the coupons in an attempt to allocate gasoline efficiently and fairly, but gasoline consumers wanted more coupons than they received and were willing to pay for them.

According to Joseph Valachi, in testimony before the U.S. Senate, a major supplier of extra coupons was the Cosa Nostra (popularly known as the Mafia). Valachi claims that this organization found it profitable to acquire coupons—either by burglarizing OPA offices or, in many cases, by directly purchasing them from OPA employees—and then sell them to garage and gas station owners who used the coupons to cover the gas they had sold at illegally high prices to consumers without coupons. From mid-1942 to 1945, Valachi personally made about $200,000 from the sale of gas-rationing coupons. And Valachi described himself as a relatively minor participant in this racket.

Note: For more detailed information, see Peter Maas, *The Valachi Papers* (New York: G.P. Putnam's Sons, 1968), pp. 185–90.

controls—price ceilings placed on rents—provide interesting illustrations of all these responses to a price ceiling.

Although many examples of rent controls could be chosen, a particularly well-documented case occurred in Stockholm, Sweden, where "temporary" rent controls were established in 1942. Because these controls created a shortage of housing, an official queue was established to ration available living space on a first-come, first-served basis. Some indication of the extent of the housing shortage that developed is provided by the fact that by 1963, with the temporary controls still in force, 40% of Stockholm's population, or 315,000 people, were registered in the official housing queue.[10]

As we would expect, however, individuals were able to compete for housing in other ways than patiently waiting in the queue. A survey of newlyweds fortunate enough to have their own housing indicated that only 29% had acquired their housing through the official queue. The remaining 71% owed their housing to the influence of family, friends, employers, or other connections, which resulted in favored treatment. Landlords also favored tenants who were willing to rent furniture at extremely high prices to obtain a rent-controlled apartment. Or renters could dispense with tie-in sales of this type by agreeing to pay more for the apartment than the law permitted the landlord to charge. There was also widespread evidence that landlords reduced maintenance and allowed the quality of their apartments to decline in response to the excess demand. This deterioration in housing occasionally reached its logical conclusion, as owners of rent-controlled housing and apartments demolished them to construct buildings that were not subject to rent controls.

It is interesting to question why temporary rent controls persist much longer than intended. We can gain some insight into one reason why it is difficult to discard a price control once it has been imposed by again examining the laws of demand and supply.

Until now, we have always drawn supply curves that indicate an increased willingness to supply a good as price increases. This is certainly the typical case, but it assumes that some time is provided for adjustment. An increase or decrease in the quantity supplied cannot occur instantaneously, and this is particularly true in the case of housing. So if we look at the supply curve for housing at a given point in time, it will be a vertical line at the existing quantity available. In Figure 2–13, this is shown as the vertical line above Q^*. With the demand curve for housing given by DD, the equilibrium price and quantity are P_1 and Q^*, respectively.

Now let's assume that a rent ceiling of $\bar{P}$ is imposed.[11] This will not have any immediate effect on the quantity supplied, because the existing stock of housing will remain at Q^*. We would expect a shortage to materialize quickly, how-

---

[10] The last remnants of rent controls in Sweden were finally removed in 1975. See F.A. Hayek et.al., *Rent Controls: A Popular Paradox* (Vancouver: The Frazier Institute, 1975).
[11] Obviously, in an actual rent-control situation, different ceilings would be imposed on different apartments and houses, depending on size, quality, location, and other factors. Attempting to take this complication into consideration would serve no purpose, however, given the point we wish to make.

Figure 2–13
Rent Controls and an Increasing Housing Shortage

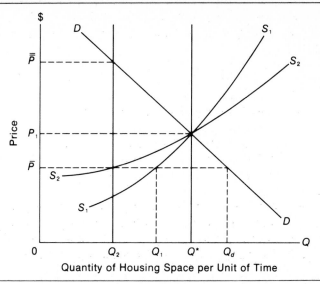

ever, as consumers should respond rapidly to the lower price by desiring additional housing space. This shortage is shown in Figure 2–13 as $Q_d - Q^*$. As the rent ceiling continues, owners of housing will have time to respond and will reduce the quantity supplied, because the return on housing will now be less relative to the return on other employments of their resources. Some people who are renting out their basements will decide that they would rather have the additional living space. Some apartment owners will convert their buildings into office space or sell them as condominiums. We can also expect owners of some older dwellings to stop maintaining them or possibly to demolish them. This means that, allowing some time for adjustment, the supply curve will be given by $S_1 S_1$ in Figure 2–13 and the quantity of housing supplied at $\bar{P}$ will be Q_1. Let even more time pass and the relevant supply curve will be $S_2 S_2$ and only Q_2 units of housing will be supplied.

Assuming that enough time has elapsed to result in the supply curve $S_2 S_2$, what would be the result from removing the rent ceiling? With Q_2 units of housing being supplied, the immediate supply curve is given in Figure 2–13 by the vertical line above Q_2. Therefore, the effect of decontrol would be an increase in rents to $\bar{\bar{P}}$, a much higher price than would have existed if controls had never been imposed. The threat of these very high rents will make it politically unpopular to remove the price ceiling. It should be noted that if the ceiling were removed, rents would eventually begin to decline below $\bar{\bar{P}}$ and would finally reach P_1 once housing suppliers had time to respond to the higher rents. But these adjustments could, and probably would, take years and would tend to be given little weight compared with the short-term effect of extremely high rents in the political decision-making process. Thus, it is possible that the longer a control is in effect, the greater the distortions and shortages it will create and the more difficult its removal.

Application: Exposing the Speculator

Speculators are generally considered to be rather unsavory characters who lack most of the virtues required to be held in high social esteem. **Speculators** do not buy commodities to meet their own consumption needs; instead, they hope to hold a commodity off the market and out of the hands of current consumers until it can be sold at a higher price in the future. Not only are speculators gamblers who risk their money on an outcome that is beyond their control, but their gamble can only pay off if society suffers from high prices for important commodities in the future. Not only do speculators reduce current supplies of valuable commodities, but they do so in the hope that these supplies will be even more restricted in the future.

But although it is unlikely that many speculators are burdened with throbbing social consciences, their self-serving motivations may perform a useful social function. In their efforts to buy commodities when their prices are relatively low and to sell them at higher prices in the future, speculators ensure that important commodities are continuously available to us over time. In fact, speculators could be characterized as farsighted individuals who are willing to take current personal risks to provide for the future well-being of society.

The implications of demand and supply analysis permit us to view speculators in such a favorable light. We will now consider a situation that permits us to use demand and supply curves to inspect the effect of speculation.

Speculation in Wheat

Agricultural crops are harvested every year, making large amounts of most crops immediately available, but no additional supplies forthcoming until the next harvest. If the crop is perishable and can be stored only at extreme cost, it is either consumed rapidly or it spoils. However, many crops can be stored, always at a cost, which means that decisions must be made as to how much of a crop is to be consumed immediately and how much is to be saved for future consumption.

To provide a specific example, let's assume that our crop is wheat and that there are two harvests a year, one every six months. Figure 2−14(a) depicts the supply and consumption demand conditions over the first three months after a harvest. The demand curve D_cD_c shows the quantity of wheat that will be consumed over the three-month interval at different prices, and the supply curve SS indicates the quantity of wheat that is available from the harvest (between harvests, the quantity supplied is not affected by price). If we were not concerned about wheat supplies beyond the first three months, the price of wheat would be $\bar{P}_1$–the price that equates the quantity demanded for consumption

Figure 2–14
Feast and Famine Consumption Patterns

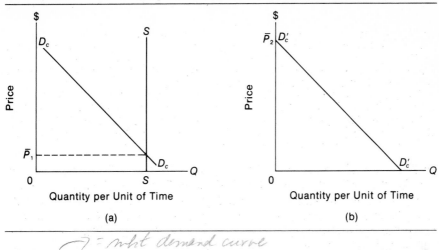

(handwritten note below figure) → = wht demand curve

with the entire harvest. If this were the case, however, then the situation over the entire interval between harvests would be represented by Figures 2–14(a) and 2–14(b). At a price of $\bar{P}_1$ during the first three months, the entire harvest would be consumed by the beginning of the second three-month period. No wheat would be available over the second three-month interval. With the demand curve over this interval, given in Figure 2–14(b) as $D_c'D_c'$, the price consumers would be willing to pay for the first bushel of wheat, if only they could get it, would be $\bar{P}_2$. Clearly, this is not a desirable pattern of wheat consumption. Satisfaction from a given quantity of wheat is not maximized by inundating consumers with it immediately after the harvest and then completing depriving them of it for a long period before the next harvest.

Such feast-and-famine consumption patterns, although undesirable, fortunately are not commonly observed because they present profitable opportunities for those who take the future into consideration. In the situation depicted in Figure 2–14, there is an opportunity to profit by purchasing wheat during the first interval at $\bar{P}_1$ per bushel, storing it until the second interval, and selling it at $\bar{P}_2$ per bushel. This would drive up the price and reduce consumption during the first interval and increase the supply and drive down the price during the second interval. As long as the price in the second interval exceeds the price in the first interval, profits can be realized by continuing to transfer wheat from the first to the second interval.[12] Only when the price is the same over both intervals will speculative buying and storage cease.

The end result of speculation is shown in Figure 2–15, where the demand

---

[12]This profit opportunity will actually be eliminated before the price in the second interval declines to the price in the first interval, due to the cost of storage and the interest cost of tying up capital in wheat rather than using it in an alternative employment. These complications will be temporarily ignored.

Figure 2-15
Demand and Supply with Speculation

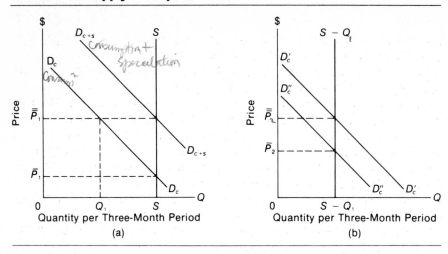

(a) Quantity per Three-Month Period

(b) Quantity per Three-Month Period

curves D_cD_c and $D_c'D_c'$ and the after-harvest supply curve SS are the same as those shown in Figure 2–14. Once demand derived from speculative activity is recognized, however, the total demand for wheat over the first interval exceeds the demand for consumption due to speculative demand. This consumption plus speculative demand is depicted in Figure 2–15(a) by the demand curve $D_{c+s}D_{c+s}$. The addition of speculative demand drives the price up from $\bar{P}_1$ (the price that would exist in the absence of speculation) to $\bar{\bar{P}}_1$. Consumers will respond to this higher price by reducing the quantity of wheat they consume over the first interval from S to Q_1. This allows $S - Q_1$ bushels of wheat to be stored and made available during the second interval. The supply curve for this interval is depicted by the vertical line over $S - Q_1$ in Figure 2–15(b). With the consumption demand curve over the second three-month interval given by $D_c'D_c'$, this supply will be entirely consumed just before the next harvest at the equilibrium price $\bar{\bar{P}}_2$, with $\bar{\bar{P}}_1 = \bar{\bar{P}}_2$.

The price of a good represents the value consumers place on an additional unit of the product, or the **marginal value** of the product. This means that our speculative solution allocates wheat over time in such a way that the value of another bushel is the same in the first interval as it is in the second. We can see that this allocation is desirable if we consider the improvements that can be made when this marginal value of wheat is greater in one interval than it is in another—say, $P_1 < P_2$. This means that another bushel of wheat is more valuable in the second interval than it is in the first, and therefore a net gain in total value can be realized by transferring a bushel of wheat from the first to the second interval. Likewise, if $P_1 > P_2$, a net gain is possible if an additional unit of wheat is consumed in the first interval at the expense of less consumption in the second interval. Only when the price of wheat is the same in both intervals—as it is in our speculative solution—have all opportunities to increase the value of the wheat through reallocation over time been exhausted.

Of course, speculative activity will not always lead to the ideal solution we obtained here. In our analysis, we had the advantage of knowing exactly what the demand curve over the second interval would be. A speculator in the market for wheat cannot be sure of this demand curve and will have to base a decision on uncertain information and estimation.[13] Obviously, mistakes may be made, and either too much or too little wheat may be carried over to the second interval. This lack of perfection, however, must be accepted, unless we know of another approach or arrangement that will improve the situation. With this in mind, some additional comments on speculation are in order.

There is no way to eliminate the uncertainty that surrounds the predictions we are forced to make about the future—or to avoid the consequences when our predictions are wrong. The most we can hope for is to motivate the decision makers to make their predictions as accurate as possible. In the case of commodity speculation, the existence of rewards (punishments) for successfully (unsuccessfully) anticipating future conditions guarantees that this motivation exists. The speculator who buys wheat at a low price and stores it for future sale at a higher price not only profits personally but also serves the useful social function of transferring an important commodity from a period where its marginal value is low to one where its marginal value is high. On the other hand, the speculator who does society a disservice by transferring wheat from a period where its marginal value is high to a period where its marginal value is low is punished by buying high and selling low. This reward and punishment structure encourages those who serve society with their predictive skills to continue to do so, but sends an unmistakable message to all others to apply their talents and resources elsewhere in the economy.

A speculator in the wheat market does not have to buy or take possession of wheat. Speculators commonly buy or sell a **futures contract** on a particular commodity. These contracts can be easily bought or sold in a number of organized markets. Major U.S. markets include the Chicago Board of Trade, the Chicago Mercantile Exchange, and the New York Coffee and Sugar Exchange, which deal in such commodities as soybeans, oats, corn, cotton, wheat, eggs, potatoes, pork, chicken, sugar, frozen orange-juice concentrate, coffee, cocoa, and pepper.

A typical futures contract will specify the commodity, the quantity, and the price on a future date at a particular location. For example, a futures contract may call for 50,000 bushels of No. 2 Red Wheat to be delivered in Chicago on November 9 of the current year at $3.50 a bushel. The $3.50 is the **futures price**. If you believe that No. 2 Red Wheat will be selling for *more than* $3.50 a bushel

---

[13]The demand curve for the second interval is not the only uncertain bit of information that is relevant to the speculator's decision. The size of the following harvest is just as important a factor and is probably harder to predict. If, for example, the next harvest is expected to be very small, ideal speculation would require some of the current supply to be carried over to the next harvest. For the purpose of exposition, however, we have ignored this possibility here and have assumed that it is desirable to consume all the current harvest before the next harvest.

in Chicago on November 9, you would buy this futures contract. When speculators buy such a contract, they take what is referred to as a **long position.** Taking a long position in this futures contract will allow you to purchase 50,000 bushels of wheat on November 9 in Chicago at $3.50 a bushel. If your expectation about the price is correct, you will be able to sell the wheat for more than $3.50 a bushel and pocket the difference. If you are wrong, you will sell the wheat for less than $3.50 a bushel and lose the difference. Few purchasers of futures contracts actually take possession of the product in question. Normally, the seller pays the purchaser the difference between the actual price on the specified date (referred to as the **spot price** on that date) and the futures price when the spot price is higher, and the purchaser pays the difference to the seller when the spot price is lower.

Note that even though purchasers of futures contracts do not physically take commodities off the market and make them available for consumption on the specified date, the effect is almost the same as if they had. If speculators become convinced that the November 9 price of wheat will be higher than the futures price, they will buy an increasing number of futures contracts on this wheat, which will drive up the November 9 futures price. Those who actually are in possession of the wheat are responsive to futures prices, and an increase in the November 9 futures price of wheat relative to today's spot price will motivate them to hold more wheat off the market until November 9. So if speculators who purchase futures contracts are correct in their future price predictions, they not only make some money themselves, but they make more wheat available at a time when, without their speculative activities, it would be relatively more scarce.

Assume, however, that you think the actions of speculators have driven the current price of wheat up too high. In other words, you believe that the price in the future (say, on November 9) will be lower than the November 9 futures price (the futures price expected by others). The difference between your price expectation and the price expectations of others is illustrated in Figure 2–15, using our two-interval example. Assume that the actions of other speculators have resulted in $S - Q_1$ bushels of wheat being taken off the market in the first interval to be held for sale in the second interval. This implies that in the collective judgment of these speculators, the future price will be $\bar{\bar{P}}_2$, so that the demand curve for the second interval will be $D_c'D_c'$. But *you* are convinced that the demand curve for the second interval will be $D_c''D_c''$ instead. If you are correct, the futures price for wheat $\bar{\bar{P}}_2$ is higher than the price that will actually materialize in the second interval $\bar{P}_2$, and too much wheat is currently being taken off the market.

Now let's assume that you act on your prediction that, say, on November 9 the price of No. 2 Red Wheat will be $3.00 a bushel rather than the futures price of $3.50. You sell a futures contract that allows you to sell, say, 50,000 bushels of this wheat on November 9 for $3.50 a bushel, but the contract obligates you to pay the November 9 spot price for it. This is referred to as taking a **short position** in wheat. If your price expectation is correct, the buyer of your futures contract will owe you $.50 for each bushel of wheat, or $25,000. You will also have helped to increase the availability of No. 2 Red Wheat at its highest marginal value. By selling the futures contract, you will have helped to lower the futures price of this wheat for November 9. And due to the decrease in this futures price relative to today's spot price, those who are physically holding wheat off the market will find it to their advantage to make more wheat available for consumption now.

So if you think speculators are performing a disservice to society by driving up the prices of important commodities, you do not have to sit idly by. You can take action to counteract this social harm by becoming a speculator yourself and, unless your concern is misplaced, you should make a nice profit in the process. If your speculations are wrong, however, you will misallocate resources, but this will leave you with less money with which to misallocate resources in the future.

Avoiding Risk by Hedging

Although we commonly think of speculators who buy and sell futures contracts as gamblers, this is often untrue. People often enter the futures market to avoid rather than to assume risk.

Consider, for example, a miller, whose business it is to mill wheat into flour. The miller is paid for the value he adds to the wheat by milling it into a more usable form. To do this, he must purchase large quantities of wheat that will not be sold as flour until some future date. If the price of wheat increases during the milling process, the price of flour will also increase and the miller will make a profit in addition to his normal profit for producing flour. But the price of wheat may also decline, in which case the miller may have to sell his flour for less than he paid for the wheat, and he will incur a loss. So the miller's return on his investment may depend more on the vagaries of the wheat market than on his ability and diligence as a miller.

This does not have to be the case, however. The miller can eliminate the effect of fluctuating wheat prices on his income by entering into the futures market for wheat. Let's assume that the miller has just purchased 50,000 bushels of wheat, which will be converted into flour and will be ready for sale on or about November 9 of the current year. By selling a futures contract for 50,000 bushels of wheat to be delivered on November 9, the miller can insure that his return for milling is largely independent of the November 9 price of wheat. To illustrate, assume that the spot price (the price the miller pays) on the day the miller purchases his 50,000 bushels of wheat is $3.45 a bushel and that the November 9 futures price is $3.50 a bushel. The difference of $.05 reflects the market judgment of the cost of storing a bushel of wheat, the forgone value of tying up capital in wheat, and so on.[14] There are now three cases to consider:

---

[14]These considerations were ignored in our graphic analysis (see footnote 12).

1. *The spot price may remain unchanged at $3.45.* In this case, the miller has the right to sell wheat, which can be bought for $3.45 a bushel on November 9, for $3.50 a bushel. Therefore, he will receive $.05 a bushel, or 50,000($.05) = $2,500, from the buyer of the futures contract. This will cover the miller's cost of storing the wheat, and his return for milling will be determined by the value he added to the wheat by milling it into flour.

2. *The spot price may go up.* If the spot price increases from $3.45 to, say, $3.60, then the miller must pay $3.60 a bushel for wheat that he will be able to sell for only $3.50 a bushel. This means that on November 9, the miller will have to pay the buyer of his futures contract 50,000($.10) = $5,000. But the miller has made a profit of $.15 a bushel on the 50,000 bushels of wheat he purchased for milling, or $7,500. This additional value will be reflected in the price of his flour. Therefore, the miller makes a net gain of $2,500 on the fluctuation in wheat prices, which just covers his storage costs. Again, the return reflects only the value added by milling wheat into flour.

3. *The spot price may go down.* If the spot price has declined from, say, $3.45 to $3.35 a bushel by November 9, the miller can sell wheat for $3.50 a bushel that he purchased for only $3.35 a bushel, thereby making $.15 a bushel on the futures contract, or $7,500. But he has lost $.10 a bushel on the 50,000 bushels of wheat he purchased for milling. So, again, the miller's net gain is the $2,500 in storage costs, and he receives only the value added by the milling process.

The miller has protected himself against fluctuations in the price of wheat by **hedging.** He offset the risks of taking a long position in the wheat used in milling flour by taking a short position in the futures market. This is referred to as a **short hedge.** In other situations, a person can reduce risk by taking a long position on a futures contract, which is referred to as a **long hedge.**

Note that even though the miller in our example has been able to protect himself against the risk of a fluctuating price, *this risk did not vanish.* As long as the future is uncertain, the risk will exist and the speculator—the one who takes only a long or a short position—will assume this risk. In our example, the speculator who bought the miller's futures contract gained when the spot increase rose above $3.50 a bushel by November 9, but lost otherwise. The futures market does not eliminate risk, but it does allow risk to be shifted from those who do not want to take it to those who are willing to take it in the hope of making a profit.

2-5 Summary

In Chapter 2, we have developed some of the theoretical background you will need to apply two of the most powerful concepts in economic analysis—the concepts of *demand* and *supply.* It is critically important to understand that a given *demand (supply) curve* assumes that everything influencing how much of a good will be demanded (supplied) is held constant with the exception of the good's price. This practice allows us to focus on the influence of the variable of prime importance by isolating its effect from the effect of other variables. Once this characteristic of demand and supply analysis is known, it becomes clear that an important distinction exists between (1) a movement along a given demand or supply curve in response to a change in price, and (2) a change in demand or supply as the entire curve shifts in response to a change in some variable other than price.

Having carefully defined demand and supply curves for a product, we will be able to discuss the important concepts of *price and quantity equilibrium* and to analyze how such an equilibrium changes in response to changes in those variables held constant along a given demand or supply curve. The comparison of the price and quantity equilibrium rates that exist before and after such changes is an important example of what economists call *comparative static analysis.*

We have used the tools of demand and supply analysis to examine the effects of attempting to control the price of a good by making it illegal to buy or sell it at a price higher than some established *price ceiling.* To the extent that the price ceiling is effectively enforced, demand and supply analysis establishes that a *shortage* of the good will be created. This shortage is the result of an inefficient allocation of resources and will produce some or all of the following conditions: long waits for the product, favoritism and discrimination in distributing the good, quality reductions, tie-in sales to disguise price increases, and *black-market transactions.*

Our final application of demand and supply analysis in this chapter was the investigation of the role of the *speculator.* We saw that the speculator can perform the essential service of removing important commodities from the consumption market when supplies are plentiful so that more of them will be available for consumption when supplies would otherwise be scarce. We saw that if critics of speculative activity are correct in their criticism, they can easily perform a socially useful service and make a profit simultaneously.

Demand and supply analysis is deceptively simple. Although the fundamental concepts are straightforward, we have seen that mistakes can easily be made unless care is exercised. Also, as simple as the analysis is, it can provide rich and robust insights into a wide variety of economic and social issues—issues that are often surrounded by widely held misconceptions. Fortunately, these misconceptions can be convincingly dispelled once the intellectual discipline required by the use of demand and supply analysis is applied.

In Chapter 3, we will develop the theoretical foundation for demand and supply analysis further and present some additional applications of this theory.

References

Barzel, Yoram. "A Theory of Rationing by Waiting." *The Journal of Law and Economics* (April 1974), pp. 73–96.

Boulding, Kenneth. "A Note on the Theory of the Black Market." *Canadian Journal of Economics and Political Science* (February 1947), pp. 115–18.

_____. *Economic Analysis, Volume I: MicroEconomics,* 4th Edition. New York: Harper & Row, 1966, pp. 159–67, Chapters 10–12.

Hayek, F.A. von, et.al. *Rent Controls: A Popular Paradox.* Vancouver: The Frazier Institute, 1975.

Tullock, Gordon. "The Transitional Gains Trap." *The Bell Journal of Economics* (Autumn 1976), pp. 671–78.

Problems

1. Assume that the government sets a price on a good and makes it illegal to charge more than this legislated price. If this price is less than the equilibrium price:
   (a) explain why some consumers will be better off because of the controls and why others will be worse off.
   (b) as a consumer, identify the characteristics that you would consider desirable to possess in this situation.
   (c) what motivations would induce both buyers and sellers to break the law?
   (d) price competition for the product will be restricted. Does this reduce competition or simply alter the form that competition for the product will take?
   (e) do you feel that the real cost of acquiring the good will be as low as the legislated price, even if the legislated price is strictly enforced?

2. In this chapter, we learned that horizontally summing individual supply curves to obtain a market supply curve is not always an appropriate procedure. But no qualifications were made about the appropriateness of horizontally summing individual demand curves to obtain a market demand curve. Describe a situation in which it might be inadvisable to use this procedure to obtain a market demand curve.

3. Assume that buying and selling wheat for current consumption is legal, but that it is against the law to purchase wheat for speculative purposes. What effect would such a law have on wheat prices between harvests?

4. Consider an occupation for which men and women are equally competent but for which women receive lower wages due to discrimination. Assume that in an attempt to eliminate the effects of this discrimination, a law is passed requiring that women be paid the same wage as men in this occupation. Since men and women are substitutes in this employment, what effect will this law have on the demand for men? If no legal restrictions are placed on the hiring practices of employers, what effect will this law have on the employment opportunities for men and women?

5. We often observe that the price of a commodity increases significantly, not because current supplies have been reduced, but because adverse

weather conditions are expected to reduce the size of future harvests. This is considered by many to be an example of unwarranted speculation and price manipulation. Do you agree? Why or why not?

6. Assume that the legal minimum imposed on the price of a good is greater than its equilibrium price. What effect would this price floor tend to have on the quality of the good? How would it tend to increase favoritism and discrimination?

7. What would happen to the current price of oil if it was announced that:
   (a) within ten years solar energy would be available at a fraction of the current cost of energy?
   (b) no further technological advances could be made to provide nonfossil fuel sources of energy?
   (c) a huge meteor was on a collision course with the earth and would obliterate our planet within ten years?
   (d) a permanent ceiling was going to be imposed on the price of oil in five years that would be lower than today's price?

8. What is the advantage of knowing that the price of a good reflects the opportunity cost of producing it? Under what conditions will the market equilibrium price reflect this opportunity cost? Explain why employing a resource where its opportunity cost is lowest is equivalent to using that resource in its highest-valued employment.

9. Assume that the cost of storing a bushel of wheat is $.03 per month and that the wheat is harvested in May and November. Explain why the following price pattern indicates a well-functioning speculative market:

MONTH	PRICE
May	$3.50
June	$3.53
July	$3.56
August	$3.59
September	$3.62
October	$3.65
November	$3.25

Now assume that the May–October prices are the same, but that the November price is $3.90. Why does this revised price pattern indicate that the speculative market is not functioning well?

10. What do you think would happen to the original price pattern in Question 9 if the government announced a price ceiling on wheat of $3.56 effective May 1? How would these effects differ from the effects of a price ceiling that were discussed in this chapter? Explain the reason for this difference.

11. Consider a demand curve that depicts the following relationship between price and rate of consumption:

PRICE	CONSUMPTION RATE
$20	5.0
18	5.5
16	6.2
14	6.9
12	6.7
10	8.0
8	9.5
6	12.0
4	15.0
2	19.0

Write the relationship between price and rate of supply that will generate an equilibrium price of $12 based on this demand curve. How many different supply curves would generate the same equilibrium price?

r

CHAPTER THREE

PRICE ELASTICITY: MEASURING RESPONSE TO PRICE

If neither the quantity demanded nor the quantity supplied were responsive to price, then there would be no advantage to price rationing. Without any response to a higher price, there would be no way to effect an equilibrium between the amount demanded and the amount supplied, and—from the perspective of resource allocation—one price would be just as good as any other. Of course, this is not the case. Quantities demanded and supplied are sensitive to changes in price, as evidenced by the downward slope of the demand curve and the upward slope of the supply curve. But knowing that decisions are responsive to price does not tell us the degree of responsiveness, and it is often useful to be able to measure just how sensitive quantities demanded and supplied are to a price change.

For example, there has been much public discussion recently about the desirability of reducing our dependency on foreign countries for petroleum. This can be accomplished by reducing the rate at which we demand oil, increasing the rate of our domestic supply, or a combination of the two. An increase in the price of oil will decrease consumption and increase production, but it is important for us to know how much of a price increase will be needed to close the gap between domestic consumption and production. Clearly, this depends on the responsiveness of demand and supply rates to the price of oil. If these rates are extremely responsive to price, then a relatively small price increase would lower the demand rate to the level of the increased supply rate and make us independent in petroleum production. In this case, establishing our energy independence would not be a particularly costly project. On the other hand, if—as evidence indicates—demand and supply rates are not highly responsive to the price of oil, then achieving energy independence would be very costly.

3-2 Demand Elasticities

A Dimensionless Measure of Responsiveness

In discussing the responsiveness of the rate of demand or supply to price, as given by the demand or supply curves, it is best to use one number to represent this information. Initially, the amount that the curve changes in the horizontal direction in response to a one-unit change in the vertical direction might seem to be the appropriate way to measure this type of responsiveness. This is the slope of the curve with respect to the vertical or price axis.[1] In Figure 3–1, this slope is obtained for the straight-line demand curve DD by considering a one-unit change in price from P_1 to $P_1 + 1$ and then measuring the resulting change in the rate of demand—the horizontal distance ΔQ, where the Δ means "change in."[2] The problem with using this slope as the sole measure of responsiveness is that it is highly sensitive to the units that are chosen for the price and quantity axes.

For example, the demand curve for petroleum might look like DD in Figure 3–1 if dollars are the unit of measure along the vertical axis and barrels are the unit of measure along the horizontal axis. But if we change our units of measure to *pennies* for price and *millions* of barrels for quantity, the demand curve will be much steeper, as shown in Figure 3–2(a). Using the slope $\Delta Q/\Delta P$ as our measure of responsiveness would lead us to the erroneous conclusion that the demand rate given by DD in Figure 3–2(a) is less responsive to a price change than the demand rate given by DD in Figure 3–1. We would be misled in the other direction if we applied our slope measure to the same curve when each unit along the price axis represented $1000 and each unit along the quantity axis represented a gallon of oil per unit of time. In this case, the demand curve would look like DD in Figure 3–2(b) and the slope measure would indicate that the demand rate is extremely responsive to price.

Thus, the slope of a demand curve with respect to the price axis is meaningless unless the price and quantity units are carefully specified. For this reason, economists do not use slope to measure the responsiveness of the demand rate to price. Instead, they use a measure that is completely independent of the price and quantity units—the **price elasticity of demand,** and which relates a percentage change in price to the corresponding percentage change in the demand

---

[1] Normally, slopes are given by the change in the vertical direction of the curve in response to a unit change in the horizontal direction. But long-established convention dictates that price and quantity per unit of time be measured along the vertical and horizontal axes, respectively, when drawing demand and supply curves. This requires us to consider the slope with respect to the vertical axis in our discussion here.

[2] Since we are dealing with a straight-line demand curve, this slope is the same everywhere on the curve and could be denoted by $\Delta Q/\Delta P$, where ΔP is any change in price and ΔQ is the corresponding change in the rate of demand. If we are dealing with other than a straight line, however, the slope will vary as we move along the curve.

Figure 3-1
Slope as a Measure of Demand Response

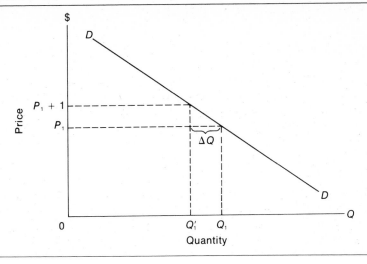

rate. Specifically, the price elasticity of demand, denoted by E, is given by

$$E = - \frac{\Delta Q/Q}{\Delta P/P} \qquad (3\text{-}1)$$

Stated in words, this means that the price elasticity of demand is equal to the percentage change in the demand rate divided by the percentage change in price and then multiplied by -1. We multiply by -1 to have the convenience of working with *positive* price elasticities of demand. Since demand curves are downward sloping, a change in the demand rate will have the opposite sign of a change in the price, so that without the minus sign in Equation (3-1), we would be dealing with a negative quantity. The advantage of working with positive price elasticities of demand is that larger numbers indicate a greater responsiveness to price than smaller numbers. Without the sign change, exactly the opposite would be true.

Several things are worth noting about our definition of price elasticity of demand. First, it can be easily seen that changing the units used to measure price and quantity has no effect on this measure. For example, if we are measuring price in units of dollars and we consider a change from $100 to $150, $\Delta P/P$ will equal 50/100 = 1/2. Changing our unit of measure to pennies will make this a change of 10,000 cents to 15,000 cents, but $\Delta P/P$ will still be equal to 1/2 (5,000/10,000). Similarly, $\Delta Q/Q$ is completely independent of the quantity units that are used. So, as claimed, the price elasticity of demand is *dimensionless:* It is independent of the dimensions used to measure price and quantity.

Figure 3-2
(a) Slope Sensitive to Units of Measure
(b) Slope Sensitive to Units of Measure

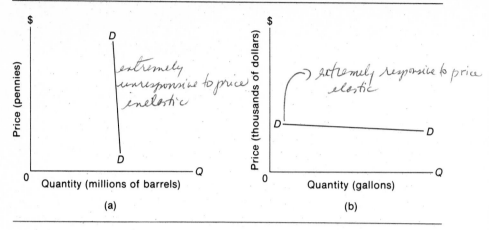

(a)   (b)

Point and Arc Price Elasticity of Demand

Some confusion may arise during the actual application of the formula for the price elasticity of demand given in Equation (3–1). In considering a change in price and the resulting change in the demand rate, changes in price ΔP and in quantity ΔQ can be easily specified. But we must decide *which* price and quantity to use to determine the percentage changes—the *initial* price and quantity or the *new* price and quantity. This choice can make a substantial difference in the value of our elasticity measure unless the changes in price and quantity are very small.

We can illustrate this point by using the hypothetical market demand curve for wheat *DD* shown in Figure 3–3. If the price of wheat drops from $6 to $2 per bushel, the demand rate will increase from 2 to 6 million bushels per year. Using Equation (3–1) for the price elasticity of demand and the *initial* price and quantity, we obtain

$$E = - \frac{\Delta Q/Q}{\Delta P/P} = - \frac{(6 - 2)/2}{(2 - 6)/6} = - \frac{4/2}{-4/6} = 3$$

However, if we use the *new* price and quantity, we obtain

$$E = - \frac{(6 - 2)/6}{(2 - 6)/2} = - \frac{4/6}{-4/2} = \frac{1}{3}$$

In each case, the changes in price and quantity are the same. But the initial values of price and quantity produce a small percentage change in price (since we compare our change with a high price) and a large percentage change in quantity (since we compare our change with a small quantity). The result is a small denominator and a large numerator in our elasticity formula—and therefore a large elasticity value. However, when we use the new values of price and quantity, we obviously obtain a larger percentage change in price and a smaller percentage change in quantity—even though the absolute changes are the same as before—and therefore a smaller measure for elasticity.

Choosing which values of price and quantity to use to determine elasticity is not much.of a problem if we are considering only small changes in price and quantity. For example, if the price of wheat is $3.50 per bushel, the demand curve *DD* in Figure 3-3 shows that the rate of demand will be 4.50 million bushels per year. If the price drops to $3.49 per bushel, the demand rate will be 4.51 million bushels per year. Using the initial price and quantity, we obtain an elasticity of

$$E = -\frac{.01/4.5}{-.01/3.5} = \frac{3.5}{4.5} = .7777$$

whereas using the new price and quantity gives us

$$E = -\frac{.01/4.51}{-.01/3.49} = \frac{3.49}{4.51} = .7738$$

This tells us that our formula for the elasticity of demand is really only appropriate for *very small* changes in price and quantity. In effect, price elasticity of demand can only be defined accurately with reference to a particular

---

Figure 3-3
Elasticity Sensitive to Reference Point

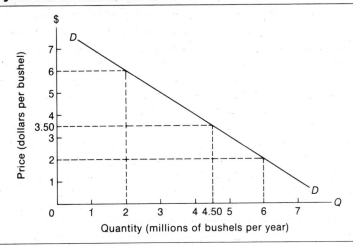

point on the demand curve. For this reason, our elasticity measure is often referred to as the **point price elasticity of demand.**

However, in certain cases, it may be desirable to consider an elasticity measure for *large* changes in price and quantity, and a price elasticity of demand formula that specifies a compromise in the choice of price and quantity has been developed for this purpose. Instead of choosing initial or new price and quantity values, the percentage changes in price and quantity are computed on the basis of the *average values* of price and quantity in these instances. To illustrate, let's consider a change in price and quantity from P_1 to P_2 and Q_1 to Q_2, respectively, as shown in Figure 3–4. The elasticity formula to be used in this case is

$$E_{arc} = - \frac{\Delta Q / \frac{1}{2}(Q_1 + Q_2)}{\Delta P / \frac{1}{2}(P_1 + P_2)} = - \frac{\Delta Q/(Q_1 + Q_2)}{\Delta P/(P_1 + P_2)} = \frac{run}{rise} \quad (3\text{–}2)$$

This elasticity, denoted by E_{arc}, is commonly referred to as the **arc price elasticity of demand.** This term is derived from the fact that this elasticity measure is defined over an arc of the demand curve. As such, it is a relatively crude measure that tells us little about the price elasticity of demand at any given point on the demand curve. Because *point price elasticity of demand* is a much sharper concept for analytical purposes, our discussion and use of elasticities will pertain to point elasticities, unless otherwise specified.

In general, point elasticity of demand varies from point to point on a demand curve. This can be easily seen if we consider a straight-line demand curve. First, we manipulate our elasticity formula[3] algebraically to obtain

$$E = - \frac{\Delta Q}{\Delta P} \cdot \frac{P}{Q} \quad (3\text{–}3)$$

which tells us that the price elasticity of demand is equal to the slope of the demand curve at a given point multiplied by the ratio of price to quantity at that point, all multiplied by -1. Since $\Delta Q/\Delta P$ is the same everywhere on a straight-line demand curve, we see that the price elasticity of demand depends only on the price–quantity ratio. Therefore, the price elasticity of demand decreases as we consider points farther down and to the right on a straight-line demand curve. The elasticity at point A, for example, on the demand curve in Figure 3–5 is greater than the elasticity at point B, since P_1/Q_1 is greater than P_2/Q_2. As we move toward point A', the ratio of price to quantity becomes arbitrarily large as the quantity approaches 0, and the elasticity also becomes

---

[3]The formula is often shown as

$$E = - \frac{dQ}{dP} \cdot \frac{P}{Q}$$

where dP/dQ represents the slope of a curve (in this case the demand curve) at a given point. This formula is more general in that it applies to nonlinear as well as linear demand curves.

Figure 3–4
Arc Price Elasticity of Demand

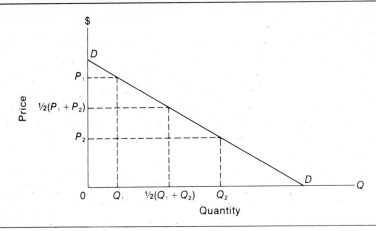

extremely large at points on the demand curve close to A'. On the other hand, as we move toward point B', the price–quantity ratio decreases to 0 as price approaches 0, and elasticity also decreases to 0 as we approach point B'. So as we progress down the demand curve from point A' to point B', the price elasticity of demand decreases from an extremely large value to 0.

Of course, there is no reason to believe that demand curves will always, or ever, be straight lines. Therefore, it will be useful to discuss how price elasticity of demand can be measured at a given point on a nonlinear demand curve. Since the slope of a nonlinear demand curve at a given point is equal to the slope of a straight line tangent to the curve at that point, we can use a linear

Figure 3–5
Change in Elasticity

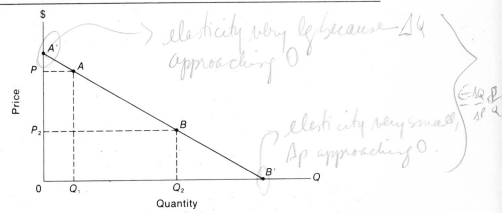

demand curve to determine the elasticities of a nonlinear demand curve. To find the elasticity of the nonlinear demand curve DD at point A in Figure 3–6, for example, we construct the linear demand curve $D'D'$, which is tangent to DD at point A. The slope $\Delta Q/\Delta P$ of $D'D'$ is equal to the corresponding slope of DD at point A. Therefore, the price elasticity of demand at point A is given by

$$E = -\frac{\Delta Q}{\Delta P} \cdot \frac{P_1}{Q_1}$$

for both the linear demand curve $D'D'$ and the nonlinear demand curve DD. *Any two demand curves that are tangent at a given point will have the same price elasticities of demand at that point.* So we can always find the price elasticity of demand for a nonlinear demand curve at a given point by finding the price elasticity of demand at the same point for an appropriately drawn linear demand curve.

In general, we will expect price elasticity of demand to vary from point to point on nonlinear demand curves, just as it does on linear demand curves. More specifically, we normally expect this elasticity to decrease as we move down the demand curve, because the price–quantity ratio will be decreasing. How-

Example 3–1

Estimated Price Elasticities of Demand

It is difficult to make an empirical measurement of the price elasticity of demand for a product. The biggest problem is to estimate the demand curve for the product, because it is difficult to separate the influence of shifts in the demand and supply curves on the price–quantity observations. This is known as the **identification problem,** and it is discussed in books that deal with regression analysis and econometrics. Once a product's demand curve has been estimated, an appropriate price must be chosen because the price elasticity will generally depend on the prevailing price. But despite these difficulties, researchers have estimated the price elasticity of demand for different products, and the resulting values have not been out of line with informed intuition. The price elasticities of demand for selected products follow.

We would expect foreign travel to be a strongly discretionary item for most people and therefore very sensitive to price. And the estimated elasticity for this item indicates that a 1% change in price causes a 4.1% change in the amount demanded. It is also to be expected that the quantity demand of a particular fruit–say, peaches–will be more sensitive to price than the quantity demand of all fruit, since fruits other than peaches will be a good substitute for peaches. Nor is it surprising to find that items that most people consider essential, such as milk, are not highly sensitive to price and display low price elasticities of demand.

Figure 3-6
Elasticity of Linear and Nonlinear Demand Curves

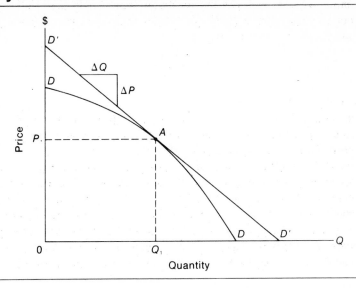

brought about by a 1% change in price

Foreign travel by U.S. residents	4.1	(H)
Medical care and hospitalization insurance	3.6	(H)
Fresh green peas	2.8	(S)
Canned green peas	1.6	(S)
Peaches	1.5	(W)
All fruit	1.1	(W)
Radio and television repair	1.0	(H)
Automobiles	.8 — 1.5	(W)
Electric power for residential use	.2 — 1.0	(W)
Milk	< 1	
Eggs	< 1	
Funeral and burial expenses	< 1	
Gasoline and oil	< 1	

(H) H.S. Houthakker and L.D. Taylor, *Consumption Demand in the United States: 1929–1970* (Cambridge: Harvard University Press, 1966).
(S) D.B. Suits, *Principles of Economics* (New York: Harper & Row, 1970).
(W) L.W. Weiss, *Case Studies in American Industry* (New York: John Wiley & Sons, 1967). Reported in D.A. Worcester, "On Monopoly Welfare Losses: Comment," *American Economic Review,* Vol. LXV, No. 4 (December 1975), pp. 1015–23.

ever, this is not necessarily true of a nonlinear demand curve, since the slope $\Delta Q/\Delta P$ will be changing also. As we will see in the next section, it is easy to construct demand curves that have the same price elasticity of demand everywhere.

Price Elasticity Related to Total Revenue

There is an important relationship between the price elasticity of demand for a good and the effect on **total revenue** (Price × Quantity) of changing the price of the good, which will be useful in subsequent chapters. When the price elasticity of demand for a good is greater than 1, a decrease in price will increase the rate of demand enough to increase the total revenue received by sellers of the good. When the price elasticity of demand is equal to 1, a small change in price in either direction will not affect total revenue. And finally, when the price elasticity of demand is less than 1, a reduction in price will cause a decrease in total revenue.[4]

It is useful to justify this result intuitively. Recall that our formula for the price elasticity of demand given in Equation (3–1) is

$$E = - \frac{\Delta Q/Q}{\Delta P/P}$$

which can be interpreted to be the percentage increase in the demand rate associated with a 1% decrease in price. Therefore, if a 1% decrease in price results in more than a 1% increase in the demand rate, then the price elasticity is greater than 1 and the revenue loss incurred by lowering the price is more than offset by the increase in sales. In other words, lowering price will increase total revenue. If a 1% price decrease causes a 1% increase in the demand rate,

---

[4]To prove this result, let's look at marginal revenue MR, or the change in total revenue in response to a change in quantity Q. Taking the derivative of $P(Q) \cdot Q$ with respect to Q, we obtain

$$\text{MR} = \frac{d\,[P(Q) \cdot Q]}{dQ} = P(Q) + \frac{dP}{dQ} \cdot Q$$

Factoring price out of the right-hand side of this equation gives us

$$\text{MR} = P \left[1 + \frac{dP}{dQ} \cdot \frac{Q}{P} \right]$$

which, because $E = - \left(\dfrac{dQ}{dP} \cdot \dfrac{P}{P} \right)$, is the same as

$$\text{MR} = P \left[1 - \frac{1}{E} \right] \qquad \begin{array}{l} > 0 \text{ if } E \; > 1 \\ = 0 \text{ if } E \; = 1 \\ < 0 \text{ if } E \; < 1 \end{array}$$

From this, it follows immediately that an increase in Q (a decrease in P) increases total revenue if $E > 1$, has no effect on total revenue if $E = 1$, and reduces total revenue if $E < 1$.

then the effects of a lower price and increased sales exactly offset one another and revenue remains unchanged. Not surprisingly, a price elasticity of less than 1 implies that lowering the price by 1% will increase sales by less than 1% and a decrease in total revenue will result.

In Figure 3–7, elasticity regions are shown for a linear demand curve. Note that price elasticity is greater than 1 ($E > 1$) at every point on the upper half of the demand curve, price elasticity equals 1 ($E = 1$) exactly halfway down the curve, and price elasticity is less than 1 ($E < 1$) at every point on the bottom half of the curve.[5] Given this information, we know that lowering the price from P_1 to P_2 in Figure 3–7 will result in more revenue because P_1Q_1 is smaller than P_2Q_2. We also know that P_4Q_4 is larger than P_5Q_5, since we have moved into the region of the demand curve where $E < 1$ and reducing price lowers revenue.

From what we have said, it should also be clear that total revenue is maximized in Figure 3–7 at price P_3, which provides a revenue of P_3Q_3. As long as $E > 1$, lowering price will increase revenue; as soon as $E < 1$, lowering price will reduce revenue. Therefore, when $E = 1$, total revenue will be at its maximum.

The region of the demand curve where $E > 1$ is referred to as the **elastic region** of the demand curve; the **inelastic region** is that part of the demand curve where $E < 1$. Normally, the upper region of a demand curve is the elastic region; then as price decreases and quantity demanded increases, price elasticity declines into the inelastic region in the lower portion of the demand curve.

---

[5]To prove this, we recognize that the equation for a linear demand curve can be expressed mathematically as

$$P = A - BQ \tag{1}$$

where P represents price, Q is quantity demanded, and A and B are positive constants. The total revenue associated with this demand curve is given by

$$PQ = AQ - BQ^2$$

The marginal revenue is obtained by taking the derivative of total revenue with respect to Q, or

$$MR = A - 2BQ \tag{2}$$

From footnote 4, we know that when marginal revenue is equal to 0, elasticity is equal to 1. From Equation (2) here, this implies that $E = 1$ when

$$A - 2BQ = 0$$

or when

$$Q = \frac{1}{2} \cdot \frac{A}{B}$$

From Equation (1) we know that when the demand curve intersects the Q axis, $P = 0$ and

$$Q = \frac{A}{B}$$

Thus, with a linear demand curve, $E = 1$ when Q is one-half the distance between $Q = 0$ and the Q that drives price down to 0. The reader is invited to prove that $E > 1$ when $Q < 1/2 \cdot A/B$, and that $E < 1$ when $Q > 1/2 \cdot A/B$.

Figure 3–7
Revenue and Elasticities

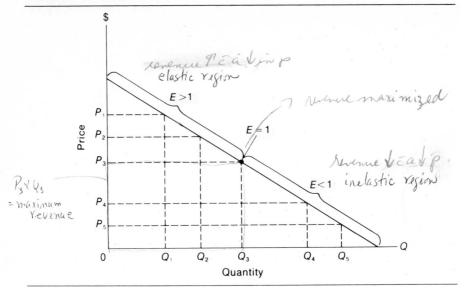

But this is not always the case. On a nonlinear demand curve, it is possible that $E > 1$, $E = 1$, or $E < 1$ *everywhere.*[6]

An interesting example is a demand curve that has a price elasticity of unity everywhere. Such a demand curve is given by the relationship $Q = A/P$, where Q is the rate of demand, P represents price, and A is some positive number. It can be easily seen that as the price goes up, the demand rate goes down. But note that this demand relation can be rewritten as $PQ = A$, which states that total revenue is always equal to the constant A. No matter what price we choose, the quantity demanded will be such that total revenue remains constant. This demand curve is shown as *DD* in Figure 3–8. As this demand curve is constructed, the revenue $P_1 Q_1$ obtained by charging a price P_1 is exactly the same as the revenue $P_2 Q_2$ obtained by charging P_2. Since, at any price, a change in price has no effect on total revenue, it follows that the price elasticity of demand is equal to 1 everywhere on this demand curve.

---

[6]It is easy to demonstrate these elasticity properties for the class of demand curves given by the relationship

$$Q = \frac{A}{P^n} = AP^{-n} \tag{1}$$

where A and n are any positive numbers. With these restrictions, we can see that the rate of demand Q is a decreasing function of the price P. To obtain the price elasticity of demand, we use the formula

$$E = -\frac{dQ}{dP} \cdot \frac{P}{Q}$$

Figure 3–8
Price Elasticity of 1 Everywhere

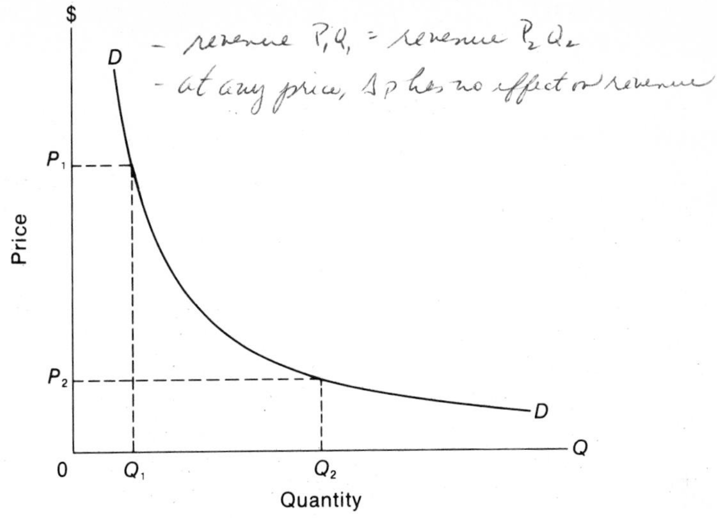
$
D
P₁
P₂
Price
0
Q₁
Q₂
Quantity
Q
D
- revenue P₁Q₁ = revenue P₂Q₂
- at any price, Δp has no effect on revenue

Price Elasticity, Substitute Possibilities, and Time

Just how responsive the quantity demanded is to the price charged depends on several factors. We have already seen that the position on the demand curve is an important consideration. In general, the higher the price and the lower the rate of demand, the larger the price elasticity of demand will be. But for a given price and rate of demand, the elasticity will vary, depending on other considerations.

The number of close substitutes that are available exerts an important influence on the price elasticity of demand for a good. For example, if ball-point pens were the only writing instrument available, the price elasticity of demand would be much lower than it is currently at prevailing ball-point pen prices. Without substitute goods, the price of ball-point pens could be increased sub-

---

To obtain dQ/dP, we differentiate Equation (1) with respect to P, which gives us

$$\frac{dQ}{dP} = -nAP^{-n-1} = -\frac{nAP^{-n}}{P}$$

Thus,

$$E = \frac{nAP^{-n}}{P} \cdot \frac{P}{Q} = \frac{nAP^{-n}}{Q}$$

But since $Q = AP^{-n}$, we have $E = n$. The price elasticity of demand is equal to the constant n, no matter which point on the demand curve we consider. If $n > 1$, then the demand curve is elastic everywhere; if $n < 1$, it is inelastic everywhere. If $n = 1$, then the demand curve exhibits unitary elasticity everywhere. The case of unitary elasticity will be discussed in the text without the aid of calculus.

U.S. postal rates
toilet paper
↳→

stantially without causing much reduction in the demand rate. Of course, we know that there are many close substitutes for ball-point pens. And if the relative price of ball-point pens increased, the demand rate would decrease noticeably, as consumers switched to fountain pens, pencils, felt-tip pens, and typewriters.

The demand rates for goods that do not have many close substitutes are relatively less price elastic. As examples, the availability of close substitutes for salt and gasoline are limited, so it is difficult to realize the benefits they provide unless these actual goods are consumed. Thus, if the price of one of these goods is increased, the choice is either to sacrifice many of the benefits resulting from its consumption or to pay the higher price.

Another important consideration that affects the price elasticity of demand for a good is the length of time that consumers have to react to a price change. If consumers have more time to adjust to a change in price, they will be more responsive to that change. For example, although there are few direct substitutes for gasoline, there are many other ways to reduce gasoline consumption. Driving a smaller car, moving closer to work, forming a car pool, and using a mass-transit system are some ways in which consumers are already economizing on gasoline. But such adjustments to a higher price take time. Immediately after a price increase, most gasoline consumers will continue their old consumption patterns, although they may cut down on Sunday driving or take shorter vacations by car. In time, however, many consumers will make major adjustments. High gasoline prices can be an important factor when purchasing

Example 3–2

Price Elasticity of Demand for Gasoline and the Oil Company "Conspiracy"

It is often heard that gasoline is a necessity and that consumers cannot reduce their gas consumption greatly, if at all, in response to increasing prices. In other words, the price elasticity of demand for gasoline is very low, if it is not 0. Although evidence strongly refutes the view that this elasticity is 0, studies by Houthakker and others (see footnotes to Example 3–1) consistently indicate that it is less than 1. So casual cocktail-party conversations dealing with the price elasticity of gasoline do have some basis in fact.

But casual conversations about gasoline are not confined to price elasticity. Many consumers believe that U.S. oil companies have been reducing their gasoline production to increase their prices and maximize their profits for some time now. Public-opinion polls indicate that most people not only believe that such a conspiracy exists, but also that it is quite successful. But if there is a conspiracy in the oil industry, has it successfully maximized the combined profits of those companies that comprise the oil a new car, for instance. Drivers will not trade their big gas guzzlers for economy cars as soon as gas prices begin to increase, but higher gasoline prices will make smaller cars more attractive to new-car buyers. Or when people move, they may purchase new homes or rent apartments closer to work, school, and mass-transit routes. As more time elapses, the gas-saving responses to higher gas prices will increase. Of course, the same principle is true of a price decrease. If the price of gasoline happened to drop significantly (don't count on it), people would not change their life styles in order to consume more gasoline immediately. But in time, consumers would respond to lower gasoline prices by increasing their consumption.

What is true of gasoline demand is also true of the demand for other goods. The more time consumers have to respond to a price change, the more price elastic the demand will be. In some cases (for example, bubble-gum purchases) the full response will be achieved in a short period of time. In the case of goods such as gasoline, whose consumption is tied to major purchases and adjustments, months or even years may be required for consumers to respond fully to a price change.

Figure 3–9 illustrates the effect of time on the response of the demand rate to an increase in the price of a good. There, D_1D_1, D_2D_2, and $D_{12}D_{12}$ represent the appropriate demand curves one month, two months, and one year, respectively, after a change in the initial price of P_1. At price P_1, the demand rate is shown as Q. As price increases from P_1 to P_2, the demand rate decreases to Q_1 after one month, Q_2 after two months, and Q_{12} after a year. The

industry? The answer has to be no if the common view on the price elasticity of gasoline is correct.

If the price elasticity of gasoline is less than 1, the oil industry cannot be charging a price that maximizes industry profits. We have seen that if the price elasticity is less than 1, then total revenue will be increased by increasing price. But an increase in price not only increases total revenue, it also reduces total cost, since less of the product will be sold at the higher price. Profit (Total revenue − Total cost) can always be increased by raising price if the price elasticity is less than 1. Of course, this means that if consumers are correct in their view that gas consumption is highly insensitive to price, then they cannot be correct in believing that the oil industry is pricing gas to maximize industry profits.

This does not imply that oil companies do not wish to maximize their profits. Naturally, investors in oil companies, like the rest of us, prefer to receive a higher rather than a lower return on their investments. What protects us, as consumers, against an effective oil-company cartel is not the good will of the oil industry but market forces that make it difficult for companies in any industry to successfully monopolize the industry. This subject will be examined in detail in Chapter 10.

Figure 3–9
Price Elasticity Increases Through Time

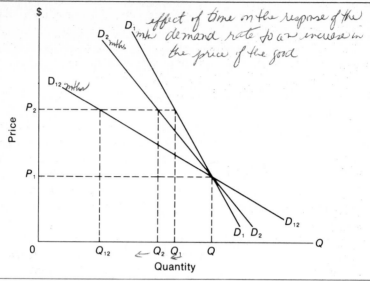

same demand curves also show that if price decreases below P_1, the demand rate will increase as more time elapses. The more time we allow for consumer response, the greater the price elasticity of demand will be.

Cross-Price Elasticity and Income Elasticity of Demand

In Chapter 2, we discussed the relationship between substitute and complementary goods. Our major point of emphasis was that some goods are related to each other in terms of the consumption process in such a way that the price of one has a significant effect on the demand for the other. The measure that economists use to record the direction and the strength of this relationship between two goods is called the **cross-price elasticity of demand** and is the percentage change in the amount demanded of one good divided by the percentage change in the price of the other good.

If, for example, we want to know how the rate of coffee consumption will respond to a change in the price of tea, the appropriate cross-price elasticity of demand is given by

$$E_{C,T} = \frac{\Delta Q_C / Q_C}{\Delta P_T / P_T} \qquad (3\text{–}4)$$

Two things are notable about this formula. First, it only provides an accurate measure for small changes in the price of tea. For large changes in price and quantity, this elasticity measure—like the price elasticity of demand—is sensitive to our choice of quantity and price. Related to this problem is the fact that cross-price elasticity will vary from one price–quantity point to another. If, for example, the price of tea is 1 cent per tea bag, the rate of coffee demand at this tea price may be quite sensitive to a change in that price. However, at a tea price of $100 per bag, we would expect a greater quantity of coffee to be demanded, but this quantity would not be very sensitive to a change in the price of tea. (At $100 per tea bag, all but the most devoted tea drinkers would have already switched to coffee.) So when we discuss cross-price elasticity of demand, we are talking about a *point elasticity.*

The second thing to note is that there is no minus sign in front of the cross-price elasticity formula. Cross-price elasticities can be positive or negative, and it is important to know their sign. In our example, we would expect the cross-price elasticity of demand between tea and coffee to be *positive,* indicating that these two goods are *substitutes;* an increase in the price of tea results in an increase in the rate at which coffee is demanded. If the cross-price elasticity of demand between two goods is *negative,* this indicates that goods are *complements.* For example, we would expect the cross-price elasticity of demand between tires and gasoline to be negative. If the price of gasoline goes up, people will drive less and therefore reduce the rate at which they wear out and demand tires.

So the *magnitude* and the *sign* of the cross-price elasticity of demand between any two goods provide useful information about the demand relationship that exists between these goods. The magnitude of this elasticity indicates how sensitive the quantity demanded of one good is to the price of the other good, and the sign tells us whether the goods are complements or substitutes. Of course, the cross-price elasticity of demand between many goods will be so close to 0 that it will be considered 0. As examples, the cross-price elasticity between tuna fish and back scratchers, economic texts and raincoats, or file cabinets and track shoes, will be extremely small—if not 0—indicating that no important demand relationships exist between these goods. Some nonzero estimations of cross-price elasticities appear in Table 3–1.

It is also worth noting that time is an important consideration in determining the size of the cross-price elasticity of demand between two goods. When the price of one good changes, it will take some time for the demand rate to respond fully to that change. This means that a period of time will have to elapse before the change in the price of one good has its full impact on the consumption of complementary and substitute goods. The more time consumers have to respond to a price change, the larger the absolute value of the cross-price elasticity of demand will be.

Not surprisingly, the rate at which many goods are consumed is sensitive to changes in consumer incomes. Some goods, such as foreign vacations, are highly sensitive to income changes; others, such as salt, are not very responsive to increases or decreases in income levels. Also, the consumption of some goods will increase with an increase in consumer income, whereas the consumption of other goods will decrease.

Table 3–1
Estimated Cross-Price Elasticities of Demand
for Some Common Commodities

COMMODITY	CROSS-PRICE ELASTICITY WITH RESPECT TO PRICE OF	CROSS-PRICE ELASTICITY
Margarine	Butter	.81
Butter	Margarine	.67
Beef	Pork	.28
Pork	Beef	.14
Flour	All animal foods	.56

— source of animal protein, pl —7.56 1g vegetable sources

SOURCE: Herman Wold, *Demand Analysis* (New York: John Wiley & Sons, Inc., 1953).

The responsiveness of the demand for a good to a change in consumer income is obtained by measuring the **income elasticity of demand,** which is given by

$$E_I = \frac{\Delta Q/Q}{\Delta I/I} \tag{3–5}$$

Stated in words, this equation tells us that the income elasticity of demand for a good is given by the percentage change in the quantity demanded $\Delta Q/Q$ divided by the percentage change in income $\Delta I/I$. As is true of the other elasticities we have discussed, the income elasticity of demand formula is more meaningful when we are considering small changes in income and quantity demanded. As with the cross-price elasticity of demand, the sign of the income elasticity of demand for a good conveys important information. If this sign is *negative,* this indicates that the demand rate for the good will decrease as income increases. Goods for which this is true are called **inferior goods,** which we described in Chapter 2 as goods for which demand decreased in response to an increase in consumer income. Of course, the income elasticity of demand for **normal goods** is positive.

Once more, it should be recognized that time is an important factor in determining the size of the income elasticity of demand. People are not likely to change their consumption patterns greatly immediately after their incomes increase, even if the increase is dramatic. But given time, increased income will cause consumption patterns to shift. The more time consumers are given to respond to an increase or a decrease in income, the larger the absolute value of the income elasticity of demand for a particular good will be. Some selected income elasticities appear in Table 3–2.

Table 3-2
Estimated Income Elasticities of Demand
for Selected Commodities

COMMODITY	INCOME ELASTICITY
Butter	.42
Margarine	−.20
Fruits and berries	.70
Cheese	.34
Meat	.35
Eggs	.37
Flour	−.36
Tobacco	1.02
Liquor	1.00

SOURCE: Herman Wold, *Demand Analysis* (New York: John Wiley & Sons, Inc., 1953).

Supply Elasticity   3-3

The concept of elasticity, as it has been developed for demand, is also a useful tool for measuring the responsiveness of the quantity supplied to changes in price. The **price elasticity of supply** is defined by the percentage change in quantity supplied divided by the percentage change in price and is given by

$$E = \frac{\Delta Q/Q}{\Delta P/P} \tag{3-6}$$

This is identical to the formula for the price elasticity of demand given in Equation (3-1), except that Equation (3-6) does not have a minus sign because it is not necessary to convert the elasticity of supply into a positive number. Since we will be dealing with upward-sloping supply curves, a change in price will always cause a change in quantity supplied in the same direction. Thus, the formula for the price elasticity of supply will always be positive, with larger elasticities signifying a greater supply response to price than smaller elasticities.

We face the same problems in using the formula for price elasticity of supply for large changes in price and quantity that we encountered earlier using demand elasticity formulas. Once more, our elasticity formula is meaningful only for small changes in price and quantity. In general, the price elasticity of supply will vary from one point to the next on a supply curve, and any attempt to characterize the responsiveness of quantity supplied to large changes in price with one number will be a crude one.

Again, as with demand elasticities, time plays an important role in determining the size of supply elasticities. In most productive activities, the more rapidly the rate of production is changed, the more costly the change is to make. New machines can be installed or old machines can be retired rapidly, but this normally costs more than it does when more time and care are taken. Often new workers can be hired quickly only if they are offered added incentives for rapid relocation and if less care is exercised in choosing the new employees; laying off workers is commonly more costly than attrition. Therefore, most firms will not expand or contract production rapidly after a price change. Instead, they will proceed cautiously, avoiding the high costs of sudden changes in their production rate. The full supply response from firms to a change in price will be known only after some period of time has elapsed.

The time element assumes an added importance when we recognize that some of the supply response to a change in product price is caused by firms entering or leaving the industry. Obviously, adjustments of this magnitude are not triggered immediately by a change in price and only occur given ample time. So just as with price elasticity of demand, the more time we allow for adjustment, the larger the price elasticity of supply will be.

refer to Class notes

It is also possible to define cross-price elasticities of supply, which are denoted by the percentage change in the amount supplied of one good divided by the percentage change in the price of another good. The discussion necessary to accomplish this would add little to our understanding of elasticities, however, and we will not pursue this subject here.

Application:
"Undesirable" Goods, Prohibition, and Law Enforcement

The consumption of some goods and services is considered so undesirable and offensive by society that their use or supply is prohibited by law. But effective prohibition of an activity is seldom achieved simply by passing a law—particularly if the activity is enjoyable, as are many of the activities that are publicly or collectively banned. Therefore, if laws prohibiting these activities are to be effective, they must be enforced and those who disobey them must be penalized.[7] Enforcement is costly; it utilizes scarce resources that have valuable alternative uses. So when an illegal activity must be reduced by a specified amount, it is reasonable to attempt to accomplish this at the least possible cost.[8]

---

[7]Even though penalties—often severe ones—are imposed on those who buy or sell illegal goods and services, the amount of money spent on these activities is enormous. In 1965, it was estimated that $350 million were spent on narcotics, $350 million on loansharking, $225 million on prostitution, $150 million on illegally produced alcoholic beverages, and $7 billion on illegal gambling. See the President's Commission on Law Enforcement and Administration of Justice, *Task Force Report: Crime and Its Impact— An Assessment* (Washington, D.C.: U.S. Government Printing Office, 1967), Chapter 3.

[8]Due to the cost of enforcement, it is impossible to eliminate an illegal activity completely. Enforcement to the point that no one could break the law would require an enormous expenditure of resources. And long before this could be accomplished, the cost of additional law enforcement would exceed the benefit that would result.

This affects the direction of enforcement efforts and the impact that outlawing a good will have on the price of the good. The implications of these effects can be analyzed with the aid of demand and supply curves.

In the absence of penalties, people would be willing to pay enough for an outlawed good to motivate suppliers to provide it. If this were not the case, there would be little point in prohibiting certain goods and services. (Society would certainly not encourage people to consume expensive concoctions designed to produce warts. Since there is no demand for such potions, however, there is no need to pass a law against them.) Therefore, in the absence of sanctions against buying and selling an illegal good, we can expect demand and supply curves for the good to be similar to those for a legal good. In Figure 3–10, the demand and supply curves for an illegal commodity in the absence of penalties are given by DD and SS, respectively. Here, the equilibrium price is P_1 and the equilibrium rate of consumption is Q_1.

If society collectively decides that the consumption of a good—say, pornographic economic textbooks—is so unsavory that it should be prohibited, enforcement of this prohibition will affect the demand and supply curves for the good. If penalties are imposed on the suppliers of these books, the costs of supplying them will increase because suppliers will then have to make an additional effort to conceal their operations and to pay the penalties they will incur if they are caught. Thus, suppliers will respond by requiring a higher price for any given quantity supplied than was charged before the prohibition; the supply will decline, and the supply curve will shift to the left—say, from SS to $S'S'$ in Figure 3–10.

Similarly, if penalties are imposed on students who insist on learning that economics is not as dismal as was once believed, some students will be dis-

Figure 3–10
Enforcing Prohibition on a Good

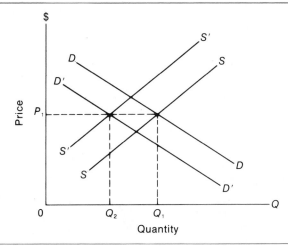

couraged from buying an X-rated economics text. Thus, the prohibition will reduce the demand and the demand curve will shift to the left. In Figure 3–10, this shift is from *DD* to *D'D'*.

Note that the reduction in demand and supply is such that the equilibrium price remains at P_1 even though the consumption rate declines from Q_1 to Q_2. Although quantity always declines, price does not always remain the same. The degree of the reduction in demand and supply depends on how effectively authorities identify and convict the users and suppliers of an illegal good and how extreme the penalties are. If, for example, suppliers are searched out and severely penalized but users are not curtailed in any way, the supply curve will shift substantially to the left–say, from *SS* to *S'S'* in Figure 3–11–but the position of the demand curve will not change. This results in an increase in equilibrium price from P_1 to P_2 and a decrease in the consumption rate from Q_1 to Q_2. It is also worth noting that the more price elastic the demand is for such a product, the more effectively this particular enforcement policy will reduce consumption. If demand is extremely inelastic, such a policy would greatly increase the price of the good but have little impact on its consumption.

The effects of enforcement are different if the users rather than the suppliers of an illegal good are subject to punishment. In this case, the demand for the good will be reduced as users become increasingly reluctant to consume the product. In Figure 3–12, this situation is depicted by a shift in the demand curve from *DD* to *D'D'* while the supply curve remains at *SS*. As in Figure 3–11, where enforcement is concentrated on suppliers, the equilibrium rate of consumption when users are penalized declines from Q_1 to Q_2 in Figure 3–12. However, the equilibrium price falls from P_1 to P_2, compared to the increase in

if ↓S > ↓D ⇒ ↑p

See Fig 3-11

if E > 1, ↑p → ↓q
→ effective enforcement

if ↓D > ↓S ⇒ ↓p

Figure 3–11
Penalizing Only Suppliers
of an Illegal Good

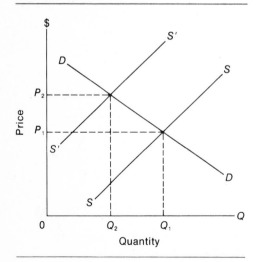

Figure 3–12
Penalizing Only Users
of an Illegal Good

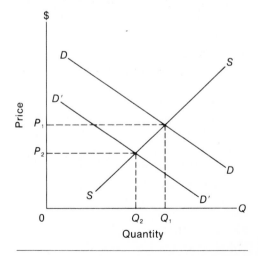

Figure 3-13
Penalizing Suppliers Versus Penalizing Users

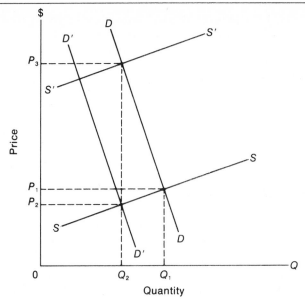

equilibrium price from P_1 to P_2 in Figure 3–11 when suppliers are penalized. Note that price elasticity again plays a crucial role in determining the effectiveness of a law enforcement policy. In this case, the policy of penalizing users more effectively reduces the consumption rate of an illegal good as the price elasticity of supply increases. If the supply curve is extremely inelastic, the primary effect of reducing demand will be to reduce price, not consumption.

What does this analysis tell us about how law enforcement resources should be employed to minimize the cost of reducing the consumption of an unlawful good by a given amount? All other factors being equal, our analysis indicates that enforcement should be directed against *users* if demand elasticity is small relative to supply elasticity, and against *suppliers* if the situation is reversed.

Casual empiricism suggests that the demand elasticity of an illegal good is likely to be small relative to its supply elasticity. Prohibited goods are often addictive (whether or not this is the case for pornographic economic textbooks is debatable!), and connoisseurs of these goods are often reluctant to reduce their consumption as price increases. On the other hand, the supply elasticities of most illegal goods are likely to be quite high, because capital requirements are normally modest and it is relatively easy for suppliers to move in or out of the industry in response to changes in price. If this analysis is accurate, it would seem more efficient to concentrate law enforcement resources on users. As Figure 3–13 shows, with relatively inelastic demand and elastic supply, a reduction in demand from DD to $D'D'$ will reduce consumption from Q_1 to Q_2

direct enforcement to the side with the smallest relative elasticity and decrease price from P_1 to P_2, assuming that supply remains at SS. If users are ignored, demand remains at DD, and all enforcement is directed at suppliers, the supply curve will have to be shifted from SS to $S'S'$, with price increasing to P_3 to obtain the same reduction in consumption. The reduction in demand necessary to reduce consumption by a given amount is much smaller than the required reduction in supply, indicating that enforcement should be focused on the users of illegal goods.

It is interesting to observe from Figure 3–13 that if law enforcement officials were to concentrate on penalizing consumers, the effect of prohibiting the consumption of an illegal good would be to reduce its price. But this seems to be at variance with what actually happens to the price of a good when it is declared illegal. Normally, the price of an illegal good will increase, which, according to Figure 3–13, indicates that enforcement is being directed primarily at suppliers.

We should not immediately conclude, however, that law enforcement resources are being poorly allocated. Remember the qualification that all other factors remain equal. This qualification permits us to ignore the difference in cost between reducing demand and reducing supply. We would expect it to be much more difficult to reduce demand than supply simply because suppliers are generally less numerous and more visible than consumers. A supplier must be visible to some degree to attract customers. Although suppliers can make their businesses more visible to potential consumers (it would be unusual for a supplier of illegal goods to advertise on billboards or television), even selective visibility makes suppliers vulnerable to police detection. On the other hand, consumers are much more difficult to detect; often they can consume the illegal goods in the privacy of their homes and may only be visible for brief periods when they make their purchases. This, coupled with the fact that normally there are many consumers for each supplier, makes it much less expensive to detect and penalize suppliers rather than users of illegal goods. Therefore, it might be possible to reduce the consumption of an illegal good more by concentrating law enforcement resources on suppliers rather than users, even though demand elasticity is low relative to supply elasticity. To analyze how a given quantity of enforcement resources should be allocated among users and suppliers to minimize consumption, we would need detailed information about both the enforcement costs and the demand and supply curves of the illegal goods.

Application: Does Crime Pay?

All our lives we have been told that crime does not pay, so does it make any sense to ask if crime does pay? To an economist it does. Economists tend to view human behavior as the rational pursuit of self-interest, and they expect individuals to engage in an activity (whether it is going to college, accepting a job, or committing a crime) only if the benefits exceed the cost—that is, only if it pays. Whether or not you accept this view of human behavior entirely (and we are not arguing that it is the only or best view, although we do argue that it can be a useful one), when many people engage in crime, it certainly makes sense to ask if crime does indeed pay.

Figure 3–14
Demand Curve for Burglary

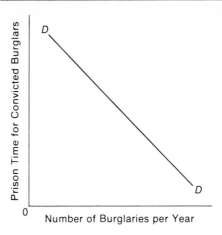

The Business of Crime

Economists have investigated the profitability of crime. This is not an easy task because it involves many factors, including such considerations as the return from the successful completion of a crime, the probability of being caught, the probability of losing the stolen goods if caught, the probability of being convicted if caught, and the cost of being convicted. Despite these complexities, it has been estimated that each act of burglary should yield a profit to the burglar of $112 above the expected cost and that the net return from an act of larceny should be $119.[9]

If, as the evidence indicates, crime does pay and if individuals who are considering a possible career in crime take the expected payoff into consideration, some interesting implications arise. For the sake of example, we could construct a demand curve for a particular criminal activity (say, burglary) and measure the amount of the activity (the number of burglaries) along the horizontal axis and some cost or price associated with the activity (the average time served in prison by convicted burglars) along the vertical axis. We would expect this demand curve for committing a burglary (shown as *DD* in Figure 3–14) to be downward sloping and look much like any other demand curve, and evidence indicates that this is the case. In 1960, the prison-time elasticity for this demand curve was estimated to be .90.[10] In other words, for every

---

[9]Isaac Ehrlich, "Participation in Illegitimate Activities: An Economic Analysis," in Gary Becker and William Landes (eds.), *Essays in the Economics of Crime and Punishment* (New York: National Bureau of Economic Research and Columbia University Press, 1974), pp. 132–33.
[10]Ehrlich, p. 97.

1% increase in the length of prison sentences there was a .90% decrease in burglaries committed.

We could construct another demand curve for burglary by replacing prison time on the vertical axis with the probability of being apprehended and imprisoned. In the study just cited, Isaac Ehrlich estimated that the probability of the imprisonment elasticity of demand for burglary was .53, indicating that a 1% increase in the probability of going to prison for burglary in 1960 reduced the number of burglaries by .53%. Thus, the demand curve for criminal activity appears to be downward sloping. Crimes can be reduced by increasing the cost of engaging in them, thereby reducing the rate of return on crime.

Capital Punishment

The conclusion that we can reduce the amount of a crime by increasing the cost of engaging in it raises an interesting and controversial question. Will capital punishment reduce the murder rate? Until economists recently began to study this question, the widely accepted answer among academics was no. There were studies to support this view—studies that showed no significant difference between the per-capita murder rates in states with capital punishment and states without it. A plausible argument to support the view that capital punishment has no impact on murder rate has also been offered. We can accept the view that potential burglars decide whether or not to burglarize after rationally weighing the costs and benefits involved, but we can reject the view

Example 3-3

Unemployment and Juvenile Delinquency

If increasing the cost of engaging in criminal activities will reduce the amount of crimes committed, then it follows that anything that reduces this cost will prompt an increase in crime. One cost associated with incarceration is the income that would otherwise have been earned through legal pursuits. Therefore, we would expect an increase in the unemployment rate (a decrease in the likelihood of finding a job) to lower the expected cost of committing a crime.

Studies that have been made on this subject are consistent with this view. One study of the relationship between juvenile delinquency and the unemployment rate in Detroit found a direct correlation between the increase in unemployment there and an increase in the number of Detroit juveniles who committed crimes. According to the study, the elasticity of this relationship ranged from .17 to .25, indicating that a 1% increase in the unemployment rate could be expected to increase juvenile delinquency .17–.25%.

The study cited here can be found in Larry D. Singell, "An Examination of the Empirical Relationship Between Unemployment and Juvenile Delinquency," *The American Journal of Economics and Sociology* (October 1967), pp. 377–86.

that potential murderers do the same thing based on the argument that murder usually results from uncontrollable emotions and not from reasoned calculation of net gain.

However, before we can determine whether this is true, we must carefully analyze whether or not capital punishment is actually carried out in states where it is a legal alternative. Most states with capital punishment have not enforced it for years. These states usually sentence murderers more leniently—often reducing the punishment a murderer faces below the penalty for murder in states without capital punishment. For example, states with capital punishment for first-degree murder typically reduce the charge to second-degree murder; this occurs less often in states where life imprisonment is the maximum sentence.

It is undoubtedly true that most murderers are motivated by emotion, not by calculation. But some potential murderers, if only a few, are influenced by the likely consequences of committing murder. Because the death penalty is considered to be the ultimate penalty, the natural conclusion seems to be that enforcing the maximum penalty against murderers will discourage at least some murderers.

Probably the most careful study of the impact of enforcing capital punishment on the murder rate has been done by Isaac Ehrlich.[11] Ehrlich estimated the elasticity of the demand curve for murder in the United States, measuring the murder rate on the horizontal axis and the probability of being executed if convicted on the vertical axis. The data indicate that this elasticity is between .06 and .065; that is, for every 1% increase in the probability of being executed if convicted for murder, there will be about a .06% decrease in the number of murders committed.[12] This evidence is quite consistent with the view that most murders are acts of passion and that the demand curve for murder is highly inelastic. But the demand curve does not appear to be vertical, indicating that increasing the probability of being executed for committing murder will reduce the murder rate. Based on Ehrlich's elasticity estimates, the trade-off between more murders or more executions is rather dramatic. His estimates, based on U.S. murder and execution rates from 1935 to 1969, indicate that increasing the number of executions by one per year during this period would have eliminated seven or eight murders each year.

This type of information may or may not affect our feelings about the desirability of capital punishment. It is important to take other considerations—particularly the possibility of executing an innocent person—into account when making a judgment on this question. But when we remember that most murder victims are innocent, studies such as Ehrlich's can give us some ideas of what the relevant trade-offs are.

---

[11]Isaac Ehrlich, "The Deterrent Effect of Capital Punishment: A Question of Life and Death," *American Economic Review* (June 1975), pp. 397–417.

[12]Note that if the probability of being executed if convicted is now 1%, an increase to 2% is *not* a 1% increase. Rather, it is a 100% increase, and these elasticities indicate that approximately 6% fewer people will be murdered if the probability of execution is raised to 2%.

3-4 Summary

In Chapter 3, we have learned that it is often useful to consider how responsive the rate of demand or supply is to changes in price. The concept of elasticity has been developed to allow information on this responsiveness to be captured in one number. This elasticity measure is independent of the units used in measuring price and rate of demand and supply. The magnitude of the elasticity measure depends on several factors, one of the most important being the length of time that economic decision makers have to respond to changes in price. The more time that is allowed for adjustments to be made following a price change, the more pronounced these adjustments will be. We have also learned that elasticities can be used to measure the demand or supply response of a good to changes in the price of related goods and to changes in income. The magnitude of these elasticities also increases as more time is allowed for adjustments to be made to these changes.

We now know that the most commonly used elasticity is the *price elasticity of demand,* which tells us the percentage increase in quantity demanded that results from a 1% decrease in price. In general, this elasticity will vary from point to point on the demand curve, becoming progressively smaller as we move into the lower portion of the demand curve. When the price elasticity of demand is greater than 1 ($E > 1$), decreases in price will increase revenue; when this elasticity is less than 1 ($E < 1$), decreases in price will decrease revenue. Therefore, revenue is maximized when the elasticity equals 1 ($E = 1$).

We have also learned to use the *cross-price elasticity of demand* to determine how the price of one good can influence the demand for another good. For example, the cross-price elasticity of demand between film and the price of film development tells us the percentage change in the quantity of film demanded when the price of development increases 1%. This cross-price elasticity is *negative* when the two goods are *complements,* as is the case with film and film development. However, when the two goods are *substitutes,* an increase in the price of one good increases the quantity demanded of the other good, and the cross-price elasticity is *positive.*

To measure the influence of an increase in income on the demand for a good, we have learned to use the *income elasticity of demand.* This elasticity tells us the percentage change in the quantity of a good demanded that results from a 1% increase in income. The income elasticity of demand is *positive* for *normal goods* and *negative* for *inferior goods.*

Although it is not used as often as the demand elasticities, we have also been introduced to the *price elasticity of supply.* This elasticity measures the percentage increase in the quantity of a good supplied that results from a 1% increase in the price of the good.

We have seen how the concept of elasticity can be applied to prohibit the consumption of "undesirable" or illegal goods. As the elasticity of *demand* for a prohibited good increases, the policy of punishing *suppliers* to reduce the supply of the good becomes more effective. As elasticity of *supply* increases, the policy of penalizing *users* of the illegal good to reduce demand becomes more effective. However, it may be sensible to concentrate law enforcement efforts against suppliers even though demand is quite inelastic, because suppliers are fewer in number and easier to identify than their customers. The observation that enforcing a prohibition against a good generally increases its price indicates that most of current enforcement efforts are directed against suppliers.

For some individuals, crime represents an opportunity to increase their income. The lower the expected cost of being caught, the more attractive it will be to commit the crime. We have found that it can be useful to analyze criminal behavior in terms of a demand curve for engaging in a criminal activity, measuring the amount of the criminal activity on the horizontal axis and some expected cost or price of being caught on the vertical axis. The elasticities of different demand curves for crime have been estimated by economists.

In Chapter 4, the economic model of consumer behavior will be developed. This model provides the theoretical foundation for the demand curves we have been considering.

References

Becker, Gary, and William Landes (eds.). *Essays in the Economics of Crime and Punishment*. New York: National Bureau of Economic Research and Columbia University Press, 1974.

Houthakker, Hendrik. *Economic Policy for the Farm Sector*. Washington, D.C.: American Enterprise Institute, November 1967, Chapter 2.

Rottenberg, Simon. "The Clandestine Distribution of Heroin: Its Discovery and Suppression." *Journal of Political Economy* (January/February, 1968), pp. 78–90.

Problems

1. Assume that the following table provides the demand curve for a product you are selling:

PRICE	QUANTITY SOLD
$100	0
90	1
80	2
70	3
60	4
50	5
40	6
30	7
20	8
10	9

(a) Use the arc elasticity of demand formula to calculate the price elasticity of demand over several different price intervals.

(b) What is the lowest price interval over which $E > 1$? What is the highest price interval over which $E < 1$?

(c) What price will maximize the revenue you receive for selling the product? Explain the relationship between your answer to (c) and your answers to (b).

2. Assume that the average price of a new car is $7,000 and that 9 million cars are sold at this price each year. If the price elasticity of demand for new cars is 1.5, what will be the effect on yearly sales if the average price of a new car declines to $6,930?

3. Assume that there is an increase in per-capita income of $150 per year in a large metropolitan area. Before this increase, per-capita income was $15,000 per year and daily ridership on the city bus system was 500,000. What will be the effect on this ridership if the income elasticity of demand for bus service is -1.5?

4. Assume that the demand curve for a product you sell is known. If your motivation is to maximize profits, explain why you will price your product so that the price elasticity of demand is greater than 1. To answer this question, what assumption did you have to make about the cost of producing your product? What elasticity would you choose if your production costs were 0? If they were negative?

5. You are the only seller of a product that costs absolutely nothing to produce and has an amazingly high income elasticity of demand of 25. After reading this chapter, you decide that you can maximize your profits by giving money away to your customers, thereby increasing their incomes and greatly increasing the demand for your product. This idea is innovative. Why is it irrational? Under what conditions would this idea be both innovative and rational?

6. Assume that for some unexplained reason the average temperature in the United States suddenly and permanently decreases 3°. Justify the prediction that the price of battery-heated clothing will increase immediately but will decline soon thereafter, although not necessarily to the level that existed before the drop in temperature.

7. Evidence supports the view that the demand for some illegal drugs is highly inelastic. There is also evidence to support the view that much of the crime in U.S. cities is committed to obtain money for drugs. If your motivation is to reduce drug use without causing an increase in the general crime rate, would you support more stringent penalties for users or suppliers? Explain your answer.

8. Over the last ten years, two convicted murderers have been executed per year on the average. Over the same ten years, the murder rate has averaged 2,000 per year. The demand for murder is highly inelastic with respect to capital punishment. Based on data during the last ten years, this elasticity figure is only .01. If one more murderer had been executed each year, how many less murders would there have been over the last ten years?

9. The price elasticity of demand for agricultural products is normally $E < 1$. Use this fact to explain why farmers generally succeed financially in years when their productivity is poor. Despite this fact, why do individual farmers strive to produce as much as possible each year?

10. A supply curve yields the following relationship between price and quantity supplied:

PRICE	QUANTITY
$0	0
1	1
2	2
3	3
4	4
5	5
6	6
7	7

What is the price elasticity of supply between prices $1 and $2? Between prices $5 and $6? Between any other two prices? Now answer the same questions for the supply curve given by

PRICE	QUANTITY
$0	0
1	5
2	10
3	15
4	20
5	25
6	30
7	35

11. Consider the following demand curve:

PRICE	QUANTITY
$10	1.00000
9	1.11111
8	1.25000
7	1.42857
6	1.66666
5	2.00000
4	2.50000
3	3.33333
2	5.00000
1	10.00000

What is the price elasticity of demand between prices $10 and $9? Between prices $3 and $2? Is it accurate to refer to the *price elasticity* of this demand curve? Explain your answer.

CHAPTER FOUR
CONSUMER BEHAVIOR

Introduction 4-1

In Chapter 1, we emphasized that microeconomic analysis is fundamentally concerned with how decision makers respond to scarcity. As consumers, we are acutely aware of the problems imposed by scarcity. Long before we become producers, our talent for consumption is well developed. In fact, we become producers largely because our aptitude for consuming desirable goods eventually overwhelms our parents' tolerance or financial resources—if not both. And no matter how large our incomes become they will always be inadequate to support our desired consumption levels. This forces us to make some hard choices—choices that result in a consumption pattern that will leave many of our desires and aspirations partially or completely unsatisfied.

In Chapter 4, we will develop a model of how consumers make their consumption choices. To do this, we will be required to make some explicit assumptions about the tastes and motivations of consumers. These assumptions will be unrealistic in the sense that they will ignore some considerations that are potentially relevant to consumer decision making. However, focusing our attention on these factors that seem to be most germane to the questions we wish to answer will help us to develop a model that is not only useful but also relatively simple to understand and apply.

Consumer Preferences 4-2

Basic Assumptions

Obviously, our tastes and preferences play a critical role in the consumption choices we make. Some people love to spend an evening at the opera or the ballet; others prefer to stay home, drink beer, and watch the football game. Some people emphasize leisurely dining and exquisite cuisine; others are content with a fast-food burger topped off with a couple of Alka Seltzers. Some people take pride in a fashionable home and have modest tastes in cars and clothing; others are willing to sacrifice all but the basics in housing so that they can drive the best and wear the latest. Individuals have variant preferences; even consumers at the same income level can be expected to exhibit quite different consumption patterns.

For the purposes of our model, we will assume that an individual's preferences are given and remain constant throughout the analysis. This ignores interesting and enormously complicated questions about how preferences are acquired and how and why they change, but allows us to focus on the aspects of preferences that are most useful for our purposes. In this regard, one of the most important aspects of preferences concerns the individual's ability to choose between different bundles of goods. Given a choice among bundles of goods, we assume that a consumer will choose to rank the bundles from the most preferred to the least preferred. For example, let's assume that two bundles of goods are available: Bundle A contains a small house, a two-month trip to Europe, and a Mercedes sports car; bundle B contains a large house, a two-week backpacking trip in the Grand Canyon, and a Datsun station wagon. We have assumed that, faced with a choice between these bundles, an individual can tell us whether A is preferred to B, B is preferred to A, or A and B are equally attractive (the individual is indifferent between A and B).

This first assumption is certainly plausible, given that people choose between different bundles of goods every time they go shopping. It should also be recognized as a crucial assumption. Unless we assume that individuals can differentiate between bundles of goods in accordance with their preferences, we have no basis on which to develop a systematic view of consumer behavior.

Our second assumption is that consumers will always prefer to have more rather than less of a commodity. If, for example, bundles A and B contain exactly the same commodities in exactly the same quantities, except that A contains an additional unit of one commodity, the consumer will always prefer bundle A. Commodities that satisfy this assumption are sometimes referred to as **goods,** indicating that consumers prefer more rather than less of them. Commodities that do not satisfy this assumption are sometimes referred to as **bads,** indicating that consumers prefer less rather than more of them.

This second assumption is really for convenience and can be ignored without damaging our analysis. It is easy to think of commodities as goods up to a certain rate of consumption and as bads beyond that point. Food is an obvious example. However, the assumption that we are dealing with goods rather than bads is not very restrictive, because, as we will see, it requires unusual circumstances for an individual to consume a commodity beyond the point where it ceases to be a good.

The third assumption we will make is that preferences are *transitive.* By **transitive preferences,** we mean that an individual who prefers a compact car to a ten-speed bike and a ten-speed bike to a skateboard will prefer the car to the skateboard. Similarly, an individual who is indifferent between a swimming pool and a tennis court or also between a tennis court and a two-month cruise on a luxury liner will be indifferent between the swimming pool and the cruise.

Many things are not transitive; the outcomes of football games provide an example. It is not uncommon for team A to beat team B, which has beaten team C, and then for team C to humiliate team A. But the assumption that preferences are transitive can be easily defended by assuming that preferences are *not* transitive. For example, suppose that an individual prefers bundle A to bundle B, bundle B to bundle C, and bundle C to bundle A. This individual initially possesses C. Since he prefers B, if you offered him B, he would be willing to give you C plus some positive sum of money in return. If you then offered him A, he would be willing to give up B and a sum of money. But since he prefers C to A, you could entice him to give up A and some money to return C to him. Then our individual would be right back where he started, minus a little money, and you could repeat the procedure all over again. In fact, as long as the individual's preferences fail to satisfy the transitivity assumption, you could continue to entice him from one bundle to the next until he spent all his money. Obviously, it would be difficult to find an individual whose preferences are not transitive, but taking the trouble to locate such an individual might well be worth the effort if you believe he or she exists.

Before the last assumption about individual preferences is stated and discussed, it will be convenient to use the assumptions we have already made to develop an important concept in the theory of consumer behavior—indifference curves.

Indifference Curves

Indifference curves enable us to represent an individual's preferences graphically as long as each bundle only contains two goods. A particular indifference curve will pass through sets of **consumption bundles** that the individual finds equally attractive. In other words, the individual has an equal preference for all bundles of goods that lie on a given indifference curve.

For example, bundle A, represented by point A in Figure 4–1, contains X_1 units of good X and Y_1 units of good Y. To obtain the indifference curve that passes through point A, we must locate all other bundles that the individual finds equally as desirable as bundle A. From our assumption that we are dealing with goods, rather than bads, we can determine the general areas in Figure 4–1 where these bundles of indifference will be located. First, consider area I, including the boundary lines. Any bundle of goods other than A represented in this area contains more of at least one good and no less of the other than bundle A does. Clearly, any such bundle is preferred to bundle A, and the indifference curve that passes through point A cannot lie anywhere in area I. Next, consider area III, including the boundary lines. All bundles except A represented in this area contain less of at least one good and no more of the other than A does. Therefore A is preferred to any bundle in area III, and the indifference curve that contains point *A* will not lie in this area. Through the process of elimination, we can conclude that the indifference curve that passes through point *A* will occupy areas II and IV, excluding the boundary lines. The logical reason that a portion of the indifference curve will occupy area II, for example, is that an individual who is presented with a bundle that contains more of good Y than bundle A does will only be indifferent between this new bundle and bundle A if the new bundle contains less of good X. Similarly, any bundle that contains less of good Y than A but is just as attractive as A must contain more of good X. We conclude that the indifference curve that passes through point *A* (curve *II* in Figure 4–1) has a downward slope. Since we chose bundle A arbitrarily, we can also conclude that an indifference curve passing through any point (in other words, *any* indifference curve) has a downward slope.

In general, an individual will view every bundle of goods as being equally attractive as some other bundles of goods. This means that an indifference curve will pass through every conceivable bundle of goods. The set of all these indifference curves represents a complete picture of a given individual's preferences. Some additional characteristics of indifference curves can be examined if we look at two indifference curves on the same graph. In Figure 4–2, $I_1 I_1$ and $I_2 I_2$ represent two of an individual's indifference curves for commodity bundles containing goods X and Y. It is important to recognize that the further northeast an indifference curve lies, the more attractive the bundles of goods it passes through will be. All bundles lying on indifference curve $I_2 I_2$, for example, are preferred to any bundle lying on indifference curve $I_1 I_1$. This follows immedi-

Figure 4–1
Downward-Sloping Indifference Curve

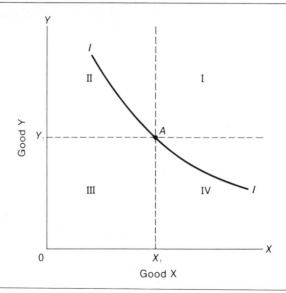

Figure 4–2
Comparing Bundles with Indifference Curves

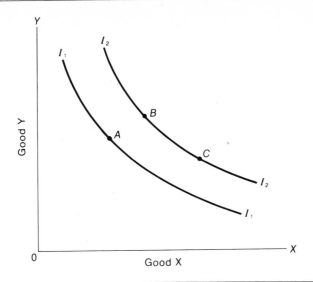

ately from the fact that bundle B is preferred to bundle A, since it contains more of both goods, and from the transitivity requirement that any bundle equally attractive to B must be preferred to any bundle equally attractive to A. From this, we know that bundle C, even though it contains less of good Y than bundle A, is preferred to A. In accordance with the consumer's preferences represented by these indifference curves, the additional units of good X contained in bundle C more than compensate for the fewer units of good Y. Without the information indifference curves provide, it would be impossible to make preference comparisons between bundles like A and C.

Another important characteristic of indifference curves is that they will never intersect. The best way to see why this is true is to assume that two indifference curves do intersect and to notice that this contradicts the assumption that preferences are transitive. In Figure 4–3 indifference curves I_1I_1 and I_2I_2 are shown to intersect at bundle A (point A). Since indifference curve I_1I_1 passes through both points A and B, it follows that the individual is indifferent between bundle A and bundle B. Likewise, bundles A and C are equally attractive, since I_2I_2 passes through both A and C. Thus, if both bundle B and bundle C are equally preferred to bundle A, the assumption of transitive preferences requires that the choice between B and C be a matter of indifference. However, this is clearly not the case, since bundle B contains more of both goods than bundle C does. Therefore, if indifference curves did intersect, the preferences they represent could not be transitive. Thus, given our assumption of transitive preferences, indifference curves cannot intersect.

Figure 4–3
Intersecting Indifference Curves
and Nontransitive Preferences

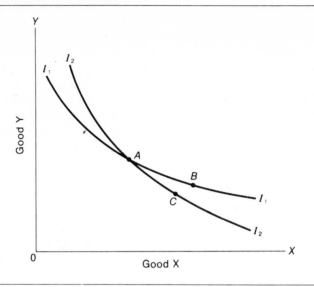

The Marginal Rate of Substitution

Until this point, the only characteristic we have established for the shape of an indifference curve is that it has a downward or a negative slope. But in constructing indifference curves, we have consistently shown that the slope also becomes progressively less negative (flatter) as we travel down a given indifference curve. Indifference curves that possess this characteristic are said to be *convex*. None of the assumptions we have already made about preferences requires that indifference curves be convex. But because, as we will see later, indifference curves are more useful when they are convex, we will introduce one more assumption concerning preferences, which will imply convex indifference curves.

Our final assumption is that the more of one good an individual consumes along a given indifference curve, the less the marginal value of that good will be relative to the marginal values of the other good. This means that as we move down a given indifference curve—increasing the consumption of good X while decreasing the consumption of good Y—the value of an additional unit of X decreases relative to Y. Another way of stating this is to say that as we move down a given indifference curve, the amount of good Y an individual would be willing to sacrifice in return for one more unit of good X becomes smaller. This assumption is certainly plausible at an intuitive level and, as we will see, implies

remember—it's
not a straight line

the widely observed behavior that individuals will allocate their expenditures over a variety of goods rather than spend their entire income on one item.

To relate this assumption to the shape of indifference curves, first we must learn how information about the value an individual places on an additional unit of a good is obtained from an indifference curve. In Figure 4–4, an individual possesses bundle A, which contains X_1 units of good X and Y_1 units of good Y. The indifference curve II passes through A. We now ask how much value does the individual place on an additional unit of good X, or how much of good Y would this individual be willing to give up for an additional unit of good X? Indifference curve II shows us that if the individual receives an extra unit of X, then $Y_1 - Y_2$ units will have to be subtracted from the new bundle of goods if bundle B is to be no more or less attractive than bundle A. Subtracting less than $Y_1 - Y_2$ units away would leave the individual at some bundle directly above B that would be preferred to B and, therefore, to A. So beginning at point A in Figure 4–4, the individual would be willing to sacrifice as many as $Y_2 - Y_1$ units of good Y to acquire an additional unit of good X. Thus, the marginal value of good X is equal to $Y_2 - Y_1$ units of good Y.

The number of units of good Y that an individual is willing to exchange for an additional unit of good X is often referred to as the **marginal rate of substitution.** However, the more precise definition of the marginal rate of substitution is -1 multiplied by the slope of the indifference curve. When goods are mea-

Figure 4–4
The Marginal Rate of Substitution

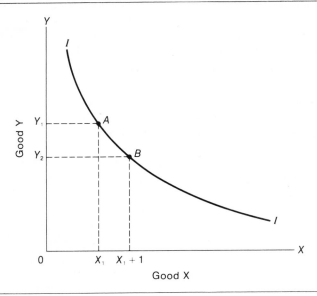

and that absolute value 'slope' curve is diminishing

sured in very small units, these two definitions provide almost identical measures of the marginal rate of substitution as well as a measure of the relative value that the individual places on the additional unit of good X.[1] This means, according to our assumption that relative marginal value diminishes with relative abundance, that the marginal rate of substitution becomes smaller and smaller as we move down a given indifference curve. Of course, this is the same as saying that the slope of the indifference curve becomes progressively less negative (flatter) as we move down the curve; that is, the shape of the curve is convex.

This declining marginal rate of substitution or convexity of indifference curves is illustrated in Figure 4–5. We will assume that an individual initially possesses bundle A (point *A*) on indifference curve *II*. Bundle A represents a consumption pattern in which the individual enjoys large quantities of food but has to eat it in a cramped corner of the kitchen in a tiny apartment. As indicated by the steep slope of the indifference curve as it passes through *A*, the individual would be willing to give a substantial amount of food intake in exchange for a small increase in living space. The marginal value of living space in terms of food is therefore quite high.

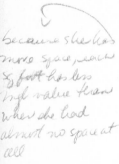

Bundle B (which our individual finds equally attractive to bundle A) is a smaller but adequate diet in an average-sized apartment or house. Having less food relative to living area, compared with bundle A, our individual will find the marginal value of housing space to be less when in possession of bundle B. This is indicated by the slope of the indifference curve at *B*, which, compared with the slope at *A*, tells us that at bundle B, our individual will not be willing to give up as much food for the same small increase in living space as was true at *A*.

Finally, we consider the trade-off that our individual would be willing to make when consuming bundle C on indifference curve *II*. Bundle C is a large home with spacious cooking and dining facilities, but meager rations. Under these circumstances, it is certainly reasonable to expect that our individual would be willing to give up very little food for an additional unit of living space, as indicated by the almost horizontal slope of the indifference curve at *C*.

The convexity of the indifference curve in this example tells us that the marginal rate at which the individual is willing to substitute housing space for food (sacrifice food for an additional unit of housing) becomes increasingly smaller as more housing space and less food are made available. Marginal rates of substitution diminish as we move up the indifference curve, as well. Moving along *II* in Figure 4–5 from bundle C to bundle A, we can easily see that the marginal rate at which the individual is willing to substitute food for housing becomes progressively smaller.

---

[1]According to the first definition, the marginal rate of substitution at *A* in Figure 4–4 is obtained by multiplying -1 by the average slope of *II* between *A* and *B*, or the slope of the straight line connecting *A* and *B*. According to the second definition, the marginal rate of substitution at *A* is given by the slope of the straight line tangent to *II* at *A* multiplied by -1. We can visualize the fact that as $X_1 + 1$ moves closer to X_1 as the units of measurement become smaller, the difference between the slopes of these two lines will diminish.

Figure 4–5
Diminishing Marginal Rates of Substitution

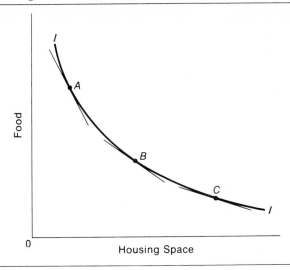

Although it is not possible to graph all of an individual's indifference curves because they are infinite in number, it is possible to provide a good description of an individual's preferences by constructing only a few indifference curves. Such a representation of preferences is often referred to as an individual's **indifference-curve map.** In Figure 4–6, two individuals' indifference-curve maps are graphed for the goods food and clothing. From the information contained in

Figure 4–6
Differences in Preferences

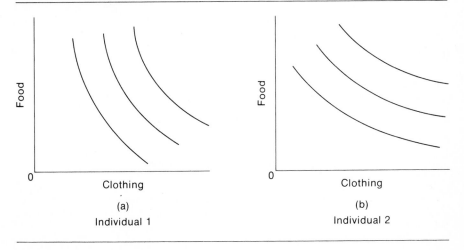

Figure 4–6, it is obvious that individuals 1 and 2 have different preferences for food and clothing. Assuming that the units of measure are identical on both graphs, individual 1's indifference curves in (a) are steeper than individual 2's curves in (b). This means that individual 1 places a higher marginal value on clothing relative to food than individual 2 does. This follows simply from the fact that when they are consuming the same bundle, individual 1 is willing to sacrifice more food for an additional unit of clothing than individual 2 is. Likewise, individual 2 places a higher marginal value on food relative to clothing than individual 1 does.

The information in Figure 4–6 leads us to believe that individual 1 is more of a dandy than 2 and that 2 is more of a gourmet than 1. However, some care must be exercised here to avoid inferring more information from indifference curves than they can actually convey. Even though individual 1 values an additional unit of clothing relative to food more than 2 does, this does not mean that 1 likes or enjoys clothing more than 2. Individual 2 may enjoy dressing up in the latest fashions but enjoys a gourmet meal even more. Therefore, 2 will be very cautious about giving up food in return for additional apparel, no matter how much individual 2 enjoys clothing. Individual 1, on the other hand, may not enjoy clothing nearly as much as 2 does but be even less enthusiastic about any food in excess of a modest diet. Therefore, individual 1 will be willing to sacrifice a large quantity of food for an additional unit of clothing. Indifference-curve maps provide important information about the preferences of individuals and the ways in which preferences differ between individuals, but they give us no indication of how much satisfaction a bundle of goods provides one individual relative to another individual.

Consumer Utility

The consumption of goods provides satisfaction, or **utility**–to use the term traditionally employed by economists. It is convenient to assign a numerical value to each bundle of goods that measures the utility an individual receives from consuming the bundle. To assign utility values that accurately reflect the individual's preferences, the only (but crucial) requirement is that the higher number be assigned to the bundle the individual prefers between any two bundles. If the individual is indifferent between two bundles, then both bundles would obviously receive the same number. This means that all bundles on a given indifference curve receive the same utility number–a fact that allows us to simply assign each indifference curve the utility value of the bundles it contains.

We know that bundles of goods on the highest indifference curve (the curve lying farthest in the northeast direction) are preferred. Therefore, the higher indifference curve will be assigned the higher utility number. An individual's indifference-curve map for goods X and Y, with utility values assigned, appears in Figure 4-7. There, we can see that the consumption of any bundle on the lowest indifference curve provides 1 *util* (unit of utility); any bundle on the next highest curve yields 53 utils; any bundle on the next highest curve, 76 utils; and 159 utils are obtained by consuming any bundle on the highest indifference curve shown.

With the exception of the restriction that higher numbers must be assigned to higher indifference curves, the numbering sequence in Figure 4-7 is totally arbitrary and tells us nothing about how much more the individual prefers a bundle on one indifference curve to a bundle on another curve. We cannot say, for example, that bundle B is 53 times as preferable as bundle A, that bundle C is 76 times as preferable as bundle A, or that the individual prefers bundle D three times more than bundle B. We do know that D is preferred to C, which is preferred to B, which is preferred to A, but we have no information about the degree of preference. The difference between utility numbers means nothing. Any other assignment of utility numbers would be just as acceptable, as long as it maintained the same ranking of bundles by assigning progressively higher numbers to bundles on higher indifference curves. For example, the utility numbers in parentheses in Figure 4-7 describe the individual preferences just as adequately as the original numbers do.

If utility numbers cannot be used to determine how much more a given individual prefers one bundle to another, then they cannot be employed to determine whether one individual likes a given bundle of goods more than another

Figure 4-7
The Acceptability of Different Utility Assignments

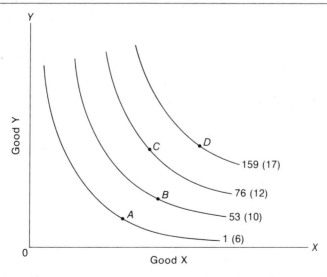

individual does. Consider the indifference-curve maps for individuals 1 and 2 in Figures 4–8(a) and (b), respectively. According to the utility numbers that have been assigned, if individuals 1 and 2 consume bundle A, 1 will receive 300 utils but 2 will receive only 2 utils. Does this permit us to conclude that individual 1 enjoys consuming bundle A more than individual 2 does? Of course not. We can assign another set of perfectly acceptable utility numbers that will allow individual 2 to receive the most utility from consuming bundle A. For example, the numbers in parentheses in Figures 4–8(a) and (b) appropriately rank the bundles of goods in accordance with each individual's preferences, but show individual 2 receiving 5 utils from A and individual 1 receiving only 3 utils from A. Utility numbers are used only to rank bundles of goods from those most preferred to those least preferred by an individual; they provide no information about the comparative enjoyment two individuals will derive from the same bundle. Economists refer to this as the inability to make interpersonal utility comparisons.

Can't compare one's satisfaction related to another

Example 4–1

Experimentally Determined Indifference Curves

An experiment to determine the characteristics of an individual's indifference curves was performed by K.R. MacCrimmon and M. Toda with seven students from the University of California at Los Angeles. The seven students were asked to construct indifference curves for money and ball-point pens and for money and pastries. A separate experiment was conducted for each indifference curve. Each experiment began with an initial reference point, or bundle, containing a given amount of money, measured along the horizontal axis, but none of the other good. The student was then presented with bundles containing varying amounts of money and the other good and asked whether each new bundle was preferred or not preferred to the initial bundle. After repeating this a number of times, a rather concise area remained that contained bundles the student found just as attractive as the initial bundle. The student then constructed his or her indifference curve within this area. This experiment was repeated seven times for the money–pen choices and four times for the money–pastry choices, and each experiment was begun with a different amount of money. So each student constructed seven indifference curves for money and pens and four indifference curves for money and pastries.

To motivate students to give thoughtful and honest answers, one of the bundles that had been considered was randomly chosen after each indifference curve was constructed. If it had been preferred to the initial bundle, the student received it; otherwise, the student received the initial bundle containing only money. In the experiments dealing with money and pastries, the student had to eat all the pastries in the bundle received before the money was awarded.

Ordinal Versus Cardinal Utility

Utility numbers provide an *ordinal ranking* of bundles of goods and are therefore referred to as **ordinal utilities.** In general, an **ordinal ranking** is any numerical measure that orders items from, for example, hard to soft, smooth to rough, friendly to unfriendly, or gorgeous to not-so-hot, without attaching any real significance to the scale employed or to the magnitude of the difference between the numbers assigned to any two of the ranked items.

In its current state of development, the economic theory of consumer behavior is based exclusively on ordinal utilities. This has not always been the case. The first economists to construct a specific model of consumer behavior in the late nineteenth and early twentieth centuries made a much stronger assumption about the measurability of utility than we have. They assumed that the utility an individual receives from the consumption of a bundle of goods could be measured in the same sense that a person's height or weight can be measured.

The resulting indifference curves were checked to see if they exhibited the characteristics that economists attribute to indifference curves. The indifference curves for each student were overlaid on the same graph to see if any of them intersected. They did not. The money–pen indifference curves and the money–pastry indifference curves were nonintersecting for all students. (The money–pastry indifference curves for three students did merge together as they moved out over the money axis.)

Also, as expected, the money–pen indifference curves were downward sloping. Students would give up money only in return for more pens, and vice versa. In other words, both money and pens were considered goods, not bads. This was not true of the money–pastry indifference curves. When the bundles being considered contained only a few pastries, male students would give up a little money to obtain another pastry so that their indifference curves were downward sloping. But after consuming about three pastries, they would consume another pastry only if they received more money. At this point, pastries became a bad, and the indifference curves became upward sloping. For the two women in the experiment, even the first pastry was a bad, and their money–pastry indifference curves were upward sloping from the beginning.

With only one minor exception, the indifference curves were convex everywhere. This is in keeping with the assumption of a diminishing marginal rate of substitution. On the upward-sloping portions of the money–pastry indifference curves, this convexity meant that the more pieces of pastry that were consumed, the more money would be required to encourage a subject to consume another pastry.

Based on K.R. MacCrimmon and M. Toda, "The Experimental Determination of Indifference Curves," *The Review of Economic Studies* (October 1969), pp. 433–51.

Figure 4–8
The Inability to Make Interpersonal Utility Comparisons

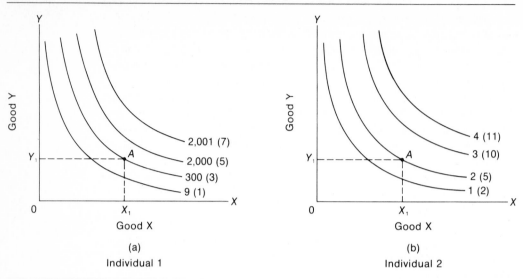

(a)

Individual 1

(b)

Individual 2

Given this assumption, utility numbers associated with different consumption bundles cannot be selected arbitrarily; each individual's preferences are described by the unique set of utilities he or she actually receives from the consumption of different bundles of goods. According to these utilities, if an individual receives, say, 15 utils from consuming bundle A and 30 utils from consuming bundle B, then the individual receives twice as much satisfaction from B than from A. A numerical measure with these characteristics is called a **cardinal measure,** and the utilities that most early economists worked with were **cardinal utilities.**

The concept of *marginal utility* is fundamental to the cardinal-utility approach to consumer behavior. **Marginal utility** is the change in total utility that results when an individual increases the consumption of a commodity by one unit. For example, let's assume that one ice-cream cone yields a total of 10 utils, the second cone increases the utility level to 16, the third increases utility to 20, and the fourth increases utility to 21. The marginal utility of the second cone is 6 (16 − 10) and the marginal utility of the third cone is 4 (20 − 16), but the marginal utility of the fourth cone is only 1 (21 − 20). The consumption of a fifth cone would probably precipitate severe indigestion and lower total utility to, say, 16. Thus, the marginal utility of the fifth cone would be − 5, and ice-cream cones would cease to be a good and would become a bad.

The marginal utility of cones diminishes as consumption expands, which is consistent with our intuitive belief that the continued consumption of almost any good will eventually result in progressively smaller increments of additional satisfaction, or diminishing marginal utility. The assumption of diminishing marginal utility has played an important role in the development of cardinal-utility consumer theory, because it explains why individuals spend their income on a wide variety of commodities and do not spend it all on one item. Earlier in this section, we said that the convexity of indifference curves, or the assumption of a diminishing marginal rate of substitution, explains why individual consumers do not concentrate their spending on one commodity. A common belief is that diminishing marginal rate of substitution is explained by the assumption of diminishing marginal utility, but this is not the case.

First, the assumption of a diminishing marginal rate of substitution is based on the shape of indifference curves derived from ordinal utility rankings, and the concept of marginal utility—diminishing or otherwise—has no meaning when we are dealing with ordinal utility. The concept of marginal utility attaches significance to the *difference in utility* that results from moving from one consumption bundle to another. But we already know that the difference between ordinal-utility numbers attached to different bundles is arbitrary and meaningless.

Second, if we assume cardinal utility and apply the concept of marginal utility, a diminishing marginal rate of substitution can result even if marginal utility is increased. Assume, for example, that as we move down an indifference curve, consuming more of good X and less of good Y, the marginal utility associated with good X is actually increasing. This is still consistent with being willing to give progressively less of good Y for each additional unit of good X if the marginal utility of Y is increasing more rapidly than the marginal utility of X, which is a completely acceptable possibility. The relationship between marginal utilities and the marginal rate of substitution will be discussed in greater detail in the next section.

It should be clear that the assumption of cardinal utilities is much stronger than the assumption of ordinal utilities. When ordinal utilities are used, the only assumption is that individuals are able to rank bundles of goods in accordance with their preferences. When cardinal utilities are used, a further assumption is that individuals can measure the utility they actually receive from the consumption of difference bundles to determine how much more or less they prefer one bundle to another. Also, as we learned in the previous section, ordinal utilities provide no justification for making utility comparisons between individuals to determine who obtains the most satisfaction from consuming a given bundle of goods. The assumption that cardinal utilities can actually be measured obviously encourages us to attempt to make utility comparisons between individuals, just as we would compare peoples' heights or weights.

The assumption of cardinal utility is certainly questionable and is rarely employed by economists today. But economists have not discarded this assumption simply because it is questionable or unrealistic. Economists and anyone else who works with theoretical models constantly employ unrealistic assumptions to ensure that their theories will be manageable and useful. But constant efforts are being made in all theoretical disciplines to develop new models that provide useful explanations and insights with more realistic or less restrictive assumptions. In the case of consumer theory, almost all the conclusions that follow from the assumption of cardinal utility can also be derived from the ordinal-utility assumption, and the ordinal approach provides some insights that are obscured by the cardinal approach. Thus, the fact that cardinal utility is a dubious assumption is not the only reason why it is no longer employed.

The Utility Function

When ordinal utilities have been assigned to all the bundles that an individual can potentially consume, this results in a functional relationship that we refer to as the individual's **utility function**–an ordinal utility function that serves simply to rank all bundles of goods in accordance with the individual's preferences. Such a utility function is not a unique description of the individual's preferences, because any of an infinite number of possible utility functions that maintained the same ranking would describe the same preference structure. But it is useful to use one of these functions as the individual's utility function.

Continuing with our two-good analysis, this utility function can be expressed as

$$U = U(X,Y) \qquad\qquad (4-1)$$

where U represents utility and X and Y are the quantities of goods X and Y, respectively. Once this utility function is specified, it is possible to obtain marginal utilities for goods X and Y. Since we are working with an ordinal-utility function, an individual marginal utility is of no important significance. But we will soon see that the slope of an indifference curve can be expressed as the ratio of these marginal utilities–an expression that will be useful when we examine the conditions that characterize consumer equilibrium.

In general, the marginal utility of good X depends on the quantity of goods X and Y being consumed. When the individual is consuming $\bar{X}$ units of good X and $\bar{Y}$ units of good Y, the marginal utility of good X can be expressed as

$$\mathrm{MU}_x\,(\bar{X}, \bar{Y}) = U\,(\bar{X} + 1, \bar{Y}) - U(\bar{X}, \bar{Y}) \qquad\qquad (4-2)$$

or the change in total utility when one more unit of good X is consumed. Likewise, we can express the marginal utility of good Y as

$$\mathrm{MU}_y\,(\bar{X}, \bar{Y}) = U(\bar{X}, \bar{Y} + 1) \;\; - U(\bar{X}, \bar{Y}) \qquad\qquad (4-3)[2]$$

Normally, these marginal utilities are expressed as simply MU_x and MU_y, but we should always remember that a marginal utility will vary from one consumption bundle to another.

The equation for any indifference curve can also be written after an accept-

---

[2]When dealing with extremely small units, the marginal utility of good X can be expressed more precisely as the partial derivative of $U(X,Y)$ with respect to good X, or $\mathrm{MU}_x = \partial U/\partial X$. Likewise, the marginal utility of good Y is given by $\mathrm{MU}_y = \partial U/\partial Y$.

able utility function has been specified. For example, the indifference curve that passes through all consumption bundles that provide a utility of 45 is given by

$$U(X,Y) = 45 \qquad (4\text{–}4)$$

By definition, all combinations of X and Y that satisfy this equation lie on the same indifference curve.

If the specific consumption bundle $(\bar{X},\bar{Y})$ lies on the indifference curve $U(X,Y) = \bar{U}$, where $\bar{U}$ is some specified level of utility, then we can increase the consumption of good X above $\bar{X}$ and remain on the same indifference curve only if the consumption of good Y is reduced below $\bar{Y}$. If we let ΔX be the increase in good X, the resulting increase in utility can be approximated by multiplying ΔX by the marginal utility of good X, or $\Delta X MU_x$. Similarly, the reduction in utility that results from a decrease in good Y, denoted by ΔY, is approximated by $\Delta Y MU_y$. If we are to remain on the same indifference curve, these changes in utility must *exactly* offset one another, or ΔX and ΔY must satisfy the equation

$$\Delta X MU_x + \Delta Y MU_y = 0 \qquad (4\text{–}5)$$

Since the changes in X and Y that satisfy this equation allow us to remain on the same indifference curve, we can subject Equation (4–5) to some simple algebraic manipulation to obtain an expression for the slope of the indifference curve:

$$\frac{\Delta Y}{\Delta X} = -\frac{MU_x}{MU_y} \qquad (4\text{–}6)$$

The ratio of the marginal utility of good X to the marginal utility of good Y multiplied by -1 gives us the slope of the indifference curve.[3]

---

[3]This result can be easily developed by using calculus. Consider the equation of an indifference curve.

$$U(X,Y) = C$$

where C is a specified constant. If a value is specified for X, we have one equation and one unknown Y, which can be solved for a specific value of Y. If we vary X, we must also vary Y to continue to satisfy the equation (to remain on the indifference curve). Therefore, Y can be considered a function of X, or $Y = Y(X)$, and the indifference curve equation can be written

$$U[(X, Y(X)] = C$$

Taking the total derivative of the left-hand side of this equation with respect to X has no effect on the value of the function, because of the way $Y(X)$ is defined. Thus

$$\frac{\partial U}{\partial X} + \frac{\partial U}{\partial Y}\frac{dY}{dX} = 0$$

Solving for dY/dX, the slope of the indifference curve, we obtain

$$\frac{dY}{dX} = -\frac{\partial U/\partial X}{\partial U/\partial Y}$$

or $-MU_x/MU_y$, the notation we will use here.

Since the marginal rate of substitution is obtained by multiplying -1 by the slope of the indifference curve, the marginal rate of substitution is equal to MU_x/MU_y. This is an intuitive result, given that the marginal rate of substitution measures the number of units of good Y that the consumer is willing to sacrifice to obtain an additional unit of good X. Assume, for example, that $MU_x = 8$ and $MU_y = 2$. This means that the marginal rate of substitution is 8/2, or 4: The individual will sacrifice 4 units of good Y for another unit of good X. This is reasonable, since the additional unit of good X increases utility by 4 times as much as the sacrifice of a unit of good Y reduces it. It is worth noting that the significant number here is 4, which results from the ratio of the marginal utilities. No matter what acceptable ordinal-utility function is chosen, each indifference curve will remain unchanged (although the utility designations will change). Bundles that have the same utility number in conjunction with one utility function will be assigned equal utilities by any other acceptable function. Therefore, the slope of an indifference curve—or the ratio of marginal utilities—does not depend on the particular utility function or on the individual marginal utilities.

4-3   The Budget Constraint

Much of our discussion of individual preferences has centered around the question of trade-offs: How much of one good is an individual willing to sacrifice to obtain additional amounts of another good? Now instead of asking what consumption trade-offs the individual is willing to make, we turn to another important question: What consumption trade-offs are possible? To answer this question, we must consider the relationship between the individual's income, the prices of the goods being purchased, and the collection of consumption bundles it is possible for the individual to purchase.

The individual would like to consume large quantities of almost all desirable commodities. Unfortunately, the individual's income limits how much can be spent, so that income becomes an important consideration in determining which consumption bundles the individual will choose. The prices of goods are also of concern here. With a given money income, the lower the prices, the greater the quantities of all goods that can be purchased.

Still assuming that only two goods are available, the relationship between an individual's income, the prices of the goods purchased, and the amount of each good the individual can buy is given by the equation

$$P_xX + P_yY = I \qquad (4-7)$$

where X is the quantity of good X purchased, Y is the quantity of good Y purchased, P_x is the price of good X, P_y is the price of good Y, and I is the individual's income.[4] This relationship, known as the **budget constraint,** is diagrammed

---

[4]The individual could refrain from spending all income on consumption and save some part of it. If this possibility were being considered, Equation (4–7) would be rewritten

$$P_xX + P_yY \leq I$$

However, the treatment of saving would require a multiperiod analysis, which would com-

**Figure 4–9
The Budget Constraint**

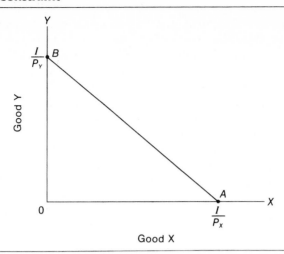

Good X

in Figure 4–9. Given the consumer's income and the prices that must be paid, this budget constraint runs through every bundle of goods that can be purchased.

Two consumption bundles lying on the budget constraint can be easily located. First, a consumer who spends all income on good X will be able to buy I/P_x units of good X and no units of good Y. For example, if the consumer's weekly income is $200 and the price of X is $5, then 200/5 = 40 units of good X can be purchased if no units of good Y are bought. In Figure 4–9, the obtainable bundle of goods, which contains nothing but good X, is shown as point *A*. This point is commonly referred to as the *X intercept* of the budget constraint. Similarly, the consumer who spends all income on good Y will be able to purchase I/P_y units of good Y and no units of good X. In Figure 4–9, this second bundle lies on the budget constraint at point *B*, or at the *Y intercept.*

The slope of the budget constraint is obviously negative, indicating that the consumer can only purchase additional units of good X by reducing the consumption of good Y. More precisely, the slope is given by multiplying − 1 by the distance 0*B* divided by the distance 0*A*, or − P_x/P_y. A plausible assumption at this point is that the prices are constant as far as the individual consumer is concerned. This means that the price ratio P_x/P_y is constant, and therefore the slope of the budget constraint is constant, as shown in Figure 4–9.

Multiplying the slope of the budget constraint by − 1 tells us how many units of good Y must be given up to purchase one more unit of good X. Therefore, it is not surprising that multiplying this slope by − 1 yields P_x/P_y. For

plicate the discussion and would add little to our understanding of the fundamentals of consumer theory. This complication will be considered in the appendix to this chapter, after we have developed the fundamental theory.

example, if $P_x = \$10$ and $P_y = \$2$, it is clear that if one more unit of X is purchased, the amount of good Y that can be bought is reduced by $P_x/P_y = 5$ units.

How consumers respond to changes in their incomes and in the prices they pay is of major interest in the theory of consumer behavior. To investigate these questions, we have to know how changes in income and prices affect the budget constraint. An increase in income will permit the consumer to purchase more of one good without purchasing less of the other good, thereby shifting the budget constraint up and to the right. This will be a parallel shift, because prices remain the same, so that the slope of the constraint does not change. The effect of income changes on the budget constraint is illustrated in Figure 4–10. With an income of I_2 and prices P_x and P_y, the budget constraint is given by the line connecting the Y intercept I_2/P_y and the X intercept I_2/P_x (line A in Figure 4–10). If income increases from I_2 to I_3, the X and Y intercepts also increase to I_3/P_x and I_3/P_y, respectively, and the new constraint is line B. If income decreases from I_2 to I_1, the X and Y intercepts also decrease and C is the new budget constraint.

If the price of good X changes but the price of good Y and the consumer's income remain the same, the X intercept of the budget constraint will change but the Y intercept will not. This causes the budget constraint to pivot on the Y intercept. Figure 4–11 illustrates the effect of a change in the price of good X. With prices P_x and P_y and income I, the budget constraint is line A. If the price of good X decreases from P_x to P_x', the X intercept moves to the right,

Figure 4–10
Shifts in the Budget Constraint Caused by Income Changes

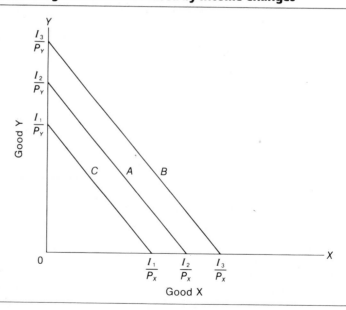

Figure 4–11
The Effect of a Price Change on the Budget Constraint

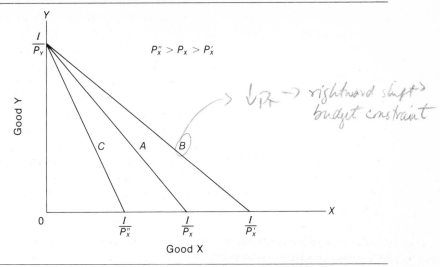

the Y intercept remains the same, and the new budget constraint is line B. If the price of good X increases from P_x to P_x'', the X intercept moves to the left, the Y intercept is still unaffected, and the budget constraint is line C. Similar reasoning establishes that if the price of good Y changes, but the price of good X and the consumer's income remain constant, the budget constraint will pivot on the X intercept.

Consumer Optimization   4–4

We have examined all the concepts we need to develop a model of consumer behavior. In our discussion of consumer preferences, we considered what trade-offs the consumer is willing to make. We then examined the budget constraint, concentrating on the trade-offs the consumer can make. Now we are ready to combine these two considerations to construct a model that will allow us to predict what the consumer will do.

Consumer Rationality

Before we can develop our model, however, it is necessary to make an assumption about the motivation of the consumer. We assume that the consumer is motivated to spend his or her limited income to achieve maximum personal benefit—that is, to reach the highest indifference curve possible. According to economists, the *rational* consumer attempts to reach the highest indifference curve (maximize utility) consistent with his or her budget constraint. This assumption energizes the model; without some assumption about consumer motivation, there would be no way for us to use the concepts we have developed to predict how consumers will behave.

The meaning that economists attach to the term "rational" is quite different from the meaning we commonly encounter. An individual who is observed drinking crank-case oil or purchasing a face drop from a plastic surgeon is not thought of as behaving rationally. Here, the use of the word "rational" refers to the individual's preferences. As economists employ the term "rational," they would not necessarily conclude that such an individual is irrational, although they would quickly agree that he exhibits rather strange tastes. According to the economist's concept of **consumer rationality,** consumers are perfectly rational, no matter how peculiar their preferences may be, as long as they behave in a way that is consistent with maximizing their utility (as they define it) subject to the constraints imposed by their budgets. In other words, unless this individual pays a higher price for the oil he drinks and for his saggy face than he has to, we cannot say that he is irrational in the sense that economists define the term.

Applying the term "rational" to preferences and tastes presents a problem: From any given individual's perspective, almost everyone else's behavior is irrational. This is not necessarily bad, since it is common to derive satisfaction from comparing your preferences to other people's preferences and smugly concluding that you are more rational than most. But in our analysis of consumer behavior, we will have to be a little more restrained and charitable in our use of the term "rational."

Consumer Equilibrium

We know that the consumer wishes to pick the consumption bundle that lies on his or her budget constraint and on the highest indifference curve possible. Given this information, it is possible to predict the consumption bundle that will be chosen.

A consumer's budget constraint and three indifference curves are shown in Figure 4–12. Of these three indifference curves, the consumer would prefer indifference curve I_3, but every bundle on I_3 lies above the budget constraint and is therefore unobtainable. This is not true of all the bundles on indifference curve I_1, since any bundle between A and C on this curve can be purchased. But the consumer can also afford bundle B, and since this bundle lies on indifference curve I_2, it is more attractive than any bundle on curve I_1. Furthermore, since every bundle on I_2, with the single exception of B, lies above the budget constraint, I_2 is the highest indifference curve that can be attained, and it can be reached only by choosing bundle B. So the consumer will maximize utility subject to the budget constraint by choosing bundle B. This is the point of **consumer equilibrium,** and it occurs where the budget constraint is tangent to an indifference curve.

To attain consumer equilibrium, the slope of the consumer's indifference curve at the selected bundle must be equal to the slope of the budget con-

Figure 4–12
Consumer Equilibrium

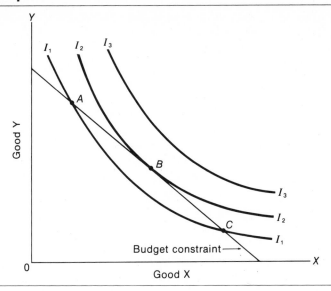

straint.[5] It is quite easy to see the rationale behind this equal-slope condition if we consider the opportunities that are available when it is not satisfied. At point *A* in Figure 4–12, the slope of the indifference curve *I,* is steeper than the slope

---

[5]This tangency condition can be derived mathematically by maximizing the consumer's utility subject to the budget constraint, or by maximizing the $U(X,Y)$ with respect to X and Y, subject to $P_x X + P_y Y = I$. This constrained maximization problem can be carried out by forming the Lagrangian function

$$L = U(X,Y) + \lambda \, (I - P_x X - P_y Y)$$

where λ is known as a *Lagrangian multiplier,* and maximizing it with respect to X and Y and minimizing it with respect to λ. The necessary conditions are

$$\frac{\partial L}{\partial X} = \frac{\partial U}{\partial X} - \lambda P_x = 0 \tag{1}$$

$$\frac{\partial L}{\partial Y} = \frac{\partial U}{\partial Y} - \lambda P_y = 0 \tag{2}$$

$$\frac{\partial L}{\partial \lambda} = I - P_x X - P_y Y = 0 \tag{3}$$

Equation (1) can be divided by equation (2), which, after simple algebraic manipulation, yields

$$-\frac{\partial U/\partial X}{\partial U/\partial Y} = -\frac{P_x}{P_y}$$

The left-hand side of this equation is -1 multiplied by the ratio of the marginal utility of good X to the marginal utility of good Y, or the slope of the indifference curve. The right-hand side is -1 multiplied by the ratio of the price of good X to the price of good Y, or the slope of the budget constraint.

The equality of these two slopes is dependent on the assumption that the consumer will consume positive quantities of both goods. Later in this chapter, we will consider the possibility that the consumer may maximize utility subject to the budget constraint by deciding to consume none of one of the goods.

of the budget constraint. This means that when consuming bundle A, the consumer is willing to sacrifice more units of good Y than necessary to obtain an additional unit of good X. In other words, the cost of additional units of good X in terms of good Y is less than the consumer is willing to pay. Therefore, the consumer will be better off by moving down the budget constraint from *A* by purchasing more of good *X*. This continues to be true until bundle B is reached, at which point the slopes of the indifference curve and the budget constraint are equal.[6] If the consumer had started at bundle C in Figure 4–12, then the consumer would have been willing to give up more units of good X than necessary to obtain an additional unit of good Y and would have moved up the budget constraint until point *B* was reached. From this, it is possible to characterize consumer equilibrium as occurring at the point where the consumer's willingness to sacrifice one good for another is exactly equal to the sacrifice required.[7]

(> in terms of money spent ltd qty of other goods forfeited)

Nonconvex Indifference Curves and Corner Solutions

Thus far, all of the indifference curves we have studied have been convex due to our assumption of a diminishing marginal rate of substitution. One of the justifications for this assumption was that the individual consumer purchases

---

[6]There can be no indifference curve tangent to the budget constraint between A and B. If there were such a curve, its convexity would require that it intersect indifference curve I_2, thereby contradicting our assumption that preferences are transitive.

[7]We can provide another intuitive rationale for the required condition for consumer equilibrium. Starting with the tangency requirement

$$\frac{MU_x}{MU_y} = \frac{P_x}{P_y}$$

we can obtain the equivalent condition

$$\frac{MU_x}{P_x} = \frac{MU_y}{P_y}$$

by simple algebraic manipulation. Verbally, this means that the consumer receives the same increase in utility from spending $1 more on good X as would be received from spending $1 more on good Y. We can see that this condition is necessary if utility is being maximized subject to the budget constraint by assuming that the condition is not satisfied. Assume, for example, that

$$\frac{MU_x}{P_x} > \frac{MU_y}{P_y}$$

This tells us that if $1 less is spend on good Y, utility will not decline as much as it will increase if $1 more is spent on good X. Therefore, the consumer can increase total utility without increasing expenditures by reducing the consumption of good Y and increasing the consumption of good X. This will continue to be true until the equality is restored, which will happen eventually as MU_y increases relative to MU_x. In a similar manner, we can argue that the consumer will move toward the equilibrium condition if we assume that

$$\frac{MU_x}{P_x} < \frac{MU_y}{P_y}$$

a variety of commodities, rather than spending everything on a single good. Now it will be useful to investigate the characteristics of consumer equilibrium when indifference curves are *nonconvex,* or *concave.*

Three concave indifference curves are shown in Figure 4–13. Concave indifference curves become more steeply sloped as we move down them, indicating an increasing, rather than a decreasing, marginal rate of substitution. In Figure 4–13, I_3 is the highest indifference curve that can be reached on the budget constraint, and this can occur only at bundle A where all of the consumer's income is spent on good Y. At point *A,* the slope of the budget constraint is steeper than the slope of the indifference curve I_3. This tells us that purchasing the first unit of X will require a larger sacrifice of good Y than the consumer is willing to make. Therefore, moving down the budget constraint by purchasing units of good X will detract from the consumer's well-being. This continues to be true of any consumption bundle along the constraint between bundles A and C (for example, at bundle B). Beyond point *C* on the constraint, the situation is reversed and the consumer is willing to give up more of good Y than necessary to obtain an additional unit of good X until bundle D is reached. This means that a move along the budget constraint in either direction from bundle C increases the consumer's utility. Therefore, when indifference curves are concave, the point at which the budget constraint is tangent to an indifference curve (point *C* in Figure 4–13) is the point at which utility is minimized subject to the constraint. Under these circumstances, the maximizing bundle will always be at a corner (*A* or *D* in Figure 4–13), total income is spent on one good. When the solution to the consumer problem or any maximization problem occurs at such a corner, it is referred to as a **corner solution.**

If indifference curves are concave, the maximizing solution will never call for the purchase of more than one good, no matter how many goods are being considered. In the case of convex indifference curves, it is possible to find a maximizing solution that requires the purchase of only one good, but this is extremely unlikely when many goods are available. However, even though indifference curves are convex, it is quite probable that to obtain the bundle that maximizes a utility subject to the budget constraint, the consumer will be willing to spend nothing on at least a few goods. This can be illustrated, graphically, even though we can only represent two commodities in our two-dimensional diagrams.

In Figure 4–14, *X* represents a particular good and *Y* represents a composite bundle of all other goods.[8] Here, the consumer maximizes utility, given the budget constraint, by spending all income on good Y and buying none of good X. This does not mean that the individual does not place a high value on good X. We can all identify things that we would enjoy enormously and that we could afford if we chose, but we do not purchase them because to do so we would have to sacrifice other goods that are even more desirable. This is the situation

---

[8]We could use the utility maximization approach to determine the composition of good Y. For our purposes here, we assume that this composition is given, and we will concern ourselves only with the consumer's choice over different bundles of X and Y.

Figure 4–13
Corner Solution with
Concave Indifference Curves

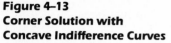

Figure 4–14
Corner Solution with
Convex Indifference Curves

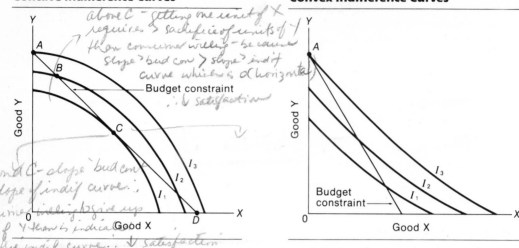

(handwritten: above C – getting one unit of X requires > sacrifice of units of Y than consumer willing – because slope > bud con > slope > indif curve which is ∝ horizontal) ∴ ↓ satisfaction

(handwritten: beyond C – slope > bud con > ∠ slope of indif curve. ∴ Consumer willing to give up more of Y than is indicated by the indif curve. ∴ ↓ satisfaction)

depicted in Figure 4–14. At consumption bundle A, the consumer is willing to give up quite a lot of good Y to obtain the first unit of good X (as indicated by the steep slope of the indifference curve at point *A*) but is not willing to give up the amount of good Y that is required to purchase the first unit of X (this required sacrifice is indicated by the even steeper slope of the budget constraint). Therefore, the rational choice is to devote all income to the purchase of good Y and to do without good X entirely.

(handwritten: measured the budget cost of X is > utility cost of Y, so, I don't trade off)

Application: The Scarcity of Priceless Goods

We have all heard people refer to some goods as "priceless." The idea they are conveying is that the value of a **priceless good** is so great that it is impossible to conceive of a price high enough to measure this value; the good is simply too valuable to be defined in crass economic terms. When people wish to solicit private or public support for a good or service, they bolster their argument by referring to the good as priceless. For example, we hear such statements as "Fine music is a priceless component of our cultural life, so please support your local symphony" or "Obviously human life is priceless, so more should be spent on medical services." If such things were truly priceless, then more support should always be given, since the value obtained from giving this support would exceed the mere economic sacrifice required. But people place definite limits on how much they are willing to spend on music, medical attention, and other "priceless" goods. And since, as economist Frank Knight once said, "People always act more intelligently than they talk," we are justified in questioning whether "priceless" goods are as commonplace as some would have us believe.

To justify our skepticism, we recall that when the consumer is in equilibrium, the price of good X relative to the price of good Y reflects the value of an additional unit of X in terms of Y (how much Y the consumer would willingly give up to obtain an additional unit of X). Therefore, saying that good X is priceless is, to an economist, the same as saying that the value of X in terms of Y is infinitely large. The consumer will be willing to sacrifice an infinite amount of Y to obtain an additional unit of X. Keeping this in mind, we can now describe the indifference curves of an individual who honestly considers a particular good to be priceless. Then we will assess whether these indifference curves actually describe people's preferences: Do consumers ever behave as if a good is really priceless?

In Figure 4–15, we assume that good X is considered priceless and that good Y is any other good or collection of goods. These indifference curves are vertical (have an infinite slope), indicating that the consumer is not willing to give up any of good X no matter how much of good Y is offered as an enticement. Relative to good X, the value of good Y is entirely insignificant. The consumer is equally satisfied with bundle A, which contains X_1 units of good X and no units of good Y, and with bundle B, which contains exactly the same amount of good X but Y_1 units of good Y. The only way to increase the individual's well-being (to move the individual to a higher indifference curve) is to increase his or her consumption of good X, irrespective of how much of good Y is provided. It is worth noting that these indifference curves will be vertical to the X axis no matter what good Y happens to be. If good X is priceless, the consumer will not be willing to relinquish any of good X in return for any finite quantity of good Y, no matter what good or combination of goods Y happens to be. This means that it is impossible for one individual to consider two or more goods priceless. The

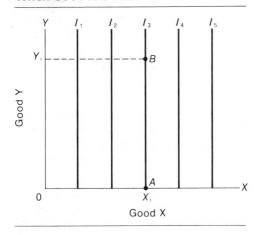

Figure 4–15
Indifference Curves
When Good X Is Priceless

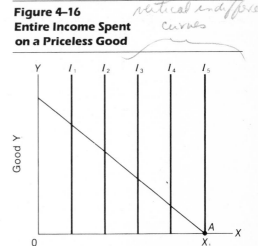

Figure 4–16
Entire Income Spent
on a Priceless Good

same individual cannot consider good X infinitely more valuable than good Y and Y infinitely more valuable than X at the same time. An individual who asserts that music is priceless is simply speaking imprecisely. But if the same individual also claims that health care is priceless, he or she is speaking nonsense.

If an individual really does consider a particular good to be priceless, we can easily predict his or her consumption choice among goods with positive prices. In Figure 4–16, the vertical indifference curves reflect the consumer's view that good X is priceless. The downward-sloping budget constraint reflects the fact that both goods X and Y have positive prices: The consumer can only obtain more of good X by sacrificing some of good Y. The highest indifference curve that the individual can reach and remain on the budget constraint is indifference curve I_5. The maximizing bundle of goods is bundle A, and all of the consumer's income is spent on good X. The only good or goods that the individual would consume in addition to good X would have to have a price of 0. If, for example, good Y in Figure 4–16 did not cost anything, then the budget constraint would be vertical at X_1 and additional units of good Y could be consumed without giving up any of good X. Only in this case could the consumer who considers a good to be priceless maximize utility while consuming something other than the priceless good.

This result is certainly not surprising. An individual who actually considers good X to be priceless is certainly not going to pay a positive price for any other good, because this would require the sacrificing of some of good X and no finite quantity of Y is worth the smallest sacrifice of X if X is truly priceless. So we can conclude that an individual who honestly considers a particular good to be priceless and behaves rationally will devote his or her entire income to the purchase of that good. Since we rarely, if ever, observe consumers acting in this way, we have every reason to believe that truly priceless goods are indeed scarce.

We should conclude our discussion of priceless goods with an important caveat. To an economist, the price of a good reflects the value *of an additional unit of the good*–not the value of the entire quantity of the good that is consumed. Therefore, the price of a good can be modest, reflecting the fact that consumers will not willingly sacrifice much to obtain an additional unit of that good, but the entire quantity of the good that is consumed can be of enormous value. Water is a good example of such a good, and people often consider this type of good to be priceless. Fortunately, few decisions must be made on an all-or-nothing basis (we do not have to sacrifice all of our water consumption to obtain more of some other good); instead, most decisions involve marginal trade-offs. This is why the economist's definition of price based on the marginal value of a good is so useful in describing economic decision making, which is predominately marginal in nature.

The value of the total quantity of a good is of some interest, however, and it is worthwhile to consider the relationship between the marginal value and the total value of a good with the aid of an indifference curve. If the individual is consuming bundle A on the indifference curve in Figure 4–17, then the value of the marginal unit of good X is small, as indicated by the shallow slope of the

Figure 4–17
Total Value and Marginal Value

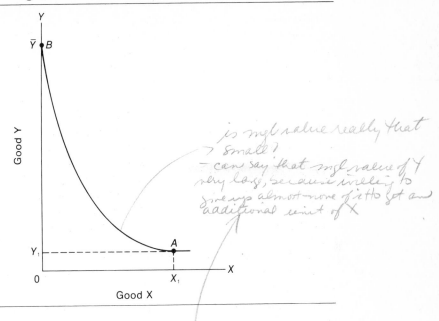

is mgl value really that small?
— can say that mgl value of Y very large, because willing to give up almost none of it to get an additional unit of X

indifference curve at point A. This individual would be willing to sacrifice very little of good Y to obtain another unit of good X when X_1 and Y_1 units of X and Y, respectively, are being consumed. However, the marginal value of good X when the individual is consuming X_1 units tells us nothing about the total value that this individual places on the consumption of all units of X_1. To determine this total value, we note that the individual's well-being is the same whether bundle A or bundle B is consumed, since the same indifference curve passes through both bundles. This means that starting at B, where the consumption of goods X and Y is equal to 0 and $\bar{Y}$, respectively, the individual is willing to sacrifice $\bar{Y} - Y_1$ units of Y to consume X_1 units of X. The total value of X_1 units of X in terms of Y is equal to the distance $\bar{Y} - Y_1$. Although we are limited as to how high we can place the intersection $\bar{Y}$ of the indifference curve and the Y axis in this graph, in actuality this can be an enormous distance.[9] Thus, we can easily see that a good whose total value is extremely large can be, and often is, consumed in quantities at which its marginal value is very small.

[9]It is possible to conceive of an indifference curve that approaches the axes *asymptotically* (comes closer and closer to but never touches the axes). In such a case, $\bar{Y}$ would occur at infinity and the total value of any positive quantity of good X could be unlimited. Also, for sufficiently small quantities of good X, the indifference curve would, in effect, be vertical, making the good priceless by our definition. Although such indifference curves may reasonably characterize preferences for some essential goods, such as water and food, these essentials are normally consumed in quantities at which they are not priceless but actually have quite low values placed on the marginal unit.

→ the mgl value is small wrt Y as no Y forfeited for more X

Application: Capturing the Consumer's Surplus

The price that a consumer pays for a good reflects the value that he or she places on an additional unit of the good. Since the price normally applies uniformly to all units of the good purchased and the consumer generally values the last unit consumed less than the units consumed previously, the consumer values the total consumption of a good at more than the amount paid for this consumption. The gap between what a consumer is willing to pay rather than do without a good (the *total value* placed on the good) and what the consumer actually pays is referred to as the **consumer's surplus.** Obviously, suppliers prefer that consumers pay more rather than less for a good and are anxious to capture as much consumers' surplus as possible. We can employ indifference-curve analysis to show how suppliers use different pricing schemes to encourage consumers to pay more for a given quantity of a good than they would if the good were uniformly priced.

Conceptually, the simplest way for a supplier to capture the total consumer's surplus of an individual would be to charge a different price for each unit consumed and to price each unit at the maximum amount the consumer is willing to pay for that unit. But such a pricing policy would be enormously difficult to implement. The supplier would have to obtain detailed information about all consumers' preferences. Also, consumers who place a relatively small value on the good and therefore purchase it for less, would have to be prevented from selling the good to consumers who value it more highly. Otherwise, low-demand consumers would be able to buy the good at a relatively cheap price and profitably undercut the price that the supplier is charging the high-demand consumers.

A final and related difficulty is that the more competitors a supplier has, the more difficult it is to charge the same customer different prices for different units or to charge different customers different prices. Although a consumer may be willing to pay the only supplier of a good more for the first unit than the second unit, more for the second unit than the third unit, and so on, this is not necessarily true when the consumer can choose among several suppliers. A consumer will not be willing to pay one supplier any more for a particular unit of a good than is being charged by an alternative supplier. The consumer still values the first unit of the good more than the second unit, but competition among several suppliers makes it difficult for any one supplier to take advantage of this fact by imposing a different pricing strategy on each consumer and charging each consumer a different price for each unit purchased. However, relatively crude or simple price-discrimination schemes can be implemented that allow suppliers to capture more of the consumer's surplus than they could under a uniform pricing policy.

Such a price-discrimination scheme is illustrated in Figure 4–18 with the aid of an individual's indifference-curve map. We assume the individual is initially at $\bar{Y}$, consuming $\bar{Y}$ units of good Y and no units of good X. Indifference curve I_1 indicates the consumer's level of satisfaction for this consumption bundle. Given an opportunity to purchase good X at a uniform price, reflected in the slope of

Figure 4–18
Two-Part Pricing

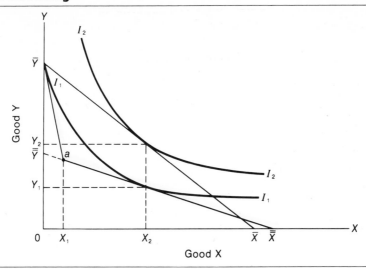

budget constraint $\overline{Y}\overline{X}$, the consumer will purchase X_2 units and increase satisfaction by reaching the higher indifference curve I_2. Increased satisfaction
is derived because less is being paid for the X_2 units than they are worth to
the consumer. The total value of the X_2 units to the consumer is given in Figure
4–18 by the distance $\overline{Y} - Y_1$, which is the maximum amount of good Y the consumer is willing to sacrifice to obtain X_2 units. (The consumer is indifferent
between $\overline{Y}$ units of Y and no X and Y_1 units of Y and X_2 units of X.) But given the
budget constraint $\overline{Y}\overline{X}$, the consumer only has to sacrifice $\overline{Y} - Y_2$ units of Y to
obtain X_2 units of X. The distance $Y_2 - Y_1$ measures the consumer's surplus
associated with the consumer's ability to buy good X at a uniform price.

The supplier is interested in whether a relatively simple pricing strategy will
capture some of this consumer's surplus. The supplier's objective is to raise
the price and still have the consumer purchase the same quantity of good X. If
the supplier raises the price uniformly, however, the budget constraint will pivot
to the left around point $\overline{Y}$, and the consumer can be expected to purchase fewer
units of good X.[10] But what will happen if the supplier imposes a **two-part
pricing policy,** which allows the consumer to purchase good X at a lower price
if a specified number of initial units of X are purchased at a higher price?
Assume, for example, that the consumer faces the budget constraint $\overline{Y}a\overline{\overline{X}}$ in
Figure 4–18. If the first X_1 units of good X are purchased at the higher price
reflected by the budget constraint segment $\overline{Y}a$, then the consumer can buy

---

[10]In Chapter 5, we will analyze the remote possibility that a higher uniform price can lead
to the purchase of a larger quantity of the good.

additional units of good X at the much lower price indicated by segment $a\bar{\bar{X}}$ of the budget constraint. Faced with such a pricing policy, the consumer will be willing to sacrifice $\bar{Y} - Y_1$ units of good Y, to buy X_2 units, thereby dissipating all of the consumer's surplus.[11]

Two-part pricing strategies in the real world are not usually calibrated accurately enough to capture all of an individual's consumer's surplus. Also, the same two-part pricing policy normally applies to everyone, even though preferences—and therefore indifference curves—vary from consumer to consumer. Thus, any given two-part pricing strategy will capture more consumer's surplus from some than from others. However, such a strategy generally allows suppliers to motivate consumers to pay more for a given quantity of a good than they would under a uniform pricing policy.

eg 2 for 1 steak sales – we pay more than we would under uniform policy because under uniform policy we wouldn't buy at all

Given the advantage that suppliers can realize from a two-part pricing strategy, it is not surprising that different variations of such pricing strategies are often encountered. For example, suppliers of electricity almost universally employ at least a two-part pricing schedule, so that the first few kilowatts of power used during the billing period cost the consumer more than subsequent kilowatts. A variation on two-part pricing is the membership fee—an initial charge that entitles the consumer to purchase a product at a lower price. As shown in Figure 4–18, this produces the same effect as straight two-part pricing. Assume that on paying an initial fee of $\bar{Y} - \bar{\bar{Y}}$, the consumer can buy all the units of X desired at the reduced price, reflected in the budget constraint $\bar{\bar{Y}X}$. We can see that the consumer will respond to this pricing policy by paying the fee and purchasing X_2 units of good X, allowing the supplier to capture all the consumer's surplus. Automobile-rental firms use a form of this pricing policy when they impose a daily charge plus a per-mile charge. Computer time is commonly obtained by paying a lump-sum rental, which then entitles the individual to use the computer at a low hourly charge. Amusement parks usually charge an entry fee and then attach no marginal charge to the rides. Surely you can think of other examples of two-part pricing policies.[12]

Application: Charity Versus Corner Solutions

The underlying assumption that individuals are motivated to maximize their own utility may leave the impression that there is no room in our analysis for concern for others. This is not true. The indifference-curve approach to utility maximization can be used to explain *charitable behavior.*

Nothing in our analysis prevents an individual's utility from being influenced by the consumption of *others* as well as by his or her own consumption. For

---

[11]Actually, the consumer is indifferent between buying no X and buying X_2 units of X. But if the consumer buys any of good X at all, it will be X_2 units, and only the slightest decrease in the price of good X along either segment of the budget constraint will make the purchase of X the most attractive alternative.

[12]In Chapter 9, we will examine this type of price discrimination from the point of view of the supplier.

example, let's assume that we are considering two individuals–individual D (the donor) and individual R (the recipient)–and that D's utility is a function not only of his own consumption but of R's as well. D's preferences can be expressed with indifference curves showing combinations of D's and R's consumption that provide D with the same utility. Two such indifference curves are shown in Figure 4–19. These curves indicate that when D has a high income relative to R's income, D is willing to transfer some income to R. As expected, however, as D's income declines relative to R's income, the slope of the indifference curves becomes more shallow, indicating that D is willing to sacrifice less income to increase R's income by an additional dollar. And if R's income increases too much relative to D's income, envy sets in and individual R's income becomes a bad to D. This is shown by the upward-sloping portions of the indifference curves. Once envy sets in, D's income will have to be increased before he is willing for R's income to increase.

Now let's assume that D can transfer income costlessly to R, or that R receives an additional dollar for each dollar D gives up. This is reflected in Figure 4–19

Figure 4–19
Sometimes It's Better to Give Than to Receive

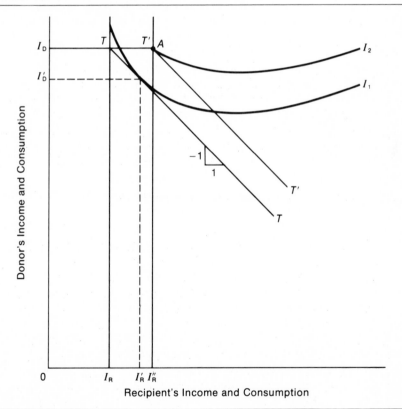

by -1 slope of TT, which shows the different income combinations that D can realize by transferring income to R. (Here I_D and I_R represent D's and R's initial incomes, respectively.) Subject to this constraint, D attempts to maximize his utility through charitable contributions, reaching indifference curve I_1 by donating $I_D - I_D'$ dollars to R. This increases R's income from I_R to I_R'.

Next we will assume that R's income increases to I_R'' without any transfers from D. The relevant constraint D faces in donating income to R is now given by $T'T'$ in Figure 4–19. But with this constraint, D maximizes utility by *not* donating any income to R. At point A, the constraint is steeper than the indifference curve, resulting in a corner solution. D does not donate any income increase to R: The first dollar that D donated would increase R's income by a lesser amount than is required to make D willing to sacrifice $1 of income.

Application: Charity and Paternalism

Few organized charities, either public or private, simply transfer income to the needy due to an underlying fear that the recipients will not spend the money in their best interests. Instead of money, **charitable contributions** normally consist of particular goods and services that the donors believe the recipients should have. It will be helpful to use the indifference-curve approach to consumer behavior to analyze the effect of these **in-kind gifts** in terms of the intent of the donors and the utility of the recipients.

The three indifference curves I_1, I_2, and I_3 in Figure 4–20 belong to an individual who is to be the recipient of a donated good–say, bus transportation. Before the donation, the individual's budget constraint with respect to bus transportation and all other goods is defined by line BC. Given this constraint, the individual will maximize utility by choosing bundle A (point A) and consuming bus rides at the rate of X_1 per week. Now we will assume that this individual qualifies for public relief, which takes the form of free bus transportation–something the transit authorities feel people should be encouraged to consume. Letting $\bar{X}$ be the quantity of free bus transportation received, the budget constraint becomes BDE. Beyond point D, the slope of this budget constraint is the same as BC, reflecting the fact that the regular price must be paid for bus transportation in excess of $\bar{X}$. Faced with this new budget constraint, the consumer will maximize utility by choosing bundle D, point D at the kink in the constraint. Consumption of bus transportation will increase from X_1 to $\bar{X}$, and utility will also increase because the individual moves from indifference curve I_1 to I_2.

Two objectives have been accomplished by this contribution. First, the recipient's well-being was improved; second, the recipient's consumption of bus transit was increased – something those controlling the contribution thought was important. It is worth noting that these two objectives are somewhat in conflict with one another. For example, if the only objective had been to increase the recipient's well-being as much as possible, the contribution would have been made in form of money or some other form of general pur-

Figure 4–20
In-Kind Charitable Contributions

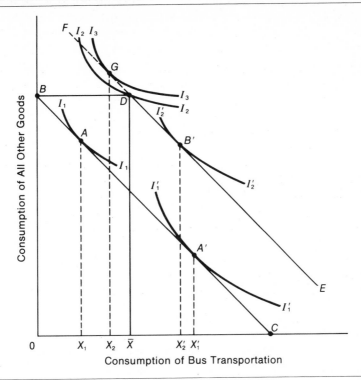

chasing power. If instead of $\bar{X}$ bus tokens, the recipient had received enough *money* to buy $\bar{X}$ bus tokens, then the budget constraint would have been *FDE*. Given this constraint, the individual would have chosen bundle G at point *G*, consumed only X_2 units of bus transportation, and reached indifference curve I_3, thereby attaining a higher utility level than that achieved when the in-kind gift of bus rides was given. Of course, this increase in utility would have been attained at the expense of the people who felt that the individual actually needed $\bar{X}$ units of bus transportation.

Next, we will consider an individual who, before the receipt of $\bar{X}$ units of free bus transportation, was consuming a greater quantity than that. The preferences of this individual are represented in Figure 4–20 by indifference curves I_1' and I_2'. Before the gift, *BC* is the budget constraint and the individual maximizes utility by choosing bundle A' at point *A'* and consuming X_1' units of bus transportation. But after the receipt of $\bar{X}$ units of bus transit, the budget constraint shifts to *BDE* and the consumer maximizes utility by choosing bundle B' at point *B'* and reducing consumption to X_2' units of bus transportation. The individual reduced bus-service consumption when this service was given free of charge. This can only occur if the individual regards bus service as an inferior good, which most people do. The gift increases the recipient's real income and motivates a reduction in the consumption of an inferior good as long as the relative price of that good remains constant. And since we assumed that the individual was consuming more than $\bar{X}$ before the gift, the relative price of the marginal unit consumed is not affected by the gift. In this case, you cannot even give the gift away. The effect of giving the recipient $\bar{X}$ units of bus transportation is the same as giving the individual enough money to purchase that much bus service.

This analysis can be applied to the current food-stamp program in the United States. As that program is now structured, people who qualify are given food stamps in specific dollar amounts that can be redeemed for food. If the dollar value of the stamps exceeds the amount the recipients are spending on food, then the program can be expected to motivate a larger increase in food consumption than would result from an equivalent income transfer. But if more money was being spent on food before the program was initiated than the dollar value of the food stamps received after the program is begun, then there is no effective difference between providing recipients with food stamps or with equivalent amounts of cash.

4–5 Summary

In Chapter 4, we have developed a model of consumer behavior that is designed to provide insights into the consumer's problem of allocating a limited income between different goods. To construct any model, some simplifying assumptions have to be made. Beginning with the basic building block of the model–*consumer preferences*–we assumed that individual preferences are given and remain constant throughout the analysis. We also assumed that individuals rank bundles of goods in accordance with their preferences, that we are dealing with commodities that consumers desired (*goods*, not *bads*), and that preferences are *transitive*. We learned that, given these assumptions, an individual's preference can be represented with downward-sloping, nonintersecting *indifference curves*. Each indifference curve passes through a set of *consumption bundles* that the consumer finds equally attractive. We imposed a further restriction on the shape of indifference curves by assuming that, along a given indifference curve, the relative value of a good decreases as its relative quantity increases. This is the assumption of a *decreasing marginal rate of substitution* and implies that the indifference curves are *convex*.

We have found that indifference curves are ranked numerically according to the consumer's preferences. Each indifference curve is assigned a number that can be thought of as the *utility* provided by any consumption bundle on that curve. We now know that between any two indifference curves, this utility ranking will always assign the highest number to the curve containing the preferred bundles. Since these numbers are only used to rank bundles of good, they are *ordinal utilities;* any other assignment of utilities is perfectly acceptable as long as the correct *ordinal ranking* is maintained. Thus, the differences between the utilities associated with different consumption bundles tells us nothing about the degree to which one bundle is preferred to another. This is in contrast with the *cardinal utilities* employed by earlier economists, which assume the utility difference between any two bundles of goods indicates how much one bundle is preferred to the other. Once ordinal utilities have been assigned, the relationship that then exists between consumption bundles and the utility numbers is an ordinal utility function that provides a description of the individual consumer's preferences.

The consumer's *utility function* tells us what the consumer is willing to do. The consumer's *budget constraint* determines what the consumer can actually do. The budget constraint supplies information about the consumer's income and the prices of the goods available, and shows us all the combinations of consumption bundles that can be purchased.

After developing both a utility function (with corresponding indifference curves) and a budget constraint, we learned that it is possible to predict how the consumer chooses the preferred consumption bundle from among alternative selections. Crucial to this prediction, however, is the assumption that the consumer is motivated to maximize utility, subject to his or her budget constraint. Given this motivation, we concluded that the consumer would choose the point on the budget constraint that is tangent to an indifference curve. At this point, the consumer—given his or her limited income and the prices of the goods to be purchased—has reached the highest indifference curve possible, or *consumer equilibrium.*

Having developed the condition that describes consumer equilibrium, we then investigated the effect of *concave (nonconvex)* indifference curves on this equilibrium. When indifference curves are concave, the consumer maximizes utility subject to the budget constraint by purchasing only *one* good. In general, at this *corner solution,* the budget constraint will not be tangent to the indifference curve. The point where the budget constraint is tangent to an indifference curve, when indifference curves are concave, will be the point at which the consumer minimizes utility subject to the budget constraint. Only when indifference curves are convex does our analysis predict that each consumer will allocate his or her limited income over a variety of goods. Obviously, this prediction conforms to observed behavior. But even when the indifference curves are convex, our analysis is consistent with an individual electing not to consume any of some goods.

We then used our model of consumer behavior to describe precisely what is meant by a *priceless good.* To do this, we had to focus on the information conveyed by price to reflect marginal value, which proved useful in emphasizing the importance of distinguishing between *marginal value* and *total value.* Goods that have a very high total value are often referred to as "priceless" when their marginal values at the quantities at which they are consumed are very modest because they are in ample supply. If an individual actually considered a good to be priceless—to have an infinite marginal value—we would expect that individual to devote his or her entire income to the purchase of that good. As such behavior is seldom, if ever, observed, it is reasonable to conclude that priceless goods are definitely rare.

In another application of our model of consumer behavior, we considered the concept of the *consumer's surplus* and the attempts of suppliers to capture some of this surplus. Under ideal circumstances, a supplier can capture the entire consumer's surplus of an individual by charging a different price for each unit of the good that is purchased. In actuality, such a finely calibrated pricing policy would be impossible. However, we demonstrated with indifference-curve analysis that a properly constructed, simple *two-part pricing policy* can allow a supplier to appropriate all of a consumer's surplus. Although such a complete confiscation is unlikely in practice, a supplier can often expect to gain more from a two-part pricing policy than from charging uniform prices.

We have also seen how our consumer model can be used to analyze certain aspects of *charitable contributions.* If one individual's utility is affected positively by another individual's consumption, a transfer from the first individual to the second may be required to maximize utility. It is likely, however, that utility maximization will call for a corner solution. Although the donor may be legitimately concerned about the recipient, contributing the first dollar may require a larger sacrifice than the donor is willing to make. In this case, no charitable contribution is made and a corner solution prevails.

Charitable contributions and transfers are often made in the form of specific goods, rather than money, not only to increase the recipient's utility but also to increase his or her consumption of a certain good. If cash were transferred, the recipient might spend it on items that the donor does not consider necessary. But if the amount of the good transferred is not greater than the amount of the good that was being consumed before the transfer, there is no effective difference between the *in-kind gift* and the gift of an equivalent amount of cash. Furthermore, if the good being transferred is inferior, the effect of giving less of the good than the recipient originally consumed will be to reduce its consumption.

In Chapter 5, we will continue to make use of our model of consumer behavior to gain additional insights into the concepts of value and demand. Our prime consideration will be to investigate the relationship between the concepts developed in this chapter and the demand curve discussed in Chapters 2 and 3.

References

Alchian, Armen A. "The Meaning of Utility Measurement." *American Economic Review* (March 1953).

Buchanan, James M. "The Theory of Monopolistic Quantity Discounts." *Review of Economic Studies* (1952–1953), p. 199.

Henderson, James, and Richard Quandt. *Microeconomic Theory,* Revised Edition. New York: McGraw-Hill, 1971, Chapter 2.

Oi, Walter Y. "A Disneyland Dilemma: Two-Part Tariffs for a Mickey Mouse Monopoly." *Quarterly Journal of Economics* (February 1971).

Stigler, George J. *The Theory of Price,* Third Edition. New York: Macmillan, 1966, Chapter 4.

Problems

1. Assume that you have a friend whose preferences conform to the indifference curves shown in Figure 4–3. How could you convince your friend to give you most of his money without depriving him of his well-being as measured by his own preferences?

2. Explain why the indifference-curve map is completely unaffected by a change in the ordinal-utility function as long as the change does not alter the preference ranking of the alternative consumption bundles.

3. Use an indifference-curve map to show how a supplier who offers an all-or-nothing choice to a consumer could convince the consumer to pay more for a given quantity or to buy more units of the good at a given price than would be the case if the consumer could purchase any quantity desired at a uniform price.

4. If the consumption of a commodity increases beyond the point where it is a good, so that the good becomes a bad, what will happen to the slope of the indifference curves? Is it possible for the price of the commodity to be such that an individual will voluntarily increase his or her consumption beyond the point where the good becomes a bad?

5. Convex indifference curves permit us to describe preferences that are consistent with a good that has an enormous total value and a very low marginal value (see Figure 4–17). It should not be difficult for you to think of examples of such goods. In what sense is life itself an example of this type of good? If we assume that indifference curves are concave, we can describe preferences that are consistent with a good that has an infinite marginal value (a priceless good) but a very modest total value. Construct an indifference curve to describe the preferences for such a good. Can you give any examples of such a good?

6. An individual whose income decreases while the prices of all goods consumed remain constant will clearly be in a worse economic position than before. On the other hand, if the price of one of the goods the individual is consuming declines while income and all other prices remain the same, the individual's economic position will improve. If both of these events occur simultaneously, the consumer's economic position will be better or worse, depending on the relative magnitude of the changes. Use the analysis developed in this chapter to show how you can determine whether an individual will be in a better or a worse economic position after a simultaneous decrease in income and in the price of one of the goods being consumed.

7. (a) Assume that two goods are perfect substitutes for each other (the consumer has an equal preference for both goods). Construct indifference curves to describe the consumer's preferences for these goods. Given these indifference curves and a budget constraint, what can you say about the consumer's sensitivity to changes in the relative prices of the two goods?

   (b) Assume that two goods are rigid complements (they are only useful in a certain proportion, such as a right shoe and a left shoe). Construct indifference curves for these goods, and comment on the sensitivity of consumption choice to changes in the relative prices of the two goods.

8. What is the price elasticity of demand for a priceless good? What is the income elasticity of demand? What is the cross-price elasticity of demand with respect to the price of another good?

9. Assume that the objective of the food-stamp program is to encourage the disadvantaged to consume more low-cost, highly nutritional foods, such as beans, potatoes, and hamburger. You are called in as a consultant to suggest ways to achieve this objective. What advice will you give if you know that the income elasticity of demand for these foods is less than one?

10. Consider five bundles of goods A, B, C, D, and E. Let U be an acceptable utility function for an individual with $U(A) = 5$, $U(B) = 7$, $U(C) = 7$, $U(D) = 500$, and $U(E) = 500.5$. Now consider five different utility functions U_1, U_2, U_3, U_4, and U_5, where

$U_1(A) = .001$	$U_2(A) = 900$	$U_3(A) = 1$	$U_4(A) = 1$	$U_5(A) = 6$
$U_1(B) = .002$	$U_2(B) = 901$	$U_3(B) = 2$	$U_4(B) = 8$	$U_5(B) = 7$
$U_1(C) = .003$	$U_2(C) = 901$	$U_3(C) = 3$	$U_4(C) = 8$	$U_5(C) = 7$
$U_1(D) = .004$	$U_2(D) = 10,000$	$U_3(D) = 4$	$U_4(D) = 7$	$U_5(D) = 9$
$U_1(E) = .005$	$U_2(E) = 100,000$	$U_3(E) = 5$	$U_4(E) = 6$	$U_5(E) = 15$

Which one of these utility functions is also acceptable?

APPENDIX

THE OPTIMAL CONSUMPTION PATTERN OVER TIME

Introduction 4A-1

In Chapter 4, we have examined the considerations that an individual faces when choosing among different combinations of two goods that must both be consumed immediately. We analyzed this choice process by using indifference curves to represent the consumer's preferences. We can use the same approach to investigate the considerations that a consumer must make when choosing between consuming more goods now and consuming more goods in the future. An individual can increase consumption in the future by reducing current consumption and saving money. Or an individual can increase current consumption, either by borrowing or by reducing savings, at the expense of future consumption. Obviously, many different consumption time patterns are possible, but some will provide the consumer with more utility than others. In this appendix, we will examine the considerations that motivate the consumer to choose the particular consumption time pattern that will maximize his or her utility.

Time Preference 4A-2

Most people who have to choose between a benefit now and an equivalent benefit a year from now would choose the benefit now. Most of us discount the future—and although the future is important, discounting it is a sensible thing to do. The future is always uncertain, and a benefit to be received later may never be received at all. Also most people are impatient and are anxious to reap their rewards as soon as they can.

When we are considering desirable experiences, the preference for earlier rather than later benefits is referred to as **time preference.** This time preference is reflected in the indifference curves that represent an individual's preferences with respect to current and future consumption. The indifference curve

133

in Figure 4A–1 displays all combinations of current (period 1) and future (period 2) consumption that will provide the same utility that $15,000 of consumption in each period would provide. This indifference curve is convex, reflecting the fact that there is a diminishing marginal rate of substitution between current and future consumption. The individual whose consumption pattern is represented by point *A* will have plenty of future consumption but little current consumption. The steep slope of the indifference curve at this point tells us that the individual is willing to sacrifice a lot of future consumption for an additional dollar of current consumption. As the individual increases current consumption relative to future consumption, the slope becomes less steep, indicating a decreased willingness to sacrifice future consumption for current consumption.

At point *B* in Figure 4A–1, the individual is spending an *equal* amount on consumption in each period. Presumably, this means that the benefit from an additional dollar of consumption in period 2 will be valued the same in period 2 as the benefit from an additional dollar of consumption in period 1 will be valued in period 1. But the indifference curve is constructed from the perspective of period 1, and the benefit from the dollar increase in consumption in period 2 is therefore discounted. This discounting is reflected by the fact that the slope of the indifference curve at point *B* is steeper than −1. When the same amount is to be spent on consumption in each period, the consumer is willing to sacrifice *more* than $1 of future consumption to obtain $1 of current consumption.

As we move down the indifference curve in Figure 4A–1 to point *C*, the slope indicates that the individual is willing to sacrifice *less* than $1 of future con-

Figure 4A-1
Indifference Curve
Between Current and Future Consumption

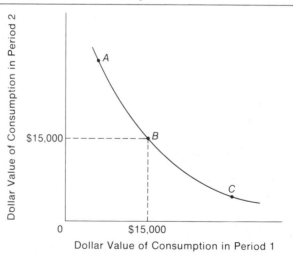

sumption to obtain $1 of current consumption. At point C, it may appear that the individual is no longer discounting the future, but this is not the case. When the individual's future consumption is very small relative to current consumption, the value of an additional dollar of future consumption is large relative to an additional dollar of current consumption. Therefore, even though the value of the future consumption is discounted, this discounted value can still be greater than the undiscounted value of current consumption. Note that the individual's *subjective* value of consumption is being discounted here.

The Interest Rate and the Budget Constraint   4A–3

We have just discussed the individual's *willingness* to sacrifice consumption in one period in return for consumption in another period. We will now turn our attention to the sacrifice that an individual *must make* in one period's consumption to increase consumption in another period. The interest rate is the important consideration in this case, because an individual can increase current consumption in period 1 by borrowing against income to be earned in period 2. But for every $1 borrowed in the first period, $1 *plus the interest rate* must be paid back in the second period (deducted from consumption in period 2). On the other hand, future consumption can be increased by reducing current consumption in order to loan money at the interest rate. Then for every $1 of consumption sacrificed in the first period, consumption in the second period can be increased by $1 plus the interest rate.

It is useful to illustrate this trade-off between current and future consumption graphically. We will assume that there is a prevailing yearly interest rate r at which the consumer can either borrow or lend. In Figure 4A–2, all of the possible combinations of current and future consumption are indicated by line BB', given the interest rate r and incomes in period 1 and period 2 of I_1 and I_2, respectively. (We will assume that each period is one year in length.) We can consider line BB' to be the budget constraint with respect to current and future consumption. Two points are of particular interest in determining the position of this budget constraint—the points at which BB' intersects the vertical and the horizontal axes.

The first point B is found by asking how much could be spent on period 2 consumption if nothing were spent on period 1 consumption. If I_1 (all income in period 1) is saved at the interest rate r, then the individual will be paid back the savings plus the interest amounting to rI_1, or a total of $(1 + r)I_1$, in period 2. This, coupled with the income in period 2, of I_2, provides the individual with $I_2 + [(1 + r)I_1]$ dollars to spend on consumption in period 2. This possibility is shown as point B in Figure 4A–2. An individual who decides to forgo all consumption in period 2 to obtain the maximum consumption in period 1 can borrow against the income in period 2. However, the amount that must be paid back in period 2—the amount borrowed plus the interest payment—cannot

Figure 4A–2
A Possible Combination
of Current and Future Consumption

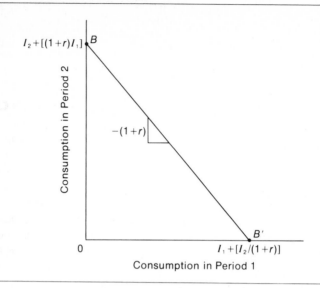

exceed I_2. The maximum that the individual can borrow in period 2 can be represented by C, where

$$C + rC = I_2$$

or $(1 + r)C = I_2$. Solving for C, we see that the individual can borrow as much as $I_2/(1 + r)$ in period 1. Therefore, an individual who intends to spend nothing in period 2 can spend $I_1 + [I_2/(1 + r)]$ in period 1. This possibility is shown as point B' in Figure 4A–2.

When the interest rate is constant, the trade-off between current and future consumption is the same everywhere and the budget constraint is a straight line. The slope of this line is obtained by dividing the vertical distance $I_2 + [(1 + r)I_1]$ by the horizontal distance $I_1 + [I_2/(1 + r)]$ and, since the slope is negative, multiplying by -1. Then only some simple algebraic manipulation[1] is required to determine that the slope is equal to $-(1 + r)$, as shown in Figure

[1]Dividing the vertical intercept by the horizontal intercept and multiplying by -1 yields

$$-\frac{I_2 + [(1 + r)I_1]}{I_1 + [I_2/(1 + r)]}$$

Multiplying both the numerator and the denominator by $1 + r$ then gives us

$$-(1 + r)\frac{I_2 + [(1 + r)I_1]}{I_2 + [(1 + r)I_1}= -(1 + r)$$

4A–2. This is not surprising, given that the slope of the budget constraint indicates how much consumption in period 2 must be sacrificed to obtain an additional dollar of consumption in period 1. If the consumption in period 1 is financed by borrowing, then for every dollar borrowed in period 1, $1 + r$ dollars must be paid back in period 2. But even without borrowing, every dollar of consumption in period 1 will cost $1 + r$ dollars of consumption in period 2. The dollar spent in period 1 could have been saved to support $1 + r$ dollars of consumption in period 2.

Optimal Consumption Pattern Over Time   4A–4

We can now determine the conditions that must be satisfied if the consumer is to choose the **optimal consumption pattern over time**–a pattern of consumption that maximizes utility subject to the budget constraint. Both the budget constraint and the highest indifference curve attainable are shown in Figure 4A–3. There, utility is maximized at point A, where this indifference curve is tangent to the budget constraint. At point A, the amount of future consumption the individual must sacrifice to obtain additional dollars for current consumption is exactly equal to the amount the individual is willing to sacrifice, or $1 + r$.

To maximize utility in Figure 4A–3, the individual should borrow $C_1 - I_1$ dollars in period 1 to spend C_1 on current consumption and pay back $I_2 - C_2$ dollars in period 2, leaving C_2 dollars available for consumption in period 2. We

---

Figure 4A-3
Utility-Maximizing Consumption Pattern over Time

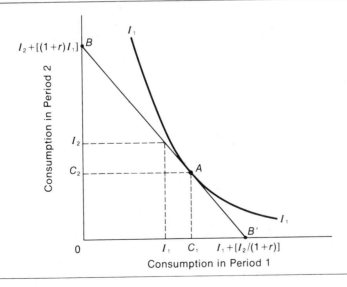

could easily construct an indifference-curve map showing the individual maximizing utility by saving in period 1 instead. Clearly, the individual will decide whether to borrow or save based on the shape of the indifference curve, the size of income in period 1 relative to income in period 2, and the interest rate. It is straightforward to show that as the interest rate increases, the amount that is borrowed will decrease (the amount saved will increase) in period 1.[2]

At this point, it is pertinent to ask what determines the interest rate. At any given interest rate, some individuals will find it advantageous to save and others will increase their utility by borrowing. If the interest rate is such that the total amount savers want to save is greater than the total amount borrowers want to borrow, then the interest rate will not be the equilibrium rate. Some of the plans individuals make in response to the interest rate will be frustrated, since some lenders will not be able to find borrowers for all that they would like to save. This frustration will exert a downward pressure on the interest rate that will remain active until the amount borrowers want to borrow is equal to the amount savers want to save. The interest rate will then be at its equilibrium rate. Similarly, if the interest rate is lower than its equilibrium rate, desired borrowing will exceed desired saving and an upward pressure will be exerted on the interest rate.

---

[2]Increasing the interest rate will cause the price of current consumption to increase relative to the price of future consumption. In Chapter 5, we will use indifference-curve analysis to consider how increasing the price of a good will affect the quantity demanded. By assuming that people will choose to consume more as their income increases, this analysis will establish that current consumption will decrease when the interest rate increases.

CHAPTER FIVE

THE THEORY BEHIND THE DEMAND CURVE

In Chapter 4, we developed the fundamentals of the theory of consumer behavior. Our objective was to acquire some insights into the problem of allocating a limited income among different products in such a way that consumer utility is maximized. To the extent that consumers are motivated by the desire to maximize their utility, our model of consumer behavior helps us to understand how and why consumers' expenditure decisions respond to changing market conditions.

For example, in Chapter 2, we simply assumed that demand curves are negatively sloped. At the time it was made, this assumption had little to recommend it other than an intuitive plausibility. This plausibility rested on the implicit assumption that individuals are motivated by a desire to maximize their well-being when they make economic decisions and on the reasonable notion that achieving this objective requires consuming more of a good when its relative price declines. Now that we have made the objective of utility maximization an explicit assumption and have considered some of the implications of this assumption in Chapter 4, we are in a position to look more carefully at the theory behind the demand curve. In particular, we will determine what conditions ensure that the demand curve will be downward sloping, and we will identify the circumstances that can theoretically produce a demand curve that contains an upward-sloping portion.

After we have used the theory of consumer behavior to develop and analyze the theoretical underpinnings of the demand curve more fully, we will be able to broaden our discussion to include some interesting aspects of the concept of *value*—a subject that has intrigued philosophers and economists for centuries. But to lay the groundwork for the development of the main points that we will examine in this chapter, we must consider some of the mechanics of determining how consumer equilibrium changes with changes in the budget constraint.

5-2 Consumer Response to Changes in the Budget Constraint

Changes in Money Income

In this section, we will examine the effect that a change in the consumer's money income will have on the choice between different bundles containing goods X and Y. In Chapter 4, we learned that an increase in money income will shift the budget constraint up and to the right, parallel to the initial constraint, assuming that the prices of good X and good Y remain constant. Similarly, a decrease in the consumer's money income will cause the budget constraint to shift down and to the left, retaining the same slope. Therefore, given a change in money income, the consumer will be faced with a different budget constraint and will have to choose a different consumption bundle to maximize utility. To determine the impact of an income change, we must compare the consumption choices in the new equilibrium bundle with those in the original equilibrium bundle.

In Figure 5–1, we assume that the consumer's money income and the prices of goods X and Y are such that the budget constraint is given by *AA*. Given this income constraint and the consumer's preferences, represented by indifference curves I_1, I_2, and I_3, consumption bundle A' (point A') will be chosen and

Figure 5-1
**The Effect of Changes in Money Income
on Consumer Equilibrium**

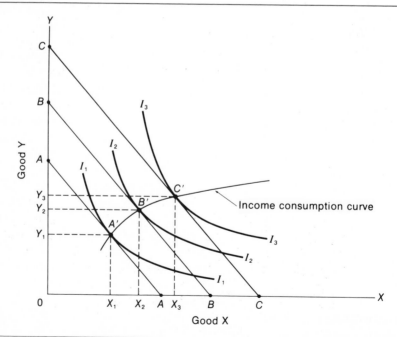

X_1 units of good X and Y_1 units of good Y will be consumed. If the consumer's money income is increased, the budget constraint will shift outward to BB in Figure 5–1. Here, the consumer's preferences are such that the additional money is used to purchase more of both goods. At the new equilibrium position B', the consumption of good X has increased from X_1 to X_2 and the consumption of good Y has increased from Y_1 to Y_2. A third increase in money income will result in the additional consumption of both goods, as indicated by the consumer equilibrium position C' associated with the budget constraint CC.

A line connecting the consumer equilibrium position associated with all levels of money income, when prices are held constant, is known as an **income consumption curve.** In Figure 5–1, this curve passes through the three equilibrium points A', B', and C'. The upward or positive slope of this income consumption curve indicates that the consumption of both goods increases when income increases. This is not surprising. We would all consume more of a large number of goods if only we had more money.

We would also consume less of some goods if our money income increased while all prices remained the same. In Chapter 2, we used the term *inferior goods* to define these commodities, which include such items as home-cooked meals, hamburger, do-it-yourself haircutting kits, second-hand automobiles, neckties from Goodwill, and mail-order dentures. Whether or not an individual considers a particular good inferior depends primarily on income level and preferences. Someone who lives in extreme poverty will probably consume more hamburger as income increases (a normal good). But if income rises above a certain level, the same individual will probably substitute porterhouse steaks and lobster tails for hamburger, which has now become an inferior good. On the other hand, an individual may simply love hamburger and never reduce consumption of it no matter how wealthy he or she becomes.

In Figure 5–2, good X is a normal good at lower incomes but becomes an inferior good at higher incomes. We can see that an increase in income necessary to shift the budget constraint from AA to BB motivates the consumer to increase consumption of good X from X_1 to X_2. However, a further increase in income to the level associated with budget constraint CC will cause the consumer to reduce consumption from X_2 to X_3. At an income level a little higher than that given by budget constraint BB, good X becomes an inferior good. This occurs at the point at which the income consumption curve bends back and becomes negatively sloped.

Changes in Price

In this section, we will analyze the effect that a change in the price of one good will have on the consumer's purchases when both money income and the price of the other good are fixed. This analysis is the first step toward using the theory of consumer behavior to derive an individual's demand curve for a product.

Figure 5–2
A Normal Good Becomes an Inferior Good

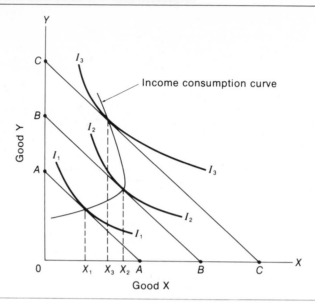

We begin with budget constraint *AA* in Figure 5–3. At point *A'*, the consumer maximizes utility subject to this constraint by consuming bundle *A'*, which contains X_1 units of good X and Y_1 units of good Y. But what happens to this equilibrium position if the price of good X decreases while the price of good Y and money income remain constant? In Chapter 4, we learned that this decrease in price causes the budget constraint to pivot to the right around point *A* on the vertical axis. Assuming that the decrease in the price of good X is sufficient to pivot the budget constraint to *AB* in Figure 5–3, the new consumer equilibrium position becomes *B'*, indicating an increase in the consumption of good X from X_1 to X_2 and an increase in the consumption of good Y from Y_1 to Y_2. Returning to the original budget constraint *AA*, we can investigate the effect of an increase in the price of good X by noting that an increase in this price will pivot the budget constraint to the left to a position similar to *AC* in Figure 5–3. Given the shape of the indifference curves, the increase in price results in a new consumer equilibrium position *C'*, where the consumption of good X has decreased from X_1 to X_3 and the consumption of good Y has increased from Y_1 to Y_3.

If we connect the different points of consumer equilibrium associated with all the possible prices of good X, we obtain what economists call a **price consumption curve.** The price consumption curve in Figure 5–3 passes through the equilibrium points *C'*, *A'*, and *B'*. It should be clear that the position of a price consumption curve depends on the assumed values of the consumer's

Figure 5-3
The Effect of Changes in Price on Consumer Equilibrium

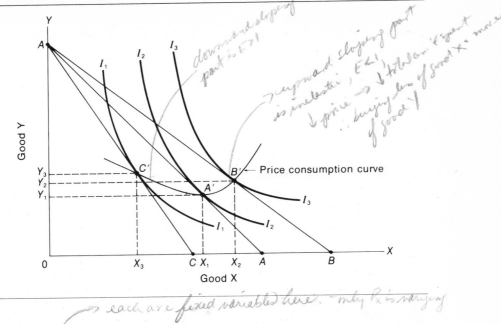

[handwritten annotations: downward sloping part is t>1; upward sloping part is inelastic, E<1; ↓ total expent ↓ price → ↓ total expent; buying less of good X & more of good Y; each are fixed variables here. only Px is varying]

money income and the price of good Y. The shape of the consumer's indifference curves or preferences are also important in determining the shape of a given price consumption curve. We could easily construct indifference curves for which the price consumption curve would be shaped quite differently, although we will see that there is a certain plausibility to the shape of the curve shown in Figure 5–3. We could also have derived a price consumption curve by varying the price of good Y, holding the price of good X and money income constant. It should be clear how this would be done.

The Consumer's Demand Curve   5–3

Deriving the Demand Curve

From Chapter 2, we know that an individual's demand curve for a good shows the quantities that he or she wishes to consume of that good at different prices, given the prices of all other goods and a specified level of money income. In developing the price consumption curve in the preceding section, we were able to determine the quantity of good X that an individual would consume at different prices, holding money income and the price of good Y constant. For example, we know from Figure 5–3 that when the price of good X is such that the relevant budget constraint is *AA*, the consumer will purchase X_1 units of good

X. Letting P_1 in Figure 5–4 denote the price associated with budget constraint *AA* in Figure 5–3 allows us to place point *A* on the consumer's demand curve for good X. As shown in Figure 5–4, this indicates that X_1 units of good X will be demanded when the price is P_1. At the lower price P_2 associated with budget constraint *AB*, we can see from Figure 5–3 that X_2 units of good X will be demanded, and this gives us point *B* on the demand curve in Figure 5–4. Finally, an increase in price from P_1 to P_3–the increase necessary to pivot the budget constraint from *AA* to *AC* in Figure 5–3–will reduce the quantity of good X demanded to X_3, and we can place point *C* on the demand curve in Figure 5–4. We could continue this process until any desired number of points were obtained. The line connecting all these points would be the demand curve *DD* shown in Figure 5–4.

The fact that demand curve *DD* (or any demand curve, for that matter) is appropriate only for a specified money income and price of all other goods deserves emphasis. We could consider, for example, what would happen to demand curve *DD* in Figure 5–4 if the consumer's income increased. Again, without cluttering Figure 5–3 with additional lines, we can visualize a parallel shift to the right in budget constraint *AC* as money income increases and the price of goods X and Y remain the same. Assuming that X is a normal good close to the equilibrium point *C* in Figure 5–3, we know that this shift in the budget constraint will cause an increase in the consumption of good X. Therefore, the new demand curve *D'D'* associated with the higher money income will show

Figure 5–4
Determining the Demand Curve and Shifts
in the Demand Curve from Price Consumption Curves

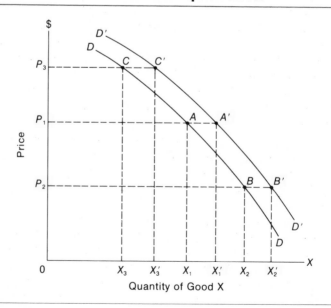

that good X is consumed at a greater rate at price P_3 than the original demand curve DD in Figure 5-4 indicates. By relating the consumption rate X_3' to the price P_3, we obtain point C' on the new demand curve $D'D'$.

The increase in money income will also produce an outward parallel shift in budget constraints AA and AB in Figure 5-3, which will cause the consumption of good X to increase at prices P_1 and P_2 if we continue to assume that X is a normal good. This is illustrated in Figure 5-4, where consumption rates X_1' and X_2' are related to prices P_1 and P_2, respectively, producing equilibrium points A' and B'. As before, we can determine any desired number of points and connect them to obtain the new demand curve associated with the higher money income. It should be noted that this procedure will also yield a new price consumption curve, which will be associated with the new demand curve.

If X is an inferior good, we can use the conceptual procedure we just outlined to show that an increase in money income will cause the demand curve to shift down and to the left. We should also be able to determine the effect that a change in the price of good Y will have on the demand curve for good X, money income being held constant.

The Price Consumption Curve and Price Elasticity

We have just used the information provided by the price consumption curve to determine the shape and position of the demand curve. Once the demand curve is constructed, we can determine one of its important and useful characteristics—the *price elasticity* at different points on the demand curve. Fortunately, we can obtain information about the price elasticity of the demand curve directly from the price consumption curve.

Referring again to Figure 5-3, we can see that the decrease in the price of good X required to pivot the budget constraint from AC to AA causes the consumption of good X to increase from X_3 to X_1 and the consumption of good Y to decrease from Y_3 to Y_1. Since the price of good Y remains the same, the consumer is spending less money on Y after the decline in the price of X. Since the consumer's money income also remains the same, we have to conclude that the decline in the price of good X causes the consumer to increase the amount spent on X. This implies that the price elasticity of demand for good X over the range of prices considered is greater than 1, because we know from Chapter 3 that the price elasticity is greater than 1 ($E > 1$) if a decrease in the price increases the total amount spent.

Now if we consider the price decrease required to pivot the budget constraint in Figure 5-3 from AA to AB, we can see that the consumer increases the consumption of good X from X_1 to X_2 and also increases consumption of good Y from Y_1 to Y_2. The increase in the consumption of Y given a constant price of Y means that the consumer is spending more on good Y after the price of good X declines. The decrease in the price of good X therefore results in a reduction in the consumer's expenditure on good X, so that the price elasticity of demand for X is less than 1 ($E < 1$).

From this discussion, it should be clear that a downward-sloping segment of the price consumption curve corresponds to an **elastic region**—a region where the price elasticity is greater than 1—on the demand curve. Similarly, an upward-sloping segment of the price consumption curve corresponds to an **inelastic region** on the demand curve. Clearly, the price elasticity of demand is equal to 1 when the slope of the price consumption curve is equal to 0 (when the slope is horizontal). The price consumption curve in Figure 5–3 is downward sloping at first and then upward sloping, so that the elasticity of the corresponding demand curve is greater than 1 at higher prices and decreases until it becomes less than 1 at lower prices. As we learned in Chapter 3, a common—although not a necessary—characteristic of demand curves is that price elasticity decreases as price declines.

Income and Substitution Effects

In analyzing the question of why a consumer will change the desired consumption rate of a good in response to a change in the price of that good, it is useful to distinguish between the two independent effects of a price change. For the sake of example, let's consider a reduction in the price of a good. If the price of a good decreases and the prices of all other goods remain the same, all individuals who consume that good will experience an increase in their real income even though their money income will remain constant. By an increase in real income, we simply mean the ability to reach a higher level of satisfaction—a capability that obviously exists if the price of one good declines and all other prices remain constant. An increase in the consumer's real income will have an effect on the rate at which he or she wishes to consume a particular good; we refer to this effect as the **income effect.** As we saw in Section 5–2, an increase in real income will cause an increase in the desired consumption of a normal good and a decrease in the desired consumption of an inferior good.[1] In the case of a normal good, we say that the income effect is *positive;* in the case of an inferior good, we say that the income effect is *negative.*

Independent of the income effect is the fact that a decrease in the price of one good will reduce the price of that good relative to the prices of all other goods, if all other prices remain constant. This makes it less costly to substitute the good whose price has declined for other goods and, as we will see, always has the effect of increasing the consumption of the good that is cheaper. This effect is referred to as the **substitution effect.** The substitution effect is always negative because, if we consider only this effect, a decrease (increase) in price causes an increase (decrease) in desired consumption.

It is possible to use the graphic techniques we have developed here and in Chapter 4 to isolate the income and the substitution effects, so that we can examine each effect more carefully. To do this, we will assume that the initial

---

[1]In Section 5–2, we examined the effects of changes in money income. However, when these changes are considered in the absence of any changes in price, an increase (decrease) in *money income* is identical to an increase (decrease) in *real income.*

Figure 5–5
Separating the Income and the Substitution Effects

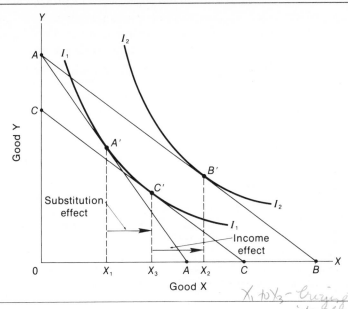

Good X

X₁ to X₃ — buying more X simply cause its cheaper now
→X(x)

budget constraint is *AA* in Figure 5–5 and that the point of consumer equilibrium is *A′*. At this equilibrium, the individual will consume X_1 units of good X.
Now if the price of good X declines while the price of good Y and money income
remain constant, the budget constraint will pivot to *AB*. The consumer equilibrium point will then be *B′*, and X_2 units of good X will be consumed. This increase
in the quantity of good X demanded is the combined result of the income and
the substitution effects. To determine the individual contributions of these
effects, we will graphically eliminate the income effect.

The fact that a decrease in price increases the consumer's real income is
reflected by the shift in consumer equilibrium from indifference curve I_1 to
indifference curve I_2 in Figure 5–5. To eliminate the income effect, in conjunction with the decrease in price we reduce money income to the point required
to shift the budget constraint back to *CC*. This constraint is parallel to *AB* and
therefore reflects the lower price for good X, but this position does not improve
the consumer's well-being because *CC* is tangent to indifference curve I_1. Thus,
the shift in equilibrium from *A′* to *C′* and the corresponding increase in the
consumption of good X from X_1 to X_3 reflects only the substitution effect. Since
the combined substitution and income effects increase the consumption of good
X from X_1 to X_2, the income effect must cause the increase in consumption
from X_3 to X_2.

Note that we can determine the substitution effect of a decrease in the price
of good X without considering the income effect. If the price of X declines, the
slope of the budget constraint will become less steep. Ignoring the income effect,

drop a budget constraint parallel to the new real income one, but, tangent to the previous indifference curve.

↳ more X for every unit of Y

the new equilibrium position will be the point at which a budget constraint with a more shallow slope is tangent to the indifference curve containing the consumption bundle that the consumer desired before the price decrease. Referring to Figure 5–5, we move directly from budget constraint *AA* and consumer equilibrium *A'* to budget constraint *CC* and equilibrium *C'*. Since the indifference curves are convex, becoming less steep as we move down them, reaching a tangency position with a less steeply sloped budget constraint will *always* require moving to a bundle on the indifference curve that contains more of good X. This proves our earlier claim that the substitution effect is *always negative:* A decrease in price causes an increase in consumption, when real income is held constant.

As we have constructed the graph in Figure 5–5, the income effect associated with the decrease in the price of good X is positive. The increase in real income, represented by the additional money income required to shift the budget constraint from *CC* to *AB*, causes an increase in the consumption of good X from X_3 to X_2. When, as in this case, the income effect is positive, it reinforces the negative substitution effect and both effects work together to increase consumption when price declines or to decrease consumption when price rises. However, we know that in the case of inferior goods, the income effect will be negative and will therefore tend to offset the influence of the substitution effect when the price of the good changes.

Example 5–1

How Smart Do You Have to Be to Behave Rationally?

Economic models are based on the assumption that economic decision makers behave rationally. In the case of consumer theory, which we have been developing in Chapters 4 and 5, we have assumed that individuals are capable of making consumption decisions that will maximize their utility subject to market constraints. A common criticism of economic theory is that people really do not behave rationally–that we simply do not have the information or the intelligence to calculate where our tangency positions are. This is certainly true. And no economist believes that consumers are constantly making the complicated calculations that are required to actually maximize utility. But most economists believe that consumers are rational in the sense that they are constantly motivated to reject choices that will not improve their well-being in favor of choices that will. This rationality permits economists to use consumer theory to make highly accurate predictions regarding consumer responses to changes in relative prices.

Apparently, you do not have to have a computer-like mind or even be very smart to respond to changes in economic variables in exactly the way our model predicts that the rational consumer will respond. White, male, albino rats–animals not known for their intellectual exploits–seem to have sufficient IQs to behave just like the economist's rational consumer. Under *when good X is an inferior good*

Figure 5-6 illustrates the opposing influences of the income and the substitution effects that result from a decrease in the price of good X. Beginning with budget constraint AA and equilibrium A' and taking into consideration only the substitution effect that results from the price decrease, we shift to budget constraint CC and equilibrium C'. This substitution effect increases the consumption of good X from X_1 to X_3. Adding the income effect by increasing money income until the budget constraint shifts out to AB, the new consumer equilibrium becomes B' and the consumption of good X is reduced from X_3 to X_2. Because we are dealing with an inferior good, the income effect is negative. Thus, when real income increases due to a price decline, the negative income effect partially offsets the negative substitution effect. The total increase in the consumption of good X resulting from a reduction in the price of X is $X_2 - X_1$, which is less than the increase resulting from only the substitution effect $X_3 - X_1$.

flatter slope
$\downarrow p \rightarrow \uparrow X/Y$

Giffen Goods

Although it is extremely unlikely, it is theoretically possible for the negative income effect arising from a decrease in the price of an inferior good to more than offset the negative substitution effect. If this happens, a decrease in the price of the good will cause a decrease, rather than an increase, in the quantity

---

experimental conditions, two rats were given the opportunity to consume root beer or Collins mix by pressing one of two levers. Each rat was given a specific number of presses to allocate between the two levers; the prices of the two beverages were determined by the number of presses required to obtain a .05 ml dipper cup of the chosen drink. The rats were initially given an "income" of 300 lever presses per day, with the price of each drink being one press. These conditions were maintained for 14 days (food and water were always available), and both subjects exhibited a stable pattern of consumption that favored root beer. After 14 days, the price of the root beer was doubled and the price of Collins mix was halved. The "income" was adjusted so that each rat could continue to consume the same beverage combination it had chosen before the price changes. Both rats responded by substantially increasing their consumption of Collins mix, and Collins mix became the most heavily consumed beverage in both cases.*

Rats may not be very smart, but they apparently have no difficulty responding to changes in relative prices in a rational way.

*For a complete discussion of this experiment, as well as other experiments that have provided results consistent with the predictions of the consumer model, see John H. Kagel et al., "Experimental Studies of Consumer Demand Behavior Using Laboratory Animals," *Economic Inquiry* (March 1975), pp. 22-38.

Figure 5–6
Income and Substitution Effects with an Inferior Good

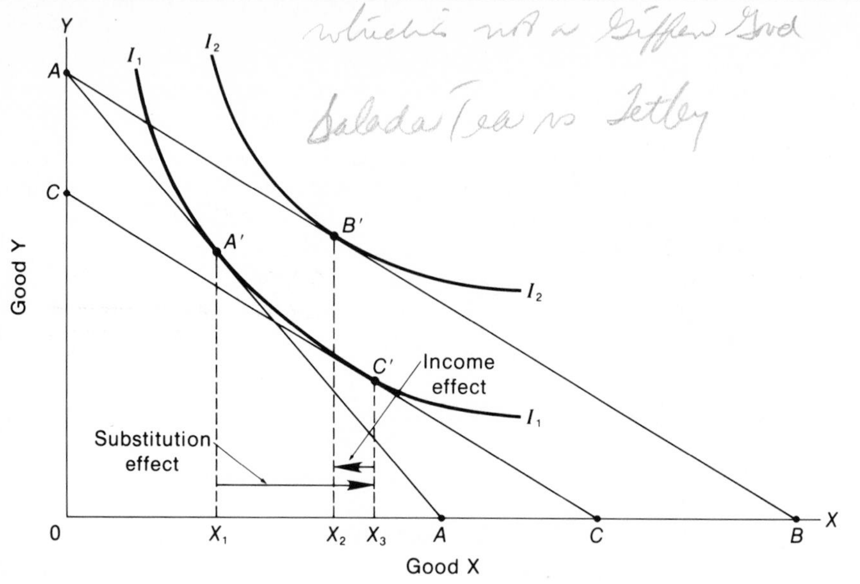

(handwritten annotations in the figure:) which is not a Giffen Good
Salada Tea vs Tetley

(handwritten annotations in left margin:) Rayon is a Giffen good $\uparrow p \rightarrow \downarrow q$ because income effect offsets substitution effect

the consumer demands. Likewise, a price increase will be accompanied by an increase in the quantity consumed. This theoretical possibility is illustrated in Figure 5–7.

Beginning with budget constraint *AA* and consumer equilibrium *A'*, the substitution effect of a decrease in the price of good X is to shift the equilibrium to *C'* on constraint *CC* and to increase the consumption of good X from X_1 to X_3. Including the income effect, however, shifts the budget constraint from *CC* to *AB*, establishing a new equilibrium at *B'* and, through a negative income effect, reducing the consumption of good X from X_3 to X_2. As shown in Figure 5–7, this negative income effect more than offsets the substitution effect, so that the net effect of the price decrease is a reduction in the quantity of good X demanded from X_1 to X_2.

The result is referred to as **Giffen's paradox,** and any good for which this result applies is called a **Giffen good.**[2] Note that only an inferior good can be a Giffen good, although an inferior good will not necessarily be a Giffen good. In fact, it is unclear whether a Giffen good has ever been empirically sighted. This is not surprising when we consider the rather unlikely conditions that would have to be satisfied for a good to be a Giffen good.

---

[2]Robert Giffen, a nineteenth-century British statistician and economist, provided the great Cambridge economist Alfred Marshall with aggregate demand data for bread that seemed to indicate that the demand curve for bread among the poor was positively sloped.

Figure 5–7
The Giffen Good Case

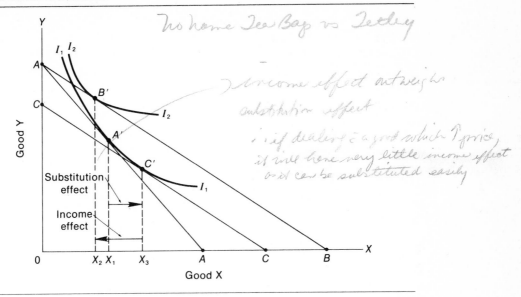

[Handwritten annotations on figure: "No home Tea Bag vs Tetley", "— income effect outweighs substitution effect", ": if dealing w a good which ↑ price, it will have very little income effect as it can be substituted easily"]

A Giffen good must be an inferior good so that the income effect will be negative. But if we are dealing with a good that comprises only a small percentage of
the consumer's budget, an increase in the price of this good will have an *[handwritten: inelasticity?]*
insignificant effect on the consumer's real income. In such a case, the negligible
negative income effect will do little to offset the negative substitution effect:
The substitution effect will not be influenced by the percentage of income spent
on the good. Therefore, to be a Giffen good, a good must be an inferior good on *[handwritten: not really — it can apply to my tea budget]*
which the consumer spends a major percentage of his or her income. This leads
us to conclude that the Giffen paradox may apply only to very poor consumers
(only a poor consumer would spend a large proportion of income on an inferior
good). This is the reasoning behind what economists most commonly accept as
a plausible example of a Giffen good.

Consider an extremely poor individual whose limited budget is devoted almost
entirely to food. With the exception of a little meat, most of this consumer's food
budget is spent on the cheapest form of nutrition available—the potato. Now
assume that the price of potatoes increases. Obviously, since potatoes comprise such a large portion of the budget, our poor consumer is now noticeably
poorer. This price increase could force the consumer to give up meat entirely
and to fill the resulting nutritional deficit with additional potato consumption.
Then the negative income effect would more than cancel out the negative substitution effect, and more potatoes would be consumed in response to an
increase in their price.

Although it is theoretically possible for a Giffen good to exist, it is extremely improbable that such a good will exist. And even if a given individual were to consider a particular good a Giffen good, most consumers would not, and the market demand curve for the good would be downward sloping, despite the fact that one consumer's demand curve was upward sloping. Therefore, for the purpose of predicting market behavior, it is sensible to ignore the possibility of Giffen goods, which we will do in the remainder of this book.

The Demand Curve and the Consumer's Surplus

In Chapter 4, we were introduced to the concept of the *consumer's surplus—* how much more the consumer is willing to pay to consume a given quantity of a good than it is necessary to pay. There, we learned to use the consumer's indifference curves and the budget constraint to measure the consumer's surplus from buying good X in terms of an alternative good, or a composite of goods, Y. In this section, we will develop the relationship that exists, given certain conditions, between the consumer's surplus and the demand curve.

A consumer's indifference curves are graphed in Figure 5–8, with good X on the horizontal axis and money income, which represents all other goods, denoted by Y on the vertical axis. We will assume that the consumer initially has $\bar{Y}$ dol-

Figure 5–8
Measuring the Consumer's Surplus from the Indifference Map

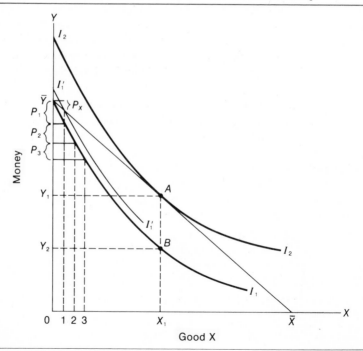

Good X

lars. The budget constraint that shows the different combinations of money and good X the consumer can have is given by $\overline{Y}\overline{X}$. Since the slope of this budget constraint multiplied by -1 is equal to the amount of money that must be sacrificed to obtain an additional unit of good X, this slope multiplied by -1 is equal to the price of good X.[3] In the initial position before the consumer has purchased any of good X, the consumer is on indifference curve I_1 at $\overline{Y}$. Given the opportunity to purchase good X at the price indicated by the budget constraint, however, the consumer will move to equilibrium point A, buying X_1 units of good X at a cost of $\overline{Y} - Y_1$ dollars, and reach indifference curve I_2. We can see from Figure 5–8, however, that the consumer would have been willing to pay as much as $\overline{Y} - Y_2$ dollars for X_1 units rather than do without good X entirely (paying $\overline{Y} - Y_2$ dollars for X_1 units would place the consumer at point B on the initial indifference curve I_1.) Thus, $Y_1 - Y_2$ represents the consumer's surplus received from buying X_1 units of good X at the indicated price.

Now let's relate the information contained in Figure 5–8 to the consumer's demand curve for good X to see what we can learn about the consumer's surplus from the demand curve. But first we must make the very important assumption that the income effect on the consumption of good X is 0: An increase or decrease in the money available to the individual will have no effect on the amount of good X that is purchased. For this to be true, all of the consumer's indifference curves have to be vertically parallel to one another; that is, for a given quantity of good X, all of the consumer's indifference curves must have the same slope. This is true of the indifference curves in Figure 5–8, where, for example, the slope of indifference curve I_2 at point A is the same as the slope of indifference curve I_1 at point B. As we reduce the consumer's income from $\overline{Y}$, the budget constraint moves downward and to the left in a parallel manner. If we continued to reduce $\overline{Y}$ until the lower budget constraint and indifference curve I_1 were tangent, the tangency would have to occur at point B because the slopes of I_1 at B and I_2 at A are identical. The reduction in income would have no effect on the quantity of X consumed.

At the initial position, with $\overline{Y}$ dollars and no units of good X, the consumer would be willing to pay the highest price on the demand curve to obtain the first unit of X. We know that we can determine this amount by multiplying the slope of the indifference curve by -1. Therefore, the absolute value of the slope of indifference curve I_1 at $\overline{Y}$ tells us how much money the consumer is willing to pay for the first unit of good X. This slope is approximated by P_1 in Figure 5–8. In Figure 5–9, P_1 is shown on the demand curve as the price the consumer is willing to pay for the first unit of good X.[4]

---

[3]From Chapter 4, we know that the slope of the budget constraint is $-P_x/P_y$, where P_x represents the price of good X and, in this case, P_y is the price of money. It is obvious, of course, that the price of money is 1 ($1 costs $1). This means that the slope of the budget constraint is equal to $-P_x$ (-1 multiplied by the price of good X).
[4]The demand curve in Figure 5–9 exhibits steps because we are considering rather large discrete units of good X, so that we can develop the relationship between the demand curve and the consumer's surplus as clearly as possible. When, as is normally the case, we consider extremely small units of good X, the steps disappear and the demand curve becomes smooth.

Figure 5–9
Measuring the Consumer's Surplus from the Demand Curve

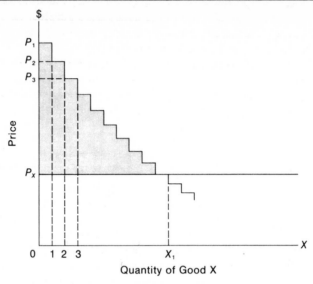

Quantity of Good X

Of course, the consumer does not have to pay P_1 for the first unit of good X. The consumer is required to pay only P_X for any unit of X; as shown in Figure 5–8, P_X is the decline in the budget constraint associated with a one-unit increase in good X. Price P_X also appears in Figure 5–9, where the horizontal line at P_X reflects that P_X is the price for all units of good X. The consumer is therefore willing to pay $P_1 - P_X$ more than is necessary to obtain the first unit, which means that $P_1 - P_X$ represents the consumer's surplus for the first unit of X.

To determine the consumer's surplus for the second unit, we need to find out the maximum amount that the consumer will pay for this second unit. In doing this, we would normally recognize that when only P_X instead of P_1 is paid for the first unit, the consumer moves to a higher indifference curve (I_1' in Figure 5–8). So the slope of indifference curve I_1' is now relevant in determining willingness to pay for the second unit. But because we are assuming that the income effect is 0, we can ignore this complication and continue to use indifference curve I_1, since I_1 has the same slope at each unit of X that all other indifference curves do. Thus, we can see from Figure 5–8 that the consumer is willing to pay P_2 for the second unit–the price associated with the second unit on the consumer's demand curve in Figure 5–9. Given this demand curve, the consumer's surplus from purchasing the second unit is $P_2 - P_X$. Similarly, the maximum the consumer is willing to pay for the third unit is P_3 and, given the demand curve in Figure 5–9, the consumer's surplus from purchasing the third unit is $P_3 - P_X$.

We can continue this process until we account for the consumer's surplus on each unit consumed, or on X_1 units. In Figure 5–8, we can see that the accumulation of each P_X (the amount paid for each unit) from 0 to X_1 is equal to $\overline{Y} - Y_1$, and that the accumulation of $P_1, P_2, P_3, \cdots, P_X$ (the amount the consumer is willing to pay for each unit) is equal to $\overline{Y} - Y_2$. The difference $Y_1 - Y_2$ between these two accumulations is the consumer's surplus. This difference is also equal to the shaded area between the demand curve and the price line P_X that extends from 0 to X_1 in Figure 5–9. So, in the absence of an income effect, the consumer's surplus can be determined directly from the demand curve. The area under the demand curve from 0 to the amount consumed represents the total value the consumer receives from the good. Subtracting the amount paid for the good from the total value received from the good gives us the consumer's surplus.

Willingness to Pay Versus Compensation Required

We have used indifference-curve analysis to conceptually measure the net value that a consumer receives from purchasing a given amount of a good at a specified per-unit price. We have defined this consumer's surplus as the maximum amount that the consumer is *willing to pay* in excess of what actually needs to be paid to consume a given quantity of the good. In Figure 5–10, the value of the consumer's surplus received from consuming X_1 units of good X at the price indicated by the budget constraint $\overline{YX}$ is $Y_1 - Y_2$, where $\overline{Y} - Y_2$ is the maximum the consumer is willing to pay and $\overline{Y} - Y_1$ is what the consumer actually pays.

Figure 5–10
Willingness to Pay Versus Compensation Required

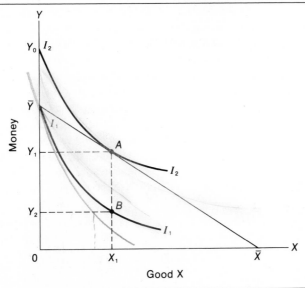

Although an individual's maximum willingness to pay is an extremely plausible measure of value, it is not the only plausible measure. It can certainly be argued that the minimum amount an individual will accept in return for giving up a good represents the value he or she attaches to that good. In other words, the *minimum compensation required* to sacrifice a good is as plausible a measure of the good's value as the *maximum willingness to pay* for the good.

Figure 5–10 provides a means of measuring the minimum compensation required to convince our consumer to voluntarily sacrifice the opportunity to purchase X_1 units of good X at the price indicated by budget constraint $\overline{YX}$. Beginning with income $\overline{Y}$ and no units of good X, the consumer will be able to improve well-being by moving down budget constraint $\overline{YX}$, giving up income in order to consume units of good X, until bundle A is reached. At point A, the consumer reaches the highest obtainable indifference curve I_2 and pays $\overline{Y} - Y_1$ for X_1 units of good X. But what is the opportunity to move from position $\overline{Y}$ to position A worth to the consumer (what is the consumer's surplus at A) in terms of the minimum compensation required to convince the consumer to voluntarily sacrifice this opportunity? Note that if our consumer stopped consuming good X by moving up indifference curve I_2 until point Y_0 was reached on the Y axis, the consumer's utility would not change. In other words, the consumer would be willing to sacrifice the opportunity to consume X_1 units of good X at the price specified by the budget constraint in return for an increase in income to Y_0. This tells us that $Y_0 - \overline{Y}$ is the minimum increase in income that the consumer would accept in exchange for sacrificing the purchase of X_1 units of good X.

Figure 5–10 therefore provides two different measures of the value the consumer attaches to the consumption of X_1 units of good X at the specified price, or the consumer's surplus received from this consumption. In terms of the maximum willingness to pay, this value is measured by $Y_1 - Y_2$; in terms of the minimum compensation required, this value is measured by $Y_0 - \overline{Y}$. Under what conditions will these two measures of value be identical? When they are not identical, is there a basis for determining which value will be the larger?

The answers to these questions are critically dependent on whether we are considering a normal good (positive income effect), an inferior good (negative income effect), or a good with an income effect of 0. First, we will consider a good for which there is no income effect, implying that the slope of indifference curve I_1 at B is identical to the slope of indifference curve I_2 at A in Figure 5–10.[5] If we further assume that the income effect is 0 for all prices of good X (for all possible slopes of the budget constraint), then the slopes of indifference curves I_1 and I_2 are equal over all quantities of good X. This implies that the vertical distance between the two indifference curves I_1 and I_2 is the same

---

[5] Recall that an income effect of 0 for good X means that a parallel shift in the budget constraint will be tangent to higher or lower indifference curves at the same consumption level for X. Since the slope of the budget constraint remains the same as it shifts, this implies that the slopes of all the indifference curves are the same above the equilibrium value of good X.

see fig 5-8

everywhere. In particular, the distance $A - B$ or $Y_1 - Y_2$ in Figure 5–10 is exactly the same as the distance $Y_0 - \bar{Y}$. Therefore, our two measures of value are identical when the income effect is 0.

Next, we will consider the case when X is a normal good at all prices of X. This means that the slope of I_2 is steeper than the slope of I_1 for every quantity of good X between 0 and X_1 and the income effect is positive.[6] It therefore follows that the vertical distance between I_2 and I_1 becomes larger as we retrace our position from X_1 to 0. Thus, the distance $Y_0 - \bar{Y}$ in Figure 5–10 is greater than the distance $Y_1 - Y_2$. So we can conclude that for a normal good, the value of the consumer's surplus in terms of the minimum compensation required is greater than it is in terms of the maximum willingness to pay.

Finally, we will consider the case when X is an inferior good at all prices. This means that the income effect is negative[7] and the slope of I_1 is steeper than the slope of I_2 for every quantity of good X between 0 and X_1. This implies that the vertical distance between the two indifference curves diminishes as we move from X_1 to 0, so that $Y_0 - \bar{Y}$ is less than $Y_1 - Y_2$. Thus, we can conclude that for an inferior good, the value of the consumer's surplus will be greater if it is measured by the willingness-to-pay criterion than it will be if it is measured by the compensation-required criterion.

With a little thought, it becomes clear that the result of this analysis is exactly what could be intuitively expected. It is appropriate to measure the value of the consumer's surplus in terms of the willingness to pay before the consumer actually purchases good X and in terms of the compensation required after the consumer purchases good X. Since the purchase is motivated by the fact that it enhances the consumer's well-being (places the consumer on a higher indifference curve), real income is greater after the purchase than it was before. This increase in real income makes a normal good relatively more valuable, so that, not surprisingly, the consumer will require more compensation to give up the good after it is purchased than the maximum amount he or she was willing to pay initially. Conversely, the increase in real income that results from purchasing an inferior good makes it less valuable relative to other goods. Therefore, once it has been purchased, the consumer is willing to sacrifice an inferior good for less than the maximum he or she was willing to pay initially.[8]

---

[6]If this were not true, then the new budget constraint would not be tangent to the higher indifference curve at a larger quantity of good X when income is increased.

[7]Of course, X can be an inferior good at some prices and a normal good at other prices. In this case, we cannot generalize about the relative slopes of indifference curves I_1 and I_2 for all quantities of good X. Although we can still make a straightforward comparison of the two measures of value, the connection between their relative sizes and the distinction between normal and inferior goods becomes somewhat blurred.

[8]At this point, the enterprising student may be weighing the prospects of selling an inferior good at the maximum an individual is willing to pay, buying it back for the minimum compensation required, and repeating this process until either the customer (victim) goes broke or becomes so poor that the good becomes a normal good. A little thought should have a calming influence, however. If you sell a good, inferior or not, at the maximum that an individual is willing to pay, the individual's real income will be the same after the purchase as it was before. Therefore, once the good is purchased, the minimum compensation required to give up the good *is equal to* the maximum willingness to pay.

The increase in real income associated with most purchases is usually quite small. When a consumer buys a can of peas, a soft drink, or an undershirt, the effect on real income is generally so small that it can be ignored. This means that there will be no meaningful difference between the value of the consumer's surplus in terms of willingness to pay versus compensation. The distinction between these two measures of value can be significant, however, in the case of a large purchase, such as an automobile or a house.

5-4   The Productivity of Exchange

Most people think that to be productive, an activity must generate a tangible product; cabinet making, assembly-line work, farming, and masonry are commonly considered to be productive activities. For economists, however, the concept of productivity has a broader meaning. Viewed from the perspective of economic analysis, a **productive activity** is any activity that increases consumer utility. This allows us to enlarge our range of examples of productive activities to include such things as looking at a beautiful landscape, visiting friends, entertaining an audience by telling jokes, and sinking a side-hill, 22-foot putt on national television to win the Master's Golf Tournament.

A list of productive activities would be grossly incomplete without including one of the most productive of all activities—the activity of *exchange.* Exchange increases the value of goods by allocating them among consumers in such a way that they provide greater utility. The explanation for this productivity of exchange is quite straightforward. When two individuals engage in an exchange, they are both motivated by the possibility of giving up something that they value less to obtain something else that they value more. The exchange does not increase the amount of goods in existence, but the well-being of both parties in the exchange is improved. The goods are *reallocated* so that they both provide more utility than they did before, and the exchange is therefore productive.[9] However, this does not mean that, in retrospect, all exchanges are mutually advantageous. We can all recall exchanges we have made that we regretted after the fact. But people learn from their experiences, and only the most accomplished incompetents would consistently engage in voluntary exchanges that detracted from their well-being.

It will be useful to give a simple numerical example of how two individuals can both increase their utility through exchange. Let's assume that initially individual A and individual B both have 20 cigarettes and 20 chocolate bars. We will further assume that A would be willing to give up as many as 3 cigarettes to obtain an additional chocolate bar and that B would willingly sacrifice up to 3 chocolate bars to obtain an additional cigarette. This means that A is indiffer-

---

[9]Another very important aspect of the productivity of exchange should be noted. The possibility of exchange allows people to specialize in their productive activities and therefore to produce more than they would if exchange did not exist and each individual had to produce everything he or she wanted to consume.

ent between a bundle containing 20 cigarettes and 20 chocolate bars and a bundle containing 17 cigarettes and 21 chocolate bars. And individual B finds a bundle containing 20 of each good and a bundle containing 21 cigarettes and 17 chocolate bars equally desirable.

Obviously, A and B place different relative values on cigarettes and chocolate bars and, because of this, both individuals can gain from an exchange. For example, A may offer B 2 cigarettes in exchange for 2 chocolate bars. This is clearly a productive exchange for A, since A is willing to offer 3 cigarettes to obtain only 1 chocolate bar. And B will consider A's offer generous, since only 1 of the 2 cigarettes A is offering is worth 3 chocolate bars to B. The gain that both A and B will realize from the proposed exchange is given in Table 5−1. After the exchange, A's bundle will contain 18 cigarettes (Cig) and 22 chocolate bars (CB), which A will clearly prefer to the bundle containing 17 cigarettes and 21 chocolate bars, since it provides more of both goods. But we know that A is indifferent between the bundle containing 17 cigarettes and 21 chocolate bars and the initial bundle containing 20 of each good. Thus, by *transitivity*, we know that A prefers the bundle after the exchange to the initial bundle; the exchange has increased A's utility. Applying the same reasoning to the effect of the exchange on B, we can see from Table 5−1 that B's utility is also higher after the exchange than it was before.

After the exchange, we will assume that A is willing to give up 2 cigarettes to obtain an additional chocolate bar and that B is willing to sacrifice 2 chocolate bars to obtain an additional cigarette.[10] Thus, both A and B can further increase their utility through exchange. For example, an exchange in which A gives B 1 cigarette in return for 1 chocolate bar increases both A's and B's well-being, as you should be able to show. The possibility of a mutually advantageous exchange continues until the number of cigarettes that A is willing to give up to obtain an additional chocolate bar is exactly equal to the number of cigarettes that will compensate B for the loss of a chocolate bar. At this point, A's and B's marginal rates of substitution for the two goods will be equal and all possible gains from the exchange will have been realized.

Table 5−1
Gains from Exchange of Cigarettes and Chocolate Bars

	AFTER EXCHANGE			BEFORE EXCHANGE	
A	[18 Cig, 22 CB]	P	[17 Cig, 21 CB]	I	[20 Cig, 20 CB]
B	[22 Cig, 18 CB]	P	[21 Cig, 17 CB]	I	[20 Cig, 20 CB]

P denotes "preferred to."
I denotes "indifferent to."

---

[10]Note that this example illustrates *diminishing* marginal rates of substitution. Both A and B have *convex* indifference curves.

Examples are instructive, but the productivity of exchange can be more generally illustrated by using indifference-curve analysis. When the indifference curves of two individuals are used to indicate the benefits they will both derive from an exchange, these curves must be positioned in a particular way with respect to each other. Figure 5–11 is an indifference-curve map for the productivity of exchange from our cigarette–chocolate bar example. This figure contains a lot of information and requires some explanation. The southwest corner of the box 0_A represents the origin for individual A; with respect to this origin, A's indifference curves are represented by I_{1A}, I_{2A}, I_{3A}, and I_{4A}. Likewise, the northeast corner of the box 0_B is the origin for individual B; B's indifference curves, with respect to this origin, are represented by I_{1B}, I_{2B}, I_{3B}, and I_{4B}.

The width of the box in Figure 5–11 is equal to the total quantity of chocolate bars available, and the height of the box indicates the total availability of cigarettes. Moving horizontally to the right along the bottom of the box represents an increase in the number of chocolate bars given to A and corresponds to a decrease in the number of chocolate bars available to B. Similarly, moving vertically down the right-hand side of the box corresponds to an increase in B's consumption of cigarettes and a decrease in cigarette consumption for A. Each point within the box represents a particular distribution of the available chocolate bars and cigarettes between A and B. For example, at point D in Figure 5–11, A is receiving 20 chocolate bars and 20 cigarettes (measuring from 0_A) and B is receiving the remaining 20 chocolate bars and 20 cigarettes (measuring from 0_B).

We can now use the information contained in what economists call the *Edgeworth box diagram*[11] to demonstrate how exchange can increase the value of the goods by distributing them so that the utility of both A and B is increased. We begin by assuming that the initial distribution is given by position D in the box. Given this allocation, A's utility is represented by indifference curve I_{2A} and B's utility is represented by indifference curve I_{2B}. The intersection of I_{2A} and I_{2B} at point D indicates that both A and B can improve their situation through an exchange. The steep slope of I_{2A} at D tells us that A is willing to give up a large number of cigarettes to obtain an additional chocolate bar, and the shallow slope of I_{2B} at D reflects B's willingness to give up a large number of chocolate bars to obtain an additional cigarette. Obviously, A can sacrifice a smaller number of cigarettes for additional chocolate bars than A is willing to sacrifice and still more than compensate B for the loss of chocolate bars.

A direct way of seeing the gains from exchange that are possible at point D is to consider exchanges that move along indifference curve I_{2A} from D to f. Although this is no improvement for A, since A remains on the same indifference curve, B's position is clearly improved by moving from indifference curve I_{2B} to the higher curve I_{3B}. In this case, B receives all the gains from the exchange. Alternatively, we could consider a move from D to g, in which case

---

[11]Named after the English economist F.Y. Edgeworth, who used this technique to analyze exchange in the nineteenth century.

Figure 5–11
The Productivity of Exchange

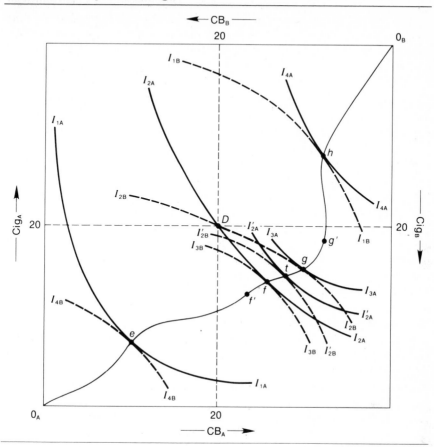

A receives all the gains from the exchange. Normally, both parties in an exchange expect to receive some of the gains. In other words, an exchange usually results in a distribution somewhere between points f and g, such as t in Figure 5–11. This rules out the possibility of an exchange that would result in a distribution at, say, point f' or g', where one individual would be in a worse position after the exchange than before and therefore would not voluntarily agree to the exchange.

It should be noted that all the exchanges we have considered have led to a point where one of A's indifference curves is tangent to one of B's indifference curves. Only at such a point is A's willingness to sacrifice one good for another exactly equal to B's (A's and B's marginal rates of substitution are equal), so that all gains from trade have been exploited. Starting from any distribution point where A's and B's indifference curves are tangent, we can see from Figure 5–11 that any redistribution will place at least one individual in a worse position. All of these tangency points have been connected in Figure 5–11, resulting in the line $0_A 0_B$. This curve is traditionally referred to as the **contract curve;** however, economist Kenneth Boulding more descriptively labeled it the **conflict curve.** The conflict arises from the fact that once the distribution point lies on this curve, the only way to improve one individual's position is to worsen the position of the other individual. Any distribution of goods that lies on this curve is referred to as a **Pareto-efficient distribution.**[12] This distribution is efficient in the sense that all possibilities of improving the well-being of one individual without reducing the well-being of the other individual have been realized. We will examine the Pareto-efficient criterion more fully in Chapter 12 in conjunction with judging the desirability of different allocations of goods and resources.

It is tempting to conclude from our example of A trading cigarettes to B in return for chocolate bars that A likes chocolate bars better than B does and that B enjoys cigarettes more than A does. But this conclusion does not follow in any way from our analysis. What we have said is entirely consistent with, for example, B enjoying both chocolate bars and cigarettes much more than A. A may not care very much for chocolate bars but may enjoy smoking cigarettes even less. Therefore, at distribution point D in Figure 5–11, A is willing to reduce cigarette consumption by a substantial amount to obtain an additional chocolate bar. On the other hand, B may tingle all over at the very thought of devouring chocolate bars, but this pleasure pales in comparison to the enjoyment experienced when smoking. Therefore, at point D we find that B is willing to sacrifice several precious chocolate bars for the greater pleasure of one more smoke. Exchange is mutually advantageous when the marginal rates of substitution for two goods differ between the two individuals. But a comparison of marginal rates of substitution between two individuals tells us nothing about the degree to which each individual enjoys a particular good.

A related point is that a comparison of marginal rates of substitution provides no basis for determining which individual receives the greater gain from an exchange. If we assume, for example, that an exchange moves the distribution point from D in Figure 5–11 to a point on the contract curve just slightly to the northeast of f, then B might appear to be receiving most of the gains and A's utility might seem to be increasing very little. But we have no basis for this conclusion. All we can say is that both A and B have increased their utility by moving to a higher indifference curve. In Chapter 4, we learned that we cannot attach any meaning to the differences between utility levels when we are working with ordinal utilities. Furthermore, recalling our discussion of the hazards of making interpersonal utility comparisons from Chapter 4, we know that we have no basis on which to compare a given increase in A's utility with an increase in B's utility. We can say that the exchange has allowed both A and B to increase their utility, but we cannot know how much benefit one individual has received relative to the other.

---

[12]Named after the Italian economist V. Pareto.

Application: An Introduction to Benefit–Cost Analysis

In the case of most goods, it is not of great importance to know the total value a good provides to determine what quantity of the good to make available. As long as the good can be supplied incrementally, only the marginal value is of concern to us. The supply of the good should be expanded as long as its marginal value is greater than its marginal cost. For some goods, however, production decisions must be made on an all-or-nothing basis. Either you construct the canal or the dam, or you do not.[13] Therefore, to determine whether or not the project is desirable, its total value and its total cost have to be compared. In cases where it is not completely unreasonable to ignore the income effect, it is useful to estimate the demand curve for a project and then to consider the area under the curve to be an approximation of the total value.

Let's assume, for example, that the U.S. Army Corps of Engineers has constructed a dam to create, among other things, a reservoir suitable for recreational activities. It is important to consider the value of this reservoir in assessing the total benefits and the total cost of the dam—something the Corps wants to do to justify some existing and proposed projects. If the demand curve for the reservoir can be estimated, then the recreational value of the reservoir can be approximated by the area under this curve if the income effects are assumed to be insignificant. It is not easy to estimate the demand curve for a reservoir, since it is usually impossible to observe the demand response to a change in the price of the use of the reservoir. But techniques are available that can provide a rough approximation of such a demand curve. Probably the most accurate approach is to let travel cost represent willingness to pay for visitor days to the recreational area. By comparing the higher travel costs and the fewer per-capita visitor days for populations living far away from the reservoir to the lower costs and the greater per-capita visitor days for populations living near the reservoir, we can estimate the demand curve.[14]

Once the value of a project has been approximated, it can be compared with the cost of the project to determine whether or not the project is worthwhile. If the value of the benefit exceeds the cost—if the *benefit–cost ratio* exceeds 1—there is strong support to undertake the project. But if the benefit–cost ratio is less than 1, then the value of the resources needed for the project will be greater if they are devoted to another project. Unfortunately, this procedure is not as simple as it may sound. Once the project has been completed, it will provide benefits not just for one year but for many years, and it is the value *over the entire life of the project* that is important. But the total value of a project is not simply determined by adding up the yearly benefits. A benefit received one year from now is not as valuable as the same benefit received now. Therefore, before

---

[13]There may be some flexibility in determining the size of such a good, but the range of this choice will probably be small compared to the total size of any reasonable project.

[14]This estimation procedure is more complicated than we have indicated here. For a detailed discussion of this procedure, as well as its problems and limitations, see Chapter 5 of M. Clawson and J. Knetsch, *Economics of Outdoor Recreation* (Baltimore: Johns Hopkins Press, 1966).

adding up the future benefits of a project, they must be discounted to their *present value.*[15]

Determining the present value of a future benefit is a relatively straightforward procedure once a discount rate has been determined. To provide a simple example, we may be interested in the present value of a $1,000 benefit that we will receive one year from now. What is the minimum amount we would accept now in lieu of $1,000 one year from today? Assuming we discount the future at 10% per year, we feel that any benefit received now provides 10% more value than the same benefit will provide a year from now. This means that we are indifferent between receiving X dollars now and 10% more, or $X + .1X = (1.1)X$ dollars, next year. Therefore, if PV_1 is the present value of $1,000 a year from now, then

$$(1.1)PV_1 = \$1,000$$

or

$$PV_1 = \left(\frac{1}{1.1}\right)\$1,000 = \$909.09$$

If the $1,000 is not to be received for two years, then we will have to wait one year for it to have a present value of $(1/1.1)\$1,000$. The present value of $1,000

Example 5-2

The Recreational Value of a Reservoir

In 1959, the travel-cost approach was used to estimate the demand curve for Lewis and Clark Lake—a large reservoir created by the Gavin Point Dam on the Missouri River in South Dakota. The relationship between the different hypothetical charges for using the lake and the estimated number of visits to the lake in 1959 is given below.

ENTRANCE FEE	ATTENDANCE
$ 1	198,000
3	136,000
5	95,000
10	48,000
15	25,000
20	18,000

This relationship is plotted as the estimated demand curve for Lewis and Clark Lake in Figure 5–12. The area under this demand curve provides a useful approximation of the total value of the Lewis and Clark Lake during 1959.

[15]In the Appendix to Chapter 4, we used indifference curves to analyze the effect of discounting the future on an individual's consumption choices over time.

two years from now, or PV_2, is therefore the present value of receiving $(1/1.1)\$1,000$ one year from now, or

$$(1.1)PV_2 = \left(\frac{1}{1.1} \right) \$1,000$$

and

$$PV_2 = \left[\frac{1}{(1.1)^2} \right] \$1,000 = \$826.45$$

So, discounting the future at the rate of 10% a year, we would be indifferent between having $826.45 now and waiting until two years from now to receive $1,000. In general, at a discount rate of r, the **present value** of V dollars to be received n years from now is

$$PV_n = \frac{1}{(1 + r)^n} V$$

We are now able to determine the present value of a sequence of benefits received over time. We will let the estimated value of a proposed reservoir i

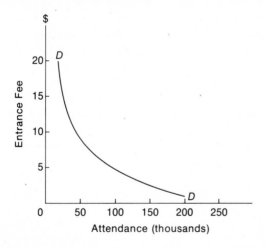

Figure 5–12
The Estimated Demand Curve for Lewis and Clark Lake

Data Source: M. Clawson and J. Knetsch, *Economics of Outdoor Recreation* (Baltimore: Johns Hopkins Press, 1966), p. 81.

years from now by V_i and the discount rate be r. If the expected life of the reservoir is N years, then the estimated present value of the benefits to be received from the reservoir PV_B is the sum of the estimated present values of the benefits to be received each year over the expected life of the reservoir, or

$$\text{PV}_B = \frac{V_1}{1+r} + \frac{V_2}{(1+r)^2} + \frac{V_3}{(1+r)^3} + \cdot \cdot \cdot + \frac{V_N}{(1+r)^N}$$

Similarly, we can obtain a useful measure of the estimated cost of the reservoir by summing the estimated present values of the costs to be incurred each year over the expected life of the reservoir. Letting C_i be the estimated cost i years from now, the present value of the reservoir's cost can be expressed as

$$\text{PV}_C = \frac{C_1}{1+r} + \frac{C_2}{(1+r)^2} + \frac{C_3}{(1+r)^3} + \cdot \cdot \cdot + \frac{C_N}{(1+r)^N}$$

Having done this, we can determine the **benefit–cost ratio**

$$\frac{\text{PV}_B}{\text{PV}_C}$$

Although the mechanics of determining benefit–cost ratios are fairly straightforward, confidence should be placed in these ratios only with great caution. The procedures used to estimate demand curves are very crude, and even when the demand curve is estimated precisely, an accurate estimate of value depends on how close the income effect is to 0. Measuring the costs of a project is generally less difficult than measuring its benefits. But the prevalence with which the realized costs greatly exceed the estimated costs of government projects indicates how difficult it is to make accurate cost projections. Also, we should not dismiss the possibility of a systematic bias on the part of the government agency constructing approved projects to overstate benefits and to understate costs. And even if the benefits and costs associated with a particular project are accurately estimated, it is still difficult to obtain an unequivocal measure of the project's benefit–cost ratio, because this ratio can be highly sensitive to the choice of a discount rate.

A typical government project requires large initial cost outlays during the construction stage, but operations and maintenance costs are relatively modest after the project is finished. On the other hand, no benefits are received from the project until what is often a long construction stage is completed. The higher the discount rate we apply in this case (the more we discount the future), the less weight we attach to future periods in which benefits will exceed costs relative to the early periods in which costs will exceed benefits. Similarly, the lower the discount rate, the more weight we attach to periods that produce positive net benefits relative to the periods that generate positive net costs. It is therefore not surprising that most government projects will have larger benefit–cost ratios when smaller discount rates are applied.

To illustrate, we will assume that a potential project will yield no benefits until the fifth year and that it will provide $50,000 in benefits each year thereafter until the end of year 10. At the end of each of the first four years, construction costs will be $50,000, and operations and maintenance costs will run $5,000 per year thereafter. These benefits and costs appear in Table 5–2, where the sum of the undiscounted benefits is shown to be $300,000 and the sum of the undiscounted costs is shown to be $230,000. But we are concerned with comparing the *present value* of these benefits and costs, and the result of this comparison is sensitive to the choice of a discount rate. We can see from Table 5–2 that if a 4% discount rate is chosen, the present value of the benefit stream is $224,050 and the present value of the cost sequence is $203,899. This provides a benefit–cost ratio of almost 1.1–a clear signal to go ahead with the project.

Table 5–2
Discounting Benefits and Costs

| | BENEFITS | | |
End of Year	Undiscounted	4%	8%
1	$ 0	$ 0	$ 0
2	0	0	0
3	0	0	0
4	0	0	0
5	50,000	41,096	34,029
6	50,000	39,516	31,508
7	50,000	37,996	29,174
8	50,000	36,535	27,013
9	50,000	35,129	25,012
10	50,000	33,778	23,160
	$300,000	$224,050	$169,896

| | COSTS | | |
End of Year	Undiscounted	4%	8%
1	$ 50,000	$ 48,077	$ 46,296
2	50,000	46,228	42,867
3	50,000	44,450	39,692
4	50,000	42,750	36,751
5	5,000	4,107	3,403
6	5,000	3,952	3,151
7	5,000	3,800	2,917
8	5,000	3,654	2,701
9	5,000	3,513	2,501
10	5,000	3,378	2,316
	$230,000	$203,899	$182,595

But if a discount rate of 8% is selected, the present value of the project's benefits becomes $169,896 and the present value of the project's costs becomes $182,595. This results in a benefit–cost ratio of .93—an argument against developing the project.

To minimize the complexity of our example, we have restricted the life of the project to 10 years. However, most government projects generate a stream of benefits and costs that extend far beyond 10 years, and the longer the useful life of a project, the more sensitive the benefit–cost analysis will be to the choice of a discount rate. Government agencies, such as the Bureau of Reclamation and the Army Corps of Engineers, which have a vested interest in constructing large public projects, consistently employ low discount rates to increase the benefit–cost ratio of proposed projects. The Narrows dam and irrigation project in eastern Colorado is one example of an attempt to inflate the apparent desirability of a project. Selecting a low discount rate of 3¼% and somewhat generous benefit figures, the Bureau of Reclamation estimated a benefit–cost ratio of 1.6 over the 100-year expected life of the project. Using the same benefit figures but applying a higher discount rate of 6⅜%, the benefit–cost ratio declines to .86 over 100 years.[16]

Application: Total Value Versus Marginal Value

In Chapter 4, we used indifference curves to contrast the *marginal value* of a good to an individual with the *total value* that individual receives from the good. Given the analysis provided in this chapter, we can use the demand curve for the good to pursue this contrast further (still assuming a negligible income effect).

For a long time, economists puzzled over the fact that water, although essential to life, can be purchased at a trivial price in comparison to the price paid for diamonds, an item of doubtful usefulness. This observation has led some people to conclude that economic values are distorted and have little relation to "real" value. This puzzle, or distortion, is often referred to as the *diamond–water paradox*. As puzzling as this paradox may have been to early economists—and as unjustifiable as it may appear to most people today—the careful reader of the last few pages should have little difficulty explaining why this economic phenomenon is not a paradox or a distortion.[17]

The price of a good reflects only the value that consumers place on a marginal unit of the good—the value they are willing to sacrifice to obtain one more unit of the good. This should be clear from the way we derived the demand curve in Figure 5–9 from the indifference curve I_1 in Figure 5–8. Therefore, if a good

---

[16]For a more detailed examination of the benefit–cost aspects of the Narrows project, see Charles W. Howe, "U.S. Water Policy and Its Implications for Agriculture, Energy, and Water Quality in the Colorado River Basin" (Boulder, CO: University of Colorado, Economics Department, April 1977), *mimeograph.*

[17]The resolution of the diamond–water paradox is also implied in our discussion of priceless goods in Chapter 4 (pages 118–121).

is in abundant supply, as water is, the marginal unit of the good may not be very valuable, and its price may be low even though the total value of the good is enormous. On the other hand, a good in less abundant supply, such as diamonds, may have a high marginal value and price but may not have a very high total value.

To illustrate this point, we will let DD represent the demand curve for water in Figure 5–13(a) and S_W represent the quantity of water available. Given this demand and supply, the price of water is P_W. If we were to measure the total value of a good by multiplying its price by the quantity consumed, then we could conclude that the total value of water is given by the darker tinted area P_W0S_WA in Figure 5–13(a). But we know that the total value of the water consumed is approximated by a much larger area under the demand curve from 0 to S_W—an area so large that it can be only partially shown in Figure 5–13(a). The demand curve for diamonds is DD in Figure 5–13(b), where S_D represents the quantity of diamonds available. This establishes the price of diamonds at P_D, which is a much higher price than the price of water P_W. The total value of diamonds P_DS_D, or the darker tinted area P_D0S_DB in Figure 5–13(b), may even exceed the total spent on water, or P_W0S_WA in Figure 5–13(a). However, we know that multiplying price by quantity tells us nothing about the total value of diamonds or of any other good. The total value of diamonds is given by the area under the demand curve for diamonds between 0 and S_D, or area $D0S_DB$ in Figure 5–13(b). The total value of water is much greater than the total value of diamonds, despite the fact that the price or marginal value of diamonds is much greater.

Figure 5–13
The Diamond–Water Paradox Resolved

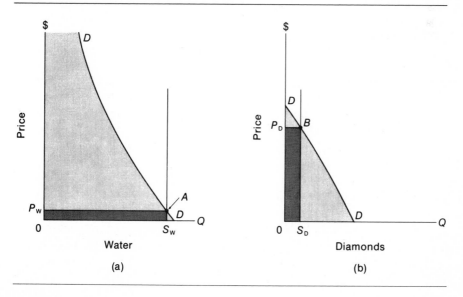

The economist's care in distinguishing between marginal value and total value
is useful to avoid a confusion that is not unrelated to the diamond–water paradox. In Chapter 3, we learned that if the price elasticity of demand for a good is
less than 1 ($E < 1$), a decrease in the quantity available will result in more being
spent on the good. The price elasticity of demand for many agricultural products–wheat, for example–is less than 1, thereby providing an explanation for
the well-known fact that the revenues of wheat farmers are larger in years when
the wheat harvest is small than they are in years when the harvest is large.
This is illustrated in Figure 5–14, where the total amount spent on wheat is
given by the area $P_2 0 S_2 B$ when S_2 units of wheat are available but by the area
$P_1 0 S_1 A$ when the supply of wheat is reduced to S_1. Since $P_1 0 S_1 A$ exceeds
$P_2 0 S_2 B$ by the area $P_1 P_2 CA - CS_1 S_2 B$, a greater amount is being paid
for S_1 units than for S_2 units of wheat.

It is tempting to conclude from this economic analysis that less wheat is of
greater value than more wheat. But this temptation is based on the erroneous
view that value is price multiplied by quantity. Once we recognize that the total
value of a good is more accurately measured by the area under the demand
curve, it becomes obvious that economic theory fully accepts that more of a
desirable good is better than less. In terms of Figure 5–14, the total value of S_2
units of wheat is greater than the total value of S_1 units by an amount equal to
the tinted area $AS_1 S_2 B$.

Application: In Appreciation of the Middleman

Now that we have studied the productivity of exchange in Section 5–4, we
should be able to resolve what must to some people be considered another
paradoxical situation. If we were asked to prepare a list of highly respected
occupations, few of us would think of including the "middleman." In fact, many
people view the middleman with a certain degree of hostility, which seems to
be rooted in the belief that although the middleman's activities are unproductive, his or her earnings lower the prices paid to the original suppliers of the
good and raise the prices consumers must pay to obtain the good. The paradoxical aspect of this view is that if the middleman's services are unproductive, why do people voluntarily pay for this service? There are no laws requiring
the general use of middlemen. Certainly, we have all eliminated the middleman
at one time or another. In fact, if we really believed everything we were told in
advertisements, we might be surprised to discover that there are any middlemen left at all. Yet the number of middlemen is increasing. Why is this happening if middlemen are unproductive?

Clearly, middlemen are productive, as we know from our discussion of the
productivity of exchange. But middlemen are productive in a way that is not
apparent to those who have a narrow view of what constitutes productive
activity. Middlemen are productive in the sense that they make it easier for
buyers and sellers to increase their utility through exchange. Therefore, most

Figure 5-14
Value Versus the Amount Paid

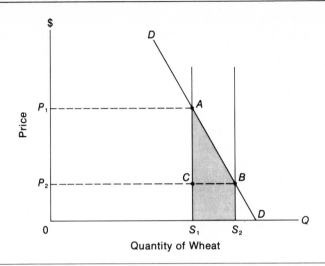

people find that they can improve their economic position by paying for the middleman's services rather than doing without them.

For example, consider the middleman services provided by your campus bookstore. In the past, you have undoubtedly entertained less than compassionate thoughts about the bookstore after finding out that a "good as new" used book you returned for one-half the original sales price was resold for much more. You might wonder what the bookstore did to deserve the high markup it received on your used book. Well, for one thing, it probably saved you a lot of trouble and expense. You could have checked with friends, posted notices on bulletin boards, and paid for a classified ad in the school newspaper, offering to sell your book for less than the bookstore would charge but for more than the store would pay you. If you had located someone who needed your book the following term, an exchange would probably have occurred. But if you deducted the value of the time, trouble and money you expended to find your customer from the price you received for your book, you might have discovered that you would have made more money by accepting the lower price offered by the bookstore. This is certainly true when, as is often the case, the book you wish to sell is not being used on your campus next term. In this situation, accepting the bookstore's low offer is the price you pay for being able to take advantage of the store's connections with used-book dealers who sell to students on other campuses. In effect, the bookstore makes a mutually advantageous exchange possible between you and some unidentified student on another campus at less cost to you than you would incur if you attempted to arrange the exchange by yourself.

Similar considerations hold if you want to purchase, rather than sell, particular books. You could attempt to locate people who want to sell these books in the hopes of buying them for less than the bookstore charges. But, in most cases, the service the bookstore provides by stocking the books you want in one convenient location is worth the additional price you pay when you buy them there.

We could cite many other examples of middlemen who perform the productive and worthwhile service of facilitating exchange between buyers and sellers. Although it is not normally considered in this light, one institution with which you are very familiar serves to a large extent as a middleman—your college or university. Professors, as experts in their subjects, are anxious to sell their knowledge to others by lecturing, giving assignments, leading discussions, and monitoring student progress. Students are anxious to acquire knowledge by purchasing these services from professors. Exchange between professors and students is therefore mutually advantageous, and any institutional arrangement that facilitates this exchange is a productive one. So the productivity of colleges and universities largely results from the fact that they provide much the same type of service as your local used-car lot or real estate agency.

5-5 Summary

In Chapter 5, we have used the basic model of consumer behavior that we developed in Chapter 4 to conduct a careful investigation of the theory underlying the consumer's demand curve. The groundwork for this investigation required us to consider the effect of an increase in the consumer's *money income* on the utility-maximizing consumption bundle. To do this, we had to develop the *income consumption curve,* which connects the consumer equilibrium positions generated by changes in money income when relative prices are held constant. When an increase in money income causes a decrease in the consumption of a good, we refer to it as an *inferior good*; otherwise, we refer to the good as a *normal good.*

Our next step in examining the underlying theory of the demand curve was to analyze how a change in the price of one good affects the consumer's choice of consumption bundles. We learned to develop the *price consumption curve,* which connects all the points of consumer equilibrium associated with the possible prices of one good. The slope of this curve provides information about the *price elasticity of demand* for that good. We then used the information we obtained from the price consumption curve to determine the demand curve for the good whose price is being varied.

We now know that when the price of a good changes, the quantity demanded changes in response to two separate effects. A decrease (increase) in price increases (decreases) the consumer's real income, which generates an *income effect.* A price decrease (increase) also makes the good less (more) costly relative to all other goods, which causes a *substitution effect.* We learned to separate these two effects on an indifference-curve map by removing the income effect of a price decrease by shifting the *budget constraint* from its position after the price decrease to a parallel position tangent to the initial indifference curve. Doing this establishes that the substitution effect is *always negative;* a decrease (increase) in the price of a good will always cause an increase (decrease) in the quantity demanded when real income is held constant. The income effect is *positive*—an increase in real income motivates an increase in consumption—for normal goods and *negative* for inferior goods.

We have seen that it is theoretically possible, but extremely unlikely, for the demand curve of a good to have an upward-sloping segment, which would indicate that an increase in the price of the good causes more of the good to be consumed. Such a good is referred to as a *Giffen good.* To be a Giffen good, a good must be inferior and must have a pronounced negative income effect that more than offsets the negative substitution effect. Since it is possible for a good to have a negative income effect that does not offset the substitution effect, inferior goods are not necessarily Giffen goods.

Given the analysis just discussed, we were able to relate the concept of the *consumer's surplus* (introduced in Chapter 4) to the demand curve. We learned that if we are considering a good with an income effect of 0, then the total value of the good is given by the area under the demand curve between 0 and the quantity consumed, and the consumer's surplus is equal to this area minus the amount paid for the good. This result provides the rationale in *benefit–cost analysis* for approximating the total social value of a good or project by the area under the market demand curve. This is an important first step in determining the advisability of constructing many large projects. But it is only a first step, because *benefit–cost ratios* are sensitive to choice of the *discount rate* as well as to measurements of benefit and costs.

The *total value* of a good is commonly considered to be equal to the consumer's *maximum willingness to pay* for the good. But an equally plausible measure of value is the *minimum compensation required* to convince the consumer to voluntarily relinquish the good. Using indifference-curve analysis, we have shown that these two measures of value will be equal only when the income effect for a good is 0. For normal goods, the maximum willingness-to-pay measure is less than the minimum compensation-required measure; the reverse is true for inferior goods.

After establishing the relationship between indifference curves, demand curves, and the total value of a good, we learned how to use demand curves to make the important distinction between *marginal value* and *total value.* Making this differentiation permits us to explain why, for example, the price of diamonds is greater than the price of water, even though water is more valuable than diamonds.

Anticipating the discussion of productivity in Chapter 6, we have also discussed the economist's rather broad view of *productivity* as anything that increases consumer utility. This view of productivity recognizes the worth of many activities that are commonly regarded as unproductive. A notable example of a productive activity is *exchange.* With a specific numerical example, we employed general indifference-curve analysis to show how exchange is productive in the sense that it allows two consumers to increase the utility that each receives from a given bundle of goods. Once the productivity of exchange is recognized, we have seen that it becomes possible to take a charitable view toward the *middleman*—the intermediary who receives a cut of the consumer dollar for performing the productive service of facilitating exchanges between buyers and sellers. We learned that your campus bookstore is a good example of a middleman that keeps customers coming back because the service it provides is worth more than the cut it receives.

References

Clawson, M., and J. Knetsch. *Economics of Outdoor Recreation.* Baltimore: Johns Hopkins Press, 1966.

Friedman, Milton. "The Marshallian Demand Curve." *Journal of Political Economy* (December 1949).

Howe, Charles W. "U.S. Water Policy and Its Implications for Agriculture, Energy, and Water Quality in the Colorado River Basin." Boulder, CO: University of Colorado, Economics Department, April 1977, *mimeograph.*

Kagel, John H. et al. "Experimental Studies of Consumer Demand Behavior Using Laboratory Animals." *Economic Inquiry* (March 1975), pp. 22–38.

Mishan, E.J. *Economics for Social Decisions: Elements of Cost–Benefit Analysis.* New York: Praeger, 1973.

Radford, R.A. "The Economic Organization of a P.O.W. Camp." *Economics* (November 1945).

Stigler, George J. *The Theory of Price,* 3rd ed. New York: Macmillan, 1966, Chapter 4.

Problems

1. Assume that there are only two goods and that each is a perfect substitute for the other. Determine the demand curve for one of these goods. What is the price elasticity of demand at prices less than the price that discourages all consumption?

2. In this chapter, we established that there is no income effect when the indifference curves are vertically parallel. But in answering Problem 1, you may have noted that there can be a positive income effect in the case of perfect substitutes, even though that case requires the indifference curves to be vertically parallel. What is the difference between the case considered in this chapter and the case of perfect substitutes that explains this contradiction?

3. Explain how the following could happen. A consumer is given a choice between paying $5,000 for a cruise around the world or a brand new Chevrolet and chooses the Chevrolet. However, just as she is about to pay for the Chevy, the consumer is informed that she does not have to pay— she can have her choice at no charge. Given this information, she promptly changes her mind and chooses the around-the-world cruise.

4. Construct an indifference-curve map, presenting two goods as normal goods. Can you also construct the indifference curves so that both goods

are inferior goods? What difficulty will you encounter in attempting to do this?

5. You have two goods that are useful only when they are consumed in combination with each other in fixed proportions, such as one right shoe and one left shoe or one car and four tires (ignoring the insurance value of a spare tire). Construct an indifference-curve map for two such perfect complements. Using this graph and the techniques developed in this chapter, identify both the income and the substitution effects of a price change.

6. Construct an indifference-curve map for the goods *leisure* and *income*. An individual who chooses the preferred combination of leisure and income is constrained by the budget constraint that relates income earned to leisure forgone (time worked). Use the analysis developed in this chapter to show the income and the substitution effects of a change in the individual's wage rate. Construct the indifference-curve map in such a way that leisure increases (time worked decreases) in response to an increase in the individual's wage rate.

7. Evidence seems to indicate that as a country's per-capita income increases, its birth rate decreases. Assuming that preferences remain constant, does this mean that children are inferior goods? Explain your answer.

8. The following graph relates the productive possibilities between output and leisure for a farmer. If the farmer works around the clock (consumes no leisure), he can produce *A* units of output; if he produces no output, he can "produce" 24 hours worth of leisure. This serves as the constraint under which the farmer maximizes utility at point *B*.

    Now assume that the farmer starts a new job that pays a fixed hourly wage and that he can choose how many hours per day he wants to work at this wage. If the wage allows the farmer to consume the same combination of leisure and output as before (combination *B*), determine graphically whether the farmer will work more or less hours on the new job than he did before.

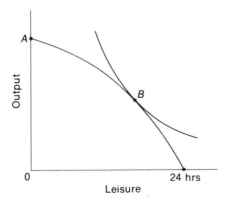

9. Assume that General Motors can make a car that provides $2,000 worth of benefits for every year of its expected life. Further assume that GM can manufacture a car that will last any number of years that the customer specifies, but that the car costs $1,000 for every year that it lasts. For example, a car that lasts 5 years will cost $5,000. If you have to pay cash for the car when you buy it, how long do you want it to last if you discount the future at a rate of 7%?

    The following information will help you to solve this problem. The left-hand column lists the number of years you have to wait for $1, and the right-hand column gives the present value of $1 at a discount rate of 7%.

Years to Wait	Present Value
1	$.93
2	.87
3	.82
4	.76
5	.71
6	.67
7	.62
8	.58
9	.54
10	.51
11	.48
12	.44
13	.41
14	.39

10. Instead of selling a property outright, people occasionally lease the right to use the property for 99 years. Interestingly enough, the price for a property is almost exactly the same whether it is sold outright or leased for 99 years. Explain why this is to be expected.

11. When a consumer's income is $100, the price of good X is $5, and the price of good Y is $10, the consumer buys 10 units of X and 5 units of Y. If the price of good X increases to $7, the price of good Y increases to $15, and income increases to $145, explain how you know that the consumer will respond by buying more than 10 units of good X.

CHAPTER SIX

PRODUCTION

We have just learned that a large body of economic theory underlies the simple notion of the demand curve. The concept of the supply curve is also based on a theoretical foundation, which is called **production theory.** In many respects, production theory is similar to demand theory, and we will employ several of the techniques we developed to help us understand demand theory again in this examination of production theory.

Production is the rearrangement of existing resources into a new relationship. The production process creates a *good* or a *service.* Goods are **tangible** items—physical things that we can touch, such as cars, shirts, and steaks; services are **intangible** things, such as medical examinations, transportation, and concerts.

Factors of Production   6–2

Inputs are combined and transformed to create goods or services. When we consider the production of a simple item, such as a paper clip, we can immediately think of some of the inputs that would be required—the factory building and the land on which it is located, steel wire, wire-bending machines, packaging machines, machine operators, shipping clerks, and managers, to name a few. These inputs are called **factors of production,** and they are divided into four categories:

1. gifts of nature, such as the factory site
2. the mental and physical input of people, such as the machine operators and managers
3. the mechanical input of the machines used to produce paper clips, such as the wire-bending machine
4. inputs, such as the steel wire, that were the outputs of some other firm.

177

This last category encompasses what we call **intermediate products,** which are not final goods and services but are produced solely to be used as inputs for some other production process. However, if we trace these intermediate inputs back to their origin, we find that they are ultimately a result of the combination of the first three types of inputs. For example, the steel wire was originally produced from iron ore, human labor, and machines.

Thus, we can see that there are three primary factors of production. These factors are generally referred to as *land* (gifts of nature), *labor* (the physical and mental input of people), and *capital* (a factor produced by other factors of production). Today, economists consider this traditional classification of the factors of production to be inadequate for certain forms of analysis. For example, traditionally labor is viewed as the physical input of people, but most individuals seeking employment today offer an additional input to physical labor—the skills they have acquired through previous training. Leisure and consumption had to be sacrificed to achieve this training, just as a craftsman forgoes leisure and consumption to acquire a set of tools. This training is therefore functionally indistinguishable from the tools. Modern economists refer to the input that results from training as **human capital.** Throughout most of this analysis of production theory, however, the simpler (if somewhat naive) classification of factor inputs as either land, labor, or capital will be sufficient for our purposes.

The economic theories of production we will construct in Chapters 6 and 7 will not pertain to a specific production process, such as the process of producing paper clips, but are general in nature and applicability. One way in which we will achieve this generality is to categorize all factor inputs as either *land, labor,* or *capital.* We will not deal with the myriad of subcategories related to the three primary factors of production. In addition, we will assume that each factor of production can be employed in *infinitely divisible amounts.* For example, we will not limit ourselves to a choice between 3 or 4 units of labor; if we wish, we will work with, say, 3.14159 units. Furthermore, we will assume that all units of a given factor input are identical or *homogeneous,* so that any unit is perfectly interchangeable with any other unit of the same factor. Instead of imposing limitations on our analysis, these abstractions will allow us to construct simple economic models that can be applied to a wide range of production processes—models that will satisfy two of the criteria for positive economic theories, simplicity and fruitfulness, that we established in Chapter 1.

When the demand for a firm's output changes from an anticipated level, the firm will adjust its output to conform to the new set of circumstances. Factor inputs such as raw materials, energy, and labor can be decreased or increased within a short time period (as long as all other firms are not attempting to decrease or increase output at the same time). The quantity of the firm's capital input, which is comprised of such things as the factory, warehouse, and machines, cannot be varied as readily. The period of time over which the firm finds it *impossible* to vary at least one of its inputs—usually capital—is called the **short run.** Inputs that can be altered in the short run are called **variable**

factors of production; inputs that cannot be altered in the short run are called **fixed factors of production.**

In the **long run,** all factors are variable: There are no fixed factors of production. It should be noted that the time required to vary all inputs is not specified. In practice, it depends on the characteristics of the firm and the magnitude of the benefits the firm anticipates receiving from the change. For some firms (Hula-Hoop manufacturers, for example), the time required to vary all inputs may be quite short—say, two to four weeks. On the other hand, automobile manufacturers may require three to five years to vary all inputs. The complexity of a firm's production process is not the only factor that dictates the time required to vary all inputs. The expected rewards for making the changes are also influential, because the time required to vary fixed inputs such as production facilities can be shortened if the firm is willing to pay such added costs as overtime pay for engineers and construction workers to speed up production. Obviously, the willingness of the firm to incur these additional expenses depends on the magnitude of the benefits it expects to receive when its products are offered on the market.

A firm can expand output in the short run only by increasing the quantity of its variable factors. For example, a plant manager who believes that an increased demand for output will be very temporary may increase the number of work hours per week and pay the workers overtime. On the other hand, if the increased demand for output is expected to continue for a considerable period of time, it may be more desirable to add another work shift. Precisely how the firm combines its variable inputs with its fixed inputs depends on the nature of the increased demand as perceived by the firm and on the characteristics of the firm. Eventually, however, the fixed factors of production will be used to their utmost capabilities, and the firm's output will increase to a *maximum.* Beyond this point, any additional amounts of the variable factors will only decrease total output, because they will interfere with one another. Before the firm reaches its maximum productive capabilities, the owners will probably start planning to increase the firm's capital. For this reason, the long run is often referred to as the **planning horizon** of the firm. In the long run, the firm will construct a plant that will be of an *economically optimal size.* The exact meaning of a firm's economically optimal size will be developed in Chapters 6 and 7.

The Production Function 6-3

We now know that the firm combines factors of production, or inputs, to produce goods and services. These inputs are not combined in a haphazard manner. For any given *state of technology,* there is a relationship between the *quantity* of inputs and the *maximum output* obtainable from these inputs. This relationship is called the **production function** and can be expressed by means of a table, a mathematical equation, or geometric curves specifying the maximum output that can be achieved for any given combination of inputs.

Production with One Variable Input *(labour)*

We will consider the simplest possible production function first—a function in which there is only one variable input. Suppose that the quantities of a firm's land and capital are fixed. In this case, labor is the only variable input: Employees can be hired in varying quantities. Given the fixed factors of production and the state of technology, a production schedule indicating the firm's labor input possibilities appears in Table 6–1. However, a production schedule can indicate output for only a few labor input possibilities. This drawback can be overcome if we graph the production function by drawing a smooth curve through the points given in Table 6–1, as shown in Figure 6–1. This curve is called the **total product TP curve.** The existence of the smooth curve through these points is justified by our assumption that fractional units of labor can be employed. It is well worth reemphasizing here that the output indicated in Figure 6–1 is the *maximum* output for any given input.

In addition to the information represented on the production schedule and graph relating the firm's input to its **total product**—the firm's total output provided by the production process—we are also interested in the average product and the marginal product of the variable input. The **average product** of the variable input is the total product divided by the quantity of the variable input. If we let TP represent the total product and L represent the units of labor input, then the production function is given by

$$TP = f(L) \tag{6-1}$$

which is read simply as "total product is a function of labor input." The average product of labor AP_L can be expressed as

$$AP_L = \frac{TP}{L} \tag{6-2}$$

The average product of labor calculated from the data given in the production schedule in Table 6–1 appears in the third column of Table 6–2.

Table 6–1
Production Schedule for a Firm with Labor as the Only Variable Input

UNITS OF LABOR	UNITS OF OUTPUT
0	0
1	1.0
2	4.0
3	7.25
4	9.0
5	10.0
6	10.5
7	10.5
8	10.1

Figure 6–1
A Production Function with One Variable Input

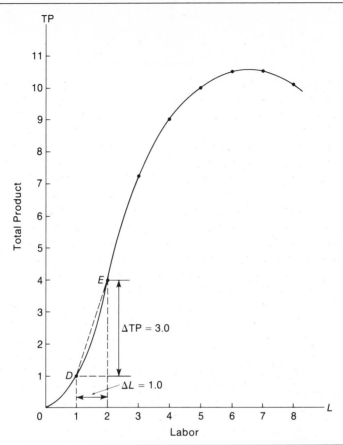

The **marginal product** of the variable input is the number of additional units of output ΔTP that can be produced by one additional unit (the *marginal unit*) of the variable input. In this example, the variable input is labor and the marginal unit of labor is symbolized by ΔL. The marginal product of labor MP_L can therefore be expressed as

$$MP_L = \frac{\Delta TP}{\Delta L} \qquad\qquad\qquad (6\text{–}3)$$

The marginal product of labor calculated from the data given in the production schedule in Table 6–1 appears in the fourth column of Table 6–2.

An examination of Table 6–2 reveals that both the average and the marginal products of labor increase in value initially, reach a maximum, and then dimin-

Table 6–2
Production Schedule of the Average and Marginal Products of Labor

UNITS OF LABOR L	TOTAL PRODUCT TP	AVERAGE PRODUCT AP	MARGINAL PRODUCT MP
0	0	–	–
1	1.0	1.0	1.0
2	4.0	2.0	3.0
3	7.25	2.417	3.25
4	9.0	2.25	1.75
5	10.0	2.0	1.0
6	10.5	1.75	0.5
7	10.5	1.5	0.0
8	10.1	1.263	−0.4

ish. The fact that both of these products eventually diminish is a common characteristic of all production functions and is not peculiar to the particular function we are using here.

This universal characteristic, called the **law of diminishing returns,** states that if we increase the quantity of a variable factor while simultaneously holding the remaining factors constant, both the average and the marginal products of the variable factor will eventually decrease.

The average and the marginal products can be computed directly from the graph of the production function. To determine AP_L at any point on the total product curve, we select a point (say point g in Figure 6–2) and draw the ray $0G$ from the origin through point g. As we can see in Figure 6–2, the slope of ray $0G$ is 1.5 and is equal to AP_L at point g, since $2.25/1.5 = 1.5$. Note that ray $0G$ also intersects the total product curve at point j, so that AP_L must also be 1.5 when 7.0 units of labor are employed.

In addition to ray $0G$, rays $0A$ and $0B$ have been drawn through points a and b, respectively, in Figure 6–2. The slopes of these rays reveal that AP_L is 1.0 when the labor input is 1.0 and 2.417 when the labor input is 3.0. Now observe that starting from 0 labor input, the slopes of the rays increase until we reach a labor input of 3.0 units. At this point (point b on the total product curve), AP_L reaches its maximum of 2.417, as indicated by the slope of ray $0B$, which is just tangent to the total product curve. Therefore, point b must be the **point of diminishing average returns** *to the variable labor input,* because AP_L will decline if we increase labor input beyond this point.

The average product of labor derived from the total product curve in Figure 6–2 is graphed in Figure 6–3(b). The total product curve in Figure 6–2 is redrawn in Figure 6–3(a) with the corresponding AP_L curve graphed below it in Figure 6–3(b). Points on the AP_L curve that correspond to points on the total product curve are labeled with primes. Thus, point a' on the AP_L curve represents the average product that prevails at point a on the total product curve. Note that the AP_L curve indicates that the average product is the same at 1.5

Figure 6–2
Determination of the Average Product
from the Total Product Curve

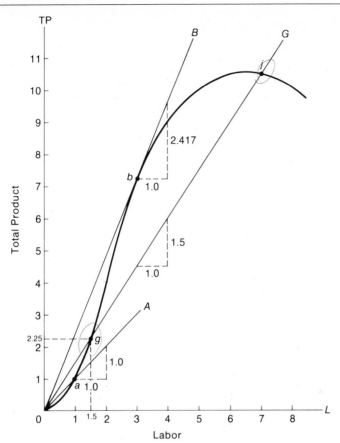

and 7.0 units of input (points g' and j', respectively). This conforms to what we concluded previously about points g and j in Figure 6–2.

When we calculated the marginal product of labor in Table 6–2, we did not calculate the marginal product at a particular point on the total product curve. We actually calculated the marginal product between two points on the total product curve. We made this calculation under the implicit assumption that the total product curve was a straight line between these two points. For example, the slope of the straight line connecting points D and E in Figure 6–1 is equal to $\Delta TP/\Delta L = 3.0$. This is the marginal product given in Table 6–2 when labor is increased from 1 to 2 units. But we are more often interested in the marginal product of the variable factor at a specific point on the total product curve— the marginal product when the increase in the variable input approaches 0. This is easily determined by drawing a straight line tangent to the total product curve

Figure 6–3
Relationship Between the Total Product, the Average Product,
and the Marginal Product Curves

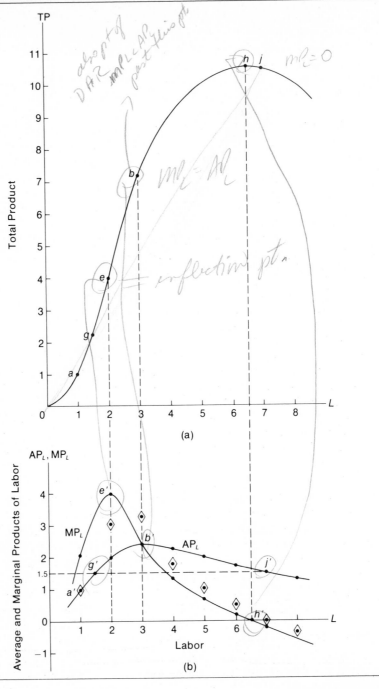

(a)

(b)

at the point where we wish to know the value of the marginal product. The slope of this line is the marginal product at that point, since this tangency line would result if we were to connect the initial and the final points on the total product curve as we allowed ΔL to approach 0.

The total product curve in Figure 6–1 appears in Figure 6–4 with tangency lines drawn at points $d, e, b, h,$ and k. The slopes of these lines are equal to the marginal product of labor at the respective points. As we move to the right along the total product curve in Figure 6–4, note that the slope of the tangent lines increases between the origin and point e. This obviously means that we are in a region of increasing MP_L. This occurs because the total product curve is *convex* when viewed from below. At point e, however, the curvature of the total product curve reverses, and the curve to the right of point e is *concave* when viewed from below. We call such a point the **inflection point.** Beyond point e, the slope of the lines drawn tangent to points on the total product curve will begin to diminish. Thus, MP_L increases between points 0 and e, reaches a maximum at point e, and then begins to diminish. For this reason the inflection point (point e in this example) is called the **point of diminishing marginal returns.**

The slope at point b in Figure 6–4 is of particular interest because, at this point, the line drawn tangent to point b coincides with the ray drawn from the origin to point b. This means that the average and the marginal products must be equal at this point. Note that point b in Figure 6–4 is identical to point b in Figure 6–2. Also note[1] that $MP_L > AP_L$ to the left of point b and that $MP_L < AP_L$ to the right of point b.

---

[1]Since

$$TP = f(L)$$

and

$$AP_L = \frac{TP}{L}$$

we can state that

$$AP_L = \frac{f(L)}{L}$$

By definition, the marginal product of labor is

$$MP_L = \frac{dTP}{dL} = \frac{df(L)}{dL}$$

The average product will be at a maximum when

$$\frac{dAP_L}{dL} = 0$$

or

$$\frac{d(TP/L)}{dL} = \left(\frac{dTP}{dL} - \frac{TP}{L} \right)\frac{1}{L} = \left(MP_L - AP_L \right)\frac{1}{L} = 0$$

Therefore, when AP_L is at a maximum, MP_L equals AP_L. Also note that when $MP_L > AP_L$, the slope of the AP_L curve will be positive, and when $MP_L < AP_L$, the slope of the AP_L curve will be negative. Thus, $MP_L > AP_L$ to the left of point b' in Figure 6–3(b) and $MP_L < AP_L$ to the right of point b' in Figure 6–3(b).

Figure 6–4
Determination of the Marginal Product
from the Total Product Curve

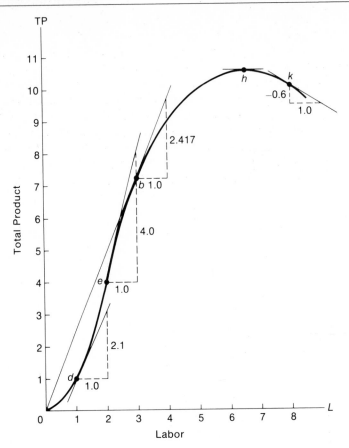

These important conclusions are illustrated in Figure 6–3(b), where both the MP_L and the AP_L curves are graphed. There, we can clearly see that MP_L reaches a maximum at point e' when 2 units of labor are employed. This point corresponds to point e–the inflection point–in Figure 6–3(a) on the total product curve. We have already proven that AP_L and MP_L are equal at point b, and this is indicated by their intersection at point b' in Figure 6–3(b). Therefore, $MP_L > AP_L$ to the left of point b', and $MP_L < AP_L$ to the right of point b'.

The last point of special interest in Figure 6–4 is point h. At point h, the total product curve has reached its maximum. The line drawn tangent to point h is horizontal, and its slope is therefore 0. Thus, MP_L must also be 0 at point h,

**Example
6–1**

Fertilizer Application and Potato Production

By holding all other factors constant, agricultural economists have been able to determine the effects of varying applications of fertilizer on crop output.* One particular experiment investigated the effect of fertilizer applications on potato production. The data from this experiment are displayed in Figure 6–5. The total product curve generated in Figure 6–5(a) is very similar to the total product curve assumed in Figure 6–3(a). However, due to the fact that the smallest application in this experiment was 500 pounds of fertilizer per acre, the experimental data only reveal diminishing marginal and average products. Thus, the AP and MP curves in Figure 6–5(b) exhibit only negative slopes. This result does seem to indicate, however, that diminishing returns are apt to be established fairly quickly in most agricultural production processes.

**Figure 6–5
The Effect of Fertilizer Applications on Potato Production**

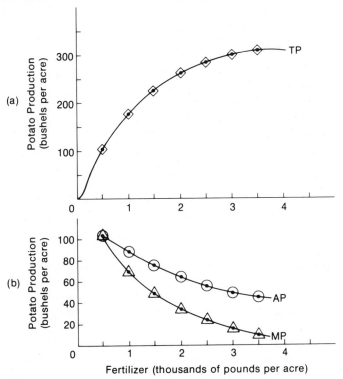

*SOURCE: Earl O. Heady, *Economics of Agricultural Production and Resource Use* (Englewood Cliffs, NJ: Prentice-Hall, 1952), p. 36.

as shown by point h' in Figure 6–3(b). To the right of point h, MP_L is negative. In other words, if more than 6½ workers are hired, they will interfere with each other's work and total output will decline.

The graphically determined AP_L and MP_L curves and their relation to the critical points on the total product curve are jointly summarized in Figure 6–3. At this stage, you should be able to take any total product curve and sketch the general shapes of the AP_L and MP_L curves in proper relation to one another.

The points surrounded by diamonds in Figure 6–3(b) are the plotted points of the calculated arc MP_L given in Table 6–2. The extent to which these points do not lie on the MP_L curve measures the error that results when we use arc measures instead of point measures of marginal change to calculate MP_L.

Application: Agriculture and Diminishing Returns

We have just learned that every production process encounters diminishing returns at some point. This unavoidable fact may have profound implications for the future. For example, we can consider the implication of the law of diminishing returns for a country with a fixed quantity of farmland and a growing population. As this country's population increases, labor will become the variable input applied to the fixed factor—land.[2] For a given level of technology, the average and the marginal products of labor will eventually decline. This means that the quantity of food per capita will start to decline at some point and will continue to decline as long as the population increases. At some stage, the decreasing number of calories per capita will produce a reduction in the population growth rate until eventually growth ceases and the population attains a level of real per-capita income just great enough to maintain the population. This level of income is called the **subsistence level** of income.

This line of reasoning, based on the law of diminishing returns, formed the cornerstone of Thomas Malthus' pioneering work on population growth almost 200 years ago. The Malthusian Theory can be easily understood if we assume the initial conditions of a given level of technology, a fixed quantity of farmland, and a population size such that the level of income is exactly equal to the subsistence level. Malthus asked what would happen if technological progress occurred and the point of diminishing returns moved to the right. His answer was that the technological advance would initially raise the standard of living above the subsistence level, which would lead to an inexorable growth in population. Due to diminishing returns, however, the population would eventually decrease to the point that the income level and the subsistence level were again equal. This certainly was not a very cheerful forecast for the human condition,

---

[2]Obviously, capital could also be increasing, but ignoring this possibility will not invalidate the conclusions we draw here.

and the Malthusian Theory led critics to label economics the "dismal science."

To date, Malthus' predictions have not proved to be correct in countries that are considered to be industrialized nations. There are several reasons for this. First, the quantity of farmland has not remained fixed. Vast agricultural areas in North and South America, Australia, and Africa have been cultivated in the last 200 years. Second, the quality of farmland that existed in Malthus' time has been greatly improved due to advances in agricultural science, increased use, improvements in farm machinery, and a decrease in the relative prices of artificial fertilizers. In other words, the point of diminishing returns has been moving to the right at a faster rate than the population has been growing. And finally, Malthus was wrong in his fundamental assumption that rising real income would inevitably result in population growth. Historical evidence indicates that over the last 200 years, the population growth rate has *decreased* in countries where per-capita income has significantly risen. Some demographers now estimate that the population growth of the industrialized nations will average to 0 by the end of the twentieth century.

If it were not for this last factor, it would be difficult to deny the eventual validity of Malthus' predictions. Whether or not the Malthusian Theory will prove to be true in the nonindustrialized world remains to be seen. Modern advances in the industrialized nations have led to relatively low-cost improvements in public health. These benefits have been transferred to the nonindustrialized nations, greatly reducing their death rates and increasing their population growth rates. Contrary to popular opinion, however, real per-capita output in almost all developing nations has been greater than 0, as shown in Table 6–3. In fact, nations with the highest population growth rates have also experienced the highest growth in real output per capita on the average. If this trend continues, we can expect a decline in the birth rate of these nations similar to the earlier decline in the birth rates of the first nations to industrialize.

Finally, it should be pointed out that there is no law of diminishing returns with respect to technology:

> The law of diminishing returns, properly understood, is a static proposition about returns to varying factor proportions under given technological knowledge, having nothing to do with the dynamic problem of an actually growing population working a given land area under conditions of constantly improving technology.[3]

It is therefore possible for technological change to forestall the effects of the law of diminishing returns indefinitely.

[3]Mark Blaug, *Economic Theory in Retrospect*, 3rd ed. (Cambridge: Cambridge University Press, 1978), p. 72. Blaug also convincingly argues that Malthus' theory of population growth is metaphysical rather than scientific, because it lacks the property of falsifiability discussed in Chapter 1.

Table 6-3
The Growth of Real Output per Capita, 1950/1952-1967/1969

	POPULATION GROWTH						
Under 2% per Year		2-2.4% per Year		2.5-2.9% per Year		3% per Year or More	
Algeria	0.7	Africa	1.6	Cambodia	2.5	Brazil	2.3
Angola	1.5	Chile	1.5	Ceylon	1.6	Colombia	1.5
Argentine	1.5	Congo		Egypt	2.6	Costa Rica	1.4
Bolivia	0.5	(French		Ghana	1.1	Dominican	
Burma	2.3	Kinshasa)	−0.2	Guiana	0.7	Republic	0.6
Ethiopia	2.7	India	1.4	Iran	5.1	Ecuador	1.6
Haiti	−0.4	Indonesia	−0.3	Korea (South)	4.0	El Salvador	2.0
Jamaica	5.1	Malawi	1.2	Morocco	0.1	Guatemala	1.4
Mozambique	1.7	Nigeria	1.4	Paraguay	0.7	Guinea	4.7
Uruguay	1.0	Pakistan	1.7	Peru	1.6	Honduras	1.9
		Tanzania	0.9	Sudan	1.2	Hong Kong	6.3
		Tunis	1.7	Syria	1.1	Iraq	5.3
				Uganda	0.9	Jordan	6.4
				Zambia	1.4	Kenya	0.9
						Malaysia	2.1
						Mexico	3.0
						Nicaragua	2.3
						Panama	3.4
						Philippines	1.9
						Rhodesia	1.7
						Surinam	2.3
						Taiwan	5.1
						Thailand	3.5
						Trinidad	4.2
						Venezuela	2.2
Average % per year	1.7		1.1		1.8		2.8

SOURCE: Colin Clark, *Population Growth: The Advantages* (Santa Ana, CA: Life Quality, 1975), p. 84. Reprinted by permission.

Production with Two Variable Inputs

We will now consider a production function in which both capital K and labor L are variable inputs, or

$$Q = f(L,K) \tag{6-4}$$

where Q is the quantity produced.[4] The technique we developed to analyze the

---

[4]The marginal product of labor MP_L is $\partial Q/\partial L = \partial f/\partial L$. The marginal product of capital MP_K is $\partial Q/\partial K = \partial f/\partial K$.

production function with one variable input is somewhat cumbersome to apply when there are two variable inputs. We will therefore develop a new technique here that is based on what are known as *isoquants*.

An **isoquant curve** traces all combinations of two inputs that generate a specified level of output according to the production function. Three isoquant curves, out of an infinite number, are drawn in Figure 6-6 for the case when labor and capital are both variable inputs. Such a graph of a production function is called an **isoquant map**. The isoquant curves in this figure are labeled $Q = 20$, $Q = 30$, and $Q = 40$, referring to the number of units (quantity) of output Q that each curve represents. For example, the isoquant curve labeled $Q = 20$ gives us all possible combinations of labor and capital that will produce 20 units according to the production function.

Characteristics of Isoquant Curves   Isoquant curves are analogous to the consumer indifference curves we studied in Chapter 4. Isoquant curves and indifference curves possess similar characteristics, although their economic interpretations are different.

Since an isoquant expresses the different combinations of two variable inputs (labor and capital, in this example) that will produce a given output, specified by the production function, it follows that a characteristic of isoquant curves is that they *cannot intersect.* If two isoquants did intersect, the same quantities of labor and capital would produce two different levels of output at the point of intersection. This is clearly impossible, because the production function specifies

Figure 6-6
An Isoquant Map

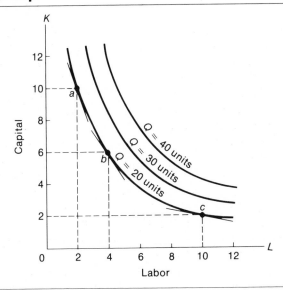

**Example
6-2**

Obtaining Zero Population Growth

Many of us erroneously believe that there should be an average number of 2 children per family to achieve zero population growth. This is incorrect because only 95% of women who marry do so before the end of their child-bearing years, and only 93% of these women become mothers. Since most unwed mothers eventually marry, we can reasonably assume that the fertility of women who never marry is negligible. For these reasons and others that will be explained here, for every 1,000 women who marry and have children, the total number of children born must equal 2,390 to maintain a constant population level. In other words, every ever-married mother must have an average of 2.4 children.*

This figure is so high because the women in the 15–44 age bracket must replace themselves to maintain a stable population. Each of these women must bear one fertile daughter on the average. Out of every 1,000 daughters born, however, 30 will die before reaching age 15, 70 will not marry, and 72 of those that marry will not be able to have children due to their own or their husbands' infertility. Therefore, every 1,000 married women must have 1,000 baby girls to replace themselves, plus 30 baby girls to replace the girls who will die before child-bearing age, plus 70 baby girls to replace the women who will not marry, plus 72 baby girls to replace the women who will not be able to have children—for a total of 1,172 baby girls. The story does not end here, however, because for every 1,000 girls born, 1,060 boys will be born, which is providence's way of compensating for the higher death rate among males. This means that for every 1,172 girl births, there will be 1,242 boys for a grand total of 2,414 births per 1,000 married females, or 2.4 births per married female. Since some families will have 0, 1, or 2 children, other families must have 3, 4, or 5 children to maintain an average of 2.4 children per family.

*Love/Life/Death/Issues, Vol. 3, No. 2 (June 10, 1977), Newsletter of the Human Life Center, St. John's University, Collegeville, MN, pp. 2–3. The slight discrepancy in the number of births per ever-married mothers is due to the fact that the first figure (2,390) is based on U.S. census data and the second (2,414) is derived from British census data.

the *maximum* output obtainable from any combination of inputs. The isoquant curve that represents the smaller quantity of output therefore cannot exist at the point of intersection.

To produce a constant level of output, the technical aspect of production requires that labor be substituted for the capital that is taken away. Due to this requirement of **technical substitution,** isoquant curves will *always have a negative slope;* that is, they will slope downward from left to right.[5]

[5]We will soon learn that this is not always the case. However, for our purposes here—and in most instances—this is the only relevant situation in which we will be interested.

The average number of babies that each woman (instead of each family) must have over a lifetime to maintain a constant population is 2.1. With the exception of the Republic of Ireland, however, the actual fertility rate for every country in western Europe and the United States in 1978 was below 2.1, as shown in Table 6–4. If these rates are maintained, the populations of these countries will eventually decline. The population of West Germany is already declining absolutely and is projected to decrease from 57 million in 1978 to 39 million by 2030.† To offset these trends, the governments of France, West Germany, and Sweden are subsidizing families that have more children.

†Alan L. Otten, "People Shortage," *The Wall Street Journal*, Vol. CI, No. 38 (August 23, 1979), pp. 1 and 24.

Table 6–4
The Average Number of Babies per Woman
over Her Lifetime in 1978 (replacement rate = 2.1)

Austria	1.6
Belgium	1.6
Denmark	1.7
France	1.8
West Germany	1.4
Ireland	3.5
Italy	2.0
Holland	1.5
Norway	1.8
Sweden	1.6
Switzerland	1.5
Britain	1.7
United States	1.8

SOURCE: Alan L. Otten, "People Shortage," *The Wall Street Journal*, Vol. CI, No. 38 (August 23, 1979), pp. 1 and 24.

Isoquant curves are also *convex* with respect to the origin—a characteristic that results from the fact that although technical substitution can occur between labor and capital, this substitution is not perfect. This means that as we reduce the quantity of capital by constant amounts, the quantity of labor required to maintain a constant output must be increased by ever-increasing amounts. For example, if we reduce the quantity of capital required to produce 20 units of output from 10 to 6 units, as shown in Figure 6–6, we must increase the quantity of labor from 2 to 4 units. A 4-unit reduction in capital is offset by a 2-unit increase in labor. Now suppose that we again reduce the quantity of capital by 4 units, this time from 6 to 2 units. Since technical substitution between labor and capital is not perfect, a greater increase in labor input will be required. From Figure 6–6 we know that this increase must be 6 units of labor, because the total required labor input increases from 4 to 10 units. We can clearly see that this limited degree of substitution is what makes the isoquant curves convex.

Another way to state this result is to say that for a constant level of output, the amount of capital for which an additional unit of labor can be substituted will decrease as this substitution progresses. This characteristic of the production process is called the principle of the **diminishing marginal rate of technical substitution.** The value of the marginal rate of technical substitution of labor for capital at any point on an isoquant curve in Figure 6–6, for example, is given by the absolute value of the slope of the isoquant curve at that point. If we consider points *a, b,* and *c* in Figure 6–6, we see that the absolute value of the slope of the isoquant curve for $Q = 20$ declines as we move from point *a* to point *b* and from point *b* to point *c.* This relationship will continue as we progress down an isoquant curve, so we say that the *marginal rate of technical substitution of labor for capital* MRTS_{LK} is diminishing.

Technical Substitution and Marginal Product   The marginal rate of technical substitution of labor for capital can be shown to be equal to -1 multiplied by the ratio of the marginal product of labor to the marginal product of capital.

$$= -1 \times \frac{mP_L}{mP_K} \quad - \quad \text{Similar to } -1 \times \frac{P}{Q}$$

Example 6–3

The Empirical Estimation of Isoquants

An elaborate experiment was conducted in Iowa to determine the effects of different applications of nitrogen and phosphate on the amount of corn yielded per acre.* The following two-variable input production function was statistically estimated:

$$Q = -5.682 - 0.316N - 0.417P + 6.3512\sqrt{N} + 8.5155\sqrt{P} + 0.3410\sqrt{PN}$$

where

        Q = bushels of corn yielded per acre
        N = pounds of nitrogen applied per acre
        P = pounds of phosphate applied per acre

Holding Q constant, it is possible to calculate the various combinations of phosphate and nitrogen required to generate isoquants for the desired level of corn production per acre. Isoquants for five different levels of corn production are drawn in Figure 6–7. We can see that the shape of these isoquants is similar to the shape of the isoquants in Figure 6–6.

*Earl O. Heady, "An Econometric Investigation of the Technology of Agricultural Production Functions," *Econometrica* (April 1957), pp. 249–68.

The proof of this statement is given in Figure 6–8, where the isoquants for outputs of Q_1 and Q_2 are drawn. Suppose that initially we are using K_1 units of capital and L_1 units of labor to produce output Q_2 at point A. Holding labor constant at L_1, we now reduce the level of output to Q_1 by reducing the capital input from K_1 to K_2. By definition, the marginal product of capital is

$$\text{MP}_K = \frac{Q_2 - Q_1}{K_1 - K_2} = \frac{\Delta Q}{\Delta K} \qquad (6-5)$$

Now, holding capital constant at K_2, we increase the quantity of labor from L_1 to L_2. By definition, once again, the marginal product of labor is

$$\text{MP}_L = \frac{Q_1 - Q_2}{L_1 - L_2} = \frac{\Delta Q}{\Delta L} \qquad (6-6)$$

Then we divide Equation (6–6) by Equation (6–5) to obtain

$$\frac{\text{MP}_L}{\text{MP}_K} = \frac{Q_1 - Q_2/L_1 - L_2}{Q_2 - Q_1/K_1 - K_2} = \frac{K_1 - K_2}{L_1 - L_2} = \frac{\Delta K}{\Delta L} \qquad (6-7)$$

An inspection of Figure 6–8 reveals that the ratio of the marginal products is equal to the slope of line AC and is an approximation of -1 multiplied by

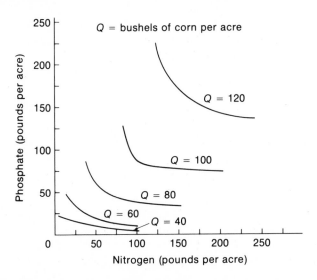

Figure 6-7
An Empirically Estimated Corn Production Function

SOURCE: Earl O. Heady, "An Econometric Investigation of the Technology of Agricultural Production Functions," *Econometrica* (April 1957), p. 253.

Figure 6-8
The Relationship Between MRTS and MP

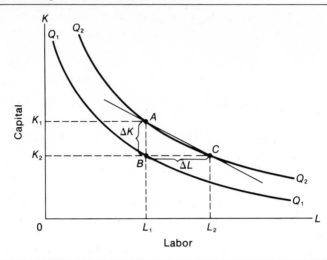

MRTS_{LK} at point B. For increasingly smaller ΔKs and ΔLs, points A and C will move closer together and the slope of the line connecting these points will become an increasingly closer approximation of the slope at point B. When ΔK and ΔL are infinitesimally small, it follows that

$$\text{MRTS}_{LK} = -\frac{\text{MP}_L}{\text{MP}_K} \tag{6-8}$$

Here, we multiply the ratio of the marginal products by -1 because we previously defined MRTS_{LK} with an absolute value.[6]

---

[6]The total differential of the production function is

$$dQ = \frac{\partial f}{\partial L} dL + \frac{\partial f}{\partial K} dK$$

Because output is constant along an isoquant curve, $dQ = 0$ and we can write

$$\frac{\partial f}{\partial L} dL + \frac{\partial f}{\partial K} dK = 0$$

or

$$\frac{dK}{dL} = -\frac{\partial f/\partial L}{\partial f/\partial K}$$

Since

$$\text{MRTS}_{LK} = \frac{dK}{dL}$$

we can write

$$\text{MRTS}_{LK} = -\frac{\text{MP}_L}{\text{MP}_K}$$

The Relevant Region of Production   Until this point, we have examined only isoquant curves that are everywhere downward sloping. In general, however, this will not be the case. Isoquant curves for most production functions will eventually assume a positive slope. Although this contradicts the characteristics of convexity and negative slope previously discussed, we will show why this will not pose a significant problem in our analysis.

Isoquant curves with positively sloped portions are illustrated in Figure 6-9(a). For any given isoquant, the points at which the curve assumes positive slope are indicated by the points of tangency between the isoquant and the dashed vertical or horizontal lines in the figure. The two curved lines 0A and 0B that pass through these points of tangency, called **ridge lines,** partition the production function into rational and irrational regions of production. No rational firm—that is, a firm that always produces a given level of output at the least cost—would ever plan to operate above ridge line 0A or below ridge line 0B. This would constitute irrational behavior because if one input is increased at a given output, the other input must also be increased, which would automatically increase cost without increasing output.[7] Considering this from a slightly different viewpoint, if we operated above 0A or below 0B, we could maintain the same level of output and simultaneously reduce the quantities of both inputs. Because it is irrational for a firm to operate in these portions of the production function, they are referred to as the **irrelevant** or **uneconomic regions of production.** We will ignore these regions in our analysis.[8]

A total product curve for either capital or labor can be easily derived from the isoquant map. Suppose we wish to derive the total product curve for labor, assuming that capital is fixed at $\bar{K}$. In Figure 6-9(a), a horizontal line is drawn through the isoquant map at $\bar{K}$. At every point that this line intersects an isoquant, we know the labor input and its total product. These points are plotted in Figure 6-9(b), and the total product curve for labor when $K = \bar{K}$ is then constructed by drawing a smooth curve through these points. A total product curve for capital could be constructed in a similar manner by holding the labor input constant.

Note that at point C' in Figure 6-9(b), the total product is at a maximum and that to the right of point C' the marginal product of labor is negative, which corresponds to the uneconomic region of production to the right of point C in Figure 6-9(a). Also observe that the marginal product of labor is increasing from the origin to point E' in Figure 6-9(b), but that this increase corresponds to production occurring to the left of ridge line 0A in Figure 6-9(a), so that it is an uneconomic range of production. The reason production is uneconomic as output increases from 0 to Q_3 is that there is too much capital in relation to the amount of labor employed. In other words, if we were to vary the quantity of

---

[7]The implicit assumption here is that both inputs are costly. This is generally true of the inputs of labor and capital.

[8]It should not be inferred from this that economic analysis always ignores the regions outside the ridge lines. For some very short-run situations, it may be necessary to determine the least *uneconomical* point of operation. The analysis of these problems is beyond the scope of this text, however.

Figure 6-9
The Relationship Between Isoquant Curves and the Total Product Curve

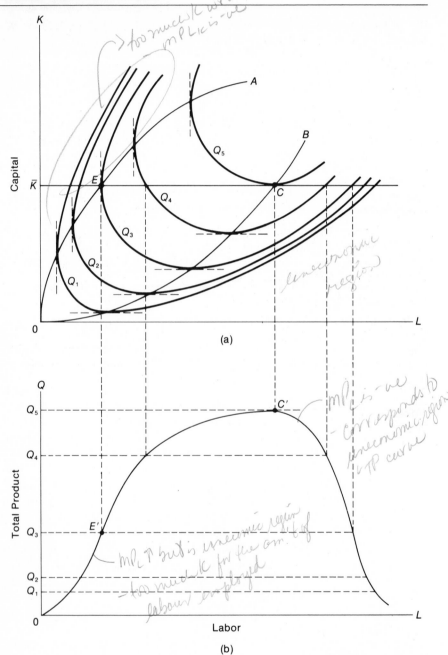

(a)

(b)

capital by a small amount, its marginal product would be negative. Thus, the regions outside the ridge lines can be considered regions of declining total product, thereby justifying the term *uneconomic regions of production.*

Returns to Scale   6–4

Suppose a generalized production function specifying *all* inputs is given by

$$Q = f(X_1, X_2, X_3, \cdots, X_n) \tag{6–9}$$

where each of the factor inputs is measured in a *specific* quantity and Q is a certain number of units of output produced. Now suppose we increase all factor inputs by a multiple of β. This will change the *scale* of our operation, and total output will now be given by

$$\alpha Q = f(\beta X_1, \beta X_2, \beta X_3, \cdots, \beta X_n) \tag{6–10}$$

Assuming that we are operating within the economic region of production, output will increase by α multiplied by the original output. When $\alpha > \beta$, we say that we have **increasing returns to scale** in production; when $\alpha < \beta$, we say that we have **decreasing returns to scale.** When $\alpha = \beta$, **constant returns to scale** in production are said to exist.

Isoquant curves can be used to demonstrate the concept of returns to scale. Three different isoquant maps, representing three different production functions, appear in Figure 6–10. The ray $0R$ is drawn in each figure. Movement along such rays on an isoquant map means that both factor inputs are being varied

Figure 6–10
Returns to Scale

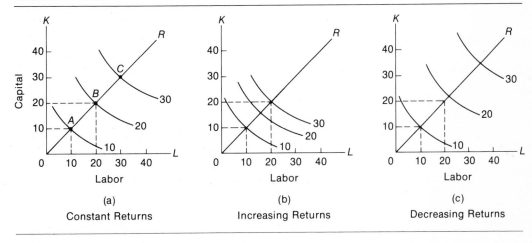

| (a) | (b) | (c) |
| Constant Returns | Increasing Returns | Decreasing Returns |

proportionately. In other words, at Point A on ray OR in Figure 6–10(a), we are employing 10 units of capital and 10 units of labor. If we increase both inputs such that $\beta = 2.0$, then we will move to point B on ray OR, where we will be employing 20 units of capital (10 × 2.0) and 20 units of labor (10 × 2.0). Since 10 units of output are produced at point A and 20 units are produced at point B, it follows that $\alpha = \beta$, indicating that there are constant returns to scale between points A and B. Now if we construct our isoquant map such that for *every* isoquant *drawn*, the difference between the output quantity of each adjacent isoquant is a constant, then the distance separating isoquants along a given ray must also be constant to maintain constant returns to scale along that ray. This can be seen by comparing point C with points A and B in Figure 6–10(a). At point C, we are employing exactly three times as much labor and capital as we are at point A, so that we are producing three times the output. Thus, $\alpha = \beta = 3.0$, and there are constant returns to scale between points A, B, and C along ray OR. The distance OA is exactly equal to AB, which is exactly equal to BC. If this condition were to exist for *every* possible ray drawn through the isoquant map, then we would say that the production function itself possessed constant returns to scale.

In the case of increasing returns to scale, the isoquants bunch up; that is, the distance between the isoquants will decrease as we move from the origin along a ray, because doubling inputs will *more than* double output. This condition is illustrated in Figure 6–10(b). On the other hand, in the case of decreasing returns to scale, shown in Figure 6–10(c), the distance between the isoquants will increase as we move from the origin along a ray, because doubling inputs will *less than* double output. Should one of these conditions prevail for any ray, then we would say that the production function possessed increasing or decreasing returns to scale.

A production function may be characterized totally by increasing, decreasing, or constant returns to scale, but it is more likely to exhibit all three characteristics at different stages of production. Initially, low levels of output can be expected to produce increasing returns to scale. Next, constant returns to scale are encountered. Finally, high levels of output will produce decreasing returns to scale.

6–5 Technological Progress

We have previously pointed out that the production function relates inputs to output at a given level or state of technology. **Technological progress** results in a change in the production function such that for a given quantity of inputs, total output is increased.

We can use isoquant curves to illustrate the concept of technological progress. We will assume that prior to the technological change, our production function is given by Equation (6–4):

$$Q = f(L,K)$$

The solid isoquant curves in Figure 6–11 correspond to this production function. At point *A*, for example, it is possible to produce 150 units of output by employing 20 units of capital and 10 units of labor.

Now suppose that a machine is developed that can operate twice as fast as the machine it has been designed to replace. Our new production function will be

$$Q = g(L,K) \qquad\qquad (6-11)$$

The isoquant curves for this new function (the dashed curves in Figure 6–11) shift inward toward the origin. Due to technological progress, 150 units of output can now be produced using *less* labor and *less* capital than before, as indicated by point *B*, which lies below and to the left of point *A* on the isoquant map.

The slope of a ray drawn from the origin to a point on an isoquant measures the ratio of capital to labor that must be employed to produce the output indicated by that isoquant. For example, if the firm's original point of operation prior to the technological change is point *A* in Figure 6–11, then the **capital–labor ratio** being used by the firm would be given by the slope of ray 0*A*. If the firm's point of operation shifts to point *B* after the technological change, the capital–labor ratio will decrease. This is indicated by the fact that the slope of ray 0*B* is less than the slope of ray 0*A* in Figure 6–11. The effect of technological progress on the capital–labor ratio adopted by a

**Figure 6–11
Technological Progress**

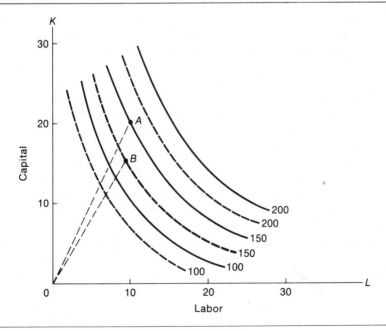

firm will determine whether that firm's demand for labor will increase or decrease relative to capital. We will examine the firm's behavior under such conditions in more detail in Chapter 11 when we examine the effect of technological progress on the distribution of income between the factor inputs.

Application: Constructing a Production Function

Not all production functions are as divorced from reality as the ones we have studied here. In this application, we will construct an isoquant map for a production function that is relevant to everyday living.

Figure 6–12 graphs the technological relationship between gasoline consumption and speed for a large American automobile. At very low speeds, it is clear that the automobile is not operating most efficiently. The number of miles per gallon increases until 30 miles per hour is reached. Beyond a speed of 30 miles per hour, the number of miles per gallon decreases at an increasing rate, primarily due to aerodynamic drag. Now suppose that we wish to travel 1,000 miles. At each speed we might decide to drive, we can expect to travel a corresponding number of miles per gallon of gas. By dividing this number into the distance of the trip, we can calculate the amount of gasoline required to travel 1,000 miles at this speed. The speed at which we decide to travel will also

Figure 6–12
The Relationship Between Gasoline Consumption
and Speed for a Large American Automobile

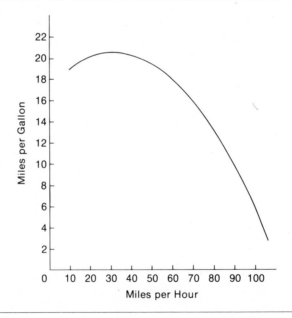

Table 6–5
Driving Time and Gasoline Consumption
for a 1,000-Mile Trip

MILES PER HOUR (mph)	MILES PER GALLON (mpg)	DRIVING TIME (hours)	GASOLINE CONSUMPTION (gallons)
10	19.0	100.0	52.63
20	20.2 *highest*	50.0	49.50
30	20.7	33.33	48.31 *lowest*
40	20.3	25.0	49.26
50	19.5	20.0	51.28
60	18.0	16.67	55.56
70	16.0	14.29	62.50
80	13.25	12.5	75.47
90	10.0	11.11	100.0

determine the total driving time, which we can obtain simply by dividing the distance of the trip by the speed traveled. These calculations for a 1,000-mile trip appear in Table 6–5. The data in the first two columns are taken from Figure 6–12. The third and fourth columns of the table provide calculated trade-off between driving time and gasoline consumption. As we would expect from Figure 6–12, the table shows that we can simultaneously reduce driving time and gasoline consumption by driving faster, *if* we are initially driving at less than 30 miles per hour. At an initial speed of more than 30 miles per hour, driving time can be reduced only by *increasing* gasoline consumption.

The points given by the data for driving time and gasoline consumption in Table 6–5 are plotted in Figure 6–13 and connected by a smooth curve labeled "1,000 miles." This isoquant curve shows the possible combinations of driving time and gasoline consumption required to travel 1,000 miles. Isoquant curves for trips of 500 and 1,500 miles are also drawn in Figure 6–13. The uneconomic region of trip production lies above the ridge line formed by ray OR. This ridge line passes through the points on these isoquants that result from driving at a steady speed of 30 miles per hour. Driving less than 30 miles per hour increases driving time *and* gasoline consumption. Our isoquant map is characterized by a single ridge line, in contrast to the two ridge lines on the isoquant map in Figure 6–9, because driving time *always* decreases as speed increases.

Now suppose we were required to make a 1,000-mile trip in an automobile that exhibited the technical characteristics graphed in Figure 6–12. At what point on the 1,000-mile isoquant in Figure 6–13 would we choose to operate our private transportation service? Clearly, we would not want to operate above point A, but any other point on the isoquant would be economically feasible.[9] We are, in fact, unable to decide where we will operate because we do not have enough

[9]For the purposes of argument, we will assume that there are no laws against speeding and that risk of collision does not increase with speed. The former would pose an upper-bound constraint, and the latter would add another variable input.

Figure 6-13
Transportation Isoquants for a Large American Automobile

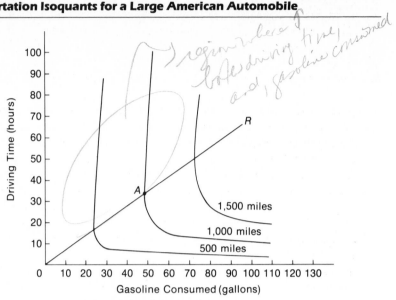

[handwritten annotations: region where both driving time and gasoline consumed; R]

Driving Time (hours) *(y-axis)*

Gasoline Consumed (gallons) *(x-axis)*

1,500 miles
1,000 miles
500 miles

information to make an economically optimal decision—we have no data pertaining to cost. Our examination of production costs in Chapter 7 will enable us to solve the problem we have just posed.

6-6   Summary

In Chapter 6, we have examined *production,* which occurs when a good or a service is created. We have learned that all of the inputs or *factors of production* that must be combined to produce a good or a service can be classified as *land, labor,* or *capital.* We now know that for a given *state of technology,* the relationship between a firm's inputs and outputs is called the *production function.* In the *short run,* one or more of the factors of production (usually capital) are *fixed;* in the *long run, all* factor inputs are *variable.* The long run encompasses the planning horizon of the firm.

If a production function has only one variable input, the relationship between output and the variable input is called the *total product curve.*

We have also learned how to calculate the *average* and *marginal products* of a production function with only one variable input. The *law of diminishing returns* states that for every production function, if one input is increased while all other inputs are held constant, the average and marginal products of that input will begin to decrease at some point. The points at which these two products begin to decline are called the *point of diminishing average returns* and the *point of diminishing marginal returns.*

[handwritten annotations: inflection pt, TP ↑ at ↓ rate, MP_L ↓ now; TP ↑ at ↓ rate, AP_L ↓ now]

We then conducted an analysis of the production function with two variable inputs by using *isoquant curves*—curves of constant output for varying combinations of the minimum required quantities of the variable inputs. Isoquant curves are analogous to indifference curves in that they cannot intersect, they are negatively sloped in the relevant region, and they are convex to the origin. In our analysis, we found that the slope at a point on an isoquant curve is the *marginal rate of technical substitution* between the two variable inputs, which is equal to the ratio of the marginal products of the inputs at that particular point. The production function can be divided into *economic* and *uneconomic* regions of production. When isoquant curves are used to graph the production function, these regions are divided by *ridge lines*. The *economic region* of production is located between the ridge lines.

We have also examined *returns to scale* in production, or the total output when *all* factors of production increase proportionately. When changes in output are more than proportionate to input, *increasing* returns to scale are said to exist; when output is less than proportionate to input, *decreasing* returns to scale exist. When output is proportionate to input, *constant* returns to scale in production exist.

We now know that *technological progress* results when a given output can be produced with less input. This is indicated by a shift in the isoquant curves toward the origin on an isoquant map. We have also seen that the *capital–labor ratio* employed by a firm can be affected when technological progress occurs.

Production theory can rule out uneconomic regions of the production function, but it cannot be used in itself to determine the economically optimal point of production. To accomplish this, the theory of production must be combined with the theory of cost, which we will examine in Chapter 7.

References

Blaug, Mark. *Economic Theory in Retrospect,* 3rd ed. Cambridge: Cambridge University Press, 1978.

Clark, Colin. *Population Growth: The Advantages.* Santa Ana, CA: Life Quality, 1975.

Heady, Earl O. *Economics of Agricultural Production and Resource Use.* Englewood Cliffs, NJ: Prentice-Hall, 1952.

Heady, Earl O. "An Econometric Investigation of the Technology of Agricultural Production Functions." *Econometrica* (April 1957), pp. 249–68.

Otten, Alan L. "People Shortage." *The Wall Street Journal,* Vol. CI, No. 38 (August 23, 1979), pp. 1 and 24.

Smith, Vernon L. *Investment and Production.* Cambridge: Harvard University Press, 1961.

Problems

1. A student was observed studying beyond the point of diminishing returns while preparing for the Graduate Record Exam in economics. Do you think that this student will make a good economist?

2. When confronted with historical evidence attesting to an increase in per-capita income over the last 200 years, modern disciples of Malthus usually respond that this trend will be reversed in the next 200 years. What does this response tell us about the scientific nature of their theory of population growth?

3. Land is usually considered to be a fixed factor of production. Can you cite some examples of land being produced?

4. What implicit, normative assumption of economics leads us to conclude that the production that occurs on a positively sloped portion of an isoquant curve is undesirable?

5. If a certain production process exhibits constant returns to scale, is this a denial of the law of diminishing returns?

6. Technological change in agriculture has tended to be capital-using. How do you think this has affected the size of the average farm? Why?

7. When the quantity of a factor input increases, why is the point of diminishing marginal returns reached prior to the point of diminishing average returns?

8. If there is only one factor of production, is it possible for constant or increasing returns to scale to exist? Explain.

CHAPTER SEVEN

PRODUCTION COST THEORY

Introduction 7-1

In Chapter 6, we developed the basic economic theory of production that relates inputs to output, but this theory did not supply enough information for us to determine exactly what combination of inputs and what quantity of output the firm would select. Here, we will extend our examination of production theory to encompass the choice of inputs, leaving the determination of the quantity of output to be produced to Chapters 8, 9, and 10. Before we can do this, however, we must make some assumption about the objective that motivates the firm to select a specific combination of inputs to produce a given level of output.

When we excluded the uneconomic regions of the isoquant map in Chapter 6, this objective was implicit: We assumed that if costs were attached to the use of labor and capital, a firm operating in an uneconomic region could reduce costs without reducing output. Now, if a firm wishes to reduce costs and therefore avoid the uneconomic regions, it follows logically that the firm will seek to produce the same quantity of output at *the lowest possible cost.* Thus, *the objective of the firm in producing any given level of output is to select the combination of inputs that minimizes cost.*

Before we examine how the firm selects the input combination that minimizes cost at a given level of output, however, it will be worthwhile to consider exactly what we mean by the word *cost.*

The Concept of Cost 7-2

To produce a good, scarce resources must be diverted from other productive activities. Therefore, if society, either privately or collectively, decides to produce more of one good (say, cake), then the production of some other good or goods (bread, for example) must be reduced to obtain the factor inputs required to produce the additional output of cake. *The cost of any good is the most valu-*

able alternative that must be sacrificed to obtain the inputs to produce the good. This concept of cost is called **opportunity cost.**

The opportunity cost of many of the inputs to a firm's production process can be measured by the individual prices that are paid for these inputs. This follows from the fact that to attract productive inputs for its operation, a firm must pay the owners of these inputs at least as much as they are worth elsewhere in the economy. For example, if a construction firm purchases 4 tons of gravel at $15 per ton, it incurs a cost of $60—the value of this gravel in alternative employments. To obtain this gravel, the firm gave up the opportunity of buying $60 worth of some other input or inputs available in the marketplace. To make this sacrifice, the firm must have considered the gravel to be worth at least $60 in its productive operation—as much as the gravel was worth anywhere else in the economy.

In this example, the calculation of the economic cost of the factor input is simple, and both economists and accountants would arrive at the same amount. Similarly, both economists and accountants would readily arrive at the same valuation of costs measured in dollars, associated with the acquisition of intermediate goods, labor services, and the rental cost of capital services provided by capital *not owned* by the firm. For these types of inputs, which are purchased directly in markets and are completely used up during the production period, all costs are said to be **explicit costs** and are therefore the easiest costs to measure.

The firm also incurs **implicit costs,** however, and the accountant and the economist diverge in their approach to and measurement of implicit costs. For example, an accountant who is asked to determine the cost of the services of a machine owned by a firm will apply a somewhat arbitrary depreciation rate to the original purchase price of the machine to compute cost per production period. From the economist's viewpoint, this method is unsatisfactory because it does not reflect the opportunity cost to the firm of using the machine. The firm's opportunity cost is the forgone rent it could have received by leasing the machine to some other firm during the production period. This lost rent is an implicit cost, and it is more difficult to calculate than an explicit cost. Nevertheless, since the opportunity cost, and not some fictitious accounting cost, should influence a firm's behavior, when we refer to the *cost of capital services,* we will mean the *explicit* rental cost of capital if it is not owned by the firm and the *implicit* rental cost of the capital if it is owned by the firm.

Another important point of divergence between economists and accountants concerns the determination of *profits.* To the accountant, profits per period are defined as the difference between revenue and explicit costs; to the economist, **profits** per period are defined as the difference between revenue and opportunity costs. Due to this definitional difference, the accountant does not consider the opportunity cost to the shareholders in the firm—the best alternative return that the shareholders could receive on their shares if they sold them and used the proceeds to buy other assets. For example, if a firm's revenue exceeds its accounting costs by an amount such that shareholders receive $.05 on every $1 they invest, the accountant would say that this firm is making a profit and that its rate of return is 5%. However, if these shareholders have the opportunity to make another investment that is *identical in all ways* to their current investment but that offers a return of 6%, then the economist would say that this firm is incurring a *loss* of 1%. The superiority of the economist's definition becomes apparent when we realize that firms that incur prolonged losses go out of business. In this example, the owners of the firm can realize a greater return on their investment by selling the assets of their firm to buy the more preferred assets of another firm, and their firm may cease to exist. We will explore the concept of the opportunity cost of profits in more detail when we examine how profits are determined and how they affect the firm's behavior in Chapters 8–11.

Throughout this book, when we refer to *cost,* we will mean the economist's concept of *opportunity cost.* With this concept of cost firmly in mind, we are now ready to turn our attention to the relationship between production and costs. To facilitate and simplify our discussion, we will assume that the firm uses only *two* variable inputs—homogeneous units of labor (measured in man hours) and homogeneous units of capital (measured in machine hours). We will also assume that the firm is *small* in relation to the economy and can therefore buy as much labor and/or capital services as it chooses without altering the prevailing market wage and rental rates. In Chapters 8–10, we will consider certain forms of market organization for which these assumptions do not prevail.

The Optimal Input Combination   7-3

In Chapter 6, we learned that when two or more inputs are employed in the production process, the firm will not operate in the uneconomic regions of production. But we also learned that this information is insufficient to determine the precise combination of inputs the firm will employ to produce a given level of output, because an infinite number of possible input combinations exist within the economic region along any given isoquant. Now we will combine production and cost theory to show how the firm makes this determination. We will assume that at any given level of output, the firm will choose the combination of inputs that minimizes production costs. A cost-minimizing combination of inputs is called an **optimal input combination.**

Isocosts

The cost of production depends on the prices of the various inputs as much as it does on the quantities employed. Assuming that we have two variable inputs, labor and capital, and that their prices per unit are P_L and P_K, respectively, then if L units of labor and K units of capital are employed, their cost $\bar{C}$ will be

$$\bar{C} = P_L L + P_K K \qquad\qquad (7\text{-}1)$$

If C is held constant, then it logically follows that if more labor is employed, less

Table 7–1
Possible Input Combinations for a Constant Cost of $1,500
(P_L = $150 P_K = $250)

UNITS OF LABOR	COST OF LABOR	UNITS OF CAPITAL	COST OF CAPITAL	TOTAL COST
L	$P_L L$	K	$P_K K$	$\bar{C}$
0	$ 0	6	$1,500	$1,500
1	150	5.4	1,350	1,500
2	300	4.8	1,200	1,500
3	450	4.2	1,050	1,500
4	600	3.6	900	1,500
5	750	3.0	750	1,500
6	900	2.4	600	1,500
7	1,050	1.8	450	1,500
8	1,200	1.2	300	1,500
9	1,350	0.6	150	1,500
10	1,500	0	0	1,500

capital will be employed, and vice versa. For example, suppose that the labor wage is $150 per worker per week and that the rental price of capital is $250 per machine per week. If the firm is spending $1,500 per week on inputs, then it can employ any of the eleven input combinations shown in Table 7–1. Actually, an infinite number of input combinations are possible, since we assume that either input can be employed in fractional units. This infinite choice possibility is illustrated in Figure 7–1, where a straight line is drawn through the plotted points given by the data in Table 7–1. Since the input cost expenditure of the firm is constant everywhere along this line, it is called an **isocost line.** If we let $\bar{C}$ represent constant total cost, then we can obtain the equation of this line by rewriting Equation (7–1) as

$$K = \frac{\bar{C}}{P_K} - \frac{P_L}{P_K} L \qquad (7-2)$$

Substituting in the assumed values for $\bar{C}$, P_K, and P_L gives us

$$K = \frac{1,500}{250} - \frac{150}{250} L$$
$$= 6 - 0.6L$$

To obtain the slope of the isoquant curve, we multiply -1 by the ratio of the price of labor divided by the price of capital, or

$$\text{Slope} = -\frac{P_L}{P_K} = -\frac{150}{250} = -0.6 \qquad (7-3)$$

Figure 7–1
The Isocost Line

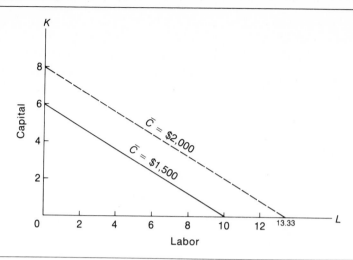

Increasing the total cost of the inputs the firm employs from $1,500 to $2,000 will not change the slope of the resulting isocost line, since the price of the inputs is assumed to be constant and the slope is determined by the ratio of input prices, as shown in Equation (7–3). The new isocost line will be parallel and to the right of the initial isocost line, as shown by the dashed isocost line in Figure 7–1. The vertical axis intercept of $\bar{C}/P_K = 2{,}000/250 = 8.0$ determines the position of the new isocost line.

In general, any isocost line for two inputs can be described by Equation (7–2), and if capital and labor are measured on the vertical and horizontal axes, respectively, then the slope of any such isocost line will be $-P_L/P_K$.

Minimizing the Production Cost of a Given Output

A fundamental assumption of the theory of the firm is that the firm wishes to maximize its profits. Therefore, the firm will always strive to produce any given level of output at the least cost. Suppose that a firm wishes to employ two variable factors of production–labor and capital–to obtain output level Q_1. The isoquant curve representing this level of production appears in Figure 7–2. Given our assumption that the firm is small in relation to other firms, the quantities of labor and capital that it employs have no impact on the markets for these inputs, so that the prices of these inputs are set by the market. In other words, the price of labor P_L and the price of capital P_K are treated as given and, for the purpose of our analysis here, fixed.

Figure 7–2
Determination of the Cost-Minimizing Input Combination

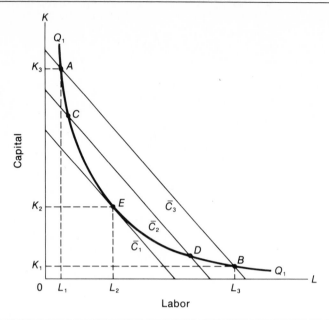

Three of an infinite number of isocost lines are also drawn in Figure 7–2. These isocost lines are parallel, since their slopes are determined by the ratio of the price of labor to the price of capital and we are assuming that these prices are constant. The position of the isocost lines is determined by the total expenditure $\bar{C}$ spent on the variable inputs. These three isocost lines represent input expenditures of $\bar{C}_1$, $\bar{C}_2$, and $\bar{C}_3$, where $\bar{C}_1 < \bar{C}_2 < \bar{C}_3$.

If the firm spends $\bar{C}_3$ on inputs, it can produce an output of Q_1 by operating at points A or B on the isoquant curve in Figure 7–2. These are feasible production points because with an expenditure of $\bar{C}_3$, the firm can employ capital and labor in quantities K_3 and L_1 at point A or K_1 and L_3 at point B, as shown by the intersection of isocost line $\bar{C}_3$ with isoquant curve Q_1 in the figure. But although this solution is feasible, is it the cost-minimizing solution? Suppose that the firm reduces its input expenditure to $\bar{C}_2$, which is less than $\bar{C}_3$. Isocost line $\bar{C}_2$ intersects isoquant curve Q_1 at points C and D in Figure 7–2, so that both of these points also represent feasible input combinations. Since total input expenditure has been reduced, either the input combination at point C or D would be preferred to the input combinations at point A or B. However, the firm has still not attained the optimal input combination because *any* point on isoquant curve Q_1 between points C and D will lie on a lower isocost line than $\bar{C}_2$. **Cost minimization** is achieved when the isoquant curve *is just tangent to* the isocost line. At this point, any further reduction in cost will result in insufficient expenditure to purchase *any* feasible input combination. Isocost line $\bar{C}_1$ is tangent to isoquant curve Q_1 at point E, and therefore the input combination K_2, L_2 is the optimal or **cost-minimizing input combination.** The optimal or cost-minimizing input combination for firms with isoquant curves that display the general characteristics studied here (illustrated by curve Q_1 in Figure 7–2) is determined by the point of tangency between an isocost line and the isoquant curve.

Since the cost-minimizing isocost line is tangent to the isoquant curve at the optimal input combination point, it follows that the slope of the isoquant curve is equal to the slope of the isocost line at this point. Recall from Chapter 6 that we defined the slope of any point on the isoquant curve as the marginal rate of technical substitution of labor for capital $MRTS_{LK}$ and we proved that

$$MRTS_{LK} = -\frac{MP_L}{MP_K} \tag{6–8}$$

where MP_L is the marginal product of labor and MP_K is the marginal product of capital. We have already proved that the slope of the isocost line is $-P_L/P_K$. Therefore at the cost-minimizing combination point, the following equality must prevail:

$$MRTS_{LK} = -\frac{MP_L}{MP_K} = -\frac{P_L}{P_K} \tag{7–4}$$

Rearranging terms, we obtain

$$\frac{MP_K}{P_K} = \frac{MP_L}{P_L} \tag{7–5}$$

which is a necessary condition if the firm is to produce a given output at the lowest possible cost. The economic common sense of the statement given by Equation (7–5) can be easily seen if we assume that the equality in Equation (7–5) does *not* hold and that

$$\frac{MP_K}{P_K} < \frac{MP_L}{P_L} \tag{7–6}$$

If production occurred under these conditions, then the marginal product of an additional dollar of capital would be less than the marginal product of an additional dollar of labor. The firm would reduce the quantity of capital employed by \$1 and maintain the same level of output by increasing the quantity of labor by *less than* \$1. Thus, the firm would reduce cost without reducing output. This trade-off of capital for labor could continue as long as the inequality prevailed. However, it cannot go on indefinitely, since the marginal product of capital will increase as less of it is used and the marginal product of labor will decrease as more of it is used. Eventually, the firm will reach equality, and the marginal product of capital for an additional dollar of capital will exactly equal the marginal product of labor for an additional dollar of labor.[1]

In general, when we are dealing with a production process with n factor inputs, $F_1, F_2, F_3, \cdots, F_n$, a necessary condition for cost minimization is

$$\frac{MP_1}{P_1} = \frac{MP_2}{P_2} = \frac{MP_3}{P_3} = \frac{MP_n}{P_n} \qquad (7\text{--}7)$$

where $MP_1, MP_2, MP_3, \cdots, MP_n$ are the marginal products of the n inputs.

7-4 Long-Run Cost

In Chapter 6, we said that the firm was operating in the *long run* if all factor inputs, including capital, were variable, so that the size of the plant constructed to produce a given level of output would be the size that minimizes cost. If we assume that we have two factor inputs—labor and capital—and that their prices remain constant as the scale of the firm's operations expands, then we can examine how the firm will behave as it increases production in the long run.

In Figure 7–3, the production function of the firm is represented by the four isoquants Q_1, Q_2, Q_3, and Q_4. Four isocost lines $\bar{C}_1, \bar{C}_2, \bar{C}_3$, and $\bar{C}_4$, are also drawn in the figure. As before, these isocost lines are parallel to one another because the ratio of the price of labor to the price of capital is assumed to be constant. These isocost lines are also drawn tangent to their respective iso-

---

[1]This conclusion can be derived mathematically. We wish to minimize the cost function

$$C = P_L L + P_K K$$

subject to the output constraint

$$Q = f(L, K)$$

The Lagrangian function is

$$Z = P_L L + P_K K + \lambda [Q - f(L, K)]$$

To produce output Q at minimum C, the quantities of L and K must be chosen such that

$$\frac{\partial Z}{\partial L} = P_L - \lambda \frac{\partial Q}{\partial L} = 0$$
$$\frac{\partial Z}{\partial K} = P_K - \lambda \frac{\partial Q}{\partial K} = 0$$

Since $\partial Q/\partial L = MP_L$ and $\partial Q/\partial K = MP_K$, solving for λ in the first of the two simultaneous equations and substituting the result for λ in the second equation yields

$$P_K - \frac{P_L}{MP_L} MP_K = 0$$

or

$$\frac{MP_K}{P_K} = \frac{MP_L}{P_L}$$

Figure 7–3
The Expansion Path of the Firm

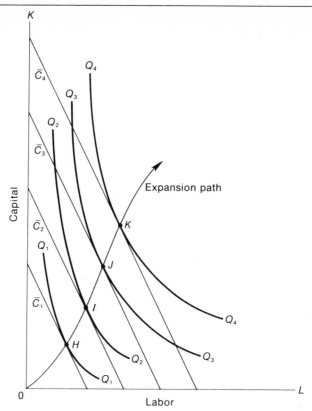

quant curves at points *H, I, J,* and *K.* A smooth curve drawn from the origin through these tangency points shows us how the cost-minimizing input combination varies as the plant is expanded to produce increased levels of output. This curve, called the **expansion path** of the firm, indicates the input combinations that will produce various levels of output at the lowest possible cost.

Long-Run Total Cost

Since the expansion path tells us the lowest possible cost for different levels of output when all factor inputs are variable, we can construct the **long-run total cost** LRTC curve by plotting these costs and their respective quantities of production. This is done in Figure 7–4(a), where point *H'* corresponds to point *H* in Figure 7–3. Point H in Figure 7–3 tells us that the lowest cost for which output Q_1 can be produced is $\bar{C}_1$. In Figure 7–4(a), point *H'* is plotted with the coordinates $(Q_1, \bar{C}_1)$. In a similar manner, points *I', J',* and *K'* are plotted based on the coordinates given in Figure 7–3 for points *I, J,* and *K,* respectively. The smooth curve drawn through points *H', I',* and *K'* in Figure 7–4(a) is the long-run total cost curve.

Figure 7–4
Derivation of the Long-Run Total Cost, Long-Run Marginal Cost, and Long-Run Average Cost Curves

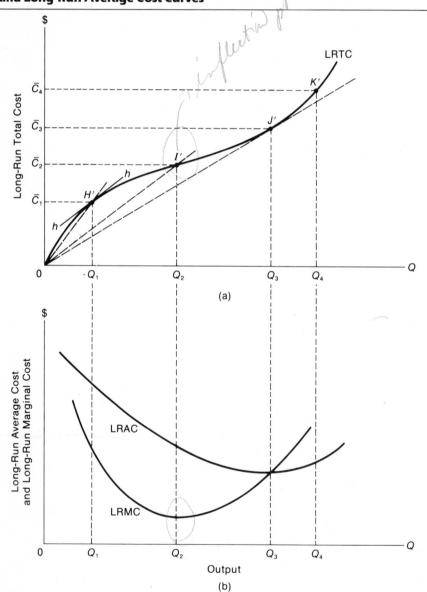

Long-Run Average and Marginal Costs

The **long-run average cost** LRAC is the total long-run cost of producing a given level of output divided by that output, or

$$LRAC = \frac{LRTC}{Q} \qquad\qquad (7\text{–}8)$$

If we draw a ray from the origin in Figure 7–4(a) to a point on the LRTC curve, then, by definition, the slope of that ray will be the long-run average cost at that point. For example, the slope of ray $0H'$ is $\bar{C}_1/Q_1$, which, in turn, is the LRAC at point H'. Rays also extend to points I' and J' in Figure 7–4(a). Given the shape of the LRTC curve, the slopes of these rays initially decline as we move to the right from the origin until we reach point J'. There, the ray $0J'$ is tangent to the LRTC curve, and rays drawn from the origin to points to the right of J' will be steeper than ray $0J'$. Thus, the slope of the rays drawn from the origin to the LRTC curve to the left of point J' will reach a minimum at point J'. In other words, long-run average cost declines as output increases until output Q_3 is reached, at which point the LRAC curve begins to rise. This is illustrated in Figure 7–4(b), where the LRAC curve is derived from the LRTC curve in Figure 7–4(a). We can readily observe that the LRAC curve initially declines, reaches a minimum at output Q_3, and then begins to rise.

A closely allied concept to long-run average cost is **long-run marginal cost** LRMC, which is defined as the addition to total cost incurred with the production of one additional unit of output when all inputs are variable, or

$$LRMC = \frac{\Delta LRTC}{\Delta Q} \qquad\qquad (7\text{–}9)$$

Graphically, the long-run marginal cost at a point on the LRTC curve is the slope of a line drawn tangent to the curve at that point. For example, line hh in Figure 7–4(a) is drawn tangent to the LRTC curve at point H', so that the slope of line hh is LRMC at output Q_1. If we compare the slope of line hh with the slope of ray $0H'$, we can see that the slope of $0H'$ is greater than the slope of hh. Thus, LRMC is less than LRAC at output Q_1. This is shown in Figure 7–4(b), where the LRAC and the LRMC curves are plotted. There we can see that the LRAC curve lies above the LRMC curve at output Q_1.

As we move right along the LRTC curve, the slopes of lines drawn tangent to points on the curve become smaller until the inflection point is reached at I' in Figure 7–4(b). Beyond I', the LRMC curve begins to increase, and we can therefore conclude that the LRMC curve reaches a minimum at output Q_2 (the output at which the point of inflection occurs), as shown in the figure. Since the slope of ray $0I'$ still exceeds the slope of a line tangent to the LRTC curve at I', it follows that LRAC must still exceed LRMC. However, at point J', LRAC reaches its minimum value, as we have already noted. But since the slope of ray $0J'$ is tangent to the LRTC curve at J', it follows that LRMC = LRAC at output Q_3. Thus, the LRMC curve must intersect the LRAC curve from below at its minimum point, as shown in Figure 7–4(b). To the right of point J', LRMC > LRAC, because the slope of the lines tangent to the LRTC curve will exceed the slope of rays drawn from the origin through the same tangency points.

7–5   Economies of Scale

The long-run average cost curve illustrated in Figure 7–4(b) displays the shape usually attributed to the LRAC curve in textbooks. The curve initially slopes downward and to the right, eventually reaches a minimum value, and then assumes a positive slope. When the LRAC declines as the size of the firm increases, **economies of scale** are said to exist. When the LRAC rises as the size of the firm increases, we say that the firm is experiencing **diseconomies of scale.** Primarily, the LRAC declines initially due to (1) division and specialization of labor and (2) technological aspects of the production process.

When the firm is very small, workers and machines perform many different tasks. Workers who perform a variety of tasks are rarely, if ever, proficient in all of them. Moreover, workers may perform some tasks so seldom that they never acquire sufficient experience to become as skillful and efficient as their capabilities permit. When machines are limited, they must also perform several operations. For example, a drill press may be used to drill holes of different diameters and depths. As the machine is readjusted and altered to complete different operations, time is lost, workers are paid to make the modifications, and there is a greater possibility that production errors, with their accompanying waste, will result. As the scale of plant operations increases, workers become more efficient due to division and specialization of labor. Specific tasks are assigned to each worker, and a worker may eventually perform only one type of task. This division of labor gives each worker an opportunity to specialize in one or more tasks that allow his or her inherent abilities to develop to the fullest.

Similarly, as the capital stock of the firm increases, machines perform fewer types of operations. Machines are often designed to perform very specific functions. As inputs become more specialized, there is an accompanying change in the technology employed. Consider, for example, the stamping of body panels for automobiles. The body panels for automobiles that are produced in small quantities, such as the Morgan, are cut from flat sheets, roughly shaped with the use of general purpose metal-bending and rolling machines, and finished by hand by skilled craftsmen called panel beaters. It requires many hours of expensive labor to form each panel, but when output is low (eight Morgans per week), it is the least expensive means of production. On the other hand, the body panels of mass-produced automobiles are stamped out in minutes by huge hydraulic presses controlled by relatively unskilled laborers. These machines and the tools and dies used to shape the panels are very costly, but the volume of production is so high that the average cost per panel is lower than it would be if it were produced by an alternative method.

Another reason technological factors produce economies of scale is that as the output capacity of machinery increases, the cost per unit of output decreases. For example, a typical one-horsepower (HP) electric motor sells for about $100. Suppose that to increase the output of each machine four-fold, we would have to increase the size of the electric motor driving the machine from 1 to 5 HP. We could do this by buying five 1-HP motors at a cost of $500 or by buying one 5-HP motor for $300. Obviously, the 5-HP motor is preferable: It would provide four times the output for only three times the motor cost. This is partially due to the weights of these motors. A 1-HP electric motor weighs 25 pounds, but a 5-HP motor weighs only 75 pounds. For technological reasons, as the output capacity of an electric motor increases, the input of copper and steel does not increase proportionally. Therefore, a 5-HP motor costs less than five 1-HP motors.

Many modern products, such as automobiles and jet airplanes, have very high initial fixed engineering and tooling costs, so that the average fixed cost component attributed to these items decreases appreciably when production runs are large. For example, the developmental costs of the General Motors X-cars (the Citation, Omega, Skylark, and Phoenix) are estimated to be $2.7 billion.[2] However, if General Motors builds 5 million X-cars, the average developmental cost per car will only be about $550.

Economies of scale can also reduce the average price as output expands by decreasing the cost of transporting the product to market. Since large bulky products, such as automobiles, occupy less space if they are shipped in parts rather than assembled, the transportation cost per disassembled automobile is less. However, this procedure becomes economical only when sales are sufficient enough to justify constructing assembly plants. The major American automobile producers maintain assembly plants in markets that are spatially separated from Detroit. An automobile manufacturer whose sales in California, for example, are insufficient to warrant constructing an assembly plant is at a distinct disadvantage. This producer must charge a competitive price, although transportation costs will be greater and the profit per sale will be smaller.

Diseconomies of scale are said to exist when the LRAC curve assumes a positive slope. This behavior is usually explained by the fact that as the firm expands beyond a certain capacity, the efficiency of its management begins to decline. Managers become further removed from actual production operations. They are forced to delegate authority to assistants who, in turn, rely on their own assistants. This lengthening of the decision-making chain decreases the quality of the information on which decisions are made and increases the time

---

[2]Charles G. Burck, "What's Good for the World Should Be Good for G.M.," *Fortune* (May 7, 1979), pp. 124–36.

**Example
7–1**

Electric Power Generation

The generation of electric power is often cited as an example of a natural monopoly, because the long-run average cost curve of the firm is believed to decline almost indefinitely. Casual empiricism seems to support this hypothesis. From 1955 to 1970, the average size of the privately owned electric power company approximately tripled, while the average cost of generating 1,000 kilowatt-hours of electricity decreased from \$7.18 to \$5.85. Such crude data have led some economists to suggest that the cost of generating electricity could be significantly reduced if the electric power industry were consolidated by nationalizing the individual firms.

In a recent study that examined the economies of scale in electric power generation, Laurits Christensen and William Greene discovered that the primary reason for the reduction in the average cost of electric power generation was due to technological change rather than to economies of scale.* In other words, the LRAC curve of the firm has shifted downward from 1955 to 1970.

Figure 7–5 summarizes the results of the Christensen–Greene study. In 1955, the minimum point on the LRAC curve occurred at an annual output of 20 billion kilowatt-hours; by 1970, the minimum point had shifted out to 32 billion kilowatt-hours. Since many firms produce electric power in the portion of the LRAC curve where average cost is declining, as shown by the size distribution scale for firms under the horizontal axis of Figure 7–5, it would seem to be possible to reduce the average cost of electric power generation if these firms could be consolidated into larger entities. Christensen and Greene calculated that if all U.S. firms produced at the minimum point of the LRAC curve (\$.473 per kilowatt-hour) in 1970, the cost

---

*Laurits R. Christensen and William H. Greene, "Economies of Scale in U.S. Electric Power Generation," *Journal of Political Economy,* Vol. 84, Part I (August 1976), pp. 655–76.

required to make decisions and to correct the inevitable mistakes that occur.[3] In addition, as managers and their assistants increase in number, the paper work, travel, and telephone calls they generate in the process of communicating among themselves adds appreciably to the firm's costs and consumes an increasing portion of their workday. All these factors contribute to reducing the efficiency of management, and as the scale of plant operations increases, the average cost of output also increases.

The concept of economies of scale serves as a useful device for categorizing various industries. Some industries are comprised of many small firms and no large ones. An example is the travel-agent industry. According to economic

---

[3]Murray Rothbard, "Ludwig von Mises and Economic Calculation Under Socialism," in Laurence S. Moss (ed.), *The Economics of Ludwig von Mises* (Mission, KA: Sheed Andrews & McMeel, 1976), pp. 67–77.

of electric power would have been 3.2% lower. It does not seem to be very realistic to assume that this saving would remain intact if electric power generating firms were nationalized and run by the government.

Figure 7–5
Economies of Scale in Electric Power Generation

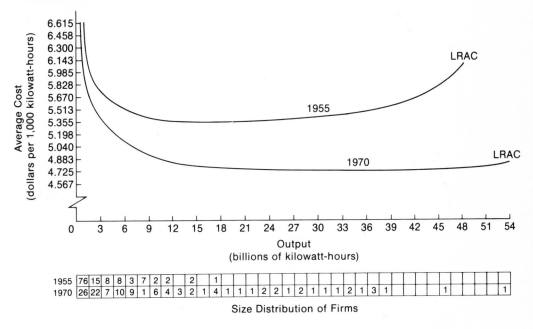

Size Distribution of Firms

SOURCE: Laurits R. Christensen and William H. Greene, "Economies of Scale in U.S. Electric Power Generation," *Journal of Political Economy,* Vol. 84, Part I (August 1976), pp. 655–76. Reprinted by permission of the University of Chicago Press.

analysis, the long-run average cost curve for travel agents would be characterized by the curve shown in Figure 7–6(a). For firms in this industry, the economies of scale are rapidly exhausted and firm size remains small. Such industries are said to exhibit **early diseconomies of scale.** In some industries, economies of scale are realized when plant size is relatively small, but diseconomies of scale are not encountered until the firm is quite large. The LRAC curve for firms in such an industry would be similar to the one shown in Figure 7–6(b). These industries exhibit **constant economies of scale.** In such an industry, both small and large firms could be expected to coexist. An example is the petroleum-refining industry, where small refineries operate within the shadow of the corporate giants. For example, 124 U.S. companies were engaged in the refining of crude oil in 1975, but only 17 of these were considered large firms capable of refining more than 200,000 barrels per day in 109 refineries.

Figure 7–6
Comparison of Economies and Diseconomies of Scale

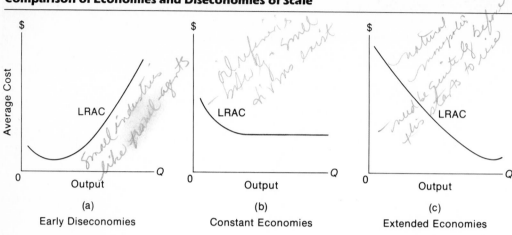

(a)
Early Diseconomies

(b)
Constant Economies

(c)
Extended Economies

Of these 17 companies, the average refining capacity per refinery of the largest company was 248,600 barrels per day; the smallest of the 17 companies refined 50,000 barrels per day. The remaining 107 small companies operated 150 refineries and their average capacity was only 22,050 barrels per day.[4] Lastly, some industries exhibit what are called **extended economies of scale.** The LRAC curves for these industries are similar in shape to the curve shown in Figure 7–6(c). Firms in these industries must be relatively large before their average costs begin to rise. Consequently, one firm is sometimes able to produce the entire output demanded for the least average cost. Such industries, called **natural monopolies,** will be examined in Chapter 9.

7–6   Short-Run Cost

In the long run, all inputs are variable. In the short run, one or more of the firm's inputs are constant. For most firms, the capital input is fixed and cannot be increased in the short run.

Short-Run Total Cost

Figure 7–7 illustrates the production function of a firm. Given this production function, the labor–capital price ratio, and a desired output of Q^*, we will assume that a plant has been constructed to produce Q^* at least cost, which occurs

---

[4]Leo R. Aulund, "Building by Small Refiners Boosts U.S. Refining Total," *Oil and Gas Journal,* Vol. 73, No. 12 (March 24, 1975), p. 14.

Figure 7–7
Production in the Short Run

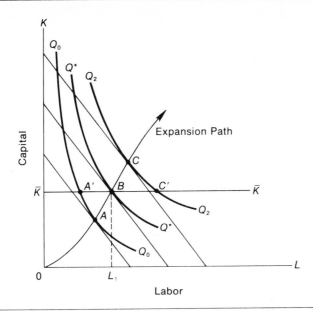

when labor input L_1 is combined with capital input $\bar{K}$. The overbar on K indicates that capital is the fixed input; we will assume that labor is the variable input. At point B, isoquant curve Q^* is tangent to the isocost line and also lies on the firm's long-run expansion path. Once the plant has been built, the firm is operating in the short run.

Short-run total cost SRTC is the cost to the firm of producing any level of output when the quantity of one or more inputs is held constant. As long as short-run output is Q^*, the short-run total cost will be equal to the long-run total cost. If the firm chooses to decrease its level of output from Q^* to, say, Q_0 and if all inputs are variable, the firm will prefer to produce at point A on the expansion path. But since capital is fixed at $\bar{K}$ in the short run, the firm will have to produce at A'. Since A' is to the right of the isocost line tangent to Q_0, it follows that the total cost of producing Q_0 in the short run must exceed the total cost of producing Q_0 in the long run. Similarly, if the firm chooses to increase its level of output from Q^* to Q_2 and if all inputs are variable, the firm would produce at point C in the long run but will produce at point C' in the short run when capital is fixed at $\bar{K}$. Since C' lies to the right of the isocost line tangent to Q_2, it follows, as before, that the short-run total cost of producing Q_2 will exceed the long-run total cost of producing Q_2.

The LRTC curve associated with the production function in Figure 7–7 is drawn in Figure 7–8. The SRTC curve when the level of output is Q^* and capital input is fixed at $\bar{K}$ also appears in Figure 7–8. We have just seen that SRTC

Figure 7–8
Comparison of Long-Run Total Cost
and Short-Run Total Cost Curves

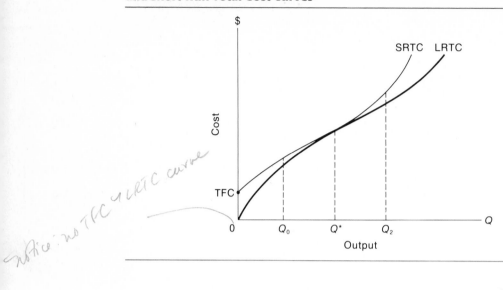

Notice: no TFC 4 LRTC curve

is equal to LRTC at output Q^*. At levels of output lower or higher than Q^*, SRTC will exceed LRTC. Also note that even if the firm produces 0 output, it must still pay for the capital that is lying idle. These costs are called **total fixed costs** TFC and are indicated in Figure 7–8 by the fact that the SRTC curve intersects the vertical axis at a positive value.

Total fixed cost can be considered a constant component of short-run total cost. This concept is illustrated in Figure 7–9, where the TFC curve is shown as a horizontal line at all levels of output. The difference between the short-run total cost and the total fixed cost is called the **total variable cost** TVC and represents the component of the short-run total cost that the firm incurs as production increases. Graphically, the TVC curve is obtained by simply subtracting the constant TFC from SRTC at all levels of output, as shown in Figure 7–9.

Short-Run Average and Marginal Costs

In later chapters, the concept of the short-run total cost curve we just derived will help us to understand the behavior of the firm. The SRTC curve can also be used to derive the equally useful concepts of *short-run average* and *marginal costs.*

Average fixed cost AFC is simply total fixed cost divided by output, or

$$AFC = \frac{TFC}{Q} \qquad\qquad (7\text{--}10)$$

The derivation of the AFC curve is depicted graphically in Figure 7–10. Rays are

Figure 7–9
Derivation of the Total Variable Cost Curve

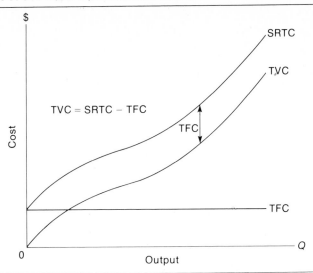

drawn from the origin to points A, B, and C on the TFC curve in Figure 7–10(a). Since the slope of these rays is their vertical distance divided by the horizontal distance of the right triangles the rays form with the horizontal axis, it follows that

$$\text{Slope } 0A = \frac{AQ_1}{Q_1} \tag{7-11}$$

and since $AQ_1 = \text{TFC}$, then

$$\text{Slope } 0A = \frac{\text{TFC}}{Q_1} = \text{AFC}$$

at point A. The value of the slope of ray $0A$ is plotted in Figure 7–10(b) at point A'. Similarly, the slopes of rays $0B$ and $0C$ give us points B' and C' in Figure 7–10(b), which are the average fixed costs at outputs Q_2 and Q_3, respectively. It is obvious from Figure 7–10(a) that as output increases, the slopes of the rays will diminish, so that the AFC curve will have a negative slope at all levels of output and will approach the horizontal axis as output approaches infinity.

We can employ the same basic technique we just used to derive the AFC curve to graph other average cost curves. Thus, we define **short-run average cost SRAC** as

$$\text{SRAC} = \frac{\text{SRTC}}{Q} \tag{7-12}$$

Figure 7–10
Derivation of the Average Fixed Cost Curve

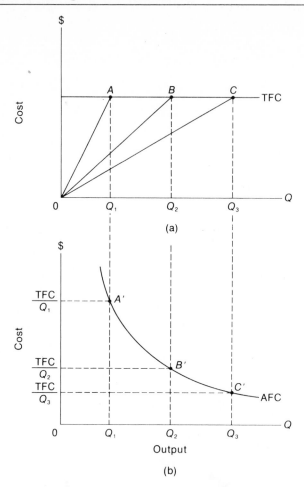

(a)

(b)

and **average variable cost** AVC as

$$\text{AVC} = \frac{\text{TVC}}{Q} \tag{7–13}$$

To derive the SRAC and AVC curves graphically, we draw rays from the origin to points on the SRTC and TVC curves, as shown in Figure 7–11(a). The slopes of these rays are equal to the short-run average cost and the average variable cost at the levels of output corresponding to the points where the rays intersect (or are tangent to) the SRAC and AVC curves. For example, ray 0*L* in Figure

Figure 7–11
Derivation of the Average Total Cost and Average Variable Cost Curves

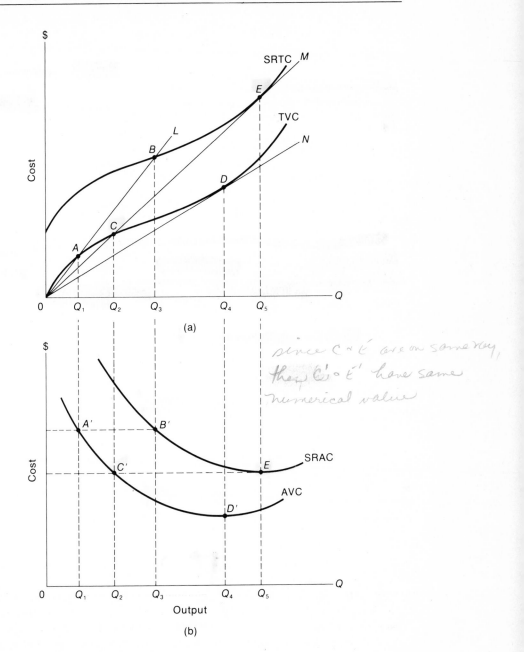

since C & E are on same ray,
they C' & E' have same
numerical value

(a)

(b)

7-11(a) intersects the TVC curve at point A and the SRTC curve at point B at outputs of Q_1 and Q_3, respectively. Therefore, AVC at Q_1 must be equal to SRAC at Q_3, as shown by points A' and B' in Figure 7-11(b). Now consider ray $0M$, which intersects the TVC curve at point C, which corresponds to output Q_2. Since the slope of $0M$ is less than the slope of $0L$, it follows that AVC at output Q_2 is less than AVC at output Q_1. This is illustrated in Figure 7-11(b), where point C' lies below A'. Also note that the ray $0M$ is tangent to the SRTC curve at point E, which corresponds to output Q_5. Since any ray drawn to any point to the left or right of point E will have a greater slope than the slope of $0M$, the SRAC curve must be at its minimum point at output Q_5. This is illustrated in Figure 7-11(b), where the SRAC curve reaches a minimum at point E'. And, since points C and E both lie on the same ray $0M$, C' on the AVC curve and E' on the SRAC curve have the same numerical value. Lastly, ray $0N$ is drawn so that it is tangent to the TVC curve at point D, corresponding to output Q_4, in Figure 7-11(a). Employing the same line of reasoning we used to establish the minimum point at output Q_5 on the SRAC curve, we can prove that the minimum point on the AVC curve occurs at output Q_4, as shown by point D' in Figure 7-11(b).

Since SRTC is always greater than TVC by a constant amount equal to TFC, the ray tangent to the SRTC curve will always have a greater slope and be tangent at a greater output than the ray tangent to the TVC curve. Thus, the minimum point on the SRAC curve will always be above and to the right of the minimum point on the AVC curve, as shown by points E' and D' in Figure 7-11(b).

The **short-run marginal cost** SRMC incurred by the firm is defined as the increase in short-run total cost when one additional unit of output is produced and is expressed mathematically as

$$\text{SRMC} = \frac{\Delta \text{SRTC}}{\Delta Q} \qquad (7\text{--}14)$$

It is also equally correct to define short-run marginal cost as the increase in total variable cost when one additional unit of output is produced, or

$$\text{SRMC} = \frac{\Delta \text{TVC}}{\Delta Q} \qquad (7\text{--}15)$$

Both definitions of short-run marginal cost are correct, because the difference between SRTC and TVC is TFC, which is a constant. Therefore, the change in SRTC will always be equal to the change in TVC for a given change in output.

The SRTC and TVC curves in Figure 7-11(a) are reproduced in Figure 7-12(a). Points A, B, D, and E are the same in both graphs. To graphically determine SRMC at any level of output Q, we simply draw a line tangent to the point on the SRTC curve or the TVC curve that corresponds to output Q. The slope of either of these tangent lines is then equal to SRMC, because, as before, the curves

Figure 7–12
Derivation of the Short-Run Marginal Cost Curve

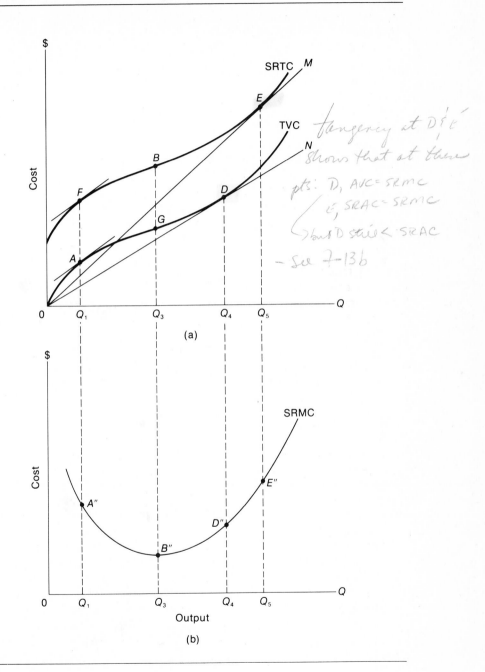

tangency at D & E
shows that at these
pts: D, AVC = SRMC
E, SRAC = SRMC
but D still < SRAC
— See 7–13b

(a)

(b)

Figure 7–13
Comparison of Short-Run Cost Curves

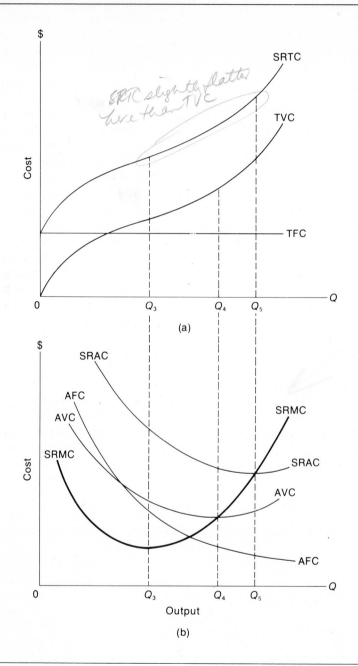

(a)

(b)

Output

differ by a constant vertical distance and, by definition, their slopes must be equal at the same level of output.

At output Q_1, the corresponding points on the SRTC and TVC curves are F and A, respectively, in Figure 7-12(a). Lines drawn tangent to these points will be parallel, and their slopes will be equal to SRMC at output Q_1. At output Q_1, SRMC is plotted at point A'' in Figure 7-12(b). The slope of lines drawn tangent to either the SRTC curve or the TVC curve as output increases will diminish until output Q_3 is reached. At output Q_3, the SRTC and TVC curves have reached their inflection points. If output increases beyond Q_3, the slope of lines drawn tangent to these curves at higher outputs will increase. Short-run marginal cost will decrease until output Q_3 is reached, and then it will increase. Therefore, the SRMC curve will be at its minimum point at output Q_3, as illustrated by point B'' in Figure 7-12(b). Similarly, the SRMC at outputs Q_4 and Q_5 are calculated and plotted as points D'' and E'', respectively, in Figure 7-12(b). Note that the tangency lines at points D and E in Figure 7-12(a) are also rays ON and OM, respectively. Therefore, SRMC at output Q_4 must be equal to AVC at output Q_4, and SRMC and SRAC must be equal at output Q_5. Recall from Figure 7-11(b) that the AVC and SRAC curves reached their respective minimums at outputs Q_4 and Q_5. To the left of point D, the slopes of lines drawn tangent to the TVC curve will be less steep than the slopes of rays drawn through these points. Therefore, for outputs less than Q_4, SRMC will be less than both AVC and SRAC. At output Q_4, SRMC will be equal to AVC but will still be less than SRAC. At output Q_5, SRMC will be greater than AVC and will be equal to SRAC. At outputs greater than Q_5, SRMC will exceed both AVC and SRAC.

Figure 7-13 summarizes the short-run cost curves we have derived in this section and their relationships to one another. The AFC curve is negatively sloped and approaches the horizontal axis as output increases. The SRAC and AVC curves are U-shaped. The SRAC curve always lies above the AVC curve at any given level of output and reaches its minimum value at a higher level of output. The SRMC curve is also U-shaped and reaches its minimum value at a level of output corresponding to the inflection point on either the SRTC curve or the TVC curve. The SRMC curve also intersects the AVC and SRAC curves from below at their minimum values.

The Relationship Between Long-Run and Short-Run Costs   7-7

The long-run total cost curve of the firm represents the minimum cost of producing any level of output when the firm has sufficient time to vary *all* inputs, assuming that relative input prices and the state of technology remain constant. Once the plant size has been determined and constructed, the relevant cost curve for the firm is the short-run total cost curve. Not surprisingly, a very definite relationship exists between the LRTC curve and the SRTC curve. We will explore this relationship in detail in this section.

The same LRTC curve for a firm is compared with SRTC curves for small, medium, and large plant sizes in Figures 7–14(a), (b), and (c), respectively. Employing the same technique we used to derive the SRAC and SRMC curves in Section 7–6, we can derive the long-run average cost LRAC and the long-run marginal cost LRMC curves graphically from the LRTC curve in Figure 7–14. The results of these derivations are illustrated in Figure 7–15.

In Figure 7–14(a), a small plant is represented by $SRTC_1$. We know that this plant is designed to produce output Q_A, since $SRTC_1$ is tangent to LRTC at this output level. Ray $0A$ in Figure 7–14(a) is drawn through the point of tangency between $SRTC_1$ and LRTC. Since the slope of ray $0A$ is equal to $SRAC_1$ and LRAC at output Q_A, it is clear that these long-run and short-run average costs must be equal at output Q_A, as shown in Figure 7–15. Rays $0B$ and $0C$ are drawn tangent to $SRTC_1$ and LRTC, respectively, which tells us that $SRAC_1$ reaches its minimum at output Q_B and that LRAC reaches its minimum at output Q_C. Quantity Q_B is therefore greater than Q_A but less than Q_C. $SRAC_1$ in Figure 7–15 exhibits these properties. From our previous discussion of the relationship of the marginal and average cost curves, we know that $SRMC_1$ must intersect $SRAC_1$ from below at its minimum value, as shown in Figure 7–15. In addition, since $SRTC_1$ and LRTC are tangent (have the same slope) at output Q_A, it follows that LRMC and $SRMC_1$ must be equal at the same level of output Q_A, as shown in Figure 7–15. We can easily see that marginal cost is less than average cost at output Q_A if we imagine that a line is drawn tangent to LRTC and $SRTC_1$ at output Q_A in Figure 7–14(a). Since the slope of this tangency line is SRMC and LRMC at output Q_A and is less steep than ray $0A$, it follows that SRMC = LRMC < SRAC = LRAC at output Q_A, as shown in Figure 7–15.

The output of the medium-size plant in Figure 7–14(b) coincides with the output at which the LRAC curve reaches its minimum point. In other words, we have chosen a plant size that will produce the firm's product at the *lowest possible cost.* The short-run total cost curve $SRTC_2$ is drawn so that it reaches its minimum average cost and is tangent to the LRTC curve at output Q_C–where the LRAC curve also reaches its minimum point in Figure 7–15. Since the marginal cost curve intersects the average cost curve at its minimum, it follows that *both* the $SRMC_2$ and the LRMC curves will jointly intersect $SRAC_2$ and LRAC at output Q_C, as shown in Figure 7–15. We can easily verify the fact that $SRMC_2$ is less than LRMC at outputs less than Q_C and greater than LRMC at outputs greater than Q_C by examining the slopes of $SRTC_2$ and LRTC in Figure 7–14(b) at outputs below and above Q_C.

Lastly, we consider the case of a large plant designed to produce a greater output than the output at which the firm's average cost is minimized. The $SRTC_3$ curve for this plant is tangent to the LRTC curve at output Q_E in Figure 7–14(c). Ray $0E$ intersects the $SRTC_3$ and the LRTC curves at their point of tangency and measures the average cost at output Q_E. Ray $0D$ is tangent to the $SRTC_3$ curve at output Q_D, so that the minimum point on the $SRAC_3$ curve in Figure 7–15 occurs at output Q_D, which is greater than output Q_C. We can see that the $SRMC_3$ curve in Figure 7–15 satisfies the properties of the short-run marginal cost curve. $SRMC_3$ intersects $SRAC_3$ from below at its minimum and is equal to

Figure 7–14
The Long-Run Total Cost Curve and the Short-Run
Total Cost Curves for Three Plant Sizes

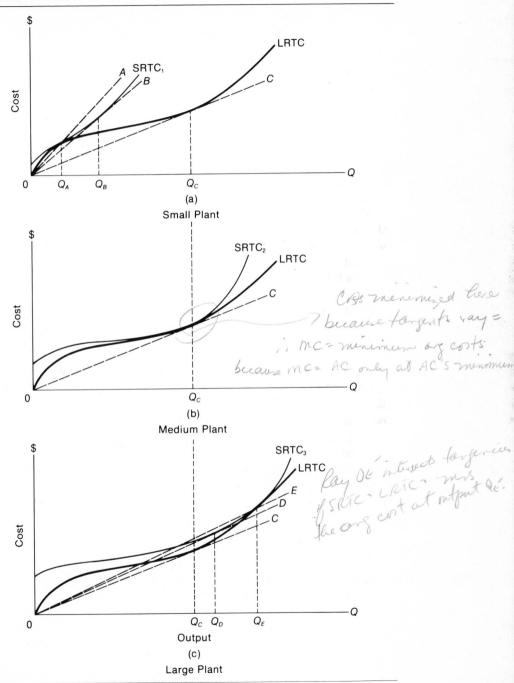

(a)
Small Plant

(b)
Medium Plant

Cost minimized here
because tangents vary =
∴ MC = minimum avg costs.
because MC = AC only at AC's minimum

(c)
Large Plant

Ray OE' intersects tangencies
of SRTC = LRTC = mrs
the avg cost at output Qe'.

Figure 7–15
Long-Run and Short-Run Average and Marginal Cost Curves

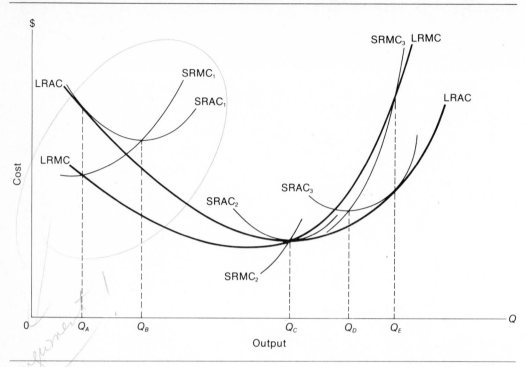

LRMC at output level Q_E—the level at which LRTC and SRTC$_3$ are tangent. The fact that SRMC$_3$ is less than LRMC at output Q_D can be verified by considering the slopes of LRTC and SRTC$_3$ at output Q_D in Figure 7–14(c).

In Figure 7–15, LRAC curve is tangent to an SRAC curve at *every* level of production. It therefore follows that we can construct a firm's LRAC curve from the SRAC curves for several plant sizes. The SRAC curves for six plant sizes are constructed in Figure 7–16. The LRAC curve can be drawn so that it never intersects but is always tangent to the SRAC curves, as shown in the figure. A curve constructed in this manner is called an **envelope curve.**

Application: The Construction of Long-Run Average Cost Curves

Using the envelope-curve technique to construct long-run average cost curves is of more than just theoretical interest. In many industrial situations it is the cheapest and fastest method to determine possible economies of scale.

Figure 7–16
Derivation of the Long-Run Average Cost Curve
from Short-Run Cost Curves

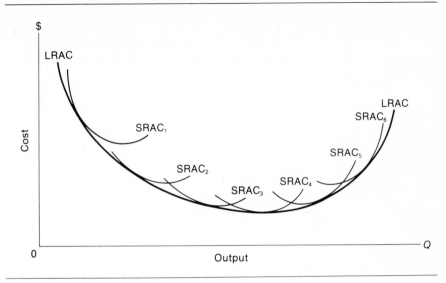

In the 1950s, for example, it became possible to greatly reduce the average cost of chicken broilers by expanding plant size. To demonstrate the economic advantages of the large-scale production of broilers, agricultural economists at the New Hampshire Agricultural Experiment Station determined the short-run average cost curves for ten plant sizes, ranging in processing capability from a low of 150 broilers per hour to a high of 10,000 per hour.[5] The results of this study are graphed in Figure 7–17, where the LRAC curve, showing the economies of scale to be achieved, is drawn as the envelope curve of the SRAC curves.

Another example of constructing a long-run average cost curve from short-run average cost curves is provided by the engineering studies that preceded construction of the trans-Alaskan pipeline. The trans-Alaskan pipeline is the largest single investment ever undertaken by private enterprise. To determine the optimal size of the pipeline, designers compared cost with throughput for given pipeline diameters. These costs are equivalent to the SRAC curves derived in this chapter, with the pipeline diameter representing a given plant size and the throughput representing the quantity produced. The results of these preliminary engineering studies are graphed in Figure 7–18. We can readily see that the short-run cost curves in this figure exhibit the characteristic shape of

[5]George B. Rogers and E.T. Bardwell, *Economies of Scale in Chicken Processing*, New Hampshire Agricultural Experiment Station Bulletin No. 459 (April 1959).

Figure 7–17
Economies of Scale in Chicken Processing

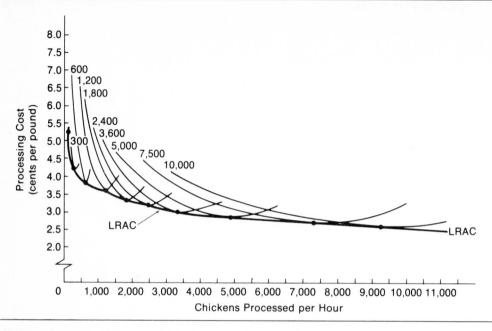

SOURCE: George B. Rogers and E.T. Bardwell, *Economies of Scale in Chicken Processing,* New Hampshire Agricultural Experiment Station Bulletin No. 459 (April 1959). Reprinted by permission.

SRAC curves and that the LRAC curve is determined by drawing an envelope curve of cost versus throughput. This LRAC curve exhibits what we have previously defined as *extended economies of scale.* (Note that the horizontal scale in Figure 7–18 is logarithmic.) One implication of this economic analysis is that it would be uneconomic for each oil company to build a pipeline to transport its own share of the estimated 1.5 million barrels of oil per day that Prudhoe Bay, Alaska, will eventually be producing. Instead, the oil companies decided to build one 48-inch pipeline and share construction and operating costs, which are passed on to the consumer in the form of lower transportation costs.

Application: Optimal Gasoline Consumption

In Chapter 6, we constructed a production function for automobile trips, assuming that the only variable inputs were driving time and gasoline consumption. This production function was illustrated in Figure 6–13 (page 204) for trips of 500, 1,000, and 1,500 miles. Using the concepts of production costs and the isocost lines developed in this chapter, we can now examine the choice of the optimal inputs for a trip of a given distance.

Figure 7–18
Relative Pipeline Costs for Fixed Pipeline Diameters
Versus System Throughputs

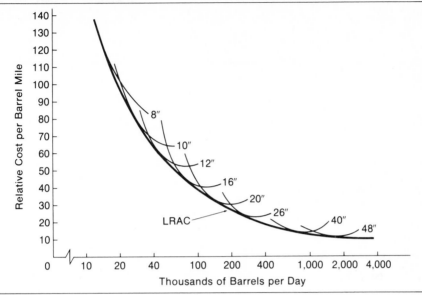

SOURCE: *Competition in the Petroleum Industry,* Exxon Company (May 1975), p. 30.

Suppose that a person wishes to make a 1,000-mile trip at the least possible cost. The production isoquant for a 1,000-mile trip is illustrated in Figure 7–19. If the price of gasoline is $1.00 per gallon and the individual's opportunity cost of driving an automobile on this trip is $4.00 per hour, then the absolute value of the slope of the budget constraint will be 1.00/4.00 = .25. The isocost line with a slope of .25, which is tangent to the 1,000-mile trip isoquant, is also drawn in Figure 7–19. The optimal combination of inputs is determined by the point of tangency between the isocost line and the isoquant curve, or point *A* in Figure 7–19.

The optimal combination of inputs given by point *A* would be a driving time of 14.0 hours and gasoline consumption of 64.0 gallons. Since the opportunity cost of gasoline is $1.00 per gallon and the opportunity cost of driving time is $4.00 per hour, the lowest possible cost of this trip, given our assumptions, is $120.00. To achieve this optimal allocation of resources, the automobile should be driven 71.43 miles per hour. This speedometer setting is determined simply by dividing the trip distance of 1,000 miles by the optimal driving time of 14.0 hours.

Now suppose that the government sets a maximum speed limit of 55 miles per hour for the stated purpose of gasoline conservation. This increases the time required to make a 1,000-mile trip from 14.0 to 18.2 hours and decreases

Figure 7-19
The Optimal Combination of Gasoline Consumption
and Driving Time for a 1,000-Mile Trip

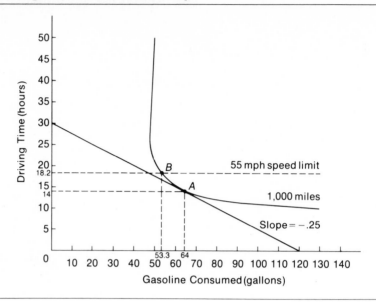

gasoline consumption from 64.0 to 53.3 gallons, as given by point B in Figure 7-19. The 55-mile-per-hour speed limit results in a net conservation of one scarce resource—gasoline—since total consumption has declined 10.7 gallons. However, the other scarce resource in this example—the individual's driving time—has increased 4.2 hours. If the opportunity cost of gasoline is $1.00 per gallon and the opportunity cost of driving time is $4.00 per hour, the 55-mile-per-hour speed limit will produce a *waste* of scarce resources amounting to

$$(4.2 \text{ hours additional driving} \times \$4.00 \text{ per hour})$$
$$- (10.7 \text{ gallons conserved} \times \$1.00 \text{ per gallon})$$
$$= \$16.80 - \$10.70 = \$6.10$$

The government's justification for imposing the 55-mile-per-hour speed limit might be based on the assumption that the price of gasoline did not reflect true opportunity costs due to such factors as the long-run depletion of petroleum resources and increasing U.S. dependency on unreliable foreign petroleum sources. If we accept this as the government's assumption, then what conclusions can we draw regarding the economic wisdom of the lowering of speed limits?

If the nation's true long-run opportunity cost of gasoline is, say, $1.25 per gallon, there will still be a net waste of scarce resources of $16.80 − $13.38

Figure 7–20
The Optimal Allocation of Resources When the Price of Gasoline Is $1.25 per Gallon

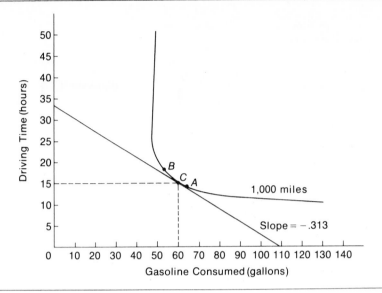

= $3.42 for the individual in our example in the form of too much time spent driving. Furthermore, the dollar value of wasted resources will be even greater for the individual whose opportunity cost of driving time is greater than $4.00 per hour (which is not much above the minimum wage). The obvious policy implication is that if the true opportunity cost of gasoline is greater than $1.00 per gallon, the government should impose a tax on currently produced gasoline to raise it to its long-run average cost and then let each individual drive at the speed that will result in the optimal allocation of all resources.[6]

For example, for the individual whose driving time is valued at $4.00 per hour, an increase in the price of gasoline from $1.00 to $1.25 per gallon will produce a budget constraint with a slope of 1.25/4.00 = .313. This budget constraint is drawn to the isoquant curve for a 1,000-mile trip at point C in Figure 7–20. Points A and B in this figure are the same as points A and B in Figure 7–19. Figure 7–20 shows that if the price of gasoline is raised to $1.25 per gallon, the individual in our example will voluntarily increase driving time from 14.0 to 15.0 hours and will reduce driving speed from 71.43 to 66.7 miles per hour. This voluntary choice will result in a net saving of 4.0 gallons of gasoline per trip. The obvious advantage of this policy proposal is that it will result in the optimal consumption of scarce resources—not just for individuals who value their time

---

[6]This policy was actually adopted by the West German government after the oil embargo of 1973 and again during the interruption of Iranian oil production in 1979.

at $4.00 per hour, but for everyone. In addition, the policy goal of reduced gasoline consumption is achieved with the *voluntary* cooperation of *all* drivers.

It should also be pointed out that the voluntary conservation of gasoline in response to higher gasoline prices will take other forms than the reduction of highway speed. Higher prices will also induce people to purchase smaller cars, make more extensive use of mass transit and car pools, move closer to where they work, and so on. These adjustments will not necessarily be made immediately after an increase in gasoline prices, but an increasing number of people will make such changes as time elapses. This is an example of the price elasticity of demand increasing with time, which we discussed in Chapter 2.

In defense of the government's 55-mile-per-hour speed limit, it is often argued that the reduction in speed saves lives. This is undoubtedly true, but for the economist an important question is could more lives be saved if the required scarce resources were expended in other ways, given the costs of increased travel time. Charles A. Lave has estimated that the cost of increased automobile travel time resulting from the 55-mile-per-hour speed limit is about $6 billion in the United States.[7] The National Highway Traffic Safety Administration estimates that about 4,500 lives are saved each year by the 55-mile-per-hour limit. Thus, it costs about $1.3 million to save one life. Is this the optimal way to save lives? Lave cites several examples to illustrate that this is not the best way. For example, the same number of lives could be saved each year if smoke detectors were placed in every home, but the cost per life saved would decrease from $1.3 million to only $50,000–80,000. Even more optimal examples include kidney-dialysis machines ($30,000 per life saved), mobile cardiac-care units ($2,000 per life saved), and highway improvements ($20,000–100,000 per life saved).

Application: Optimal Fertilizer Use

In Example 6–3 (page 194), we examined a production function for the production of corn. The two variable inputs in this production function were the amounts of phosphate and nitrogen applied per acre. If the price of nitrogen is $.36 per pound and the price of phosphate is $.24 per pound, we can determine the optimal amounts of each fertilizer required to produce a given amount of corn.

Suppose that the farmer wishes to produce 100 bushels of corn per acre. Since the slope of the isocost line is equal to -1 multiplied by the price of nitrogen divided by the price of phosphate, or $-.36/.24 = -1.5$, we can construct an isocost line having this slope and then determine its point of tangency to the isoquant curve representing 100 bushels per acre. Figure 6–7 is reproduced here as Figure 7–21, with the addition of an isocost line having a slope of -1.5 and shown to be tangent to the Q-100 isoquant curve at point A.

---

[7]Charles A. Lave, "The Cost of Going 55," *Newsweek* (October 23, 1978), p. 23.

Figure 7–21
Determination of the Optimal Fertilizer Combination

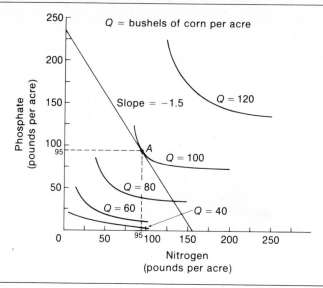

SOURCE: Earl O. Heady, "An Econometric Investigation of the Technology of Agricultural Production Functions," *Econometrica* (April 1957), p. 253. Reprinted by permission.

We can see from Figure 7–21 that the optimal combination of phosphate and nitrogen required to produce 100 bushels of corn is 95 pounds of phosphate and 95 pounds of nitrogen per acre. The total expenditure on fertilizer will therefore be

$$(95 \cdot \$.36) + (95 \cdot \$.24) = \$57.00$$

Alternatively, we could specify a given expenditure on fertilizer per acre and then solve for the input combination to obtain the maximum output. For example, if the farmer wishes to spend $57.00 per acre on fertilizer, our solution would be to use 95 pounds of each fertilizer to produce a maximum of 100 bushels of corn per acre.

Summary   7–8

In Chapter 7, we have examined how the concept of *cost* is viewed by the economist and the accountant. We have determined that the economist's definition of *opportunity cost* is more appropriate for the purposes of our analysis, although in some areas of economic calculation, the measurement of opportunity cost is based either on *explicit costs* produced by market forces or, when the opportunity cost of the firm is subjective, on *implicit costs.*

We have also developed a theory to explain how a firm decides what combination of inputs to employ to produce a given output at minimum cost. This theory builds on the theory of the production function that we developed in Chapter 6. The concept of the *isocost line* was introduced, and it was shown that at a given level of output, the *optimal* or *cost-minimizing input combination* was determined by the point of tangency between the isocost line and the isoquant curve. When input prices are held constant and the firm's total expenditure on inputs is allowed to increase, the curve connecting the points of tangency between the isocost line and the isoquant curve indicates how the firm will vary its optimal input combination as its output increases. This curve is called the *expansion path* of the firm.

We now know that when all inputs are *variable,* the firm is said to be operating in the *long run,* and the optimal input combination selected will be such that the ratio of the marginal product of an input to its price will be exactly equal to the ratio of the marginal product of every other input to its price. In this analysis, we were introduced to the concepts of the firm's *long-run total cost* LRTC, *long-run average cost* LRAC, and *long-run marginal cost* LRMC, and we learned to derive the respective curves of these concepts graphically. When the long-run average cost curve declines as the size of the firm increases, *economies of scale* in production are said to exist. When the LRAC curve rises as the size of the firm increases, *diseconomies of scale* occur. If the production process is characterized by a flat LRAC curve, *constant economies of scale* exist.

We have also learned that in the *short run,* one or more inputs (usually capital) are held *constant.* When a plant is operating at either greater than or less than its design capacity, the *short-run total cost* SRTC will exceed the long-run total cost LRTC. It follows from this that even at an output level of 0, the firm will incur costs. The difference between these costs, called *total fixed costs* TFC, and the short-run total cost is defined as the firm's *total variable cost* TVC. From the corresponding short-run total cost, total variable cost, and total fixed cost curves, we learned to derive the *short-run average cost* SRAC, *average variable cost* AVC, and *average fixed cost* AFC curves, as well as the *short-run marginal cost* curve SRMC.

Lastly, we have learned to combine the concepts of long-run and short-run costs to show that the long-run average cost curve is the *envelope curve* of an infinite number of short-run average cost curves representing various plant sizes. We have further examined the relationship between the long-run average cost and marginal cost curves and the short-run average cost and marginal cost curves and have found that specific points of tangency and intersection occur at various levels of plant size.

In Chapter 8, we will turn our attention to how the firm decides what and how much to produce. The theory of perfect competition that we will examine there forms the foundation on which the concept of the supply curve is based.

References

Aulund, Leo R. "Building by Small Refiners Boosts U.S. Refining Total." *Oil and Gas Journal,* Vol. 73, No. 12 (March 24, 1975), p. 14.

Baumol, William J. *Economic Theory and Operations Analysis,* 2nd ed. Englewood Cliffs, NJ: Prentice-Hall, 1965, Chapters 5 and 12.

Burck, Charles G. "What's Good for the World Should Be Good for G.M." *Fortune* (May 7, 1979), pp. 124–36.

Christensen, Laurits R., and William H. Greene. "Economies of Scale in U.S. Electric Power Generation." *Journal of Political Economy,* Vol. 84, Part I (August 1976), pp. 655–76.

Dantzig, George B. "Computational Algorithm of the Revised Simplex Method." RAND Report RM-1273. Santa Monica, CA: The RAND Corporation, 1954.

Ferguson, Charles E., and John P. Gould. *Microeconomic Theory,* 4th ed. Homewood, IL: Richard D. Irwin, 1975, Chapters 5–7.

Lave, Charles A. "The Cost of Going 55." *Newsweek* (October 23, 1978), p. 23.

Rogers, George B., and E.T. Bardwell. *Economies of Scale in Chicken Processing.* New Hampshire Agricultural Experiment Station Bulletin No. 459 (April 1959).

Stigler, George J. "The Cost of Subsistence." *Journal of Farm Economics,* Vol. 27 (May 1945), pp. 303–14.

Stigler, George J. *The Theory of Price,* 3rd ed. New York: Macmillan, 1966, Chapters 6 and 7.

Viner, Jacob. "Cost Curves and Supply Curves." In George J. Stigler and Kenneth E. Boulding (eds.). *Readings in Price Theory.* Homewood, IL: Richard D. Irwin, 1952, pp. 198–232.

Problems

1. A major tire manufacturer for antique automobiles uses the same molds, equipment, and techniques that were used when the tires were first produced. However, instead of being manufactured in Ohio, as before, the tires are now made in India. Why do you think the production of these tires was shifted to India?

2. Prior to the War Between the States, the unloading of ships in New Orleans was so hazardous that Irishmen, rather than slaves, were used as longshoremen. What is the economic explanation for this behavior by slaveowners?

3. Why is the use of cost-minimizing input combinations a necessary—but not a sufficient—condition for profit maximization?

4. Would a profit-maximizing firm ever employ so much of a factor input that it would be operating in the region of increasing marginal product? Of increasing average product? Of decreasing marginal product? Of decreasing average product? Of negative marginal product?

5. We often hear remarks such as, "Tom Jones' BA degree from Stanford cost his parents $20,000." A more interesting question may be how much did the degree cost Tom Jones?

6. Jacob Viner, a distinguished 20th century economist, once directed an artist to draw the long-run average cost curve so that it was tangent to the short-run average cost curves and simultaneously passed through the minimum point of each SRAC curve. When the resulting figure was published in a journal article, it did not satisfy the requirements specified by Viner. Why? (*Hint:* See the article by Viner cited in the reference section of this chapter.)

7. The assumption of cost minimization makes sense when the owner of the firm is also the manager. But is it reasonable in the case of large corporations when ownership is spread over thousands of stockholders and the managers own little or none of the stock? Why or why not?

8. If a firm could produce a product and maintain constant economies of scale at all levels of output when all inputs were variable, what would be the shape of the firm's long-run average cost curve? Would its short-run average cost curves have the same shape?

APPENDIX

LINEAR PROGRAMMING

Introduction 7A–1

The theory of optimal production presented in Chapter 7 was purposely constructed in the simplest possible manner to bring the fundamental concepts of production into sharper focus. One of the most important assumptions that we made during our analysis of production theory was the assumption that only two variable inputs—labor and capital—are to be considered. We made this assumption in order to simplify the mathematical (graphic) solution to the problem of selecting the optimal input combination. In the real world, of course, the number of possible input combinations in a production process can become quite large—so large, in fact, that the computational problem precludes the determination of the optimal input combination without a mathematical technique that allows us to solve this problem in a fairly direct manner. During World War II, a desire to compute the optimal input combination for computationally complex problems led to what is today known as **linear programming.**

The Diet Problem 7A–2

Like production theory, linear programming is best explained in terms of a very simple example. We will examine a classic example of linear programming, called the **diet problem,** which was originally formulated by George J. Stigler.[1] The basic concept of the diet problem can be easily stated. Suppose that you are raising beef cattle and that, to be marketable in the future, the cattle must consume food that meets certain minimum requirements with respect to diet. Specifically, each steer must receive a minimum daily allowance of vitamin B_1, protein, and calories. To simplify our example, we will assume that only two

---

[1]George J. Stigler, "The Cost of Subsistence," *Journal of Farm Economics,* Vol. 27 (May 1945), pp. 303–14.

available inputs—barley and corn—are used to provide these minimum dietary standards.

Linear programming assumes that the rate at which one input can be traded for another input, while maintaining the minimum daily allowance of one of the dietary requirements, is constant. This assumption is illustrated in Figure 7A–1, where all the possible combinations of barley and corn necessary to provide one steer with a minimum daily allowance of vitamin B_1 are given. Since the rate of substitution is assumed to be constant, the curve representing the vitamin B_1 trade-off is linear. Furthermore, since this line provides all the possible combinations of barley and corn that meet the minimum B_1 requirement, it is a dietary *constraint* below which the farmer cannot drop. For simplicity, we will assume that there is no maximum constraint on any of the dietary requirements in our problem, but it should be obvious that in the case of real-world diet problems, this would not be true.

The dietary constraint lines for calories, protein, and vitamin B_1 are drawn simultaneously in Figure 7A–2. The barley–corn mixture that will simultaneously meet or exceed *all* the dietary requirements appears as a boldface line in the figure. This is the **line of feasible input combinations,** which is analogous to the isoquant curve in production theory. But instead of being a smooth curve, the line of feasible input combinations is composed of linear segments. We will see shortly that this linearity is what permits us to compute the optimal input combination in linear-programming problems.

As in our previous examination of production theory, the optimal input combination is the combination of inputs that achieves the desired output at the lowest possible cost. In our diet problem, the desired output is a cattle-feed

---

Figure 7A–1
**The Combinations of Barley and Corn Needed
to Meet Vitamin B_1 Requirement**

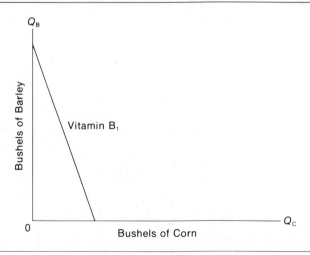

Figure 7A-2
The Line of Feasible Input Combinations

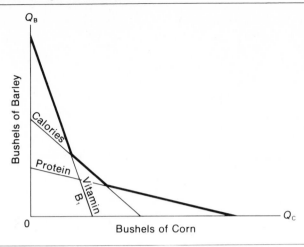

mixture that equals or exceeds the dietary requirements of calories, protein, and vitamin B_1 for a specific grade of beef. The costs of barley and corn per bushel are given, and the objective is to minimize the total expenditure C on barley and corn, which is given by

$$C = P_B Q_B + P_C Q_C$$

where

Q_B = quantity of barley
Q_C = quantity of corn
P_B = price of barley
P_C = price of corn

The slope of the **cost constraint line** is $-P_C/P_B$. Four cost constraint lines with this slope are drawn in Figure 7A-3. The line of feasible input combinations from Figure 7A-2 also appears in Figure 7A-3. Any input combination that can be purchased with an expenditure represented by cost constraint C_1 fails to meet all of the minimum dietary requirements. The input combinations on cost constraint C_4 between points E and F do exceed the dietary requirements but are not optimal, because the minimum standards can be met with a smaller expenditure than C_4 (for example, C_3). The lowest expenditure on corn and barley that will meet the minimum dietary requirements is given by cost constraint C_2, which passes through point G in Figure 7A-3 at a *kink* on the line of feasible input combinations. Thus, given the input price ratio, the optimal input quantities of barley and corn are $\bar{Q}_B$ and $\bar{Q}_C$, respectively.

Figure 7A–3
The Optimal Combination of Barley and Corn

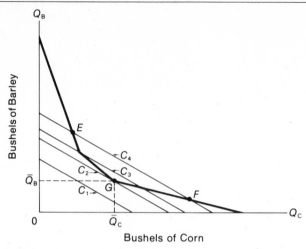

The solution illustrated in Figure 7A–3 is only one of three possible types of solutions. If we suppose that the price ratio of corn to barley is much greater than in our first example, the various cost constraints become steeper, as shown by cost constraint C_5 in Figure 7A–4. In this case, the optimal input combination is given by the intersection of cost constraint C_5 with the line of feasible combinations on the vertical axis at Q_B. In other words, if the price of corn is very high relative to barley, then the lowest–cost feed mix will be comprised solely of barley.

A third solution is also illustrated in Figure 7A–4. In this case, cost constraint C_6 has the same slope as one of the linear segments of the line of feasible input combinations, so that an infinite number of optimal input combinations are possible. However, note that the solutions given by the kinks at both ends of this line segment are also optimal.

We are now in a position to explain the importance of linear programming. Figures 7A–3 and 7A–4 demonstrate that, given a linear model, an optimal input combination will always be found at a kink on the line of feasible input combinations or at the point at which this line intersects the vertical or the horizontal axis. All such points are called *corners*. Therefore, in solving for the optimal input combination, only those solutions, called **basic solutions,** given by the corners on the line of feasible input combinations need to be considered. This conclusion is called the **fundamental theorem of linear programming.** The cost of each basic solution is computed, and the basic solution with the lowest cost is the optimal solution.

The method of optimal input selection we have just outlined may seem elementary, but its strength lies in its simplicity. Real-world optimization problems are much more complex than the examples presented here. In determining

Figure 7A-4
Other Possible Optimal Solutions

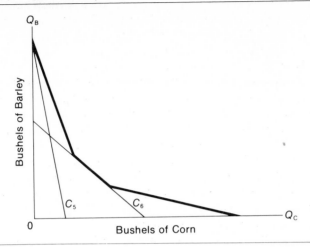

the optimal feed mix, for example, dozens of feed grains may be available and many more dietary requirements will be stipulated. It is essentially impossible to use a direct method to solve mathematically for the optimal input combination. If we used our elementary method to solve the problem, the number of basic solutions we would have to examine would be so astronomical that the number of computations required to solve the problem could not even be made by a modern computer. To make the elementary solution presented here computationally feasible, George Dantzig developed a computational method known as the **simplex algorithm**.[2] The **simplex method of linear programming** is a set of computational instructions outlining a step-by-step procedure that can be followed to obtain the optimal input solution by considering only a very small fraction of all basic solutions. In other words, the simplex method allows us to determine the optimal input combination without computing the cost of the input combinations at all the corners.[3]

Other Linear Programming Problems   7A-3

The technique of linear programming has been used in a multitude of applications. We will briefly examine two in this section.

The first problem we will describe is'called the **transportation problem.**

[2]George B. Dantzig, "Computational Algorithm of the Revised Simplex Method," RAND Report RM-1273 (Santa Monica, CA: The RAND Corporation, 1954).
[3]The theory underlying the simplex method and the computational steps involved are beyond the scope of this text. For an excellent introduction, see William J. Baumol, *Economic Theory and Operations Analysis*, 2nd ed. (Englewood Cliffs, NJ: Prentice-Hall, 1965), Chapters 5 and 12.

Suppose that a firm produces a good and stores it in several warehouses throughout the economy. The good is shipped from the warehouses to retail stores, which are also distributed around the nation. Each store orders a specific quantity of the good, and each warehouse can ship a maximum number of units of the good during each sales period. The firm wishes to determine how many units of the good should be shipped from each warehouse to each store to minimize the total shipping cost in each sales period.

The second problem we will describe is known as the **activity problem.** A firm has at its disposal given quantities of different factors of production. These factors—intermediate goods, capital, and labor—can be combined to produce one of several different goods or any combination of these goods. The firm knows how much of each factor input is required to produce each good as well as the profit that can be earned on each unit at a given output. The firm wishes to produce the quantity and mix of goods that will maximize its total profits.

We have already pointed out that the functions employed in linear programming are assumed to be linear. If this assumption is not in accord with reality, serious errors will result. For example, increasing returns (a nonlinearity) will result when a large number of very small warehouses are consolidated. If this is ignored when the transportation problem is solved, the linear-programming solution will prescribe too many warehouses. On the other hand, if diminishing returns (also a nonlinearity) occur—as would probably be the case when a firm concentrates on producing fewer items—and this is ignored when the activity problem is solved, the linear-programming solution will call for the production of a smaller number of the various goods than the number that will maximize profits. Thus, linear programming is a powerful tool of analysis, but its use will lead to suboptimal solutions if the assumptions on which it is based are violated.

CHAPTER EIGHT

PERFECT COMPETITION

Introduction 8-1

In Chapters 2 and 3, we were introduced to the fundamental concepts of supply and demand, and their usefulness in analyzing real-world problems was demonstrated. We then examined the economic theory on which the demand curve is based in Chapters 4 and 5. Chapters 6 and 7 were devoted to developing the theory of optimal production, under the assumptions that the firm knows what product it wants to produce and the rate at which it wishes to produce that product. In this chapter, we will construct a theory that explains how the firm decides what and how much to produce. As we will soon learn, this theory also forms the foundation on which the concept of the supply curve is based, and the combined interaction between supply and demand ultimately determines the behavior of the firm.

The Assumptions of Perfect Competition 8-2

In economics, the concept of *perfect competition* is very precise and must be clearly distinguished from the concept of *competition* that we use in everyday speech. When we speak of **competition,** we are usually referring to a highly *personalized* situation in which the participants in a game or a market are completely aware of one another's presence and consciously take this into consideration when they make decisions. In economics, as well as in sports, this condition is sometimes called *rivalry.* In the economist's abstract world of perfect competition, however, the essential market characteristic is absolute *depersonalization.* The participants in the market do not know or try to outsmart the other participants in the market. In **perfect competition,** market participants only respond to the depersonalized market signals of input and

251

output prices. For a depersonalized, perfectly competitive market to exist, these four conditions must prevail:

1. Each participant must be insignificant relative to the market.
2. For a given industry, the product of each firm must be identical to the product of every other firm.
3. All resources must be perfectly mobile.
4. Each participant must have perfect knowledge of all market conditions and possibilities.

We will discuss each of these assumptions in detail in this section.

Price Takers

In a perfectly competitive market, every participant in the market is so small relative to the size of the market that an individual participant cannot affect the price of any good or service that they supply or demand. Since they cannot affect prices and must therefore accept the going market price, participants in a perfectly competitive market are called **price takers.**

From the viewpoint of the producers of goods under perfect competition, this means that market participants must pay the going market price to obtain the factors of production they require. Because the size of the individual firm is so small relative to the size of the market, the price of factor inputs remains constant, regardless of what quantities of these inputs the firm decides to purchase. Similarly, the price of the product the firm produces is determined by the market as a whole. No matter how much or how little of its product the firm offers for sale, the price of the product remains constant. In other words, the firm *by itself* cannot influence the price of its product; it must accept the market price. If the firm raises its price even slightly above the market price, it will be unable to sell any of its output. If, on the other hand, the firm lowers its price, it will be unable to sell any more units of output than it could at the market price, because the firm is already selling all it wishes to sell at the market price.

In a perfectly competitive market, individual households are suppliers of labor and, via their savings, the suppliers of the funds lent to producers for the purpose of purchasing capital goods. The price that households receive for their labor (the wage rate) and the return on their savings (the interest rate) are both determined by market forces that no single household can influence. Each household must accept the going wage and interest rates. Similarly, when a household enters the market to purchase the products of firms, the prices of these products are fixed, and the household can buy any quantity of a product without influencing its price. Thus, the individual household in perfect competition—whether in its capacity as a supplier of labor and funds or as a demander of consumption goods—is, like the firm, a price taker.

Identical Product

For all suppliers and demanders in a particular market to be price takers, the product supplied by every seller in this market must be exactly *identical* to the product supplied by every other seller in the market. This condition is necessary to ensure that the demanders of the product are completely indifferent to the various suppliers from whom they purchase the product. If this were not the case—if a firm could convince a buyer that its product was better than similar products offered by other firms—then this firm could raise its price without a resulting decline in sales. The firm, since it would then be able to influence market price, would no longer be a price taker and would therefore no longer be a perfectly competitive firm.

Mobility of Factors

Perfect competition also requires that all factor inputs be perfectly mobile. **Perfect factor mobility** implies several conditions. First, factor inputs must be mobile not only among firms that produce identical products, but also among firms that produce different products. In the case of labor factor input, *perfect labor mobility* implies not only that labor must be geographically mobile to move from one firm to another in a given industry, but also that the necessary labor skills in *all* industries must be similar if labor is to be mobile between industries. *Perfect capital mobility* implies that capital must be easily adaptable to the various production processes used in all industries. Second, perfect mobility requires that there be no barriers to prevent factor inputs from leaving firms and entering firms in the same industry or in other industries. Such barriers as apprenticeship programs, licensing, and union membership, which can prevent labor from entering alternative forms of employment without cost, inhibit perfect labor mobility. Similarly, copyrights, patents, manufacturing secrets, and highly specialized manufacturing techniques restrict capital mobility.

The implications of perfect factor mobility are that (1) firms will be able to freely enter or exit any industry and (2) if factor input costs in a firm or industry increase relative to these costs in other firms or industries, the supply of these factor inputs will increase when their return is higher and decrease when their return is lower.

Complete Knowledge

Producers, consumers, and the owners of the factors of production must have *complete knowledge* of the market if perfect competition is to prevail. If producers did not know the market price of the various factor inputs, they might pay too much for these inputs, thereby invalidating the assumption of a single market-determined price for each input. If consumers were unaware of the market-determined price of a product, they might pay too high a price for that product, thereby violating the assumption of identical prices for identical products.

Similarly, if the suppliers of labor did not have complete knowledge of the wages paid per unit of labor, more than one wage might exist in the labor market. And if the owners of capital did not have complete knowledge of the rate of return on capital paid by all firms, more than one interest rate might exist in the capital market.

8-3   Demand in Perfect Competition

In Section 8–2, we stated that the price of the product produced by a perfectly competitive firm was determined by market forces, but that any individual firm could sell as little or as much as it could possibly produce without affecting the price of its product. Initially, this appears to be a contradiction of the law of demand, which states that the price of a product must be decreased to induce consumers to increase the rate at which they purchase that product. We will now examine the conditions of market and firm demand under perfect competition that allow us to make these seemingly contradictory assumptions.

Market-Determined Price

The market demand and supply curves for a product produced and sold under the conditions of perfect competition are illustrated in Figure 8–1(a). In keeping with our perfectly competitive condition that individual firms and consumers are insignificant, we will assume that there are 100,000 firms, each producing 1/100,000 of the industry's total output of this product, and that the product is currently being consumed by 10,000,000 households in each time period. The demand curve in Figure 8–1(a) represents the combined demand curves of the 10,000,000 households, and since each (or at least the overwhelming majority) of the individual demand curves has a negative slope, the horizontal summation of these demand curves also exhibits this characteristic. The supply curves of each of the 100,000 perfectly competitive firms has a positive slope,[1] and when these supply curves are horizontally summed, the resulting market supply curve also possesses positive slope. The intersection of the market supply and market demand curves in Figure 8–1(a) determines the equilibrium market price of $\bar{P}$ and market output of $\bar{Q}$.

The Firm's Demand Curve

Now suppose that a firm enters this industry and begins to produce a product that is absolutely indistinguishable from the product produced by all the other firms in the industry. Since the entry of one additional firm will increase total

---

[1]Shortly, we will examine why the slope is positive in greater detail.

Figure 8-1
Determination of a Firm's Demand Curve in Perfect Competition

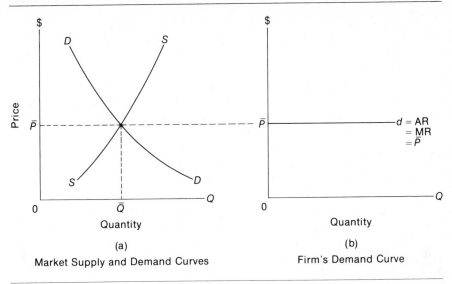

(a)
Market Supply and Demand Curves

(b)
Firm's Demand Curve

output by only 1/100,000, the new firm would be correct in assuming that the impact of its additional output on the market-determined price $\bar{P}$ will be insignificant. Thus, the demand curve of the new firm will be the perfectly horizontal demand curve d shown in Figure 8-1(b). This demand curve intersects the vertical axis at the market-determined price $\bar{P}$.

It should be emphasized here that although we have developed the concept of the demand curve faced by the firm in perfect competition assuming that the firm is a new entrant to the industry, this is not a necessary assumption. Any firm already in the industry would perceive that the effect of its remaining in or leaving the industry is insignificant and would assume that its demand curve is horizontal at the market-determined price $\bar{P}$.

The Firm's Revenue

The **total revenue** TR that any firm receives from the sale of its product is simply the price of the product multiplied by quantity sold, or

$$TR = PQ \qquad (8-1)$$

Since the price at which a firm in perfect competition can sell its product is fixed at $\bar{P}$, total revenue for a perfectly competitive firm is

$$TR = \bar{P}Q \qquad (8-2)$$

Figure 8-2
A Firm's Total Revenue in Perfect Competition

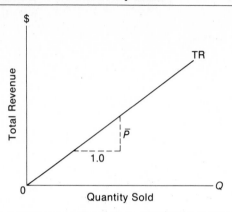

Because price is a constant, total revenue for the perfectly competitive firm is proportional to output, as shown by the total revenue TR curve in Figure 8-2. The slope of this curve is $\bar{P}$, the market-determined price of the product.

The **average revenue** per unit of output AR received by a firm is simply the total revenue divided by the quantity produced, or

$$AR = \frac{TR}{Q} \qquad\qquad (8\text{-}3)$$

Thus, for the perfectly competitive firm

$$AR = \bar{P} \qquad\qquad (8\text{-}4)$$

which is a constant, so that the firm's demand curve is also its average revenue AR curve, as shown in Figure 8-1(b).

The **marginal revenue** MR received by a firm is defined as the addition to total revenue that results from the sale of one more unit of output, or

$$MR = \frac{\Delta TR}{\Delta Q} = \frac{\Delta(PQ)}{\Delta Q} \qquad\qquad (8\text{-}5)$$

Since $P = \bar{P}$ in perfect competition, marginal revenue for a perfectly competitive firm is simply[2]

---

[2]In terms of differential calculus

$$MR = \frac{dTR}{dQ} = \frac{d(\bar{P}Q)}{dQ} = \frac{\bar{P}dQ}{dQ} = \bar{P}$$

$$MR = \frac{\bar{P}\Delta Q}{\Delta Q} = \bar{P} \qquad (8-6)$$

Thus, in perfect competition, the firm's demand curve is horizontal at the equilibrium market price and is also the firm's marginal revenue curve as well as its average revenue curve. Therefore, $MR = AR = \bar{P}$, as shown in Figure 8–1(b).

The Firm's Behavior in the Short Run   8–4

The behavior of the perfectly competitive firm is motivated by a desire to maximize profits. This does not mean that real-world firms do not occasionally pursue other objectives. But in constructing abstract theories of the firm, economists have singled out profit maximization as the most important explanatory factor in terms of firm behavior.

At this point, it may also be useful to mention that profit maximization is not always synonymous with greed and that nonprofit operation is not always altruistic. As a simple example, suppose that you decide to build and endow a children's hospital and that your entire source of income is produced by your firm (you are the sole owner). How should you operate the firm to ensure that your altruistic activity–the children's hospital–will be the best it can possibly be? The answer is that you should operate the firm to maximize profits, which can then be donated to the hospital. The point of this example is *not* to show that profit maximization by firms always results in charitable activities. Instead, this example illustrates that the criterion of profit maximization is not a normative assumption but a positive assumption, since profits can be used for either good or bad purposes.

Profit

The definition and computation of profit in the real world can be exceedingly difficult and ambiguous. Fortunately, the economist's definition of profit, on which the theories we will examine in this book are based, is simple and direct. The economist defines **profit** π as

$$\pi = TR - TC \qquad (8-7)$$

where total cost TC is the concept we defined in Chapter 7.

As long as $TR > TC$, the profits of the firm will be positive. When $TR < TC$, the firm incurs negative profits or, as they are more commonly called, **losses.**

In Figure 8–3(a), a total revenue TR curve and a short-run total cost SRTC curve are drawn for a perfectly competitive firm that is operating in the short run. We know the firm is operating in the short run because the SRTC curve intersects the vertical axis at a positive value, indicating that there are fixed costs at 0 output. In the long run, there are no fixed costs and the total cost curve intersects the origin in this situation.

Figure 8–3
Total Revenue/Total Cost Approach to Profit Maximization

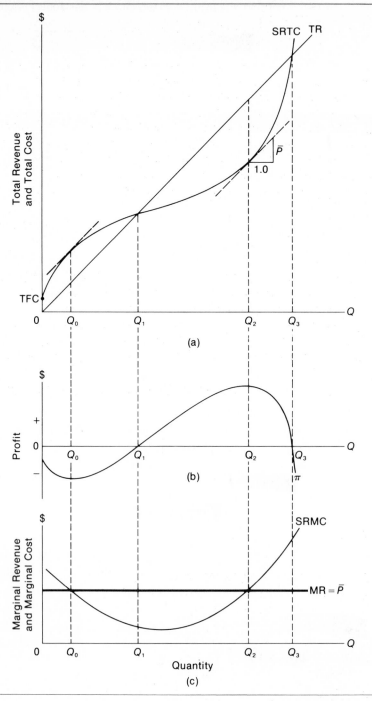

We have defined profits as the difference between total revenue and total cost. Since TR < SRTC for levels of output less than Q_1 and greater than Q_3 in Figure 8–3(a), profits π will be negative in these regions of production, as shown in Figure 8–3(b). At outputs Q_1 and Q_3, TR = SRTC and profits are 0, as shown in Figure 8–3(b). However, in the region of production between Q_1 and Q_3, TR > SRTC and profits are positive. The problem the firm faces is to determine the precise level of output between Q_1 and Q_3 at which π will be maximized. Since π = TR − SRTC, the profit-maximizing firm will produce at the level of output at which the difference between the total cost and total revenue curves in Figure 8–3(a) is greatest. This occurs at output Q_2 where the slope of the SRTC curve is just equal to the slope of the TR curve, as shown in Figures 8–3(a) and 8–3(b). At outputs between Q_2 and Q_1, the slope of the TR curve is greater than the slope of the SRTC curve, so that the vertical distance between these two curves increases as output increases. At outputs between Q_2 and Q_3, the slope of the SRTC curve is greater than the slope of the TR curve, so that the vertical distance between the two curves decreases as output increases. If we remember that at a given level of sales the slope of the TR curve is equal to the marginal revenue MR, which (in perfect competition) is equal to the market equilibrium price $\bar{P}$, and that the slope of the SRTC curve at a given level of production is equal to the marginal cost SRMC, then it follows that if a perfectly competitive firm is maximizing short-run profits,

$$\text{SRMC} = \text{MR} \qquad\qquad (8\text{–}8)$$

or

$$\text{SRMC} = \bar{P} \qquad\qquad (8\text{–}9)$$

In other words, a perfectly competitive firm will maximize profits if it produces at that level of output where the cost of producing one additional unit of output is exactly equal to the price at which that unit will sell.[3]

---

[3]To prove this statement, first we note that

$$\text{TR} = \bar{P}Q$$

Then we define total cost to be a function of output:

$$\text{SRTC} = C(Q)$$

Next, we define profits π to be

$$\pi = \text{TR} - \text{SRTC} = \bar{P}Q - C(Q)$$

Differentiating with respect to Q and equating with 0, we then obtain

$$\frac{d\pi}{dQ} = \bar{P} - \frac{dC(Q)}{dQ} = 0$$

$$\bar{P} = \frac{dC(Q)}{dQ}$$

Since $\dfrac{dC(Q)}{dQ}$ = SRMC, profits are maximized when SRMC = $\bar{P}$.

To further explain and analyze the condition of profit maximization, the marginal revenue and short-run marginal cost curves related to the total revenue and short-run total cost curves in Figure 8–3(a) are drawn in Figure 8–3(c). First, we notice that SRMC = MR = $\bar{P}$ at output Q_2, which is the profit-maximizing level of output. Second, we notice that SRMC is also equal to MR at output Q_0, but since SRTC > TR at this output level, profits are negative. Thus, we can conclude that although SRMC = MR = $\bar{P}$ is a *necessary* condition for profit maximization, it is not a *sufficient* condition. However, the slope of the SRMC curve in Figure 8–3(c) is negative at output Q_0 and positive at the profit-maximizing output of Q_2. Therefore, the necessary and sufficient conditions of profit maximization are that SRMC = MR = $\bar{P}$ and that the slope of the SRMC curve be positive.[4]

8–5 Short-Run Supply

Figure 8–4 is a graph of a firm's short-run marginal cost SRMC curve and its demand or average revenue AR curve. In pure competition, the firm's AR curve is also its MR curve. The firm's short-run average cost SRAC curve and its average variable cost AVC curve, which we derived in Chapter 7, are also drawn in Figure 8–4. The addition of the SRAC and AVC curves will allow us to determine the level of the firm's profits and to derive the short-run supply curve for the firm.

Short-Run Profits

If the market equilibrium price is $\bar{P}_2$, then the firm's AR and MR curve is given by the heavy horizontal line in Figure 8–4, which intersects the vertical axis at $\bar{P}_2$. In Section 8–4, we learned that the firm will maximize profits when SRMC = MR. This occurs at point C in Figure 8–4, where $\bar{P}_2$ = SRMC, so that the profit-maximizing output is Q_2. Since the firm's demand curve is also its AR curve in pure competition, its total revenue TR will be equal to $Q_2\bar{P}_2$, or the area $0P_2CQ_2$ in the figure. The average cost that the firm incurs by producing output Q_2 is given by point E, which corresponds to point F on the horizontal axis in Figure 8–4. Multiplying the dollar value given by point F, the average total cost of production, by the level of output Q_2 gives us the firm's short-run total cost, which is equal to the area $0FEQ_2$. The firm's profits are TR − SRTC, which is graphically equivalent to subtracting $0FEQ_2$ from $0\bar{P}_2CQ_2$. The result $F\bar{P}_2CE$ is the shaded area in Figure 8–4. Since TR > SRTC at the market equilibrium price $\bar{P}_2$, the area of the shaded rectangle FP_2CE measures the firm's positive profits.

---

[4]In terms of the mathematics of optimization, the condition MC = MR = $\bar{P}$ is said to be the *first-order condition* and $dMC/dQ > 0$ is said to be the *second-order condition of maximization.*

Figure 8–4
Derivation of a Firm's Short-Run Supply Curve

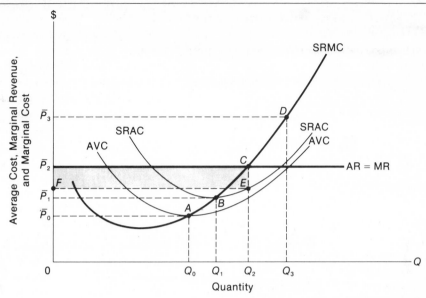

Remembering from Chapter 7 that the firm's total cost of production includes the implicit cost of the normal rate of return on capital, it is obvious that at the market equilibrium price $\bar{P}_2$, the firm's profits will be in excess of the minimum profits (in an accounting sense) that are necessary to keep the firm's capital in this industry. When this condition results, we say that the firm is making **pure profits.**

If the market price rises to $\bar{P}_3$, the firm will increase production to Q_3, since the SRMC curve now intersects the MR curve corresponding to price $\bar{P}_3$ at point D in Figure 8–4. The pure profits of the firm will be greater at output Q_3 than they were at output Q_2. Now suppose that the market price declines to $\bar{P}_1$. At this price, the firm's demand curve intersects the SRMC curve at point B and the profit-maximizing output is Q_1. However, since the SRAC curve is just tangent to the MR curve corresponding to price $\bar{P}_1$, TR = SRTC and pure profits are 0. When the firm makes no pure profits, the rate of return on the firm's invested capital is just equal to the normal rate of return on capital in general. Economists call this 0 level of profit **normal profits.** This *does not mean* that an accountant would show no profits when preparing this firm's books. On the contrary, unlike the economist, an accountant would not treat the return on invested capital as a cost and would show positive profits.

The next question we will consider is what is the lowest price that will motivate the firm to produce in the short run? At first, $\bar{P}_1$ might appear to be the lowest price, since the firm will incur negative profits at any lower price. But this is not true because fixed costs exist in the short run. At point B in Figure 8-4, the SRMC curve intersects the SRAC curve. Thus, if $\bar{P} = \bar{P}_1$, the firm's average revenue will be just equal to the sum of the firm's average fixed cost and average variable cost. If the market price were less than $\bar{P}_1$ but greater than $\bar{P}_0$, at the profit-maximizing level of output, the firm's average revenue would exceed its average variable cost but would *not* exceed the sum of the average variable cost and the average fixed cost (the average total cost). However, the profit-maximizing firm would continue to produce in the short run, because the quantity of fixed factors of production cannot be altered. *The cost of fixed factor inputs must be borne in the short run, whether or not the firm produces.* If the firm produces no output, the *entire* fixed cost must be paid out of the firm's assets. But if the firm produces the output dictated by the intersection of the SRMC and MR curves, then at least a portion of the cost of the fixed factors can be paid with the revenue in excess of the variable cost. In other words, the firm will behave in a way that will *minimize its losses.* If the firm stopped producing when the market price was between $\bar{P}_1$ and $\bar{P}_0$, the firm's losses would be greater than they would if the firm produced at an output level between Q_0 and Q_1. However, if the market-determined price were lower than $\bar{P}_0$, the firm's average revenue would not even be large enough to cover its average variable costs. In such a situation, the firm would stop producing to minimize its losses. Thus, point A on the SRMC curve corresponding to price $\bar{P}_0$ specifies the level of output Q_0 at which the firm is indifferent to continuing or ceasing production.

= shut down pt.

The Firm's Supply Curve

The minimum positive output that the perfectly competitive firm in Figure 8-4 will produce in the short run is Q_0 at price $\bar{P}_0$. If the market price is below $\bar{P}_0$, the firm will produce no output. As the market price rises, the firm's output also increases. At market prices of $\bar{P}_1$, $\bar{P}_2$, and $\bar{P}_3$, the respective outputs produced are Q_1, Q_2, and Q_3. The points corresponding to the price–quantity coordinates—A, B, C, and D—all lie on the SRMC curve, as shown in Figure 8-4. Thus, the SRMC cost curve from point A upward is the **short-run supply curve** for the firm in perfect competition. The portion of the SRMC curve in Figure 8-4 that is the supply curve for the perfectly competitive firm is illustrated in Figure 8-5.

Market Supply

Since the individual firm's supply curve is a portion of its SRMC curve, it might seem reasonable to suppose that the supply curve for the entire industry is merely the horizontal summation of the relevant portions of the SRMC curves for all firms in the industry. This may not necessarily be true, however,

Figure 8-5
The Supply Curve for a Perfectly Competitive Firm

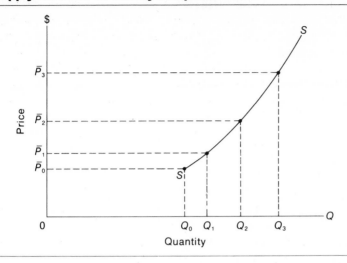

because when we derived the individual firm's SRMC curve in Chapter 7, an underlying assumption was that the cost of the variable factors of production remained constant. And although it is reasonable to assume that a single firm in perfect competition may hire as much of the variable factor inputs of production as it wishes without affecting their market price, it does not necessarily follow that *all* firms in the industry can increase their use of *all* variable inputs without affecting the price of these inputs.

If all firms attempt to purchase additional inputs, the price of one or more of these inputs may rise. When this happens, the SRMC curves of the individual firms will shift to the left, and the *actual* market supply curve will be steeper than the market supply curve derived by assuming that input prices are constant and simply summing the relevant portions of the SRMC curves.

To illustrate this thought more explicitly, we will assume that labor is the only variable input in the production of some good. For each of the various possible wages paid to labor, there will be a corresponding SRMC curve for the firm. If we horizontally summed the relevant portion of each firm's SRMC curve when the wage rate in the industry is at a given level, the resulting curve would be a *market supply curve* for that industry, assuming a constant labor input price. Four market supply curves are drawn in Figure 8–6(a) for wages of W_0, W_1, W_2, and W_3.

Now suppose that as the industry increases its total output, the wage paid to the single factor input (labor) rises according to the functional relationship shown in Figure 8–6(b). At industry outputs of Q_0, Q_1, Q_2, and Q_3, the respective wages are W_0, W_1, W_2, and W_3. Given this information, we can derive the

Figure 8–6
Derivation of the Market Supply Curve
When There Is a Rising Input Price

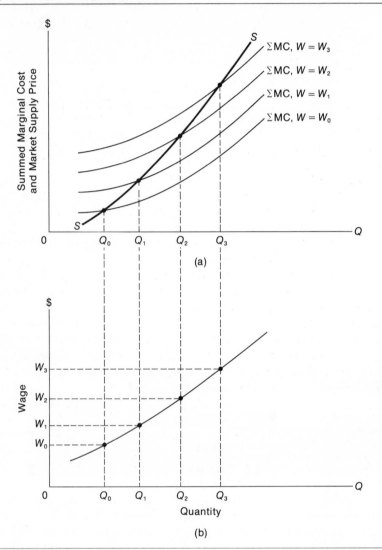

market supply curve in Figure 8–6(a) by drawing a curve through the point on each of the constant-wage supply curves corresponding to the output level for which that wage is relevant, as specified in Figure 8–6(b). The resulting market supply curve SS retains the same positive slope as the constant input price supply curves, but it is more steeply sloped and less price elastic. The important point to notice is that the market or industry supply curve will have a positive slope in the short run, as we assumed in Figure 8–1(a).

Long-Run Equilibrium   8–6

In the short run, at least one factor input is fixed. In the long run, however, *all* factor inputs are variable. In the long run, therefore, every firm can enter into whatever industry it desires, build the plant size it wishes, and employ any method of technology that is available to any other firm. When the firm does not wish to make any changes in either the quantity or the arrangement of its factor inputs, it is said to be in **long-run equilibrium.** When every firm in an industry is in long-run equilibrium and no additional firms wish to enter the industry, then we say that **long-run industry equilibrium** exists. In this section, we will examine the conditions of long-run equilibrium and the attendant implications for efficient resource allocation.

Long-Run Profit Maximization

In the long run, as in the short run, the perfectly competitive firm is assumed to be a profit maximizer. As long as the marginal revenue resulting from the sale of an additional unit of output is greater or less than the marginal cost of producing that unit, the firm is not maximizing profits. Profit maximization occurs when $MC = MR$. In the short run, we assumed that the plant size was fixed and that the relevant marginal cost was the short-run marginal cost SRMC. In the long run, however, all factor inputs are variable, the relevant marginal cost is long-run marginal cost LRMC, and profit maximization occurs when $LRMC = MR$. Since $MR = P$ in perfect competition, the profit-maximization rule in the long run is $LRMC = P$.

The firm's long-run total cost LRTC curve and its total revenue TR curve are drawn in Figure 8–7. Here, the long-run profit-maximizing level of output is Q_0, because at this level of output, the slope of the LRTC curve is equal to the slope of the TR curve, or $LRMC = MR = P$.

Because the long-run total cost curve is the planning curve for the firm, it can never represent a single plant size. In Chapter 7, we saw that the long-run average cost LRAC curve, from which the LRTC curve is derived, is the envelope curve for an infinite number of short-run average cost SRAC curves. Therefore, to make the production of output Q_0 possible, the firm must first build the scale of plant with an SRAC curve that will be just tangent to the LRAC curve at output Q_0, because this is the *only* scale of plant capable of producing output Q_0 under long-run, profit-maximizing marginal cost conditions. Since output Q_0 must be produced at the lowest possible cost if profits are to be maximized, the firm must build the scale of plant whose SRAC curve will be

Figure 8–7
Long-Run Profit Maximization

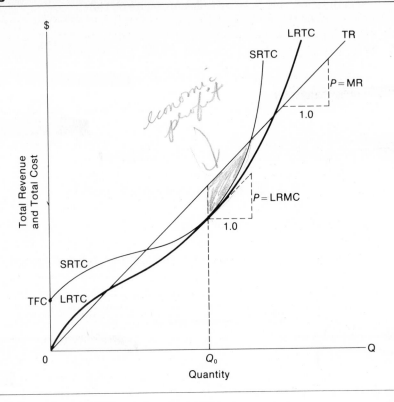

just tangent to the LRAC curve at output Q_0. The fact that the SRAC curve is tangent to the LRAC curve at output Q_0 implies that SRTC = LRTC at Q_0, since

$$\text{SRAC} = \frac{\text{SRTC}}{Q_0} = \frac{\text{LRTC}}{Q_0} = \text{LRAC} \qquad (8\text{--}10)$$

or

$$\text{SRTC} = \text{SRAC} \cdot Q_0 = \text{LRAC} \cdot Q_0 = \text{LRTC} \qquad (8\text{--}11)$$

This conclusion is shown graphically in Figure 8–7 where the SRTC curve corresponding to the scale of plant that must be built to maximize profits in the long run is drawn so that the condition SRTC = LRTC at output Q_0 is satisfied.

We can now derive an additional condition, which must be satisfied for the firm to be in long-run equilibrium. Since the short-run average cost for the scale of plant that maximizes long-run profits lies *above* the long-run average cost curve at *every* level of output greater than or less than Q_0, it necessarily follows that the SRTC curve in Figure 8–7 must lie *above* the LRTC curve at all levels of output greater than or less than Q_0. But since SRTC = LRTC at output Q_0, the SRTC curve and the LRTC curve must be tangent at output Q_0, as shown in the figure. The slopes of these two curves are therefore equal at output Q_0, and long-run profit maximization for the firm will occur when SRMC = LRMC = MR = P.

Long-Run Industry Equilibrium

We have just proved that a perfectly competitive firm maximizes profits in the long run by producing the level of output where SRMC = LRMC = P. Given the characteristics of a perfectly competitive industry, we can determine the scale of plant that each firm will construct when the industry is in long-run equilibrium.

Suppose that the initial positions of the industry and the representative firm are as illustrated in Figure 8–8. The intersection of market demand curve D_0D_0 and industry supply curve S_0S_0 in Figure 8–8(a) yields an initial market price of $\bar{P}_0$. At this price, the representative firm in Figure 8–8(b) will build a scale of plant represented by $SRAC_0$ and produce output $\hat{Q}_0$. The firm will be maximizing long-run profits, since LRMC = SRMC = MR = P. However, note that since $\bar{P}_0 = SRAC_0$, the firm will achieve no pure profits.

Now suppose that market demand increases to D_1D_1, as shown in Figure

Figure 8–8
Long-Run Industry Equilibrium

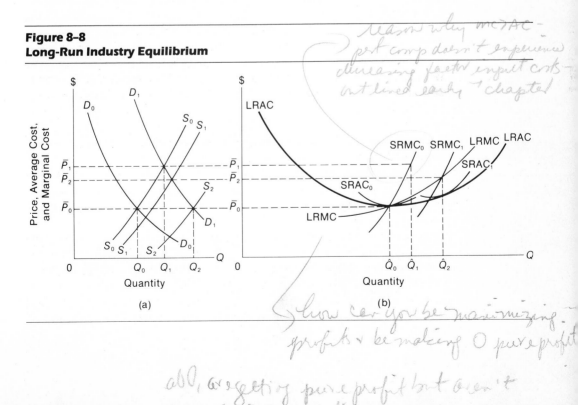

(handwritten margin note: how can you make a profit if your marg cost > avg cost?)

8–8(a), so that the market price becomes $\bar{P}_1$. In the short run, existing firms in the industry will expand output up to the point where $SRMC_0 = \bar{P}_1$. At this short-run maximizing output of $\hat{Q}_1$ in Figure 8–8(b), the firm will now make pure profits, since $\bar{P}_1 > SRAC_0$ at output $\hat{Q}_1$.

Suppose for the moment that firms outside the industry are not attracted to the industry in the long run, even though pure profits prevail. The existing firms in the industry will attempt to build a scale of plant such that $LRMC = SRMC = \bar{P}_1$ in the long run. However, as they try to accomplish this goal, the increased production capacity of each firm will shift the market supply curve to the right. If

Example 8–1

(handwritten margin note: Cartels/Producers want barriers in form of import quotas)

Taxicabs in Chicago: Part I

Pure profits in a perfectly competitive industry are short-lived because other firms will be attracted to the industry. The entry of these firms into the industry drives down the market price as supply is increased, and the pure profits disappear in the long run. This is a strong incentive for existing firms to erect barriers to entry and to transform the industry into something that is a far cry from perfect competition. A standard technique is for the existing firms to convince the local, state, or federal government to regulate the industry by means of a licensing law and to fix the number of permissible licenses at the number of firms currently existing in the industry.

An example of this practice is the licensing of taxicabs in Chicago, New York City, Baltimore, and Boston. To legally operate a taxicab in these cities, the cab owner must possess a license issued by the city, and because the total number of licenses is fixed, there is an almost total barrier to the entry of additional owners. If you wish to enter the taxicab business legally, you must purchase a license from an owner who is leaving the business. The current price of these licenses is about $40,000 in Boston and $50,000 in New York.[*] These very high entry fees reflect the capitalized value of the pure profits accrued by the first owners of the licenses. Therefore, we should not be surprised to find daring entrepreneurs either operating taxicabs without a license or providing services that are prohibited under the ordinance that regulates the industry.

By ordinance, the number of taxicab licenses in the city of Chicago is limited to 4,600.[†] Although this ordinance requires that taxicabs operate throughout Chicago, many drivers, both black and white, refuse to take passengers into the poorer black areas of the city. Chicago cab drivers argue that it is too hazardous to operate in these neighborhoods, but another

[*]Walter Williams, "Government-Sanctioned Restraints That Reduce Economic Opportunities for Minorities," *Policy Review* (Fall 1977), pp. 1–29.
[†]The data in this example pertaining to taxicabs in Chicago are taken from Edmund W. Kitch, Marc Isaacson, and Daniel Kasper, "Regulation of Taxicabs in Chicago," *Journal of Law and Economics* (October 1971), pp. 285–350.

no new firms enter the industry, the resulting supply curve will be S_1S_1 and the market price will be $\bar{P}_2$, as shown in Figure 8–8(a). At price $\bar{P}_2$, all of the original firms in the industry will build a scale of plant represented by $SRAC_1$ and produce output $\hat{Q}_2$, as shown in Figure 8–8(b). Each firm will still enjoy pure profits, since $\bar{P}_2 > SRAC_1$ at output $\hat{Q}_2$, and the conditions for long-run profit maximization for the firm prevail, since $LRMC = SRMC_1 = \bar{P}_2$. But does long-run industry equilibrium prevail?

Unfortunately, for firms in perfect competition, they cannot prevent other firms from entering the industry. The pure profits the original firms are making

important factor may be that the O'Hare Airport and downtown Loop trade is much more profitable. Since fares are uniform throughout the city and cab drivers' wages are a fixed percentage of these fares, it pays them more to work the busiest and safest portions of the city.

The lack of legally licensed taxicabs in poor black neighborhoods presents profit-making opportunities to alert entrepreneurs who are willing to operate illegally. In 1969, about 300 such illegal or "gypsy" cabs were operating on Chicago's black near-west side. There is little risk of arrest for drivers who engage in this illegal activity, however, because the ordinance is not enforced in these neighborhoods. If the taxicabs leave their neighborhood and venture into the Loop area, however, their illegal operations are no longer tolerated. These gypsy cabs operate out of such enterprises as grocery and record stores and are often dispatched by CB radios.

Another attempt to provide taxicab service in the black neighborhoods of south Chicago is centered along King Drive between about 28th and 63rd Streets. There, licensed taxicabs called "jitneys" drive up and down streets picking up passengers until they are full, thereby ignoring the group-riding ban of the Chicago taxi ordinance. Like buses, the jitneys charge a fixed fee for any distance along King Drive—a violation of the taximeter requirements of the ordinance. Unlike buses, however, for an additional fee, the jitneys will deliver passengers directly to their door if it is nearby. This service is widely used, because the jitney fare for any distance along King Drive in 1971 was $.25 (with an additional $.25 for a drop-off), compared to the $.45 fare charged by buses operated by the Chicago Transit Authority. This illegal activity is tacitly endorsed by the city. The Public Vehicle Commissioner has even gone so far as to informally request that all jitneys be painted blue and gray, so that they can be identified more easily.

This example illustrates the great difficulty of uniformly enforcing laws that are designed to reduce competition. In Chapter 9, we will see that the Chicago taxicab ordinance provides pure or *monopoly* profits for a group of individuals who control 80% of the licensed taxicab fleets in the city. Since the licensed taxicabs do not operate in the poorer black neighborhoods, illegal operations do not cut into these profits, and they are therefore tolerated—if not encouraged.

at $\bar{P}_2$ serve as a signal to firms outside the industry that are making only normal profits to shift their capital into this industry. As new firms enter in perfect
competition, the industry supply curve in Figure 8–8(a) shifts to the right, driving down the price at which the product can be sold. The supply curve will continue to shift to the right until pure profits become 0; only at this level of profits
will new firms stop entering the industry. When this happens, the result is said
to be in **long-run industry equilibrium.** This occurs in Figure 8–8(a) at the
point where industry supply curve S_2S_2 intersects market demand curve D_1D_1
at price $\bar{P}_0$. At price $\bar{P}_0$, each firm in the industry will be operating a scale of
plant represented by $SRAC_0$, and since $LRMC = SRMC_0 = \bar{P}_0$, each firm will be
maximizing long-run profits. Moreover, since $SRAC_0 = \bar{P}_0$, each firm's pure profit
will be 0. Thus, if a perfectly competitive industry is in long-run equilibrium,
then $LRMC = SRMC = P = SRAC$.

Long-Run Equilibrium of the Firm

If all firms in an industry attempt to maximize profits and there are no barriers to entry, market forces produce long-run industry equilibrium. We now
know that when the market price is such that pure profits are accrued by
existing firms, additional firms enter the industry. This shifts the market supply curve to the right and causes the market price to decline, thereby reducing
the pure profits of firms in the industry and the desire of outside firms to enter
the industry. Firms continue to enter the industry and pure profits continue to
decline until the market price is just equal to the minimum long-run average
cost and pure profits disappear. When the market price is initially *below* the
minimum long-run average cost, pure profits are *negative* and firms leave the
industry, causing the market price to rise until normal profits result.

The long-run equilibrium of a firm in a perfectly competitive industry in long-
run equilibrium is illustrated in Figure 8–9. When the market price is $\bar{P}$, the
profit-maximizing output is $\bar{Q}$, which produces only normal profits or no pure
profits. At price $\bar{P}$, firms within the industry have no desire to expand their
scale of operations and outside firms have no incentive to enter the industry.

If the market price were below $\bar{P}$, firms would sustain *pure losses* and
would leave the industry, which would cause the market supply curve to shift
to the left and the market price to rise. If the market price were above $\bar{P}$, pure
profits would result, new firms would enter the industry, and the market price
would decline. Long-run industry equilibrium exists when firms are not
entering or leaving the industry. Thus, there are no pure profits when the
industry is in long-run equilibrium. When there are no pure profits, it necessarily follows that average revenue (the market price) must be equal to the
long-run average total cost, which, under conditions of long-run industry
equilibrium, can only occur when each firm is operating at the minimum point
on its long-run average cost LRAC curve. This conclusion is shown in Figure
8–9, where at price $\bar{P}$ and output $\bar{Q}$, $LRMC = SRMC = LRAC = SRAC = MR = P$.

Figure 8–9
Long-Run Equilibrium of a Perfectly Competitive Firm

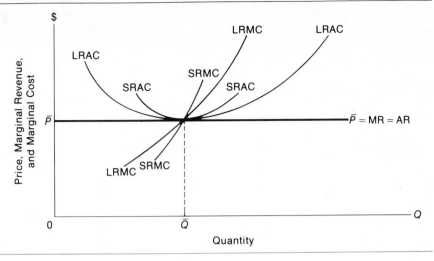

Constant-Cost and Increasing-Cost Industries   8–7

Until this point in our examination of long-run equilibrium, we have implicitly assumed that the cost of factor inputs remains constant. We will now explicitly explore the ramifications of this assumption under the condition of expanding market demand. We will also consider the effect of increasing factor input costs. The effect of decreasing factor input costs is not consistent with all of the assumptions of perfect competition made earlier in this chapter and will not be examined here.[5]

Constant-Cost Industries

Our analysis in Section 8–6 was based on the implicit assumption that the cost of the factor inputs remained the same regardless of the number and size of the firms in a given industry. Such an industry is called a **constant-cost indus-try.** Figure 8–11 illustrates a constant-cost industry that is initially in long-run equilibrium. The initial market price of $\bar{P}_1$ is determined by market supply and demand curves S_1S_1 and D_1D_1 in Figure 8–11(a). This firm is shown to be in long-run equilibrium in Figure 8–11(b), producing quantity $\hat{Q}_1$ at price $\bar{P}_1$.

Now we will suppose that market demand shifts to the right, increasing from D_1D_1 to D_2D_2 and causing the market price to temporarily rise from $\bar{P}_1$ to P_2,

[5]For a discussion of this interesting but complicated effect, see Milton Friedman, *Price Theory* (Chicago: Aldine, 1976), pp. 97–106.

as shown in Figure 8–11(a). In the short run, each firm will maximize profits by equating SRMC and P_2. The output of each firm will therefore increase from $\hat{Q}_1$ to $\hat{Q}_2$, and pure profits, indicated by the shaded area in Figure 8–11(b) will result. This outcome is only temporary, however. The existence of pure profits will attract new firms to this industry, and the market supply curve in Figure 8–11(a) will shift to the right.

Since we are considering the case of a constant-cost industry, the entrance of new firms does not result in an increase in the cost of factor inputs. Therefore, despite the fact that the number of firms in the industry has increased, both the old and the new average cost and marginal cost curves for each firm will remain constant, as shown in Figure 8–11(b).

When long-run equilibrium is finally reestablished, the market supply curve

Example 8-2

Competition and Discrimination

In the long run, a perfectly competitive firm will be making no pure profits. Any employment practice of a perfectly competitive firm that substitutes a less-qualified worker for a more-qualified worker due to discrimination on the basis of race or sex places the firm at a disadvantage with respect to firms that do not discriminate. The discriminating firm will incur higher costs because it employs less-qualified workers and will eventually be forced out of the industry. But firms that operate in markets that are not perfectly competitive, where long-run pure profits are possible, could conceivably maintain permanent discriminatory employment practices. Based on our theory of the perfectly competitive firm, we would therefore predict that racial and sex discrimination in hiring will increase as we move from more competitive to less competitive industries.

In a study to test this prediction, William G. Shepherd* examined the percentage of black white-collar employees in 46 industries in nine major U.S. cities. The lack of competitiveness in each industry was determined by the use of a four-firm concentration ratio—a ratio that measures the percentage of an industry's sales (or assets or value added) that are accounted for by the industry's four largest firms. A higher industry concentration ratio indicates a smaller amount of competitiveness in that industry. If our theory is correct, we would expect to find a negative correlation between the percentage of black white-collar workers and the industry concentration ratio.

Figure 8–10 summarizes one of the most revealing results of the Shepherd study. This graph indicates the percentage of blacks employed as officials, managers, and professionals in 46 U.S. manufacturing and service industries in 1966. Each plotted point on this graph represents one or more industries. For every additional 20 concentration points, there is a 30–40%

*William G. Shepherd, "Market Power and Racial Discrimination in White-Collar Employment," *Antitrust Bulletin* (Spring 1969), pp. 141–61.

S_2S_2 again intersects the market demand curve D_2D_2 at the initial price of $\bar{P}_1$, and each firm returns to producing quantity $\hat{Q}_1$ in Figure 8–11(b). Thus, for the constant-cost industry in Figure 8–11, the quantity supplied in the long run will always sell for price $\bar{P}_1$, and the long-run industry supply curve is the horizontal line that intersects the horizontal axis at price $\bar{P}_1$, or line S_{LR} in Figure 8–11(a).

Increasing-Cost Industries

In an **increasing-cost industry,** the cost of factor inputs increases as the number of firms in the industry increases. The rise in factor input price results from the fact that the supply of at least one production input is not infinitely price-

reduction in the black share of white-collar employment. This data verifies our prediction that racial discrimination tends to decrease as industries tend to be more competitive.

Figure 8–10
Relationship Between Industry Concentration
and Blacks Employed as Officials, Managers, and Professionals

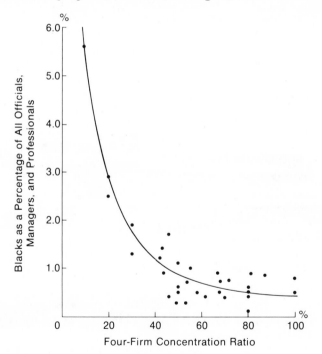

SOURCE: William G. Shepherd, "Market Power and Racial Discrimination in White-Collar Employment," *Antitrust Bulletin* (Spring 1969), p. 156.

Figure 8–11
Long-Run Adjustment in a Constant-Cost Industry

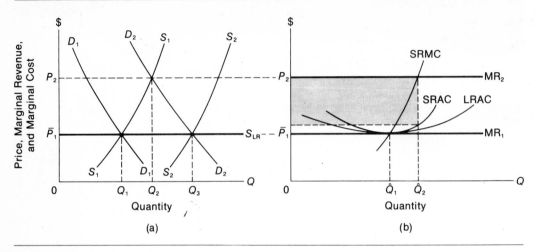

Quantity
(a)

Quantity
(b)

elastic, so that the cost of this input must rise to increase the quantity supplied to satisfy the increased demand of an increasing number of firms.

The initial long-run equilibrium conditions are illustrated in Figure 8–12. The intersection of the market supply and demand curves $S_1 S_1$ and $D_1 D_1$ in Figure 8–12(a) determines the initial market price of $\bar{P}_1$. In Figure 8–12(b), the firm is shown to be in long-run equilibrium, producing quantity $\hat{Q}_1$ at price $\bar{P}_1$.

As we did in our example of the constant-cost industry, we will suppose that market demand shifts to the right, increasing from $D_1 D_1$ to $D_2 D_2$ in Figure 8–12(a) and causing the market price to rise to P_2. As before, output increases from Q_1 to Q_2 in response to increased demand, as all firms increase output in the short run by moving upward along their short-run supply curves, represented by $SRMC_1$. This increased output in the short run generates pure profits for each firm, because average revenue exceeds average cost.

As pure profits attract new firms to an increasing-cost industry, the cost of one or more factor inputs rises, causing the short- and long-run cost curves of new as well as existing firms to shift upward. Also in the long run, the market supply curve shifts to the right as new firms enter the industry, which causes the market price to drop below P_2. The final long-run equilibrium position that results from the increase in demand produces the short-run market supply curve $S_2 S_2$ in Figure 8–12(a), which intersects demand curve $D_2 D_2$ at price $\bar{P}_3$. At price $\bar{P}_3$, which is below P_2 but *above* $\bar{P}_1$, the firm is again in long-run equilibrium, producing quantity $\hat{Q}_3$, as shown in Figure 8–12(b).

In a constant-cost industry, firms continue to enter the industry until the market price returns to its initial level, or the minimum long-run average cost of the firm. In an increasing-cost industry, the market price cannot return

Figure 8–12
Long-Run Adjustment in an Increasing-Cost Industry

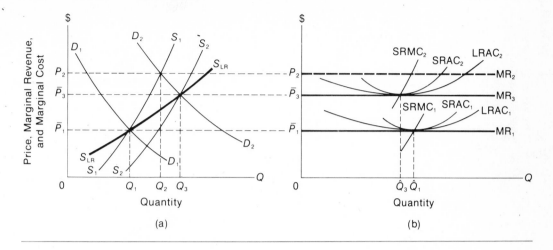

(a)

(b)

to its initial level, because the LRAC curve shifts upward in response to the increase in input costs and the minimum point on the LRAC curve shifts upward as well. Thus, the long-run equilibrium price increases in response to an increase in market demand. The long-run supply curve for the increasing-cost industry is therefore upward sloping in contrast to the horizontal long-run supply curve for the constant-cost industry. The long-run supply curve for the increasing-cost industry in this example is given by the positively sloped line S_{LR} in Figure 8–12(a).

Application: Economic Rent

One of the problems confronting British economists in the early nineteenth century was the need to provide an explanation for the rents received by land-owners. One particularly confusing aspect of this problem was that the land-lords earned dissimilar rates of profit from renting their lands and that the farmers who rented the land tended to earn the same rate of profit.

We can readily explain these issues if we relax our assumption that all factor inputs of a particular kind are equal. For example, suppose that two grades of land are available for cultivation. Grade I land is more fertile and will naturally be tilled before Grade II land. As long as some Grade I land remains uncultivated, the long-run supply curve of the food products obtained from this land will be horizontal at price $\bar{P}_1$, as shown in Figure 8–13(a). $\bar{P}_1$ is the minimum long-run average cost of production on Grade I land. Since $\bar{P}_2$—the minimum long-run average cost of production on Grade II land—is greater than $\bar{P}_1$,

Figure 8–13
Variable Factor Input Quality and Economic Rent

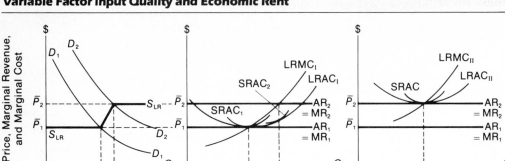

| (a) | (b) | (c) |
| Market | Grade I Land | Grade II Land |

Grade II land will not be cultivated until the market price of the food products reaches $\bar{P}_2$. As long as the market price of the food is $\bar{P}_1$, each farm will be operating at output $\hat{Q}_1$, which corresponds to the minimum point on the $LRAC_I$ curve in Figure 8–13(b). At price $\bar{P}_1$, there are no pure profits, so that the rental payments the landowners are receiving from the farmers just equal the opportunity cost of renting the land. The farmers are also receiving an income that just equals the opportunity cost of being employed in the production of food.

Now suppose that the population increases and that eventually market demand becomes equal to demand curve D_1D_1, as shown in Figure 8–13(a). The price of the food will still be $\bar{P}_1$. As soon as demand becomes greater than D_1D_1, however, the price of the food must rise, because all of the Grade I land will then be cultivated. But the cultivation of Grade II land will not be begun until demand increases to D_2D_2 and the price of the food reaches $\bar{P}_2$, because $\bar{P}_2$ is the minimum long-run average cost of production on Grade II land. Farming Grade II land when the price is less than $\bar{P}_2$ would result in pure losses, because the average revenue would be less than the average cost. Between prices $\bar{P}_1$ and $\bar{P}_2$, farms on Grade I land will expand output by moving along the $LRMC_I$ curve in Figure 8–13(b). The long-run supply S_{LR} curve between industry outputs Q_1 and Q_2 in Figure 8–13(a) therefore has a positive slope.

When demand becomes greater than D_1D_1, the average cost of farming on Grade I land becomes less than the average revenue, and long-run pure profits result because all of Grade I land, which is in absolutely fixed supply, is completely cultivated. All of the long-run pure profits will be accrued by the landowners, since competition among farmers bids up the rent they are willing to pay for Grade I land in response to the rising market price until they are receiving only normal profits from farming. The profits to landlords from renting out Grade I land now become greater than the opportunity cost of renting this land, because the landlords own a resource that is in absolutely fixed supply. Economists refer to such returns as **pure rent** or, more simply, **rent.**

When the market demand curve shifts to D_2D_2, the market price becomes $\bar{P}_2$. Each farmer on Grade I land will be operating a farm size represented by SRAC$_2$ and be producing output $\hat{Q}_2$, as shown in Figure 8–13(b). In the long run, Grade I farmland is farmed more intensively. In other words, more labor and capital will be devoted to the cultivation of the existing supply of Grade I land. As this occurs, the average farm size on Grade I land, measured in terms of its labor and capital content, will increase and operate beyond the minimum point on SRAC$_2$ in Figure 8–13(b). If demand increases beyond D_2D_2, Grade II land will begin to be cultivated and the long-run supply curve for the food produced will again become horizontal. However, this time the S_{LR} curve will be horizontal at price $\bar{P}_2$, as shown in Figure 8–13(a), as long as some Grade II land exists that is not being farmed.

If the market price does not become greater than $\bar{P}_2$, owners of Grade II land do not receive any pure rent because no pure profits result from the cultivation of this land. Both the owners and tenants of Grade II land and the tenants of Grade I land will be receiving a return just equal to their opportunity costs, or normal profits. Owners of Grade I land, however, will be receiving a return in excess of the minimum amount necessary to induce them to rent Grade I land to farmers.

Thus, the answer to the question posed by early nineteenth-century British economists concerning the dissimilar rates of return to landowners and the equal rates of return to farmers can be found in the existence of factors of production with a fixed supply. All landowners do not own the same grade of land, and the quantities of the various grades of land are fixed. Landowners with better grades of land will receive higher rates of return. Farmers, on the other hand, must compete among themselves to lease the available land. Because farmers bid up the rental price to the point at which their average cost equals their average revenue, the rate of return received by all farmers is the normal rate of return.

The basic idea that economic rent can be accrued to a factor of production (land) that is fixed in the long run has been applied by economists to factors of production that are fixed in the short run. The return on resources that are fixed in the short run is determined by the residual that is left after the variable factors have been paid; the payment of variable factors is determined by the amount that they could earn in alternative employments. Returns in excess of opportunity costs to factors of production that are fixed in the short run are called **quasi-rents.** If the factor input is only fixed or immobile in the short run, quasi-rent for that input will disappear in the long run as the quantity of the input in a given employment expands in the long run in response to greater than average rates of return.

**Example
8-3**

Short-Run Quasi-Rents to Professors

We have just pointed out that above-normal returns to a factor of production with a fixed supply in the short run are called *quasi-rents*. This situation can occur when the demand for a factor input such as labor rapidly increases but the supply of that input lags behind because a time period is required to train workers.

Such an event took place in the academic profession in the 1960s when college enrollments rapidly increased as a result of the World War II baby boom. The effect on the annual salaries of economics professors was particularly pronounced. Figure 8–14 illustrates the quasi- or short-run rents received by professors of economics beginning with the 1963/64 academic year. The salaries are in constant 1967 dollars deflated by the Consumer Price Index.

Figure 8–14 reveals that the salaries of economics professors rose rapidly in the 1960s, peaking approximately in the 1969/70 academic year, and then declined in the late 1970s to about the same median level as salaries at the beginning of the period of rapid enrollment increases. The decline in salaries resulted from an increased production of doctorates in economics, as labor factors responded to above-normal returns in the economics profession. The fact that it takes four or five years to produce a PhD economist explains the payment of quasi-rents to academic economists. Once the new PhDs began to emerge, the quasi-rents began to disappear.

Application: Long-Run Equilibrium in Agriculture

Economists often cite agriculture as an industry that approximates the assumptions of a perfectly competitive industry for the following reasons:

1. The industry is comprised of a large number of firms (farms), none of which is large enough to influence the market price of the product it produces.
2. The products produced by the farms are graded into standardized, homogeneous products (for example, No. 2 hard red winter wheat).
3. There are a large number of expert buyers of farm products in the commodity markets, where prices are established under conditions approaching perfect knowledge.
4. Barriers to entry into the farm industry are relatively minor.

In this application, we will examine the long-run behavior of agricultural firms to see if they behave in a manner consistent with the assumptions of a perfectly competitive model.

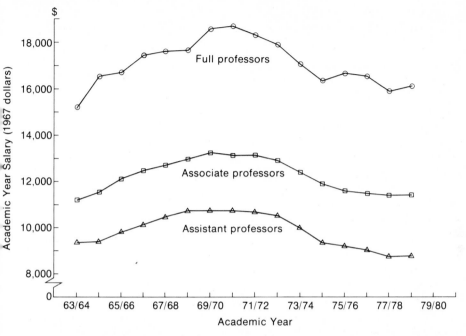

Figure 8–14
Median Real Salaries of Professors of Economics

SOURCE: Calculated from *Annual Survey of Economics Departments,* conducted by Francis M. Boddy, University of Minnesota.

In 1947, the annual income of the average farm worker was $3,029 in constant 1972 dollars, while a comparable worker in nonfarm production earned an average annual income of $7,545. The productivity per worker in nonfarm production was therefore more than twice the productivity per farmer in agriculture. These figures suggest that, in 1947, the opportunity cost of the resources being employed in agriculture on marginal farms was greater than the revenue these farms yielded. In other words, the resources employed on these marginal farms would have yielded higher incomes if they had been employed elsewhere. Because the opportunity existed for the owners of these resources to improve their economic condition, we know that the agricultural industry could not have been in long-run market equilibrium in 1947. The perfectly competitive model predicts that in situations such as this, firms (farms) will leave the industry and employ their labor and capital in other areas of economic activity that will yield higher profits. In addition, as firms leave the agricultural industry, the market supply curve will shift to the left, causing the market price to rise. This will increase the income per worker of those firms remaining in agriculture, and the spread between the annual income per worker in farm and nonfarm production will be narrowed.

Figure 8–15
The Percentage of the U.S. Labor Force Engaged in Farming, 1947–1978

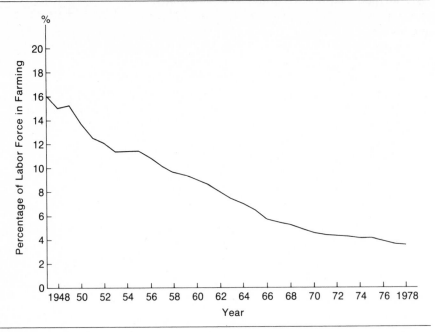

SOURCE: *Economic Report of the President 1979* (Washington, D.C.: U.S. Government Printing Office, 1979), p. 214.

Figure 8–15 shows the long-run trend of the fraction of the labor force employed in agriculture. In 1947, 16% of the labor force was engaged in farming; 30 years later, in 1978, less than 4% of all U.S. laborers were farmers. In absolute numbers, the farm workforce declined from 7,890,000 in 1947 to 3,342,000 in 1978 while the nonfarm workforce rose from 49,148,000 to 91,031,000 during the same period. These results are consistent with our perfectly competitive model. The average income produced per worker in farm and nonfarm activities from 1947 to 1978 is graphed in Figure 8–16. The spread between annual farm and nonfarm income in 1947 was $4,516, but this difference had declined to $2,864 by 1978, measured in dollars of constant 1972 purchasing power. This result is also in accordance with the predictions of our model.

Figure 8–17 graphs the number of U.S. farms during the 1947–1978 period. The total number has declined 54% from 5,871,000 farms in 1947 to 2,680,000 in 1978. Once again, this is consistent with the predictions of our model.

Finally, we would expect the marginal and least profitable farms to be the smaller farms. As these farms cease to exist, the average number of acres per farm should tend to increase, as is shown to be the case in Figure 8–18. But Figure 8–18 also indicates that the average number of acres farmed per worker has risen proportionately with the rising size of the average farm. This dramatic increase in the number of acres tilled per worker *cannot* be due entirely to the reduction in the number of farms. This increase is primarily the consequence of technological improvements that have made production methods more efficient.

The primary source of technological improvement in agricultural production has been agricultural equipment manufacturers, chemical firms, seed producers, pharmaceutical firms, and other suppliers of inputs to the farmer. A secondary source has been government-subsidized laboratories and agricultural experiment stations. Most of the technological innovations in agriculture have resulted in the replacement of labor by capital. For example, the average real value of farm-productive assets per worker (measured in 1958 dollars) rose 2⅓ times from $26,000 per worker in 1964 to $63,000 per worker

Figure 8–16
Average U.S. Farm and Nonfarm Gross Income per Worker, 1947–1978

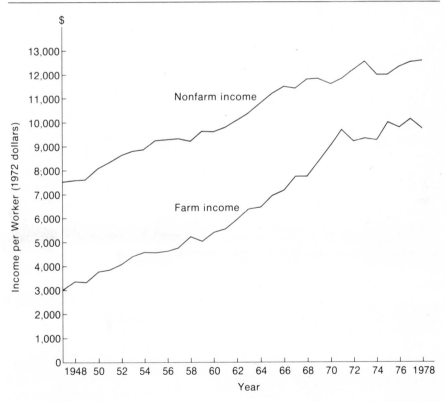

DATA SOURCE: *Economic Report of the President 1979* (Washington, D.C.: U.S. Government Printing Office, 1979), pp. 195, 214.

Figure 8-17
Number of U.S. Farms, 1947-1978

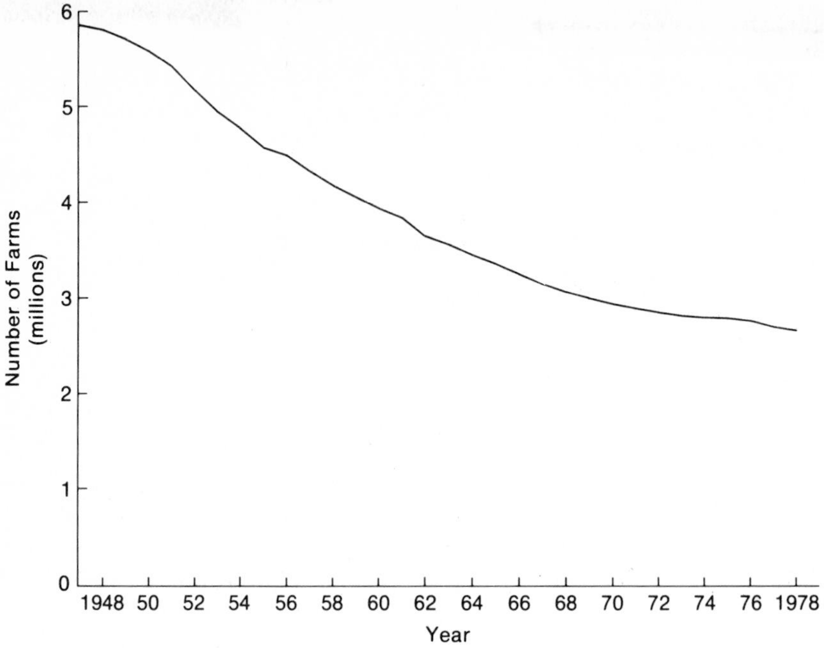

DATA SOURCE: *Statistical Abstract of the United States 1978* (Washington, D.C.: U.S. Government Printing Office, 1978), p. 686.

in 1974.[6] In terms of our model, these capital-intensive technological changes have resulted in reductions in variable input costs but have increased fixed input costs in such areas as interest payments, depreciation, and taxes. Consequently, a larger total output is necessary if the potential for a lower average cost per unit of output is to be realized, and this in turn has also contributed to the increase in the size of the average farm.

Technological improvements in farming have played an even more significant role in reducing the number of workers required per acre. This results from the fact that the demand for basic farm products as a whole has very low price- and income-elasticities, as we found in Chapter 3. Thus, an increase in the total national consumption of farm products depends primarily on the growth in the total population. Under these market conditions, if the growth in farm labor productivity occurs at a faster rate than the growth in population, fewer workers will be required over time. This conclusion can be easily shown with the aid of the identity

[6]Daniel B. Suits, "Agriculture," in Walter Adams (ed.), *The Structure of American Industry* (New York: Macmillan, 1977), p. 30.

Figure 8–18
Average U.S. Farm Size and Acres per Worker, 1947–1978

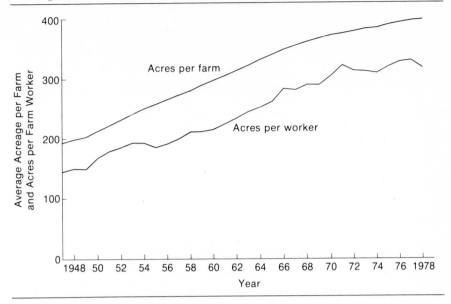

DATA SOURCE: *Statistical Abstract of the United States 1978* (Washington, D.C.: U.S. Government Printing Office, 1978), p. 686.

$$CN \equiv OW$$

where

C = per-capita consumption of farm products
N = total population
O = output of farm products per farm worker
W = total number of farm workers

This identity merely states that the total amount of farm products consumed CN must be equal to the total quantity of farm products produced OW. By rearranging this identity and assuming that the per-capita consumption of farm products is a constant and therefore unaffected by technological progress, we obtain the equation

$$\frac{W}{N} = \frac{C}{O}$$

which tells us that the fraction of the population engaged in farming W/N depends only on the per-capita consumption of farm products and on the productivity per farm worker. Because C is assumed to be unaffected by changes in agricultural technology, it necessarily follows that the ratio of farm workers to the total population must decline as the productivity of farm labor rises. In general, this has been true of U.S. farm labor. In 1947, 5.5% of the total U.S. population was employed in the agricultural industry, but by 1978 this number had declined to only 1.5%.

Thus, the forces of the competitive agricultural market during the 1947–1978 period reduced the total number of U.S. farms, increased the average size of the farms, reduced the number of farm workers, and increased the number of acres cultivated per worker. This resulted in the reallocation of productive resources of labor and capital from farm to nonfarm production, where they could be employed more efficiently, and greatly reduced the gap between the annual income per worker in farm and nonfarm production.

8-8 Summary

In Chapter 8, we have examined the economic theory of *perfect competition*. This very abstract vision of a market economy is based on the following assumptions:

1. All buyers and sellers are *price takers*.
2. In a given industry, an *identical product* is produced by all firms.
3. *Perfect factor mobility* exists within each industry; that is, all factors of production are completely mobile, and there are no barriers to entering or leaving any given industry.
4. *Complete knowledge* is available to all participants in the market.

From this set of assumptions, we have seen that although the market demand curve for an industry displays the normal characteristic of negative slope, the demand curve for the perfectly competitive firm is horizontal at the market-determined price. Because the firm's demand curve is horizontal, the *marginal revenue* and *average revenue* curves for a perfectly competitive firm are identical to its demand curve.

We have learned that the goal of the perfectly competitive firm is assumed to be the maximization of profits, where *profits* are defined as the difference between the firm's total revenue and its total cost. When profits are defined in this manner by economists, they are said to be *normal profits* if they are 0 and *pure profits* if the firm's total revenue exceeds its total cost.

Next we saw that a firm that maximizes profits in the short run will equate short-run marginal cost and marginal revenue (SRMC = MR) or, in other words, will equate short-run marginal cost and market price (SRMC $=\bar{P}$). As market price rises, the firm moves outward and to the right along its short-run marginal cost curve, so that the portion of the SRMC curve that lies above the minimum point on the average variable cost AVC curve is the *short-run supply curve* of the firm. When input prices are constant, the *market supply curve* is merely the horizontal summation of the supply curves of the individual firms that make up the industry. If input prices are a function of market supply, the construction of the market supply curve is more complex, but we demonstrated that although the slope of the market supply curve becomes steeper, it remains positive.

We have learned that *long-run equilibrium* in perfect competition is also dependent on the profit-maximizing behavior of firms. When *long-run industry equilibrium* occurs, firms desire neither to leave nor to enter the industry because all firms are receiving normal profits. This occurs in the long run, when profit-maximizing firms equate long-run marginal cost and market price and each firm operates at the minimum point on its long-run average cost LRAC curve. When this occurs, the scale of plant constructed will operate at the minimum point on the firm's short-run average cost SRAC curve and LRMC = SRMC = LRAC = SRAC = MR = AR = P.

[handwritten marginal note: 0 profit when LRMC = p at minimum LRAC]

[handwritten note: = pt Li, at S, P > SRAC = economic profit]

We have also examined the characteristics of long-run industry supply curves when market demand is allowed to vary. The two cases of *constant-cost* and *increasing-cost industries* were considered. We concluded that the long-run supply curve is horizontal for the constant-cost industry, but that it is positively sloped for the increasing-cost industry.

We have learned that the term *rent*, like *profit*, is defined very specifically by economists. *Economic rent* is a return on a factor of production that is in excess of the factor's opportunity cost and results only if the factor is in fixed supply in the long run. A factor of production that is fixed in the short run but not in the long run is said to receive *quasi-rent* when its return exceeds its opportunity cost. Quasi-rents become 0 in the long run as the supply of factors increases.

We then applied the theory of perfect competition to an examination of the agricultural industry, which closely approximates the assumptions of a perfectly competitive industry. Given the large disparity in U.S. farm and nonfarm incomes in 1947, the perfectly competitive model predicts the reallocation of resources from farm to nonfarm production and a subsequent trend toward equalization of incomes between the agricultural and nonagricultural sectors. This actually occurred in the U.S. agricultural industry during the 1947–1978 period. In addition, improvements in agricultural technology increased the size of the optimal farm and the average number of acres that could be cultivated per worker. The net result of agricultural resource allocation and technological change was an increase in the average gross income per farm worker from 40% of nonfarm income in 1947 to 77% in 1978.

References

Friedman, Milton. *Price Theory.* Chicago: Aldine, 1976, pp. 85–129.

Henderson, James, and Richard Quandt. *Microeconomics Theory.* New York: McGraw-Hill, 1958, pp. 85–125.

Kitch, Edmund W., Marc Isaacson, and Daniel Kasper. "Regulation of Taxicabs in Chicago." *Journal of Law and Economics* (October 1971), pp. 285–350.

Shepherd, William G. "Market Power and Racial Discrimination in White-Collar Employment." *Antitrust Bulletin* (Spring 1969), pp. 141–61.

Stigler, George J. *The Theory of Price,* 3rd ed. New York: MacMillan, 1966, pp. 247–56.

Suits, Daniel B. "Agriculture." In Walter Adams (ed.). *The Structure of American Industry.* New York: MacMillan, 1977, pp. 1–39.

Williams, Walter. "Government-Sanctioned Restraints That Reduce Economic Opportunities for Minorities." *Policy Review* (Fall 1977), pp. 1–29.

Problems

1. When the price of inputs rises as a perfectly competitive industry expands, we have stated that the market supply curve is positively sloped. Could the long-run market supply curve ever be negatively sloped? Explain.

2. In discussing long-run adjustment for the case of an increasing-cost industry, Figure 8–12(b) illustrates a case in which the minimum point on the firm's LRAC curve shifts to the left as costs increase. Is this always the case, or could the minimum point remain at the same level of output or shift to the right? Explain.

3. Throughout the discussion of perfect competition in this chapter, we have assumed that the LRAC curve is U-shaped. Why is this assumption necessary?

4. When there are barriers to entry in what would otherwise be a perfectly competitive market, pure profits are possible in the long-run. Does it automatically follow that all participants in this market will always receive pure profits? Explain.

5. To simplify our application of economic rent, we assumed that there were only two grades of land. What would the implications for the slope of the long-run supply curve be if this analysis were applied to the real world, where there are a great many grades of farmland?

6. In the Example 8–1, it was pointed out that in cities where the quantity of taxicabs is fixed by law, the cost of obtaining a license to operate a cab is very high. If you were to purchase an existing license and begin driving a cab, do you think that your profits would be normal or pure? Explain.

7. How is it possible for an industry to be a constant-cost industry when each firm in the industry has increasing marginal costs?

8. Suppose that a perfectly competitive industry is in long-run equilibrium and that all firms in the industry are earning no economic profits. If the market price of the industry's product begins to decline, does this mean that all firms will now leave the industry? Explain.

9. In perfect competition, we assume perfect knowledge; but in the real world, knowledge is far from perfect. Given this obvious fact, Nobel Laureate Friedrich A. von Hayek has long argued that the central problem of economics is determining the manner in which an economy should be organized in order to maximize the efficient use of the available imperfect information. Do you agree or disagree with von Hayek? Why?

10. Explain why a perfectly competitive firm might continue to produce and sell its product in the short run, even though the average revenue it received was less than its short-run average total cost.

CHAPTER NINE

PURE MONOPOLY

Introduction 9-1

In this chapter, we will examine the form of market organization that is the polar extreme of perfect competition–pure monopoly. A **pure monopoly** is said to exist when there is a single seller of a product that has no close substitutes. In other words, a given industry is comprised of only one firm, and no products from other industries can readily be used in place of this firm's product. However, we will learn that the fact that a firm is a monopoly does not guarantee that its rate of return will be greater than or equal to the normal rate.

Even though a **monopolist** is the sole firm in an industry, it is still affected by the competitive forces that exist throughout the rest of the economy. This is due to the fact that consumers are constrained with regard to what they can purchase by the finiteness of their budgets. The monopolist must therefore vie with the firms of many other industries for the consumers' expenditures. Furthermore, it is very difficult to cite examples of goods or services that have no close substitutes. For example, the telephone company is often considered to be a pure monopolist, but it only approximates this condition because close substitutes are telegrams, messenger services, mail, and radio communication. If only one firm produced insulin for diabetics, this might approximate the pure monopoly of economic theory in the real world.

Nevertheless, the study of pure monopoly can provide some useful insights into the behavior of firms as market conditions approach those of pure monopoly. These insights have proved especially helpful in establishing public policy toward such industries as the electric, gas, and water utilities that possess monopolistic characteristics.

One additional aspect of monopoly should be mentioned before we proceed. Our definition of pure monopoly states that a given industry contains only one firm. The single firm is a necessary condition, but it is not a sufficient condition to characterize an industry as monopolized. For a firm to have a monopoly–or at least to maintain it for any length of time–barriers must exist to prevent other firms from entering the industry. Otherwise, monopoly profits, if they occur, would immediately attract additional capital to the industry. Barriers to industry entry may take such forms as patents, secret manufacturing processes, and government regulations or franchises.

9-2   Monopoly Demand and Revenue

The monopolist's demand curve is the market demand curve, because the monopolistic firm is the only seller, by definition, of the product produced for that market. Moreover, since the market demand curve is negatively sloped, it follows that the monopolist's demand curve is also negatively sloped, in contrast to the horizontal curve of the perfectly competitive firm. This difference in the slopes of the demand curve of perfectly competitive and monopolistic firms results in important differences in their total revenue and marginal revenue curves.

Total Revenue

To consider these differences, we will examine the simple linear demand curve, which intersects the horizontal and the vertical axes in Figure 9–1(a). In Chapter 3, we showed that such a demand curve has the following characteristics with respect to the price elasticity of demand:

1. At the vertical intercept, the price elasticity of demand is infinite ($E = \infty$), or perfectly *elastic.*
2. Price elasticity of demand declines as we move down the demand curve, reaching the value of unity ($E = 1$) exactly halfway down the curve.
3. Price elasticity of demand is less than 1 ($E < 1$) from the midpoint of the curve to the horizontal axis and becomes 0 ($E = 0$), or perfectly *inelastic* at the horizontal axis.

Thus, demand is elastic between the vertical intercept and the midpoint of the demand curve and demand is inelastic between the midpoint and the horizontal intercept. In Chapter 3, we also examined the effect on total revenue when the price of a product is reduced. In the elastic region of the demand curve, a price reduction will increase total revenue; in the inelastic region, a price reduction will decrease total revenue. Given this information, we can now determine the shape of the monopolist's total revenue curve.

As we move down the demand curve from its vertical intercept, the lower prices of the product elicit a demand response such that the percentage increase in the quantity sold will exceed the percentage reduction in price and total revenue will increase. This result is illustrated in Figure 9–1(b) for levels of output between 0 and Q_1. At output Q_1, however, total revenue reaches its maximum,

Figure 9-1
The Relationship Between Average Revenue and Total Revenue

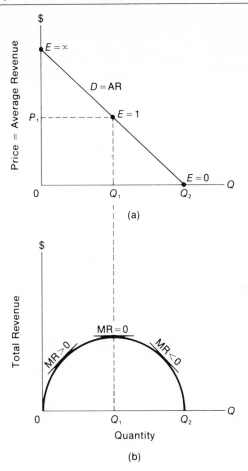

(a)

(b)

because at this point the price must be lower than P_1 to sell additional units of the product. At prices less than P_1 in the inelastic region of the demand curve, the percentage increase in the quantity sold will be less than the percentage reduction in price. Thus, total revenue will decline at outputs greater than Q_1 and reach a minimum value of 0 at output Q_2 when price is 0. This behavior of total revenue is illustrated in Figure 9-1(b) for levels of output between Q_1 and Q_2.

If we compare Figure 9-1(b) with Figure 8-2 (page 256), the difference between the monopolistic firm's total revenue curve and the perfectly competitive firm's total revenue curve becomes readily apparent. The total revenue curve of the perfectly competitive firm shown in Figure 8-2 is a straight line passing through the origin with a slope equal to the market price, whereas the total revenue curve of the monopolistic firm shown in Figure 9–1(b) is concave when viewed from below. This difference in the two curves is due to the fact that the firm in perfect competition can sell as much of its product as it wants at a constant price but that the monopolistic firm must lower its price in order to increase sales. Another way of looking at this result is to realize that the slope of a ray drawn from the origin in Figure 9–1(b) to a point on the total revenue curve is by definition the average revenue at the level of output corresponding to that point. As the points of intersection of additional rays move further to the right, the slopes of these rays must decline. Since the demand curve is also the monopolistic firm's average revenue AR curve, it follows that the condition that the total revenue curve must be concave simply means that the demand curve must have a negative slope. Similarly, it can be demonstrated that the shape of the perfectly competitive firm's TR curve implies that its demand curve must have a slope of 0.

Marginal Revenue

In Chapter 8, we learned that *marginal revenue* is defined as the addition to total revenue that results from the sale of one more unit of output. There we found that a perfectly competitive firm's marginal revenue is equal to the slope of its total revenue curve and that since the slope of its total revenue curve is a constant equal to the market price, the perfectly competitive firm's marginal revenue curve is a horizontal line equal to the market price. The marginal revenue curve of a monopolistic firm is defined in exactly the same manner but has a different shape.

Consider the total revenue curve in Figure 9–1(b). Between levels of output 0 and Q_1, the slope of this curve is positive; therefore marginal revenue MR in this region must also be positive. When output is exactly equal to Q_1, the slope of the total revenue curve is 0, so that MR must also be 0 at output Q_1. At levels of output between Q_1 and Q_2, the total revenue curve assumes a negative slope, and we can conclude that MR must be negative in this region.

Since the demand curve is downward sloping, the monopolistic firm must lower its price in order to sell one more unit. However, because this price reduction applies not only to the marginal unit but to all other units as well, the increase in revenue from selling the additional unit is less than the price charged. Therefore, the monopolistic firm's marginal revenue curve will lie *below* the demand curve. This conclusion can be clarified with the aid of a numerical example. Consider the demand schedule in Table 9–1. The price at which a given quantity of units can be sold is also the monopolistic firm's average revenue resulting from the sale of an additional unit. At a price of $9, the monopolist can sell 2 units. In order to sell 3 units per time period, the price of not only the third unit, but also of the first and second units, must be reduced to $8. Thus, while the monopolistic firm increases its revenue by $8 from the sale of the third unit, it loses $2 in revenue at the same time, because the first and second

Table 9–1
Monopoly Average and Marginal Revenues

UNITS SOLD	PRICE OR AVERAGE REVENUE	TOTAL REVENUE	MARGINAL REVENUE
1	$10	$10	$10
2	9	18	8
3	8	24	6
4	7	28	⟋
5	6	30	2
6	5	30	0
7	4	28	−2
8	3	24	−4
9	2	18	−6
10	1	10	−8

units are now selling for $8 apiece instead of $9. The monopolist's marginal revenue is therefore $6 rather than $8, or less than the firm's average revenue. If sales are expanded, marginal revenue will eventually become negative even though the price is positive. For example, if sales are expanded from 7 to 8 units, the firm will receive $3 for the additional unit sold. But since this requires a $1 reduction in the price of each of the 7 units that could have been sold for $4, the firm's total revenue will be reduced by $4.

At this stage of our discussion, we can say no more concerning the shape and the location of the marginal revenue curve. In the following section, we will learn how to derive the MR curve graphically.

Graphic Derivation of the Marginal Revenue Curve   9–3

Demand curves can be *linear* or *nonlinear*. Once we have learned how to derive the MR curve for the linear demand curve, we can readily adapt the procedure to derive the MR curve for the nonlinear demand curve.

Linear Demand

The graphic derivation of the marginal revenue curve corresponding to a linear demand curve is easy to present. From our examination of marginal revenue in Chapter 3, we know that

$$MR = P\left(1 - \frac{1}{E}\right) \tag{9–1}$$

where P is the price and E is the absolute value of the price elasticity of demand. Because the price elasticity of demand is infinite at the point of intersection of the demand curve and the vertical price axis, we know that $1/E = 0$ at the vertical price intercept and MR = P.

We have now established one point on the MR curve. Since the MR curve for a linear demand curve is also linear,[1] we need to determine only one additional point to construct the MR curve. The second point can be easily determined by setting Equation (9–1) equal to 0 and solving for E, which gives us

$$P\left(1 - \frac{1}{E}\right) = 0$$

$$1 - \frac{1}{E} = 0 \tag{9–2}$$

$$E = 1$$

Thus, when MR = 0, $E = 1$. Recall from Chapter 3 that the price elasticity of demand is equal to 1 at the midpoint of a linear demand curve. The point on the horizontal axis corresponding to $E = 1$ on the demand curve will be one-half the distance between the origin and the horizontal intersection of the demand curve. Since MR = 0 when $E = 1$, the second point on the MR curve will lie one-half the distance between the origin and the horizontal intercept of the demand curve.

Our conclusions concerning the shape and the location of the MR curve are illustrated in Figure 9–2. The linear demand curve intersects the vertical price axis at point P, and this point is also the vertical intercept of the MR curve. Halfway down the demand curve, $E = 1$ at point B, which corresponds to Q_1 on the horizontal axis. Point Q_1, in turn, is midway between the origin and Q_2, which is the horizontal intercept of the demand curve. The MR curve is the heavy dashed line connecting points P and Q_1 in Figure 9–2.

Since the MR curve and the demand curve have the same vertical intercept and the horizontal intercept of the MR curve is one-half that of the demand curve, it follows that the slope of the MR curve will be two times the slope of the demand curve.[2]

The fact that the slope of the MR curve is twice the slope of the demand curve provides us with an alternative method for graphically determining the

---

[1]This result can be shown with the aid of calculus. Given the linear demand curve

$$P = a - bQ$$

total revenue is

$$TR = PQ = (a - bQ)Q = aQ - bQ^2$$

and marginal revenue is

$$\frac{dTR}{dQ} = a - 2bQ$$

Thus, the MR curve is linear, intersects the vertical axis at a (the demand curve's intercept), and has an absolute slope two times that of the demand curve.

[2]From Figure 9–2, we know that the slope of the demand curve is P/Q_2 and the slope of the MR curve is P/Q_1. Since $Q_1 = \frac{1}{2} Q_2$, the slope of the MR curve is therefore $P/\frac{1}{2} Q_2$ or $2P/Q_2$, which is twice the slope of the demand curve. See also footnote 1.

Figure 9–2
Construction of the Linear Marginal Revenue Curve

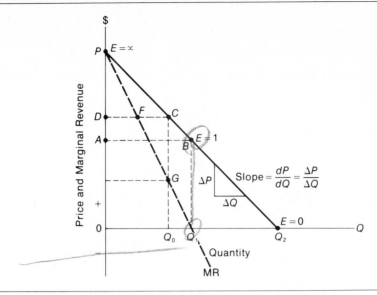

marginal revenue at any level of output. To illustrate this method, suppose that we wish to determine MR at output Q_0, which corresponds to point C on the demand curve in Figure 9–2. We accomplish this simply by drawing a horizontal line from point C to point D on the vertical axis. Bisecting the line DC gives us point F. A straight line drawn from the vertical intercept through point F has exactly twice the slope of the demand curve and is therefore the MR curve. The intersection of the MR curve with dashed line CQ_0 at point G gives us the value of the marginal revenue (read off the horizontal axis) corresponding to point C. Although this technique is somewhat laborious, it is useful in graphing the MR curve corresponding to a nonlinear demand curve.

Nonlinear Demand

When the demand curve is nonlinear, such as curve DD in Figure 9–3, the MR curve is constructed using a variation of the technique we have just learned. Essentially, we determine the marginal revenues corresponding to several points on the demand curve and then connect these points with a smooth curve to obtain the MR curve.

A line originating on the vertical axis at point V_1 is drawn tangent to point A on the demand curve in Figure 9–3. If we assume that this tangent line is a linear demand curve, then the marginal revenue of this demand curve at point A is identical to the marginal revenue of the nonlinear demand curve at point A,

Figure 9–3
Construction of the Nonlinear Marginal Revenue Curve

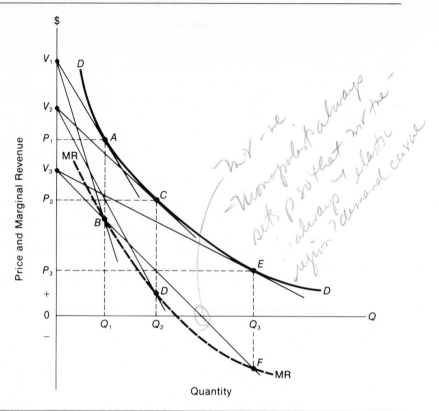

Quantity

because the slopes of the two demand curves are equal at point A and have the same corresponding price P_1 and quantity Q_1. Therefore, to determine the marginal revenue graphically, we simply draw a straight line from V_1 that bisects line P_1A. This line intersects line AQ_1 at point B, giving us the marginal revenue that corresponds to point A on the demand curve.

Point B is only one point on the MR curve associated with the nonlinear demand curve DD. To construct this MR curve, we must determine the marginal revenues that correspond to additional points on curve DD. Points D and F on the MR curve are determined for points C and E on curve DD by repeating the steps we followed to locate point B. The construction lines required to obtain points D and F are drawn in the figure, and you should verify that these points have been correctly determined.

Once a sufficient number of points on the MR curve have been located, a smooth curve drawn through these points is the graphically constructed MR curve associated with the nonlinear demand curve. Figure 9–3 shows that this MR curve is also nonlinear and lies below the demand curve.

Market Equilibrium   9–4

Thus far, we have examined the revenue conditions faced by the monopolist and contrasted them with the revenue conditions faced by the perfectly competitive firm. In terms of costs, the monopolist may or may not face the identical cost functions of the perfectly competitive firm. However, it is reasonable to assume that the general shape of the monopolist's cost curves will retain the same characteristics as the cost curves of the perfectly competitive firm. Based on this assumption, we will now analyze the profit-maximizing behavior of the monopolist.

Short-Run Equilibrium

As we did in the case of the perfectly competitive firm, we will assume that the monopolist is a profit maximizer in the short run as well as in the long run. The total revenue TR and short-run total cost SRTC curves of a monopolistic firm are depicted in Figure 9–4. We know that this figure illustrates a short-run cost function because the SRTC curve intersects the vertical axis at a positive value, indicating the existence of fixed costs.

As before, we will define *profits* as the difference between total revenue and total cost. Profit maximization occurs in Figure 9–4 at output level $\bar{Q}$, where the vertical distance between the TR and SRTC curves is at its maximum. As we showed in Chapter 8, at the profit-maximizing level of output, the slope at

Figure 9–4
The Total Revenue and Short-Run Total Cost Curves
of a Monopolistic Firm

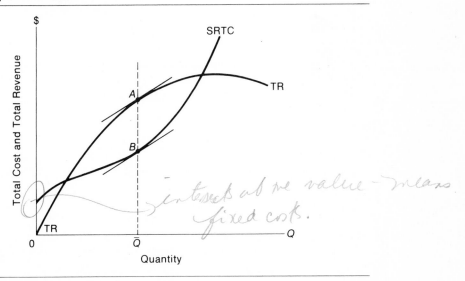

point A on the TR curve is equal to the slope at point B on the SRTC curve. Thus, a necessary condition for profit maximization is that[3]

$$MR = SRMC \qquad\qquad (9-3)$$

This is the same profit-maximizing condition we arrived at in our discussion of perfect competition—with one important difference. In pure competition, MR = P and we can state the profit-maximizing conditions as SRMC = P. But in the case of a monopoly, MR < P, since the monopolist's demand curve is downward sloping, and profit maximization requires that MR = SRMC < P.

Figure 9–5 depicts the conditions of a monopolist in short-run equilibrium. With a linear demand curve D, the monopolist's MR curve is constructed as described in Section 9–3. Equating MR and SRMC at point A yields the profit-maximizing output $\bar{Q}$. The price at which output $\bar{Q}$ can be sold is determined by moving vertically upward from point A to point C on the demand curve. The price corresponding to point C is given by $\bar{P}$ on the vertical axis.

Also included in Figure 9–5 is the short-run average total cost SRAC curve, which we can use to determine the monopolist's short-run profits. The total revenue is equal to $\bar{P}\bar{Q}$, which is equivalent to $0\bar{P}C\bar{Q}$. The total cost is equal to the average total cost multiplied by the quantity produced, or area $0DB\bar{Q}$.

---

[3]*Proof:*   The monopolistic firm's demand curve is

$$P = P(Q)$$

and its total revenue is therefore

$$TR = PQ = P(Q)Q$$

If we let the monopolist's total cost function be

$$C = C(Q)$$

profits π will be

$$\pi = P(Q)Q - C(Q)$$

To obtain the first-order condition for profit maximization, we differentiate the profit function with respect to Q and set it equal to 0 to obtain

$$\frac{d\pi}{dQ} = P(Q) + Q\frac{dP(Q)}{dQ} - \frac{dC(Q)}{dQ} = 0$$

This yields the profit-maximizing condition

$$P(Q) + Q\frac{dP(Q)}{dQ} = \frac{dC(Q)}{dQ}$$

or

$$MR = SRMC$$

since

$$\frac{d\,TR}{dQ} = \frac{d[P(Q)Q]}{dQ} = P(Q) + Q\frac{dP(Q)}{dQ} = MR$$

and

$$\frac{d\,TC}{dQ} = \frac{dC(Q)}{dQ} = SRMC$$

Figure 9–5
A Monopolist in Short-Run Equilibrium

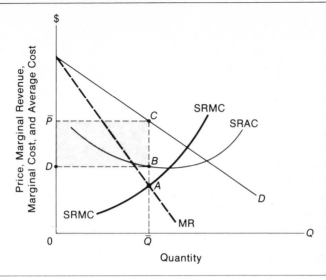

The difference between these two areas is the *monopolist's profit,* which is the tinted area $D\bar{P}CB$ in Figure 9–5. Since TR > SRTC in this example, according to the short-run equilibrium condition depicted in Figure 9–5, the monopolist is obtaining pure economic profits.

It should be pointed out at this time that the possession of a monopoly does not guarantee profits. The profitability of a monopolized industry depends on the nature of the demand for the industry's product and the costs associated with its production. For example, the revenue and cost curves in Figure 9–6 are such that this monopolist incurs short-run losses. The profit-maximizing or, in this example, *loss-minimizing* level of production is $\bar{Q}$, which is determined by the intersection of the MR and SRMC curves. The market price is $\bar{P}$, which is less than the average total cost of production ATC. The firm is therefore incurring negative profits equal to the tinted rectangle $\bar{P}ABD$ in Figure 9–6. However, because the monopolistic firm's average revenue $\bar{P}$ exceeds its average variable costs $\bar{C}$, as shown by the AVC curve at output $\bar{Q}$ in Figure 9–6, the firm is able to pay all of its variable costs plus a portion of its fixed costs. Since we are dealing with the firm in the short run, fixed costs must be paid. By remaining in operation, a portion of these costs can therefore be paid out of the firm's current revenue.

It may also prove useful to examine another facet of monopolistic behavior at this point. It is a common misconception that the monopolist's demand curve is inelastic, or that the monopolist is immune to market forces. Specifically, it is commonly believed that the monopolistic firm can raise its price without suffering a loss in total revenue, which implies that the monopolist must be

Figure 9–6
Short-Run Monopoly Losses

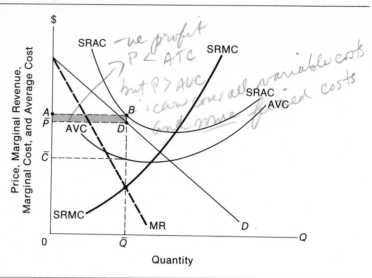

operating in the inelastic region of the demand curve. But a monopolist that
operates in this manner will not maximize profits due to the fact that since
production costs must always be positive, the MC curve must intersect the MR
curve when it is positive also. The MR curve, in turn, is only positive when

**Example
9–1**

Taxicabs in Chicago, Part II

Of the 4,600 taxicab licenses issued by the city of Chicago, 80% (3,666) are
held by the Checker or the Yellow taxicab companies.* Since both of these
companies are controlled by the same interests, they can be considered a
single dominant firm in an industry in which there are barriers to entry. In
addition, the Chicago taxicab ordinance is written so that Checker and
Yellow taxicabs can, for all practical purposes, obtain fare increases from
the Public Vehicle Commissioner whenever they choose, so that in addition
to barriers to entry, the dominant firm has the ability to vary the price
charged by all firms in the industry. In such a case, economic theory predicts that the dominant firm—Checker/Yellow—will restrict the supply of
taxicabs to drive up fares and reap monopolistic profits.

*The data in this example is taken primarily from Edmund W. Kitch, Marc Isaacson,
and Daniel Kasper, "Regulation of Taxicabs in Chicago," *The Journal of Law and Economics* (October 1971), pp. 285–350.

demand is elastic, so that a profit-maximizing monopolist will always set a price in the elastic region of the demand curve. We examined this result briefly in Example 3–2 (page 64) when we discussed the control U.S. oil companies have over the price elasticity of demand for gasoline.

Long-Run Equilibrium

Like the perfectly competitive firm, the monopolistic firm has no fixed costs in the long run. In other words, plant size is not fixed, and the firm will build and operate the scale of plant that will maximize its long-run profits. If the monopolist is incurring losses in the short run, the scale of plant that maximizes positive profits will be built, if possible. If no scale of plant can produce either normal or pure profits, then the monopolist will go out of business. If the monopolist is initially achieving pure profits in the short run, the scale of plant will be altered in the long run to increase pure profits, if they are not already at their maximum.

Long-run profits are maximized by equating marginal revenue and long-run $(LRMC = MR$ marginal cost. This is shown in Figure 9–7 by the intersection of the MR curve and the long-run marginal cost LRMC curve at point A, which yields a long-run profit-maximizing level of output $\bar{Q}$ at price $\bar{P}$. The long-run profit-maximizing scale of plant is represented by the short-run average cost curve SRAC$_1$ in Figure 9–7, which is tangent to the long-run average cost curve LRAC at point B and can therefore produce output $\bar{Q}$ at a lower average cost than any other scale of plant. Furthermore, when the long-run profit-maximizing scale of plant SRAC$_1$ is operated at the long-run profit-maximizing level of output $\bar{Q}$, profits are simultaneously maximized in the short run. This is indicated by the joint

According to Kitch, Isaacson, and Kasper, Checker/Yellow has restricted supply by operating only 2,256 taxis out of the 3,666 licensed taxis that both companies own. Moreover, on any given day, 20% of the Checker/Yellow fleet is in the shop for maintenance, so that the number of licensed Checker and Yellow taxicabs operating full time is 1,805, or about 50% of the total Checker/Yellow fleet. The small, independent Chicago cab companies own 934 licenses, and given the rate structure set by Checker/Yellow, they can maximize profits only if they operate full time, which is what they do. This means that the total number of licensed taxis operating full time in Chicago is 2,739, or about 60% of the maximum number of licensed taxicabs in the city.

Checker and Yellow are able to maximize profits by the seemingly paradoxical action of keeping 50% of their taxicab fleet idle, because this prevents the reissuance of licenses to independent operators, who would conduct their business in a competitive rather than a monopolistic manner. Kitch, Isaacson, and Kasper estimate that the value of the taxicab monopoly created by the Chicago City Council was $41,085,000 in 1971.

Figure 9-7
Long-Run Equilibrium Under Monopoly

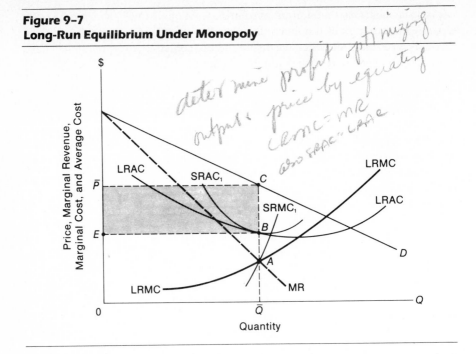

intersection of the LRMC and SRMC₁ curves with the MR curve at point *A* in Figure 9-7.

For the market demand and cost curves shown in Figure 9-7, we can see that the selling price $\bar{P}$ is greater than the long-run average cost of production LRAC at output $\bar{Q}$. Thus, this monopolist is achieving positive pure profits equal to the tinted area $\bar{P}EBC$. Unless the demand curve shifts due to changing tastes, rising incomes, or the introduction of close substitutes for the monopolist's good, the monopolistic firm will be able to achieve pure profits period after period. The monopolist is able to maintain this enviable position only because barriers exist that prevent other firms from entering the industry.

9-5 Monopoly Supply

In Chapter 8, we learned that for every quantity supplied by the perfectly competitive firm, there is a corresponding unique price determined by the short-run marginal cost SRMC curve. Therefore, the perfectly competitive firm has a short-run supply curve that is identical to its SRMC curve at all prices above the price corresponding to the minimum point on the average variable cost AVC curve. This is not the case in a monopoly, however, and we will now demonstrate that the supply curve of the monopolistic firm is not well defined.

A monopolist's SRMC curve is shown in Figure 9-8. There, two possible demand curves D_1 and D_2 are drawn such that their respective marginal reve-

Figure 9–8
Monopoly Supply

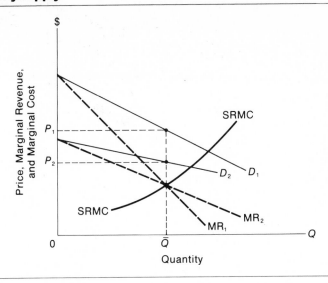

nue curves MR$_1$ and MR$_2$ intersect the SRMC curve at the same level of output $\bar{Q}$. If demand were D_1, the monopolistic firm would charge price P_1 for quantity $\bar{Q}$; if demand were D_2, it would charge price P_2 for $\bar{Q}$. Thus, the monopolist will charge no unique price for a given quantity of output. Therefore, the monopolistic firm does not have a short-run supply curve in the sense that the perfectly competitive firm has such a curve.

Multiplant Monopoly   9–6

There is no reason to suppose that a monopolistic firm will produce all of its output in a single plant. If the firm is operating in the short run or has the usual U-shaped, long-run average cost curve, it will probably be faced with the problem of profit maximization in conjunction with multiplant operation.

Short-Run Optimization

For simplicity, we will assume that our monopolist is operating two plants in the short run and that the scale of plant 1 is such that its operating costs are greater than those of plant 2. This is represented in Figure 9–9(a) by the fact that MC$_1$, the marginal cost curve for plant 1, lies above MC$_2$, the marginal cost curve for plant 2.

To maximize profits in the short run, the multiplant monopolist must produce an additional unit of output using the production facilities of the plant with

Figure 9–9
Multiplant Operation in the Short Run

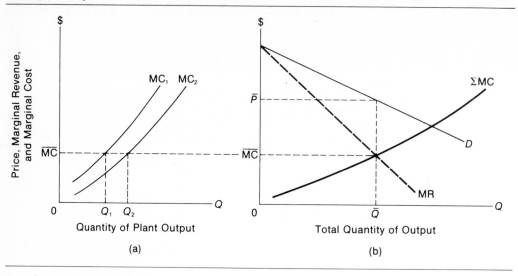

the lower marginal cost. When the monopolist is maximizing overall profits from the operations of both plants, the marginal cost of producing the output of plant 1 will just equal that of producing the output of plant 2. We can easily see that this condition must exist if profits are to be maximized if we assume that production costs are distributed between the two plants so that $MC_1 > MC_2$. In this case, output could be maintained at reduced costs, thereby increasing profits by reducing the output of plant 1 by one unit and increasing the output of plant 2 by one unit. Total output would remain constant, but total costs would decline, since the cost savings due to reduced production in plant 1 would exceed the cost increase due to additional production in plant 2. Thus, profits would increase. As long as opportunities exist to reduce total cost by increasing output in one plant and reducing it in the other, profit maximization will not occur.

The manner in which the total profit-maximizing level of output is determined and divided between plant 1 and plant 2 is explained in Figure 9–9(b), where the monopolist's demand and marginal revenue curves are drawn. The curve labeled ΣMC is the horizontal summation of the MC_1 and MC_2 curves. A very useful property of the ΣMC curve is that it indicates the lowest marginal cost at which any given amount of total output can be produced. The intersection of the ΣMC curve and the MR curve in Figure 9–9(b) therefore determines the profit-maximizing total output $\bar{Q}$ that the monopolist can sell at price $\bar{P}$. The marginal cost $\overline{MC}$ of producing $\bar{Q}$ can only be obtained when output in plant 1 is Q_1 and output in plant 2 is Q_2, as shown in Figure 9–9(a). When this condition of *joint production* occurs, $Q_1 + Q_2 = \bar{Q}$.

Determining the short-run profit-maximizing operation of a monopolistic firm that owns more than two plants is merely an extension of this technique. For

Figure 9–10
Multiplant Production with Constant Costs

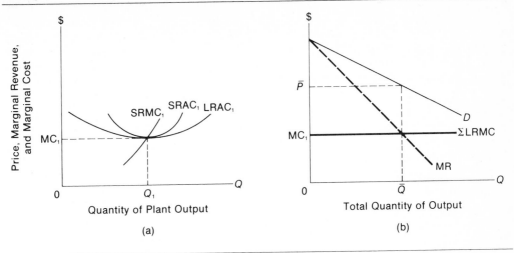

(a)

Quantity of Plant Output

(b)

Total Quantity of Output

example, the market for automobiles in the United States is widely dispersed geographically, and each manufacturer operates many assembly plants throughout the country. U.S. automobile manufacturers determine the profit-maximizing allocation of production among their plants based on the analysis developed in this section.

Long-Run Optimization

In the long-run, a multiplant monopolist will alter the number of plants to decrease or increase output. Each plant that is constructed will be scaled so that it is just tangent to the LRAC curve at its minimum point, as the $SRAC_1$ curve is in Figure 9–10(a). If the monopolistic firm is operating under conditions that permit any number of plants to be constructed and operated at constant input costs, then its long-run marginal cost curve $\Sigma LRMC$ will be horizontal, as illustrated in Figure 9–10(b).[4] The horizontal property of the multiplant LRMC curve indicates that the monopolistic firm can construct as many plants of scale $SRAC_1$ producing output $\bar{Q}$ as it desires. Since the marginal cost of producing output $\bar{Q}$ is MC_1 and all input prices are assumed to be independent of the number of plants in operation, any number of plants can be constructed such that each plant's marginal costs are also $SRMC_1$. This long-

---

[4]Of course, the horizontal $\Sigma LRMC$ curve is only a good approximation to the actual $\Sigma LRMC$ curve when Q is small relative to $\bar{Q}$. This is due to the fact that the $\Sigma LRMC$ curve is produced by joining a successive series of $SRAC_1$ curves together, so that in actuality the $\Sigma LRMC$ curve will have a scalloped shape. This is also true of the $\Sigma LRMC$ curve in Figure 9–11(b).

run multiplant adjustment produces the horizontal ΣLRMC curve. The long-run profit-maximizing output level $\bar{Q}$ is given by the intersection of the ΣLRMC and the MR curves in Figure 9–10(b). Each plant produces quantity Q_1, and all output is sold at price $\bar{P}$.

In the case of the multiplant monopolist, however, it is probably more realistic to assume that as output is increased by expanding the number of plants, input costs will also increase. Rising input prices will raise the long-run average cost curve of all plants. This is illustrated in Figure 9–11(a) by the upward movement of the long-run average cost curve from $LRAC_1$ to $LRAC_2$ that results when a monopolist increases the number of plants in operation. Since that scale of plant will always be constructed that is tangent to the LRAC curve at its minimum point, the short-run average cost curve of the minimum-cost plant will also shift upward as input costs increase, as shown by the $SRAC_1$ and $SRAC_2$ curves in Figure 9–11(a). Since increasing costs cause the minimum point on the LRAC curve for a single plant to increase as the monopolist expands the number of plants, the ΣLRMC curve will have a positive slope, as shown in Figure 9–11(b).

The long-run profit-maximizing condition is given by the intersection of the ΣLRMC and the MR curves in Figure 9–11(b). Total output is $\bar{Q}$, which sells at price $\bar{P}$. The scale of each plant operated by the multiplant monopolist is represented by the $SRAC_2$ curve in Figure 9–11(b), and each plant produces output Q_1 such that $\Sigma Q_1 = \bar{Q}$. The number of plants $\bar{N}$ that the monopolist can construct is therefore $\bar{N} = \bar{Q}/Q_1$.

Figure 9–11
Multiplant Production with Increasing Costs

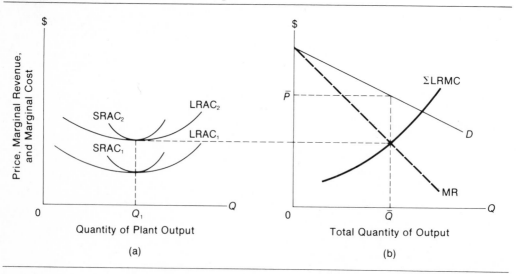

(a) Quantity of Plant Output

(b) Total Quantity of Output

Price Discrimination 9–7

Price discrimination occurs when a firm charges some customers a higher price than it charges other customers for the same product and the price difference cannot be explained by a difference in the cost of supplying the product. A firm may engage in price discrimination to (1) maximize profits from an already existing monopoly; (2) eliminate competition by bankrupting or disciplining rival firms; or (3) increase competition by reducing price to penetrate quasi-monopoly markets or to match the price reductions of competitors.

In this section, we will discuss the use of price discrimination to achieve the first two objectives. The third objective will be examined in the applications of monopoly theory to regulation at the end of this chapter.

Segmented-Market Price Discrimination

A monopoly may be able to increase its profits further if it practices **segmented-market price discrimination**–selling the same product to different customers at different prices at the same time. For example, an electric power monopoly may charge 5 cents per kilowatt-hour to manufacturing plants and 8 cents per kilowatt-hour to households. Both groups are buying the same product, and although the costs of producing and supplying the product are not identical, the difference is not great enough to justify the price differential.

Certain conditions must prevail for a monopolist to practice segmented-market price discrimination successfully. First, buyers must be segmented into different categories, based on significant differences in their price elasticities of demand. Second, the monopolist must be able to determine the demand characteristics of these buyers and to place them in the appropriate categories at a low cost. Third, buyers must not be permitted to resell the product among themselves, to prevent arbitrage between low-price buyers and high-price buyers. If these three conditions exist, the discriminating monopolist is still faced with the problems of deciding what price to charge each segment of buyers and how much of total production to allocate to each segment.

For simplicity, suppose that the market is segmented into only two categories of buyers, or two separate *submarkets*, and that the cost of supplying each submarket is the same. To maximize profits, the monopolistic firm must sell an amount of its product to each submarket such that the marginal revenues yielded by both submarkets are equal. We can readily see why this must be so if we assume that the marginal revenue of one submarket is greater than the marginal revenue of the other. In this case, the monopolist could clearly raise profits at a given level of total production by selling fewer units of output to the submarket with the lower marginal revenue and then selling the released units to the submarket with the higher marginal revenue. As the monopolist reallocates sales, however, the difference between the marginal revenues of the two submarkets will diminish. When the marginal revenues in both submarkets are equal, the monopolist will be maximizing profits and will stop reallocating sales.

A more direct method of determining the conditions of profit maximization that allows for variations in production is illustrated in Figure 9–12. There, demand curves D_1 and D_2 and their respective marginal revenue curves MR_1 and MR_2 are drawn, along with the horizontal summation of the two marginal revenue curves, designated ΣMR. The intersection of the MC curve with the ΣMR curve at point A determines the monopolist's profit-maximizing output $\bar{Q}$. To ensure that profits are actually maximized, total production $\bar{Q}$ must be divided into two portions and sold at different prices to the two submarkets. We have already shown that this must occur such that the marginal revenues received from both submarkets are equal. Graphically, this is easily accomplished by moving horizontally to the left of point A in Figure 9–12 to points C and B on the marginal revenue curves MR_1 and MR_2, respectively. The portion of output $\bar{Q}$ to be sold in submarket 1 is Q_1, which corresponds to point C on the MR_1 curve; the portion of $\bar{Q}$ to be sold in submarket 2 is Q_2, which corresponds to point B on the MR_2 curve. The price at which the monopolist's product is sold to each submarket is determined by points D and E on demand curves D_1 and D_2, respectively, which correspond, in turn, to points C and B on marginal revenue curves MR_1 and MR_2, as shown in Figure 9–12. Thus, the monopolist will sell output Q_1 at price $\bar{P}_1$ to buyers in submarket 1 and output Q_2 at price $\bar{P}_2$ to buyers in submarket 2. When more than two submarkets exist, the optimal outputs and prices are determined by an extension of the method we just employed.

Figure 9–12
Segmented-Market Price Discrimination

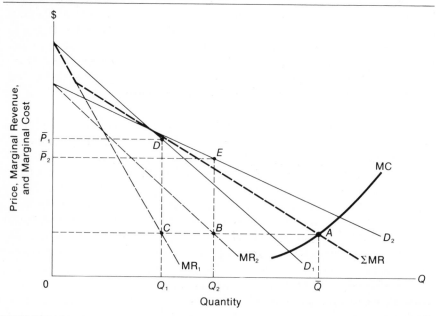

[handwritten: evening, telephone calls are elastic, p is lower]

We can now show that if two submarkets exist the profit-maximizing price in the submarket with the higher price elasticity of demand will be *lower than* the price in the submarket with the lower price elasticity of demand. Recalling Equation (9–1), which states that

$$MR = P\left(1 - \frac{1}{E}\right)$$

[handwritten: ie 9 1 2 D1 is more elastic & D2 is the lower p of P2]

if $MR_1 = MR_2$, it follows that

$$P_1\left(1 - \frac{1}{E_1}\right) = P_2\left(1 - \frac{1}{E_2}\right) \qquad (9\text{–}4)$$

Rearranging then gives us

$$\frac{P_1}{P_2} = \frac{1 - (1/E_2)}{1 - (1/E_1)} \qquad (9\text{–}5)$$

If $P_1 > P_2$, then it necessarily follows that $E_2 > E_1$ for this equality to hold.

The fact that electric power utilities charge higher prices to residential users than to commercial users can now be explained using the analysis of segmented-market pricing we just developed. The demand for electric power by large commercial users will be more sensitive to price than the demand of residential users, because low-cost substitutes for the electric power supplied by a particular utility are more readily available to commercial users than to residential users. For example, firms may be sufficiently large that they can generate their own electric power at a lower cost than the rate that the public utility charges residential users. Since the price elasticity of demand for commercial users will be higher than that for residential users, an electric power utility will maximize its profits by charging a higher price per kilowatt-hour to residential users than it charges to commercial customers.

Another example of this form of segmented-market price discrimination is found in the pricing practices of airlines. If you learn today that you must fly to London tomorrow on business and return within 24 hours, the price of your ticket will be significantly greater than the price you would pay if you were planning a two-week vacation to the same city three months in advance. In light of our discussion on price discrimination, the pricing behavior of the airline makes perfectly good sense. If you must make a business trip to London on short notice, there are no close substitutes for the service provided by the airline. If you are planning a vacation in advance, however, there are not only alternative means of travel available to you but also alternative places for you to spend your vacation. The price elasticity of demand for the business trip will therefore be relatively inelastic compared to that of the vacation trip, and the airline can increase its profits by charging higher fares on reservations made on short notice and for short durations.

[handwritten: the smaller the e, the higher the p]

Multipart Price Discrimination

We have just learned how a monopolistic firm can increase profits by placing its customers in different market segments with varying price elasticities of demand. When this form of price discrimination is employed, the price in each

**Example
9-2**

Price Discrimination in Medicine

It is a well-known fact that some physicians practice price discrimination by basing their fees on their patients' income levels. Wealthier patients are charged more than poorer patients for the identical medical service. One theory favored by physicians to explain this behavior is that by charging the rich more, doctors can provide medical services to the poor for less. In other words, this form of segmented-market price discrimination is a privately operated, income-redistribution policy instituted for charitable purposes. An alternative theory favored by economists is that these physicians are simply behaving as rational profit maximizers.

Since 79% of the 200,000 or more private physicians in the United States are engaged in either individual or two-party practice, a model based on monopolistic conditions would seem inappropriate to analyze their price behavior.* Because there are such a large number of small firms, a perfectly competitive model would be expected to yield more reliable predictions. However, other factors could offset the large number of small firms and produce conditions more closely approximating monopoly price behavior.

A primary prerequisite of perfect competition is that the buyer is *completely knowledgeable* about the product being purchased. Of course, this is never true in the real world. Medical services, in particular, are usually bought by consumers who are largely ignorant about the product. This is due to the fact that medical science is a highly esoteric and complex field in which the seller possesses much more knowledge than the buyer.

A second feature of the medical services market is inherent in the product itself. Because medical treatment is often a life-or-death proposition, the physician alone may determine what medication, hospitalization, and surgery the patient requires. In other words, the physician is in a unique position due to both the buyer's ignorance and the nature of the product. Therefore, within limits, physicians can increase the demand for the product they sell.

Consumer ignorance and the indispensability of the product are two necessary but not sufficient conditions to create a market in which segmented-market price discrimination occurs. Even given these two conditions, the desire of physicians to increase their incomes, especially when

*Elton Rayack, "The Physicians' Service Industry," in Walter Adams (ed.), *The Structure of American Industry,* 5th ed. (New York: Macmillan, 1977), p. 404.

market segment is different but all of the customers in a given market segment are charged the same price. Another form of price discrimination employed by monopolies, called **block** or **multipart price discrimination,** involves charging each customer a different price for varying amounts of the product purchased. A monopolist who charges the customer a different price for each

---

they are just beginning to establish their practices, will result in the reduction of fees to richer customers to obtain their business. This behavior, even if practiced by a small percentage of physicians initially, would eventually eliminate price discrimination in medicine.

A legal preventative to price cutting by some physicians is to make would-be price cutters an "offer they can't refuse." In the United States, the American Medical Association (AMA)† regulates the natural price-cutting inclinations of profit-maximizing physicians by means of sanctions that impose economic costs on those who fail to comply with industry price standards. First, the AMA has the power to certify hospitals as suitable or unsuitable establishments for the training of interns. For many hospitals, interns are a relatively inexpensive source of medical service inputs. Revoking a hospital's "Class A" rating would cause the hospital to lose its intern staff, resulting in higher operating costs and, in turn, the possible loss of patients. Hospitals that wish to obtain a "Class A" rating are "advised" by the AMA to employ physicians on the hospital staff who are also members of the county AMA medical society. This makes it critical for any physician who wishes to practice professionally on a hospital staff to join the county AMA medical society. And surgeons who charge flat fees for various kinds of operations could lose their memberships in the county medical society and be unable to use hospital operating rooms.

Because physicians who are just beginning to practice privately have the highest incentive to attract patients by price cutting, they are initially given only probationary memberships in county medical societies, regardless of their experience elsewhere. In this way, newcomers are kept under surveillance and are faced with the possible loss of AMA membership if they fail to comply with the pricing practices of the group.

Given the importance of hospital-staff membership in the maintenance of monopoly price discrimination, we would expect price discrimination to decline as fields of medical specialization become less and less dependent on the use of hospital facilities. For example, in the field of psychiatry, which is almost independent of the need for hospital facilities, there is little or no price discrimination. On the other hand, surgical specialists are noted for their price discrimination between the rich and the poor.

---

†Two classic studies dealing with the monopolistic practices of the AMA are Milton Friedman and Simon Kuznets, *Income from Independent Professional Practice* (New York: National Bureau of Economic Research, 1945), and Reuben A. Kessel, "Price Discrimination in Medicine," *The Journal of Law and Economics* (October 1958), pp. 20–53. The data in this example are drawn primarily from Kessel's article.

Figure 9–13
Multipart Price Discrimination

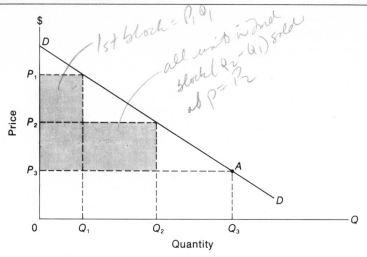

additional fractional unit of output is said to be engaged in **perfect multipart price discrimination.** In actual practice, the usual multipart pricing practice is to charge the customer a high price for the first number of units sold, a lower price for the second number of units sold, and so on.

Multipart pricing is illustrated in Figure 9–13. Given the consumer's demand curve DD as depicted in the figure, the monopolistic firm offers to sell the initial block of units from 0 to Q_1 to the consumer at a price of P_1. The consumer can purchase varying amounts of the second block of units between Q_1 and Q_2 at the lower price of P_2. Finally, at the lowest possible price P_3 at which the monopolist will sell the product, the consumer can purchase as many additional units as desired. The additional units purchased at price P_3 will be $Q_3 - Q_2$, as shown in Figure 9–13.

We are now ready to explain what motivates the monopolistic firm to engage in multipart price discrimination. Suppose that the monopolist charged only one price P_3 and that that price was determined by the intersection of the firm's MC and MR curves. The total revenue received would then be equal to the area $0P_3AQ_3$ in Figure 9–13. However, by practicing multipart pricing, this monopolist can increase total revenue by an amount equal to the tinted area in Figure 9–13 without appreciably increasing production costs. Clearly, the monopolist's profits are now greater than they were before price discrimination. Multipart pricing in effect reduces the consumer's surplus and transfers the reduction to the monopolist. We used indifference-curve analysis to illustrate the ability of a two-part pricing policy to capture the consumer's surplus in the application "Capturing the Consumer's Surplus" in Chapter 4 (page 122).

The single characteristic common to both segmented-market and multipart price discrimination is that the identical product is being sold to consumers at different prices. Since this cannot occur in perfectly competitive markets, charging different prices for the same product *may* be evidence of monopoly pricing. Of course, this may not always be the case, because the price of a product in the real world is influenced by such factors as shipping distance and volume of purchase. A common example of what seems to be multipart pricing is found in supermarkets. Bars of bath soap may sell for $.75 apiece, but a package of two bars may sell for $1.45. In other words, the first bar in the package costs $.75, and the second bar costs $.70. But is this pricing policy evidence of monopoly power? In this example, the answer is probably no. The reduction in the price of soap may merely be a cost savings in the form of less time spent by stock clerks in price marking the soap and less time spent by cashiers in totaling customer bills that has been passed on to the consumer. In economic terms, we would say that this pricing scheme economizes on transactions costs, and competition between grocery stores results in the transfer of these economies to the consumer.

Predatory Pricing

The use of predatory pricing by a firm to achieve or maintain a monopoly position is popularly believed to be a common form of monopoly behavior. **Predatory pricing** occurs when a firm deliberately cuts prices below cost in the short run to obtain profits in the long run. Prices are reduced below cost to bankrupt competitors, to "persuade" them to merge, or to encourage collusion on industry outputs and prices.

The theory of predatory pricing can best be explained by constructing a hypothetical example.[5] Suppose that firm A plans either to bankrupt firm B or to make B subservient by means of a predatory-pricing campaign and that firm A assumes its plans will be successful. It is unlikely that A will attempt to drive B out of business, because this is a very expensive course of action. Even if firm A were successful, it would probably not secure a monopoly in the industry, because when B declares bankruptcy, its fixed assets will be sold to some other firm that will reenter the market.

Since A cannot operate below cost in the long run, it will be unable to exclude successors to firm B from the market in the long run. Firm A is therefore more likely to try to convince firm B that it should enter into a merger with A or to set its prices according to the desires of firm A. In this situation, it is conceivable that firm A might initiate predatory pricing to "soften up" firm B before proposing a merger. Economic analysis discounts the likelihood of this possibility, however. Suppose that A places a value of x dollars on B's assets in the event of

---

[5]This theoretical analysis is drawn from Roland H. Koller II, "The Myth of Predatory Pricing: An Empirical Study," in Yale Brozen (ed.), *The Competitive Economy* (Morristown, NJ: General Learning Press, 1975), pp. 418–28.

Example 9-3

Multipart Pricing by Utilities

In contrast to grocery stores, public utilities much more closely approximate pure monopolies. We should therefore not be surprised to discover that multipart pricing is a common practice among public utilities.

When the use of water, for example, is metered, it is relatively easy for utilities to employ multipart pricing. A rather extreme example of this form of price discrimination was employed in the town of Normal, Illinois, where the pricing of water was broken down into the following nine parts or blocks.* (Most U.S. water utilities use fewer blocks.)

Public utilities argue that multipart pricing merely reflects the fact that it costs less to deliver a large quantity of water, gas, or electricity to a customer than it does to deliver a small amount.† This is usually true, but given the nature of the product and the lack of close substitutes for many buyers, we should consider the available evidence before accepting this explanation.

In a pioneering study, Kirby Davidson examined the pricing rates of the Consolidated Gas Electric Light and Power Company of Baltimore, Mary-

*William S. Foster, "The Block System Makes the Best Rate Schedule," in William S. Foster (ed.), *Modern Water Rates* (New York: American City Magazine, 1966), p. 63.
†*Ibid.*, pp. 53–54.

a merger and that a third firm C places a lower value of *y* dollars on the acquisition of firm B. Thus, the price A is willing to pay for B's assets will lie somewhere between *x* and *y* dollars. Is A likely to initiate predatory pricing in this situation? A knows that it cannot make B an offer below *y* dollars, and if firm C is strong financially, A might endure the cost of a price war only to be faced with a stronger competitor than before if C acquires B. Firm A will therefore seek to maximize its profits by offering B at least *y* dollars for its assets. Firm B can accept firm A's offer or incur anticipated losses from a price war, only to accept C's offer of *y* dollars in the end. Therefore, firm B's rational behavior would be to bargain with A to reach an agreement that will benefit both firms— that is, B will sell its assets to A at a price above *y* but below *x* dollars.

We could use a similar line of reasoning to show that it would be economically irrational for firm A to engage in predatory pricing to encourage firm B to enter into collusion on industry outputs and prices. Economic analysis therefore indicates that predatory pricing is unlikely when firms are seeking to maximize profits. However, the theory does *not* indicate that firms will never engage in price wars in the real world. Although such wars are uncommon, they do occur.[6] In our example, we assumed that prices *x* and *y* were known with a fair degree of certainty. Such perfect knowledge is not possible in the real world, and price miscalculations on the parts of A and B may result in a price war.

[6]For an example, see B.S. Yamey, "Predatory Price Cutting: Notes and Comments," *The Journal of Law and Economics* (October 1972), pp. 129–42.

NUMBER OF GALLONS	PRICE PER 1,000 GALLONS
First 7,000	$.93
Next 10,000	.85
Next 18,000	.76
Next 30,000	.65
Next 50,000	.55
Next 50,000	.51
Next 200,000	.47
Next 300,000	.44
Next 300,000 or more	.41

land, from 1910 to 1950.[*] Davidson tested the hypothesis that multipart pricing could be explained by "cost of service" against the alternative hypothesis that the rate structure was the result of "profit maximization." Davidson showed that the rate structure did not reflect true variations in cost and that the pricing behavior of the utility was therefore consistent only with the theory of monopolistic multipart pricing.

[*]Ralph Kirby Davidson, *Price Discrimination in Selling Gas and Electricity* (Baltimore: Johns Hopkins Press, 1955).

Perfect Competition Versus Pure Monopoly   9-8

A comparison of the long-run equilibrium conditions of pure monopoly and perfect competition serves two important functions. First, since monopoly and perfect competition represent polar extremes in the theoretical analysis of firm behavior, a comparison between these two models will illuminate their differences. Second and more important from a practical standpoint, the differences between these theoretical long-run equilibrium conditions serve as a justification for the regulation of monopoly, which we discuss in Section 9-9.

For the purposes of analysis, we will suppose that the industry we are examining initially operates under conditions of perfect competition. Later, a single firm will acquire the assets of all other firms and effectively prevent the entry of additional firms. We will also assume that the industry's demand and cost curves remain the same under conditions of perfect competition and pure monopoly.

The two long-run average cost curves $LRAC_1$ and $LRAC_2$ in Figure 9-14(a) indicate that we are dealing with an increasing-cost industry. In perfect competition, as the number of firms increases, factor input prices rise and the firm's long-run average cost curve shifts upward. The fact that the minimum point on the LRAC curve in Figure 9-14(a) also shifts to the right as the number of firms increases is merely one of three possibilities. On *a priori* grounds, we have no way of knowing whether the minimum point shifts to the right or to the left or

**Example
9-4**

The Standard Oil Case

Perhaps the most well-known example of predatory price cutting is the alleged case of the Standard Oil Company. To obtain a monopoly position in the oil refining industry, it is commonly believed that Standard Oil employed predatory price discrimination in local markets to bankrupt or shut out competitors. Price warfare was the method Standard Oil ostensibly employed to obtain and maintain this monopoly.

Examination of the facts in the Standard Oil case by John S. McGee indicates that the story of Standard Oil's predatory-pricing policies is mere myth.* McGee found "that Standard did not systematically, if ever, use local price cutting in retailing, or anywhere else, to reduce competition."† In other words, Standard Oil did not use price discrimination to obtain its monopoly position. Instead, Standard Oil obtained its monopoly position primarily

---

*John S. McGee, "Predatory Price Cutting: The Standard Oil (N. J.) Case," *The Journal of Law and Economics* (October 1958), pp. 137–69.
†*Ibid*, p. 168.

---

remains stationary.[7] Since the industry experiences increasing input costs, the industry's long-run marginal cost curve ΣLRMC slopes upward and to the right, as shown in Figure 9–14(b). In addition, since we have initially assumed that perfect competition prevails, the ΣLRMC curve is also the industry's long-run supply curve. The intersection of the ΣLRMC curve and the market demand curve D therefore determines the long-run equilibrium level of output $\bar{Q}_{PC}$ and price $\bar{P}_{PC}$.

Now we will assume that all firms in the industry are absorbed by a single firm and that this firm has the power to prevent entry into the industry. Since we have previously assumed that all costs are unaffected by monopolization, the ΣLRMC curve of the industry in Figure 9–14(b) becomes the multiplant monopolist's long-run marginal cost curve. To maximize profits, the monopolist equates ΣLRMC with the MR curve in Figure 9–14(b) to determine the optimal level of monopoly production $\bar{Q}_M$ and price $\bar{P}_M$.

We can now compare the long-run equilibrium conditions of pure monopoly and perfect competition. Our first conclusion is that the monopolistic firm will produce less of the product and sell it at a higher price than the perfectly competitive firm. Our second conclusion is that in perfect competition the price of the product is equal to the long-run marginal cost, whereas in a monopoly, product price exceeds marginal cost. In Chapter 5, we learned that the *price* of a good measures its *marginal value* to society, and the *marginal cost* of a good indicates its *marginal social cost*. Thus, we can draw a third conclusion that under conditions of perfect competition, the marginal value to society of the

---

[7]For example, the LRAC curve in Figure 9–11(a) shifted such that its minimum point remained at output level $\bar{Q}$.

by merging with other oil refineries, as economic theory predicts. However, once it obtained a monopoly, Standard Oil apparently practiced price discrimination between markets to maximize its profits.

Unfortunately, for the owners of Standard Oil, these monopoly profits proved to be short-lived. Standard's share of the refining market peaked at 88% in 1879 and was still over 82% in 1895. However, the price of kerosene per gallon sold in barrels declined from 9.125 cents in 1880 to 8.5 cents in 1885 to 7.375 cents in 1890 to 5.91 cents in 1896.[*] This price decrease was the result of Standard Oil's attempts to introduce cost-saving technological innovations in oil refining and to use price competition to maintain its share of the market. After 1896, however, gas and electric lighting became substitutes for kerosene in the home, and the discovery of petroleum in Texas, Kansas, Oklahoma, and California spawned companies that substantially reduced Standard Oil's share of the market.

[*]D.T. Armentano, *The Myths of Antitrust* (New Rochelle, NY: Arlington House, 1972), p. 77.

last unit produced is exactly equal to the marginal cost to society of producing that unit, whereas under conditions of monopoly, the value society places on the last unit produced exceeds the marginal cost of production. In other words, from the point of view of society, perhaps total welfare could be increased if the monopolist's output could be increased.

Figure 9–14
Comparison of Pure Monopoly and Perfect Competition

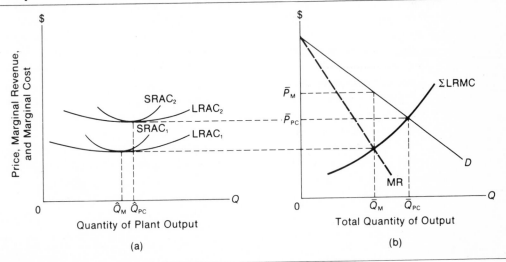

Quantity of Plant Output

(a)

Total Quantity of Output

(b)

Application: The Social Cost of Monopoly

We have just shown that in long-run equilibrium, the monopolistic firm produces less of a product and charges a higher price for it than would be the case
if perfect competition prevailed. This monopolistic behavior results in a net
welfare loss to society.

For the last 25 years economists have been intrigued with the possibility of
empirically measuring the social cost of monopoly in the United States. The first
economist to attempt this estimation was Arnold C. Harberger.[8] Harberger
assumed that in the long run and over the relevant range of production,
resources can be allocated by the monopolist in a way that will yield approximately constant returns to scale. This means that the monopolistic firm's long-
run average cost curve will coincide with its long-run marginal cost curve, and
both of these curves will be horizontal, as the LRAC and LRMC curves are in
Figure 9–15.

If the monopoly prevails, the intersection of the MR and the LRMC curves at
point A in Figure 9–15 will result in output Q_0 being produced and sold at price
P_1. Now suppose that the industry begins to function under conditions of
perfect competition, so that the LRMC curve becomes the perfectly competitive
industry's supply curve. The intersection of the industry supply curve with the
market demand curve DD at point C will therefore increase output to Q_1, and
price will decline to P_0.

Recalling our discussion of the consumer's surplus in Section 5–3 (page 152),
we can now graph the social welfare loss due to monopoly. The industry's tran-
sition from the conditions of monopoly to those of perfect competition results
in an increase in the consumer's surplus, measured by the trapezoidal area
Q_0ABCQ_1 in Figure 9–15. However, this increase in the consumer's surplus is
not equal to the benefit to society of the transformation to perfect competition,
due to the accompanying cost as output increases from Q_0 to Q_1, which is given
by the rectangular area Q_0ACQ_1 in Figure 9–15. Therefore, the *net* benefit to
society is measured by the triangle ABC in Figure 9–15, which is sometimes
referred to as the **welfare triangle.**

When Harberger estimated the social cost of monopoly in the United States,
he assumed that the price elasticity of demand was equal to 1 and then measured the welfare triangle for each manufacturing industry. Harberger obtained
the rather surprising result that welfare loss due to the existence of monopoly
in the American economy amounted to only about one-tenth of 1% of total
national income.

George J. Stigler has criticized Harberger's estimate for being too low,[9] arguing that Harberger's analysis was faulty for the following reasons:

---

[8] Arnold C. Harberger, "Monopoly and Resource Allocation," *American Economic Review*
(May 1954), pp. 77–87.
[9] George J. Stigler, "The Statistics of Monopoly and Merger," *Journal of Political Economy*
(February 1956), pp. 33–40.

Figure 9–15
The Social Welfare Loss Due to Monopoly

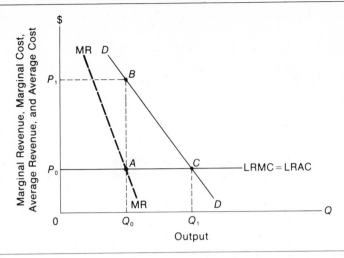

1. A profit-maximizing monopolist will produce in that region of the demand curve where elasticity of demand is greater than 1, as we showed in Section 9–4.

2. The profits reported by the industries Harberger studied may be too low, because the cost of such items as salaries and patent royalties are too high due to the monopoly.

3. Monopolistic firms may tend to exaggerate the value of intangible items in their balance sheet to increase the value of assets, thereby reducing profits as a percentage of assets.

   Later studies have attempted to refine Harberger's analysis in light of Stigler's criticisms. David Kamerschen found that estimated demand elasticities for each industry ranged between 2 and 3 and also adjusted profits to account for royalties and intangibles.[10] Kamerschen estimated that the welfare loss due to monopoly was about 6% of total national income. To further refine these estimates, Dean Worcester, Jr., using firm instead of industry data, concluded that the welfare loss due to monopoly was only about one-half of 1% of total national income.[11] Another critic of the Harberger estimate, Gordon Tullock, argues that scarce resources expended by firms in their attempt to obtain a monopoly should

---

[10]David R. Kamerschen, "An Estimate of the 'Welfare Loss' from Monopoly in the American Economy," *Western Economic Journal* (Summer 1966), pp. 221–36.
[11]Dean A. Worcester, Jr., "New Estimates of the Welfare Loss to Monopoly, United States: 1956–1969," *Southern Economic Journal* (October 1973), pp. 418–28.

also be considered in determining the social cost of monopoly.[12] Richard Posner, who attempted to incorporate the monopoly costs identified by Tullock into his analysis, concluded that estimates of the social loss due to monopoly were probably much higher than either Harberger's or Worcester's calculations, but that the social costs of government regulation were even greater than the costs of private monopoly.[13]

9-9   Government Regulation of Monopoly

Based on the theoretical analysis developed in the preceding section, the public has come to view the social welfare effects of monopoly as undesirable. Governments have therefore attempted to regulate monopolies for the stated purpose of mitigating their effects on social welfare. The two most popular methods of government regulation of monopolies are *taxation policies* and *price controls*. In this section, we will analyze the effects of these two regulatory methods in terms of the theory introduced in this chapter.

Taxation Policies

Three methods of taxation can be employed to reduce the monopolist's pure profits. One method, called a **per-unit tax,** taxes the monopolist x dollars for each unit sold. Another method, the **lump-sum tax,** simply taxes the monopolist a fixed amount regardless of how much of the product is sold. The third method is the **profits tax,** which imposes a tax on the monopolist's profits. We will examine the effects of these three methods of monopoly regulation here.

The effects of the *per-unit tax* are illustrated in Figure 9–16. Prior to the imposition of the tax, the long-run average cost curve and its accompanying marginal cost curve are represented by $LRAC_0$ and $LRMC_0$, respectively. Profit-maximizing behavior dictates that the firm produce output Q_0 and sell it at price P_0. Since the per-unit tax results in an increase in the monopolist's *total* tax as output increases, it is viewed by the firm as a variable cost of production. Therefore, *both* the firm's LRMC and LRAC curves shift upward when the per-unit tax is imposed, as illustrated in Figure 9–16 by the shift from $LRAC_0$ to $LRAC_1$ and from $LRMC_0$ to $LRMC_1$. As a result of the shift in the LRMC curve to $LRMC_1$, the monopolist now produces output Q_1 and sells it at price P_1. An examination of Figure 9–16 reveals that the monopolist's pure profits actually are reduced, but this result is accompanied by a reduction in output and an increase in price. Because this, in turn, reduces the welfare of consumers, the per-unit tax method of monopoly regulation is not generally favored by economists.

---

[12]Gordon Tullock, "The Welfare Costs of Tariffs, Monopolies, and Theft," *Western Economic Journal* (June 1967), pp. 224–32.

[13]Richard A. Posner, "The Social Costs of Monopoly and Regulation," *Journal of Political Economy* (August 1975), pp. 807–27.

Figure 9–16
Effects of a Per-Unit Tax

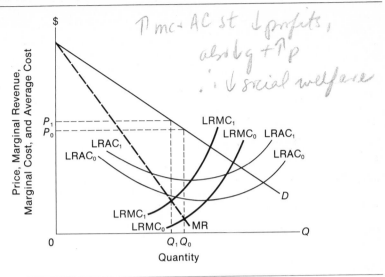

The effects of the *lump-sum tax* are illustrated in Figure 9–17. As before, the firm's initial average cost and marginal cost conditions are depicted by curves $LRAC_0$ and $LRMC_0$, respectively. Since the lump-sum tax is imposed on the firm regardless of the level of output or scale of plant, it is essentially a "fixed" cost that the firm must bear in the long run if it wishes to remain in business. The imposition of a lump-sum tax will therefore cause the monopolist's long-run average cost curve to shift upward from $LRAC_0$ to $LRAC_1$ in Figure 9–17. However, because the lump-sum tax does not alter the slope of the long-run total cost curve, the marginal cost curve at $LRMC_0$ remains unaffected. Since the marginal cost curve does not shift, in contrast to the per-unit tax, the lump-sum tax does not provide the monopolist with any incentive to reduce the level of output or to raise price. But the upward shift in the long-run average cost curve to $LRAC_1$ does reduce the monopolist's pure profits while leaving the allocation of resources unaffected.

The same general result is obtained when the regulating agency imposes a *profits tax.* Suppose that a tax rate of $t\%$ is placed on the monopolist's profits. Since $0 < t < 100$, the monopolist will retain $100 - t\%$ of the profits received prior to paying taxes. Thus, to maximize after-tax profits, the monopolist must select the price and output levels that maximize pre-tax profits. Therefore, the profits tax, like the lump-sum tax, will not affect the allocation of resources.

Because the lump-sum and profits taxes do not decrease the efficiency of resource allocation, they are preferred to the per-unit tax. Of course, this does not mean that they are the best methods of monopoly regulation.

Figure 9-17
Effects of a Lump-Sum Tax

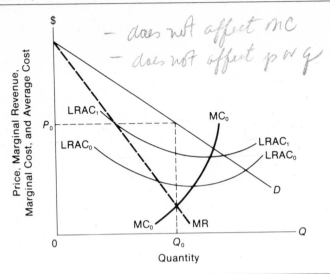

[handwritten: — does not affect mc]
[handwritten: — does not affect p or q]

Axis labels: Price, Marginal Revenue, Marginal Cost, and Average Cost — vertical; Quantity — horizontal. Curves labeled LRAC₁, LRAC₀, MC₀, MR, D. Points P_0, Q_0.

Price Controls

Price controls are normally used to regulate public utilities supplied by a single private firm. In Figure 9–18, such a monopolist, in the absence of regulation, would maximize profits by producing output Q_4 and selling it at price P_4 to acquire pure profits. The regulatory commission would therefore impose a price ceiling at some level below P_4. If the regulated maximum price is $\bar{P}$, the horizontal line $\bar{P}A$ in Figure 9–18 becomes the monopolist's effective demand and marginal revenue curves for output levels ranging from 0 to $\bar{Q}$, because any quantity of output within this range can be sold at price $\bar{P}$. Since the effective demand curve in this range is horizontal, $\bar{P} = MR$. By equating the MC curve with the effective MR curve at point A, the monopolist can now maximize profits by producing quantity $\bar{Q}$ and selling it at the regulated price ceiling of $\bar{P}$. Because point A lies on the demand curve D, supply is equal to demand and the market is in equilibrium. The regulated price ceiling has reduced the monopolist's pure profits, reduced the price of the product, and increased the total quantity sold to consumers.

The ceiling price $\bar{P}$ illustrated in Figure 9–18 was not arbitrarily selected. Suppose that the price ceiling had been placed somewhere between $\bar{P}$ and P_4—say, at P_3—instead. The effective demand curve would then be P_3E, to the left of point E, so that between outputs of 0 and Q_3, MR = P_3. At output levels greater than Q_3, the monopolist's demand curve would be its unregulated

[handwritten in left margin: because P doesn't fall, it doesn't increase; in other words P=MR]

Figure 9–18
Effects of a Price Ceiling

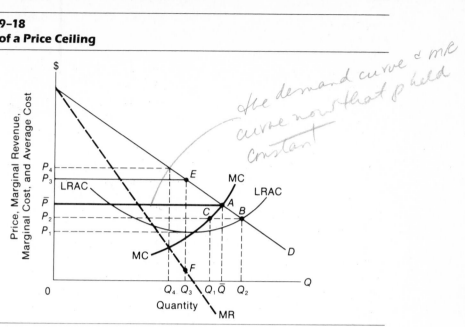

demand curve to the right of point E. Thus, the firm's MR curve at output levels greater than Q_3 would be its unregulated MR curve to the right of point F, so that the firm's MR curve at output Q_3 is discontinuous between points E and F in Figure 9–18. Since the MC curve cuts through the MR curve in this discontinuous region at output Q_3, the firm will maximize profits by producing output Q_3 and selling it at the regulated price of P_3. This course of action is preferable to setting an unregulated price, since a greater level of output can be supplied at a lower price. However, it is less desirable than setting a price of $\bar{P}$, because the price of the last unit sold exceeds its marginal cost.

Now we will consider a price below $\bar{P}$ but greater than P_1—the price that corresponds to the minimum point on the firm's LRAC curve.[14] At first glance, a likely candidate would appear to be price P_2, because quantity Q_2 would be demanded at this price. If the monopolist were to supply quantity Q_2 at P_2, price would decrease, output would increase, and no pure profits would result. However, the profit-maximizing monopolist would not voluntarily supply output Q_2, because at price ceiling P_2, the effective MR curve of the firm to the left of output Q_2 would be P_2B. Profit maximization would therefore occur at output level Q_1 corresponding to the intersection of the MC curve and the effective MR curve at point C in Figure 9–18, instead of at Q_2.

[14]At prices below P_1, the monopolist would obviously incur pure losses and stop production.

got r!

Since $Q_1 < Q_2$, there would be an excess demand for the product at price P_2, and the monopolist would have to establish a nonprice form of rationing to allocate the available output. An alternative solution might be to force the monopolist to produce at output level Q_2, but in effect this would require that the regulatory agency take over and run the industry. Experience with governmentally operated industries does not provide much justification for embracing this suggestion with enthusiasm.

where MC=D
& this determines
P

Given the alternative price ceilings illustrated in Figure 9–18, $\bar{P}$ would be the best choice, because price and pure profits are reduced, output is increased, and the quantity voluntarily supplied by the monopolist will be equal to the quantity demanded. Since the ceiling price $\bar{P}$ is determined by the intersection of the monopolistic firm's marginal cost and demand curves, this method of monopoly regulation is often referred to as **marginal cost pricing.**

Unfortunately, regulatory agencies cannot always employ marginal cost pricing to control monopolistic behavior. As an example, we will consider the monopolist depicted in Figure 9–19, whose long-run average cost curve continuously declines at all levels of output. Such a monopolist is called a **natural monopolist,** because the negative slope of the LRAC curve prevents more than one firm from efficiently meeting the demand of the entire market. It is easy to see from the figure that the cost of producing any level of output is lower when all output is produced by one firm than when two or more firms produce total

Figure 9–19
Natural Monopoly Regulation

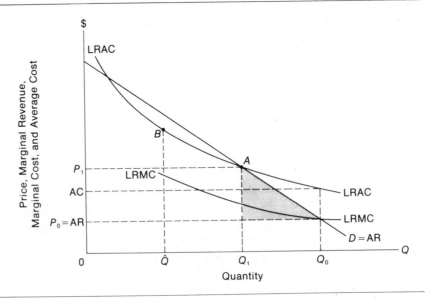

industry output. For example, if Q_1 units are produced by one firm, the average cost is given by the distance Q_1A in Figure 9–19. But if two firms produce $\frac{1}{2}Q_1 = \hat{Q}$ apiece, then the average cost of production will increase to the distance $\hat{Q}B$.

Due to the fact that the natural monopolist's LRAC curve is negatively sloped at all levels of output, the long-run marginal cost LRMC curve will always lie below the LRAC curve. Therefore, if the price ceiling is determined by the intersection of the LRMC curve and market demand D and is set at P_0, as shown in Figure 9–19, the monopolistic firm's long-run average cost will exceed its average revenue and production will cease.

In the case of natural monopolies, an alternative to marginal cost pricing is to set the price ceiling at the level determined by the intersection of the monopolist's LRAC and AR curves, which would be P_1 in Figure 9–19. At this price, the monopolist will produce output Q_1 and receive only normal profits. However, this is not the most efficient solution, since the cost to society of producing this level of output will be less than society is willing to pay. The tinted area in Figure 9–19 indicates the loss in efficiency that results from equating the natural monopolist's average cost with its average revenue. Since lowering price and increasing output clearly improves efficiency, some economists have suggested that optimal efficiency could be achieved by equating the natural monopolist's price with its marginal cost and then, providing the monopoly with a government subsidy equal to the difference between its average cost and its average revenue to keep the firm in business.

Regulatory agencies are faced with the insurmountable problem of obtaining information. In our analysis here, we have assumed that the monopolist's marginal cost is measurable and known. In the real world, accountants and economists measure marginal cost in a variety of ways. Since there is no single correct method to use to ascertain marginal cost, the regulators usually obtain the information they require from the regulated industry itself. And obviously, the regulated industry will be tempted to prejudice this information in its favor.[15]

The Application of Monopoly Theory to Government Regulation   9–10

The economic theory of pure monopoly we have examined in this chapter has served as the basis for the passage of state and federal legislation designed to control the undesirable effects produced by an actual monopoly. In this section, we will limit our attention to one of the most frequently cited antimonop-

---

[15]For a more detailed discussion of the practical problems associated with marginal cost pricing, see J. Wiseman, "The Theory of Public Utility Price–An Empty Box," *Oxford Economic Papers*, Vol. 9 (1957), pp. 56–74, and Stephen C. Littlechild, "Controlling the Nationalized Industries: *Quis Custodiet Ipsos Custodes?*," University of Birmingham (England), Faculty of Commerce and Social Science, Series B Discussion Paper No. 56 (August 1979).

oly laws—Section 2(a) of the Clayton Act of 1914 as amended by the Robinson-Patman Act of 1936. This statute makes it

> ... unlawful for any person ... to discriminate in price between different purchasers ... where the effect of such discrimination may be substantially to lessen competition or tend to create a monopoly ... or to injure, destroy, or prevent competition with any person ... who knowingly receives the benefit of such discrimination, or with customers of either of them.

However, this law does not

> ... prevent [price] differentials which make only due allowance for differences in the cost of manufacturing, sale, or delivery resulting from the differing methods or quantities in which such commodities are ... sold or delivered.

Economists raise the following questions with respect to such legislation:

1. Is the legislation being applied in cases where an actual monopoly exists?
2. Does the legislation achieve its goal of increasing competition within the regulated industry?
3. Do consumers benefit from the legislation?

In this section, we will examine three cases in which federal antimonopoly laws were allegedly applied to protect consumers from price discrimination. Although these are not textbook cases of pure monopoly, the courts and the Congress have decided that they are sufficiently similar to conditions of pure monopoly that the theoretical models we have examined in this chapter can serve as economic justification for antimonopoly law enforcement.

Application: The Borden Milk Case

In 1948, the Federal Trade Commission (FTC) charged the Borden Company with price discrimination in the form of selling the same product to different customers at different prices. Specifically, Borden was charged with packaging and selling its Borden-label brand of evaporated milk to distributors at a higher price than it sold the chemically identical product under the distributors' private label.

Borden countered the FTC suit by arguing that cost considerations allowed the company to sell the private-label canned milk at a lower price because lower clerical costs, less expensive labels and cartons, and no freight charges, storage fees, brokerage fees, or advertising expenditures were associated with the private-label milk. For these reasons and others we will refer to later in this discussion, the commissioner at the 1961 FTC hearing ruled in favor of Borden and ordered the complaint dismissed.

Despite the ruling of its own commissioner in 1962, the FTC ordered Borden to stop selling chemically equivalent canned milk at different prices. The FTC's primary argument was that due to the company's size, Borden possessed certain monopolistic powers. However, economic evidence did not support this, since Borden's share of the canned-milk market had risen from 9.9% to only 10.7% over the 1948–1962 period. Furthermore, this small increase in sales could be attributed to the fact that Borden's plants were geographically closer to the final markets than competing plants, so that its delivery prices were lower. As a result, the Circuit Court of Appeals dismissed the FTC's order in 1964. In addition to citing virtually no increase in Borden's share of the canned-milk market, the Circuit Court concluded that although an objective chemical analysis of the Borden-label and private-label milk might produce identical results, consumers subjectively considered the two products to be different, which was indicated by a willingness to pay a premium for the Borden-label milk over the private-label milk. The Circuit Court therefore ruled that the Borden-label and private-label milks legally could not be defined as the same product.

The FTC appealed the Circuit Court's decision to the U.S. Supreme Court. In 1966, in a split decision, the Supreme Court overturned the Circuit Court ruling on the basis that the intention of the Robinson–Patman Act was to treat name brands and private-label brands in the same manner if they were chemically identical. The minority opinion, however, argued that this was too narrow a definition of "like grade and quality" and that consumers in the market did not consider chemically identical name brands and private-label brands to be the same.[16]

Application: The Morton Salt Case

For many years the Morton Salt Company sold its "Blue Label" table salt according to the following pricing scheme:

1. Customers who purchased less than a carload lot of salt paid a delivery price of $1.60 per case.
2. The price per case when a carload shipment was purchased declined to $1.50.
3. Customers who bought more than 5,000 cases during a 12-month period paid a $1.40 price per case.
4. Customers buying more than 50,000 cases during any 12-month period paid the minimum price of $1.35 per case.

In 1940, the Federal Trade Commission ordered Morton Salt to stop this pricing practice, because the FTC felt that it gave retailers who could afford to buy

---

[16]The information cited in "The Borden Milk Case" and "The Morton Salt Case" applications draws heavily on the analysis found in D.T. Armentano, *The Myths of Antitrust* (New Rochelle, NY: Arlington House, 1972).

large quantities of salt an unfair advantage, thereby reducing and preventing competition in the retail grocery business.

Although Morton conceded that only four major grocery chains (American Stores, National Tea, Safeway Stores, and A&P) were able to purchase salt at the lowest price, it claimed that less than .01% of its entire sales were sold at the maximum of $1.60 per case. A large percentage of Morton's salt was sold to cooperatives that independent grocers formed to take advantage of the quantity discounts offered by the producer. For example, the National Retail-Owned Grocers, Inc., comprised of 18,917 members, purchased Morton Salt in sufficient quantities that its members paid $1.40 per case.

Morton Salt appealed the FTC decision before the Circuit Court of Appeals, which ruled 2 out of 3 in favor of Morton. The Circuit Court found that Morton's discounts were available to all purchasers and were similar to those offered by other firms that sold similar products. The Circuit Court also concluded that the FTC had not proved that Morton's pricing practice resulted in injury to purchasers who paid more than $1.35 per case. In particular, the Circuit Court pointed out that the sale of salt at the nondiscount price of $1.60 per case had actually risen during the period of investigation—a result that contradicted the FTC argument that small purchasers were being driven out of business. Finally, the majority view of the Circuit Court was that the carload quantity discounts were definitely related to cost savings, but whether or not the additional discounts were also cost-related was immaterial, since the FTC had failed to prove injury to the competition.

The FTC in turn appealed the Circuit Court's ruling to the Supreme Court, which reversed the lower court's ruling in a split decision. In essence, the Supreme Court decided that those grocers who paid higher prices for salt were obviously injured and that although the price discounts were said to be available to all customers, this was not true, since only four major chains were able to purchase salt at $1.35. Moreover, the Supreme Court took the position that the Robinson-Patman Act was designed to protect small businesses that were unable to buy salt in carload quantities. We will discuss the consequences of the Robinson-Patman Act in greater detail at the end of this section.

Application: The Utah Pie Case

In the early 1950s, many firms began to market frozen pies. Prior to 1957, the Salt Lake City frozen-pie market was principally served by three national firms— the Pet Milk Company, the Carnation Milk Company, and the Continental Baking Company. A local firm, the Utah Pie Company, was alert to changing consumer preferences and began to produce frozen pies late in 1957. Taking advantage of the low transportation costs due to its location, the Utah Pie Company was able to offer frozen pies at a lower price and attracted two-thirds of the market in Salt Lake City in 1958.

Pet, Carnation, and Continental decided to resort to price competition to regain their former shares of the Salt Lake City market, even if they had to reduce their profits per pie sold. All three companies cut the prices of their pies, so that although Utah Pie's profits continued to increase, its share of the market declined from 66.5% in 1958 to 45.3% in 1961. When the major frozen-pie producers in the Salt Lake City market reduced their prices, they were selling these pies at a lower price than they were charging customers in markets closer to their bakeries. The Utah Pie Company contested this pricing behavior, calling it discriminatory and illegal as specified under section 2(a) of the Robinson–Patman Act, and Pet, Continental, and Carnation were found guilty in a jury trial. The verdict was appealed to the Circuit Court, and the jury's decision was reversed on the grounds that insufficient evidence had been provided to prove that competition had been adversely affected by the price reductions.

The FTC then appealed the case to the U.S. Supreme Court, which reversed the Circuit Court's finding. The Supreme Court based its decision on the fact that the price of frozen pies in the Salt Lake City market had declined from 1958 to 1961 and that the national firms were responsible for this decline.[17]

Consequences of the Robinson–Patman Act

In light of the three cases we have just reviewed, we will now examine and evaluate how effectively federal antiprice discrimination legislation curbs the undesirable effects of monopoly power. In the Borden case, the Borden Company was able to increase its private-label sales by passing cost savings on to its customers. This pricing policy caused competitors' sales to decline and the prices paid by consumers to decrease. The fact that Borden's brand-name and private-label milk was chemically identical did not make the products identical, because consumers subjectively considered them to be different enough to justify a retail price differential. The actions of the Borden Company did not reduce competition, but fostered it and brought the fruits of competition–reduced prices–to the consumer. The adverse effects of Borden's marketing behavior were therefore not felt by the consumer, but were borne by the less efficient firms in the market.

In the Morton Salt case, cost savings were clearly achieved by selling carload quantities, and only one-tenth of 1% of all sales failed to qualify for this discount. Due to cooperative buying, most grocers paid $1.40 per case, so that the retail cost differential between small, nondiscount stores and the nationwide chains could not have been more than one-fifth of 1 cent per package. It is unlikely that this differential resulted in any reduction in the competitive structure of the grocery business. The purpose of the Supreme Court decision was to protect the profitability of the small, nondiscount customers of Morton Salt and to insulate them from the forces that exist in a competitive market. The Supreme Court sought to maintain the *status quo* in the retail grocery business and to prevent the consumer from benefiting from economies of scale in distribution and marketing.

---

[17]This section is based on Ward S. Bowman, "Restraint of Trade by the Supreme Court: The Utah Pie Case," *The Yale Law Journal* (November 1967), pp. 70–85.

The Utah Pie case presents perhaps the clearest example of the consequences of a misdirected regulatory policy purportedly designed to prevent the abuses of monopoly power. In this case, major pie producers reduced their prices to meet the competition of the Utah Pie Company, which is precisely the response we would expect in a competitive market. But the Supreme Court chose to view this response as evidence that Pet, Carnation, and Consolidated were violating the Robinson–Patman Act. The Supreme Court decision was based on the fact that Pet, Carnation, and Consolidated sold pies in the Salt Lake City market at prices below the prices of identical pies sold in other markets closer to their manufacturing plants. In other words, the Supreme Court ruled that these companies engaged in monopolistic price discrimination.

The unifying thread that joins the three cases cited in this section is the implication that the existence of price discrimination automatically indicates exploitation of an existing monopoly market position or the attempt to create a monopoly. The former impression is derived from the theory of segmented-market price discrimination; the latter is based on the theory of predatory price discrimination. A third reason that firms employ price discrimination is to *foster* (rather than to destroy or prevent) competition. In this situation, a firm may be acting *defensively* to protect or establish itself in the market or *offensively* to break down existing monopolies or quasi-monopolies. The three cases examined in this section provide examples of price discrimination that reflect the competitive forces passing benefits on to the consumer in the form of lower prices. In these cases the Supreme Court ruled in effect *against* competition, and these rulings are typical of the Court's approach to the problem of monopoly power. These facts raise serious questions concerning the adequacy of much federal antimonopoly legislation.[18]

In Chapter 10, we will examine economic theories that have been designed to deal with market situations similar to the ones discussed in this section.

9–11 Summary

The two extremes of the spectrum of economic models that have been constructed to explain market organization are *perfect competition* and *pure monopoly*. In Chapter 9, we have learned that a *pure monopoly* exists if there is a single seller of a product that has no close substitutes and if there are barriers that prevent other firms from entering the monopolist's market. We have seen that in contrast to the perfectly elastic demand curve of the perfectly competitive firm, the monopolistic firm's demand curve is downward sloping so that its marginal revenue curve lies *below* its average revenue curve. And we have learned to graph the marginal revenue curves for both linear and nonlinear demand curves.

---

[18]For a thorough examination of this issue, see Robert H. Bork, *The Antitrust Paradox* (New York: Basic Books, 1978).

Like the perfectly competitive firm, the monopolistic firm is assumed to be a profit maximizer that attempts to operate at the level of output at which the difference between the firm's total revenue and its total cost is the greatest. We have proved that profits are maximized at the level of output that corresponds to the condition of equality between marginal revenue and marginal cost. Because the monopolistic firm's marginal revenue curve lies below its demand or average revenue curve, the price at which the monopolist's product is sold will be greater than the marginal cost of production. We have also seen that a monopoly position in a market does *not* guarantee that a firm will receive positive profits.

We have found that whether the monopolistic firm operates in the long run or in the short run, it will maximize profits by equating its marginal cost with its marginal revenue. In the long run, however, the firm is not limited to a specific scale of plant. We now know that the profit-maximizing scale of plant is determined by the short-run average cost curve that is tangent to the monopolist's long-run average cost curve at the level of output at which long-run marginal cost is equal to marginal revenue. When the optimal scale of plant is operated at its profit-maximizing level of output, its short-run marginal cost curve will simultaneously intersect its long-run marginal cost and marginal revenue curves.

In contrast to the well-defined supply curve of the perfectly competitive firm, we have seen that the monopolist does not supply a given quantity of output at a specific price. Thus, the monopolistic firm does not have a short-run supply curve in the sense that the perfectly competitive firm has such a curve.

In the short run, we have found that the multiplant monopolist can maximize profits only if each plant is operated so that the marginal costs of production for all plants are equal. In the long run, the scale of plant for all of the monopolist's plants will be represented by the short-run average cost curve that is tangent to the firm's long-run average cost curve at its minimum point. If all costs faced by the monopolistic firm are constant, then its long-run marginal cost curve will be *horizontal*. However, if costs increase as the firm expands its number of plants, the monopolist's long-run marginal cost curve will slope upward and to the right.

In this chapter, we have also examined the reasons why firms may practice *price discrimination*. The monopolist is most likely to engage in price discrimination to maximize profits from a given monopoly position. The monopolist benefits from price discrimination when customers can be easily separated into distinct groups with different demand characteristics. Once this is accomplished, the monopolist can practice segmented-market price discrimination by charging different prices to the customers in each group and making a larger profit than would be the case if all consumers were charged the same price. *Multipart price discrimination* is another method a monopolist employs to increase profits. When this form of price discrimination is practiced, each customer is charged a different price for varying amounts of the product purchased. Still another method of price discrimination exercised by the monopolist is *predatory pricing*, in which the monopolistic firm prices its product below cost in the short run to bankrupt competitors, to "persuade" them to merge, or to encourage collusion on industry outputs and prices. Economic theory indicates that predatory pricing is unlikely to maximize monopoly profits, and empirical evidence tends to support this view due to the limited number of documented cases of predatory pricing.

We have learned that economic theory points out that pure monopoly leads to the following undesirable welfare effects compared with the welfare effects of perfect competition.

1. In a monopoly, lesser amounts of a product are sold at higher prices.
2. Price exceeds marginal cost in a monopoly. In perfect competition, marginal cost is equal to price.
3. Since the value society places on the last unit produced exceeds its cost under monopolistic conditions but is equal to its cost under perfectly competitive conditions, the welfare of society could be increased by moving from a condition of pure monopoly to one of perfect competition.

These conclusions form the theoretical basis for the government's current regulation of monopolies.

We have also examined the two most popular methods of regulating monopolies—*taxation policies* and *price controls*. Regulating monopolies by taxation usually assumes the form of a *per-unit tax*, a *lump-sum tax*, or a *profits tax*. Of these three methods of taxation, the profits tax and the lump-sum tax are preferable, because they do not reduce output and they decrease the prices paid by consumers.

Given sufficient information, the regulatory agency can choose a price ceiling that produces lower prices and greater output than the prices and output levels that result from taxation regulation. Unless the firm is a natural monopoly, the regulated price should be chosen such that marginal cost is equal to the average revenue at the regulated price. This is referred to as *marginal cost pricing*. The long-run marginal cost curve of a *natural monopolist* will be negatively sloped and will lie below the long-run average cost curve at all levels of output. If the marginal cost pricing rule is applied in this situation, the monopolist must be subsidized by the government to remain in business. An alternative way of regulating natural monopolies would be to equate demand or average revenue and average cost. In the real world, the application of theoretical pricing rules is much more difficult, and no rule can ensure an unambiguous, optimal allocation of resources.

Finally, in this chapter, we have seen that the application of monopoly theory when natural monopolies do not exist has led to Supreme Court decisions that have produced *less* competition in the marketplace, so that antimonopoly legislation such as the Robinson–Patman Act in practice has often worked against the consumer. Three cases—the Borden Milk case, the Morton Salt case, and the Utah Pie case—were cited as typical examples of the misapplication of monopoly theory.

In Chapter 10, we will examine theoretical models that have been developed to represent market conditions that are not perfectly competitive or purely monopolistic.

References

Armentano, D.T. *The Myths of Antitrust.* New Rochelle, NY: Arlington House, 1972.

Bork, Robert H. *The Antitrust Paradox.* New York: Basic Books, 1978.

Bowman, Ward S. "Restraint of Trade by the Supreme Court: The Utah Pie Case." *The Yale Law Journal* (November 1967), pp. 70–85.

Davidson, Ralph Kirby. *Price Discrimination in Selling Gas and Electricity.* Baltimore: Johns Hopkins Press, 1955.

Foster, William S. (ed.). *Modern Water Rates.* New York: American City Magazine, 1966.

Friedman, Milton. *Price Theory.* Chicago: Aldine, 1976.

Friedman, Milton, and Simon Kuznets. *Income from Independent Professional Practice.* New York: National Bureau of Economic Research, 1945.

Harberger, Arnold C. "Monopoly and Resource Allocation." *American Economic Review* (May 1954), pp. 77–87.

Hicks, John R. "Annual Survey of Economic Theory: The Theory of Monopoly." *Econometrica,* Vol. 3 (January 1935).

Kamerschen, David R. "An Estimate of the 'Welfare Loss' from Monopoly in the American Economy." *Western Economic Journal* (Summer 1966), pp. 221–36.

Kessel, Rueben A. "Price Discrimination in Medicine." *The Journal of Law and Economics* (October 1958), pp. 20–53.

Kitch, Edmund W., Marc Isaacson, and Daniel Kasper. "Regulation of Taxicabs in Chicago." *The Journal of Law and Economics* (October 1971), pp. 285–350.

Koller, Roland H., II. "The Myth of Predatory Pricing: An Empirical Study." In Yale Brozen (ed.). *The Competitive Economy.* Morristown, NJ: General Learning Press, 1975, pp. 418–28.

Littlechild, Stephen C. "Controlling the Nationalized Industries: *Quis Custodiet Ipsos Custodes?*" University of Birmingham (England), Faculty of Commerce and Social Science. Series B Discussion Paper No. 56 (August 1979).

McGee, John S. "Predatory Price Cutting: The Standard Oil (N.J.) Case." *The Journal of Law and Economics* (October 1958), pp. 137–69.

Posner, Richard A. "The Social Costs of Monopoly and Regulation." *Journal of Political Economy* (August 1975), pp. 807–27.

Rayack, Elton. "The Physicians' Service Industry." In Walter Adams (ed.). *The Structure of American Industry,* 5th ed. New York: Macmillan, 1977, pp. 401–41.

Robinson, Joan. *The Economics of Imperfect Competition.* London: Macmillan, 1933.

Stigler, George J. "The Statistics of Monopoly and Merger." *Journal of Political Economy* (February 1956), pp. 33–40.

Stigler, George J. *The Theory of Price,* 3rd ed. New York: Macmillan, 1966.

Tullock, Gordon. "The Welfare Costs of Tariffs, Monopolies, and Theft." *Western Economic Journal* (June 1967), pp. 224–32.

Wiseman, J. "The Theory of Public Utility Price—An Empty Box." *Oxford Economic Papers,*
    Vol. 9 (1957), pp. 56–74.

Worcester, Dean A., Jr. "New Estimates of the Welfare Loss to Monopoly, United States:
    1956–1969." *Southern Economic Journal* (October 1973), pp. 418–28.

Yamey, B.S. "Predatory Price Cutting: Notes and Comments." *The Journal of Law and Eco-
    nomics* (October 1972), pp. 129–42.

Problems

1. In this chapter, you learned that using marginal cost pricing to regulate natural monopolies is unsatisfactory. Is it also possible that for essentially the same reason, marginal cost pricing may not be applicable when the monopolistic firm's long-run average cost curve is a typical U-shaped curve? Explain.

2. Prove that the total revenue curve of the perfectly competitive firm implies that its demand curve has a slope of 0, whereas the total revenue curve of the monopolistic firm implies that its demand curve has a negative slope.

3. The sale of an additional unit of output has the same effect on price if it is sold by a competitive firm or by a monopoly. Why is this effect taken into consideration by the monopoly, but not by the competitive firm? Marginal revenue for a linear demand curve can be expressed as

$$MR = P + \frac{\Delta P}{\Delta Q} Q$$

where P is the price and Q is the quantity sold, should help you to answer this question.

4. In 1901, the United States Steel Corporation accounted for almost 90% of domestic steel production and could have been characterized as a natural monopoly. Today, U.S. Steel manufactures about 25% of all domestically produced steel and cannot be described as a natural monopoly. If anything, technological changes have increased the output range over which the average cost of steel production is declining. What change explains why U.S. Steel is no longer a natural monopoly? Illustrate your answer graphically.

5. Graph the demand curve and the marginal revenue curve, assuming that the price elasticity of demand is equal to 1 everywhere. If the marginal cost of production is positive, what is the profit-maximizing output for this monopolist?

6. Assume that a price-discriminating monopolist has separated his customers into two markets. The prices P and quantities Q in market 1 and market 2 are as follows:

MARKET 1		MARKET 2	
P	$\hat{Q}$	P	$\hat{Q}$
$10	1	$5	1
9	2	4.5	2
8	3	4	3
7	4	3.5	4
6	5	3	5
5	6	2.5	6
4	7	2	7
3	8	1.5	8
2	9	1	9
1	10	.5	10

If the marginal cost of production for either market 1 or market 2 is just slightly less than $2, what quantity will the profit-maximizing monopolist sell in each market? What price will this monopolist charge in each market? Which market exhibits the highest price elasticity of demand when the profit-maximizing price is being charged in both markets? Explain why this is an intuitive result.

7. Suppose that a multiplant monopolist owns two plants and that the cost of production in each plant is as follows:

PLANT 1		PLANT 2	
Q	TC	Q	TC
1	$ 5	1	$ 2
2	11	2	5
3	18	3	9
4	26	4	15
5	35	5	24
6	46	6	37
7	58	7	55
8	70	8	79
9	83	9	110
10	97	10	152

(a) If the monopolist wishes to produce 5 units of output Q, how much would be manufactured in each plant?

(b) If the monopolist wishes to produce 10 units of output Q, how much would be manufactured in each plant?

(c) How did you allocate the units of production between each plant in (a) and (b)?

8. Some so-called "singles bars" offer beverages to women at a lower price than they charge men for the same drinks. Does this segmented-market price discrimination provide the only explanation for this form of sexual discrimination?

9. Why does price discrimination tend to occur more often in the service industries than in the manufacturing industries?

10. U.S. patent laws grant monopoly rights to inventors for a maximum of 34 years. Why are these laws allowed to coexist with the antimonopoly laws? What reward would inventors receive under conditions of perfect competition?

CHAPTER TEN

IMPERFECT COMPETITION

In our examination of the economic theory of the firm thus far, we have considered the two polar extremes of perfect competition and pure monopoly. It should be obvious at this point that neither case is frequently encountered in the real world. We seldom, if ever, purchase perfectly homogeneous products that are sold by a large number of firms. Nor do we often find ourselves in the position of having to purchase a good or a service for which there is no close substitute from a single seller. In the real world, we are confronted with many large and small firms, selling heterogeneous products that have many close substitutes.

The apparent lack of correspondence between the models of perfect competition and pure monopoly and the real world began to become obvious to economists in the 1920s. Led by the pioneering works of Edward Chamberlin and Joan Robinson,[1] these economists launched an attack on the orthodox neoclassical models of the firm. In this chapter, we will examine some of the theories this literature has produced and apply them to some real-world problems.

Monopolistic Competition 10–2

In his theory of monopolistic competition, Chamberlin began the construction of what he hoped would be a more realistic model of the firm with a critical set of assumptions describing the characteristics of the firm. Foremost among Chamberlin's more realistic assumptions was that in contrast to the perfectly homogeneous product of firms in perfect competition, firms in monopolistic

---

[1]Edward Chamberlin, *The Theory of Monopolistic Competition* (Cambridge, MA: Harvard University Press, 1933); Joan Robinson, *The Economics of Imperfect Competition* (London: Macmillan, 1933).

competition sell *heterogeneous products* that are slightly *differentiated* from one another in some way. For example, consider the large number of brands of bath soap and the even further differentiation within a given brand by means of scent, color, shape, and so on. Since all products are differentiated, each firm has some control over the price at which it sells its output. In other words, in contrast to the perfectly competitive firm's horizontal demand curve, the monopolistically competitive firm's demand curve is negatively sloped like the monopolist's demand curve. However, because the product of the monopolistically competitive firm is only slightly differentiated from the products of its competitors, consumers can find many close substitutes for the product so that the monopolistically competitive firm's demand curve is highly price-elastic. Therefore, although the monopolistically competitive firm has an absolute monopoly in terms of the differentiated product it markets, this monopolistic power is severely limited by the competition from firms selling products that are close substitutes.

Monopolistic competition also differs from perfect competition in that complete information is not assumed on the part of either the sellers or the buyers. In perfect competition, it is assumed that complete information is known in the market, so there is no need for firms to expend funds on advertising. In the real world, however, firms engage in advertising, and monopolistically competitive models explicitly allow for sales promotion costs. Advertising is necessary because buyers have *imperfect knowledge* about the products sold by firms. To overcome the ignorance of buyers and to increase the demand for their products, firms advertise. As long as advertising adds more to sales revenue than to production costs, it is less than the optimal amount. Consequently, firms will increase advertising expenditures until the marginal revenue yielded by one additional dollar of advertising is just equal to $1.

The assumption of less than complete information on the part of consumers gives rise to an important corollary assumption that will play a critical part in our subsequent analysis. If a large number of firms are producing similar products, it is assumed that each firm believes that it can act to increase its share of the market *without detection by competitors.* In this regard, monopolistic competition is just like perfect competition, because firms are assumed to function independently of one another. We will soon see that this assumption gives each firm a distorted view of its true market demand curve and results in the pricing and output decisions that are characteristic of monopolistic competition.

The assumption that each firm produces a slightly differentiated product leads to the conclusion that homogeneous goods can only be produced by an individual firm. Given our previous definition that an *industry* is comprised of firms that sell a homogeneous product, this results in the unsatisfactory conclusion that each monopolistically competitive firm is an industry in itself. We are interested in the interaction of firms competing for consumer purchases in a market, but it is difficult to discuss competition within a partial-equilibrium framework if the market consists of only one firm. To solve this problem,

Chamberlin suggested grouping firms that produce similar products together— for example, all laundry-detergent manufacturers. Chamberlin called these groups of similar firms *product groups,* but we will use the more familiar, if somewhat inaccurate, term *industry* throughout our discussion of monopolistic competition.

Short-Run Equilibrium in Monopolistic Competition

In contrast to the perfectly competitive firm, which does not need to lower price to increase sales and which will lose *all* sales if it increases price, the monopolistically competitive firm exerts some influence over pricing decisions. This is because the monopolistically competitive firm's demand curve is negatively sloped. Thus, a monopolistically competitive firm's sales will increase if it reduces its price below the price of its competitors, all other factors remaining constant, and its sales will decrease, but not necessarily decline to 0, if it raises its price. In this regard, the demand curve of the monopolistically competitive firm is similar to the pure monopolist's demand curve.

However, unlike the pure monopoly which has the market all to itself, the monopolistically competitive firm shares total market demand with many other firms. In our examination of monopolistic competition, we will make the simplifying assumption that the monopolistically competitive firm has a **proportional demand curve.** In other words, if there are 100 firms in a monopolistically competitive industry (product group) and all firms in the industry are charging the same price, the output level demanded from the firm will be exactly 1/100 of total market demand. If we further assume that all firms in the industry have *identical costs,* then all firms will be of equal size. Given these assumptions, any firm in the industry can be selected to represent the behavior of all firms in the industry and is therefore called a **representative firm.**

In Figure 10−1, *DD* is the proportional demand curve faced by the representative firm in a monopolistically competitive industry. To establish the initial price and quantity conditions, we will assume that each firm in this monopolistically competitive industry is selling quantity Q_1 at price P_1, as shown in the figure.

As we pointed out earlier, one of the important characteristics of a monopolistically competitive firm is that it does not have complete information about the behavior of the other firms in the industry when it varies its price. The most important assumption of the theory of monopolistic competition is that each firm believes that if it lowers its price, its behavior will not be noticed by other firms in the industry and they will not follow suit. By lowering its price, the firm therefore believes it will obtain a larger share of the market and increase its profits. This crucial assumption of monopolistic competition is depicted by the firm's **perceived demand curve** D_p, which intersects the proportional demand curve *DD* at the assumed initial price of P_1 in Figure 10−1.

The monopolistically competitive firm's belief that it can vary its price to

Figure 10–1
Monopolistic Competition: The Firm in Disequilibrium

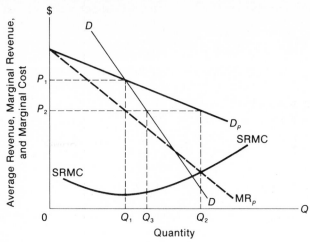

maximize profits without its competitors behaving in a similar way is erroneous, because each firm in the industry believes this and therefore all firms will reduce their prices in a vain attempt to capture more of the market. Each firm lowers its price under the mistaken belief that the other firms will be holding their prices constant. Since all firms are simultaneously lowering price, each firm's relative share of the market will remain the same, with demand curve DD specifying the actual quantity that can be sold at any price.

The manner in which the monopolistically competitive firm behaves is illustrated in Figure 10–1. The firm is initially selling output Q_1 at price P_1, and the firm perceives that its relevant demand curve is D_p and not DD. To maximize its anticipated profits based on its perceived demand curve, the firm will attempt to equate its **perceived marginal revenue curve** MR_p with its short-run marginal cost SRMC curve and produce output Q_2, as shown in the figure. This firm mistakenly believes that output Q_2 can be sold at price P_2, and it will begin to expand production in an attempt to produce Q_2. However, since all other firms also believe that their profit-maximizing output is Q_2, they will also begin to expand their production. When all firms in the industry are increasing output simultaneously, no firm can increase its relative share of the market, so that the quantity of output that each firm can sell at P_2 is Q_3, rather than the perceived profit-maximizing output of Q_2.

Since each firm will be forced to remain on its proportional demand curve DD selling output Q_3 at price P_2, the perceived demand curve will shift downward to D_p', as shown in Figure 10–2. But the firm will still not be in equilibrium because its new perceived marginal revenue MR_p' is not equal to its

Figure 10-2
Monopolistic Competition: Movement Toward Equilibrium

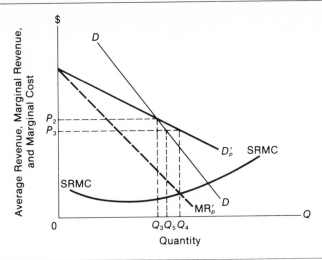

short-run marginal cost SRMC at output Q_3. Once again, the firm believes that it can increase its relative share of the market by moving down its D_p' curve and producing the perceived profit-maximizing output of Q_4, which the firm believes can be sold at price P_3. However, all other firms believe that they can also increase their profits by reducing price and increasing output quantities. As a result of this monopolistically competitive behavior by all firms, the firm's actual demand curve will still be DD, not D_p'. Since each firm will only be able to sell output Q_5 at price P_3, the firm's perceived demand curve will shift downward once more until it intersects the proportional demand curve DD at price P_3. At this point, each firm will still believe that its profits are not maximized (that $MR > SRMC$) and will continue to adjust its price and output.

The monopolistically competitive firm will be in short-run equilibrium when the perceived profit-maximizing output is equal to the output that the firm can actually sell at the perceived profit-maximizing price. Short-run equilibrium in monopolistic competition is illustrated in Figure 10-3, where the representative firm's perceived demand curve D_p intersects the proportional demand curve DD at price $\bar{P}$. The perceived profit-maximizing output, determined by the intersection of the perceived marginal revenue curve, MR_p, and the SRMC curve is $\bar{Q}$. At output $\bar{Q}$, the firm will actually be able to sell all that it produces at price $\bar{P}$, because the D_p curve also intersects the DD curve at $\bar{Q}$. Thus, perceived profit maximization will be realized and there will be no incentive for firms to make any further adjustments in price or output in the short run.

Figure 10–3
Short-Run Equilibrium in Monopolistic Competition

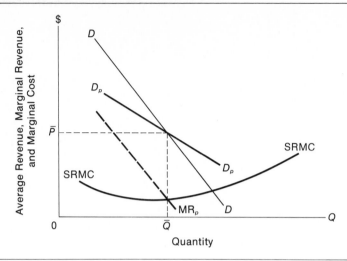

Long-Run Equilibrium in Monopolistic Competition

In the long run, a monopolistically competitive firm is able to alter its scale of plant and to enter or leave a product group. As in both perfect competition and pure monopoly, a necessary condition for long-run equilibrium is that long-run marginal cost LRMC be equal to marginal revenue MR.

The long-run equilibrium price $\bar{P}$ and output $\bar{Q}$ for the representative firm in monopolistic competition are shown in Figure 10–4. In addition to the previously stated conditions of long-run equilibrium, each firm must be earning 0 economic profits in the long run. This condition follows from our earlier assumption that outside firms are free to enter a monopolistically competitive industry, so that whenever firms in a given product group are earning pure profits, other firms will be attracted to that industry and output will expand. Furthermore, as additional firms enter the market, each firm's proportional demand curve DD will shift to the left, since the quantity demanded of each firm will become smaller at any market price. In long-run equilibrium, the long-run average cost LRAC curve will be tangent to the perceived demand curve D_p at its point of intersection with the proportional demand curve DD, as shown by point A in Figure 10–4. The intersection of the DD and D_p curves at the long-run equilibrium price $\bar{P}$ and quantity $\bar{Q}$ is another necessary condition, because if the perceived profit-maximizing price and quantity were not in accord with realizable market conditions, firms would alter price and quantity. In the long run, firms have no incentive to change price, quantity, or plant size. Figure 10–4 depicts all the necessary conditions for long-run equilibrium in monopolistic competition.

Figure 10–4
Long-Run Equilibrium in Monopolistic Competition

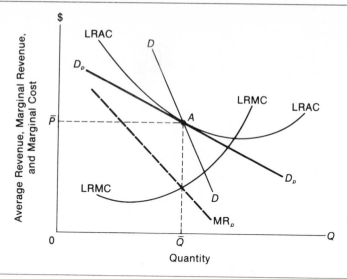

Long-Run Equilibrium: Perfect Versus Monopolistic Competition

We are now ready to compare the long-run equilibrium conditions necessary for perfect competition and monopolistic competition. In Chapter 8, we showed that in long-run equilibrium, the perfectly competitive firm will be producing at the minimum point on its LRAC curve and consequently will be producing at the minimum point on its SRAC curve at the same time. This long-run equilibrium is illustrated at the profit-maximizing output in perfect competition $\bar{Q}_{PC}$ in Figure 10–5.

The long-run, profit-maximizing level of output in monopolistic competition must lie to the left of the minimum point on the LRAC curve. This occurs because the firm's perceived demand curve D_pD_p is negatively sloped due to product differentiation and must be tangent to the LRAC curve in long-run equilibrium, which can only take place to the left of the minimum point on the LRAC curve. This conclusion is illustrated in Figure 10–5, where the profit-maximizing output in monopolistic competition $\bar{Q}_{MC}$ lies to the left of $\bar{Q}_{PC}$.

The "ideal" level of output in terms of productive efficiency occurs at the point where the long-run average cost is at its minimum. In Figure 10–5, the LRAC curve is at its minimum point at output $\bar{Q}_{PC}$. As we have just shown, however, the monopolistically competitive firm will not produce at this "ideal" output but will produce to the left of $\bar{Q}_{PC}$ at $\bar{Q}_{MC}$. The difference between the actual output and the "ideal" output in long-run equilibrium is called **excess capacity.** In the case of monopolistic competition, actual output lies to the left of "ideal" output and excess capacity is negative. Some economists therefore argue that

Figure 10-5
Comparison of Long-Run Equilibrium
Between Monopolistic and Perfect Competition

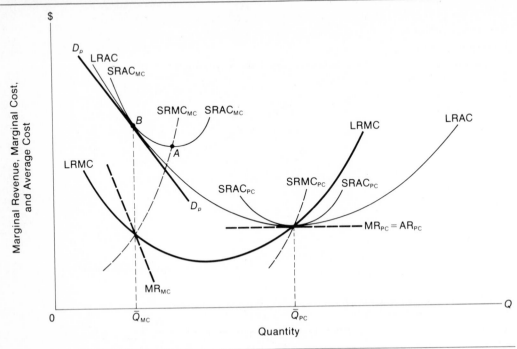

monopolistic competition reduces plant size, so that firms become too small to produce at the lowest long-run average cost, and that this in turn results in productive inefficiencies.

But not all economists view production at the lowest point on the LRAC curve as "ideal" when the value to society of having differentiated products is considered. The difference between the actual long-run average cost and the minimum or "ideal" average cost is the cost of producing differentiated products. In other words, if all facial tissue were the same color, size, scent, and texture and were packaged in brown paper boxes, than facial tissue could probably be produced at lower cost. But since consumers clearly prefer to have a choice of facial tissues, as their willingness to pay higher prices for differentiated facial tissues indicates, the difference between the production costs of identical and differentiated tissues is merely a measure of the value society places on variety.

Another observation frequently made by economists concerns the long-run equilibrium solution in monopolistic competition. In Figure 10-5, the monopolistically competitive firm builds a scale of plant represented by the SRAC$_{MC}$ curve, but instead of operating at point A (the minimum point on SRAC$_{MC}$), the firm operates to the left at point B. Some economists refer to this as *positive*

excess capacity, since the plant is being operated at less than its most technically efficient level of output. These same economists cite such evidence as
unused checkout counters in supermarkets and jet airliners flown at less than
maximum capacity to support their theoretical conclusions. Such casual empiricism ignores the important fact that the number of checkout counters in a grocery store or the number of passenger seats on an airliner is determined by
the requirements of customers at or near conditions of *peak demand.* The reason for this is that one of the most significant ways in which firms compete is
in terms of *service.* A supermarket that keeps its customers waiting in checkout lines twice as long as its competitors, all other factors being equal, will soon
lose customers until waiting times are equalized between this store and competing stores. Similarly, if one airline usually places a businessman on standby
every Friday and a competing airline does not, then the businessman will quickly
develop a preference for the competing airline. Thus, the "excess capacity" of
many firms is actually an inventory of the services that are available to customers in the form of reduced waiting time. Firms with this type of "excess
capacity" incur higher costs because they are meeting the demands of their
customers. These are not the type of costs illustrated in Figure 10-5.

Shortcomings of the Theory of Monopolistic Competition

Milton Friedman has argued that the biggest deficiency in the theory of monopolistic competition is its treatment of industries.[2] Because the hallmark of the
theory of monopolistic competition is its emphasis on product differentiation,
the definition that an industry is comprised of firms that produce a homogeneous product cannot be employed, because every firm would then be an industry. In Friedman's view, the use of Chamberlin's concept of product groups is
not a useful solution because it "introduces fuzziness and undefinable terms
into the abstract model, where they have no place, and serves only to make the
theory analytically meaningless. . . ."[3]

But perhaps a more damaging criticism of the theory of monopolistic competition is that on closer examination, most markets that initially appear to be
monopolistically competitive are found to be something else. Wherein there are
many brands in a market (for example, cigarettes and soap), the products are
often manufactured by a relatively small number of firms. Thus, a necessary
assumption of the theory of monopolistic competition—that a large number of
firms act independently of one another—does not exist, and firms that even
closely approximate monopolistically competitive firms are rare.

We will examine the economic theory that attempts to deal with industries
that are comprised of a small number of interdependent firms in Section 10-3.
This form of market organization is called *oligopoly.*

---

[2]Milton Friedman, *Essays in Positive Economics* (Chicago: University of Chicago Press,
1953), pp. 38–39.
[3]*Ibid.,* p. 38.

Example 10-1

Advertising and the Price of Eyeglasses

At the beginning of Section 10-2, we pointed out that monopolistically competitive firms are assumed to engage in advertising. For many years, economists have debated the effect of advertising on the price of the commodity sold. Some economists and psychologists have argued that firms rely on advertising to differentiate their products from the products of their competitors and to persuade consumers to buy what they produce. If this is the case, then advertising can only add to a firm's production costs and raise the price of its product. Other economists have taken the position that advertising is the firm's primary means of providing consumers with information about products and markets. This enables the consumer to locate the lowest-priced seller in a particular market and may reduce the price of the product by allowing the firm to achieve economies of scale in production and distribution. We cannot determine which view is correct purely by theoretical analysis. Empirical research is required to establish the validity of these conflicting views of the impact of advertising on product price.

Economist Lee Benham studied the effects of advertising on prices in monopolistically competitive markets by examining the pricing behavior of firms in a market where advertising is prohibited by law and then comparing this to the pricing behavior of firms in markets where advertising is permitted.* Benham specifically chose the eyeglass market because some states prohibit advertising for eyeglasses and eye examinations and other states do not.

*Lee Benham, "The Effect of Advertising on the Price of Eyeglasses," *Journal of Law and Economics* (October 1972), pp. 337–52.

10-3 Oligopoly

An **oligopoly** is a market in which there are only a *few sellers,* so that each seller must speculate on how changes in its market behavior will affect the market behavior of its competitors. In an oligopoly, there is a mutual interdependence between all firms in the industry, in contrast to the market structures of perfect and monopolistic competition in which firms in an industry are assumed to operate independently of one another.

Since each firm in an oligopoly must speculate on the reactions of its competitors, how any particular firm in the industry will respond to changing market conditions is never known precisely in advance. In some situations, predictions about competitor reaction may be highly accurate; in others, predictions will be inaccurate. When predictions about competitor reaction are good, the firm will have a fairly accurate picture of the position and shape of the

Benham found that in 1963 the average price of a pair of eyeglasses in North Carolina—a state in which there had been extensive restrictions on advertising for many years—was $37.48, whereas the average price of a pair of eyeglasses in both Texas and the District of Columbia, where there was no prohibition on advertising, was $17.98. The price differential, which Benham attributed to the cost-reducing effects of advertising, amounted to $19.50. When Benham widened the sample of states in his analysis to include states with less severe restrictions on advertising than those in North Carolina, the difference in the price of a pair of eyeglasses between states with and states without restrictions declined to $6.70—the price of eyeglasses being about 20% lower in states that allowed advertising.

In a more recent study of the eyeglass market, the Federal Trade Commission discovered that the average price of a pair of eyeglasses, including an eye examination, was $94.58 in cities where advertising was prohibited.[†] In cities where advertising was permitted, eye doctors who did not advertise charged $74.66 and those who did advertise charged $62.58. In addition to measuring price differentials, the Federal Trade Commission study also rated the quality of the examinations and the eyeglasses sold by advertisers and nonadvertisers. The Commission found that consumers were no more likely to be given an incorrect prescription by an advertiser than by a nonadvertiser and that the quality of the eyeglasses supplied by both advertisers and nonadvertisers was the same.

[†]Ronald S. Bond, John E. Kwoka, Jr., John J. Phelan, and Ira Taylor Whitten, *Staff Report on Effects of Restrictions on Advertising and Commercial Practice in the Professions: The Case of Optometry* (Washington, D.C.: Federal Trade Commission, Bureau of Economics, April 1980).

demand curve it is facing; when predictions are poor, the firm will have only a hazy description of its demand curve. Because there can be varying degrees of uncertainty with regard to competitor reactions and concomitant vagueness about market demand, there is no single theory of oligopolistic behavior. Instead, we find that a great variety of models encompass the entire spectrum of oligopolistic uncertainty. In examination of oligopoly, we will focus our attention on theories that are employed to analyze situations in which the firm's demand curve is fairly well established.

Oligopolies can be divided into two categories. **Pure oligopolies** produce homogeneous products and **differentiated oligopolies** produce differentiated products. Examples of pure oligopolies are the aluminum, copper, steel, lead, cement, kerosene, newsprint, and sheetrock industries. Examples of differentiated oligopolies include the manufacturers of automobiles, motorcycles, television sets, high-fidelity equipment, razors, toothpaste, and electrical appliances.

10-4 Unorganized Oligopoly

The firms in an **unorganized oligopoly** do not operate under explicitly established rules of behavior, although implicit behavioral guidelines may have resulted from an historical trial-and-error movement toward greater market predictability. In this section, we will consider two theories that offer explanations of implicit market cooperation among firms in an unorganized oligopoly.

The Kinked Demand Curve

In the perfectly competitive model we examined in Chapter 8, we found that changing market conditions invariably result in changes in the price of the firm's product. In the real world, however, economists have noted that prices of products in many industries tend to be "sticky" or resistant to change either upward or downward. Most economists consider these industries to be oligopolistic.

One of the best-known economic theories constructed to explain price inflexibility is Paul Sweezy's **kinked demand model.**[4] The demand curve D for an oligopolistic firm is drawn in Figure 10–6. At the prevailing market equilibrium price P_0, the firm is producing Q_0 units of output. Note that at point A the demand curve is *kinked;* that is, there is an abrupt change in the slope of the curve.

The kink in the demand curve represents the assumed reaction of competing firms to a change in the oligopolistic firm's price. Since the firm sells a differentiated product, it can raise its price above P_0 without losing all of its sales, but if the other firms in the industry hold their prices at P_0, sales will decline rapidly due to the close substitutability of products. If it raises its price above the market price, the firm's perceived demand curve will be relatively price-elastic. But if the firm reduces its price and its competitors do not, the firm will greatly increase its share of the market due to the close substitutability of products. Of course, it is highly unlikely that the remaining firms in the oligopolistic industry will sit idly by and allow their shares of the market to decline. Instead, the remaining firms in the industry would probably follow suit and match the price reduction. Thus, the firm cannot expect to increase its sales at the expense of the remaining firms in the oligopoly. Any increase in the firm's sales due to a price reduction would merely be that firm's proportionate share of the movement of all firms in the oligopoly down the market demand curve. The firm's perceived demand curve after a price reduction will therefore be steeper or relatively more price-inelastic than it will be after a price increase.

The demand curve in Figure 10–6 illustrates the characteristics of the oli-

---

[4]Paul M. Sweezy, "Demand Under Conditions of Oligopoly," *Journal of Political Economy* (August 1939), pp. 568–73. Appearing in the same year and presenting essentially the identical theory was R.C. Hall and C.J. Hitch's "Price Theory and Business Behavior," *Oxford Economic Papers* (May 1939), pp. 12–45.

Figure 10–6
The Kinked Oligopoly Demand Curve

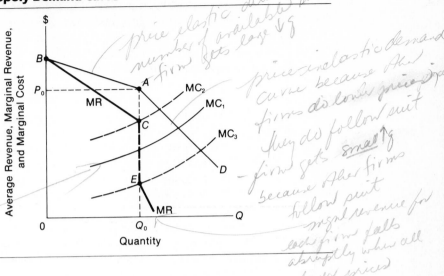

[handwritten annotations:] price elastic due to substitutes number gets large ↓ number of available firm

price inelastic demand curve because the firms do lower prices, they do follow suit

— firm gets small ↓ because after firms follow suit mgnl revenue for each firm falls abruptly when all lower prices

gopolistic firm's assumed demand. To the left of point *A*, demand curve *D* is shallow, indicating that any price increase will not be matched by the remaining firms in the oligopoly and that sales will decline rapidly. To the right of point *A*, demand curve *D* is steep, indicating that if one firm reduces its price, all other firms in the industry will follow suit and the sales of each firm will increase only slightly.

Having provided an economic rationale for the kink in the oligopolist's demand curve in Figure 10–6, we are now prepared to explain the rigidity of oligopolistic prices. The marginal revenue MR curve corresponding to portion *BA* of the demand curve in Figure 10–6 is given by the line *BC*. At point *A*, the slope of the demand curve abruptly becomes steeper, and the MR curve corresponding to the portion of the demand curve to the right of point *A* commences at point *E*. We can readily see by inspecting Figure 10–6 that the kink in the demand curve produces a discontinuity in the MR curve between points *C* and *E* at output Q_0.

A profit-maximizing oligopolistic firm will produce at that level of output where marginal cost is equal to marginal revenue (MC = MR). In Figure 10–6, the firm's marginal cost curve MC_1 intersects the MR curve in its discontinuous portion *CE*, so that output Q_0 is produced and sold at price P_0. If the MC curve shifts up or down between points *C* and *E* on the MR curve, as shown by dashed curves MC_2 and MC_3, the firm will have no incentive to alter its price or output. This demonstrates that changing cost conditions in an oligopolistic industry can occur without accompanying changes in price or output.

Suppose that an oligopolistic firm attempts to increase the demand for its product by means of more advertising or product improvement. As long as the remaining firms in the industry are perceived to respond to price increases or decreases in the manner we have just described, the firm's demand curve will be kinked at the prevailing market price P_0 and moderate shifts in the firm's demand curve will probably result in the continued intersection of the MC and the MR curves in the latter's discontinuous portion. This conclusion is illustrated in Figure 10–7, where the marginal revenue curve MR_1 corresponding to the initial demand curve D_1 is intersected by the marginal cost MC curve in the discontinuous portion of MR_1. At this point, the market price is P_0 and the firm is producing output Q_0. Now suppose that the firm is able to shift its demand curve to the right from D_1 to D_2 without appreciably increasing its costs. As drawn in Figure 10–7, the MC curve will continue to intersect the marginal revenue curve MR_2 in the discontinuous portion produced by the kink in D_2 at price P_0. Thus, although the firm increases its output from Q_0 to Q_1, the market price remains fixed at P_0.

If the firm's demand were to decrease due to advertising or product improvement on the part of its competitors, it is possible that production would be cut back but that price would be held at the initial market price. If the firm's demand curve is kinked, the price of the product could remain constant while output varied.

A theoretical problem associated with the kinked demand theory is that although it can explain price rigidity at the equilibrium price, it cannot explain

Figure 10–7
A Shift in the Kinked Demand Curve

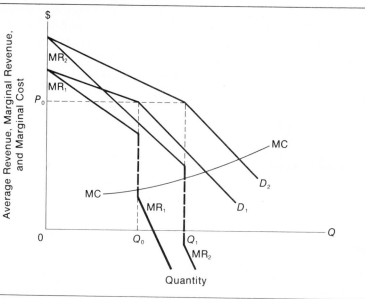

how this price is determined. A primary purpose of price theory is to explain the determination of the market equilibrium price. Since the kinked demand theory cannot do this, it is no more than an *ex post* rationalization of price rigidity.

Price Leadership

The kinked demand theory we have just examined could not explain how the initial market price is established. A class of models of oligopolistic markets that overcome this shortcoming are called **price-leadership models.** In this section, we will consider *low-cost* and *dominant-firm price-leadership models.*

In Figure 10–8, market demand curve D is jointly faced by two oligopolistic firms producing the same homogeneous product. The two firms are depicted by their short-run average cost curves $SRAC_1$ and $SRAC_2$. Since $SRAC_2$ lies below $SRAC_1$, $SRAC_2$ represents the low-cost firm and $SRAC_1$ depicts the high-cost firm.

Both firms are faced with the economic problem of determining what price to charge for their product. The theory of **low-cost price leadership** assumes that each firm has tacitly agreed to share the total market equally, so that the demand curve faced by each firm is demand curve *d* in Figure 10–8. The marginal revenue MR curve for each firm along with each firm's marginal cost curve MC_1 and MC_2, also appear in the figure. In the absence of some additional assumption, however, our model will be incomplete, because if each firm equates MC with MR, the low-cost firm will set its price at P_0 and the high-cost firm will set its price at P_1. This is not a solution to the problem of oligopolistic

Figure 10–8
Low-Cost Price Leadership

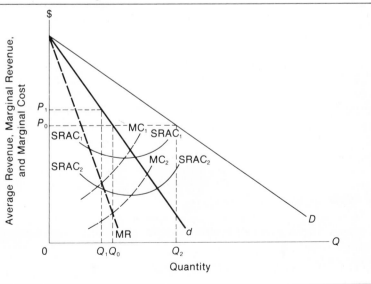

Example
10-2

The Pricing Behavior of Oligopolists

If the demand curve of an oligopolistic firm is kinked, we have shown that variations in demand for the firm's product and in the firm's production costs within specific limits are consistent with a single profit-maximizing price. However, any variation in either the monopolist's marginal revenue or marginal cost results in a new profit-maximizing price. We should therefore expect prices in oligopolistic industries to be more rigid than prices in monopolistic industries. Furthermore, the kinked demand theory assumes that when an oligopolist lowers its price, competitors will follow suit, but that when an oligopolist raises its price, rival firms will not match the increase. Thus, according to the theory, oligopolistic prices should decline more often than they rise.

The assumed differences in pricing behavior between oligopolists and monopolists and between oligopolists and other oligopolists lend themselves to empirical testing. George J. Stigler compared the stickiness of prices in oligopolistic industries with that of prices in monopolies.* According to the kinked demand theory, we would expect the prices charged by monopolists to be more variable than the prices charged by oligopolists. Stigler's analysis refuted the kinked demand theory. He discovered that prices in the monopolistic industries he examined were more rigid than those in oligopolistic industries. In addition to testing the theory, Stigler also tested the hypothesis that price changes in oligopolistic industries were more likely to be downward. He examined pricing behavior in seven industries that were considered to be highly oligopolistic (anthracite coal, automobiles, cigarettes, dynamite, oil, potash, and steel), and found that contrary

*George J. Stigler, "The Kinky Oligopoly Demand Curve and Rigid Prices," *Journal of Political Economy* (October 1947), pp. 432–49.

market sharing and pricing, since the high-cost firm will be able to sell Q_1 at price P_1, but the low-cost firm will price its output at P_0 and sell Q_0. This will leave a segment of the market demand equal to $Q_2 - (Q_0 + Q_1)$ that will be unable to purchase the product at price P_0. In other words, if both firms set prices that will maximize their profits, this will result in an excess market demand of $Q_2 - (Q_0 + Q_1)$, which will lead the low-cost firm to believe that its market-sharing demand and marginal revenue curves lie to the right of the MR and d curves in Figure 10–8. In its effort to maximize profits, the low-cost firm will therefore expand production, and its share of the market will increase at the expense of the high-cost firm.

To maintain oligopolistic market sharing, the price-leadership model assumes that the high-cost firm will charge the same price for its product that the low-cost firm charges. Each firm therefore sets its price at P_0 and sells $Q_0 = \frac{1}{2}Q_2$, which is one-half the total quantity demanded at P_0.

to the kinked demand theory, competitive firms were just as likely to match price increases as price decreases. Stigler concluded that the empirical evidence did not support the kinked demand theory of oligopoly.

Stigler's analysis was not readily accepted in all economic quarters, however. Two main criticisms were leveled at his study. First, the type of interindustry comparisons Stigler used suffer from the shortcoming that different industries established specific customs and conditions for conducting their business and that the industries Stigler selected to represent monopolistic industries might have had sticky prices even if they were composed of many instead of a few firms. Second, the definition of an industry is largely a matter of subjective choice or convention. Two of the industries that Stigler chose to represent monopolies were aluminum and nickel. If the firms that comprise these industries had been lumped together into the category of "nonferrous metals" instead, Stigler would have treated them as oligopolists rather than monopolists and would have attributed the stickiness of their prices to oligopoly.

In an attempt to overcome these objections, Julian L. Simon examined the advertising prices of the trade magazines published for various industries.† The number of magazines serving the various trade groups varied from one to 29. Simon assumed that a trade magazine's degree of advertising monopoly power increased as the number of magazines catering to that trade decreased. According to the kinked demand theory, we would expect flexibility in advertising prices to increase as the degree of monopoly increased. Simon's analysis resulted in the opposite conclusion, supporting Stigler's earlier work. Simon found that as a magazine grouping became more monopolized the degree of price inflexibility increased.

†Julian L. Simon, "A Further Test of the Kinky Oligopoly Demand Curve," *American Economic Review* (December 1969), pp. 971–75.

If there are additional firms in the market and they are approximately the same size and can agree to share the total market equally, the low-cost price-leadership model provides a solution to the problem of determining the market price. In many oligopolistic markets, however, a few large firms and many smaller firms appear to coexist. The theory of **dominant-firm price leadership** is one explanation of how the market price is determined and the total market is shared by all firms in such a situation.

To simplify our analysis, we will assume that we are dealing with a market that is comprised of one large firm and many smaller firms, all producing the same homogeneous product. In this case, we will make the fundamental assumption that the dominant firm sets the market price, allows the smaller firms to sell as much as they wish at that price, and then sells the residual demand.

Since the market price is fixed by the dominant firm, each small firm will behave as if it were in a perfectly competitive market, because it can sell whatever quantity it wishes at the going price. In other words, the demand curve faced by each small firm will be perfectly price-elastic at the price set by the dominant firm. Furthermore, since the small firms' marginal revenue curves will coincide with their demand curves, profit maximization for each small firm will occur when it produces at the level of output at which its marginal cost is equal to the price set by the dominant firm.

As in perfect competition, the aggregate supply curve for the small firms will be equal to the horizontal summation of their marginal cost curves. The aggregate supply curve for the small firms ΣMC appears in Figure 10–9, along with the market demand curve DD that is faced jointly by the small firms and the dominant firm. We can now construct the demand curve for the dominant firm. The small firms' supply curve ΣMC intersects the market demand curve DD at price P_3. According to our assumption, if the dominant firm sets its price at P_3, the small firms will produce quantity Q_4 and supply the entire market. Therefore, at price P_3 the dominant firm's demand curve D_{DF} must intersect the vertical axis, because its sales will be 0 when the combined sales of the smaller firms equal Q_4. If the dominant firm sets the market price at P_1, then the total quantity demanded will be Q_7 and the smaller firms will supply Q_2. This will permit the dominant firm to sell the difference between Q_2 and Q_7, which is Q_5. Thus, the demand curve for the dominant firm D_{DF} must pass through point A in Figure 10–9 when the market price is P_1. By selecting other possible market prices, we could determine various points on the dominant firm's demand curve to construct curve D_{DF} in Figure 10–9.

Figure 10–9
Dominant-Firm Price Leadership

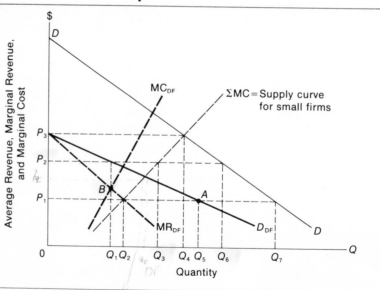

The dominant firm's marginal revenue curve MR_{DF} is derived from its demand curve D_{DF}. The dominant firm maximizes profits by equating its marginal revenue curve MR_{DF} with its marginal cost curve MC_{DF}, which occurs at point B in Figure 10-9. Consequently, the dominant firm will produce output Q_1, which it will sell at price P_2. At price P_2, the market demand is Q_6, so that the difference between Q_1 and Q_6 is the output Q_3 that the small firms will be willing to produce at price P_2. Like the dominant firm, each small firm will perceive that it is maximizing profits, and the market price set by the dominant firm will therefore be agreeable to each small firm.

The dominant-firm theory of price leadership can be expanded to incorporate the addition of two or more large firms producing in a market with many small firms. Under these market conditions, the small firms may follow the price leadership of one of the large firms. Such a firm is sometimes referred to as the **barometric firm,** since it is usually the first firm to make a price change and all other firms traditionally follow its example. The other large firms may tacitly agree to share the portion of the market that remains after the small firms produce their desired levels of output. As in the case of the low-cost model of price leadership, the barometric firm may be the low-cost firm among the large firms in such a market. Additional variations of the dominant-firm model of price leadership are possible, and if product differentiation is permitted, the number of possible permutations of the simple theories we have examined here becomes quite large. Instead of exploring all of the models that are based on the assumption of tacit agreement between firms, at this point we will move on to the more fruitful examination of the market conditions under which explicit cooperation between firms is posited to exist.

Administered Pricing

In contrast to the neoclassical models of price and output determination in oligopolistic industries that we have examined thus far, alternative theories have been developed based on an entirely different paradigm in which the supplier is assumed to control not only supply but also demand. In this "new view" of **administered pricing,** prices are "administered" by the management of the oligopolistic firms, instead of being determined by the interplay of supply and demand. The foremost expositor of this "new view" of oligopoly pricing is John Kenneth Galbraith,[5] whose views are summarized here.

> In the last two or three years, the argument on oligopoly has been carried a further step forward. . . . It holds that the market power of oligopoly is not an aspect of profit maximization under the ultimate power of the market, but of industrial planning. This planning, impelled by the technology, market deficiencies, and large capital and organizational requirements of modern industry, seeks to secure as many as possible of the parameters—costs and supplies of important materials and components, capital supply, product prices—within which the industrial firm functions. And this planning goes beyond the market for products to organize the needed consumer response. In

[5]John Kenneth Galbraith, *The New Industrial State* (Boston: Houghton Mifflin, 1967).

consequence, where the oligopolist in pursuit of maximum profits was subordinate to the instructions of the market and the consumer beyond, the modern firm takes the market in hand and, to the extent possible, instructs the consumer. The old market sequence, in which the sovereign consumer expressed his wishes in the market and there through to the producer, is paralleled by a new reverse sequence in which the producer puts prices at a level appropriate to its needs and goes on to persuade the consumer as to what he should do.[6]

This administered-pricing approach employs one of two primary theories to explain oligopolistic pricing behavior. The first theory is referred to as the *full-cost pricing mechanism;* the second is the *target-return pricing mechanism.*

The **full-cost pricing** theory simply states that price is the average variable cost of production at the planned level of output multiplied by a fixed multiple or *markup,* so that

$$P = (1 + \lambda)(\text{AVC}_N) \qquad\qquad (10\text{--}1)$$

where

P = price
λ = markup
AVC_N = average variable cost of production at the planned level of output

The amount of the markup is a policy decision made by the firm and will be the same for all similar or slightly differentiated products manufactured by the firm. Price will only be altered if there is a change in average variable cost, and since most manufacturing processes are characterized by constant returns to scale over a wide range of output levels, the same price will prevail over large variations in output. Thus, this pricing equation is consistent with the belief that oligopolists tend to hold their prices constant as output varies.

The full-cost pricing equation can be reconciled with the traditional pricing theories based on profit maximization in the long run if we assume that the firm's production function is characterized by constant returns to scale over a wide range of output in the long run. If this is the case—and many empirical studies tend to support that it is—then the oligopolist's LRAC curve will be horizontal and coincide with its LRMC curve in this range of output. If we recall from Chapter 9 that

$$\text{MR} = P\left(1 - \frac{1}{E}\right) \qquad\qquad (9\text{--}1)$$

if $E = \partial$, $MR = P$

since MR = LRMC when profits are maximized, we obtain

$$\text{LRMC} = P\left(1 - \frac{1}{E}\right) \qquad\qquad (10\text{--}2)$$

---

[6]John Kenneth Galbraith, "Memorandum on the Automobile Industry: A Case Study in Competition—A Statement by the General Motors Corporation," *Planning, Regulation, and Competition: Automobile Industry, 1968* (Washington, D.C.: U.S. Government Printing Office, 1968), pp. 910–12.

Now, if we assume that there are constant returns to scale, LRMC = LRAC, so that we can express the profit-maximizing price P as

$$P = \left(\frac{E}{E-1} \right) LRAC \qquad \textit{higher part} \qquad (10\text{–}3)$$

As we pointed out in Chapter 9, to maximize profits, a firm will set P so that it is operating in the elastic portion of the demand curve. Therefore, since $E > 1$, then $E/E - 1$ will also be greater than unity (1) and will be equal to λ, the profit-maximizing markup.

The somewhat more sophisticated concept of **target-return pricing** is a pricing equation that yields the price that will meet the firm's goals for a desired or targeted rate of return on invested capital and planned level of output. Algebraically, the target-return pricing equation is

$$P = \frac{rK}{Q_N} + AVC_N \qquad (10\text{–}4)$$

where

$r =$ targeted rate of return
$K =$ capital employed to produce the product being priced
$Q_N =$ planned level of output
$AVC_N =$ average variable cost of production at the planned level of output

According to this pricing equation, price will rise (decline) if the average variable cost rises (declines) and if the planned level of output declines (rises). Since the "new view" of pricing assumes that firms can persuade consumers to purchase their planned level of output, the pricing policy pursued by oligopolistic firms that employ the target-return pricing equation should also be characterized by inflexible prices.

Organized Oligopoly   10–5

Over 200 years ago Adam Smith observed: "People of the same trade seldom meet together, even for merriment and diversion, but the conversation ends in a conspiracy against the public, or in some contrivance to raise prices."[7]

Conditions have not changed since Smith wrote those words. Many firms still attempt to drive up their prices and profits by entering into collusive agreements to reduce the amount of the product sold in a market. In this section, we will examine the manner in which a *cartel* can increase the profits of its members by controlling output and price, and we will discover why such agreements are unstable.

---

[7]Adam Smith, *An Inquiry into the Nature and Causes of the Wealth of Nations,* reprinted ed. (Chicago: University of Chicago Press, 1976), p. 144.

**Example
10–3**

Testing Administered Pricing Theory

Tests of the predictive abilities of the full-cost and target-return pricing equations have been conducted. Unfortunately, some investigators have used such highly aggregated data that their results are suspect.* To avoid this problem, Paul L. Burgess and Fred R. Glahe have used disaggregated data derived from production costs of the Ford Motor Company to test these equations.† The average variable costs for three slightly differentiated 1966 Ford four-door sedans with base V-8 engines, along with the prices paid by the automobile dealer are provided in the following table.☆ Dividing these average variable costs by the prices paid by the dealer gives us the markup λ on each model which also appears in the table.

AUTOMOBILE MODEL	AVERAGE VARIABLE COST AVC	PRICE TO DEALER	MARKUP $\lambda = \lambda'$
Custom	$1,432.26	$1,773.05	0.238
Custom 500	1,440.03	1,845.55	0.282
Galaxie 500	1,475.38	1,947.97	0.320

We already know that if a firm is using full-cost pricing, its markup λ for slightly differentiated products will be constant. The three automobile models in this table are essentially the same. Their product differentiation is the result of internal and external trim changes—the Custom being the plainest and the Galaxie 500 being the most luxurious sedan. Since Ford's markup on these three sedans increases as the product becomes more luxurious, and since similar results can be demonstrated for other Ford automobiles and optional equipment, it is apparent that the Ford Motor Company does not employ full-cost pricing.

To test the target-return pricing equation, Burgess and Glahe employed a pseudo markup λ' that could be calculated from target-return determined prices. This can be accomplished by substituting λ' for λ in Equation (10–1) and equating Equation (10–1) with Equation (10–4) to obtain

$$(1 + \lambda')\,(AVC_N) = \frac{rK}{Q_N} + AVC_N \qquad (10\text{–}5)$$

*For example, see Otto Eckstein and Gary Fromm, "The Price Equation," *American Economic Review* (December 1968), pp. 1159–83.
†Paul L. Burgess and Fred R. Glahe, "Pricing in the American Automobile Industry and the Galbraith Hypothesis," *Rivista Internazionale di Scienze Economiche e Commerciali* (December 1970), pp. 1176–86.
☆*Ibid.*, p. 1183.

Since the three automobiles being considered are all produced on the same assembly lines, the amount of capital K used in their production is equal to the fraction of total production required to produce each model multiplied by the total capital employed to produce the three models, or

$$K = \frac{Q_N}{Q_T} K_T \qquad (10\text{--}6)$$

where

Q_T = total production of all models
Q_N = production of a particular model
K_T = total capital employed to produce all models

Substituting the right-hand side of Equation (10–6) into Equation (10–5) and simplifying and rearranging gives us

$$\lambda' = \frac{rK_T}{Q_T \text{AVC}_N} \qquad (10\text{--}7)$$

Since r, K_T, and Q_T are constants, Equation (10–7) can be rewritten as

$$\lambda' = \frac{C}{\text{AVC}_N} \qquad (10\text{--}8)$$

where

$$C = \frac{rK_T}{Q_T}$$

Equation (10–8) tells us that if the target return pricing equation is used, then as AVC_N increases as more expensive variants of the same model are produced, the pseudo markup λ' will decline. But as we can clearly see from the table, λ' increases as more costly variants are produced. Thus, these data do not support the hypothesis that target-return pricing is used by the Ford Motor Company. If we make the reasonable and intuitively appealing assumption that the price elasticity of demand becomes more inelastic as we move from the cheapest to the most expensive automobile model, then according to Equation (10–3) a profit-maximizing automobile firm will increase its markup as it increases the luxuriousness of its product. Since this is what we observe in the table, we can conclude that Ford's pricing behavior in this example is consistent with traditional microeconomic theory but is not consistent with the theory of administered pricing.

Cartel Profit Maximization

A **cartel** is an organization of oligopolistic firms within an industry that is formed for the specific purpose of creating a collective monopoly. In its most perfect form, the members of a cartel follow the instructions of a centralized agency that seeks to maximize the profits of the cartel as a whole.

To illustrate, initially we will suppose that perfect competition prevails, that an industry is comprised of 1,000 firms, all producing homogeneous products, and that these firms are equally efficient. Each firm's long-run average cost and long-run marginal cost curves under this set of conditions are illustrated in Figure 10–10(a). Assuming, for convenience, that this industry is a constant-cost industry, the long-run market supply curve of the perfectly competitive industry would be a horizontal line at price P_1 in Figure 10–10(b). (See Section 8–7, pp. 271–75, for an explanation of long-run supply in perfect competition.)

Due to the assumption of initial perfect competition, each firm will consider its individual demand curve to be perfectly elastic at price P_1, so that its initial marginal revenue curve MR_{PC} will be horizontal at price P_1. Under these conditions, the firm will maximize its profits by equating MR_{PC} with LRMC to produce output $\hat{Q}_1$ in Figure 10–10(a). Because $\hat{Q}_1$ is 1/1,000 of Q_1–the output that the market demands at P_1 in Figure 10–10(b)–and the industry is comprised of 1,000 identical firms, total industry output will be equal to Q_1. At price P_1 and output $\hat{Q}_1$, long-run average cost is at its minimum point and

Figure 10–10
The Creation of Pure Profits by a Cartel

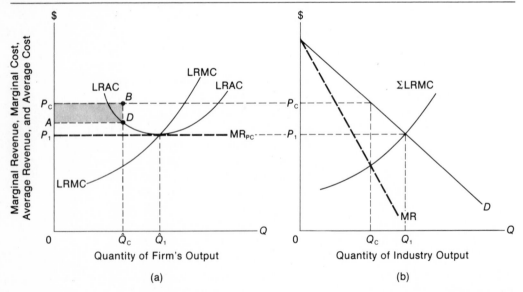

(a) Quantity of Firm's Output

(b) Quantity of Industry Output

is equal to average revenue, so that there is no incentive for additional firms to enter the industry, since there are no pure profits.

Now suppose that these 1,000 firms decide to form a cartel and set up a central headquarters to coordinate the pricing and production of each firm in the industry. The cartel's objective is to maximize the profits of the cartel, thereby increasing the profits of the member firms. To accomplish this goal, the cartel's management behaves as if it were a multiplant monopolist, producing the level of output at which the sum of the individual firms' long-run marginal cost curves ΣLRMC is equal to the industry's revenue curve MR. In our example, this occurs at output Q_C in Figure 10–10(b).

The cartel can raise the price of its product from P_1 to P_C by reducing total industry output from Q_1 to Q_C. The impact that this has on the profits of the individual firm is illustrated in Figure 10–10(a). Prior to the formation of the cartel, the firm received only normal profits. Now each firm receives pure profits, because its total revenue, measured by the rectangle $0P_C B\hat{Q}_C$, exceeds its total cost $0AD\hat{Q}_C$. The pure profits earned by each firm are therefore equal to the tinted area $AP_C BD$ in Figure 10–10(a). Clearly, all firms are in a better position after the formation of the cartel than they were before. Since this is true, we will now turn our attention to the question of why there are so few cartels in the real world.

Why Cartels Fail

Despite the fact that cartels are able to increase the profits of member firms, they have a history of unsuccessful long-run operation unless they are supported and protected by government. The reason for this paradoxical result can be found in Figure 10–11, where the long-run marginal and average cost curves are the same as those in Figure 10–10(a). The cartel-established price P_C and firm output $\hat{Q}_C$ are also indicated in Figure 10–11. If the firm produces $\hat{Q}_C$ and sells it at P_C, its pure profit will be equal to the lighter tinted area in the figure.

Once the cartel is formed and in operation, the demand curve of an individual firm will remain perfectly price-elastic, as it was prior to joining the cartel, except that it will now be the cartel price P_C. Under these conditions, a single firm will probably assume that if it increases production in excess of $\hat{Q}_C$, it can sell the additional output at the cartel-established price, because it believes that all other 999 firms in the cartel will comply with the cartel's directive to reduce their output to $\hat{Q}_C$. Therefore, the marginal revenue curve for the individual firm now becomes a horizontal line at the cartel price P_C. Thus, after the cartel is in operation, the individual firm can increase its profits by *cheating* on the cartel agreement by increasing its production beyond $\hat{Q}_C$. The optimal amount of cheating on the cartel agreement will occur at the level of production that corresponds to the intersection of the firm's long-run marginal cost curve and its new marginal revenue curve. This is illustrated in Figure 10–11 by the intersection of the LRMC curve with the $MR_{cheater}$

Figure 10–11
The Incentive to Cheat in a Cartel

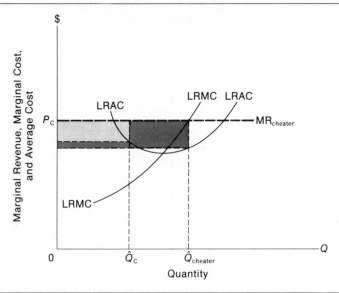

curve at output $\hat{Q}_{cheater}$. The incentive for a firm to cheat is equal to the additional profits that will result from increasing its output. These additional profits are measured by the darker tinted area in Figure 10–11.

Since every firm realizes that it can increase its profits by cheating, most firms will probably begin to increase output in excess of $\hat{Q}_C$ soon after the cartel establishes this production limit. Each firm will rationalize that the other firms are engaging in a little bit of undetected cheating and that they will be at a disadvantage if they refrain from doing the same. Clearly, if almost all firms in the industry are cheating a "little" bit, even if it is to such a slight degree that it is difficult for the cartel headquarters to detect, the overall effect on the market will be to shift the aggregate supply curve in Figure 10–10(b) to the right. This increase in market supply will result in an excess supply of output at the cartel price P_C, the inventories of member firms will begin to increase, and the pure profits these firms enjoyed in the early days of the cartel will begin to decline.

This situation will provide member firms with an incentive to engage in another form of cheating on the cartel agreement. Firms will quickly recognize that one way to reduce their unwanted buildup of inventories is to make "secret" price discounts or rebates to buyers. The problem with such a policy, of course, is that it is impossible to keep these discounts and rebates a secret, and buyers will quickly inform sellers about what is happening within the market. Firms that have been conducting their business according to the rules of the cartel will suddenly learn that they are at a distinct disadvantage in the marketplace and will quickly abandon the cartel rules and regulations. In a short time, all firms will find that their position has reverted back to the situation that existed prior to the formation of the cartel, and they will be achieving no pure profits. At this point, it is highly likely that the firms will realize that their position in the market has worsened as a result of cheating, and the cartel will probably be reorganized in the hope that cheating will be avoided in the future. However, as history demonstrates and as we will learn in the applications that follow this section, the hope of establishing a voluntary cartel without cheating is a vain one, and the sequence of events that resulted in the collapse of the cartel will repeat itself.

But a cartel will also fail even if none of its members resort to cheating, because a successful cartel produces pure profits, which attract outside firms to the industry. If new firms are admitted to the cartel, pure profits will eventually decline to 0 as the industry supply curve ΣLRMC in Figure 10-10(b) shifts outward and to the right. Before this occurs, however, the decline in pure profits created by the original members of the cartel will encourage cheating, and the cartel will meet its demise in short order.

The conclusions we have reached concerning the theoretical instability of the cartel formed in an industry originally in perfect competition also holds true when there are only a few firms in the industry. For example, suppose there are only two identical firms in an industry and that they decide to form a cartel to maximize profits. Profit maximization will occur at that level of cartel output where the sum of the marginal cost curves of both firms is equal to the marginal revenue of the cartel. When this condition prevails

$$MC_1 = MC_2 = MR_C \qquad\qquad (10\text{–}9)$$

where

MC_1 = marginal cost of firm 1
MC_2 = marginal cost of firm 2
MR_C = marginal revenue of the cartel

When the sum of the marginal costs of both firms is equated with the cartel's marginal revenue, the profit-maximizing price of the cartel P_C is determined. Since the two firms are identical, cartel profits are maximized when

$$MC_1 = MC_2 = P_C\left(1 - \frac{1}{E_C}\right) \qquad\qquad (10\text{–}10)$$

where E_C is the price elasticity of demand faced by the cartel at price P_C.

The cartel will tend to be unstable because firm 1, for example, will correctly perceive that the price elasticity of demand E_1 that it faces at P_C is greater than E_C, so that its marginal revenue is

$$MR_1 = P_C \left(1 - \frac{1}{E_1} \right) > P_C \left(1 - \frac{1}{E_C} \right) = MR_C \qquad (10\text{--}11)$$

From Equation (10–9), we know that $MC_1 = MR_C$, so that

$$MR_1 > MC_1 \qquad (10\text{--}12)$$

[handwritten margin notes: "& expands output 'cause"]

[handwritten margin notes: "& believe E is > Ec"]

which tells us that firm 1 can increase its profits by cheating if it expands its output beyond the limit set by the cartel. Firm 2 will view the situation in the same way. Thus, both firms will have an incentive to cheat on the cartel agreement, and if this occurs, the cartel will collapse.

[handwritten margin notes: "can keep down only by controlling Q"]

The instability of cartel agreements quickly became apparent to cartel organizers. Thus far, the most successful way to eliminate this instability has proved to be the government enforcement of cartel agreements. We will now examine a few of the many instances in which government regulation has been employed to maintain pure profits for extended periods of time.

10-6 Cartels in Action

Strong incentives exist for firms in an oligopolistic industry to establish a cartel to maximize their joint profits. Once the cartel is organized, however, strong incentives exist for firms to cheat on the cartel agreement to obtain even higher profits than they were achieving by following cartel regulations. Because firms expect to receive rewards from violating the cartel agreement, we argued in Section 10–5 that cartels can be expected to be highly unstable unless cartel agreements are made legally binding by government regulation. In this section, we will examine cases of cartel operation and the role the government plays in each.

Application: The Great Electrical "Conspiracy"

Perhaps the most famous recent example of price collusion among U.S. firms occurred in the late 1950s in the electrical equipment industry. This industry manufactures such items as electric meters, generating turbines, generators, electrical transformers, circuit breakers, switchgear, and power transformers for sale to electric power companies and other industrial firms. There are thousands of firms in this industry, but it is dominated by a few corporate giants, including General Electric, Westinghouse Electric, Allis-Chalmers, and Carrier. Another important characteristic of the electrical equipment industry is that the design of most of the items produced by firms in this industry are standard-ized by the industry's trade association. These items are listed in catalogs, and extensive inventories result in "off the shelf" sales of many items.

The big firms are the leaders in the industry because they expend large amounts of money for research and development and incur large overhead expenses, or fixed costs, that must be met regardless of a short-run decline in sales. Because there are such a large number of firms in the electrical equip-ment industry and, although many are small in size, competition is fierce, and because the total volume of sales rises and falls concurrently with the busi-ness cycle, the industry tyically finds itself in periods of either "feast" or "famine." During periods of recession in the 1950s, there was intensive pressure within the industry to cut prices below the stated catalog prices to maintain produc-tion and meet fixed costs. For example, in the wake of the 1953–1954 recession, the price of electrical switchgear was being discounted from the catalog price by as much as 40–50%, and switchgear discounts reached 60% during the 1957–1958 recession.[8]

Given the intense competition in the electrical equipment industry, it is not surprising that some attempt was made to establish a cartel to maintain prices and to define market shares. Ironically, the institutional setting for the estab-lishment of this cartel had resulted from World War II government price con-trols instituted by the Office of Price Administration (OPA), which had sanctioned formal meetings among the electrical manufacturers for the purpose of coordi-nating and increasing needed production for the war effort. In addition, these meetings provided electrical manufacturers with an opportunity to discuss the ways and means of convincing the OPA to raise its price ceilings on their equip-ment. When these price ceilings were finally removed after the war, the estab-lished electrical manufacturers continued to meet to discuss the problems of declining profits as new firms became attracted to the industry. The intent of these meetings was to fix prices and to divide up the market.[9]

From the very beginning of the electrical equipment cartel, cheating occurred. An executive at General Electric remarked, "No one was living up to the agree-ment, and we at G.E. were being made suckers. On every job, someone would try to cut our throat."[10] As predicted by economic theory, the electrical equip-ment cartel was unstable. Members would agree on prices and market shares, someone would begin to cheat, a price war would ensue, firms that were forced to sell below cost would be badly damaged, and the cartel would reorganize in the vain hope that its members had learned the lesson that as a group they would benefit by adhering to the cartel agreement.

---

[8]U.S. Congress, Senate Committee on the Judiciary, Subcommittee on Antitrust and Monopoly, *Price Fixing and Bid-Rigging in the Electrical Manufacturing Industry,* Parts 27 and 28, 87th Congress, 1st Session (April–June 1961), p. 16740.
[9]Richard Austin Smith, "The Incredible Electrical Conspiracy," *Fortune,* Part I (April 1961), pp. 132*ff* and Part II (May 1961), pp. 161*ff.*
[10]*Ibid.,* Part I, p. 171.

After the 1957–1958 switchgear price war, General Electric, Westinghouse, Allis-Chalmers, and Federal Pacific I-T-E decided to reorganize the cartel. As in previous unsuccessful cartel agreements, the firms decided to coordinate sealed bids to electric power companies, so that a selected member of the cartel would be the low bidder and receive the contract. However, the Tennessee Valley Authority became suspicious and reported the coincidence of identical bids with one exception—the low bidder—to the Department of Justice. In the resulting investigation, executives involved in the cartel acknowledged their attempts to fix prices and market shares. On February 6, 1961, the firms belonging to the cartel and some of their executives were found guilty of violating federal anti-trust law. Seven executives went to jail, 23 more received suspended sentences, and the firms were fined almost $2 million and were required to pay millions more in damages to their customers.

From an economic aspect, what concerns us here is not the acknowledged fact that business executives conspired to raise prices, but the question of whether or not they were able to accomplish their goal. From their sworn testimony, it is clear that they were not. Typical of this testimony is the following exchange between Horace L. Flurry, a Senate counsel, and H. Frank Hentschel, the general manager of General Electric's medium-voltage switchgear department, regarding the collusion between firms engaged in the manufacture of medium-voltage switchgear:

> *Mr. Flurry:* I understood you to say that this [attempt at collusion] broke off some time before 1959?
> *Mr. Hentschel:* That is right, sir.
> *Mr. Flurry:* What was the cause of that break-off?
> *Mr. Hentschel:* Basically, the thing wasn't working. In other words, everybody would come to the meeting, the figures would be settled, and they were only as good as the distance to the closest telephone before they were broken. In other words, so the thing just wasn't working.[11]

It could well be argued that such testimony was self-serving and therefore unreliable. Because price fixing and bid-rigging were not in full force in the electrical equipment industry until 1956, a comparison between the rates of return on invested capital and sales in the 1950–1955 period and the 1956–1959 period should reveal an improvement in the profitability of cartel members in the later period. But as we can readily see in the following table,[12] both the percentage profit on invested capital and the percentage profit on sales in *all* cases are *lower* in the 1956–1959 period than they are in the 1950–1955 period. We can therefore conclude that the most famous domestic U.S. cartel in the twentieth century was an economic failure.

---

[11]U.S. Congress, *op. cit.,* p. 16884.
[12]Table data from D.T. Armentano, *The Myths of Antitrust* (New Rochelle, NY: Arlington House, 1972), p. 160.

FIRM	1950−1955		1956−1959	
	Profit on Capital	Profit on Sales	Profit on Capital	Profit on Sales
General Electric	20.5%	5.9%	20.1%	5.8%
Westinghouse	10.8	5.1	7.0	3.0
Allis-Chalmers	11.3	5.1	6.6	3.7
Carrier	12.9	4.4	7.9	3.5

Application: The Railroad Cartels

The economic history of the American railroad industry in the nineteenth century provides us with a classic case study of the instability of cartels when the association among firms is voluntary.

Competition among railroads in the United States after the Civil War was very intense, because many more railroad routes became available to shippers. In addition, there was a rapid growth in railroad mileage during the last quarter of the nineteenth century. In an effort to reduce this competition, financier J. Pierpont Morgan carried out an extensive program of mergers and consolidations among existing lines, but his efforts were unsuccessful due to the entry of new firms into the industry.

In an attempt to increase profits, numerous cartels—or "pools," as they were called then—were formed. A typical pool was the cartel of the major eastern railroads, which was formed in 1874 under the direction of William H. Vanderbilt of the New York Central Railroad and included the Erie and the Pennsylvania railroads. This initial arrangement lasted only six months, however, primarily due to the fact that the Baltimore & Ohio Railroad did not join the cartel and cut its rates when the cartel members attempted to raise theirs.[13]

In the spring of 1877, the eastern cartel was reactivated after three years of rigorous competition. This time, the arrangement lasted less than four months due to rate violations by the Grand Trunk Line of Canada. Undaunted, cartel members met in July of 1877 to establish the Joint Executive Committee under the direction of Albert Fink. In less than five months, however, the Wabash Railroad and the Grand Trunk Line of Canada were cutting rates. By March of 1878, the cities of Peoria, Toledo, Cincinnati, Louisville, and Columbus were outside the cartel. Despite a complete failure to prevent freight rates from declining, the Joint Executive Committee continued to meet. However, between 1879 and 1882, railroad mileage increased from 105,000 to 141,000 miles with no corresponding increase in the volume of goods transported.[14] The result was an

---

[13]Gabriel Kolko, *Railroads and Regulation: 1877–1916* (Princeton, NJ: Princeton University Press, 1965), pp. 8–9.
[14]*Ibid.,* p. 19.

increase in competition for the available business. Railroads serving Philadelphia and Baltimore cut their rates, thereby diverting freight that would otherwise have gone to New York City. In March of 1881, the Joint Executive Committee responded to this traffic diversion by cutting the rates of all members in the cartel to the lowest rate prevailing among competitors. Between July and October of 1881, railroad freight rates declined by 50% in the eastern United States and by an almost equal amount in the West.[15] As a result of this and the 1883–1884 rate war between Jay Gould's West Shore Line and the New York Central, which involved the entire eastern railroad system, the Joint Executive Committee ceased to have any power or authority.

The pattern of the failure of the eastern railroad cartel was to be repeated in all other regions of the United States. All of these cartels were utter failures due to their inherent instability. Despite the objective of these cartels to raise prices, the freight revenue per ton-mile received by the railroads decreased from 1.88 cents in 1870 to 1.22 cents in 1880, .94 cents in 1890, and .73 cents in 1900.[16]

The railroads were not unaware of the dismal performance of voluntary cartel agreements, and the presidents of many lines, along with farmers and businessmen, quickly became leading advocates of government intervention in the railroad industry. The upshot of this political and economic unrest was the Act to Regulate Commerce of 1887, which created the Interstate Commerce Commission (ICC).

The railroads were not totally in accord when the Act to Regulate Commerce was debated in Congress. Many lines were strongly opposed to the act and lobbied against it.[17] However, there is little doubt that once the act became law and the ICC was established, the railroads sought to turn the intervention of the government to their own advantage.

A major objective of the Act to Regulate Commerce was to ensure that railroads would no longer be able to practice price discrimination by means of secret rate reductions. The large trunk-line railroads that provided the long-distance traffic routes between the East and the Midwest were quick to take advantage of this portion of the law. These railroads agreed to share the shipping tonnage, as they had so often done in the past, but they now openly posted discounts to bring their relative shipping shares into line with the agreed on cartel shares.[18] After the establishment of the ICC, the cartel was much more stable because the Act to Regulate Commerce greatly reduced the profits from cheating for two reasons. First, according to the law, any reduction in rates had to be applied to both long- and short-haul customers, so that the expected

---

[15]*Ibid.*, p. 19.
[16]*Ibid.*, p. 7.
[17]Edward A. Purcell, Jr., "Ideas and Interests: Businessmen and the Interstate Commerce Act," *The Journal of American History* (December 1967), pp. 576–78.
[18]Paul W. MacAvoy, *The Economic Effects of Regulation: The Trunk-Line Railroad Cartels and the Interstate Commerce Commission Before 1900* (Cambridge, MA: M.I.T. Press, 1965), pp. 123–24.

profits from price-cutting the more lucrative long-haul business would be offset by losses to short-haul customers. Second, the fact that rate reductions had to be publicized in advance shortened the time period over which a disloyal cartel member could receive larger profits.

The seven-year period from 1887 to 1893 was characterized by strong regulation on the part of the ICC. But beginning in 1892, court decisions began to seriously weaken the regulatory power of the ICC.[19] During the period of strong government regulation, the railroad cartel was able to maintain stable rates at higher levels than the rates the railroads had unsuccessfully strived for prior to 1887.[20] The market value of the stock of cartel members rose rapidly between 1887 and 1894, indicating the success of the cartel in generating pure profits for its members when assisted by the legal authority of the state.[21]

During the period of weak regulation from 1894 to 1903, the profitability of the railroads declined. Strong regulation was returned to the ICC in 1903, when Congress passed the Elkins Bill. The basic concept of this bill was initially written in 1901 by James A. Logan, the general solicitor of the Pennsylvania Railroad.[22] The Elkins Bill achieved two of the railroads' primary goals. First, it declared the granting of rebates illegal and subject to a fine of up to $20,000 for each offense. Second, although the bill did not recognize the legitimacy of cartels, it did allow identical rates to be filed with the ICC. Once filed, these rates became the legal rates from which any departure was considered a violation of the law. This provision for rate maintenance accomplished the same goal that the railroad cartels had sought for 30 years.[23]

Application: The Oil Cartel

In 1960, the primary oil-producing countries in the less developed nations of the world formed the Organization of Petroleum Exporting Countries (OPEC).[24] At that time, seven major U.S. oil companies owned the capital used for oil exploration and production in the OPEC countries and operated under concessions granted them by the host countries.

As a result of the discovery of large oil reserves between 1950 and 1970 in the OPEC countries and despite efforts on the part of domestic producers in the United States to limit oil imports to the United States, the price of oil in constant 1967 dollars per barrel declined, as shown in the following table.[25] By 1975, however, the real cost of oil had risen almost 300%.

---

[19]*Ibid.*, p. 153.
[20]*Ibid.*, p. 201.
[21]*Ibid.*
[22]Kolko, *op. cit.*, p. 97
[23]*Ibid.*, p. 100.
[24]Saudi Arabia, Iran, Iraq, Venezuela, Libya, Nigeria, Kuwait, and Indonesia produce 85% of all OPEC oil.
[25]Table data from Walter J. Mead, "An Economic Analysis of Crude Oil Price Behavior in the 1970s," *The Journal of Energy and Development* (Spring 1979), p. 214.

YEAR	PRICE OF OIL IN CURRENT DOLLARS	PRICE OF OIL IN 1967 DOLLARS
1950	$ 2.51	$3.07
1960	2.88	3.03
1970	3.18	2.88
1975	13.93	7.96
1976	13.48	7.37
1977	14.53	7.48
1978 (June)	14.54	6.94
1979 (Jan.–Mar.)	15.00–22.00	6.76–9.91

The historical events associated with this marked increase in U.S. oil prices are well-known. During the Arab-Israeli War, the Arab members of OPEC imposed an oil embargo in the latter part of 1973. A large percentage of the West's oil imports were cut off, and the price of oil rose sharply. When the embargo was lifted, the OPEC countries decided to sell their oil at a higher price. Light Arabian crude oil from Ras Tanura, Saudi Arabia, which had been selling for $1.30 per barrel freight on board (f.o.b.) in 1970, therefore rose to $10.72 per barrel in 1975,[26] causing the price of an average barrel of oil in the United States to increase from $3.18 in 1970 to $13.93 in 1975, as shown in the table.

The conventional explanation for this rapid increase in oil prices is that OPEC is a cartel that has reduced its output and raised its prices, so that its members can achieve pure profits. If this view is correct, the alert reader may wonder why this cartel—in contrast to other cartels throughout history—has been stable and successful since 1974. The answer is often given that countries such as Saudi Arabia, Kuwait, Libya, and the United Arab Emirates are able to cut back their oil production because they are so-called "saver countries." Their cutbacks then compensate for the increased oil production of the other members of the OPEC cartel. Unfortunately, this theory does not coincide with the data. In 1974, total OPEC production was 30,746,000 barrels per day, and the market share produced by the "saver countries" was 46.3%. In 1977, total OPEC production had *risen* to 31,215,000 barrels per day, and the market share produced by the "saver countries" had *increased* to 48.9%.[27]

An alternative hypothesis to explain the stability of higher world oil prices since 1974 is based on the unconventional view that OPEC is *not* a cartel. One of the foremost defenders of this view is Walter J. Mead.[28] Mead has calculated the price path of oil over time that would maximize the present value of OPEC's nonrenewable resource. Assuming that the real rate of return is 2% and that the future price of large quantities of oil derived from oil shale would sell for $40.00 per barrel, Mead calculated that the present value of a barrel of OPEC

---

[26]Salah El Serafy, "The Oil Price Revolution of 1973–1974," *The Journal of Energy and Development* (Spring 1979), pp. 273–90.
[27]Mead, *op. cit.*
[28]*Ibid.*

oil in 1978 was $14.86, which is very close to the actual world price prevailing at that time ($14.54).

Mead feels that the sudden jump in the price of OPEC oil in 1974 is the result of the effective transfer of the ownership of the oil fields from the U.S. major oil companies to the OPEC countries when this property was nationalized. The oil companies perceived the eventuality of nationalization in the 1960s, which motivated them to maximize short-run profits by pumping as much oil as possible before the oil fields were nationalized. From 1960 to 1970, the annual rate of growth in oil production in the Middle East was 10.9%; from 1970 to 1973, it increased to 15%.[29] As a result of these high growth rates, the price of U.S. oil declined in real terms. By the end of 1973, however, the host countries had completed the nationalization process, and U.S. oil companies were merely serving as product distributors. Once the oil fields became the property of the OPEC countries, the optimal marketing strategy was switched from maximizing profits in the short run to long-run profit maximization over time. To achieve this, the OPEC countries had to increase the price of oil until it was equal to the prices of alternative energy sources and had to reduce the growth rate in oil production to almost 0%.

Summary   10–7

In Chapter 10, we have examined some of the economic theories of the firm that operate within the forms of market organization that lie between perfect competition and pure monopoly. First, we considered Chamberlin's *theory of monopolistic competition*, which assumes that an industry is comprised of many firms, each producing a slightly differentiated product. Due to this *product differentiation*, we now know that the monopolistically competitive firm is faced with a demand curve that, although not perfectly price-elastic, is highly elastic because competitors within the industry can supply a large number of very close substitutes. We have also found that unlike the theories of perfect competition and pure monopoly, the theory of monopolistic competition is based on the more realistic assumption that buyers have imperfect *knowledge* about the products sold by firms, making *advertising expenditure* a necessary business cost. The assumption of less-than-perfect knowledge plays an additional, critical role in the theory of monopolistic competition because it serves as the basis for the corollary assumption that each firm believes it can increase its share of the market *without detection by competitors*. Each monopolistically competitive firm thinks that when it reduces its price, none of the competing firms will follow suit, so that the *perceived demand curve* of the representative firm in monopolistic competition will be more price-elastic than its *proportional demand curve*. The firm believes that its profits will be maximized by producing the level of output at which its *perceived marginal revenue* is equal to its marginal cost.

---

[29] *Ibid.*, p. 222.

We have seen that as a result of each firm's desire to capture more of the market, all firms will lower their prices in the short run until the perceived profit-maximizing price is equal to the market equilibrium price. In the long run we have found that a monopolistically competitive firm will be in equilibrium when its profits are 0 and it is producing at the level of output and scale of plant determined by the tangency of the firm's perceived demand curve with its long-run average cost curve. Some economists have argued that since this point of tangency lies to the left of the minimum point on the firm's LRAC curve, monopolistic competition results in the inefficient use of resources. This argument was shown to be questionable when the advantages of product differentiation were considered. However, the most damaging criticism of the theory of monopolistic competition has been that it is only slightly more realistic than the theory of pure competition, because monopolistically competitive firms are as rare in the real world as perfectly competitive firms.

We have also studied the movement toward more realistic initial assumptions in forming an economic theory of firm behavior characterized by *oligopoly theory*, which assumes that there are only a small number of mutually interdependent firms in an industry. Oligopolies can be divided into two categories: *unorganized oligopolies* in which pricing and production decisions are implicitly coordinated among firms, and *organized oligopolies*, in which firms employ explicit collusion to coordinate prices and market shares. Within each of these categories, a further subdivision into pure and differentiated oligopolies is possible. In *pure oligopolies*, each firm produces a homogeneous product; in *differentiated oligopolies*, the product is differentiated as it is in monopolistic competition.

In the context of oligopoly theory, we have also discussed the *kinked demand theory*, which assumes that each firm believes that if it raises its price, its competitors will not follow suit, but if it lowers its price, its competitors will cut their prices as well. This assumption results in a demand curve that has a sharp bend or *kink* at the market equilibrium price, so that the marginal revenue curve is discontinuous at the level of output corresponding to the kink. Since the profit-maximizing output is determined by the intersection of the firm's marginal revenue and marginal cost curves, the MC curve can rise or fall within the discontinuous region of the MR curve without a resulting change in the firm's output or price. The same price rigidity was also shown to be possible when the firm's demand curve increases or decreases. Thus, the kinked demand model offers one explanation for the observed price stickiness in oligopolistic industries. Unfortunately, the kinked demand theory does not hold up under empirical testing, which tends to reveal that oligopolistic firms are just as likely to raise price as to lower price and also that, contrary to the kinked demand theory, oligopolistic firms exhibit greater price flexibility than monopolistic firms do.

We have also examined another form of implicit coordination found in oligopolistic industries called *price leadership*. The two types of price leadership models we considered were the *low-cost* and the *dominant-firm models*. When all firms in an industry are approximately the same size, the market price is determined by the low-cost firm, and this price is met by all the remaining firms.

fig 10-8   fig 10-9

When an industry is comprised of one large firm and several small firms, it is assumed that the dominant firm sets the price and allows the small firms to sell as much as they desire at the established price. The residual demand then constitutes the sales of the dominant firm. Since the small firms behave as perfectly competitive firms under dominant-firm price leadership, it is possible to construct their aggregate supply curve at various prices, which will provide the residual demand curve for the dominant firm. We have seen that the dominant firm maximizes its profits by producing at the level of output determined by the intersection of its marginal cost curve and its marginal revenue curve as derived from its residual demand curve. This output determines the price set by the dominant firm, and the small firms charge the same price. A nontraditional view regarding pricing in oligopolistic industries is based on the concept that firms in these industries have such great economic power that they can control demand as well as supply. Such firms are said to be able to *administer* the price and the output level of their products. Two commonly cited pricing mechanisms that these firms supposedly employ are the *full-cost pricing* formula and the *target-return pricing* formula. However, we have seen that there is little empirical evidence to support this view.

In this chapter, we have also examined *cartels*–organizations of oligopolistic firms that have joined together for the explicit purpose of collusion to fix prices and market shares within an industry. In a centrally directed cartel composed of identical firms, the cartel will behave as if it were a multiplant monopolist and set total cartel output equal to the amount corresponding to the intersection of the sum of the individual firms' marginal cost curves and the industry's marginal revenue curve. The price at which this output is sold is then determined by the market demand curve. Price and profits will be higher and output will be lower than they will be in the absence of the cartel agreement. We have seen that despite the fact that cartels are able to increase profits, they tend to be unsuccessful if they are established as voluntary associations, because the incentive to cheat to achieve even greater profits than those secured by the cartel agreement is ever-present. Unless supported and protected by government regulation, cartels will be unstable and generally ineffective in their attempts to garner pure profits.

Finally, we have studied three major cartels in action. In the first application, attempts by cartels in the electrical equipment industry to fix prices met with only limited success in the short run. As economic theory predicts, cheating was commonplace and the various cartel arrangements proved to be highly unstable. In the second application, as long as the railroad cartels were voluntary associations, they also proved to be unstable and unable to produce pure profits for their members. In contrast to the electrical equipment industry, however, the railroads were able to capitalize on political sentiment supporting the government regulation of their industry. The creation of the Interstate Commerce Commission in 1887 and further legislative extensions permitted the railroads to enforce previously unobtainable shipping rates. As a result, the downward trend in shipping rates and railroad profits was reversed. In the first case, the government's role in making such price fixing illegal did not stop, as

Adam Smith predicted, attempts by firms to "conspire against the public," but it did act as a barrier against government support and encouragement of the cartel. In the second case, through attempts to extend the role of government into the workings of the market economy, government itself became the tool whereby the goals of the cartel could finally be achieved. The third application we have studied in this chapter—the so-called OPEC oil cartel—thus far has defied the prediction that cartels are unstable arrangements that quickly collapse. One explanation for the continued high price of OPEC oil is that OPEC is not a cartel in the sense that we have used the term in this chapter.

In Chapter 11, we will construct economic theories that explain how the proceeds of the total product of the firm are distributed among the factor inputs of land, labor, and capital. We will also explore the implications of government legislation that is designed to alter this distribution.

References

Armentano, D.T. *The Myths of Antitrust.* New Rochelle, NY: Arlington House, 1972.

Benham, Lee. "The Effect of Advertising on the Price of Eyeglasses." *Journal of Law and Economics* (October 1972), pp. 337–52.

Bond, Ronald S., John E. Kwoka, Jr., John J. Phelan, and Ira Taylor Whitten. *Staff Report on Effects of Restrictions on Advertising and Commercial Practice in the Professions: The Case of Optometry.* Washington, D.C.: Federal Trade Commission, Bureau of Economics, April 1980.

Burgess, Paul L., and Fred R. Glahe. "Pricing in the American Automobile Industry and the Galbraith Hypothesis." *Rivista Internazionale di Scienze Economiche e Commerciali* (December 1970), pp. 1176–86.

Chamberlin, Edward. *The Theory of Monopolistic Competition,* 8th ed. Cambridge, MA: Harvard University Press, 1962.

Chamberlin, Edward. *Toward A More General Theory of Value.* Cambridge, MA: Harvard University Press, 1957.

Eckstein, Otto, and Gary Fromm. "The Price Equation." *American Economic Review* (December 1968), pp. 1159–83.

El Serafy, Salah. "The Oil Price Revolution of 1973–1974." *The Journal of Energy and Development* (Spring 1979), pp. 273–90.

Friedman, Milton. *Essays in Positive Economics.* Chicago: University of Chicago Press, 1953.

Galbraith, John Kenneth. "Memorandum on the Automobile Industry: A Case Study in Competition—A Statement by the General Motors Corporation." *Planning, Regulation, and Competition: Automobile Industry, 1968.* Washington, D.C.: U.S. Government Printing Office, 1968, pp. 910–12.

Galbraith, John Kenneth. *The New Industrial State.* Boston: Houghton Mifflin, 1967.

Hall, R.C., and C.J. Hitch. "Price Theory and Business Behavior." *Oxford Economic Papers* (May 1939), pp. 12–45.

Kolko, Gabriel. *Railroads and Regulation: 1877–1916.* Princeton, NJ: Princeton University Press, 1965.

MacAvoy, Paul W. *The Economic Effects of Regulation: The Trunk-Line Railroad Cartels and the Interstate Commerce Commission Before 1900.* Cambridge, MA: M.I.T. Press, 1965.

Mead, Walter J. "An Economic Analysis of Crude Oil Price Behavior in the 1970s." *The Journal of Energy and Development* (Spring 1979), pp. 212–28.

Purcell, Edward A., Jr. "Ideas and Interests: Businessmen and the Interstate Commerce Act." *The Journal of American History* (December 1967), pp. 561–78.

Robinson, Joan. *The Economics of Imperfect Competition.* London: Macmillan, 1933.

Simon, Julian L. "A Further Test of the Kinky Oligopoly Demand Curve." *American Economic Review* (December 1969), pp. 971–75.

Smith, Adam. *An Inquiry into the Nature and Causes of the Wealth of Nations,* reprinted ed. Chicago: University of Chicago Press, 1976.

Smith, Richard Austin. "The Incredible Electrical Conspiracy." *Fortune,* Part I (April 1961), pp. 132*ff,* and Part II (May 1961), pp. 161*ff.*

Stigler, George J. *Five Lectures on Economic Problems.* London: Longman's Green, 1949.

Stigler, George J. "The Kinky Oligopoly Demand Curve and Rigid Prices." *Journal of Political Economy* (October 1947), pp. 432–49.

Sweezy, Paul M. "Demand Under Conditions of Oligopoly." *Journal of Political Economy* (August 1939), pp. 568–73.

U.S. Congress, Senate Committee on the Judiciary, Subcommittee on Antitrust and Monopoly. *Price Fixing and Bid-Rigging in the Electrical Manufacturing Industry,* Parts 27 and 28. 87th Congress, 1st Session (April–June 1961).

Problems

1. List the assumptions of perfect competition and monopolistic competition. In what respects are these assumptions similar and dissimilar?

2. Given that every firm has identical cost functions, compare the long-run equilibrium condition that prevails in perfectly competitive and monopolistically competitive industries.

3. What are some of the techniques that fast-food restaurants employ to differentiate their products?

4. Does monopolistic competition lead to excess advertising expenditures and unnecessary product differentiation?

5. Explain the sudden popularity of "generic foods" in terms of monopolistic competition and in terms of perfect competition. Which explanation is more consistent with the facts?

6. Is competition, as it is commonly understood, greater in perfect competition or in an oligopoly?

7. Draw a kinked demand curve and construct its corresponding marginal revenue curve. Explain why variations in marginal cost might not be accompanied by changes in the price of the product.

8. If the dominant firm in an oligopolistic industry is the price leader, what does this imply about the behavior of the rest of the firms in the industry?

9. Given the overwhelming evidence contesting the validity of Sweezy's kinked demand theory, why do you think it is such a popular topic in economics textbooks? Can you think of a rejected scientific theory in physics or chemistry that still enjoys such popularity?

10. Between 1920 and 1933, the consumption of alcoholic beverages was prohibited by law in the United States. In order to supply the demand for alcohol, entrepreneurs called "bootleggers" violated the law. In the city of Chicago, the two major bootleggers were Alphonse "Scarface Al" Capone and George "Bugs" Moran. Capone and Moran agreed to share the Chicago market equally and divided the metropolitan area into geographic territories. On Saint Valentine's Day in 1929, members of the Capone gang, dressed as policemen, machine-gunned down seven members of the Moran gang. This event was called the "Saint Valentine's Day Massacre." Explain the Saint Valentine's Day Massacre in terms of the economic theory of cartels developed in this chapter.

11. In Chapter 8, we asserted that if all perfectly competitive firms have identical costs, they will all be the same size. Would this be true in monopolistic competition?

CHAPTER ELEVEN

MARKET DISTRIBUTION

Introduction 11-1

In our study of the foundations of modern microeconomic theory thus far, we have developed the theories of supply and demand, which jointly explain the determination of market price. In the process of deriving this theory of price, we have assumed that the cost of productive inputs is given. Since the cost, or price, of productive inputs is also determined in the marketplace, we will not be able to construct a complete theory of price until we can also explain how factor input price is determined.

Fortunately, the determination of the price of factor inputs is analogous to the determination of the price of commodities. The significant difference in the case of determining factor input price is that firms are now the demanders and individuals are now the suppliers. Business firms are the demanders of productive input services, while landowners, capitalists, and workers supply the services of land, capital, and labor respectively. Since the total output of goods and services in an economy—the *national income*—is the result of the employment of the nation's land, labor, and capital, if we can determine the price of the services of these factor inputs, we will also be able to determine how national income is distributed.

The Demand for Inputs Under Perfect Competition 11-2

The underlying assumption of our theory of the demand for the services of factor inputs is that the firm seeks to maximize its profits. Thus, if the employment of a marginal unit of a factor input adds more to the firm's revenue than to its cost, the firm will profit by employing the additional unit of input. Profit maximization will therefore take place when the revenue yielded by the employment of the last marginal unit of a factor input is just matched by the cost of that

375

input. Since the theory of factor input demand that we will develop and explore in this chapter is based on the marginal productivity of the inputs, it is usually referred to as the **marginal productivity theory of input demand.**

Although this theory is generally applicable to all kinds of factor inputs, its most readily apparent application is to the study of the demand for labor. We will therefore tend to limit our theoretical examples to the case of labor demand, but the reader should constantly be aware that the theory and examples presented here are equally applicable to the demand for any productive service.

One-Variable Input Demand

We know that one of the characteristics of perfect competition is that each firm is so small in relation to the size of the market that it can sell any desired level of output at the market-determined price. Table 11–1 provides us with a numerical example. The firm represented here is assumed to be operating under the conditions of perfect competition. This is indicated by the fact that the price P at which the firm can sell its product is a constant $10 per unit and the wage W at which it can purchase a unit of labor is a constant $30 per unit. This means that the firm can sell all the output it desires at $10 per unit and hire as much labor as it wishes at $30 per unit.

For our first example, we will assume that the firm's only variable input is labor. The problem faced by the firm of course is familiar to us by now—determining the decision rule for maximizing profits. When we approached this problem in Chapter 8, we were interested in determining the level of output at which profit maximization occurred. In this chapter, we will approach the problem from a slightly different perspective: We now wish to determine the number of units of labor (or any other productive input) that the firm should purchase in order to maximize its profits.

The first three columns in Table 11–1 provide information concerning the relationship between the number of units of labor employed L, listed in column (1), and the resulting total physical output or **total product of labor** TP_L, given in column (2). Column (3) tells us what the physical product of each additional unit of labor, or the **marginal product of labor** MP_L will be. Since the price at which the firm can sell each unit is constant at $10, if we multiply this amount by the marginal product of each unit of labor, we will obtain the **value of the marginal product of labor** VMP_L at various levels of labor employment. The results of these calculations appear in column (5) of Table 11–1.

We have already pointed out that if the employment of an additional marginal unit of labor adds more to a firm's total revenue than to its total cost, the firm will profit from purchasing additional units of labor until its addition to revenue is equal to its addition to cost.

VMP_L is the measure of the addition to the firm's total revenue that each marginal unit of labor contributes. To maximize profits, the firm simply deter-

Table 11–1
Determination of the Profit-Maximizing Labor Employment Level

(1)	(2)	(3)	(4)	(5)	(6)	(7)
	TOTAL	MARGINAL	PRICE OF	VALUE OF	PRICE	MARGINAL
UNITS	PRODUCT	PRODUCT	PRODUCT	MARGINAL	PER UNIT	FACTOR
OF LABOR	OF LABOR	OF LABOR	PER UNIT	PRODUCT	OF LABOR	COST
			OF LABOR	OF LABOR		OF LABOR
L	TP_L	MP_L	P	VMP_L	W	MFC_L
0	0	0	$10	$ 0	$30	$30
1	13	13	10	130	30	30
2	24	11	10	110	30	30
3	33	9	10	90	30	30
4	40	7	10	70	30	30
5	45	5	10	50	30	30
6	48	3	10	30	30	30
7	49	1	10	10	30	30

mines at what level of labor employment VMP_L is equal to the **marginal factor cost of labor** MFC_L. Due to our assumption of perfect competition, this can be easily accomplished: Since the firm can hire as much labor as it wishes at $30 per unit, MFC_L is constant and equal to $30 per unit, as shown in column (7) of Table 11–1. Clearly, profit maximization for the firm in our example will occur when 6 units of labor are employed, since $VMP_L = MFC_L = \$30$ at this level. If the firm employs only 5 units of labor, then $VMP_L = \$50 > \$30 = MFC_L$ and profits can still be increased by purchasing additional units of labor. If 7 units are employed, then $VMP_L = \$10 < \$30 = MFC_L$, and the opposite condition prevails.

Figure 11–1 provides the graphic solution to the profit-maximizing level of labor input for the data given in Table 11–1. If we assume that units of labor are infinitely divisible, we can draw the VMP_L and MFC_L curves in Figure 11–1 through the plotted points obtained from the data in Table 11–1. The point at which these two curves intersect provides the profit-maximizing quantity of labor, which is 6 units.

The VMP_L curve in Figure 11–1 is negatively sloped, because in Table 11–1 we assume diminishing marginal productivity for all levels of factor input. Given a continuously diminishing marginal product and a constant product price, VMP_L must also be continuously diminishing. On the other hand, the MFC_L curve in Figure 11–1 is horizontal, because the firm can purchase as many units of labor as it desires at a constant price of $30. Therefore, for the firm in perfect competition, the MFC_L curve is the **labor supply curve** S_L faced by the individual firm.

Now we will assume that market forces cause the price of labor W to increase from the initial $30 to $60, as indicated by the shift in the labor

Figure 11-1
Profit-Maximizing Level of Labor Employment

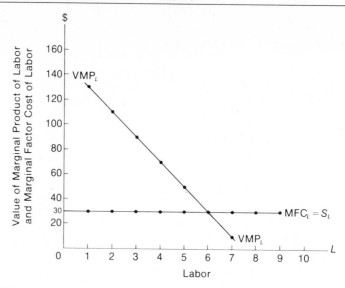

supply curve from S_{L_0} to S_{L_1} In Figure 11-2. The VMP_L curve in this figure is the same as the VMP_L curve in Figure 11-1. As we can see in Figure 11-2, the number of units of labor the firm will employ at a price of $60 per unit declines from 6 to 4.5. If the labor supply curve shifts again from S_{L_1} to S_{L_2}, the firm will further reduce its labor employment from 4.5 to 3 units at a price of $90 per unit.

We have been shifting the labor supply curve in Figure 11-2 simply to show that the value of the marginal product of labor curve VMP_L is also the firm's **labor demand curve** D_L, as indicated in the figure. This is clearly evident from the fact that whenever we vary the cost of the labor input, the profit-maximizing quantity of labor is determined by the VMP_L curve. Thus, the labor demand curve is negatively sloped, due to our assumption that the marginal product of labor is diminishing. Of course, in some situations, the marginal product of labor will increase and the firm's labor demand curve will be positively sloped, but this will occur only at relatively low levels of output associated with the negative, long-run marginal products of factors that remain fixed in the short run. Since negative marginal products are not consistent with long-run profit maximization, operation by the firm in the region of increasing marginal product of labor would be short-lived.[1]

---

[1]For an extended discussion of this point, see Charles W. Baird, *Prices and Markets: Microeconomics* (St. Paul, MN: West Publishing, 1975), pp. 66–69.

Figure 11–2
Derivation of the Labor Demand Curve

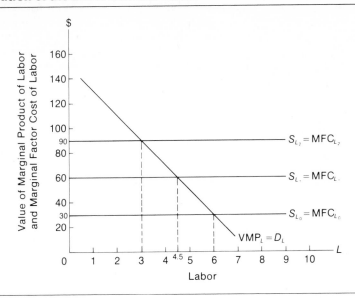

Two-Variable Input Demand

When two or more different kinds of the firm's inputs are variable, the derivation of the firm's demand curve for one of the inputs is more complicated, primarily because the value of the marginal product of the factor input whose price
is being varied is *no longer the firm's demand curve for that factor*. Changing
the price of one kind of input produces changes in the quantities of the other
inputs employed and, in turn, causes the marginal product curve of the input
whose price was initially varied to shift.

To illustrate, we will consider a firm that has two variable inputs–labor and
capital. To derive this firm's labor demand curve, we will vary the price of labor
P_L and measure the change in the quantity of labor L demanded while we hold
the price of capital P_K constant, but allow its quantity K to vary.

To analyze the effect of a reduction in the price of labor P_L on the quantity of
labor demanded L when the price of capital P_K is held constant, we must consider the firm's production function. In Figure 11–3, the initial price of labor to
price of capital ratio P_L/P_K is given by the slope of the isocost line that is tangent to isoquant curve Q_0 at point A. At output Q_0, K_0 units of capital and L_0
units of labor are demanded. The total change in the quantity of labor
demanded when the price of labor declines can be broken down into three
effects: (1) the substitution effect, (2) the output effect, and (3) the profit effect.

The **substitution effect** in production theory is similar to the substitution

Figure 11–3
Changes in the Quantity of Labor Demanded
When the Price of Labor Declines

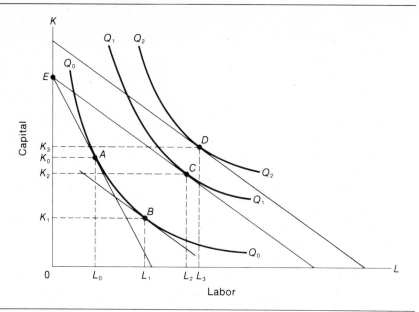

effect in consumer theory, which we examined in Chapter 5. If output is held constant at its initial value of Q_0 and the price of labor is reduced, the isocost line will become less steep and the *least-cost combination* of inputs will be given by tangency point B on isoquant curve Q_0 in Figure 11–3. Labor is substituted for capital and increases from L_0 to L_1, while the quantity of capital utilized decreases from K_0 to K_1, so that output is held constant.

However, a profit-maximizing firm will probably not wish to hold output constant at Q_0. If costs are held at their initial level, the isocost line will rotate counterclockwise around point E and become tangent to isoquant curve Q_1 at point C in Figure 11–3. A movement such as the one from point B to point C is called the **output effect.** In contrast to consumer price theory, however, a profit-maximizing firm is not constrained in the same way as an individual. The firm is willing to expand its total expenditures on labor and capital if its profits can still be increased. In Figure 11–3, an increase in the firm's total expenditure on labor and capital is indicated by a parallel shift in the isocost line outward and to the right, so that it is now tangent to isoquant curve Q_2 at point D. A movement such as the one from point C to point D is called the **profit effect.**

The net result of the firm's profit-maximizing process illustrated in Figure 11–3 is to increase the quantity of labor demanded as the price of labor

declines.[2] Thus, we can conclude that the labor demand curve will be negatively sloped if there are two variable inputs.[3] This conclusion also holds when
there are three or more variable inputs.

The Demand for Inputs Under Imperfect Competition   11–3

Like the firm in perfect competition, the firm in imperfect competition seeks to
maximize its profits. One major difference, however, between perfect and
imperfect competition is that the perfectly competitive firm can sell as much of
its product as it wishes at a constant price, but the imperfectly competitive firm
must lower its price to sell additional output. This difference results from the
fact that the firm's demand curve is horizontal in perfect competition, whereas
it is negatively sloped in imperfect competition. We will now examine the
significance of this difference in demand for the firm's output on the demand
for the firm's factor inputs.

One-Variable Input Demand

The first three columns in Table 11–2 are identical to the first three columns in
Table 11–1, which indicates that the production functions for our representative firms in perfect and imperfect competition are identical. This means that
any difference in the demand for factor inputs we discover will result from differences in the demand for the output of each firm.

Because the firm illustrated in Table 11–2 is assumed to be operating under
conditions of imperfect competition, the price at which this firm can sell a given
amount of output *decreases* as the quantity of output sold increases, as shown
in column (4). In contrast, the perfectly competitive firm represented in Table
11–1 can sell any amount of output it desires at the constant price of $10.00.
Since the imperfectly competitive firm also desires to maximize profits, it will
purchase additional units of labor as long as a marginal unit of labor adds more
to the firm's revenue than its cost. Due to the fact that the imperfectly competitive firm faces a downward-sloping demand curve for its output, the calculation of the marginal revenue obtained from employing an additional unit of labor
is slightly more complicated than it is under conditions of perfect competition.
This is illustrated in Table 11–2, where *total revenue* TR at various levels of
production is calculated in column (5). Dividing the change in total revenue as

---

[2]In this example, the total quantity of capital demanded also increased, but it is not necessary that this result occur.
[3]In contrast to the theory of consumer behavior, which does not exclude the possibility of
Giffen goods, it can be shown that the labor demand curve will *always* be negatively
sloped, but the proof is long and tedious. See Charles E. Ferguson, "Production, Prices, and
the Theory of Joint-Derived Input Demand Function," *Economica* (November 1966), pp.
454–61.

Table 11–2
Calculation of the Marginal Revenue Product

(1)	(2)	(3)	(4)	(5)	(6)	(7)	(8)
	TOTAL	MARGINAL	PRICE OF			MARGINAL	MARGINAL
UNITS	PRODUCT	PRODUCT	PRODUCT	TOTAL	MARGINAL	REVENUE	FACTOR
OF LABOR	OF LABOR	OF LABOR	PER UNIT	REVENUE	REVENUE	PRODUCT*	COST
			OF LABOR			OF LABOR	OF LABOR
L	TP_L	MP_L	P	TR	MR	MRP_L	MFC_L
0	0	0	$11.50	$ 0	$ 0	$ 0	$30
1	13	13	10.00	130.00	10.00	130	30
2	24	11	8.64	207.36	7.03	77	30
3	33	9	7.80	257.40	5.56	50	30
4	40	7	7.19	287.60	4.31	30	30
5	45	5	6.80	306.00	3.68	18	30
6	48	3	6.58	315.84	3.28	10	30
7	49	1	6.42	314.58	−1.26	−1	30

*Rounded to the nearest dollar.

each additional unit of labor is employed by the change in output produced by the additional unit of labor gives us the *marginal revenue* MR from the increased output for each additional unit of labor employed, which appear in column (6) of Table 11–2.

The **marginal revenue product of labor** MRP_L is defined to be the marginal revenue multiplied by the marginal product of a marginal unit of labor, or

$$MRP_L = MR \cdot MP_L \qquad (11\text{–}1)$$

The results of these calculations, rounded to the nearest dollar, appear in column (7) of Table 11–2. Since MRP_L is the addition to the firm's total revenue when one additional unit of labor is employed, it follows that a profit-maximizing firm will purchase additional units of labor until the marginal revenue product of labor MRP_L is just equal to the **marginal factor cost of labor** MFC_L given in column (8). Table 11–2 indicates that with $MFC_L = \$30$, this occurs when the firm has hired 4 units of labor.

If the price of labor is $50 per unit, then the imperfectly competitive firm represented in Table 11–2 will only hire 3 units of labor. The MRP_L curve based on the data given in Table 11–2 and drawn in Figure 11–4 is the imperfectly competitive firm's labor demand curve. We can see that it is negatively sloped, like the labor demand curve for the perfectly competitive firm. To illustrate the difference between the demand for labor input of the perfectly and imperfectly competitive firms represented in Tables 11–1 and 11–2, respectively, the VMP_L

Figure 11–4
Comparison of Profit-Maximizing Levels of Labor Employment

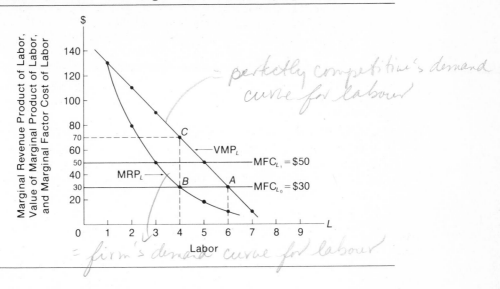

curve for the perfectly competitive firm is also drawn in Figure 11–4. As we can see, the MRP_L curve for the imperfectly competitive firm lies to the left of the VMP_L curve, so that at any given price per unit of labor, the imperfectly competitive firm in our example will purchase fewer units of labor. In general, if a perfectly competitive industry could somehow be transformed into an imperfectly competitive one, the outcome would be a reduction in output and an accompanying reduction in the employment of factor inputs. This is consistent with the conclusions we reached in Chapter 9.

Another important difference between the purchase of factor inputs by perfectly and imperfectly competitive firms produces what is commonly referred to as **monopolistic exploitation,** which occurs when the payment to the factor input is less than the value of its marginal product. To explain this concept more fully, we will consider the labor input in Figure 11–4. Suppose that the market-determined marginal factor cost of labor is $30 per unit, which is represented by the MFC_{L_0} curve in the figure. Under conditions of perfect competition, the firm will purchase 6 units of labor and the wage of $30 per unit of labor will be exactly equal to the value of the marginal product the labor produced, as shown by the intersection of the VMP_L and MFC_{L_0} curves at point A in Figure 11–4. However, if the firm is a monopolist, the profit-maximizing labor input will be 4 units, which is determined by the intersection of the MFC_{L_0} and MRP_L curves at point B in Figure 11–4. However, if 4 units of labor are employed, the value of the last unit of labor to the firm is $70, as given by point C in Figure 11–4, although labor only receives a return of $30 per unit. The difference of $40 is a measure of the amount of monopolistic exploitation.

Example
11-1

Estimates of the Demand for Labor

In a study of employment behavior in terms of man-hours in U.S. manufacturing industries, Roger N. Waud estimated the elasticity of demand for
production workers.* This elasticity of demand is the ratio of the percentage change in the number of man-hours of labor demanded to a corresponding percentage change in the hourly wages of production workers. The
statistically significant elasticity estimates from Waud's study are provided
in the following table.†

We are interested in the sign of the wage elasticity of demand for workers, because it tells us whether the slope of the demand curve is positive
or negative. The estimates in this table have not been multiplied by −1.
The sign of every one of these elasticity estimates is negative, which implies
that the labor demand curve in these industries must be negatively sloped.

*Roger N. Waud, "Man-Hour Behavior in U.S. Manufacturing: A Neoclassical Interpre-
tation," *Journal of Political Economy* (May/June 1968), pp. 407–25.
†*Ibid.*, pp. 416–17.

The word "exploitation" takes on normative implications when we realize that
the market price of an input is a measure of its social value. Under monopolistic exploitation, the input is worth more to society at the margin than society
pays for it. This occurs in imperfect competition because, as we explained in
Chapter 9, output is restricted, which is not the case in perfect competition. Of
course, this does not mean that workers in imperfectly competitive industries
are paid less than workers in perfectly competitive ones. As long as there is
mobility of labor between all industries in the economy, the same wage rates
will tend to prevail for equivalent jobs in all firms and industries, whether they
are perfectly or imperfectly competitive.

Two-Variable Input Demand

As in the case of perfect competition, when two or more different kinds of an
imperfectly competitive firm's inputs are variable, the derivation of the firm's
demand curve for one of the inputs becomes more complicated. Our analysis of
the imperfectly competitive firm's behavior when there is a reduction in the price
of labor would follow the same general pattern that we employed in Section
11–2 for the perfectly competitive firm. The only significant departure would
be in the determination of the profit effect. However, this difference would not
alter our major conclusion that in imperfect competition, a reduction in the price
of labor results in an increase in the quantity of labor demanded. Thus, the labor
demand curve for an imperfectly competitive firm is also negative sloped, and
this conclusion holds regardless of the number of kinds of variable inputs.

For example, a 1% increase in the hourly wage of production workers in the petroleum industry will result in a 1.527% decrease in the number of production man-hours.

INDUSTRY	$\%\Delta W/\%\Delta L$
Food	−0.506
Paper	−0.613
Chemicals	−0.654
Petroleum	−1.527
Rubber and Plastics	−1.334
Stone, Clay, Glass	−1.967
Fabricated Metals	−2.366
Nonelectrical Machinery	−2.103
Electrical Machinery	−2.142
Instruments	−1.692
Miscellaneous	−1.364

Market Demand for Factor Inputs   11–4

The usual way to construct a market demand curve for a good or service is simply to sum up the quantity demanded by each participant in the market at all possible prices. The resulting aggregate demand curve is the *market demand curve*. Unfortunately, we cannot employ this relatively simple method to construct the market demand curve for a factor input, because as additional units of an input are employed, more output is produced, which in turn affects the price of the product and consequently the derived demand for the input.[4]

This rather complicated argument can be clarified by considering Figure 11–5. The firm in Figure 11–5(a) is initially in equilibrium at point A on labor demand curve $D_{\hat{L}}D_{\hat{L}}$ at the initial wage of W_0. Since each firm is demanding $\hat{L}_0$ units of labor, multiplying $\hat{L}_0$ by the number of firms in the market gives us L_0, the quantity demanded by the market at wage W_0, and yields point A' on the market labor demand curve $D_L D_L$ shown in Figure 11–5(b).

Now, we will suppose that the labor wage declines from W_0 to W_1, so that each firm, as previously shown, will employ additional labor and produce a greater quantity of the product. Although an increase in one firm's production will have no impact on product price, when all firms increase production, the market supply curve will shift to the right and product price will decline. Since the firm's demand for labor is a derived demand, a decline in the price of the product produced will also reduce each firm's demand for labor. This

---

[4]The analysis and conclusions presented in this section are valid whether the firm has one or more variable inputs.

Figure 11–5
Derivation of the Market Labor Demand Curve

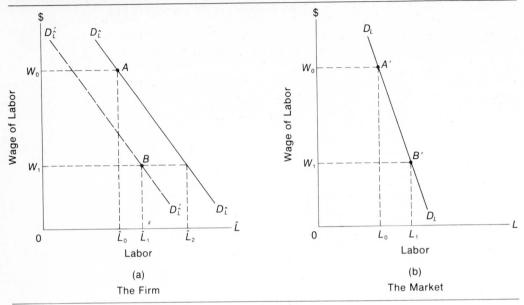

(a)

The Firm

(b)

The Market

is shown in Figure 11–5(a) by the leftward shift in the firm's labor demand curve from $D_{\hat{L}}D_{\hat{L}}$ to $D'_{\hat{L}}D'_{\hat{L}}$. At wage W_1, the firm will now maximize its profits by employing $\hat{L}_1$ units instead of $\hat{L}_2$ units of labor.

The total quantity of labor employed in the market L_1 at wage W_1 is obtained by multiplying the number of firms in the market by $\hat{L}_1$ units of labor. Thus, at wage W_1, the market labor demand curve D_LD_L passes through point B' in Figure 11–5(b). By selecting other possible market wages, any additional number of points like A' and B' can be obtained in Figure 11–5(b), and connecting these points will provide the market labor demand curve D_LD_L.

11–5 The Supply of Factor Inputs

All variable supplies of factor inputs can be classified into three categories: natural resources, intermediate goods, and labor. *Natural resources,* such as agricultural land and minerals, are usually not suitable factors of production in their native state and must be altered by a production process before they can be used as inputs themselves. For example, minerals must be mined before they can be refined, so that the short-run supply curve for minerals is positively sloped, like the supply curves of other manufactured commodities we examined in Chapter 8. *Intermediate goods* are simply goods that are produced by one firm to be sold to other firms that use them to produce commodities for sale to other firms or to final consumers. Since intermediate goods are the outputs of the firms that produce them, these goods also exhibit positively sloped supply curves in the short run.

In this section, we will restrict our examination of the supply of factor inputs to the supply of labor input, which exhibits a more interesting supply curve than other productive inputs for two reasons. First, as we will soon see, it is not possible to state the sign of the slope of the labor supply curve unequivocally. Second, the supply of labor plays a particularly important role in public policy debates, and we will consider some applications of the theory of labor supply to current problems in the labor market.

Individual Labor Supply

An individual can allocate time in one of two ways—work or leisure. The individual is faced with the problem of deciding how much of the total available time in a given period (a day, week, month, or longer) should be devoted to work and how much should be devoted to leisure. We assume that individuals prefer leisure to work and that income must be received from working if leisure is to be forgone. The extent to which an individual is willing to trade off leisure for work depends on the shape and position of his or her indifference curves.

Indifference curves I_1, I_2, I_3, and I_4 in Figure 11-6 describe how a hypothetical individual feels about the trade-off between leisure and income. The time period we are considering in this analysis is one day, so that the increments on the horizontal axis begin at 0 hours at the origin and end at a maximum of 24 hours. Since, by definition, all time must be spent in either leisure or work, if we subtract the number of hours the individual spends in leisure activities from 24, the difference must be the number of hours worked. A second horizontal axis is therefore drawn under the leisure axis in Figure 11-6. The increments on the second axis range from 24 to 0 hours and measure the number of hours the individual worked during the day.

If we know the wages W paid per hour of work, then we can easily compute the daily earnings or income Y the individual receives for working H hours, since

$$Y = WH \qquad\qquad (11-2)$$

Equation (11-2) is *linear* and is drawn in Figure 11-6 for four different hourly wages. All of these lines originate at the right end of the horizontal axis, because if leisure equals 24 hours, then work must equal 0 hours, so that Y will also be equal to 0 regardless of the hourly wage. For example, if the hourly wage is $1.00, then the straight line depicting Equation (11-2) originates at the right end of the horizontal axis where 0 hours are worked per day, because $Y = 0 \cdot \$1.00 = 0$ and intersects the vertical axis at a daily income of $24.00, since $Y = 24 \cdot \$1.00 = \$24.00$. For any number of hours worked between these two extremes, the daily income can be read from this line. If, say, 18 hours are worked per day and the hourly wage is $1.00, we would be at point J on the $1.00-per-hour line in Figure 11–6 and the daily income on the vertical axis would be $18.00. As the hourly wage rises, the lines depicting Equation (11–2) intersect at increasingly higher points on the vertical axis measuring daily income, but the horizontal axis intercept remains at 24 hours of leisure per day. Thus, the hourly wage determines the slope of the straight lines, which economists call **constraint lines.** Each of these lines geometrically represents a wage constraint under which the individual maximizes utility.

Utility maximization will occur at the point where an indifference curve is tangent to its corresponding wage constraint line. For example, when the hourly wage is $.50, the highest possible indifference curve that can be reached is curve I_1, which is just tangent to the $.50-per-hour wage constraint line at point A in Figure 11–6. Faced with working for this hourly wage, our hypothetical individual chooses to work 6 hours per day and earn a daily income of $3.00. Now suppose that the hourly wage is raised to $1.00 per hour. Our individual will then maximize welfare by moving to point B, where indifference curve I_2 is just tangent to the $1.00-per-hour wage constraint line, and will work 9 hours and earn $9.00 per day. The individual's utility-maximizing choices when offered hourly wages of $1.50 and $2.00 are similarly designated by points C and D, respec-

Figure 11–6
Indifference-Curve Analysis of an Individual's Behavior Toward Leisure and Work

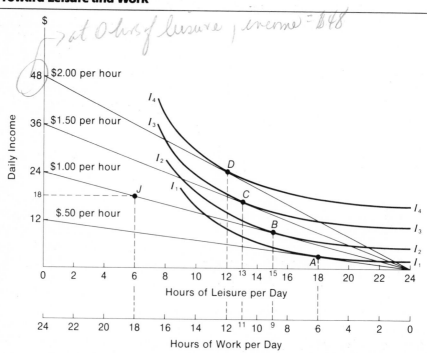

Figure 11–7
The Labor Supply Curve for an Individual

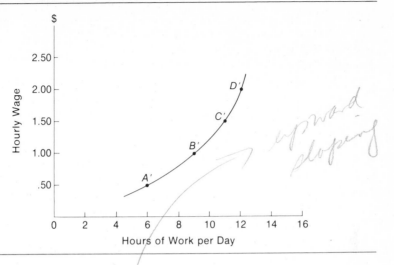

tively, in Figure 11–6. By varying the hourly wage in this manner, we can deter-mine the number of hours our individual will work each day at any hourly wage.

The data we derived in Figure 11–6 is plotted in Figure 11–7 to provide the **individual's labor supply curve.** The hourly wage is measured on the vertical axis, and the hours of work per day are measured on the horizontal axis. If the hourly wage is $.50 in Figure 11–6, then the individual will choose to be at point *A*, working 6 hours per day. Point *A'* in Figure 11–7 corresponds to point *A* in Figure 11–6, given the difference that the vertical axis in Figure 11–7 measures the wage per hour rather than the income per day. Similarly, points *B'*, *C'*, and *D'* in Figure 11–7 correspond to points *B*, *C*, and *D* in Figure 11–6. The curve drawn through points *A'*, *B'*, *C'*, and *D'* in Figure 11–7 is the individual's labor supply curve. By changing the time span under consideration, an individual's labor supply curve can be derived for a week, a month, a year, or an even longer period of time.

Backward-Bending Supply

Although the labor supply curve we derived in Figure 11–7 has an exclusively positive slope, this may not be true for every individual. In some cases, an indi-vidual's labor supply curve may have a positive slope initially, but the slope of the curve will reverse and become negative at a particular wage. Such a curve is called a **backward-bending labor supply curve.**

The indifference curves of an individual whose labor supply curve is backward-bending are drawn in Figure 11–8. Initially, as wage increases from $.50 to $1.00 to $1.50 per hour, the individual is willing to work additional hours

Figure 11–8
The Backward-Bending Labor Supply Curve

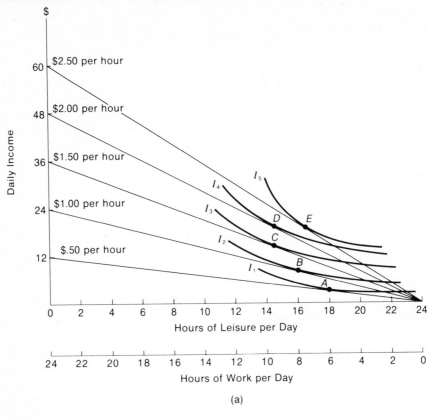

(a)

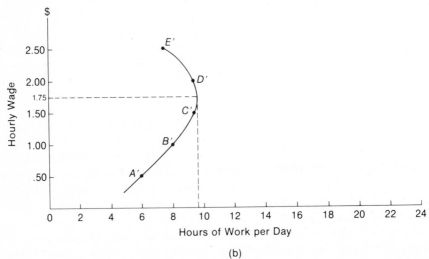

(b)

to obtain a higher income. However, when the wage is raised from $1.50 to $2.00 per hour, there is no change in the quantity of labor supplied, and when the wage increases to $2.50 per hour, the number of hours worked per day actually begins to diminish. This is more clearly illustrated in Figure 11–8(b), where the labor supply curve corresponding to the data given in Figure 11–8(a) is constructed. The backward-bending curve in Figure 11–8(b) reveals that the individual will work the maximum number of hours per day when the wage is $1.75 per hour. At wages higher than $1.75 per hour, the number of hours of labor supplied will begin to diminish.

We can explain the backward-bending labor supply curve in terms of the interaction between the *income* and *substitution effects* first introduced in Chapter 5. In terms of our analysis in this section, the *substitution effect* indicates the change in the quantity of labor supplied in response to varying wage rates when the individual's utility is held constant. The *income effect* isolates the change in the quantity of labor supplied as income is increased, holding the wage rate constant.

In Chapter 5, we showed that the substitution effect is *always negative*–that is, that an increase in price will always cause a decrease in consumption. The wage rate of the individual in our example here corresponds to price, and leisure is the good that the individual is "buying" by foregoing income that could be earned. Thus, the substitution effect implies that when wages are increased, consumption of leisure will be decreased (the number of hours worked will increase) if the individual's utility remains constant. Now, if we make the reasonable assumption that leisure is a *normal good* (that its consumption increases as income increases), then the income effect will *always be positive*. This means that as income increases, the consumption of leisure will increase if the wage rate is held constant. Since a wage increase incorporates both the income and substitution effects and since these effects operate in opposite directions, the labor supply curve's switch from positive to negative slope must be the result of the income effect overwhelming the substitution effect.

Figure 11–9 is a graphic presentation of what we have just stated about the income and substitution effects. If the initial wage is $1.00 per hour, the individual in Figure 11–9 will be maximizing utility at point A on indifference curve I_1 and working 12 hours per day. If the wage is raised to $2.00 per hour, the individual will prefer point C on indifference curve I_2, thereby reducing the amount of work supplied from 12 to 10 hours per day. To separate out the income and substitution effects, we employ the same techniques that we were introduced to in Chapter 5. First, we construct a new constraint line that is parallel to the $2.00-per-hour constraint line but tangent to the initial indifference curve I_1. This new constraint is tangent to I_1 at point B in Figure 11–9. This point of utility maximization could be achieved in practice by taxing the individual $14.00 per day after the wage is raised to $2.00 per hour. Since utility is held constant, the movement from point A to point B is the substitution effect, which–as Figure 11–9 shows–is negative. Thus, when the price of leisure (the hourly wage) rises, less leisure (more work) will be consumed when the individual is constrained to the original indifference curve. However, since leisure is a normal

Figure 11-9
The Income and Substitution Effects

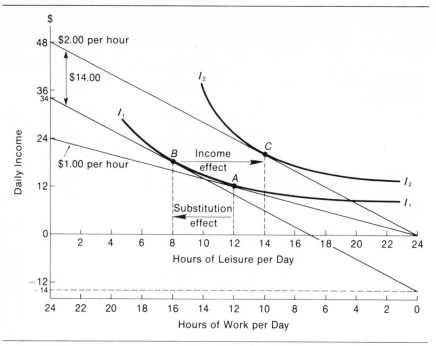

good, the income effect—the movement from point B to point C in Figure 11–9— will always be positive and may be greater in absolute magnitude than the substitution effect. Point C—the utility-maximizing point when a tax is not imposed— lies to the right of point A, and the number of hours of work the individual supplies per day declines when the hourly wage is increased from $1.00 to $2.00 per hour. Therefore, when the labor supply curve is positively sloped, the magnitude of the substitution effect is greater than the magnitude of the income effect; when the labor supply curve is negatively sloped, the opposite is true.

Application: Overtime Pay

The hourly wages of many workers increase after a specified number of hours per day or week have been worked. This type of wage increase is usually referred to as **overtime pay** and is an almost universally stated condition in wage contracts between labor unions and firms. Although it may seem surprising, overtime pay is earned just as frequently in the nonunion sector of the labor market. In this application, we will learn why such an arrangement is to be expected.

To illustrate, we will consider the individual whose indifference curves are drawn in Figure 11–10. Initially, at a wage of $1.00 per hour, this individual is willing to work 8 hours per day, as shown by point A on indifference curve I_1.

Figure 11–10
The Effect of Overtime Pay on Labor Supply

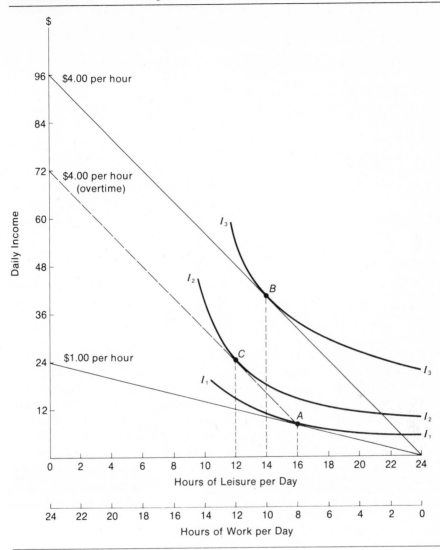

Now suppose that the employer wants the employee to work more than 8 hours per day. One alternative would be to raise the hourly wage to $4.00 per hour. If this occurs, the worker would move from point A on indifference curve I_1 to point B on indifference curve I_3 in Figure 11–10 and work an additional 2 hours per day. Or the employer can offer to pay the worker $1.00 per hour for the first 8 hours worked and $4.00 per hour thereafter for *each additional hour worked*. Under these conditions, our individual will move to point C on indifference curve I_2 in Figure 11–10.

Example
11-2

The Supply Curve of Physicians' Services

In a study of the health services market, Martin S. Feldstein statistically estimated the supply curve of physicians' services.* Feldstein's study revealed that the price elasticity of supply for physicians' services was between $-.67$ and $-.91$. In other words, the physicians' supply curve was backward-bending.

In his study, Feldstein argued that physicians set their fees so that there is an excess demand for their services and then select only those cases for treatment that they find most interesting out of all the patients demanding their services. If Feldstein is correct, then the presence of a backward-bending physicians' supply curve has important policy implications.

Figure 11-11(a) illustrates the market supply and demand curves for physicians' services when supply is less price-elastic than demand. In this figure, physicians price their services at P_1, which is *below* the market equilibrium price $\bar{P}$, in order to create excess demand. If government regulations are enacted to lower the price of physicians' services to P_2, the excess demand for these services will increase, thereby creating a greater shortage of doctors than before. On the other hand, if the demand for physicians' services is less price-elastic than the supply, which Feldstein believes to be

*Martin S. Feldstein, "The Rising Price of Physicians' Services," *The Review of Economics and Statistics* (May 1970), pp. 121-33.

The employer's benefit from the overtime payment is now obvious. The worker will supply an additional 4 hours of work per day at an average of $2.00 per hour instead of $4.00, so that 12 hours of work will be supplied at a total cost of $24.00 per day. Obviously, this is preferable to paying the worker $4.00 per hour to work 10 hours at a cost of $40.00 per day, and the employer has benefited from this overtime arrangement by receiving the additional hours of work desired. But the worker has also benefited, since point C is preferable to point A, even though point B would provide an even greater benefit. The reason that overtime payment results in a greater number of additional work hours supplied than an overall increase in the worker's hourly wage is because the substitution effect is large and the income effect is small, since the wage increase applies only to overtime hours.

Application: The Negative Income Tax

Many economists have long recognized that existing "welfare" programs designed to alleviate poverty also provide a strong disincentive to work. In this application, we will examine why current welfare programs create such a large work disincentive and we will examine a possible remedy for this social problem.

In our analysis, we will assume that the existing welfare system is equivalent to a program that guarantees a minimum level of income to all citizens, the case, then physicians will set their price at P_4 in Figure 11–11(b), which is *above* the market equilibrium price $\bar{P}$. In this case, if regulations are enforced to lower the price of physicians' services to P_3, then the excess demand for their services will decrease, thereby reducing the shortage of doctors. If price is depressed below $\bar{P}$, there will be an excess supply of services and consumers will be able to pick and choose their physicians.

Figure 11–11
The Effect of Regulation on the Excess Demand for Physicians

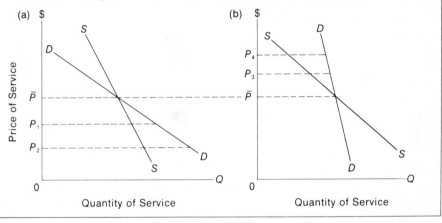

whether they work or not. Although the existing welfare system does *not* exactly correspond to this oversimplification, it is a sufficiently accurate description for our purposes here.

First, we will consider the effects of a **guaranteed minimum income** on the individual represented in Figure 11–12. This worker's wage before taxes is $1.50 per hour, but income and Social Security taxes reduce earnings to $1.25 per hour. With an after-tax income of $1.25 per hour, the individual maximizes welfare by working 10 hours per day and earning $12.50 per day. This is illustrated in Figure 11–12 by the tangency of the after-tax constraint line with indifference curve I_1 at point A.

Now suppose that a welfare system is introduced that guarantees a minimum daily income of $24.00 per day. Any individual who earns less than this amount will be supplemented by the welfare system for the difference between their after-tax income and $24.00. The individual represented in Figure 11–12 will therefore receive the difference between $12.50 and $24.00, as shown by the distance between points A and B, which will be made up by the welfare system. In other words, by working 10 hours the individual will receive $12.50 in after-tax wages and a cash payment of $11.50 to raise the total daily wage to $24.00. However, if leisure is always preferred to work, then point B on indifference curve I_2 is clearly not the worker's optimal position, since the individual can work no hours and receive an income supplement of $24.00 per day at point C on indifference curve I_3.

Figure 11–12
The Effect of Minimal Income Maintenance
on Labor Supplied: Case I

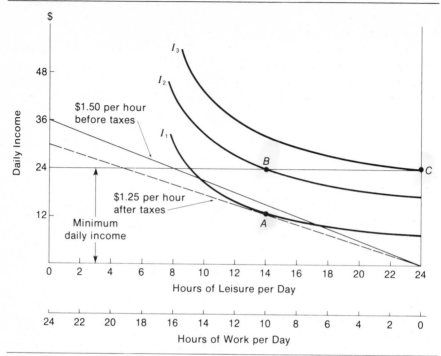

The conclusion we have reached in this analysis is an intuitive one. If a person can receive the same income by not working as by working, then given our assumption that leisure is preferred to work, it logically follows that the individual will not spend any time working. In our analysis, we can also show that even when their after-tax daily income lies *above* the guaranteed minimum income level, some people will still prefer not to work. Such an individual is represented in Figure 11–13. Before a guaranteed minimum daily income was established, this individual maximized welfare at point *A* on indifference curve I_1 in Figure 11–13, working 12 hours per day at $2.50 per hour and earning an after-tax daily income of $24.96. But after a minimum income-maintenance level of $24 per day is established, our individual will prefer not working at point *B* on indifference curve I_2 to working at point *A* on indifference curve I_1, because the 12 hours of leisure gained from not working more than offset the decrease in income of $.96 per day.

Due to the excessive work disincentive that minimum income-maintenance programs appear to provide, some economists have devised alternative welfare policies to moderate this drawback. Milton Friedman's so-called **negative income tax** is one policy that has been proposed to alleviate the work disin-

Figure 11-13
The Effect of Minimal Income Maintenance
on Labor Supplied: Case II

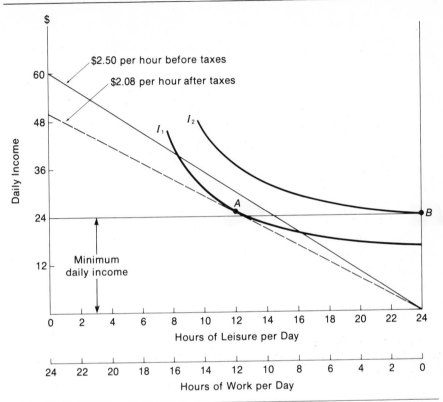

centive.[5] To understand how such a system would function, we will consider the individual represented in Figure 11-14. As before, we will assume that every individual is guaranteed a minimum daily income of $24.00 per day. Prior to the institution of any welfare program, the individual will choose to work at point A on the after-tax constraint line tangent to indifference curve I_1. The establishment of a guaranteed minimum daily income of $24.00 per day will simply result in the same movement to the no-work condition at point B on indifference curve I_2 that occurred in Figure 11-13.

Under the negative income tax policy, the guaranteed minimum income of $24.00 per day is maintained, but to provide an incentive to work, a **break-even level of income** is established *above* the guaranteed minimum. Below this break-even level, take-home pay exceeds earnings (taxes are negative); above it,

[5]Milton Friedman, *Capitalism and Freedom* (Chicago: University of Chicago Press, 1962), pp. 190–95.

Figure 11–14
The Negative Income Tax and Labor Supplied: Case I

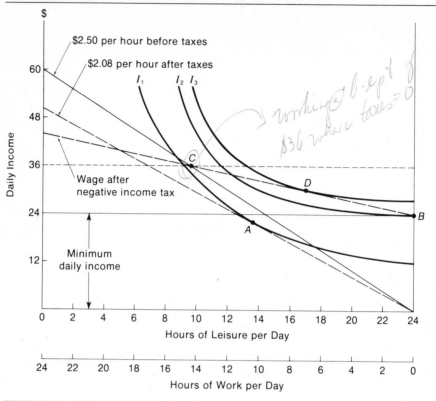

take-home pay is less than earnings (taxes are positive). In Figure 11–14, the break-even level of income is $36.00 per day. Therefore, if an individual works 14.4 hours at a wage of $2.50 per hour, after-tax daily income is $36.00 ($2.50 per hour × 14.4 hours), because the individual is working at the break-even point where taxes are 0. The individual is at point C in Figure 11–14 under these conditions. On the other hand, if the individual works 0 hours per day, the negative income tax will be $24.00 because a minimum daily income of $24.00 is guaranteed. This position is indicated by point B in Figure 11–14. Thus, we can construct the new negative income-tax constraint line by drawing the straight dashed line through points B and C in Figure 11–14. This line tells us how much a worker will receive per day at a wage of $2.50 per hour when taxes are negative to the right of point C and positive to the left of point C.

Given this new negative income-tax constraint line, the individual will now prefer to work at point D in Figure 11–14 working 7 hours per day at $2.50 per hour. The advantages to society of the worker's position represented by point D compared with point B should now be obvious. At point B, the individual is

Figure 11-15
The Negative Income Tax and Labor Supplied: Case II

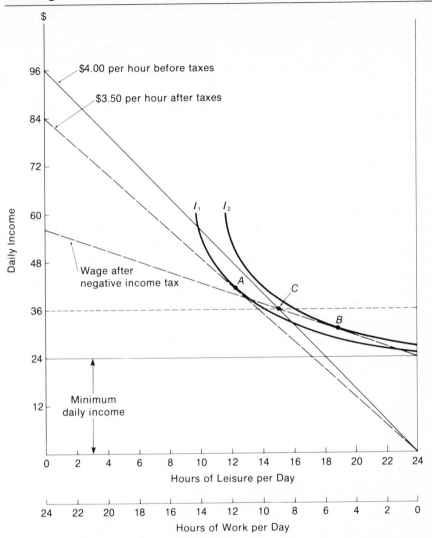

receiving $24.00 per day in tax revenue and is producing nothing for the benefit of society. However, at point *D*, the individual is being paid $17.50 per day ($2.50 per hour × 7 hours) by the employer and is receiving a negative income-tax subsidy of $12.50 per day for a total daily wage of $30.00. Clearly, this is preferable to society, since its payment to the individual has decreased from $24.00 to $12.50 per day and the individual is also contributing to the economy's output by working 7 hours per day. Therefore, in this case, the negative income tax provides greater output at a lower cost compared with the standard minimum income-maintenance welfare program. However, we cannot say that from society's viewpoint, the condition represented by point D is preferred to that of point A in Figure 11–14, because positive taxes had to be imposed on other individuals to move our individual from point A to point D. There is no scientific way to determine whether the utility gained from moving the individual in Figure 11–14 from indifference curve I_1 to I_3 is greater than the utility lost by imposing positive taxes on other individuals. However, we can say that given society's desire to provide a guaranteed minimum daily income for all individuals, the negative income-tax program would be preferable to a minimum income-maintenance plan if the only individuals affected by the negative income tax are already earning less than the guaranteed minimum daily income.

Unfortunately for advocates of the negative income tax, individuals who are making less than the guaranteed minimum daily income are not the only ones affected by the program. For example, consider the individual in Figure 11–15 (page 399). Prior to the establishment of any welfare program, this individual is at point A on indifference curve I_1, earning $41.00 per day by working 11.7 hours at $3.50 per hour after taxes. The establishment of a guaranteed minimum income of $24.00 per day does not affect this individual's work/leisure decision. However, if we introduce a negative income tax that establishes a break-even point at point C in Figure 11–15, the individual will maximize utility by moving to point B on indifference curve I_2, which will result in a *decline* in the number of hours worked from 11.7 to 5.25 per day. Furthermore, when at point A, the individual was a positive taxpayer, whereas at point B, the individual receives a subsidy in the form of a negative income tax.

When individuals like the worker represented in Figure 11–15 are considered, our prior conclusion that the negative income tax is superior to a guaranteed minimum income-maintenance program ceases to be valid. To determine which policy would impose the *least cost* on society, both of these programs must be evaluated on the basis of empirical data acquired from implementing experimental programs in the real world.

Application: Income-Maintenance Experiments

We have seen that economic theory can be employed to predict the direction of choice between work and leisure when income-maintenance programs are initiated, but we know little about the *magnitude* of these choices. Rough estimates of the annual cost of implementing a national income-maintenance program range from $5–10 billion.[6] Since even small improvements in the operating efficiency of such a program would save hundreds of millions of dollars every year, the federal government has initiated several experiments to explore the work-disincentive effects of various programs.

---

[6]Robert Ferber and Werner Z. Hirsch, "Social Experimentation and Economic Policy: A Survey," *Journal of Economic Literature*, Vol. XVI (December 1978), pp. 1379–1414.

The income-maintenance programs in these experiments are generally of the form

$$w = M - rY \qquad (11\text{–}3)$$

where

w = weekly welfare payment
M = income-maintenance level
r = rate of welfare-payment reduction as income is earned by working
Y = weekly income earned before taxes

For the purposes of our analysis, however, equation (11–3) can be expressed in the more useful form

$$Y_d = M + [(1 - r)WH] \qquad (11\text{–}4)$$

where

Y_d = weekly disposable income (income after taxes are paid and income-maintenance payment is received)
$1 - r$ = rate of earned income that is retained
W = hourly wage
H = hours worked per week
$WH = Y$

For example, suppose that the income-maintenance level M = $50 per week, W = $1 per hour, and $0 \le r \le 1.0$. If we let r = 1.0, then no matter how much an individual earns by working, weekly disposable income will remain at $50. This is illustrated in Figure 11–16 by the horizontal line that intersects the vertical axis at $50. If r is reduced to .5, then the worker will retain one-half of every dollar earned by working an additional hour. In Figure 11–16, the line that intersects the vertical axis at $134 ($50 + $168 ÷ 2) graphs the relationship between hours worked per week and weekly disposable income when r = .5. If r = 0, then the weekly disposable income is simply the number of hours worked H multiplied by the hourly wage W plus the income-maintenance level M. At an hourly wage of $1 and a $50 income-maintenance level, the line that intersects the vertical axis at $218 ($50 + $168) provides the weekly disposable income as a function of the number of hours worked per week when r = 0. Lines like those in Figure 11–16 are the individual's constraint lines for a set of initial conditions M and W as r is varied. We can clearly see that as r is reduced, the constraint lines rotate clockwise. Similarly, if we raised (lowered) the income-maintenance level, the constraint line would undergo a parallel shift upward (downward) at a given rate r. Given this information, we can now theoretically examine the work disincentives that result from programs of the form characterized by Equation (11–3).

Figure 11–16
The Effect of the Rate of Welfare-Payment Reduction
on Disposable Income

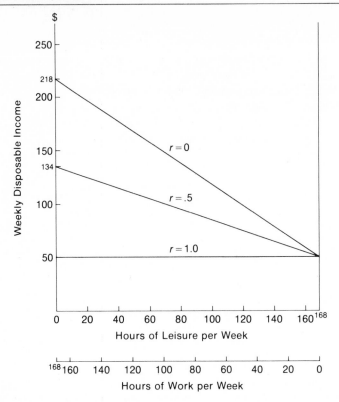

Figure 11–17 illustrates the work/leisure choices of an individual when all factors are held constant *except* the income-maintenance level M, which is raised in three steps from M_0 to M_3. This causes the individual's constraint line to shift upward to a position parallel to the initial constraint line. Earlier in this section, we used this parallel shift in the constraint line to explore the income effect of an individual's work/leisure choices. If we make the realistic assumption that leisure is a normal good and if the income-maintenance level is increased (income is increased), then on theoretical grounds we would expect more leisure to be consumed and the individual to work fewer hours per week. This is illustrated in Figure 11–17 by the fact that the tangency points of the indifference curves move toward the right as M is increased. We can therefore conclude that increasing the income-maintenance level and holding all other factors constant does produce a work disincentive.

In Figure 11–18, the income-maintenance level M is held constant while the rate of welfare-payment reduction r is reduced in four successive steps from r_4

Figure 11–17
The Effect of the Income-Maintenance Level
on Hours Worked

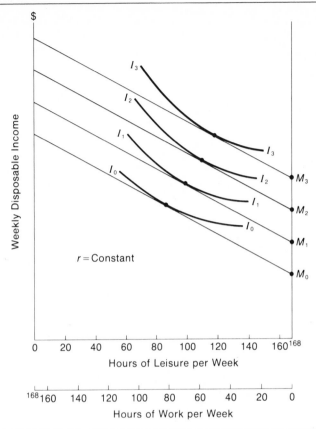

to r_0. As r is reduced, the price of leisure rises. If we ignore income effects, we know that as the price of any good increases, less of the good will be consumed due to the substitution effect. However, we also know that as r is reduced, weekly disposable income increases and the individual will choose to increase the number of leisure hours due to the income effect. Therefore, the individual's work/leisure choices in Figure 11–18 are influenced by both the income and substitution effects working in opposite directions. Note that this is the reverse of the situation we examined in Chapter 5, where the income and substitution effects were reinforcing for a normal good.

As the rate of welfare-payment reduction is lowered from r_4 to r_2 in Figure 11–18, the number of hours that the individual works per week increases. However, for values of r less than r_2, the number of work hours decreases. This increase followed by a decrease in the number of work hours as r is reduced is the result of the interaction of the income and substitution effects. At values of

Figure 11–18
The Effect of the Rate of Welfare-Payment Reduction
on Hours Worked

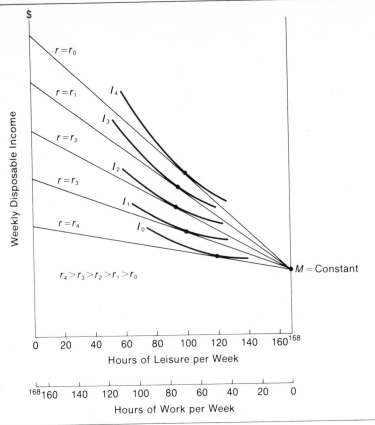

r approaching unity, the income effect of a reduction in r will be very small and less than the substitution effect. Thus, the individual's desire to increase the number of hours worked as a result of the substitution effect will overpower the desire to increase the number of leisure hours produced by the income effect, and the net effect will be an increase in the number of hours worked. However, as r becomes smaller, the *magnitude* of the income effect becomes greater and eventually predominates, so that the overall effect is a reduction in the number of hours worked. Thus, our theoretical analysis of the effect on work disincentive of a reduction in the value of r results in an ambiguous conclusion. Over some ranges, a reduction in the value of r will produce an increase in the number of hours worked; over other ranges, a reduction in r will cause a reduction in the number of hours worked.

We have just seen that although the theoretical analysis of a particular form of income-maintenance program is very useful in making qualitative predictions about the work disincentives such a program would induce, this analysis is of little help in selecting the particular values of r and M that will maximize the program's efficiency. For this reason, the federal government has been funding social experiments over the past decade to determine the effects of various values of r and M on work disincentive.

Four major income-maintenance experiments have been conducted to date. These experiments are usually referred to by geographic location as the New Jersey/Pennsylvania, the rural North Carolina/Iowa, the Denver/Seattle, and the Gary experiments. In these experiments, the income-maintenance level M was varied from 50% to 150% of the poverty income level within each region. The rate of welfare-payment reduction r was also varied between .3 and .8 within each region.[7]

In the New Jersey/Pennsylvania experiment, the change in the average number of hours worked per week by husbands after they enrolled in the experiment varied according to the ethnic group investigated. The average number of hours worked per week declined 2.4 hours for whites and 7.3 hours for Spanish-speaking men, but increased for blacks. For wives, the average number of hours per week worked outside the home declined 20% after they enrolled in the program. For the average family unit, when $r = .5$, the average number of hours worked per week after enrollment declined 7%.[8]

Unfortunately, the New Jersey/Pennsylvania experiment contained many shortcomings and its conclusions were limited, if not questionable.[9] The Denver/Seattle experiment was undertaken to overcome these problems. This experiment involved 4,800 families and is the largest that has been conducted thus far. The general findings of the Denver/Seattle experiment supported the results of the New Jersey/Pennsylvania experiment—namely that for workers included in these experiments, there is a decrease in the number of work hours supplied and this decrease is substantial for secondary earners. More specifically, for each additional $1,000 in the income-maintenance level M per year, husbands worked 5% fewer hours per week, wives worked 22% less hours, and other females worked 11% less hours. Each 10% reduction in disposable income at the mean wage due to increasing values of r produced a reduction of 1 hour per week for husbands, 2 hours per week for wives, and 1 hour per week for female heads of households.[10]

Although the Denver/Seattle experiment cost hundreds of millions of dollars, we can expect additional social experiments to be conducted in the future due to the very high cost of implementing a comprehensive nationwide welfare program. For example, the total cost of all income-maintenance experiments from 1967 through 1977 amounts to only about 1–2% of the projected cost of operating a nationwide welfare program for one year.[11]

---

[7] In two subexperiments in the Denver/Seattle experiment, r was also a function of Y according to the equations $r = .7 - .0254Y$ and $r = .8 - .025Y$.
[8] *Ibid.*, p. 1384.
[9] *Ibid.*
[10] *Ibid.*, p. 1387.
[11] *Ibid.*, p. 1391.

Figure 11–19
Determination of the Factor-Market Equilibrium Wage Rate

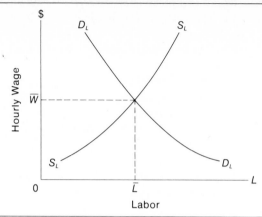

11–6   Market Input Supply and Factor-Market Equilibrium

We derived the individual's labor supply curve earlier in Figure 11–7 (page 389), and we found that this curve can become backward-bending at sufficiently high wage rates. The market supply curve for a given occupation or profession cannot be backward-bending, however, because additional workers will be attracted to the market as wages in that market increase relative to wages in other labor markets. Therefore, even though the number of hours worked per period might decline for some workers in that occupation, the total number of hours supplied will increase. All other variable factor inputs are the commodity outputs of other firms, and we showed in Chapter 8 that their supply curves are positively sloped. Thus, the market supply curves of all variable factor inputs will be positively sloped.

Combining the market labor demand curve $D_L D_L$, which we derived earlier in Figure 11–5, with the market labor supply curve $S_L S_L$ under competitive conditions determines the **factor-market equilibrium.** This is accomplished in Figure 11–19, where the intersection of the $D_L D_L$ and $S_L S_L$ curves determine the equilibrium wage rate $\overline{W}$ and employment level $\overline{L}$.

Application: The Economic Effect of Illegal Aliens[12]

There have been illegal aliens in the United States ever since laws were enacted to restrict their entry. At present, the number of illegal aliens in the United States is estimated to be somewhere between 2 and 12 million. The

---

[12]The data presented in this section are based in part on Barry R. Chiswick, "Immigrants and Immigration Policy," in William Fellner (ed.), *Contemporary Economic Problems, 1978* (Washington, D.C.: American Enterprise Institute for Public Policy Research, 1978), pp. 285–325.

number of deportable aliens apprehended in the United States each year has grown rapidly since 1960: 71,000 in 1960; 110,000 in 1965; 345,000 in 1970; 767,000 in 1975; and in excess of 1 million in 1977. Most of the apprehended aliens are Mexican nationals; in 1975, they comprised 89% of the total apprehended. The reasons for this growth in illegal Mexican immigration are:

1. the rapid population growth in Mexico
2. the relatively low growth rate of the Mexican economy
3. the end of the contract farm labor (*bracero*) program in 1964
4. the establishment of numerical limits by the United States on immigration from the Western Hemisphere
5. the recent prospect of amnesty for illegal aliens already residing in the United States.

Part of any rational policy for dealing with these illegal aliens must be the evaluation of the economic impact they have on American citizens.

We can analyze some of the aspects of this problem in terms of the simple factor-market equilibrium model we have just constructed. Suppose that the American labor market is similar to the market presented in Figure 11–20. The demand for labor curve D_L is also the value of the marginal product of labor VMP_L. Prior to immigration, the labor supply curve is S_L and is assumed to be fixed in the short run, so that the wage rate is W_0. Total aggregate *labor* income is simply the wage rate W_0 multiplied by the number of units of labor supplied L_0, or area $0W_0BL_0$ in Figure 11–20. Total aggregate *national* income is the area under the VMP_L curve, or area $0ABL$. If we assume that there are

Figure 11–20
The Economic Effect of Immigration

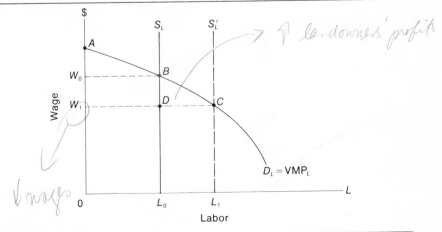

only two factors of production—labor and capital—then the return to the owners of capital is area $W_0 AB = 0ABL_0 - 0W_0 BL_0$.

Now suppose that workers with no capital immigrate to the United States.
This will cause the labor supply curve to shift to the right to S_L', so that wages
decrease to W_1 and labor employed increases to L_1. The aggregate labor
income of the immigrants is then area $L_0 DCL_1$, and the labor income of the
native population therefore declines from $0W_0 BL_0$ to $0W_1 DL_0$. Income received
by the owners of capital increases by the area $W_1 W_0 BC$, so that the net gain
to the native population—the owners of capital and the workers—increases
by the area BCD in Figure 11–20. Although this net increase in national
income produces an increase in the average income of the total population,
it is accompanied by a redistribution of income that favors the owners of
capital.

This simple analysis provides insight into the debate and interest concerning immigration policy among various groups within the economy. If the total
capital stock were evenly distributed among all workers, then workers would
gain from an open-door immigration policy even though their wages would
decline because they would receive an increased return on their capital. On the

**Example
11–3**

Occupational Licensing and Factor Mobility

An important implication of our model of factor-market equilibrium is that
if wage rates are higher in one region of the country than another, laborers
will migrate from the lower-wage to the higher-wage region. This factor
mobility of labor inputs will increase the supply of labor and reduce wages
in the higher-wage region and decrease the supply of labor and raise wages
in the lower-wage region. Eventually, wage rates will equalize and factor
mobility will cease.

The equalization of wage rates for the same type of labor input in all
regions of the country will not occur if there are barriers to factor mobility.
The most common barrier to labor mobility in the United States is the
requirement by many state governments that an occupational license must
be acquired for various professions. For example, 32 licensing boards in
the state of Illinois regulate 100 professions with approximately 500,000
practitioners.

A professional considering the possibility of establishing practice in
another state must determine whether or not a license will be required and,
if so, how difficult it will be to obtain. In some professions, such as pharma-
cology, optometry, architecture, veterinary medicine, and private medical
practice, most state licensing boards practice reciprocity; that is, they
recognize one another's licensing standards as equivalent and individuals
in these professions merely fill out an application to receive the new license.
In other professions, such as law and dentistry, however, there are significantly fewer reciprocity arrangements.

other hand, if capital ownership were concentrated in the hands of a few, a political conflict would arise over immigration policy: Owners of capital would support immigration, and workers would oppose it. Since capital ownership is concentrated, it should not be surprising to learn that the landowners, who are engaged in the production of labor-intensive agricultural products, lobby for a return to the pre-1964 *bracero* program and that the farm labor unions such as La Raza Unidad, which represent predominantly Spanish-speaking American citizens, oppose the entrance of ethnically similar immigrants into the United States and support the efforts of the United States Immigration Service to apprehend and deport illegal aliens.

Monopsony 11-7

In our analysis of factor-market equilibrium thus far, we have assumed that employers in both perfectly and imperfectly competitive industries believe that their individual hiring decisions will have no impact on the labor market. In other words, employers believe that for their particular firm, the supply of workers is *infinitely elastic* at the going wage rate. This situation does not always occur,

---

B. Peter Pashigian examined the effect of occupational licensing on the interstate mobility of lawyers and dentists in the United States.* Pashigian found that the number of lawyers who would migrate over a five-year period would increase 5% if reciprocity were practiced in the profession; for dentists, migration would increase 3–4% with reciprocity. Elimination of all licensing requirements raises the percent of professionals who would migrate over a five-year period 16–18% for lawyers and 12–16% for dentists. Without any licensing requirements, Pashigian concluded that the percentage of lawyers and dentists who would migrate across interstate lines each year would be approximately equal to the percentages currently prevailing for nonlicensed, nonacademic professionals, such as geologists, biologists, and chemists.

The economic impact of state licensing requirements on the dental profession was studied by Lawrence Shepard.† By comparing fees and incomes between the 15 states that are reciprocally bound to endorse each other's licenses with the fees and incomes of the 35 states that have no reciprocity agreements, Shepard found that the price of dental services and the mean income for dentists are 12–15% higher in states without reciprocity agreements. Shepard estimated that this represented an overall additional cost to consumers of $700 million per year.

*B. Peter Pashigian, "Occupational Licensing and the Interstate Mobility of Professionals," *Journal of Law and Economics* (April 1979), pp. 1–25.
†Lawrence Shepard, "Licensing Restrictions and the Cost of Dental Care," *Journal of Law and Economics* (October 1978), pp. 187–201.

however. In rare cases, there are only a few employers of a factor input, such as labor, and these firms are called **oligopsonists.** In even rarer cases, only one firm purchases a certain input, and that firm is called a **monopsonist.** When either oligopsonists or monopsonists decide to increase their utilization of the factors that make the firm an oligopsonist or monopsonist, they realize that their actions will alter the market-determined price of those factor inputs and they behave differently than they would if this were not the case.

For simplicity, we will consider only the behavior of monopsonists in this section. The conclusions we draw here, however, are also applicable to most oligopsonists.

Marginal Factor Cost

The market supply curve of most factor inputs is positively sloped. Because the monopsonist is the only employer of its factor inputs, the monopsonist's factor input supply curve is also positively sloped. To hire one additional unit of input, therefore, in the case of labor, the monopsonist must pay a higher wage to attract one additional worker. However, since all workers previously hired by the monopsonist must now be paid this higher wage as well, the *marginal factor cost* of hiring an additional worker is greater than the marginal cost of the worker.

To better grasp the significance of marginal factor cost, we will consider the example in Table 11–3, where seven different levels of factor input intensity are listed in column (1). Since we are dealing with a monopsonist, the cost of employing additional units of labor increases as each worker is hired. This is indicated in column (2) by the fact that the wage of each additional unit rises as more units are employed. However, we have just pointed out that the cost of hiring an additional unit exceeds the wage increase that must be paid to the last worker hired, because all other workers previously hired by the monopso-

Table 11–3
Calculation of Marginal Factor Cost Under Monopsony

(1)	(2)	(3)	(4)
			MARGINAL
UNITS	WAGE PER	TOTAL WAGES	FACTOR
OF LABOR	UNIT	PAID	COST
	OF LABOR		OF LABOR
L	W	LW	MFC_L
1	$ 2	$ 2	$ 2
2	4	8	6
3	6	18	10
4	8	32	14
5	10	50	18
6	12	72	22
7	14	98	26

Figure 11-21
The Marginal Factor Cost of Labor

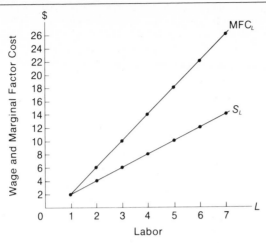

nist must now be paid the higher wage. This total cost of employing various levels of labor is calculated by multiplying the number of units of labor by the corresponding wage necessary to employ that quantity of labor. The results of these calculations appear in column (3) of Table 11-3. The marginal factor cost to the monopsonist of employing an additional unit of labor input is then computed by subtracting the total wage at the previous input level from the total wage at the input level under consideration. For example, if we wish to determine marginal factor cost of labor MFC_L of moving from 4 units to 5 units, we subtract the total wage at 4 units, or $32, from the total wage at 5 units, or $50, to obtain the marginal factor cost of $18. The results of these calculations for the various input levels are given in column (4) of Table 11-3. Note that with the exception of the first unit of labor, MFC_L is always greater than the wage per unit of labor W.

Figure 11-21 is a graph of the data contained in Table 11-3. The figure illustrates that MFC_L exceeds the W and that this difference becomes greater as the number of units of labor increases. In other words, the MFC_L curve lies above and to the left of the labor (input) supply curve S_L, as shown in Figure 11-21.

Factor Price and Employment

A profit-maximizing firm, whether or not it is a monopsonist, will continue to hire additional units of factor input as long as the input's marginal revenue product MRP exceeds its marginal factor cost MFC, since each additional input will add more to the firm's revenue than to its cost. Profit maximization therefore occurs when MRP = MFC, as we have already proved earlier in this chap-

Figure 11-22
Determination of the Wage Rate
and the Employment Level for a Monopsonist

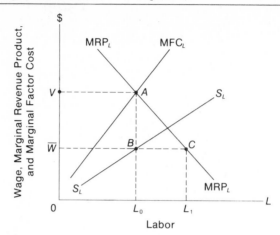

ter. However, although the profit-maximizing condition is the same for both the monopsonist and the nonmonopsonist, the determination of their equilibrium input prices and quantities differs.

The determination of the wage rate and the employment level of the labor input for a monopsonist is illustrated in Figure 11-22. At point A, $MFC_L = MRP_L$ and the profit-maximizing employment level is L_0. However, because the monopsonist's MFC_L curve lies to the left and above its labor supply curve $S_L S_L$, the equilibrium wage is not determined at point A, but at point B on the $S_L S_L$ curve. Thus, $\overline{W}$ is the equilibrium wage paid by the monopsonist.

In Section 11-3, we said that exploitation of a factor input occurs when the payment for the input is less than the value of its marginal product. If the firm in Figure 11-22 produces a product that is sold elsewhere in a perfectly competitive market but the firm itself is located on a small island state, where it is the major employer, then the firm's MRP_L curve will also be its value of the marginal product of labor VMP_L curve. In this situation, the factor input—labor—will be paid $\overline{W}$, which is less than the value V of the marginal product of labor in Figure 11-22. Labor will therefore be exploited solely as the result of the monopsony. This type of exploitation is called **monopsonistic exploitation.**

In addition to being a monopsonist, suppose that the firm in Figure 11-22 also has some control over the price at which its output is sold. Then the firm's MRP_L curve will lie below its VMP_L curve (not drawn in the figure), and the factor input—labor—will be exploited from both directions. Once again, we must emphasize that "exploitation" used in this context does not mean that workers, capital, or land are being paid less than similar factor inputs in alternative and accessible employments. The word "accessible" is used here because in our example of labor monopsony on a small island state, the continuance of the monopsony hinges on the immobility of labor. Thus, although the single firm on the island may pay a lower wage than workers receive elsewhere, it must still pay as high a wage as the wages offered by alternative employments on the island. In fact, the lower wage level probably attracted the firm to the island in the first place. And, since the existence of the firm will greatly increase the demand for labor, this monopsonist will drive up all wages on the island and increase the islanders' welfare.

Application: The Effects of Minimum-Wage Legislation

The effects of minimum-wage legislation on labor markets has been a source of controversy in the United States ever since the first minimum-wage laws were passed in the 1930s. The economic theory we have developed in this chapter provides us with two models to employ to predict these effects: the **nonmonopsonistic model** – or, as it is sometimes called, the **competitive model** – and the **monopsonistic model**.

First, we will consider the predictions of the nonmonopsonistic model. In Figure 11–23, the equilibrium wage rate $\overline{W}$ and employment level $\overline{L}$ are determined by the intersection of the labor demand curve $D_L D_L$ and the labor supply curve $S_L S_L$ at point A. If a law is passed setting the minimum wage at W_0, which is above the equilibrium wage $\overline{W}$, then the quantity of labor supplied

Figure 11–23
The Effects of Minimum-Wage Legislation
on a Nonmonopsonistic Labor Market

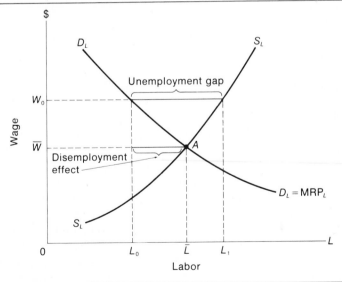

Figure 11–24
The Effects of Minimum-Wage Legislation
on a Monopsonistic Labor Market

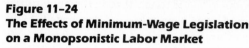

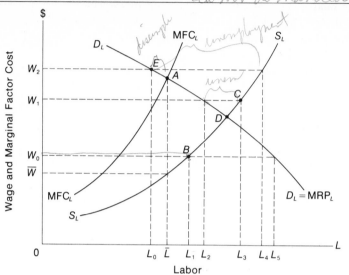

Labor

L_1 will exceed the quantity of labor demanded L_0.[13] As indicated in Figure 11–23, this excess supply of labor at W_0 is called the **unemployment gap.** The actual number of workers who will lose their jobs as a result of the minimum wage is $\bar{L} - L_0$ in Figure 11–23, and this is called the **disemployment effect.** From this analysis of a nonmonopsonistic market, we can predict that setting a minimum wage above the market equilibrium wage will create unemployment, because the number of workers seeking employment will increase and the number of jobs will decrease.

Under conditions of monopsony, the results of effective minimum-wage legislation may differ from the predictions of the nonmonopsonistic model. To illustrate, we will consider the monopsonistic model in Figure 11–24. Prior to the establishment of a minimum wage, the equilibrium employment level $\bar{L}$ is determined by the intersection of the labor demand curve $D_L D_L$ with the marginal factor cost of labor MFC_L curve at point A in Figure 11–24. However, the equilibrium wage $\bar{W}$ is determined by the labor supply curve at $S_L S_L$ at $\bar{L}$ units of labor. A minimum-wage law establishes an effective labor supply curve that is perfectly elastic (horizontal) at the minimum wage out to the point where it intersects the positively sloped labor supply curve $S_L S_L$. Since the effective labor supply curve is horizontal, the effective marginal factor

---

[13]We will consider only minimum wages in excess of the equilibrium rate here, since minimum wages below the equilibrium rate will have no effect on the market.

cost curve in this region will also be horizontal and will coincide with the effective labor supply curve out to the point where it also intersects the $S_L S_L$ curve.

We will now consider the effects of minimum wage-legislation in three individual cases. In case I, we will assume that the minimum wage is set at W_0, which is slightly above the equilibrium wage $\overline{W}$. The effective labor supply curve faced by the firm is now horizontal at W_0 out to point B in Figure 11–24. The firm's effective marginal factor cost coincides with this labor supply curve out to point B. Beyond point B, marginal factor cost jumps up to the MFC_L curve, because the labor supply curve now exceeds the minimum wage. If the firm could hire all the labor it desired at W_0, it would hire L_5 units. But since workers will not supply more than L_1 units of labor at the minimum wage W_0, the firm is only able to hire L_1 units. The results in case I contradict the nonmonopsonistic model. The establishment of an effective minimum wage has raised the level of employment above the equilibrium level $\overline{L}$, and all workers who want jobs can find them.

In case II, the minimum wage is set at W_1. The firm's effective $S_L S_L$ labor supply and MFC_L curves are now horizontal out to point C in Figure 11–24. In case II, unlike case I, the minimum wage W_1 is above the intersection of the $D_L D_L$ and $S_L S_L$ curves at point D, and the firm can hire all the labor it desires at the minimum wage. The actual quantity of labor the firm hires is L_2 units, as shown in Figure 11–24. Thus, raising the minimum wage from W_0 in case I to W_1 in case II increases the number of workers employed from L_1 to L_2. However, in contrast to case I, the quantity of labor supplied L_3 is greater than the quantity demanded, so that the minimum wage has created unemployment in the form of a disemployment effect.

In case III, the minimum wage is set at W_2, which is higher than the wage corresponding to the intersection of the MFC_L and $D_L D_L$ curves at point A in Figure 11–24. The firm in case III employs that level of labor L_0 determined by the intersection of the horizontal MFC_L curve for the minimum wage and the $D_L D_L$ curve at point E. The effects of case III are therefore identical with the nonmonopsonistic model: Fewer workers are hired after the imposition of a minimum wage than were hired before, and the unemployment gap $L_4 - L_0$ exceeds the disemployment effect $\overline{L} - L_0$.

Thus, the *nonmonopsonistic model* predicts that an effective minimum wage will cause some workers who were employed prior to the minimum wage to lose their jobs, so that an even greater number of workers will be seeking jobs. The *monopsonistic model* can yield one of three possible predictions:

1. When the minimum wage is only slightly above the equilibrium wage, employment will increase and there will be no unemployment.

2. At a higher minimum wage, employment will increase but will now be accompanied by unemployment.

3. At a sufficiently high minimum wage, the total number of jobs will actually decrease and a large unemployment gap will result.

**Example
11-4**

The Impact of Minimum-Wage Laws

Studies conducted to investigate the effects of minimum-wage laws usually focus on discernible groups of workers who tend to be low-wage recipients. Youths, women, minorities, students, and older workers are the overlapping groups within the work force that are most likely to be directly affected by increases in the minimum wage. These workers comprise 10–25% of the U.S. labor force.*

The earliest empirical studies examined changes in employment in low-wage industries. One of the first was conducted by Albert Ford Hinrichs, who studied the employment effects of the initial minimum-wage legislation in low-wage relative to high-wage hosiery plants. Employment in the low-wage plants decreased relative to the high-wage plants, and the lowest-wage plants underwent an absolute decline in employment.† John M. Peterson extended Hinrichs' study to include employment in sawmills and men's cotton-underwear production from 1938 through 1950.☆ Peterson's results were in accord with Hinrichs' findings: Employment decreased in low-wage plants relative to high-wage plants. Peterson also discovered that the same relative decline in employment existed between low-wage and high-wage cities and regions.

Recent empirical studies have concentrated on the unemployment effects in low-wage demographic groups, such as teen-agers and minorities. In an important study, Masanori Hashimoto and Jacob Mincer examined unemployment effects over the 1954–1969 period, when the minimum wage was raised four times from $1.15 per hour to $1.60 per hour.** Their findings revealed statistically significant reductions in employment for white and nonwhite teen-agers, for white and nonwhite males aged 20–24, for white males aged 65 and over, and for white and nonwhite females aged 20 and over. Hashimoto and Mincer also obtained data that–although not statistically significant–suggested that raising the minimum wage reduced employment for white and nonwhite males aged 25–64 and for nonwhite males aged 65 and over. Another important effect revealed by this study was that two-thirds of the workers who lost their jobs due to the rising minimum wage dropped out of the labor force. The official unemployment

*Finis Welch, *Minimum Wages: Issues and Evidence* (Washington, D.C.: American Enterprise Institute for Public Policy Research, 1978), p. 15.
†Albert Ford Hinrichs, "Effects of the 25-Cent Minimum Wage on Employment in the Seamless Hosiery Industry," *Journal of the American Statistical Association,* Vol. 35 (March 1940), pp. 13–23.
☆John M. Peterson, "Employment Effects of Minimum Wages, 1938–1950," *Journal of Political Economy,* Vol. 65 (October 1957), pp. 412–30.
**Their results are summarized in Jacob Mincer, "Unemployment Effects of Minimum Wages," *Journal of Political Economy,* Vol. 84, part 2 (August 1976), pp. S87–S104.

rate therefore understates the actual unemployment created by raising the minimum wage.

In a study conducted for the Joint Economic Committee of the U.S. Congress, Walter Williams examined the unemployment effects of minimum-wage legislation on black youths.†† Williams' ratios of black unemployment to white unemployment for males aged 16–17, 18–19, and 20–24 from 1948 to 1978 are provided in Table 11–4 (page 418). This table is significant because it shows that for male teen-age workers, whose wages tend to be among those most affected by increases in the minimum wage, the ratio of black to white unemployment has approximately doubled since 1948, while the unemployment ratio of black to white adults aged 20–24 has remained fairly constant. One of the reasons for this increasing relative rate of unemployment among black teen-agers is the extension of minimum-wage coverage from 53.4% of all nonsupervisory employees in private, nonagricultural work in 1953 to 83% in 1976.☆☆ This extended coverage, in conjunction with increases in the minimum wage, has had a major disemployment effect on teen-agers who have low skill levels–especially on black teen-agers, whose average skill level is lower than that of white teen-agers.

Williams' study also suggests that the higher unemployment rate among black teen-agers compared with white teen-agers may partially result from racial discrimination. This should not surprise us, since minimum-wage laws also reduce the cost to employers of discriminating on the basis of race, sex, religion, length of hair, or some other prejudice. The fact that discrimination in employment is considered morally and legally wrong provides us with another reason–in addition to the economic ones we have examined here–to abolish all minimum-wage laws.

The results of these studies and numerous others support the predictions of the nonmonopsonistic model. Due to the ambiguous predictions of the monopsonistic model, the empirical results cited here do not contradict the predictions of case III. However, the fact that no accepted empirical study indicates that an increase in employment results from the establishment of or subsequent increase in the minimum wage casts a grave doubt as to the relevance of the monopsonistic model to the American economy. The available empirical evidence overwhelmingly suggests that minimum-wage legislation reduces employment among low-wage earners–particularly teen-agers and minorities.

††Walter Williams, *Youth and Minority Unemployment,* Joint Economic Committee, U.S. Congress (Washington, D.C.: U.S. Government Printing Office, July 6, 1977).
☆☆Welch, *Minimum Wages: Issues and Evidence,* p. 3.

Table 11–4
Ratio of Black Youth Unemployment to
White Youth Unemployment

Year	Ages 16–17	Ages 18–19	Ages 20–24	Year	Ages 16–17	Ages 18–19	Ages 20–24
1948	.92	1.11	1.83	1964	1.61	1.72	1.70
1949	1.18	1.20	1.61	1965	1.84	1.77	1.58
1950*	.90	1.51	1.64	1966	1.80	2.30	1.93
1951	.92	1.43	1.86	1967*	2.26	2.23	1.90
1952	.73	1.43	1.84	1968*	2.16	2.31	1.80
1953	.93	1.14	1.80	1969	1.98	2.40	1.83
1954	.96	1.13	1.72	1970	1.77	1.93	1.62
1955	1.21	1.24	1.77	1971	1.95	1.93	1.72
1956*	1.40	1.54	1.97	1972	2.14	2.11	1.73
1957	1.37	1.79	1.79	1973	2.28	2.21	1.94
1958	1.81	1.62	1.66	1974*	2.41	2.31	1.97
1959	1.48	2.09	2.17	1975*	2.29	2.15	2.08
1960	1.55	1.86	1.58	1976*	2.06	2.29	2.05
1961*	1.89	1.58	1.53	1977	2.20	2.78	2.33
1962	1.45	1.72	1.83	1978**	2.59	2.47	2.25
1963*	1.52	1.93	1.99				

SOURCE: Walter Williams, "Government Sanctioned Restraints that Reduce Economic Opportunities for Minorities," *Policy Review,* revised reprint (Washington, D.C.: Heritage Foundation, July 1978), p. 9. Reprinted by permission.

*Year there was a change in the federal minimum-wage law.
**March 1978.

To assess the relevancy of the nonmonopsonistic and monopsonistic models with respect to the economic effects of minimum-wage legislation, economists have resorted to analyzing the empirical data generated by actual minimum-wage legislation. Unfortunately, these data are not easily interpreted. For example, in the real world, labor is not the homogeneous input that we assume it to be in economic theory. Each individual has a different set of skills to offer in the labor market, and a positive correlation tends to be exhibited between wage rates and skill levels. Thus, the effects of a nationwide minimum wage will have no immediate impact on highly skilled workers, who are already being paid a wage in excess of the minimum wage. These effects will be confined to less skilled, low-wage workers.

11–8   The Distribution of Income

Economists have always been intrigued by the question of the *distribution of income* produced by a society. More specifically, they have been concerned with defining the economic factors that determine what fractions of total output are

Figure 11–25
Aggregate Shares of Labor and Capital

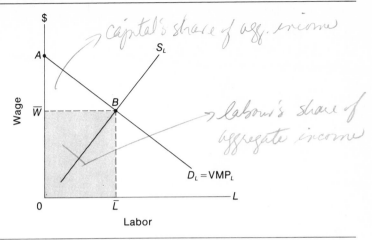

allocated to land, labor, and capital. Nobel Laureate Sir John Hicks launched modern distribution theory in 1932 with his book *The Theory of Wages,* which provided a systematic explanation of the economic forces that determine the distribution of income in a competitive society.[14]

Labor and Capital Shares

We will assume that we have a simple, perfectly competitive economy with only two input factors—labor and capital—and that total output or income can be described by a constant returns to scale production function of the form

$$Q = f(L,K) \qquad\qquad (11-5)$$

Holding capital stock K constant, the share of national income distributed to labor Y_L is given by

$$Y_L = WL \qquad\qquad (11-6)$$

The wage of labor $\overline{W}$ and the quantity of labor employed $\overline{L}$ are determined by the intersection of the labor demand and labor supply curves at point B in Figure 11–25. Labor's share of aggregate income Y_L is therefore the shaded area $0\overline{W}B\overline{L}$ in the figure. Since we are assuming that constant returns to scale exist and that there are only two factors of production, the triangular

---

[14]John R. Hicks, *The Theory of Wages* (London: Macmillan, 1932).

area $\overline{WAB}$ in Figure 11–25 measures capital's share of aggregate income Y_K, which is equal to

$$Y_K = RK \tag{11-7}$$

where R is the rental price of a unit of capital.[15]

Since we are dealing with an aggregate production function, if we let P equal the average price of aggregate output Q, then the total value of aggregate output or national income will be $Y = PQ$. Labor's share of national income will then be

$$\frac{Y_L}{Y} = \frac{WL}{PQ} \tag{11-8}$$

and capital's share of national income will be

$$\frac{Y_K}{Y} = \frac{RK}{PQ} \tag{11-9}$$

Dividing Equation (11–8) by Equation (11–9) gives us the *relative share* of labor to capital

$$\frac{Y_L}{Y_K} = \frac{WL}{RK} \tag{11-10}$$

If the ratio expressed in Equation (11–10) increases, this means that labor's share of national income is increasing; if the ratio declines, it means that capital's share is increasing. Because we are assuming that perfect competition exists, each factor of production will be paid the value of its marginal product, or

$$W = \text{VMP}_L = P(\text{MP}_L) \tag{11-11}$$
$$R = \text{VMP}_K = P(\text{MP}_K) \tag{11-12}$$

Thus, the share of income being distributed to each factor can be written as

$$\frac{Y_L}{Y} = \frac{P(\text{MP}_L)L}{PQ} = \frac{(\text{MP}_L)L}{Q} \tag{11-13}$$

$$\frac{Y_K}{Y} = \frac{P(\text{MP}_K)K}{PQ} = \frac{(\text{MP}_K)K}{Q} \tag{11-14}$$

---

[15]The theorem stating that if each factor earns the value of its marginal product, then the sum of all factor payments will exactly equal the total product is sometimes referred to as the Clark–Wicksteed theorem, after the American economist J.B. Clark and the English economist Phillip H. Wicksteed. However, the first proof was offered by A.W. Flux when he reviewed Wicksteed's *Essay on the Coordination of the Laws of Distribution.* For Flux's proof, see Mark Blaug, *Economic Theory in Retrospect,* 3rd ed. (London: Cambridge University Press, 1978), pp. 463–64.

Equations (11–13) and (11–14) reveal that the **distribution of income** depends only on the level of output, the amount of each factor input employed, and the marginal productivity of each factor input. If the exact specification of the aggregate production function given by Equation (11–5) were known, the factor shares could then be determined.

The Elasticity of Substitution

If the stock of capital or the supply of labor were to change, then the prices paid for the use of their services would probably change also. These changes in factor prices would, in turn, produce changes in the distribution of income. To predict how labor and capital shares will change when their prices change, we will employ Sir John Hicks' concept of the *elasticity of substitution*.[16]

Like all other elasticity measurements, the elasticity of substitution is the ratio of two percentages. Specifically, the **elasticity of substitution** σ is the percentage change in the capital–labor ratio K/L divided by the percentage change in the marginal rate of technical substitution of labor for capital MRTS_{LK}. Algebraically, the elasticity of substitution is given by

$$\sigma = \frac{\Delta(K/L)/K/L}{\Delta\text{MRTS}_{LK}/\text{MRTS}_{LK}} \qquad (11\text{–}15)$$

From Sections 6–3 and 7–3, we know that in equilibrium

$$\text{MRTS}_{LK} = \frac{\text{MP}_L}{\text{MP}_K} = \frac{P_L}{P_K} = \frac{W}{R} \qquad (11\text{–}16)$$

since $P_L = W$ and $P_K = R$. The elasticity of substitution σ can therefore be expressed as

$$\sigma = \frac{\Delta(K/L)/K/L}{\Delta(W/R)/W/R} \qquad (11\text{–}17)$$

We wish to know what happens to relative income shares when the price of labor changes relative to the price of capital. To illustrate, suppose that W/R increases by 5%. Since labor is now more expensive relative to capital, firms will increase their use of capital inputs relative to labor inputs and the capital–labor ratio K/L will rise. The extent to which K/L increases will depend on the elasticity of substitution of the production function. If $\sigma > 1$, then according to Equation (11–17), K/L will increase by a greater percentage–say, 10%. If we now rewrite Equation (11–10) as

$$\frac{Y_L}{Y_K} = \frac{W/R}{K/L} \qquad (11\text{–}18)$$

---

[16]Hicks, *op. cit.*, Chapter VI.

Table 11–5
Factor Shares and the Elasticity of Substitution

DIRECTION OF CHANGE IN FACTOR PRICE RATIO		VALUE OF THE ELASTICITY OF SUBSTITUTION		
		$\sigma < 1$	$\sigma = 1$	$\sigma > 1$
$\dfrac{W}{R}$	increases	Labor's share increases.	Factor shares remain constant.	Labor's share decreases.
		Capital's share decreases.		Capital's share increases.
$\dfrac{W}{R}$	decreases	Labor's share decreases.	Factor shares remain constant.	Labor's share increases.
		Capital's share increases.		Capital's share decreases.

then with W/R increasing by 5% and K/L increasing by 10%, it follows that Y_L/Y_K will decline. Therefore, labor's share of national income will decrease and capital's share will increase. On the other hand, if $\sigma < 1$ and W/R increases by 5%, as before, then it follows from Equation (11–17) that K/L will increase by less than 5%–say 2%. Thus, from Equation (11–18), labor's share of national income will increase and capital's share will decrease. This analysis has been expanded to encompass all possible cases, and the results are summarized in Table 11–5.

Technological Progress

We were introduced to the concept of *technological progress* in Chapter 6. To review, when technological progress occurs, the production function is altered so that for a given quantity and combination of factor inputs, total output will be greater after the change than before. Graphically, this is equivalent to the isoquant curves shifting inward toward the origin. We will now categorize the ways in which technological progress occurs and relate this to the subsequent effect it will have on the distribution of income.

Sir John Hicks developed a method for classifying technological progress that has been widely adopted by economists.[17] Hicks categorized technological progress as *capital-using, labor-using,* or *neutral,* according to whether the marginal rate of technical substitution of labor for capital decreases, increases, or remains the same when a constant capital–labor ratio is maintained.

---

[17] *Ibid.*

To better understand Hicks' classification system, we will begin by considering Figure 11–26. Prior to the innovation that produces the technological progress, the production function is represented by isoquant curve QQ. Given the factor price ratio W/R, the slope of the constraint line is determined to be the solid line tangent to the pretechnological progress isoquant curve QQ at point A in Figure 11–26. Thus, the cost-minimizing combination of capital and labor required to produce output $Q = 100$ is known. Recall that the slope of a ray drawn from the origin to point A measures the capital–labor ratio K/L, and that movement along this ray represents various levels of output that can be produced with a constant capital–labor ratio. Now suppose that technological progress occurs and that isoquant curve QQ, representing 100 units of output, shifts inward toward the origin to $Q'Q'$ which also represents 100 units of output. If we assume that the factor price ratio W/R remains constant, then the new cost-minimizing combination of capital and labor is given by point B on isoquant curve $Q'Q'$ in Figure 11–26. The ray drawn from the origin to point B shows that the capital–labor ratio has increased. This illustrates **capital-using technological progress.** Now note point C on isoquant curve Q' in Figure 11–26. Point C lies on ray $0A$, which measures the original K/L ratio, and the marginal rate of technical substitution of labor for capital MRTS_{LK} at point C is *less than* MRTS_{LK} at point A. We can confirm this by a visual inspection of Figure 11–26, if we recall that the slope at a point on an isoquant is equal to MRTS_{LK} at that point. Since the slope of isoquant curve $Q'Q'$ at point C is less than the slope of isoquant curve QQ at point A, it follows that technological progress

Figure 11–26
Capital-Using Technological Progress

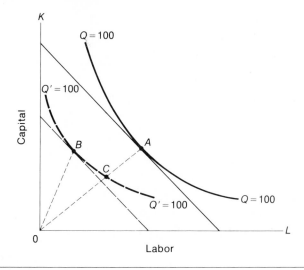

that results in a diminished MRTS_{LK} at the original K/L ratio is capital-using according to Hicks' classification system.

Now consider the technological progress illustrated in Figure 11–27. The original cost-minimizing K/L ratio is given by the slope of ray $0A$, which intersects isoquant curve QQ at point A. After technological progress occurs, the new production function is represented by isoquant curve $Q'Q'$, which intersects ray $0A$ at point C. The slope at point C on $Q'Q'$ is greater than the slope at point A on QQ. Thus, MRTS_{LK} is greater at C than it is at A, and Hicks would classify the technological progress that occurred as labor-using. This can be easily verified by noting that at the initial factor price ratio, the cost-minimizing combination of inputs is given by point B on isoquant curve $Q'Q'$ in Figure 11–27. The K/L ratio is less at point B than it is at point A, so that the quantity of labor relative to the quantity of capital has increased as a result of the technological change.

Finally, we will examine the case of neutral technological progress illustrated in Figure 11–28. The optimal combination of capital and labor required to produce 100 units of output is determined by the tangency of the constraint line with isoquant curve QQ at point A. The initial K/L ratio is given by the slope of ray $0A$. After technological progress occurs, isoquant curve $Q'Q'$ intersects the original K/L ratio given by $0A$ at point B. Figure 11–28 clearly shows that since $Q'Q'$ is tangent at point B to a constraint line that is parallel to the initial constraint line, MRTS_{LK} at point B must be the same value it is at point A.

Figure 11–27
Labor-Using Technological Progress

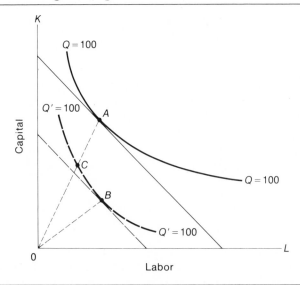

Figure 11–28
Neutral Technological Progress

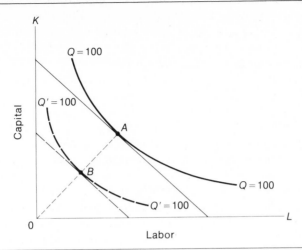

Thus, according to Hicks' classifications, the technological progress illustrated in Figure 11–28 is neutral. In other words, if the factor price ratio W/R remains constant, the K/L ratio employed will not change.

We are now in a position to examine how technological progress can affect the distribution of income. First, we will consider the case of neutral technological progress, which, as we have just seen, occurs when the K/L ratio remains constant at the given factor price ratio W/R. Since there is no change in the denominator or the numerator of Equation (11–18), labor's income share remains constant relative to capital's income share when neutral technological progress occurs.

In the case of labor-using technological progress, the K/L ratio will decline at a constant factor price ratio. This means that the numerator of Equation (11–18) will not change, but the denominator will decrease. Labor's income share will therefore increase relative to capital's income share when technological progress is labor-using.

Similarly, we can easily prove that capital-using technological progress will result in a decrease in labor's income share relative to capital's income share.

Summary   11–9

In Chapter 11, we have concentrated on the construction of microeconomic theories to explain the pricing of factor inputs. The *demand* for factor inputs is based on the marginal productivity of the inputs and is derived from the final demand for the goods and services produced in the economy. The *supply* of factor inputs results from a desire on the part of the owners of these inputs to consume the goods and services produced in the economy.

For the perfectly competitive firm, we have seen that the demand curve for a factor input when there is only one variable input is the same as the *value of the marginal product* VMP curve of the variable input. When two or more inputs are variable and the price of one input is reduced, we were shown that an increased quantity of that input will be employed and its demand curve will be negatively sloped. In either a single-variable or a multivariable input situation, the demand curve for a particular input will be negatively sloped.

Under conditions of imperfect competition, we have learned that the firm must reduce the price of its product in order to sell additional units of output. When there is only one variable input, its *marginal revenue product* MRP curve, rather than its value of marginal product curve, is the firm's demand curve for that input. The marginal revenue product curve will lie below the value of marginal product curve, so that for a given factor input price, the imperfectly competitive firm will employ fewer units of input than the perfectly competitive firm and pay less per unit than the value of the input's marginal product. When less is paid for a factor input than the value of its marginal product, the difference is called *monopolistic exploitation.* When there is more than one variable input and the price of one input is reduced, an increased quantity of that input will be employed. Therefore, the imperfectly competitive firm's demand curve for factor inputs, like that of the perfectly competitive firm, will be negatively sloped.

For both perfectly and imperfectly competitive firms, we have found that if the firm's demand for a particular input is small relative to the market demand for that input, then the input supply curve faced by the firm will be horizontal. Since the firm will be able to employ as many units of the input as it desires at a constant price, the *marginal factor cost* of an additional unit of the input will be a constant and the supply curve of the input will also be the same as the marginal factor cost MFC curve of the input.

In contrast to the market demand for final goods and services, we have seen that the *market demand for factor inputs* is not merely the horizontal summation of the demand of individual firms at various factor prices. As the price of an input declines, the firm will not only employ more units of that input but will also increase production of its output. As all firms increase their output, the market supply of output will increase and product price will decline, thereby reducing the value of the input's marginal product. When there is only one variable input, the market demand curve for that input will be negatively sloped and steeper than its value of marginal product curve. When there is more than one variable input, all that can be said about the market demand curve on theoretical grounds is that it will be negatively sloped.

We have also learned that the *supply of factor inputs* is usually positively sloped. However, the labor supply curve can be positively or negatively sloped, depending on the relative magnitudes of an individual's income and substitution effects as wages increase. For a wage increase, the *substitution effect* will always increase the supply of labor and the *income effect* will always reduce the supply of labor. At sufficiently high wages, the income effect will exceed the substitution effect in absolute magnitude and the individual's labor supply curve will become negatively sloped, producing what is called a *backward-bending labor supply curve.*

The income and substitution effects associated with an individual's labor supply curve were then shown to play key roles in several applications of the theory. We found that *overtime pay* is the least costly method for the firm to employ to increase the quantity of labor supplied, because the substitution effect resulting from overtime pay is large relative to the income effect.

We have also examined the strong work disincentives produced by welfare programs that provide a *guaranteed minimum income* for workers earning less than or slightly above the minimum income. In an effort to reduce these work disincentives, Milton Friedman has proposed the *negative income tax*, but theoretical analysis does not indicate that the negative income tax would necessarily overcome work disincentives any more efficiently than current welfare programs. Due to the ambiguity of theoretical analysis, the federal government has conducted several vast social experiments to determine the magnitude of the work/leisure choices of individuals when income-maintenance programs are instituted. Initial results from these experiments reveal that a guaranteed minimum income for low-income workers results in a reduction in the number of work hours supplied and that this reduction is substantial for secondary earners in the household.

Under competitive conditions, the price paid for each unit of a factor input is determined by the intersection of the market demand and supply curves for that input. When we applied this analysis to the problem of the migration of illegal aliens, we concluded that landowners would be in favor of liberalizing immigration laws and that agricultural unions would oppose them.

In this chapter, we have also examined the economic implications when one firm is the only employer of a factor input. Such a firm is called a *monopsonist,* and as it varies the quantity of the input employed, it alters the input price. We have seen that the marginal factor cost MFC curve for the monopsonist's input will lie above and to the left of the input's supply curve. The monopsonist maximizes profit by purchasing inputs up to the point where its marginal revenue product is equal to its marginal factor cost (MRP = MFC). But because the input's marginal factor cost curve lies above its supply curve, the payment for the input will be less than the value of its marginal revenue product. This difference is called *monopsonistic exploitation.*

We have also discussed the effects of minimum-wage legislation on employment that are predicted by economic theory, based on both nonmonopsonistic and monopsonistic models of the labor market. The *nonmonopsonistic model* always predicts disemployment when an effective minimum wage is imposed;

the *monopsonistic model* predicts either disemployment or increased employment. Empirical evidence strongly indicates that significant disemployment effects occur in labor markets where the minimum wage exceeds the market wage.

Finally, the *distribution of income* was shown to depend solely on the level of output, the amount of each factor input employed, and the marginal productivity of each factor input. When the factor price ratio of labor to capital increases, labor's income share relative to capital's income share increases, remains constant, or decreases, depending on whether the *elasticity of substitution* is less than, equal to, or greater than unity. *Technological progress* was shown to be *capital-using, labor-using,* or *neutral,* depending on whether $MRTS_{LK}$ decreases, increases, or remains the same at the initial capital–labor ratio. Labor's income share relative to capital's income share will increase, decrease, or remain the same, depending on whether technological progress is labor-using, capital-using, or neutral.

Thus far, we have limited ourselves to partial-equilibrium analysis. In Chapter 12, we will study general-equilibrium analysis and employ it to examine the problem of economic efficiency as it relates to the welfare of individuals and to society as a whole.

References

Baird, Charles W. *Prices and Markets: Microeconomics.* St. Paul, MN: West Publishing, 1975.

Blaug, Mark. *Economic Theory in Retrospect,* 3rd ed. London: Cambridge University Press, 1978, Chapter 11.

Chiswick, Barry R. "Immigrants and Immigration Policy." In William Fellner (ed.) *Contemporary Economic Problems, 1978.* Washington, D.C.: American Enterprise Institute for Public Policy Research, 1978, pp. 285–325.

Feldstein, Martin S. "The Rising Price of Physicians' Services." *The Review of Economics and Statistics* (May 1970), pp. 121–33.

Ferber, Robert, and Werner Z. Hirsch. "Social Experimentation and Economic Policy: A Survey." *Journal of Economic Literature,* Vol. XVI (December 1978), pp. 1379–1414.

Ferguson, Charles E. "Production, Prices, and the Theory of Joint-Derived Input Demand Function." *Economica* (November 1966), pp. 454–61.

Friedman, Milton. *Capitalism and Freedom.* Chicago: University of Chicago Press, 1962, Chapter 11.

Hicks, John R. *The Theory of Wages.* London: Macmillan, 1932.

Hinrichs, Albert Ford. "Effects of the 25-cent Minimum Wage on Employment in the Seamless Hosiery Industry." *Journal of the American Statistical Association,* Vol. 35 (March 1940), pp. 13–23.

Mincer, Jacob. "Unemployment Effects of Minimum Wages." *Journal of Political Economy,* Vol. 84, Part 2 (August 1976), pp. S87–S104.

Pashigian, B. Peter. "Occupational Licensing and the Interstate Mobility of Professionals." *Journal of Law and Economics* (April 1979), pp. 1–25.

Peterson, John M. "Employment Effects of Minimum Wages, 1938–1950." *Journal of Political Economy,* Vol. 65 (October 1957), pp. 412–30.

Shepard, Lawrence. "Licensing Restrictions and the Cost of Dental Care." *Journal of Law and Economics* (October 1978), pp. 187–201.

Waud, Roger N. "Man-Hour Behavior in U.S. Manufacturing: A Neoclassical Interpretation." *Journal of Political Economy* (May/June 1968), pp. 407–25.

Welch, Finis. *Minimum Wages: Issues and Evidence.* Washington, D.C.: American Enterprise Institute for Public Policy Research, 1978.

Williams, Walter. "Government Sanctioned Restraints that Reduce Economic Opportunities for Minorities." *Policy Review,* revised reprint (Washington, D.C.: Heritage Foundation, July 1978).

Williams, Walter. *Youth and Minority Unemployment.* Joint Economic Committee, U.S. Congress. Washington, D.C.: U.S. Government Printing Office, July 6, 1977.

Problems

1. Show that for all individuals, the substitution effect will be greater than the income effect at low wages so that the labor supply curve will initially have a positive slope.

2. Show that it is possible for an individual to choose to be employed under a guaranteed minimum income-maintenance system of welfare but to prefer to be unemployed when a negative income tax system is introduced.

3. How would the supply of labor be affected if the government instituted a welfare program of the type specified by Equation (11–4) on page 401 that incorporated a negative marginal income tax ($r < 0$)?

4. Federal law exempts workshops established to train blind people to work in private industry from minimum-wage legislation. How could such an exemption be modified to alleviate teen-age minority unemployment?

5. If a firm is a monopsonist in its employment of labor, can the firm's labor demand curve be derived? Explain.

6. If it were legal to own slaves, provided they were guaranteed a minimum income, what would a slave's work/leisure choice be? What would the slaveowner's work/leisure choice with respect to the slaves be? How could the divergence in their desires be resolved?

7. Do physicians earn high wages because their supply is restricted? Or do their high salaries partially reflect the fact that they work long hours? Why might a physician who is a highly trained specialist work longer hours than a general practitioner?

8. Why has the determination of income distribution always been a primary concern of economists?

9. If there are two variable inputs and the price of one input declines, show that the quantity of the other input that is employed may increase, decrease, or remain constant.

10. Under what conditions will the wage paid to labor be equal to the marginal factor cost of labor? When will it be less than MFC_L?

11. Explain why it is logical to call a technological change *capital-using* when the marginal rate of technical substitution of labor for capital decreases as the capital–labor ratio is held constant.

CHAPTER TWELVE

WELFARE ECONOMICS AND GENERAL EQUILIBRIUM

Introduction 12-1

Until this point, we have been primarily interested in constructing models to aid us in predicting and explaining the response of economic decision makers to scarcity. We have been concerned with how consumers allocate their limited incomes when they must choose among different consumption bundles and with how a firm determines what combination of inputs to use to produce a given quantity of output. And we have closely examined the question of how a firm's output and pricing decisions are affected by consumer demand in different market structures. Although we have occasionally referred to the desirability or the undesirability of the allocative decisions predicted by the analysis, evaluation has not been our main focus.

In this chapter, we will develop criteria that can be used to evaluate the desirability of resource allocation decisions. Obviously, this is necessary if economists are to use the ability to predict and explain economic behavior to make policy recommendations that are designed to influence this behavior in certain directions. The branch of microeconomics that is concerned with evaluating the desirability of different resource allocation decisions is called **welfare economics.**[1]

Although we are only at the introductory stage of our discussion, it is prudent to preview some of the difficulties we will encounter in the study of welfare economics. First, as we discussed in Chapter 4, there is *no scientific basis for making interpersonal utility comparisons*. Because changes in economic activity invariably increase the well-being of some at the expense of others, if we cannot compare the utility increases of those who benefit from an economic change with the utility decreases of those who do not, it is impossible to deter-

---

[1]To avoid confusion, it should immediately be pointed out that welfare economics is *not* a study of government welfare programs.

mine unequivocally whether or not the change was a net improvement. For example, assume that a technological advancement makes it cheaper to construct housing by substituting machinery for labor. This will result in lower purchase prices for new houses, but many construction workers will be forced to seek alternative employments that pay lower wages and owners of existing houses will suffer capital losses because the market value of their houses will decline. Although there are reasons for approving such technological advancements, there is simply no way to add up the utility increases experienced by the gainers and compare the result with the sum of the utility decreases suffered by the losers.

The inability to make interpersonal utility comparisons not only makes it impossible to determine whether or not a given economic change results in a net increase in social well-being but also makes it extremely difficult to conclude that one income distribution is more desirable than another. If someone feels that the existing distribution of income is undesirable, this is another way of saying that a net gain in well-being will result if money is taken from some and given to others. This may or may not be the case, but there is no way to determine this on the basis of scientific reasoning. As we will see, the marginal conditions that we will develop to define an ideal or efficient allocation of resources can be satisfied for any distribution of income. However, since we will not be able to conclude that one income distribution is better than another, we will not be able to say that the efficient allocation of resources associated with one income distribution is more desirable than the efficient or even an inefficient allocation of resources associated with another income distribution.

A second, less serious difficulty we will encounter in assessing the welfare implications of economic activity stems from the *interdependencies* that exist in an economy. A change may be considered desirable in one market, but it must always be recognized that this change will have impacts in other markets that should also be evaluated. For example, if it is considered desirable to increase the size of our railroad system to facilitate the shipment of agricultural output, either more steel will have to be produced or the use of steel in other sectors of the economy will have to be reduced. If more steel is to be produced, then more coal will be required by the steel industry, which in turn will increase the production of the inputs used by the coal industry. Of the many inputs required to produce coal, railroad transportation must be recognized as an important one. Many changes throughout the economy are therefore required to increase the rail transportation of agricultural products—including an even larger increase in railroad capacity than was initially desired.

The attempt to explicitly consider the implications of a change in one market on all other markets in the economy is known as **general-equilibrium analysis.** This is in contrast to *partial-equilibrium analysis,* which we have relied on so heavily in the development of the economic theory we have examined thus far. Of course, partial-equilibrium analysis does not ignore the effects that decisions in one market have on other markets. It should always be kept in mind that when economists talk about the *cost* of expanding output in one market, they are talking about the *opportunity cost*—the value that is foregone by using available resources for this expansion that could otherwise be employed in valuable alternative uses. Thus, the cost and supply curves that play such an important role in partial-equilibrium analysis provide the link between the market under investigation and the rest of the economy. But general-equilibrium analysis makes the connections among the different sectors of the economy more explicit than partial-equilibrium analysis does.

We can see then that it is extremely difficult to determine that one position in the economy or one allocation of resources is better than other positions or allocations. In fact, it is impossible to do this at all without reverting to value judgments. However, it is possible to compare alternative resource allocations with minimal reliance on value judgments. The value judgment that is central to welfare economics is that any change that improves the well-being of one individual without reducing the well-being of anyone else is a desirable change. Any change that satisfies this condition is referred to as a **Pareto-efficient change**.[2] When all opportunities to take advantage of Pareto-efficient changes have been exhausted, a **Pareto-efficient allocation of resources** is said to have been reached. Armed with the value judgment imbedded in the Pareto criterion and the tools of economic analysis, we are now in a position to examine the concept of welfare economics.

Economic Efficiency   12-2

Previously Developed Efficiency Conditions

Economists use the term *efficient* (or *Pareto efficient, optimal,* or *Pareto optimal*) to describe an **efficient allocation of resources** such that it is impossible to increase the utility of one individual without reducing the utility of someone else, or an allocation in which all opportunities to make Pareto-efficient changes have been taken. In this chapter, we will describe the conditions that must be fulfilled for resources to be allocated efficiently within the framework of a general-equilibrium model. First, however, it will be useful to elaborate on some of the conditions for an efficient resource allocation that were developed within the framework of partial-equilibrium analysis in previous chapters.

An obvious requirement for efficiency is that the production process generate *as much output as is technically possible* from the input combination in use. We discussed this requirement in Chapter 6. If this condition is not satisfied, it is possible that someone's position could be improved without making anyone

---

[2]The reader should recall our discussion of *Pareto efficiency* in conjunction with the productivity of exchange (Section 5–4, pages 158–72). It is of interest to note that if two or more individuals in the economy envy someone else's good fortune, it may be impossible to increase the well-being of one person without placing someone else in a worse position, even though it may be possible to increase the consumption level of one individual without reducing the consumption level of others.

else any worse off simply by increasing the output being produced by the inputs already in use. It is this type of technical or engineering consideration that most people have in mind when they think of efficiency. To the economist, however, the term *efficiency* means more than just obtaining the maximum output from a given combination of inputs.

Another requirement for economic efficiency is to select the *least-cost input combination* that will produce a given quantity of output. The necessary conditions for a least-cost input combination were developed in Section 7–3 (pages 209–14), where we learned that the input combination should be chosen so that the slope of the isoquant curve is equal to the price ratio of the two inputs being considered. Unless this condition is satisfied, it is possible to move along the isoquant curve (maintaining constant output) in such a way that the cost of the input combination in use declines. Again, unless output is being produced with the least-cost input combination, it is possible to increase the well-being of at least one individual without reducing the well-being of others. By moving to the least-cost input position, someone can realize a savings without anyone having to reduce their consumption of goods.

But there is more to achieving economic efficiency than producing output with the least-cost input combination. What quantity of output to produce must be determined, since it is possible to produce too much or too little of a good. Ideally, we know that the production of a good should be expanded as long as the value of the marginal unit is greater than the value sacrificed to produce it. Since the market price of a good reflects its marginal value, it follows that the price of the good at the quantity produced should equal the marginal cost of producing the good. In Section 8–4, we saw how perfectly competitive markets lead to output rates that satisfy the condition of *price being equal to marginal cost.* If this condition is not met, it is possible to reallocate resources between different employments so that at least one person's utility is increased without reducing anyone else's well-being. For example, if the price of a pencil sharpener is $6 and its marginal cost is $5, then someone is willing to pay $1 more for a pencil sharpener than the value of what has to be sacrificed to produce it. Clearly, the $1 gain from producing the pencil sharpener can be used to improve one person's position without worsening another's.

Finally, after the conditions for the efficient production of a good are satisfied, it is desirable to distribute the good in such a way that it is available to consumers who value it most highly. Of course, this immediately poses problems, because we are unable to make interpersonal utility comparisons. In trying to decide whether individual A should receive more of a product than individual B, we simply cannot tell whether A or B will derive the most benefit from the product. It is possible, however, to develop a criterion against which to judge the desirability of a distribution of two or more goods among individuals. In fact, we did this in Section 5–4 when we established that an exchange between two individuals can improve the position of one or both of them without placing anyone in a worse position as long as the marginal rates of substitution (the slopes of the individual indifference curves) remain unequal. Only when the *marginal rates of substitution* of one good for another *are equal* for all buyers do we have a Pareto-efficient distribution of the two goods among consumers. More will be said about distributional efficiency in Section 12−3.

Waste as a Violation of Efficiency Conditions

It is useful to think of waste as the inefficient allocation of resources. If our resources are being used in such a way that opportunities to improve the positions of some without jeopardizing the positions of others are being passed up, then referring to this as *waste* is certainly consistent with our intuitive notion of the term. Also, this concise definition of waste will guard against more common but misleading usages of the term.

For example, when a particular resource is considered to be of prime importance, there is a tendency to regard any activity as wasteful that employs more of this resource when less could have been used. The commonly held view toward energy resources provides one of the most obvious examples of this. The focus on energy resources often obscures the fact that other things are also valuable, and if less energy is used, it is always at the expense of sacrificing some of those other things. You do not necessarily avoid waste by using less energy. In fact, using less energy will be wasteful if the value of the items that must be sacrificed as a consequence are more valuable than the energy that is saved. In the application "Optimal Gasoline Consumption" in Chapter 7, we saw that enforcing the 55-mile-per-hour speed limit can reduce the quantity of gasoline needed for a given trip—but possibly at the expense of sacrificing time that is worth more than the value of the gas saved. By keeping the consumer from using the least-cost combination of gas and time required for a given trip, the 55-mile-per-hour speed limit can be increasing waste, not reducing it. We hasten to add that the 55-mile-per-hour speed limit may be justified on the basis of safety considerations. But to support the 55-mile-per-hour speed limit because it avoids waste by forcing a reduction in gasoline consumption is to take a view of waste that ignores the obvious fact that gasoline is not the only valuable resource in use.

But if we view waste as the inefficient allocation of resources, it takes more to eliminate waste than producing a given quantity of a good using the least-cost combination of inputs. Even with this requirement for efficiency satisfied, waste can still exist because too much or too little of the good can be produced. In our discussion of price controls in Section 2−3, we referred to the inappropriate allocation of resources in response to a price ceiling. Such an allocation is inappropriate because additional production of the price-controlled good ceases at an output level where consumers are willing to pay a greater price than the marginal cost of production. According to our definition, this is wasteful, because it violates an efficiency requirement. The only way to eliminate this waste is to reallocate resources from alternative employments and use them in the production of the price-controlled good until the price consumers are willing to pay is equal to the marginal cost of production. Of course, the incentive to do this that would normally exist is eliminated by the price ceiling.

Another cause of waste is the government's provision of as much of a good as consumers will demand at 0 price—this provision being financed through taxation. With the direct cost of consuming one more unit being 0, each consumer will find it to his or her advantage to consume the good until its marginal value is also 0. Unfortunately, the marginal cost of providing the good will not be 0. Therefore, the resources devoted to the production of this "free" good would generate more value if they were employed elsewhere. Free national health care and nominal entrance fees into national parks are examples of government policies that may encourage the excessive use of a particular good at the expense of other goods that are not subsidized.[3]

There is one interesting possibility of providing whatever amount of a good consumers demand at 0 price without wasting or misallocating resources. If the price elasticity of demand for the good is 0, then consumers will demand no more of the good at 0 price than they will at the price that is equal to the marginal cost of the good, so that giving the good away will not motivate wasteful consumption. For example, it is unlikely that a government policy of providing standardized burial services at no cost for all consumers who satisfied the "stiff" qualifications would result in an increase in the number of burials demanded. Generalizing from the extreme case of a 0 price elasticity of demand, it follows that it will be less wasteful to subsidize a commodity with a low price elasticity of demand than a commodity with a high price elasticity of demand. Based on this line of reasoning, a better case could be made for providing open-heart and brain surgery free of charge than for providing people with all the physical exams, psychiatric treatment, and cosmetic surgery they would demand at 0 price. However, it should be pointed out that the excessive demands motivated by "free" health care can crowd out emergency medical care. A hospital in Britain, which provides health care at no charge under the country's National Health Service, once had 20 unconscious patients on its admissions waiting list and "sent a trained health visitor round to assess the priority of these cases, presumably to see who was the most unconscious."[4]

---

[3]It should be acknowledged that even though these policies may result in the inefficient use of resources, they may be justified on the basis of other considerations. It is also possible that subsidizing the consumption of some goods will bring us closer to an efficient allocation of resources, because not all of the benefits derived from consuming the good are passed on to the individual consumer. Consumption of the good may generate *positive externalities*—a concept that we will examine in Chapter 13.

It is also possible that the government will not provide as much of a good at a low or 0 price as consumers desire at that price. This could mean that the efficient quantity of the good will be provided, but since it will be rationed through some nonprice mechanism, it is doubtful that it will be efficiently distributed among consumers. On this point, see James M. Buchanan, "The Inconsistencies of the National Health Care System," *Occasional Paper* (November 1965). This article also appears in James M. Buchanan and Robert D. Tollison (eds.) *Theory of Public Choice* (Ann Arbor: University of Michigan Press, 1972).

[4]Quoted from the *British Medical Journal* (March 22, 1975), p. 678, by Harry Schwartz in R. Emmett Tyrell, Jr. (ed.) *The Future That Doesn't Work: Social Democracy's Failure in Britain* (Garden City, NY: Doubleday, 1977), p. 30.

Efficiency and Perfect Competition in a   12-3
General-Equilibrium Model

In this section we will consider all of the conditions of economic efficiency introduced in Section 12–2 within the framework of a model that explicitly examines the relationships between different sectors of the economy. To keep the analysis as simple as possible, we will assume that our economy consists of only two industries, two productive inputs, and two consumers. This oversimplification will help to clarify the following analysis at the expense of little in terms of the insights provided, because the results can be generalized to include any number of industries, inputs, and consumers.

Production Efficiency

We will assume that one of the two industries in our economy is in the entertainment business. This industry, referred to as Industry F, produces fun and frolic. Since consumers want to look their best when they engage in fun and frolic, the second industry in our economy, Industry C, produces clothing. The two productive inputs required by both industries are capital and labor. For production to be efficient, the available capital and labor must be allocated among the two industries in such a way that it is impossible to increase the output of one industry without reducing the output of the other industry.

To graphically develop the condition required to achieve this production efficiency, we will construct a diagram that places the isoquant curves of the two industries in a useful configuration with respect to each other. In Figure 12–1, the southwest corner 0_F of the box represents the origin for industry F, and the isoquant curves for industry F (represented by F_1, F_2, and F_3) are referenced with respect to this origin. Similarly, the isoquant curves for industry C (represented by C_1, C_2, and C_3) are referenced with respect to the origin 0_C, which is positioned at the northeast corner of the box. The width of the box $0_F L$ is determined by the total quantity of labor available, and the height of the box $0_F K$ is determined by the amount of capital available.[5] Moving to the right along a horizontal axis indicates that more labor is employed by industry F and less is employed by industry C. Similarly, moving up along a vertical axis indicates an increase in the use of capital by industry F and a corresponding decrease in the capital available to industry C. Each point within the box diagram represents a distribution of the two inputs between the two industries.

The condition required to achieve production efficiency is most easily visualized by considering an inefficient allocation of inputs between the two industries, such as the one represented by point g in Figure 12–1. Allocation g is inefficient because the inputs can be reallocated in such a way that the output of at least one of the industries can still be increased without reducing the output of the other industry. For example, if inputs were reallocated from g to h in

---

[5] This is an *Edgeworth box diagram* for production, which is analytically identical to the Edgeworth box diagram we developed in Section 5–4 to analyze the productivity of exchange.

Figure 12–1
Production Efficiency

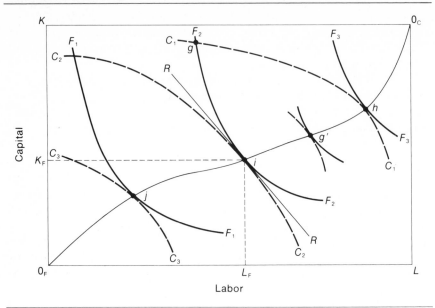

Figure 12–1, the output of industry F would increase (it would move from iso-quant curve F_2 to isoquant curve F_3) with no corresponding reduction in industry C's output. If the inputs were reallocated from g to i, then the output of industry C would increase with no offsetting reduction in the output of industry F. Or we could consider a reallocation from g to an allocation between i and h such as g', which would increase the output of both industries.

Notice that each reallocation we have considered moved us from a point where the isoquant curves for the two industries have different slopes (their marginal rates of technical substitution are different—as we saw in Section 7–3) to a point where their isoquant curves are tangent or have the same slope.

Only when the inputs are allocated between the two industries in such a way that their marginal rates of technical substitution are equal will it be impossible to increase the output of one industry without reducing the output of the other. To illustrate, we will reconsider the allocation represented by point g, where the marginal rate of technical substitution of labor for capital $MRTS_{LK}$ is larger for industry F than it is for industry C (that is, the slope of F's isoquant at g is greater than the slope of C's isoquant at g). For the sake of being specific, we will assume that at g $MRTS_{LK}$ is 3 for industry F and ½ for industry C. This means that industry F could give up 3 units of capital and still maintain the same level of output if it received an additional unit of labor. Industry C would have to sacrifice 1 unit of labor in return for only ½ unit of capital to maintain the same output. An obvious response in this situation is to transfer 1 unit of labor from industry C to industry F, thereby reducing the amount of capital F needs to maintain a constant level of output by 3 units. Since industry C requires only ½ unit of this capital to maintain its current output, the output of both industries can be maintained at the original levels and 2½ units of capital will be left over–capital that can be used to increase output in one or both industries.

From this example, it is clear that as long as the marginal rates of technical substitution for the two industries are different, it will still be possible to reallocate inputs between them to increase the output of one or both industries without reducing the output of either. Once the marginal rates of technical substitution become equal, this is no longer possible. In this situation, the amount of capital one industry can sacrifice in return for an additional unit of labor is exactly equal to the additional capital the other industry will require if it gives up a unit of labor, as long as the outputs of both industries remain constant. At this point, it is impossible to increase the output of one industry without reducing the output of the other. The line $0_F 0_C$ in Figure 12–1 intersects all the points of tangency between the isoquant curves for the two industries, or all the points where their marginal rates of technical substitution are equal. This line maps out all of the efficient resource allocations that are possible and is often referred to as the **contract curve.**[6]

The Production Possibility Curve

Another way to represent efficiency in the production of two goods is to show the maximum amount of one good that can be produced given a specified output of the other good. For example, we might determine the maximum amount of fun and frolic that can be produced given an output level of clothing C_3 (the output level associated with isoquant curve C_3 in Figure 12–1). As Figure 12–1 shows, given this output of clothing, it is most efficient to operate at the input allocation represented by point j and produce a maximum of F_1 units of fun and frolic. If the two consumers in our economy are willing to sacrifice some clothing and production is reduced to C_2, then the maximum quantity of fun and frolic that can be produced will increase to F_2. Similarly, a maximum of F_3 units of fun and frolic can be obtained when C_1 units of clothing are produced. Of course, all of the input allocations that generate the maximum output for industry F, given the output level for industry C, lie on the contract curve.

If we plotted the levels of output of fun and frolic and clothing associated with every point on the contract curve, we would construct the **production possibility curve** for our simple two-commodity economy. This has been done in Figure 12–2, where the outputs of industry F and industry C are measured on the vertical and horizontal axes, respectively. For every possible level of output for industry C, this production possibility curve indicates the maximum

---

[6]Recall from Section 5–4 that the curve mapping out all of the efficient allocations of goods between the two consumers was also referred to as the *contract curve*.

Figure 12-2
The Production Possibility Curve

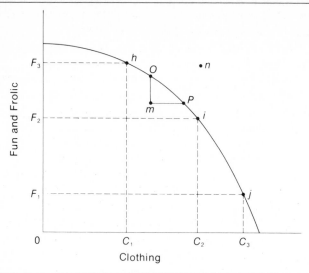

output of F that can be produced, and *vice versa*. The production possibility curve is usually bowed outward (concave from below), as shown in the figure. The reason for this is that some inputs are more productive in one industry than in the other. For example, if all of the available inputs were devoted to the production of *F*, an input combination more suited to the production of *C* than to the production of *F* could be transferred to industry C, which would result in a large increase in C's output but only a small decrease in F's output. As this process continues, we find increasingly that input combinations that are more favorable to the production of *F* than *C* must be transferred to industry C if its output is to be expanded. The result is that the production of an additional unit of *C* requires larger and larger sacrifices of *F*, as shown by the increasingly steep slope of the production possibility curve as we move right along the *C* axis.[7] This slope multiplied by -1 is referred to as the **marginal rate of transformation** of clothing for fun and frolic MRT_{CF} and tells us how many units of fun and frolic have to be sacrificed to obtain an additional unit of clothing.

Notice that it is possible to produce the output combination given by point *m* in Figure 12–2. Obviously, it would be inefficient to do so, however, since a reallocation of inputs would allow production to occur somewhere on the production possibility curve between points *O* and *P*, so that more of at least one good would be produced without reducing production of the other good. Any

---

[7]A more rigorous explanation of the conditions that produce a production possibility curve that is concave from below would require consideration of the increasing or decreasing returns to scale for the two production functions, which we discussed in Chapter 6. This more detailed analysis will not be pursued here.

point *inside* the production possibility curve represents *inefficient* production. On the other hand, given the state of technology and the available resources, there is no way to produce the output combination represented by point *n*. Any point lying *outside* the production possibility curve represents an output combination that is technologically impossible to produce.

Consumption Efficiency

In Section 5–4 (pages 158–72), we used an Edgeworth box diagram to analyze the gains that could result from allowing two consumers to exchange two goods among themselves. It was shown that it was impossible to increase the utility of one consumer without reducing the utility of the other only when the marginal rates of substitution for the goods were the same for both consumers. Therefore, to allocate goods efficiently between two consumers, their marginal rates of substitution must be equal, or they must lie somewhere on the contract curve.

In our previous discussion of the efficient allocation of goods, we assumed that the quantities of the two goods were fixed. We can now relax this assumption and recognize that any combination of the two goods that lies on the production possibility curve can be chosen. For example, if point *h* is chosen in Figure 12–2, C_1 units of clothing and F_3 units of fun and frolic will be produced. Given this output combination, the Edgeworth box we would employ to consider exchange between these two consumers is $0C_1$ units wide and $0F_3$ units high. If the output combination *i* is chosen instead, then the width of the appropriate Edgeworth box is $0C_2$ units and the height is $0F_2$ units. When output combination *j* is selected, the Edgeworth box is $0C_3$ units wide and $0F_1$ units high.

In Figure 12–3, the Edgeworth box associated with the output combination at point *i* on the production possibility curve in Figure 12–2 is constructed. The indifference curves for the two individuals in our economy, Len and Sue, are drawn within the dimensions of this box. Len's indifference curves L_1, L_2, and L_3 are referenced with respect to origin 0; Sue's indifference curves S_1, S_2, and S_3 are referenced with respect to origin *i*. Every distribution of the two goods that falls on the contract curve 0*i* is efficient. Every distribution that does not fall on the contract curve is inefficient, since this indicates that a reallocation of the two goods can still be made that will increase the utility of at least one individual without reducing the utility of the other.

The Efficient Output Combination

Assume that the distribution of income between Len and Sue is such that the efficient allocation of goods that exhausts both of their incomes is given by point *E* on the contract curve in Figure 12–3. At this point, Len's and Sue's marginal rates of substitution of clothing for fun and frolic MRS_{CF} are both equal to the slope of the line *PP* (or, more accurately, the marginal rates of substitution are equal to the slope of *PP* multiplied by -1). As Figure 12–3 is constructed, the

Example

12–1

Watering Down Efficiency with Water Pricing

When two or more prices are charged for the same product, inefficiency will probably result. The pricing of water provides us with an informative example. In Example 9–3 on multipart pricing by utilities, we saw that the price of water commonly varies with the quantity consumed. For example, there are nine different price categories for water in Normal, Illinois, and the price per unit of water there declines as use increases. In some cities (Los Angeles, for example), you will pay a lower price for water if you are using it for irrigation than if you are using it for a shower.

    The inefficiency results from the fact that consumers will choose consumption bundles that equate the marginal rate of substitution between two goods with the price ratio of those goods. Assume, for example, that a large family uses a lot of water and pays a price per unit of water that is $1/10$ the

slope of PP is equal to the slope of TT, so that the common marginal rate of substitution of C for F is equal to the marginal rate of transformation of C for F at output combination i. This is an important condition, and unless it is satisfied, we will not have chosen an efficient output combination; that is, it will still be

Figure 12–3
Consumption Efficiency and Choice of Output Combination

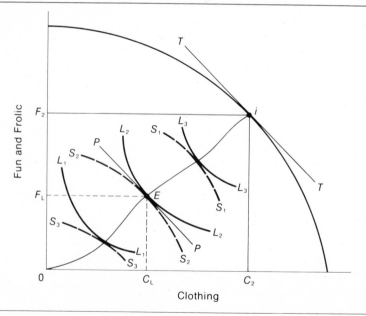

price paid for soap. The small family next door pays a price per unit of water that is $1/7$ the price paid for soap. If the units of measure are 1,000 gallons of water and 1 bar of soap, the large family will, under conditions of consumer equilibrium, be willing to sacrifice 10,000 gallons of water to obtain an additional bar of soap, but the small family will only give up 7,000 gallons of water to obtain an extra bar of soap.

Clearly, the positions of both families could be improved by reallocating water and soap. If a member of the small family came to the large family's door with a bar of soap and a big, big bucket and offered to trade the soap for 8,000 gallons of water, both families would benefit from the exchange.[*]

[*]For a very complete discussion of water allocation problems, see J. Hirschleifer, J. Milliman, and J. DeHaven, *Water Supply* (Chicago: University of Chicago Press, 1960). See also C. Howe and F. Linaweaver, Jr., "The Impact of Price on Residual Water Demand and Its Relation to System Design and Price Structure," *Water Resources Research*, Vol. 3 (first quarter, 1967), pp. 12−32.

possible to increase the utility of at least one individual without reducing the utility of the other.

To illustrate this, we will assume that we have chosen an output combination for which the marginal rate of transformation of C for F is different from the common marginal rate of substitution of C for F. To be specific, we will assume that $MRS_{CF} = 3$ and that $MRT_{CF} = 1$. This means that both Len and Sue will be willing to sacrifice 3 units of F to obtain an additional unit of C. It is possible to produce an additional unit of C at the expense of only a one-unit reduction in F, so that Sue could obtain an additional unit of C, for example, by sacrificing only 1 unit of F. This would obviously benefit Sue, since she is willing to sacrifice 3 units of F to obtain the additional unit of C, and would not harm Len, since his consumption bundle would remain the same.[8] Continuing this type of reallocation will increase MRT_{CF} and, assuming that consumption efficiency is maintained, reduce the common MRS_{CF}. Only when they are equal will an efficient output combination be reached. A similar line of reasoning applies if we begin at an output combination where MRS_{CF} is less than MRT_{CF}.

Efficiency and Perfect Competition

We have now seen that three marginal conditions must be satisfied for resource allocation to be efficient:

1. The marginal rates of technical substitution of labor for capital must be equal for both productive units.

[8]After this occurs, it will be possible for further gains to be made, since Sue's MRS_{CF} will have changed and will no longer be equal to Len's MRS_{CF}. This presents the opportunity for productive exchange, which moves us back to the contract curve.

2. The marginal rates of substitution of one good for the other good must be equal for both consumers.

3. The common marginal rate of substitution of one good for the other must equal the marginal rate of transformation of that good for the other.

It will now be shown that in a perfectly competitive environment, all of these conditions will be satisfied as a consequence of consumers maximizing utility and firms maximizing profits.

In Chapters 7 and 8, we learned that to maximize profits, the firm will choose the least-cost combination of inputs to produce a given level of output, which requires equating the marginal rate of technical substitution for any two inputs with their price ratio. In terms of our simple economy, industries C and F will both equate $MRTS_{LK}$ to P_L/P_K, where P_L is the per-unit price of labor and P_K is the per-unit price of capital. Furthermore, in a perfectly competitive environment, the price of labor and capital will be the same for both industries, which means that $MRTS_{LK}$ will be the same for both industries. Therefore, profit maximization in a perfectly competitive environment results in the satisfaction of marginal condition 1.

In Chapter 4, we learned that the consumer who maximizes utility subject to his or her budget constraint will choose a consumption bundle that equates the marginal rate of substitution for the two goods being considered to the price ratio of these two goods. In our two-person, two-good economy, this means that both Len and Sue will consume at the point at which $MRS_{CF} = P_C/P_F$, where P_C is the per-unit price of clothing and P_F is the per-unit price of fun and frolic. Under conditions of perfect competition, the price of both goods will be the same for Len and for Sue. Thus, their MRS_{CF} will be identical as a consequence of their utility-maximizing behavior, which satisfies the marginal condition 2.

To explain how perfect competition leads to the satisfaction of marginal condition 3, we need to look a little more closely at the slope of the production possibility curve. We have already seen that the absolute value of this slope is equal to the marginal rate of transformation of C and F (that is, the amount of F that must be sacrificed for another unit of C to be produced). With a little thought, we can see that this is equal to the ratio of the marginal cost of C to the marginal cost of F, or MC_C/MC_F. Assume, for example, that $MC_C = \$10$ and that $MC_F = \$5$, giving us a marginal cost ratio of 2. If the economy is on the production possibility curve (using both inputs as efficiently as possible), the only way to obtain the additional $\$10$ worth of inputs required to produce one more unit of C is to reduce the production of F by 2, or MC_C/MC_F. So the ratio $MC_C/MC_F = MRT_{CF}$, or the marginal rate of transformation of C for F. In Chapter 8, we learned that the perfectly competitive firm will expand output until price equals marginal cost. In our simple economy, this means that $P_C = MC_C$ and $P_F = MC_F$, or $P_C/P_F = MC_C/MC_F$. But with $MC_C/MC_F = MRT_{CF}$, we have $P_C/P_F = MRT_{CF}$. Furthermore, since each consumer equates MRS_{CF} with the price ratio P_C/P_F, it follows that for each consumer, $MRS_{CF} = MRT_{CF}$. The common marginal rate of substitution of C for F is equal to the marginal rate of transformation of C for F, and perfect competition has led to the satisfaction of the third marginal condition for efficiency.

The fact that perfect competition will channel the behavior of independent decision makers in such a way that their actions will result in an efficient allocation of resources is an important one. However, several qualifications must be kept in mind. As our discussion in Section 12-4 will reveal, many different resource allocations satisfy all three marginal conditions for efficiency, and we have no objective basis for considering one efficient allocation superior to another. Imperfections also prevent the satisfaction of all three efficiency conditions. These problems will be discussed in this chapter and in Chapter 13.

Economic Interdependence

Our examination of efficiency conditions makes it clear that production and consumption decisions cannot be made independently of each other. The desirability of different production options is influenced by the decisions of individual consumers. Perhaps what is less clear from the preceding discussion is that consumption decisions are influenced by production choices.

For example, consider the solution given in Figure 12-3, where C_2 units of clothing and F_2 units of fun and frolic are being produced and the distribution of this output is given by point E. At this distribution level, Len is purchasing C_L and F_L units of C and F, respectively, and Sue is buying the remainder. We know that the total income earned from producing output $C_2 F_2$ is equal to the amount required to purchase this output,[9] but is the distribution of this income between Len and Sue such that each can afford the bundle that point E indicates they are consuming?

To answer this question, we have to know how many units of the income-earning inputs each individual owns and something about the per-unit price of each of these inputs. The distribution of the inputs between the two individuals is conveniently assumed to be given. However, the prices paid for the inputs cannot be assumed to be given, because they are determined as a consequence of the behavior implied by our economic model. We have assumed that point i on the production possibility curve in Figure 12-3 represents the output combination that is actually produced. The particular distribution of inputs between industries C and F required to produce this output combination is given by point i in Figure 12-1 (page 438). At this point, F_2 and C_2 units are being produced by industries F and C, respectively, with industry F employing L_F units of labor and K_F units of capital and industry C employing the remaining labor and capital.

Once we know the efficient input combination required to produce the chosen output combination or bundle, we can determine the ratio of one input price to the other. Returning to Figure 12-1, we can see that the slope of the produc-

---

[9] Income can be measured in terms of claims on output, and the production of a given output generates a claim on that output.

tion isoquants (the marginal rate of technical substitution of labor for capital $MRTS_{LK}$) is given by the absolute value of the slope of line RR. Since we know that $MRTS_{LK}$ is equal to the ratio of the price of labor to the price of capital P_L/P_K, it follows that P_L/P_K is equal to the slope of line RR multiplied by -1.[10] Once the input price ratio and the quantities of labor and capital each individual owns are known, we can determine Len's and Sue's relative incomes. For example, assume that P_L is twice as high as P_K, that 100 units of labor are available (Len and Sue each provide 50 units), and that capital availability is 150 units (100 units belong to Len and 50 units are owned by Sue). This being the case, the ratio of Len's income to Sue's income is 4/3.[11]

We now return to Figure 12–3, where we observe that at point E, which represents the distribution of goods between Len and Sue, the slope of their indifference curves L_2 and S_2 is given by the slope of the line PP. Since the absolute value of this slope equals the common marginal rate of substitution of C for F, which is equal to the ratio of the price of C to the price of F, we know that P_C/P_F is equal to the slope of PP multiplied by -1. Knowing this ratio and the quantities of the two goods being consumed by Len and Sue, we can determine the ratio of the expenditure required for Len to purchase his consumption bundle to the expenditure required for Sue to purchase her bundle. Only if this ratio is the same as their income ratio will the solution we have been discussing be consistent. The solution will be consistent if the chosen output combination generates an income distribution that provides both Len and Sue with the exact incomes they need to purchase the consumption bundles that equate their marginal rates of substitution with each other and with the marginal rate of transformation.

If the income ratio does not equal the expenditure ratio, then we will have to seek another solution. When we do arrive at a solution and these ratios are equal, it will be a consistent solution. If this solution also satisfies the three marginal conditions of efficiency as well, then it represents both an efficient and a consistent allocation of resources.

The Inefficiency of Monopoly Revisited

In Chapter 9, we discussed the pricing and output decisions of a monopolist. There, we learned that because the marginal revenue of a monopolistic firm is less than the price of its product, the monopolist's profit-maximizing output will be reached when its product price is greater than its marginal cost;

---

[10]Note that this information does not allow us to determine a unique set of values for P_L and P_K. As we are about to see, this does not pose a problem in determining whether or not the solution under consideration is consistent. The solution is consistent if it results in an income distribution between Len and Sue that allows them to afford the consumption distribution indicated by point E in Figure 12–3.

[11]Len's income is $50P_L + 100P_K$ and Sue's income is $50P_L + 50P_K$. Since $P_L = 2P_K$ by assumption, we can write the ratio of Len's income to Sue's income as

$$\frac{100P_K + 100P_K}{100P_K + 50P_K} = \frac{200P_K}{150P_K} = \frac{4}{3}$$

that is, profits will be maximized when marginal revenue is equal to marginal cost. Given that the product price reflects the value of the marginal unit of output and that the marginal cost is equal to the value forgone when producing an additional unit of output, it follows that increasing production beyond the monopoly's level of output would be desirable. Monopoly pricing is therefore *inefficient*.

It is possible to use the framework of the general-equilibrium model developed in this chapter to examine monopoly-induced inefficiency. Returning to the simple economy we have been discussing, we will assume that industry F is perfectly competitive and that industry C is a monopoly. Since it is now a monopoly, industry C's product price is no longer equal to its marginal cost, so that we will not be operating on the production possibility curve where $MRT_{CF} = P_C/P_F$. Since $MRT_{CF} = MC_C/MC_F$, with $MC_C < P_C$ and $MC_F = P_F$, this means that $MRT_{CF} < P_C/P_F$, or the ratio P_C/P_F is greater than the absolute value of the slope of the production possibility curve at the output combination being produced. This is illustrated in Figure 12-4, where production is taking place at point d on the production possibility curve and the absolute value of the slope of line TT is equal to the price ratio P_C/P_F. At point d, industry C is producing $\bar{C}$ units and industry F is producing $\bar{F}$ units, so that the Edgeworth box is given by $0\bar{F}d\bar{C}$. Since both consumers are responding to the price ratio P_C/P_F, they will be consuming at a point on the contract curve $0d$ where their marginal rates of substitution are both equal to this ratio. This position is represented by point B in Figure 12-4, where Len and Sue are on indifference curves L and S, respectively, and the slope of $T'T'$ is the same as the slope of TT.

Figure 12-4
Inefficient Monopoly Pricing by Industry C

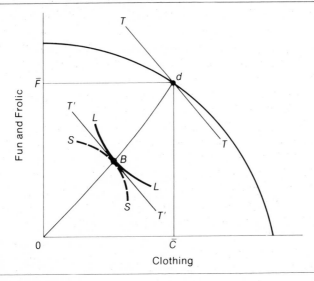

Clothing

The problem with the resource allocation in Figure 12–4 is that the common marginal rate of substitution of C for F is greater than the marginal rate of transformation of C for F. Thus, the absolute value of the slope of $T'T'$ (and therefore TT) is greater than the absolute slope of the production possibility curve at point d. This means that both Len and Sue are willing to sacrifice more units of F to obtain an additional unit of C than it is necessary to sacrifice. Clearly, both consumers could improve their utility by moving to a point on the

Example 12–2

Trucking Regulation:
The Political Popularity of Waste and Inefficiency

The Interstate Commerce Commission (ICC) regulates interstate trucking, in the United States by limiting entry into the trucking industry to below what it would be in the absence of regulation. This results in a *welfare loss* to society, because resources are prevented from flowing into the trucking industry when it is worth more to use them in this industry than in alternative employments. An interesting–but unfortunate–aspect of this inefficiency is that the ICC policy that creates it can become more and more politically entrenched as the inefficiency increases.

To illustrate, we will assume that an individual believes the most efficient use of his resources is to purchase some trucks and go into the business of hauling freight cross-country. You may think that this individual will simply buy some trucks and equipment, advertise the availability of his service, and start hauling freight. Unfortunately, the procedure is not that simple. Before freight can be trucked across state lines, a certificate of public convenience and necessity must be acquired from the Interstate Commerce Commission. Each certificate specifies the product that the trucker is permitted to carry and the route over which the freight can be moved. The aspiring trucker can obtain the necessary certificates either by requesting them from the ICC or by purchasing existing certificates from established trucking firms.

It is very unlikely, however, that individuals who wish to start a trucking firm will be able to obtain certificates from the ICC. Existing firms in the trucking industry can heavily influence ICC decisions. And existing firms are highly sensitive to what they consider "excessive" competition for hauling important products over profitable routes. So if our potential trucker is anxious to haul sea water between Florida and Texas, he will have a better chance of getting his certificates of public convenience and necessity than he will if he wants to carry furniture and other household belongings from North Carolina to New York. Therefore, when a potential trucker attempts to enter the trucking business, the necessary certificates usually must be purchased from existing trucking firms–and buying these certificates can be very costly. The certificates of a trucking firm that went bankrupt a few years ago were auctioned off for $21 million. Economist Thomas Moore has production possibility curve where more C and less F is being produced than at point d. This is consistent with the conclusion we reached in Chapter 9 that under conditions of monopolistic pricing, a monopolistic industry will produce too low a level of output. As a natural consequence of this conclusion, we can now recognize the corollary that under conditions of monopolistic pricing a nonmonopolistic industry will produce too high a level of output.

estimated that the market value of all outstanding trucking certificates and permits is between \$2.1 and \$3 billion.* (Permits, rather than certificates, must be granted to truckers who make contract deliveries for firms that hold certificates.)

The prices of these certificates and permits reflect one of the major inefficiencies of ICC policy in the trucking industry. A positive certificate price indicates how much more the purchaser thinks his or her resources will be worth in the trucking industry than they would earn in the best alternative employment. As the certificate price increases, the net gain derived from transferring more resources into the trucking industry becomes greater. Ideally, productive inputs should be transferred into the industry until resource owners no longer receive greater returns from trucking than they could receive from alternative employments. If this happens, as it tends to in unregulated markets, the value of the certificates will be driven down to 0.

But high trucking certificate prices reflect more than the waste from ICC regulation. The market value of these certificates is a major asset of trucking firms, and the prices of trucking certificates and permits provide a measure of the political opposition that an attempt to deregulate the trucking industry will encounter. By eliminating the value of the certificates, deregulation of the trucking industry would impose an enormous loss on certificate owners. The desire to avoid this loss effectively motivates members of the trucking industry to organize and exert political pressure against deregulation. The greater the inefficiency of ICC regulation (the higher the certificate prices), the larger the loss the trucking industry will experience from deregulation and the more political opposition deregulation attempts will encounter.

It is true that consumers would gain from deregulation. But this gain would be distributed to millions and millions of consumers, and few (if any) individuals would benefit enough to be motivated to support deregulation politically.

*Most of the data presented in this example can be found in Thomas G. Moore, "The Beneficiaries of Trucking Regulation," *The Journal of Law and Economics* (October 1978), pp. 327–43. The remainder of the data were supplied personally by Professor Moore.

12-4   The Problem of Comparing Efficient Allocation Positions

The Grand Utility Possibility Curve

Nothing we have said in our discussion thus far rules out the possibility that all the efficiency conditions may be satisfied at a point where one of the consumers is receiving most, if not all, of the economic benefits. This can be shown by constructing the **grand utility possibility curve,** which indicates the maximum utility that one consumer can receive at each possible utility level for the other consumer.

To construct such a curve for our simple economy, first we pick a point on the production possibility curve—say, point i in Figure 12–3 (page 442). Associated with this point is the contract curve $0i$. Each point on this curve tells us the maximum utility that can be received by one consumer, given a specified utility level for the other consumer. In Figure 12–5, each of the utility combinations associated with contract curve $0i$ is plotted, with Len's utility U_L measured along the horizontal axis and Sue's U_S measured along the vertical axis. The resulting curve, shown as heavy line ii in Figure 12–5, is a utility possibility curve, but it only applies when the output combination i is being pro-

Figure 12-5
The Grand Utility Possibility Curve

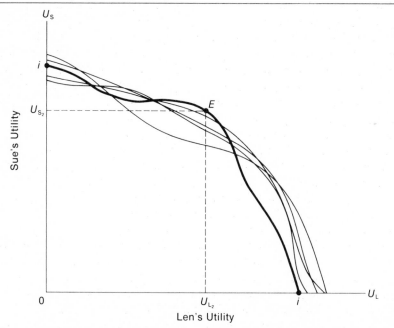

duced. Its downward slope follows from the fact that the only way to increase the utility of one consumer along any contract curve is to reduce the utility of the other consumer. Point E on this curve corresponds to point E in Figure 12–3, where Len and Sue are on indifference curves L_2 and S_2, respectively.

To construct the grand utility possibility curve, we continue to select points on the production possibility curve and to construct the utility possibility curve associated with each point. In Figure 12–5, several of these curves are shown in addition to ii. Like all utility possibility curves, each of these curves is downward sloping. Over some intervals, a few curves will lie outside (northeast of) curve ii, indicating that the common marginal rate of substitution is not equal to the marginal rate of transformation at all points along ii. This being the case, we have seen that it is possible to increase the utility of both consumers by producing a different output combination. In Figure 12–5, note that no curve lies to the northeast of ii at point E, because at this point the common marginal rate of substitution is equal to the marginal rate of transformation, and there is no way to increase the utility of both individuals.

Once all the utility possibility curves are drawn, the outer bound of these curves will be the grand utility possibility curve. This curve will indicate the maximum possible utility for one consumer relative to each utility realized by the other consumer if all of the efficiency conditions are satisfied. In Figure 12–6, this grand utility possibility curve is shown as gg'. The maximum utility that the economy can provide Sue is $0g$, but this can occur only if Len receives nothing and his utility is 0. Similarly, Len can receive a maximum utility of $0g'$,

Figure 12–6
Comparing Positions on the Grand Utility Possibility Curve

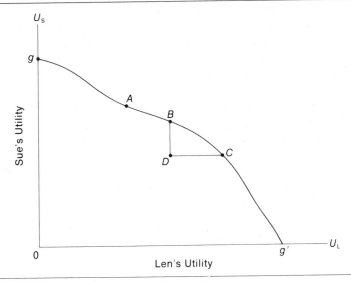

but only by completely depriving Sue. Because every point on the grand utility possibility curve represents a Pareto-efficient distribution of resources, this curve will be downward sloping everywhere, since the only way to increase the utility of one consumer is to decrease the utility of the other.

Allocative Efficiency Versus Distributional Considerations

Until this point, our analysis has allowed us to identify some allocations as Pareto-efficient and some as Pareto-inefficient but has not provided us with any criteria for determining that one efficient allocation is superior to other efficient allocations. In fact, as we are about to see, it can even be difficult to determine that efficient allocations are superior to some inefficient allocations.

The problems we encounter in this area of our analysis result from our reluctance to make interpersonal utility comparisons. Consider a move from Pareto-efficient point A to Pareto-efficient point B in Figure 12–6. This move represents a redistribution of income between Sue and Len: Sue's utility decreases and Len's utility increases. Since we cannot compare the value of one individual's utility with the value of another individual's utility, we have no way to determine whether this redistribution is a social improvement or not. The small decrease in Sue's utility that results from the move from A to B may or may not be more significant than the larger increase in Len's utility due to the move.

Next, we will consider the Pareto-inefficient allocation represented by point D in Figure 12–6. From this position, Pareto-efficient moves can be made that will position Len and Sue on the grand utility possibility curve. A move from D to any point on the curve between points B and C will be a Pareto-efficient move, because it will improve the utility of at least one consumer without reducing the utility of the other. Therefore, any point on the curve from B to C is Pareto-superior to point D. But is the efficient position represented by point A Pareto-superior to position D? It is clear that Len will answer negatively, and he will be correct. The move from D to A will not be Pareto-superior, because it increases Sue's well-being at Len's expense. The Pareto criterion that a reallocation is unequivocally efficient only if it increases the well-being of one consumer without reducing the well-being of anyone else is regarded as a weak one; it cannot establish that an efficient position is better than some inefficient positions.

Economists have attempted to develop criteria that are stronger than the Pareto criterion but that avoid introducing value judgments regarding the relative virtue of different income distributions. The best-known criterion was developed in the 1930s by two British economists, Nicholas Kaldor and Nobel Laureate John R. Hicks. According to the **Kaldor–Hicks criterion,**[12] a reallo-

---

[12]Nicholas Kaldor, "Welfare Propositions in Economics and Interpersonal Comparisons of Utility," *Economic Journal* (September 1939), pp. 549–82; and John R. Hicks, "The Foundation of Welfare Economics," *Economic Journal* (December 1939), pp. 696–712.

cation of resources is efficient if those who gain from it obtain enough to fully compensate those who lose from it. To illustrate, we will reconsider the move from D to A in Figure 12–6. If this move is made, Len could be compensated by a move along gg' from A to B, which could leave him with the same utility he had before the move, and Sue would acquire more utility than she had at D. Note that moving from A to D would not permit Len to maintain a higher utility level than he received at A *and* to compensate Sue adequately for her loss. Unfortunately, it is possible to conceive of situations when a change is an improvement according to the Kaldor–Hicks criterion, but once the change is made, a change back to the original position is also an improvement according to this criterion. To avoid this difficulty, economist Tibor Scitovsky suggested that a change only be considered an improvement when making the change is a Kaldor–Hicks improvement but reversing the change is not.[13]

Note that even given the Kaldor–Hicks and Scitovsky criteria, we are left with the question of whether or not a move to or along the grand utility possibility curve can be considered an improvement unless the suggested compensation is actually made. If we argue that compensation is not a prerequisite for the change to be an improvement, we are in essence making value judgments about the value of one consumer's utility relative to another consumer's utility. If we argue that the compensation must be made for a change to constitute an improvement, we are bound by the Pareto criterion, which only permits utility improvements that are not made at someone else's expense. But the Pareto criterion provides no guideline to follow to determine the *preferred* Pareto-efficient point. Thus, we must conclude that only by making value judgments about the desirability of the trade-off between one consumer's utility and another's can we choose the superior Pareto-efficient position.

Recognition of this point led economist Abram Bergson to consider the merits of a **social welfare function** that contains an explicit value judgment regarding the importance of one consumer's utility relative to another's.[14] Such a function provides **social indifference curves** that map out utility combinations that are considered to be equally desirable. Two social indifference curves for our two-consumer economy appear in Figure 12–7, along with the grand utility possibility curve gg'. These social indifference curves are convex, indicating that when Sue is receiving a large amount of utility relative to Len, society is willing to reduce Sue's utility a lot to increase Len's utility a little. However, as we move to positions on the grand utility possibility curve gg' where Sue's utility is smaller relative to Len's, society will accept less of a decrease in Sue's utility to obtain a given increase in Len's utility.

---

[13]Tibor Scitovsky, "A Note on Welfare Propositions in Economics," *Review of Economic Studies* (November 1941), pp. 77–88.
[14]Abram Bergson, "A Reformulation of Certain Aspects of Welfare Economics," *Quarterly Journal of Economics* (1937–1938), pp. 310–34.

Figure 12-7
Social Indifference Curves and the Preferred Point
on the Grand Utility Possibility Curve

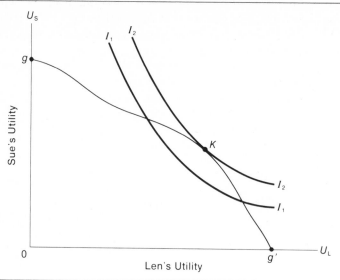

Although it is customary to construct social indifference curves in this way, convexity is not a requirement, because we have imposed no restrictions on the type of value judgments underlying these curves. The social welfare function can reflect the value judgments of Sue, Len, a social planner, a dictator, or a legislative body. What we must keep in mind is that definite value judgments, regardless of whose judgments they are, are reflected in any social welfare function and the corresponding social indifference curves—and, more importantly, that value judgments are *not* and *cannot* be scientifically determined.

But if we accept a social welfare function and its underlying value judgments, it becomes possible to choose a particular point on the grand utility possibility curve as preferable to all other points on that curve. As Figure 12–7 shows, the highest social indifference curve that can be reached along gg' is social indifference curve I_2, on which the maximum obtainable social welfare subject to the constraint given by the grand utility possibility curve gg' occurs at point k. At this constrained welfare maximum, the social indifference curve I_2 is tangent to the grand utility possibility curve.[15] Having chosen the preferred point on the grand utility possibility curve, we will know the utility levels for each consumer. In general, this will permit us to determine the point on the

---

[15]Since there is no requirement that the grand utility possibility curve be concave (as shown in Figures 12–6 and 12–7, the curve has both concave and convex segments) or that the social indifference curves be convex, it is possible for one social indifference curve to be tangent to gg' at more than one point. We will ignore this possibility, however, and consider only one tangency point in our discussion here.

production possibility curve that allows these respective utility levels to be reached such that each consumer's marginal rate of substitution is equal to the marginal rate of transformation. And once this point on the production possibility curve has been determined, we will be able to select the distribution of inputs required for the efficient production of the combination of goods represented by this point. If we are willing to choose a social welfare function, it is possible to choose a most preferred resource allocation *if all other data are known.*

Arrow's Impossibility Theorem

The existence of a social welfare function allows us to rank different resource allocations and to designate a particular Pareto-efficient allocation as superior to all others. Unfortunately for those of us who feel that an acceptable social welfare function should reflect the individual preferences and priorities of a broad spectrum of the community, no social welfare function that satisfies certain plausible conditions can be democratically determined.

The impossibility of the existence of such a democratically based social welfare function has been established by Nobel Laureate Kenneth Arrow.[16] The four conditions that Arrow believes should hold if social welfare choices are to reflect individual preferences are summarized here:

1. Social welfare choices must be transitive. (If A is preferred to B and B is preferred to C, then A has to be preferred to C.)

2. A social welfare choice that moves up in the rankings of one or more individuals and does not move down in the ranking of any individual cannot move down in the social welfare choice ranking.

3. Social welfare choices cannot be implied or dictated by one individual inside or outside the community.

4. The ranking of one social welfare option relative to another is independent of alternative options. (If A is preferred to B and B is preferred to C, then A will still be preferred to B in the absence of option C.)

Assuming that everyone does not have the same preferences with respect to the available social welfare options, it is impossible to rank these choices democratically without violating at least one of Arrow's four conditions. A very simple example will illustrate how the first condition of transitivity can be violated. In Table 12–1, we consider how three individuals I, II, and III feel about three options A, B, and C. The table indicates that individual I considers A the first choice, B the second choice, and C the third choice. For individual II, C is the first choice, followed by A and then B. Individual III ranks B first, C second, and A third. Assuming that the majority rules, a vote between A and B will result in A being preferred, since I and II will vote for A and III will vote for B. The choice between B and C will result in B being preferred 2 to 1, since I and III will vote for B and II will vote for C. Thus, A will be preferred to B and B will be preferred

---

[16]Kenneth Arrow, *Social Choice and Individual Values* (New York: John Wiley & Sons, 1951).

Table 12-1
Majority-Rule Voting and Intransitive Social Choices

Individual	OPTION		
	A	B	C
I	1	2	3
II	2	3	1
III	3	1	2

to C. But if there is a vote between A and C, option C will be preferred to A, since II and III will vote for C and I will vote for A. In this example, majority-rule voting results in *intransitive* social welfare choices.

Given the wide diversity of tastes and preferences found in a community, it is not surprising that any collective attempt to choose a particular resource allocation meets formidable obstacles. In Chapters 13 and 14, other problems involved in making collective decisions will be discussed.

12-5 The Theory of the Second Best

In Section 12-3, we found that three conditions must be satisfied for the economy to be operating at a Pareto-efficient position. Since it may be impossible to satisfy one or more of these conditions, however, it is interesting to consider the requirements for achieving a "second-best" position in the economy. The natural inclination may be to assume that when one of the efficiency conditions cannot be satisfied, the best alternative is to ensure that the remaining efficiency conditions are satisfied. Unfortunately, the **theory of the second best** shows that there is no guarantee that satisfying the remaining efficiency conditions will make things better rather than worse.[17]

It is possible to illustrate graphically how satisfying one efficiency condition can make things worse if another efficiency condition is not satisfied. Figure 12-8 depicts the production possibility curve TT, with the quantity of clothing produced represented on the horizontal axis and the quantity of fun and frolic produced represented on the vertical axis. Curves I_1, I_2, and I_3 are social indifference curves.[18] As the figure shows, the best position for the economy is at point L, where TT is tangent to the highest possible social indifference curve I_3. However, we will assume that position L cannot be reached because

[17]See Kelvin Lancaster and Richard G. Lipsey, "The General Theory of the Second Best," *Review of Economic Studies,* Vol. 24 (1956–1957), pp. 11–32.

[18]Note that these social indifference curves are constructed with output levels measured along the axes rather than utility levels, which we measured in Section 12-4. Given a set of social indifference curves with utility levels measured along the axes, it is possible to determine their corresponding social indifference curves with output levels measured along the axes. However, this procedure is complicated and will be ignored here.

Figure 12–8
The Theory of the Second Best

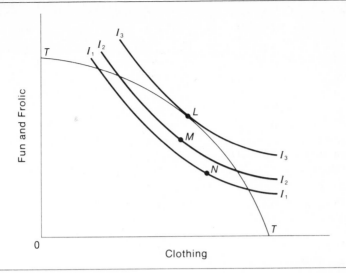

industry C (clothing) is paying a lower price for one input than industry F (fun and frolic) is paying and this situation cannot be corrected. This means that the economy will be operating somewhere below the production possibility curve, since the marginal rates of technical substitution for the two inputs will not be the same for both industries.

Moreover, we will assume that industry C is a monopolist and that industry F is perfectly competitive. In Section 12–3, we saw that this results in the violation of the efficiency condition that the common marginal rate of substitution must equal the marginal rate of transformation. By itself, this inefficiency would cause industry C to produce too little relative to industry F, but the first inefficiency at least partially offsets this tendency for industry C to underproduce, since industry C is paying less than industry F for one of the inputs. We will assume that the combined effect of these two inefficiencies places the economy at position M on social indifference curve I_2 in Figure 12–8.

Since we cannot eliminate the inefficiency that results from paying different prices for the same input (the inefficiency that keeps us below the production possibility curve), it is tempting to argue that we could at least improve matters by eliminating the inefficiency that results from the monopoly. But restructuring industry C to make it competitive may only make the situation worse. If industry C becomes competitive, C's output will increase relative to F's output, but the remaining inefficiency will still prevent the economy from operating on the production possibility curve. Therefore, removing the monopoly inefficiency could result in a shift from M to N in Figure 12–8, which would position the economy on social indifference curve I_1 and reduce social welfare.

Given the input pricing inefficiency, the economy is in a better position with the monopoly inefficiency than without it. If the best position for the economy cannot be reached because one of the efficiency conditions is irrevocably violated, some of the remaining efficiency conditions may have to be violated as well to achieve the second best position.

The theory of the second best cautions against attempts to improve economic performance by isolating one sector of the economy and improving its efficiency without taking into account what is happening in other sectors. Once again, we are reminded of the interdependence that exists throughout the economy. To the extent that one sector is independent of other sectors, isolated attempts to improve the overall efficiency of the economy by improving the efficiency of that one sector are justified. For example, policies that promote competition in the pharmaceutical industry may be worthwhile, even though inefficiencies remain in the motion-picture industry. However, interdependencies among different sectors of the economy are more pervasive than is commonly realized. In the next section, we will consider a model that explicitly deals with these interdependencies.

12-6 Input–Output Economics

Economists have long been aware of the interdependencies that exist in the economy. In 1874, the French economist Leon Walras constructed one of the first general-equilibrium models of the economy, which explicitly recognized that changes in one market affected other markets.[19] More recently, Nobel Laureate Wassily Leontief has constructed a general-equilibrium model that can conceivably be used as a guideline for economic policy.[20] Leontief's model is known as the *input–output model*.

The underlying concept of the input–output model is that the output of one industry is produced not only for final consumption but also for use as an input by other industries and that the outputs of some of these other industries provide the necessary inputs for the industry's own production. Having recognized this industry interdependency, it becomes clear that to obtain a specific amount of each industry's output for final consumption, each industry must produce enough to satisfy not only its final consumption demands but also the input demands of other industries, including itself. (In general, an industry will employ its own output as an input. For example, the steel industry uses steel as an input in its production process.) Input–output economics provides a systematic method of cutting through these enormously complicated interdependencies to determine exactly what output pattern is necessary to support a given consumption pattern.

---

[19]Leon Walras, *Elements of Pure Economics*. William Jaffe (translator) (Homewood, IL: Richard D. Irwin, 1954). The original version appeared in French in 1874.
[20]Wassily Leontief, *The Structure of the American Economy* (New York: Oxford University Press, 1951).

The Underlying Assumptions of Input–Output Economics

Not surprisingly, the ability of input–output economics to reduce a complicated problem to manageable size results from the use of some simplifying assumptions. First, we will assume that we are dealing with only the *aggregate quantities* supplied or demanded by each industry (not with how industry totals are allocated among firms and particular consumers). This reduces the number of variables and equations that we will have to deal with and therefore simplifies the computations required to reach a solution.

Second, we will assume that final consumption demands are *independent* of the solution reached. This assumption obviously ignores the role of the demand theory we have developed in earlier chapters. It also ignores the affect of decisions made in the productive sector on income and income distribution—and therefore on what and how much is demanded.

Finally, most crucial to the manageability of the input–output model is the assumption that each production process utilizes inputs in a *fixed* proportion and that there are *constant* returns to scale. This means that the same increment of each input is required to produce another unit of the output and that this relationship is the same at all output levels. For example, if 1 barrel of petroleum, 20 pounds of coal, and 7 man-hours of labor are required to produce 10 gallons of gasoline, it will take 10 barrels of petroleum, 200 pounds of coal, and 70 man-hours of labor to produce 100 gallons of gasoline. This assumption clearly disregards the input substitution possibilities motivated by changes in relative input prices and represented by isoquant curves. Over short periods of time, however, this assumption may not be too much at variance with reality and, as we will see, makes it relatively easy to solve a problem that otherwise could not be solved for all practical purposes.

A Simple Example

To illustrate the input–output approach, we will consider a very simple two-industry model. Much larger input–output models are constructed to represent real economies (a model that includes 450 industries has been developed for the economy of the United States), but a basic understanding of input–output economics can be achieved without tackling the computational complexities that a larger model would require.

We will assume that our simple economy consists of a manufacturing industry and an agricultural industry. We will also assume that the total outputs of both industries are distributed as indicated in Table 12—2. The 100 in the manufacturing row and the manufacturing column indicates that 100 units of manufacturing output are used by the manufacturing industry as an input.[21] The 400 in the manufacturing row and the agricultural column tells us that 400 units

---

[21]The physical units chosen for measurement here are arbitrary. It is also possible to construct an input–output model by using monetary units of measurement.

Table 12-2
Input-Output Relationships in a Two-Industry Economy

PRODUCING INDUSTRY	USING INDUSTRY		HOUSEHOLD DEMAND	TOTAL OUTPUT
	Manufacturing	Agricultural		
Manufacturing	100	400	500	1,000
Agricultural	300	300	1,400	2,000

of manufacturing output are used by the agricultural industry as an input. Similarly, the agricultural row indicates that the manufacturing industry uses 300 units of agricultural input and that 300 units of agricultural output are also used as agricultural input. The household demand column shows that 500 units of output from the manufacturing industry and 1,400 units of output from the agricultural industry are being consumed by households. Adding up these demands gives us 1,000 units of total output for the manufacturing industry and 2,000 units of total output for the agricultural industry.

At this point, it is interesting to determine what additional demands would be placed on the two industries if the household demand for manufacturing output increased from 500 to, say, 700. Even when only two industries are being considered, we can appreciate the complexities involved in making this determination if we attempted to casually trace through the interdependencies in our example.

To make this determination using the more systematic input–output approach, we must first determine what we call the **input coefficients,** which indicate the proportion of output from one industry that is required as an input to obtain each unit of output from another (or the same) industry. From Table 12–2, we can see that 100 units are required from the manufacturing industry to produce the 1,000 units of total manufacturing output, so that the input coefficient is $100/1{,}000 = .1$. It takes .1 unit of manufacturing output as a manufacturing input to produce 1 unit of manufacturing output. Similarly, from Table 12–2, we can see that $400/2{,}000 = .2$ unit of manufacturing output is required to produce 1 unit of agricultural output, $300/1{,}000 = .3$ unit of agricultural output is required to produce 1 unit of manufacturing output, and $300/2{,}000 = .15$ unit of agricultural output is required to produce 1 unit of agricultural output.

Given these input coefficients, the total requirements for manufacturing output M and agricultural output A can be expressed as

$$M = .1M + .2A + 500 \qquad (12\text{–}1)$$

$$A = .3M + .15A + 1{,}400 \qquad (12\text{–}2)$$

Equation (12–1) tells us that the manufacturing output is equal to $.1M$ (the amount that is returned to the manufacturing industry as an input) plus $.2A$ (the amount that is required as an input to the agricultural industry) plus the

500 units to satisfy household demand. The explanation for Equation (12–2) is the same.

Equations (12–1) and (12–2) are two linear equations with two unknowns (M and A), which can be solved using well-known techniques.[22] In our case, the solution is $M = 1,000$ and $A = 2,000$. Of course, this result is not surprising, since we knew before we formulated our problem in equation form that manufacturing and agricultural outputs were 1,000 and 2,000, respectively, as shown in Table 12–2. But putting our problem into equation form has not been just an idle exercise. It is now easy to determine what additional demands will be placed on our industries if household demand for manufacturing output increases from 500 to 700. We simply change household demand in Equation (12–1) from 500 to 700 and solve the resulting system of equations:

$$M = .1M + .2A + 700 \qquad\qquad (12\text{–}3)$$

$$A = .3M + .15A + 1,400 \qquad\qquad (12\text{–}2)$$

The solution is $M = 1,241$ and $A = 2,085$, or a 241-unit increase in manufacturing output and an 85-unit increase in agricultural output.[23]

The system of equations we have developed here can be used to determine the required output for the manufacturing and agricultural industries for any combination of household demands. In general, letting D_M and D_A represent the household demands for manufacturing and agricultural goods, respectively, the output is given by solving the system of equations

$$M = .1M + .2A + D_M \qquad\qquad (12\text{–}4)$$

$$A = .3M + .15A + D_A$$

Without worrying about the computational procedure, the general solution to this system of equations is

$$M = 1.206D_M + .284D_A$$

$$A = .426D_M + 1.277D_A$$

Having expressed our solution in this form, we can easily determine the manufacturing and agricultural outputs necessary to satisfy interindustry demands and household demands for any combination of household demands.

The importance of the assumption that each industry utilizes inputs in a fixed proportion should now be clear from the way we have developed our example. This assumption allows us to determine the input coefficients and to consider them constant at different levels of output. These constant input coefficients

---

[22]With a large number of equations and unknowns, the computations required to obtain a solution become practically impossible without the use of a computer. Even small systems of equations can result in complex computational problems.
[23]This solution will not exactly satisfy Equations (12–3) and (12–2) due to rounding errors.

result in linear equations that can be solved with straightforward computational techniques. Without the assumption of constant input proportions, these equations would be nonlinear and, for all practical purposes, impossible to solve.

The Usage of Input–Output Economics

The primary appeal of input–output economics lies in its ability to express extremely complicated interdependencies in the economy in relatively simple terms. This potential has prompted many input–output studies of real-world economies. All of these studies begin with a somewhat arbitrary division of the economy into different industries and estimates of the appropriate input coefficients. The input coefficients for the economy of the United States have been estimated by the U.S. Department of Commerce for the years 1947, 1958, and 1963.

Once the appropriate input coefficients have been estimated, input–output models can be employed in a wide variety of ways. In anticipation of war-time mobilization, input–output analysis has been used to forecast the industry output pattern that would be required to meet the demands exerted by the military. Input–output models have been used to estimate the overall economic impact of the 1973 Arab oil embargo. Input–output models have also been developed that include pollution as an output and provide information on the environmental impacts of changing economic conditions. Numerous states and municipalities as well as foreign economies have constructed input–output models based on their economies for a variety of purposes.

Despite the potential usefulness of the input–output model, care should always be exercised when employing this method of analysis to predict very far into the future. We know that technological advancements, relative scarcities, and other changes will alter the relative prices of inputs. And in response to these changes in relative prices, there will be a change in the input combinations used to produce a given output. This obviously violates the key assumption in input–output economics–that input proportions remain constant over time.

Application: The Welfare Cost of Excessive Medical Care

Medical care is clearly a desirable service, but just like any other good that can only be produced at a cost, we can reduce our well-being if we consume too much of it. In Section 12–2, we discussed the waste or welfare loss that would result if the federal government made medical care available at a 0 price. If the government provides all that consumers will demand at no price, then individuals will consume medical care until its marginal value is 0, which will be less than the marginal cost of providing it. This means we will be devoting resources to medical care that provide less value in this employment than these resources would generate in other employments.

Excessive medical care can also be motivated by insurance programs, which reduce the marginal cost of purchasing this care. It should be pointed out immediately that insurance provides a social gain by reducing the risks each individual must face by spreading unavoidable risks over a large population. But economist Martin Feldstein has argued that we are overinsured against rather routine medical problems in the United States. A primary reason for this overinsurance is the tax rule that excludes employee benefits in the form of medical insurance from taxable income. For example, an employee who pays $.25 in taxes on each additional $1 earned would prefer that the employer provide him or her with an additional $1 of nontaxed medical insurance rather than another $1 in wages, even if the $1 of insurance is worth only $.76 to the employee. Therefore, employers—who are competing against each other to attract competent workers—are motivated to provide their employees with medical insurance that is worth less than it costs. Also when a high percentage of their medical care is covered by insurance, consumers will demand more expensive medical treatment. This results in still higher prices for medical care—a compelling reason to extend insurance coverage even more.

The welfare loss from excessive medical care due to extensive medical insurance coverage is illustrated in Figure 12–9. The demand for medical care is given by DD, and the marginal cost is P_1, which is also the marginal price of medical care. In the absence of medical insurance, Q_1 patient days will be demanded, and the net value to society is given by the area under the demand curve DD between 0 and Q_1 minus the cost area of $0P_1AQ_1$. This net value appears in Figure 12–9 as the triangular area P_1DA. Once medical insurance is

Figure 12–9
Medical Insurance and the Value of Medical Care

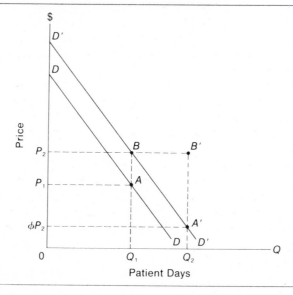

introduced, the cost of medical care will increase as people demand more and more expensive treatments, and because the care is better, the demand curve will shift up and to the right. In Figure 12–9, the post-insurance marginal cost is P_2 and the new demand curve is $D'D'$. But because the treatment is insured, the marginal price paid by the consumer is only $\phi\%$ of the marginal cost, or ϕP_2. At this price, Q_2 patient days of medical care will be demanded. But now the net value of medical care is lower than it was when the consumer had no insurance. Up to quantity Q_1, the marginal value exceeds the marginal cost and the net gain is given by the triangular area $P_2D'B$. But from Q_1 to Q_2, the marginal cost of medical care is greater than its marginal value, and providing this additional care generates a net loss equal to the triangular area $BB'A'$. Thus, with medical insurance, the net value of medical care is $P_2D'B - BB'A'$, and the value of medical care without medical insurance exceeds the value of this care with insurance by the area $P_1DA - (P_2D'B - BB'A')$. In other words, this area represents the welfare loss associated with the excessive consumption of medical care motivated by health-insurance coverage.

Economist Martin Feldstein has estimated the size of this welfare loss, while taking into consideration an estimate of the welfare gain that the insurance provides by reducing the risk of major medical expenses. Based on what he considers conservative estimates of demand parameters, Feldstein concludes that increasing the percent of medical care costs that consumers pay from 33% to 50% or 67% would result in a net gain to society of $2–3 billion per year. Feldstein suggests that health insurance coverage be restructured so that consumers pay a much higher percentage of their small and moderate medical bills, with their insurance providing more protection against major medical expenses.[24]

Application: Blue Whales and Marginal Cost Pricing

We have found that efficiency requires that everyone must pay the same price for a good or an input and that this price must be equal to the marginal cost of this good or input. A further discussion of this requirement in conjunction with a consideration of the plight of the Blue Whale will help to reinforce our understanding of the important role of prices in promoting economic efficiency.

Our analysis of both consumer and producer behavior indicates that a purchaser will buy units of a product only up to the point where the value received from the marginal unit of a good is equal to its price. By charging everyone the same price, we prevent some people (those who would otherwise pay lower prices) from purchasing additional units of a product when the marginal unit of the good is worth less to them than it is to people who are paying higher prices for it. But charging all consumers the same product price is not a sufficient condition for economic efficiency. Unless the price reflects the value forgone to make an additional unit of the product available (the marginal cost), ineffi-

---

[24]See Martin Feldstein, "The Welfare Loss of Excess Health Insurance," *Journal of Political Economy* (March/April 1973), pp. 251–80.

ciencies will arise. As the previous application on medical insurance empha-sized, if the product price is less than the marginal cost, consumers will be motivated to purchase the good even though the marginal unit is worth less than what has to be sacrificed to make it available, thereby resulting in a wel-fare loss.

Unfortunately, the case of the Blue Whale can be cited as a relevant example of the economic inefficiency that results when prices do not reflect the mar-ginal cost of the product. The Blue Whale is being killed at a rate that may, if continued, soon result in the extinction of this majestic species—the largest of all mammals. It has been estimated that at one time a population of 2,000,000 Blue Whales existed. By 1930, this population had been reduced to 100,000, and almost 30,000 Blue Whales were killed in the same year. Although 1930 was the peak year for killing Blue Whales, harvesting has continued at a very high rate, and today fewer than 10,000 Blue Whales remain.[25]

The explanation for this excessive and rapid exploitation of the Blue Whale is rooted in economic analysis. It must be recognized that it would be extremely difficult, if not impossible, to establish and enforce private property rights for Blue Whales. But if Blue Whales could be privately owned, then each owner would be motivated to consider the future as well as the current value of his or her whales when deciding whether to harpoon them now, harpoon them later, or use them for breeding stock. An individual owner would refrain from har-pooning a whale today if the value he or she would receive for the whale car-cass would be less than the value that could be realized from harvesting the whale or its offspring in the future. No one else could harpoon one of the owner's whales without compensation, and you can be sure that the owner would insist on a price that reflected the whale's value in its most valuable alternative use. Since this alternative value would be the *opportunity cost* of harpooning an additional whale now, the product price would reflect the marginal cost. Thus, whales would be harvested only as long as the marginal benefit exceeded the marginal cost of doing so. Because private ownership and a price that reflects the marginal cost of the product characterize the markets for animals such as cows, pigs, horses, and chickens, these animals will not be excessively exploited and driven to extinction.

But because the Blue Whale cannot be privately owned, the whaler who first sights a Blue must compensate no one for the value forgone by harpooning it and will gain nothing from not harpooning it. Each whaler knows that any whale that is not harpooned today will almost surely be harpooned by someone else tomorrow. Whales are therefore harpooned even when the whale carcasses generate much less value than would result if the whales were left in the ocean to mature and breed. The problem is that without private property rights, there will be no price on Blue Whales to reflect the marginal cost of harvesting them. So the waste and inefficiency resulting from the excessive carnage of Blue Whales is the consequence of violating one of the basic requirements for eco-nomic efficiency—that product price be equal to marginal cost.

---

[25]See *Environmental Quality: The Third Annual Report of the Council on Environ-mental Quality* (Washington, D.C.: U.S. Government Printing Office, August 1972), p. 95.

Application: More on Price Controls

We discussed the consequences of price controls in Chapter 2. Using simple demand and supply analysis, we argued that if the price ceiling on a good is below the market equilibrium price, then shortages, waste, discrimination, tie-in sales, and black markets will result. In taking another look at price controls here, we will concentrate on the waste—or welfare loss—that results when prices are held below their market equilibrium levels. Our analysis will show that the welfare loss that results from a price ceiling will generally be higher in situations where it is widely believed that price controls are needed most.

To illustrate, we will consider demand curve $D'D'$ and supply curve $S'S'$ in Figure 12–10, where the market clearing or equilibrium price is $\bar{P}$ and the equilibrium quantity is $\bar{Q}$. At quantity level $\bar{Q}$, the cost of producing one more unit is exactly equal to the value of the additional unit, which follows from the interpretation of demand as the marginal value curve and supply as the marginal cost curve. But at all output levels less than $\bar{Q}$, the marginal value exceeds the marginal cost and a positive net value is realized when an additional unit is produced. The sum of all these net values when $\bar{Q}$ units are being produced is equal to the area between the demand and the supply curves from 0 to $\bar{Q}$, or the triangular area SDB in Figure 12–10, which provides a measure of the total net value provided by the good. We can reach the same conclusion by recogniz-

Figure 12–10
Welfare Loss Due to a Price Ceiling

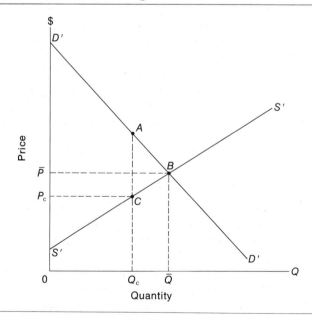

ing that total value can be measured by the area under the demand curve between 0 and $\bar{Q}$ (assuming, as we are, that the income effect is insignificant) and that total cost can be measured by the area under the supply curve between 0 and $\bar{Q}$.

Now assume that a price ceiling is imposed below $\bar{P}$ at P_c in Figure 12–10. Suppliers will respond to this price ceiling by reducing output from $\bar{Q}$ to Q_c. At this reduced output level, the net value realized from the good is given by area SDAC, and the net value sacrificed is given by the area ABC. Area ABC represents the welfare loss due to the price ceiling.

For goods with a low price elasticity of demand, the demand curve is very steep and the potential for a large price increase is great. Given such a demand curve, a small decrease in supply will result in a large price increase. It is also true that goods with a very low price elasticity of demand are commonly considered to be "necessities," since the quantities of these goods that are demanded will decrease only slightly in response to a large price increase. For these reasons, it is argued that price ceilings on "basic necessities" are justifiable because they protect consumers from paying high prices for goods that they cannot consume in reduced quantities. An example that comes readily to mind is the imposition of price ceilings on energy products. Although this may seem to be a plausible argument, it is simple to show that as the demand for a good becomes less price-elastic, the welfare loss resulting from price controls becomes greater.

Two demand curves are drawn in Figure 12–11. DD represents the *inelastic* demand for good I, and D'D' represents the *elastic* demand for good E. For

Figure 12–11
Price Elasticity of Demand and the Welfare Loss
Due to Price Controls

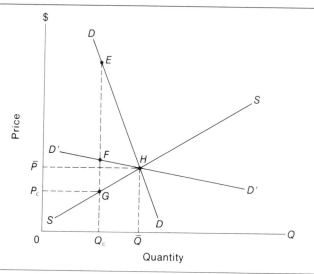

convenience, the equilibrium price and quantity for both goods are given by $\bar{P}$ and $\bar{Q}$, respectively, and SS is the supply curve for both goods. Thus, the important difference here is the difference reflected in the different price elasticities of the two goods. Now we will consider the welfare effects of imposing a price ceiling of P_c on both goods. As we can see in Figure 12–11, the quantity of both goods that is supplied will decline from $\bar{Q}$ to Q_c. But the resulting welfare loss is much greater for good I than it is for good E. For good I, the price ceiling causes the welfare loss given by area GEH, whereas the price ceiling on good E generates the welfare loss given by GFH, which is a much smaller area. Thus, all other factors remaining constant, as the price elasticity of demand becomes smaller, the waste created by a price ceiling becomes greater.

The implication here is rather clear. Greater sacrifices are associated with reductions in the available quantities of products that are more essential and have fewer close substitutes (products with lower price elasticities of demand). When a product is not particularly essential and plenty of close substitutes are available (when the product has a high price elasticity of demand), a great loss will not be associated with a reduction in the quantity of the good that is supplied. If price ceilings are to be selectively imposed on some products, clearly such important and price-inelastic goods as food and energy products should not be among them. If we must place price controls on some items, we can minimize the damage these controls cause by confining our efforts to such items as battery-powered yo-yos, souvenirs, false teeth from Disneyland, and musical salt and pepper shakers.

12–7 Summary

In Chapter 12, we have been concerned with *welfare economics*–the branch of microeconomics that permits us to evaluate the desirability of resource-allocation decisions while explicitly recognizing the interdependencies that exist in the economy.

We have examined the concept of *economic efficiency,* or *Pareto-efficiency,* which provides the fundamental criterion against which the desirability of a particular allocation of resources is judged. We have learned that in a *Pareto-efficient allocation of resources,* it is impossible to increase one individual's utility without reducing someone else's utility. The partial-equilibrium analysis we have developed in earlier chapters establishes certain guidelines for economic efficiency. First, the economy is not operating efficiently unless *as much output as is technically possible* is being produced by the input combination in use. Also, economic efficiency requires that the *least-cost input combination* be used. In addition, the production of each good should be expanded until the product's *marginal cost is equal to its marginal value.* Finally, economic efficiency requires that the good be distributed among consumers in such a way that their *marginal rates of substitution are equal.*

We have found that it is useful to think of waste as the inefficient allocation of resources. Once we considered waste in these terms, it became apparent that simply using more of a resource−say, an energy resource−when less could be used does not necessarily constitute waste. It also became clear that price controls can create waste by motivating inefficient resource allocations and that waste can result from government programs that provide services to individuals at no direct personal cost.

Keeping the efficiency conditions we derived in partial-equilibrium analysis in mind, we then found it useful to construct a model that explicitly examines the relationships between different sectors of the economy, or a *general-equilibrium model*. Assuming a simple, two-input, two-output, two-consumer economy, we considered the requirement for production efficiency first. Only when the marginal rates of technical substitution between the two inputs are the same for both industries is there *production efficiency*−a situation where it is impossible to increase the output of one industry without reducing the output of the other industry. Many different input allocations, all of which lie on the relevant *contract curve*, satisfy the production efficiency requirement. The output combination that results from each input combination along the contract curve provides us with the output combinations that lie along the production possibility curve. The *production possibility curve* shows the maximum amount of one good that can be produced, given a specified level of output for the other good. Under reasonable conditions, the production possibility curve will be concave from below.

Once an output combination is produced, we have seen that *consumption efficiency* requires that it be distributed among consumers in such a way that the marginal rates of substitution of one good for the other are equal for all consumers. Only when this is the case is it impossible to increase the utility of one consumer without reducing the utility of another consumer. Many different distributions, all lying along the consumer contract curve, satisfy this efficiency condition.

To achieve efficiency, we have also learned that the proper combination of goods must be produced. This requires that the common marginal rate of substitution of one good for the other good be equal to the *marginal rate of transformation* of that good for the other good. Unless this condition holds, each consumer will be willing to give up more of one good to obtain an additional unit of the other good than is required.

These three requirements for economic efficiency were then shown to be satisfied under conditions of perfect competition in our simple, two-industry economy. In perfect competition, the price of a given input is the same for everyone. Therefore, since each industry will minimize the cost of producing a given output by equating the marginal rate of technical substitution between inputs to the input price ratio, the marginal rate of technical substitution will be the same in both industries, thereby fulfilling the first efficiency requirement. Perfect competition also guarantees that the price of each good will be the same for all consumers. We now know that when each individual is maximizing utility subject to his or her budget constraint, every consumer will choose a consumption bundle that equates the marginal rate of substitution between the two goods with the input price ratio. Since this price ratio will be common to all consumers, the second efficiency condition is satisfied: The marginal rates of substitution between the two goods are the same for all consumers. In perfect competition, the third efficiency condition is met as the result of the fact that each industry operates at the point where marginal cost is equal to product price. Since the ratio of the marginal cost of one good to the marginal cost of the other good is equal to the marginal rate of transformation of one good for the other good, it follows that the marginal rate of transformation is equal to the input price ratio under conditions of perfect competition. But from the second efficiency condition, this implies that the marginal rate of transformation is equal to the common marginal rate of substitution, thereby satisfying the third efficiency condition.

In addition to providing a means of exhibiting these efficiency conditions, we have seen that the framework of the general-equilibrium model brings out the *economic interdependencies* that exist between production and consumption decisions. For example, the relative incomes of consumers are dependent on the output combination chosen and therefore the appropriate consumption pattern may be inconsistent with consumer incomes. So it is not sufficient to satisfy the conditions of economic efficiency; these conditions must be satisfied at a position where the interrelated production and consumption decisions are consistent with each other.

We have seen that many internally consistent positions can satisfy the conditions of economic efficiency. Each of these positions will provide the maximum possible utility for one consumer, given the utility level for the other consumer. The curve that traces out these utility levels is referred to as the *grand utility possibility curve*. The efficiency criterion, although very useful, provides no justification for designating one point on the grand utility possibility curve as superior to any other Pareto-efficient point. Economists have attempted to circumvent their reluctance to make interpersonal utility comparisons to some extent by arguing that a move is desirable if those who gain from it obtain enough to fully compensate those who lose from it. This is known as the *Kaldor–Hicks criterion*. But at best, this criterion allows us to make comparisons between Pareto-inefficient and Pareto-efficient positions. The only way to select the most desirable Pareto-efficient position is to be willing to make a *value judgment* regarding the value of one consumer's utility relative to another's. Having done this, we have found that it is possible to determine a *social welfare function* and the corresponding *social indifference curves* in utility space that can be used in conjunction with the grand utility possibility curve to select the "superior" Pareto-efficient position. However, *Arrow's impossibility theorem* demonstrates that a democratically based social welfare function that satisfies certain plausible conditions does not exist.

We have also learned that attempts to improve the efficiency of the economy by satisfying efficiency conditions in one sector but allowing inefficiencies to remain elsewhere can, according to the *theory of the second best,* make economic conditions worse rather than better. In general, when all of the conditions for economic efficiency cannot be satisfied, we have seen that there is no justification to support policies aimed at satisfying only some of these conditions. The more interdependent the different sectors of the economy are, the more relevant the theory of the second best becomes.

In this chapter, we have also examined *input–output economics,* which deals explicitly with interdependencies in the economy. The input–output model considers the implications of the fact that each industry both supplies inputs to and uses outputs from other industries. By making some simplifying assumptions–the most important being that inputs are used in a *fixed proportion* within each industry–we were able to use input–output analysis to determine the total output required from each industry to accommodate a specified pattern of final demand. This technique has been used to estimate the economy-wide impact of such actions as wartime mobilization and the Arab oil embargo.

We have concluded this chapter with three applications related to welfare economics. In the first application, we learned that attempts have been made to measure the actual welfare loss that results when some of the conditions of economic efficiency are not being satisfied. Specifically, we considered economist Martin Feldstein's attempt to estimate the welfare loss due to the excessive demand for medical care created by medical insurance, which lowers the price of medical care below its marginal cost. Feldstein's estimates indicate that the welfare loss resulting from excessive medical care is $2–3 billion per year.

Although the authors do not know of any estimates of the actual welfare loss created by the excessive exploitation of the Blue Whale, this loss is certainly not insignificant. In the second application, we learned that the excessive slaughter of Blue Whales results from the fact that no price is imposed on harpooning these whales to reflect the marginal cost of reducing the Blue Whale population. When animals are privately owned–an arrangement that cannot be seriously considered for the Blue Whale–the prices charged for them reflect their most valuable use, and there is no need to be concerned about their exploitation and possible extinction.

In the final application, we found that the welfare loss resulting from a price ceiling can be represented by the area under the demand curve minus the area under the supply curve, if we consider only the areas under these curves that lie between the price-controlled output and the equilibrium output. Using this measure of the waste caused by a price ceiling, we saw that when the demand for a good is less price-elastic, the welfare loss that results from imposing a price ceiling will be greater. An interesting aspect of this conclusion is that price controls are most often applied to goods for which the demand is less price-elastic.

In Chapter 13, we will turn our attention to considerations that result in violations of the efficiency conditions that have been developed in this chapter. This will lead us to an examination of the rationale for the collective economic decision making that characterizes much economic activity.

References

Arrow, Kenneth. *Social Choice and Individual Values.* New York: John Wiley & Sons, 1957.

Bator, Francis. "The Simple Analytics of Welfare Maximization." *American Economic Review* (March 1957), pp. 22–59.

Bergson, Abram. "A Reformulation of Certain Aspects of Welfare Economics." *Quarterly Journal of Economics* (1937–1938), pp. 310–34.

Buchanan, James M., and Robert D. Tollison (eds.). *Theory of Public Choice.* Ann Arbor: University of Michigan Press, 1972.

Environmental Quality: The Third Annual Report of the Council on Environmental Quality. Washington, D.C.: U.S. Government Printing Office, August 1972, p. 95.

Feldstein, Martin. "The Welfare Loss of Excess Health Insurance." *Journal of Political Economy* (March/April 1973), pp. 251–80.

Graff, J. de V. *Theoretical Welfare Economics.* London: Cambridge University Press, 1957.

Hicks, John R. "The Foundation of Welfare Economics." *Economic Journal* (December 1939), pp. 696–712.

Hirschleifer, J., J. Milliman, and J. DeHaven. *Water Supply.* Chicago: University of Chicago Press, 1960.

Howe, C., and F. Linaweaver, Jr. "The Impact of Price on Residual Water Demand and Its Relation to System Design and Price Structure." *Water Resources Research,* Vol. 3 (first quarter, 1967), pp. 12–32.

Kaldor, Nicholas. "Welfare Propositions in Economics and Interpersonal Comparisons of Utility." *Economic Journal* (September 1939), pp. 549–82.

Lancaster, Kelvin, and Richard G. Lipsey. "The General Theory of the Second Best," *Review of Economic Studies,* Vol. 24 (1956–1957), pp. 11–32.

Leontief, Wassily. *The Structure of the American Economy.* New York: Oxford University Press, 1951.

Little, I.M.D. *A Critique of Welfare Economics.* Oxford: Clarendon Press, 1950.

Moore, Thomas G. "The Beneficiaries of Trucking Regulation." *The Journal of Law and Economics* (October 1978), pp. 327–43.

Scitovsky, Tibor. "A Note on Welfare Propositions in Economics." *Review of Economic Studies* (November 1941), pp. 77–88.

Scitovsky, Tibor. *Welfare and Competition.* Homewood, IL: Richard D. Irwin, 1951.

Tyrell, R. Emmett, Jr. (ed.). *The Future That Doesn't Work: Social Democracy's Failure in Britain.* Garden City, NY: Doubleday, 1977.

Walras, Leon. *Elements of Pure Economics.* William Jaffe (translator). Homewood, IL: Richard D. Irwin, 1954.

Winch, D.M. *Analytical Welfare Economics.* Baltimore: Penguin Books, 1971.

1. Explain how all three conditions of economic efficiency can be satisfied when all industries are monopolies. How is this explanation related to the conclusion reached by the theory of the second best?

2. The importance of the interdependencies that exist within the economy is rooted in the problem of scarcity. Explain how all the economic interdependencies that exist within the general-equilibrium model we developed in Section 12–3 would either vanish or become inconsequential in the absence of scarcity. What significance would be attached to the conditions of economic efficiency in a world without scarcity?

3. Under what conditions do you believe partial-equilibrium analysis is more appropriate than general-equilibrium analysis? Do your conditions justify ignoring the implications of the theory of the second best?

4. In Table 12–1 (page 456), the alternatives of three individuals under majority-rule voting were shown to lead to intransitive social choices. Still assuming majority-rule voting, explain how this intransitivity might be eliminated if people were permitted to buy or sell their votes.

5. Consider the following input–output relationships in a two-industry economy:

PRODUCING INDUSTRY	USING INDUSTRY		HOUSEHOLD DEMAND	TOTAL OUTPUT
	A	B		
A	35	105	175	315
B	17.5	70	122.5	210

Use the information provided in this table to determine the four input coefficients. Then express the two linear equations that, when solved simultaneously, will yield the output requirements that industries A and B must meet to satisfy input demand and household demand.

6. Assume that apples and grapefruits are distributed between Tom and Mary in such a way that Tom's marginal rate of substitution of apples for grapefruits is 3 and Mary's marginal rate of substitution of apples for grapefruits is ½. In which direction should trade take place? How can this trade increase both Tom's and Mary's utilities?

7. Assume that the common marginal rate of substitution of apples for grapefruits is 2 and that the marginal rate of transformation of apples for grapefruits is ½. How should resources be reallocated in this situation? How can this reallocation increase everyone's well-being?

8. Explain the logic behind the following statement:

We cannot expect government decisions to result in Pareto-efficient changes, because these decisions are usually made on the basis of majority-rule voting.

9. Consider a rent-subsidization program that varies the price of a particular type of house for different consumers, thereby moving the economy below the production possibility curve. Can you justify this program on the basis of Pareto efficiency? Can you justify the program on the basis of a social welfare function? Is there any conceivable program you could not justify on the basis of some social welfare function?

10. Assume that the contract curve in Figure 12–1 (page 438) is a straight line from 0_F to 0_C and that both production functions exhibit constant returns to scale. What will the shape of the production possibility curve be in this case?

CHAPTER THIRTEEN

PUBLIC GOODS, EXTERNALITIES, AND POLLUTION

Introduction 13-1

Many economic decisions are made collectively or through political processes, rather than by individuals. Until now, there has been little in our discussion to indicate why this is so. In this chapter, we will correct this deficiency by using economic theory to understand the necessity for and the problems involved in collective economic decision making. But before we can proceed, we must identify and relax two assumptions that have been implicit throughout much of the discussion in this book.

The first assumption concerns an attribute of the goods that individuals consume and exchange. Thus far, our implicit assumption has been that as more of a given quantity of a good is consumed by one individual, less of that good becomes available for others to consume. This assumption has remained implicit primarily because it is obviously true for the vast majority of goods that we consume. We cannot increase our consumption of clothing, food, housing, toothpaste, or automobiles, for example, without reducing their availability to other consumers. When the availability of a good for consumption can be exhausted through use, the good is referred to as a **private good.**

With a little thought, however, we can see that not all goods are private goods. Some goods, once they are made available for the benefit of one consumer, are equally available to all consumers. Our consumption of such a good is in no way diminished because the number of consumers of the good increases. The classic example of such a good is national defense. The fact that only a given amount of national defense is available does not make us feel more vulnerable to the threat of foreign invasion each time a birth increases the number of people who are consuming that defense. When the availability of a good is not reduced through consumption, the good is referred to as a **public good.** Other examples of public goods include flood protection, television broadcasts, and a beautiful, sunny day.

It is often, although not necessarily, the case that once a public good is provided, it is difficult, if not impossible, to selectively exclude individuals from the benefits the good provides. The military cannot let an invader obliterate your house in a nuclear attack and prevent your next-door neighbor's home from being damaged at the same time. It is also difficult to imagine a flood-control district letting a flood wash away the properties of specific individuals while protecting other properties in the area from flood damage. On the other hand, some public goods can be selectively distributed. Television sets can be equipped with scrambling devices that prevent a viewer from receiving a TV broadcast unless a sufficient amount of coins are deposited. Up to the point where the stadium is full, a football game closely satisfies the requirements of a public good. But high stadium walls with only a few gates selectively deprive would-be onlookers of the benefits of watching the game.

A second assumption that has been implicit in our discussions throughout this book is that whenever an exchange occurs, all the costs and benefits resulting from that exchange are accrued only by those who voluntarily agree to the exchange. For example, when a landlord rents an apartment, it is reasonable to assume that he or she will incur all of the costs associated with maintaining the apartment and will receive a rental payment. Similarly, the tenant will normally pay the entire rent and will receive all of the services provided by the apartment and the landlord.

Clearly, the costs and benefits of a transaction are not always confined to the parties who are directly involved in the transaction. For instance, a voluntary exchange can occur between you and the local gas and electric company: The company provides you with electricity in return for a monthly payment based on your usage rate. But the cost of providing the electricity you consume may not be entirely reflected in your monthly bill if the generation of the electricity results in a large quantity of smoke and air pollution. This imposes an involuntary cost on others who do not receive any of the benefits from your electricity consumption. In effect, these people are subsidizing part of your consumption of power.[1] Since this cost is external to those who are voluntary participants in the exchange, economists call it an **external cost.** Another way of referring to this phenomenon is to say that the production and consumption of electricity generates a **negative externality.**

Not all externalities are negative. For example, you may engage in an exchange with the local nursery that results in your yard being beautifully landscaped. To the extent that neighbors and passers-by appreciate aesthetically appealing yards, much of the benefit from this exchange between you and the nursery will be an **external benefit** or, equivalently, a **positive externality.**

The concepts of public goods and externalities are not unrelated. There are advantages, however, in discussing them separately. First, we will focus our attention on public goods and the resource allocation problems that they cre-

---

[1] If you also suffer from the air pollution generated by the gas and electric company, then you subsidize a small portion of the power consumption of the rest of the community as well.

ate. Following this discussion, we will direct the analysis toward an understanding of the problems associated with externalities. The problems that result from both public goods and externalities will then be explained in terms of inadequately defined and enforced property rights. Providing such an explanation will give us an understanding of the importance of property rights in the efficient allocation of resources. Finally, a section on environmental pollution will provide us with an opportunity to apply the concepts of public goods and externalities to better understand an all too relevant problem. Fortunately, this understanding will not only generate insights into why the problem of pollution exists but will also provide suggestions for effective responses.

Public Goods   13-2

The Market Demand Curve and the Efficient Quantity

In Chapter 2, we saw that the market demand curve for a private good is obtained by summing the individual consumer demand curves horizontally. The resulting demand curve tells us how much of the good all individuals will want to consume at each price. In Chapter 5, we found that the demand curve also indicates what value consumers attach to an additional unit of the good at all possible quantities. With horizontal summation, this value is equal to the value each consumer places on an additional unit of the good. This is appropriate because if another unit of the good is made available, only one individual can consume it.

Unlike a private good, however, if an additional unit of a public good is provided, *everyone* can consume that unit. This means that the value of the additional unit is equal to the sum of the values that all consumers receive from the unit. For example, if additional national defense is provided, its value is equal to the sum of the values that all individuals in the nation place on it. To reflect this cumulative marginal value, the market demand curve for a public good must be obtained from the *vertical* summation of each consumer's demand curve.

Figure 13-1 illustrates the vertical summation of the individual demand curves to obtain the market demand curve for a public good. For simplicity, we will consider only two individuals, since it is a straightforward procedure to generalize the process to any number of consumers. The horizontal axis in Figure 13-1 measures the quantity of the public good. The value of the public good is measured in money along the vertical axis. Consumer 1's demand curve for the public good is D_1D_1, and consumer 2's demand curve is D_2D_2. By adding the height of D_1D_1 to the height of D_2D_2 for each quantity, or by vertically summing the two demand curves, we obtain the market demand curve DD_2, which indicates the marginal value of the good at each possible quantity.

Consider, for example, the marginal value society places on the good when $\bar{Q}$ units are available. We can see from Figure 13-1 that when $\bar{Q}$ units are consumed, the value that consumer 1 places on the marginal unit is P_1

Figure 13-1
The Optimal or Efficient Quantity of a Public Good

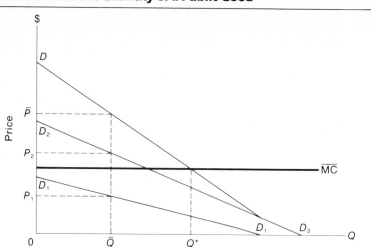

and the value that consumer 2 places on the marginal unit is P_2. Since both individuals will be able to consume the additional unit of the public good if it is provided, the value society (in this case, a two-consumer society) places on the additional unit is given by $\bar{P}$, which is equal to $P_1 + P_2$.

Once we have constructed the market demand curve for a public good, it is possible to determine the socially optimal or *efficient quantity* of the good if we know the marginal cost of providing it. In Figure 13-1, we let $\overline{MC}$ represent the marginal cost of providing the public good. (For simplicity, we will assume that marginal cost is constant.) As we can see, at any quantity of the good less than Q^*, its marginal value exceeds its marginal cost and net gains can be realized by expanding output. At quantities greater than Q^*, the marginal value of the good is less than its marginal cost and net gains can be achieved only by reducing output. Only at Q^*, where the marginal value society places on the good is equal to its marginal cost, is the net benefit from providing the public good maximized. Q^* is therefore the optimal or *efficient quantity* of the good.

In Chapter 12, we saw that the efficient quantity of a private good is being produced when everyone's marginal valuation of the good is the same and this common marginal valuation is equal to the marginal cost of providing the good. The marginal rate of substitution is then equal to the marginal rate of transformation. The optimality of this condition results from the facts that each consumer can vary his or her consumption of a private good *independently* of the consumption decisions of other consumers and that the marginal value society places on a private good is only equal to the marginal value that each individual who consumes the good attaches to it. The optimality condition we have just developed for a public good is a somewhat altered version of the optimality condition for a private good. The optimal quantity of a public good is being produced when the marginal value of the good is equal to the marginal cost of supplying it, but the marginal value of a public good will be equal to the sum of the marginal values attached to it by all those who are consuming it. When the efficient quantity of a public good is produced, it will generally be true that the marginal value of the good will differ among consumers. The explanation for this is that consumers will have preferences for the public good which cannot be accommodated with different consumption rates; everyone has to consume the same quantity of a public good.

Market Incentives and Suboptimal Consumption

When a private good is sold, all consumers contemplate the purchase of the good with the full awareness that they will only benefit from what they buy. No consumer can expect to benefit from the units of the good that someone else pays for and consumes. Therefore, when the price of a private good is equal to its marginal cost, each consumer will be motivated to purchase the quantity at which his or her marginal valuation of the good is equal to its marginal cost, and the total quantity consumed is the optimal or efficient quantity.

Unfortunately, things do not work out quite so smoothly when public goods are being considered. When an individual contemplates the purchase of a public good, he or she realizes that it is possible to benefit from the units of the good that are purchased by someone else. This provides an incentive for each person to be a "free-rider" by not buying any of the good and hoping to benefit from the purchases that others make.[2] Thus, the social value of a public good can far exceed its cost, but consumers will still not want to pay anything to obtain it.

Figure 13–2 illustrates the point we have just made. We will assume that a community contains four individuals, all of whom have the same demand curve D_1D for a public good. Vertically multiplying this demand curve by 4 yields the community demand curve DD for the public good. With $\overline{MC}$ representing the marginal cost of providing the good, the efficient quantity of the public good is Q^*. Up to output Q^*, the marginal value of the good to the community exceeds its marginal cost. However, if the good is priced at its marginal cost, we can see that no one individual will be motivated to purchase the first unit of the good. Even though all four individuals will benefit if they collectively contribute to the

---

[2]The free-rider problem is eliminated if nonpayers are excluded from the benefits provided by the public good. It is sometimes possible to selectively exclude people from enjoying certain public goods. When this occurs, these goods are often privately supplied, as in the case of cable TV. However, unless otherwise stated, our discussion will proceed on the assumption that selective exclusion is impractical. For a discussion of pricing possibilities when nonpayers can be prevented from consuming a public good, see Dwight R. Lee, "Discrimination and Efficiency in the Pricing of Public Goods," *The Journal of Law and Economics* (October 1977).

Figure 13–2
A Public Good: Everyone Wants It–No One Will Pay for It

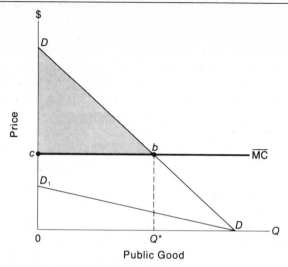

purchase of the good, none of the good will be purchased if we rely on their individual motivations.

The conclusion that none of the public good will be demanded is overly pessimistic when the number in the community is small. First of all, when only a few people are involved, the cost of negotiating and enforcing an agreement requiring each individual to contribute a specific amount to purchase the public good can be small relative to the gains that can be realized from taking collective action to provide the public good. In Figure 13–2, for example, if the four individuals take collective action to acquire Q^* units of the good, their net gains are represented by the tinted area bcD.[3] If the cost of reaching an enforceable agreement obligating each individual to share in the cost of acquiring Q^* units is less than this net gain, then it is reasonable to presume that an agreement will be reached. An example is the provision of fire protection through volunteer fire departments in small communities.[4]

Even if a collective agreement is not reached, some of the public good may still be provided, especially if the number of individuals who wish to acquire the public good is small. In a small community, at least one individual will probably benefit sufficiently from the public good relative to its cost to justify pur-

---

[3]Any time we use the area under the demand curve to measure the total value of a good, we should recall from Chapter 5 that we are assuming that the income effect is insignificant.

[4]Although fire protection does not qualify as a pure public good, it has some characteristics of a public good. Providing the capacity to put out your neighbor's fire certainly extends some protection to you, even if it is only to prevent the fire from spreading to your property.

chasing some of the good, even if no one else contributes. This possibility is illustrated in Figure 13–3, where it is *not* assumed that everyone's demand for the public good is the same. Individual 1 exhibits a high demand D_1D for the public good, and five other members of the community each have a lower demand D_2D for the good. The marginal cost of providing the good is given by $\overline{MC}$. In the absence of a collective agreement, it is clear that none of the low demanders will feel it is in their interest to acquire any of the good. But this is not true of individual 1. Even without the help of the low demanders, individual 1 will find it advantageous to acquire Q_1 units of the good. Once these Q_1 units are available, the five low demanders will benefit from the public good at no cost to themselves, and at this point, they will have even less incentive to acquire additional units individually than they did before. Therefore, only Q_1 units of the good will be consumed. Although this is less than the socially optimal quantity Q^* (DD being the vertical summation of all demand curves), it is better than having none of the good at all.

We have just demonstrated the likelihood that when a public good provides different benefits to different consumers, those with low demands for the good may be able to benefit at no cost from the public good acquired by those who have the most to gain from consuming the good. The United Nations provides us with an example. The mission of the UN is to attempt to provide a very desirable public good—world peace. The fact that one country benefits from world peace in no way reduces the benefits that other countries receive from it. Yet it can be argued that the economically advanced, industrial countries have a larger stake in international tranquility than less developed countries do. Therefore, it is quite natural for the more advanced countries to be motivated to contribute

Figure 13–3
Suboptimal Consumption of a Public Good

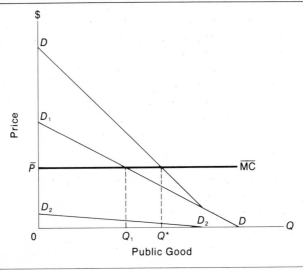

Example 13-1

Privately Supplying a Public Good: The Lighthouse Case

Next to national defense, the lighthouse is the most commonly cited example of a public good. Once a lighthouse is constructed and is in operation, the beacon it provides is available to guide all passing ships. The fact that one ship realizes a navigational advantage from the lighthouse does not reduce the advantage the lighthouse provides to other ships. In addition, because it would be difficult to exclude nonpayers from taking advantage of a lighthouse once it is made available, it is commonly believed that it would be unprofitable for a private firm to go into the lighthouse business.

But any time the value of a service exceeds the cost of providing it, we should not be surprised to find private firms searching for a way to capture enough of that value to make a profit. And this is exactly what happened to

to a peace-keeping organization like the UN, regardless of the contributions of other nations. Of course, in the absence of adequate contributions by the less developed countries, the quantity of peace-keeping activities will be suboptimal. Certainly, this analysis is consistent with complaints that countries like the United States contribute a disproportionate share to maintain the UN and that too little is allocated to efforts to promote international harmony.[5]

Thus, we have seen that when a relatively small number of people are involved, a positive quantity of a public good will probably be provided, either through a negotiated agreement or the unilateral actions of at least one party. However, as the number of people involved increases, the chances that an agreement will be reached decreases. This is because as more people become involved, each individual's contribution becomes less and less significant, and the chance that a failure to contribute will be noticed and criticized by others correspondingly decreases. This obviously increases the difficulty of arriving at a broad agreement obligating everyone to contribute. Also, when the group is large, each person's share of the total benefits will be small, and it is very unlikely that one individual will find it advantageous to acquire any of the public good without some assurance that others will also contribute. This produces a rather paradoxical situation: When more people will benefit from a public good, it is less likely that any of that good will be provided in response to individual demands.

We will return to the classic example of a public good—national defense—here, because it illustrates our point well. It is difficult to imagine an entrepreneur providing national defense to a large country in response to individual demands. Although everyone may be willing to contribute to national defense rather than do without it, people know that individual contributions will not

[5]This example is borrowed from M. Olson, *The Logic of Collective Action*, rev. ed. (New York: Schocken Books, 1971), pp. 35–36. It provides an example of what Olson refers to as the "exploitation of the strong by the weak."

the lighthouse. Private individuals constructed and operated lighthouses along the English coast during the seventeenth, eighteenth, and nineteenth centuries. Ships paid lighthouse tolls in ports, and these tolls were collected by lighthouse agents, some of whom represented several lighthouses. A ship's toll depended on its size and how many lighthouses it passed. These charges were cataloged in published books, which listed the lighthouses passed and the fees imposed for different voyages. In 1820, 22 of the 46 lighthouses operating in England were operated by private individuals or organizations, and 34 of the 46 lighthouses had been constructed by private individuals. Private profit had motivated the private supply of a public good.*

*For more on this example, see Ronald Coase, "The Lighthouse in Economics," *The Journal of Law and Economics* (October 1974), pp. 357–76.

measurably frighten a foreign enemy and that they will be protected against foreign aggressors by the contributions of others whether they chip in or not. Therefore, a private supplier of national defense would not find enough consumers who would voluntarily pay for this service to remain in business, no matter how valuable the service of national defense is relative to its cost. For this reason, many public goods like national defense and flood protection are provided by the government and financed by taxes, which—as we all know—are involuntary payments.

Providing Public Goods Through Collective Action

The desire of large groups to obtain certain public goods and the lack of incentive to acquire these goods through individual action provides a rationale for acquiring public goods through government or collective action. The government can enable individuals to obligate not only themselves but everyone else in the community to a given course of action.[6] It is difficult to motivate people to support the provision of a public good individually when each person knows that his or her support—or lack of support—will have no influence on the behavior of others. The political process provides a motivation for individuals to agree, through voting, to contribute toward a public good, since this agreement, if widely enough shared, obligates the rest of the community to contribute.

The political process not only provides a means of motivating individuals to incur obligations that will benefit the overall community. Ideally, it also gener-

---

[6]There are obvious and necessary restrictions on the use of this coercive power that are reflected in the voting rules and the procedures of representative democracy. For an economic analysis of different voting rules and different forms of political representation, see J.M. Buchanan and G. Tullock, *The Calculus of Consent* (Ann Arbor: University of Michigan Press, 1962); and A. Downs, *An Economic Analysis of Democracy* (New York: Harper & Row, 1957). In Chapter 14, we will examine the economic analysis of political decision making in some detail.

ates accurate information about the preferences of individuals for public goods. We do not simply want the government to supply desirable public goods; we want the government to supply these goods at near optimal levels. As we saw earlier in this section, to choose the optimal or efficient quantity of a public good, we must acquire information about individual demands for the good. The problems involved in the political determination of how much of a public good to provide are worth considering here—not only to better understand the workings of the political process, but also to draw a useful comparison between this process and the market process.

We will now consider an example in which it is easy to determine what quantity of a public good to provide. In Figure 13–4, four individual demand curves for a public good—D_1D, D_2D, D_3D, and D_4D—represent the demands of individuals 1, 2, 3, and 4, respectively. Assuming that four individuals comprise the entire community, the vertical summation of these four demand curves DD is the community demand curve for the public good. Given a marginal cost of $\overline{MC}$, the efficient quantity of the good is Q^*.

If this public good is provided through government action, the good will be paid for with revenues obtained from taxing the four individuals. Given his or her demand curve, the quantity of the good that each individual desires will depend on how much an increase in the quantity provided will cost the individ-

Figure 13–4
Everyone Wishes to Obtain the Same Quantity
of a Public Good

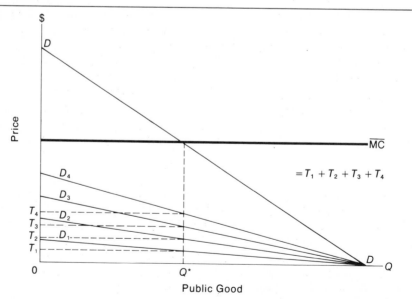

ual in additional taxes. In other words, each individual is concerned with his or her personal marginal tax-cost of the public good. We will assume that the tax structure is such that T_1, T_2, T_3, and T_4, respectively, in Figure 13−4 represent the marginal tax-cost of the good to individuals 1, 2, 3, and 4. If this is the case, we can see that the value each individual places on the marginal unit of the good exceeds the marginal tax-cost until Q^* units are provided. Therefore, each individual will wish to obtain the efficient quantity of the good, and the task of determining how much of the good to provide will be uncontroversial. Generally stated, this indicates that it is desirable to pay for a governmentally provided public good with a tax that imposes a marginal cost on each individual that is equal to the marginal value received from the good at its efficient level of output.

The problems of implementing such a regulation are by no means insignificant. Obtaining accurate information about each individual's preferences is a particularly difficult task. If people believe that their share of the tax needed to finance the public good will be based on their demand for that good, then each individual will find it profitable to understate his or her desire for the good to lower the tax bill. The lower tax is a gain that is captured solely by the individual, whereas the loss in terms of less of the public good being provided will be spread over everyone in the community.

It is worth noting that when faced with the purchase of a private good, a consumer gains nothing from distorting his or her preferences. Given the supply conditions for a private good, its price will be established by the cumulative demands of numerous consumers, and the consumption decision of any one person will have no significant influence on this price. The decision each individual must make is how much of the private good to purchase at the market price. Since a consumer will not benefit from the units that other consumers purchase, each individual will find it advantageous to buy the good as long as its marginal value exceeds its price. Under these conditions, individuals would realize no advantage from pretending to receive less benefit from the good than they actually do.

In this regard, we can observe a very important difference between providing a good through the political process and supplying it through markets. Self-interest dictates that individuals openly reveal their preferences for goods by deciding what quantities of the goods being provided in private markets they will purchase. Without this information about individual preferences, there would be only the remotest hope that efficient quantities of goods would be made available. And because preferences for goods provided through the political process are generally not honestly revealed, there is reason to be less than optimistic that this process will result in the production of optimal quantities. In part, this problem results from the fact that many of the goods made available through the government are public goods. Yet, as we will see in the next section, the provision of private goods through the political process can produce problems that would not be encountered if their supply was confined to private markets.

The Controversy Over Public Goods

Because it is so difficult to determine individual preferences for a public good, we do not expect the marginal tax-cost of a public good to be distributed in such a way that everyone will wish to consume the same quantity of the good. Such factors as income level and the value of property holdings determine the amount that individuals pay in taxes to support a public good—not how much they happen to value that good. An implication of this fact is that there will be little, if any, agreement about what quantity of a public good to provide.

This point is illustrated in Figure 13–5, where D_1D_1 and D_2D_2 represent the respective demands of individuals 1 and 2 for a public good—mosquito control— in a simple two-person community. The vertical summation of these two demand curves provides the community demand DD_2, so that given the marginal cost of $\overline{MC}$, Q^* is the optimal quantity of mosquito control. But Q^* is not the level of mosquito control desired by either individual 1 or 2. Individual 1 exhibits a relatively small demand for this control, possibly because he is an avid indoorsman or because his body fragrance cannot be penetrated by even the most insensitive mosquito. However, individual 2's demand for mosquito control is strong, possibly because she is fond of outdoor activities or because she has a painful reaction to mosquito bites. Despite 1's lower demand for control, he may earn a higher taxable income and therefore pay more for mosquito control than individual 2 does. In Figure 13–5, the marginal tax-cost for individual 1 is T_1,

Figure 13–5
Controversy Over the Quantity of a Public Good
to Be Provided

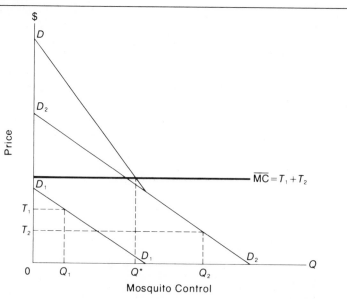

and the marginal tax-cost for individual 2 is T_2. The marginal value of mosquito abatement to individual 1 exceeds his marginal cost only up to level Q_1. Consequently, Q_1 is all the mosquito control that individual 1 will want. On the other hand, individual 2 desires a control level of Q_2.

Unfortunately, only one level of mosquito control can be selected, and both individuals must benefit from and pay for the chosen level. Given the tax structure, there is no way to reach a decision that will be agreeable to both parties, and controversy will certainly be evident during the political process required to determine how much mosquito abatement to provide. This controversy will probably be intensified by the fact that both individuals will be motivated to distort their preferences. We have already seen that the individual can create a tax advantage by understating his or her demand for a public good when marginal tax-cost is based on this demand. In the case we are considering now, however, where marginal tax-cost is fixed independently of preferences, some people will be motivated to exaggerate their desire for the good. For example, individual 2 will realize that if preferences are accurately assessed, Q^* units of control will be provided, which is less control than she desires. Therefore, if individual 2 can convince political decision makers that her demand is greater than it actually is, she may obtain more than Q^* control and improve her personal well-being. Of course, individual 1 will feel that it is in his interest to understate any benefit he receives from mosquito control, hoping to convince the government to provide less than Q^*.[7]

We have seen here that participants in the political process tend to exaggerate their differences to gain an advantage. The polarization of opinion and controversy that results arises from the very nature of public goods and is a commonly observed aspect of the political process.

It is therefore not surprising that one of the best examples of a public good—national defense—is also a very controversial good. Everyone in the country must pay for and consume about the same quantity and quality of national defense, even though we hold differing opinions as to its importance. Many people believe that our national security is in grave jeopardy and feel strongly that the government should expand national defense expenditures. Others feel just as strongly that current levels of military spending pose a threat to world peace and that the threat of war would be reduced if the government spent less on national defense. It is hard to imagine how this controversy, as well as the strife surrounding the provision of other public goods, could be eliminated. Unfortunately for domestic peace and harmony, as long as public goods must be provided to people who have different opinions about the worth of these goods, controversy will continue to be a visible feature of the political process.

A major advantage in dealing with private goods is that diverse preferences

---

[7]We are justified in asking what claim Q^* has to optimality when no one in the community personally views it as the desirable quantity. The answer is that Q^* is the only output level that both individuals could desire and still collectively pay the tax required to cover the cost of the good. This will always be true of the efficient or optimal quantity. For this agreement to occur, of course, each individual's marginal tax-cost must equal his or her marginal value at Q^*.

for them can be accommodated without controversy and polarization, simply because one consumer can choose a consumption level for a private good that is independent of the consumption choices made by other consumers. It is possible to negate this advantage, however, by providing private goods through the political decision-making process as if they were public goods. For example, imagine what would happen if a community decides that the determination of a proper diet is simply too important to be left up to each individual. Instead, the "best" diet is to be politically determined (fully considering the advice of dietary experts, of course) and then made available to everyone at the taxpayers' expense. It is hard to imagine a better prescription for encouraging community strife and generating ill will. Before this "progressive" policy is instituted, the individual who liked to fill up quickly at a fast-food restaurant could exercise this preference without interfering with the gourmet who lives down the block. By eliminating this consumption independence, however, the new policy makes it impossible for one individual to pay for the diet he or she desires without denying someone else this advantage. Friends have been turned into adversaries, and another barrier has been erected in the path of social tranquility.

13–3 Externalities

Externalities and Inefficiencies

Every time you consume a good or a service, you are imposing a cost on those who have devoted their resources and efforts to make the product available to you. In many cases, this cost is entirely reflected in the price you pay for the good or service, and it is to your advantage to consume the item only if you feel it is worth at least as much as it cost you. When you go to a restaurant, for example, you impose a cost on the owner, who has to pay for the food you eat and the people who prepare and serve it. When you are deciding whether or not to go out to eat, you take this cost into consideration because you know it will be reflected in the bill. You will decide to go to the restaurant only if you feel that the value you will receive from dining out will exceed the cost.

However, people sometimes engage in activities that do not require them to compensate those who bear the costs imposed by these activities. Suppose, for example, that you enjoy listening to your favorite hard-rock recording at a decibel level, which borders on inflicting pain. If the people who live next door delight in the softer sounds of Beethoven and Bach and hate hard rock, then your consumption of music is imposing a cost that you do not have to consider when you are deciding how much rock music to consume. The cost is external to your decision-making process and is referred to as an *external cost* or a *negative externality*. Of course, not all externalities impose costs; some convey benefits. If your neighbors also enjoy listening to hard rock at the same decibel level you enjoy, then your consumption of rock music will generate a positive externality. In this case, you will be providing a benefit for which you are not compensated.

When externalities exist, individuals usually do not have enough information about the costs and benefits of their consumption decisions to know the socially efficient or optimal consumption rate (the rate that equates social marginal costs with social marginal benefits). Even having complete cost-benefit information would provide individuals with little motivation to weigh external costs or benefits the same as they weigh the costs and benefits that have a direct personal impact on themselves. Therefore, if all the benefits from an activity are internal or private (completely accrued by those engaged in the activity) but some of the costs of the activity are external, we would expect the activity to be pursued beyond the socially efficient point. Conversely, when all the costs of an activity are internal but the activity generates benefits that are external to those engaged in it, in general we would expect there be too little participation in the activity. In this regard, the connection between a positive externality and a public good is quite direct. We have seen that a public good will tend to be undersupplied and underconsumed, because once it is available, people can receive its benefits whether or not they compensate those who provided it. In other words, those who purchase a public good for their own consumption will be engaging in an activity that generates a positive externality.

A useful illustration of the inefficiencies that result from externalities can be provided by taking another look at the model of the competitive firm. In Chapter 8, we saw that the competitive firm equates marginal cost to product price in order to maximize its profits. In Chapter 12, we also found that this results in the production of the socially efficient or optimal quantity of the good, since output is expanded to the point where the marginal value society places on the good (the price) is equal to the marginal value society sacrifices to produce the good (the marginal cost). An implicit assumption for this result to be considered efficient, however, is that the entire cost of producing the good is internal to the firm. If this is not the case—if the firm is creating loud noises or polluting a river—then the private marginal cost that the firm takes into consideration will be less than the social marginal cost, and the firm will produce a greater than optimal output. The marginal value society places on the good will then be less than the marginal cost to society.

This result is graphically depicted in Figure 13−6, where the market price is $\bar{P}$ and the private marginal cost function is MC_p. Profit maximization dictates that this competitive firm produce output $\hat{Q}$. However, if part of the production cost is external to the firm, the social marginal cost function will be higher than MC_p at MC_s. (The vertical distance between these two curves represents the marginal external cost.) The firm's efficient output is achieved at the point where the social marginal cost curve MC_s intersects the price level $\bar{P}$, or Q^* in the figure. Due to the negative externality, this firm is producing more than the efficient output.

To analyze the inefficiencies associated with a positive externality, we will return to the model of the monopolistic firm discussed in Chapter 9. Recall that the revenue the monopolist receives from selling the marginal unit is less than the product price. Since the price reflects the value of the marginal unit, this means that the monopolistic firm is not capturing the total value it is pro-

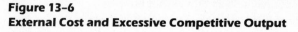

Figure 13–6
External Cost and Excessive Competitive Output

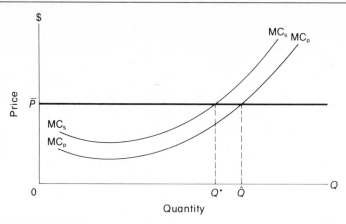

viding by producing an additional unit of its product. More concisely, the monopolist is generating a positive externality. This positive externality provides another explanation for the suboptimal output that we expect from the monopolist. This result is illustrated in Figure 13–7, where *DD* is the monopolist's demand curve, MR is the marginal revenue curve, and MC_p is the monopolist's private marginal cost curve. The profit-maximizing monopolist will operate at output $\hat{Q}$, where marginal revenue MR is equal to private marginal cost MC_p. Ideally, however, the monopolist should expand output until demand curve *DD*, which represents the marginal value of the product, intersects the private marginal cost curve MC_p (assuming for the moment that there are no negative externalities). Price is equal to private marginal cost at output rate Q^*, which exceeds $\hat{Q}$, and the monopolist is therefore producing at a suboptimal output rate at $\hat{Q}$.

The monopolistic firm is not necessarily confined to the generation of a positive externality. Its activities may produce negative externalities as well. For example, a monopolistic firm may emit smoke, create loud noises, or simply look unlovely, thereby imposing uncompensated costs on others. As we have seen, the existence of these negative externalities will motivate the firm to produce quantities in excess of the optimal output rate, which will offset the influence of the positive externality to some extent. If MC_p represents the private marginal cost of a monopolistic firm that is generating an external cost, then the social marginal cost curve MC_s will lie above the MC_p curve, as shown in Figure 13–7, and the monopolist's socially efficient output rate is now Q^{**}. We can expect the firm to ignore the external cost, however, and continue to maximize its profits by equating private marginal cost MC_p with marginal revenue MR and producing $\hat{Q}$ units of output. We have constructed the graph Figure 13–7 so that the influence of the negative externality does not entirely offset

Figure 13-7
The Monopolist as a Generator of Externalities

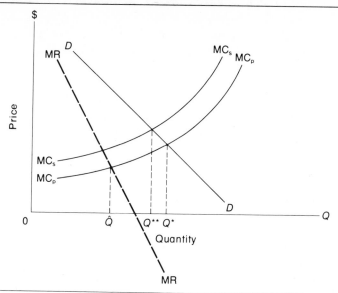

the influence of the positive externality, and therefore the monopolist's profit-maximizing output $\hat{Q}$ is still less than the efficient output Q^{**}. However, a sufficiently large external cost will raise the social marginal cost curve high enough so that the efficient output rate will fall below $\hat{Q}$. When an activity produces both positive and negative externalities, we cannot determine *a priori* whether the firm will engage in too much or too little of the activity.

There Are Externalities and There Are Externalities

We have just seen that when externalities exist, individual decision making does not necessarily lead to socially optimal choices. It is also true that most activities impose some external benefits or costs (although, in many cases, these are slight). Someone can be expected to receive a benefit as a result of someone else smiling, applying an adequate amount of deodorant, having a face lift, wearing a pretty dress, allowing the aroma of freshly brewed coffee to drift through a kitchen window, landscaping a yard, or asking an intelligent question in class. Conversely, negative externalities can be generated by many activities, such as frowning, forgetting to brush after every meal, taking your dog out for a walk, lighting a cigarette, and snoring in class.

Although it may be theoretically possible in each of the examples cited here to engage in some type of collective action that would modify people's behavior in a socially efficient direction, the cost of doing this would probably exceed the benefits we would derive. The real world is full of imperfections, and in many cases, it is wise simply to accept them. This is certainly true of many of the imperfections that result from the existence of externalities.

Unfortunately, some of the consequences of externalities are too important to be ignored. The benefits provided by an education can be cited as an example of an externality that is considered too positive to ignore. It has long been argued that when an individual receives an education, many of the benefits are accrued not only by that individual but also by everyone in society. It cannot be denied that when an individual becomes more productive, is capable of making more informed political decisions, and improves social skills as a result of education, many other people benefit from that education. Since this is true, it can

Example 13-2

Eliminating Externalities Through Business Arrangements

Many business activities require a team effort. The profits from such an activity depend on everyone's contribution to a common objective. In these situations, every individual is tempted to reduce his or her contribution, since the advantage derived from doing this will be captured entirely by the individual but the cost will be spread over everyone in the organization. In other words, the cost of reduced effort is largely an external cost. Of course, all participants will be worse off if everyone neglects their responsibilities than they will be if each individual performs diligently. Therefore, we would expect people entering into a business arrangement to attempt to reduce the possibility that the negligence of some will impose a cost on others.

An example of this can be found in franchise agreements. A franchise agreement is a contract between two parties—the franchiser and the franchisee. The franchiser is the firm that has control over the product, and the franchisee is a firm that makes this product available in a particular area. Your neighborhood McDonald's is an example of a local business (the franchisee) that has entered into a franchise agreement with the parent firm, the McDonald's Corporation (the franchiser). Almost all franchise agreements require that the franchisee pay some specified percentage of sales to the franchiser and that the franchisee must purchase productive inputs from either the franchiser or a supplier approved by the franchiser. It is commonly believed that these requirements are designed to allow the franchiser to take advantage of the franchisee. For example, it would appear that the restriction on input supply places the franchiser in a monopoly position with respect to the franchisee. But there are reasons to believe that these requirements are part of the franchise agreement because they reduce external costs and are therefore beneficial to both parties.

When an individual enters into a franchise agreement with, for example, the McDonald's Corporation, he or she is doing more than investing in a be argued that an individual, when faced with the entire expense of obtaining an education, will ignore some of the benefits of pursuing an education and will tend to purchase too little education when judged from a broader, social perspective. This argument provides the justification for subsidizing an individual's education from taxes levied against the community at large.

There are also externalities that are too disruptive and costly to be ignored. Unabated automobile exhaust, sulfur-dioxide emissions from the smokestacks of an electric power plant, and untreated waste discharged into a river are all too familiar examples. All of these negative externalities can be grouped under the general heading of *environmental pollution*—a topic that requires the application of economic analysis to be adequately understood. The concepts

hamburger joint. The franchisee is investing in the McDonald's trademark. This trademark is valuable because it provides information to hungry people. If you are on the road and getting hungry, you might be able to find a better hamburger for the money than McDonald's offers, but you would probably spend a lot of time and trouble in the attempt. You pull into McDonald's because you feel confident that the golden arches indicate the availability of hamburgers and fries of consistent quality. In other words, the owner of one McDonald's gets more business because the owners of other McDonald's serve quality food. But this presents each McDonald's owner with the opportunity to cut expenses by reducing the quality of his or her food a little and spread the cost, in terms of reduced business, over all McDonald's owners. Since a reduction in quality generates an external cost, business will decline and all franchisees as well as the franchiser will suffer. Obviously, any arrangement that reduces the external cost associated with food-quality decisions will increase the value of a McDonald's franchise.

Now we can understand the advantage of the requirements of a franchise agreement mentioned earlier in this example. Because the franchiser receives some percentage of the sales from each franchisee, he or she has an interest in maintaining the sales of *all* franchisees—not just one. Therefore, by letting the franchiser determine the quality of the product by exercising control over inputs, the external cost associated with a decline in product quality is greatly reduced. If the franchiser allows product quality to decline at one franchise, he or she will incur a cost in the terms of the reduced sales at all franchises. Such a quality-control arrangement, which internalizes an important cost, benefits all franchisees by protecting their sales against the irresponsible actions of others and thereby increasing the value of their franchisees.*

*For a more complete discussion of franchise agreements, see Paul Rubin, "The Theory of the Firm and the Structure of the Franchise Contract," *The Journal of Law and Economics* (April 1978), pp. 223–33.

of public goods and externalities are particularly applicable to the question of why pollution has become a problem and to the evaluation of alternative responses to this problem. But before we apply the theory to an analysis of environmental pollution, it will be useful to consider the importance of property rights in the efficient allocation of resources.

13–4 Property Rights

When private property rights are well-defined and easily enforced, there is little or no need to be concerned about the inefficiencies caused by externalities. If you own a house, for example, the rights and obligations associated with this ownership are well-defined. Ownership entitles you to use the house in a lawful manner for your benefit. In addition, you have control over the use that others make of your house. No one else can legally use the house you own without your permission. But ownership also imposes certain obligations. As the owner, you must bear the cost of the house. This cost is the value of the house in its best alternative use. If you paid for the house, its cost is obvious, because you must have paid at least as much as other buyers were willing to pay or your offer would not have been accepted. But the cost of ownership is the same even if the house has been given to you. By using the house yourself, you are sacrificing the amount of money that someone else would be willing to pay for it. Because you own the property rights to the house, you receive its benefits and bear its costs, which provides you with a strong motivation to put the house to its best use. You will keep the house only as long as you feel it is worth more to you than others are willing to pay. But if someone else believes that your house is worth more than the value you attach to it, you will be willing to sell it to him or her.

Transaction Costs, Property Rights, and Efficiency

Of course, privately owned resources are not always put to their most valuable uses. Even if someone values your house more than you do, several other conditions must be met before an exchange can take place. First, the two of you must identify each other as potential trading partners and get together. Second, you must negotiate the price and other terms of the exchange. Finally, you must devise some mechanism for enforcing the terms of the agreement. Satisfying the requirements for a transaction can be costly. Valuable resources have to be expended to locate potential trading partners, negotiate with them, and enforce the agreement. Economists refer to these costs as **transaction costs,** and when they are higher than the gains to be realized from an exchange, no exchange will occur. For example, people may leave their home for several weeks while they are away on vacation. While they are gone, they can receive less value from the use of their house than others can, and if the transaction costs were 0, they would rent the house to someone else for the duration of their vacation. This does not happen because the transaction costs are greater than the gains from the exchange (renting the house). When people are going to be gone for several months or more, however, the gains from renting their homes exceed the transaction costs, and houses are not left unoccupied for long periods of time. Any activity that lowers transaction costs will increase the number of exchanges that move resources into higher-valued uses and is therefore a productive activity. As we discussed in Chapter 5, middlemen perform a valuable service because their activities lower transaction costs and facilitate exchange.

Because positive transaction costs can prevent desirable exchanges from taking place, the assignment of property rights can be an important factor in the attempt to achieve efficiency. For example, who should be assigned the property right to proceed at a railroad crossing when a conflict arises—train or automobile traffic? Since it would be very costly for people riding in an automobile to negotiate an exchange with the people on an incoming train, there is little chance that the right to proceed will be subject to trade once it is assigned. It is therefore desirable to assign this right to the party to whom it is most valuable, or the party who would end up with the right if the transaction costs were 0. Since it is much more expensive to stop and start a train than an automobile, it is plausible to assume that in most cases the right to proceed at railroad crossings is more valuable when it is assigned to trains. And, of course, this procedure is commonplace.

It should be emphasized that in the absence of transaction costs, it would make no difference how property rights were assigned. If automobiles had the right to proceed at railroad crossings and there were no transaction costs, a train would simply purchase the right to proceed as long as this right was worth more to the train than to the car. For example, if the people in the car collectively valued the right to continue nonstop through the crossing at $2 and the people on the train collectively valued the right to proceed at $20, the train would purchase the right by offering the car between $2 and $20 for it. There would be no haggling or holding out for a higher price on the part of the car, because that would constitute a transaction cost—something we have assumed away. Of course, if the property right had been assigned to the train, the train would retain this right, since the car would not be willing to offer as much to obtain it as the right to proceed would be worth to the train. This result—that efficiency will always be realized in the absence of transaction costs, no matter how property rights are assigned—is known as the **Coase Theorem,** after economist Ronald Coase.[8]

A useful way to consider the Coase Theorem is to recognize that there can be no external costs or benefits in the absence of transaction costs. If you are engaged in an activity, such as playing your stereo at a high volume, that imposes a cost on your neighbors, they will be willing to pay you to turn your stereo

---

[8]The importance of transaction costs and property right assignments in the promotion of efficient exchanges is developed in Ronald Coase, "The Problem of Social Cost," *The Journal of Law and Economics* (October 1960), pp. 1–45.

Example 13–3

Establishing Property Rights

Defining and enforcing property rights is not costless. It requires the use of resources that could be productively used elsewhere. It is therefore not always efficient to establish property rights to a resource. Although property rights would promote the more valuable use of the resource, this gain could be more than offset by the cost of enforcing these property rights. We can weigh the interesting implications that this suggests against what we observe in the real world. For example, if a common property resource becomes more valuable, the motivation to establish property rights to this resource should increase. We would also expect property rights to be extended if the costs of enforcing them diminishes. History provides interesting accounts of both occurrences.

Throughout the seventeenth century, the Montagnes Indians lived in a large region near Quebec, Canada, hunting fur-bearing animals for food and keeping an occasional fur pelt for personal use. During this period, there was no attempt to assign property rights to these animals. This provided hunters with little motivation to consider the effect that their hunting had on others, but since the demand for fur-bearing animals was limited relative to their availability, this externality did not cause significant problems. However, at the beginning of the eighteenth century, traders arrived in the area who were willing to pay attractive prices for furs. This immediately increased the value of the fur-bearing animals and resulted in more extensive hunting. At this point, the hunting externalities became significant, which greatly increased the advantages to be realized from establishing property rights to the animals. Because the valuable fur-bearing animals confined their wanderings to relatively small distances, the costs of establishing effective property rights were low. It was therefore efficient to

down if there are no transaction costs. If quiet is worth more to them than the loud music is worth to you, your neighbors will offer you enough money to make you willing to reduce the volume. If not, you will keep the volume turned up.[9] But notice that even if you do keep the volume turned up, the cost you are imposing on others is no longer external to you. Free exchange serves to *internalize* externalities. By continuing to play loud music, you are sacrificing an amount equal to the cost being imposed on your neighbors–the amount they would pay you if you turned the volume down. Similarly, in the absence of transaction costs, there would be no external benefits. You could deny individuals the benefits they would receive if you turned down your music unless they

---

[9] Of course, many people in the surrounding area would undoubtedly be willing to pay for the privilege of not listening to your music. With no transaction costs, these people could costlessly get together, and each would be willing to pay what peace and quiet is worth; there would be no free-riders.

establish these rights, and that is exactly what the Indians did. Hunting land was divided into areas, usually about two leagues square, and a particular family was assigned the exclusive hunting rights to each area.*

There are also historical examples of the establishment of property rights in response to a reduction in the cost of enforcing them. One can be drawn from the American West during the last century. Due to the scarcity of precipitation over large areas of the Great Plains, grazing livestock was the most valuable use of much of the land. However, a large area was required to support each animal, the livestock roamed widely, and it was difficult for ranchers to control their herds. Property rights to livestock were not completely absent, of course. Cattle were branded, and harsh penalties were imposed on those who ignored or altered these brands. Enforcement was difficult, but even if enforcement had been absolute, the property rights provided by branding were incomplete. Although brands enabled owners to identify their cattle during a roundup, there was insufficient control to provide special food and to breed their animals selectively. But it suddenly became much cheaper to extend property rights to livestock in 1874 when barbed wire was introduced and the cost of fencing large areas of land declined dramatically. In 1874, 10,000 pounds of barbed wire were sold; by 1880, over 80,500,000 pounds were sold. As fencing expanded rapidly, the response was the establishment of more complete property rights to livestock and the beginning of livestock management in the West.†

*This example is borrowed from Harold Demsetz, "Toward a Theory of Property Rights," *American Economic Review* (May 1967), pp. 347–59.
†For a more complete account of property rights in the American West, see Terry Anderson and J.P. Hill, "The Evolution of Property Rights: A Study of the American West," *The Journal of Law and Economics* (April 1975), pp. 163–79.

compensated you for your efforts. Not surprisingly, when there are no transaction costs, efficiency will always prevail no matter how property rights are assigned.

When Property Rights Do Not Exist

But transaction costs are never 0. In some cases, in fact, property rights cannot be effectively enforced because transaction costs are prohibitive. When this is the case, productive exchanges do not take place, and resources are not directed to their most valuable employments, thereby creating negative externalities. An example of a resource for which the transaction costs are prohibitive is the air. It would make little sense to talk about property rights to the atmosphere.[10] It

[10]Although, as we will see in the following applications, some moves can be usefully made in this direction.

would mean nothing if someone claimed ownership over the air that surrounded them, since there would be no way for them to exercise control over their "property." Because individuals cannot enforce an agreement that prevents others from using their air without compensation for the cost imposed, no exchanges will put air to its most valuable uses and exclude its less valuable uses. Another way to state this is to say that those who use the air as a waste-sink for polluting activities (which includes all of us) are imposing negative externalities on others, and excessive air pollution will result.

We can think of other examples of negative externalities that lead to the excessive use of resources because property rights to these resources cannot be established. It is difficult, for example, to enforce property rights to water contained in large lakes, rivers, and oceans. The result is excessive water pollution. In an application in Chapter 12, we discussed the excessive slaughter of the Blue Whale. Because it is difficult, if not impossible, to enforce property rights to Blue Whales, there is little to motivate individuals to refrain from harpooning as many as possible, because much of the cost of killing another Blue Whale is an external cost. The near extermination of the American buffalo and many species of African wildlife can also be explained in terms of inadequate property rights. Resources such as our atmosphere, our waterways, and our wildlife, which are not subject to well-defined property rights, are referred to as **common property resources.** In the absence of property rights, it is not surprising that these resources are exploited.

Inadequate property rights can also serve to explain the existence of positive externalities. When an individual plants and cultivates a beautiful garden, he or she often has less than complete control over who enjoys the result of this personal effort. Because the property right to the garden is incomplete, the gardener cannot charge those who benefit from looking at the garden, and he or she generates a positive externality. Similarly, the problems associated with public goods can be explained in terms of incomplete property rights. If an individual who provides a public good could selectively deny others the benefit it generates, then consumers of the good could no longer be free-riders.[11] The problems associated with public goods arise because those who provide public goods cannot effectively enforce the property rights to the benefits that these goods generate.

Substantial expenses are frequently incurred to reduce transaction costs and thereby improve the enforcement of property rights. For example, building a wall around a football field or a beautiful garden and controlling entry through a

---

[11]It has been argued that even if you could selectively deny individuals the use of a public good unless they paid for it, the efficient price should be zero. Once a public good is provided, according to this argument, the additional consumption of one individual imposes no cost on anyone else. Therefore, any positive price will discourage consumption that is available at no marginal cost, which is inefficient. But recall that in Section 13-2 it was argued that efficiency would be achieved if each consumer had to pay a marginal price (tax) equal to the marginal value he or she received from the good when the optimal output level was produced. While reconciling this apparent conflict is beyond the scope of this chapter, the interested student is referred to Dwight R. Lee, "A Note on the Optimal Pricing of Public Goods," *Public Finance Quarterly* (October 1978), pp. 503–11.

few gates makes it easy to identify and charge those who will benefit from the good being provided. The same function is also served by checkout counters at the supermarket and the campus bookstore. It is costly for business to construct such barriers and costly for consumers to wait in lines to pass through them. But because they help to enforce property rights, these barriers are worth more than they cost.

Application: Environmental Pollution

Concern over the quality of the environment has become a major political and economic issue in recent years. As we will soon see, this concern is not misplaced and reflects serious inefficiencies in the methods we employ to allocate some of our important environmental resources.

Environmental Quality as an Economic Good

Why our environmental resources are important requires little explanation. Air is rather nice to have around for breathing. Those of us who live in Los Angeles and Denver occasionally consider how nice it would be to have air that you could see through. Water is, of course, useful for drinking, bathing, swimming, boating, fishing, ice skating, and other recreational activities. And most of us still enjoy the aesthetic appeal of an unspoiled natural landscape. However, if we made a list of all the important uses of our air, water, and land, it would be grossly incomplete if it did not mention the importance of the environment as a waste-sink. The ability of the environment to assimilate and disperse waste products is just as essential to the maintenance of life as its ability to provide us with oxygen and water. Every activity we engage in—from breathing in and out to producing steel—generates by-products that have to be discharged into the environment.

Unfortunately, the absorptive capacity of the environment is limited. If we rely as much as we wish on the environment to absorb our waste products, we will have to sacrifice some of the amenities that clean air, unpolluted water, and unspoiled landscape provide. Conversely, we can reduce pollution and increase environmental quality only by sacrificing valuable alternatives. For example, the U.S. Department of Agriculture has estimated that if pollution from pesticides was eliminated by banning the use of insecticides, U.S. crop and livestock yields would be reduced 25–30%. Attacking air pollution by making automobile-emission standards more stringent can reduce fuel efficiency. Poisonous sulfur dioxide in the atmosphere can be reduced by converting from coal production in the eastern United States to coal production in the West, but only by increasing the use of strip mining—an activity that can scar large expanses of our landscape.

Without continuing our list of the trade-offs that exist between environmental quality and other desirable alternatives, we should be able to recognize that we face some tough choices. Obviously, we all want to live in a cleaner environment. But at the same time, we want warm homes, good food, convenient and safe transportation, modern medicine, fast-acting detergents, fashionable clothing, and many other creature comforts. And we cannot have more of one of these desirable things without giving up some of the others. It is simply not very useful to argue that environmental quality is good, so let's have more of it. This ignores the really interesting and relevant problem of choosing an acceptable combination of all desirable goods while recognizing that environmental quality is much like any other economic good—it is highly desirable, but it is not free.

The Optimal Level of Pollution

This raises an important question: What is the desirable quantity of environmental quality? Another way of phrasing this question is to ask: How much environmental quality are we willing to sacrifice by engaging in polluting activities? As offensive as this may seem to some, we are suggesting that the optimal level of pollution is positive.

To illustrate the underlying concept of the optimal level of pollution, we construct the marginal benefit and the marginal cost curves for pollution, as shown in Figure 13–8. The MB curve represents the value of the benefits that result from increasing pollution an additional unit. The first few units of pollution provide enormous benefits to the polluter. Just go around for a few hours without polluting and then see what an enormous benefit you receive from the first little bit of polluting you do. But as more and more pollution occurs, the advantage of being able to pollute an additional unit can be expected to diminish, as is reflected in the negative slope of the MB curve. Of course, pollution imposes

Figure 13–8
The Optimal Level of Pollution

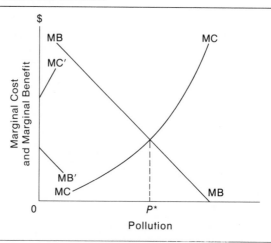

a cost in terms of sacrificed environmental quality, and the MC curve in Figure 13-8 represents the marginal cost of pollution. At low levels of pollution, the cost associated with another unit of pollution will generally be small. However, as pollution increases, the damage caused by polluting an additional unit also increases. For example, at very low concentrations, a small increase in carbon monoxide will produce no noticeable effect. But at sufficiently high levels, an increase can mean the difference between a severe headache and death. Therefore, the MC curve is constructed with a positive slope.

As the marginal benefit and marginal cost curves are constructed in Figure 13-8, the optimal level of pollution is given by P^*. At pollution levels less than P^*, the benefits gained from polluting an additional unit are more valuable than the benefits sacrificed, and a net gain results from expanding polluting activities. Exactly the opposite is true if pollution levels are greater than P^*, and a net gain results from reducing polluting activities.

The optimal level of pollution P^* in the figure is positive. This is undoubtedly the case for most, if not all, types of pollution. However, it is certainly possible for the optimal level of some types of pollution to be 0. This would be the case if the marginal costs of the very first unit of this pollution exceeded its marginal benefits. This situation is represented in Figure 13-8 by the marginal benefit and marginal cost curves MB' and MC', respectively. The waste from plutonium and other types of radioactive material would be examples of this type of pollution. An implicit assumption in the policy to ban the use of DDT is that the marginal cost of discharging the first unit of DDT into the environment is greater than the marginal benefit of doing so.

It should be pointed out that determining the exact location of the MB and the MC curves for a given type of pollution is no easy task. This is particularly true of the marginal cost curve. The cost of additional pollution is the value that people place on the environmental quality that is sacrificed. But environmental quality can be considered a public good, since once a given level of environmental quality has been provided for one individual, it is equally available to all members of the community. Therefore, it is extremely difficult to determine what value people place on environmental quality for the same reasons that individuals do not openly reveal their preferences for any public good, which we discussed in Section 13-2. And without knowing what value to attach to environmental quality, it is difficult to determine the costs of pollution. Although the concepts of the marginal costs and benefits of pollution are useful in considering the pollution problem, they do not allow us to pinpoint the optimal level of pollution.

Even if we could determine the optimal pollution level, most people would probably not consider this level desirable. Some individuals will receive large marginal benefits from pollution and will attach a low marginal cost to high pollution levels. An individual who works for an electric power plant and who smokes five packs of cigarettes a day is a likely example. The polluting activities of the plant provide him with a good income, and he may think that the thick layer of tar in his lungs is protecting him against air pollution. This individual will desire more pollution than the optimal level P^* in Figure 13-8. Other individuals will consider the marginal benefits from an additional unit of pollution to be very low and the marginal costs to be quite high. For example, a college student who is very aware of environmental pollution and who receives no income from those firms near campus that are large polluters will view P^* as an excessive pollution level.

This leads us to suspect that much controversy surrounds issues dealing with pollution and environmental quality—a suspicion that casual observation will indicate is well-founded. The problem we encounter here is the same one that always arises when a community is determining how much of a public good to provide, and one we have already discussed in Section 13–2. Everyone in a given area consumes about the same amount of environmental quality (or, on the negative side, pollution), although each person attaches different benefits and costs to this good.

The Economic Explanation for Excess Pollution

Thus far, we have established that there is an optimal level of pollution—albeit a controversial one—and that this level will generally be positive. Another question now arises: What reasons do we have to believe that the actual pollution level is greater than the optimal level? We address this question here and conclude that there are compelling reasons for believing that the current pollution level is excessive.

When an individual or a firm wishes to use a resource, it usually must be acquired from someone who owns it. The price that is paid for the resource will tend to reflect its worth in the most valuable alternative use, since the owner will probably not direct a resource into one employment unless the compensation equals or exceeds what could be received from other employments. Since the price reflects the opportunity value of the resource, it will be purchased only by those who feel that the use they will make of it is at least equal to its value in alternative employments. Therefore, the resource tends to be allocated to its most productive and valuable uses.

The assimilative capacity of the environment is an important resource that is not privately owned. The very nature of our waterways and airsheds makes it practically impossible to conceive of dividing up ownership rights to them and then enforcing these rights. Due to this lack of ownership, there are no prices attached to these resources to reflect their value in their most productive employments, and as we discussed in Section 13–4, market exchanges will not direct these environmental resources to their most valuable employments. If people want to use the environment as a waste-sink to produce electricity, refine petroleum, publish a book on environmental decay, or simply drive their car to the supermarket, they use it and it costs them nothing.

Of course, we know that there is a cost associated with discharging waste into the environment that is borne by everyone in the affected area. Therefore, the individual who engages in a polluting activity is creating a negative externality. Recalling our discussion of negative externalities, we know that this means that polluting activities will be engaged in beyond the optimal pollution level.

The bias toward excess pollution is graphically illustrated in Figure 13–9, where again the MB curve represents the marginal benefits of pollution and the MC curve represents the marginal cost of pollution. As these curves are constructed, the optimal level of pollution is P^*. However, when the personal cost that each individual pays for increasing his or her polluting activities is effectively 0, pollution will be expanded until the marginal benefits of pollution are 0. Under these conditions, the pollution level is $\bar{P}$, which is a level clearly in excess of the optimal pollution level P^*. The cost of polluting, being largely external to the polluter, is ignored, whereas the benefits of polluting are fully considered since they are received directly by the polluter. It is not surprising then that pollution is pushed beyond the point where its marginal benefits are equal to its marginal cost.

It is also useful to view the problem of excess pollution as the result of inadequate incentives to engage in pollution abatement activities. If an individual incurs a personal cost by reducing the pollution generated by his or her activities, then that individual will be providing a benefit in the form of a slightly cleaner environment that everyone in the community will receive. The personal benefit to the pollution abater will be only a small percentage of the total benefit to the community. Based on our earlier discussion of public goods, we can see that pollution abatement is the same as the purchase of a public good. From our discussion of externalities, it follows that pollution abatement generates a positive externality. And we know that there is inadequate motivation to purchase public goods or to generate positive externalities.

Figure 13–9
The Bias Toward Excess Pollution

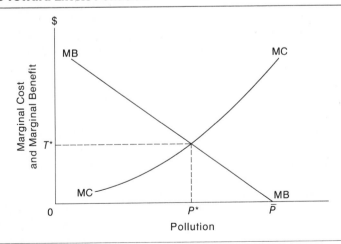

Pricing Pollution

We will now turn our attention to the problem of improving environmental quality by motivating people to reduce pollution below existing levels. The most common response to the question of how to reduce pollution is to suggest that the government impose direct regulations and controls on polluting activities. These controls usually involve having all polluters in a given area reduce pollution by a specified percentage and/or install particular types of pollution abatement devices. However, our discussion of the economic explanation of the pollution problem suggests an alternative approach to environmental management that has some significant advantages over the direct government regulation and control of polluters.

The fact that the environment is overused as a waste-sink because nothing has to be paid for this use suggests that imposing a price on polluting would produce a desirable reduction in pollution. Returning to Figure 13–9, we will assume that a tax of T^* is imposed on each unit of waste that is discharged into the environment. Once this pollution tax is imposed, the marginal cost of polluting to each polluter is T^*, which is greater than the marginal benefit of polluting beyond P^*. Therefore, the pollution tax T^* will motivate a reduction in polluting until the optimal pollution level P^* is reached. Ideally, the tax level should be determined so that the marginal tax is equal to the marginal cost of polluting at P^*. A pollution tax would serve the same function as the establishment of property rights to the absorptive capacity of the environment in that it would require those who use this resource to pay a price that reflects the cost of their use.

Before continuing our discussion of the pollution tax, it should be made clear that this approach to pollution management is not as simple as we might have indicated thus far. Different pollutants will impose different social costs when emitted into the environment. Ideally, a different tax should be levied on each pollutant to reflect its particular cost. Also, the same pollutant discharged in one area will often have a different impact than it will when it is discharged somewhere else. Dumping sewage upstream of a popular swimming and fishing area will impose a greater environmental cost than a downstream discharge. Ideally, a pollution tax should take these differences into consideration. After determining a set of pollution taxes, some mechanism for monitoring the emissions of polluters and levying the appropriate tax would then have to be established.

Obviously, there is no way to achieve a perfect pollution taxation. The tax on a particular pollutant will probably not be set at the precise point that will motivate people to reduce their polluting activities to the socially optimal level. And no matter what tax is levied, it undoubtedly can and will be avoided to some extent. The point to be made here, however, is that analogous problems exist when attempts to reduce pollution are made through direct government regulation and control. Regulators cannot be expected to know exactly what limits to place on each of the different types of pollutants or what abatement device is most appropriate for a particular polluter to use. And once these decisions are made, the problems of monitoring and enforcement still remain.

It seems reasonable to conclude that neither pollution taxation nor direct government regulation and control has a clear administrative advantage and that neither approach will allow us to achieve the optimal level of pollution. It makes sense, therefore, to compare these two approaches to environmental management on the basis of how efficiently a given reduction in pollution is realized. There are strong reasons to support the belief that a given amount of environmental improvement can be achieved more efficiently (at less cost) by employing pollution taxation than it can by instituting and enforcing direct controls and regulation.

The Advantages of Pollution Taxation

Once a pollution tax is imposed, it will motivate the polluter to (1) reduce pollution as cheaply as possible and (2) reduce pollution until the marginal benefit of polluting is equal to the marginal tax.[12] Even when the pollution tax is not set at the optimal level, substantial advantages will be realized from these motivations.

Minimizing the Abatement Costs of Each Polluter   Once it has been decided to reduce pollution by a specified amount, it is obviously desirable to do this as inexpensively as possible. Faced with a pollution tax, it becomes profitable for each polluter to do just that. The pollution tax not only provides polluters with the incentive to reduce their polluting activities at the least possible cost to themselves but also gives them the freedom to do so. This can be a major advantage compared with the common form of direct regulation, which is to rely on the Environmental Protection Agency (EPA) to specify the type of devices that must be used for pollution abatement. In general, as we have already said, the best way of abating a particular pollutant in one situation will not be the best way of abating that pollutant in another situation. The EPA has little detailed information about these relevant differences, however, and it is common for the agency to require that everyone discharging a particular pollutant use one type of abatement procedure. This seldom, if ever, is the least-cost approach to abatement and frequently fails to result in the anticipated pollution reduction.

As an example, in an effort to reduce the sulfur-oxide emissions from coal-fired electric power plants, the EPA is requiring that all of these plants install very expensive stack scrubbers—a device designed to precipitate harmful pollutants out of the smoke discharged by these plants. However, it is cheaper for some power plants located near deposits of low-sulfur coal to reduce their sul-

---

[12]Since costs are the same as forgone benefits, the cost of reducing a unit of pollution is equal to the benefit that would have been derived from the polluting activity if it had not been reduced. Therefore, the marginal benefit MB curve in either Figure 13–8 or 13–9 represents the marginal cost of reducing pollution.

fur emissions by burning this coal—which is more expensive per equivalent energy unit than high-sulfur coal—than by installing stack scrubbers. But because they are required to install scrubbers, these plants are provided with little motivation to incur the additional expense of using the low-sulfur coal. And in some cases, burning the high-sulfur coal with scrubbers emits more sulfur oxide than burning low-sulfur coal without scrubbers.

Achieving the Least-Cost Pattern of Abatement   To reduce pollution to a specified level as cheaply as possible, not only must each polluter use the least-cost method of abatement but the total abatement must be distributed among polluters in a particular way. Some polluters can reduce their polluting activities more cheaply than others, and it is clearly desirable to have the low-cost abaters reduce their pollution levels more than the high-cost abaters. The advantage of being able to do this is rarely, if ever, achieved by direct regulation, which usually takes the form of requiring all polluters in an area to reduce pollution by a given percentage. Again, the problem is a lack of information. The EPA simply does not have enough data to determine each polluter's relative abatement cost and therefore cannot assess what the relative abatement of each polluter should be to minimize the total cost of the desired reduction in pollution.

It is in this area that the employment of a pollution tax is highly advantageous. If the same marginal pollution tax is imposed on all polluters, each polluter will respond independently in such a way that the distribution of abatement over all polluters will be the least-cost distribution. This can be achieved without accomplishing the impossible task of informing the EPA about the abatement costs of literally thousands of different polluters. This result follows from the consideration mentioned earlier that each polluter will be motivated to reduce pollution until the marginal benefit of polluting is equal to the marginal tax.

To illustrate this advantage of pollution taxation, we will consider the marginal benefits of two firms that discharge a pollutant into the environment. The marginal benefit curves MB_1 and MB_2 are illustrated in Figures 13–10(a) and 13–10(b) for polluters 1 and 2, respectively. Without any restrictions, each polluter will expand polluting activities until the marginal benefit of doing so is 0, which will produce P_1 and P_2 units of pollution. Now we will assume that the EPA issues a mandate that environmental quality be improved by (as is normally the case) requiring all polluters to reduce their pollution levels by the same percentage. Thus, polluter 1 will reduce pollution to $\bar{P}_1$, and polluter 2 will reduce pollution to $\bar{P}_2$. Unfortunately, this is not the least-cost method of achieving the desired reduction in pollution. As we can see in Figure 13–10, polluter 2's marginal cost of pollution abatement (the sacrificed marginal benefit of the polluting activity) is MC_2 at $\bar{P}_2$, which is higher than polluter 1's marginal cost of abatement MC_1 at $\bar{P}_1$. Clearly, the same amount of abatement can be realized at less cost by requiring polluter 1 to reduce its pollution level by an additional unit, thereby increasing costs by MC_1, and allowing polluter 2 to increase its pollution level by an additional unit, thereby reducing costs by MC_2.

Figure 13–10
The Least-Cost Pattern of Pollution Abatement

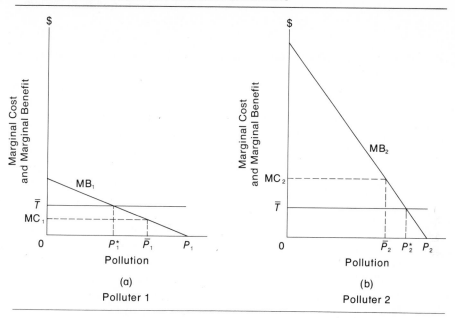

(a)

Polluter 1

(b)

Polluter 2

If, for example, $10 worth of benefit must be sacrificed by polluter 2 to reduce 2's level by an additional unit but polluter 1 can reduce its pollution by an additional unit by sacrificing only $5, then the same level of pollution abatement can be achieved at a cost of $5 less by having 1 reduce pollution by 1 unit and 2 expand pollution by 1 unit. This reduction in the cost of achieving the same level of environmental quality can be continued until the marginal cost of abatement is the same for both polluters. The least-cost pattern of abatement is reached when polluter 1 has reduced its pollution level to P_1^* and polluter 2 has increased its pollution level to P_2^*, as shown in Figure 13–10.

If instead of requiring both polluters to reduce pollution by the same percentage, the EPA had imposed a marginal pollution tax of $\bar{T}$, in this example, as shown in the figure, then the least-cost pattern of pollution abatement would have resulted because each polluter would have found it advantageous to reduce pollution until its marginal abatement cost was equal to the common marginal pollution tax.

The advantage of pollution taxation in this regard is further illustrated by a study of the Delaware estuary.[13] According to the study, cleaning up this estuary to the point that it contains 3–4 parts per million of dissolved oxygen would cost $20 million per year if uniform pollution-reduction percentages were

---

[13]See the *Report on the Effluent Charge Study* (Washington, D.C.: Federal Water Pollution Control Administration, 1966).

required of all polluters. However, the same improvement in the estuary could be achieved for only $12 million per year if the marginal abatement cost were the same for all polluters, as it would be if a uniform pollution tax were levied.

Incentives for Improved Technology When a resource can be employed at no cost to the user, there will be little incentive to invest in the development of techniques to conserve this resource. So it is not surprising that there has been little, if any, improvement over the years in our ability to produce a given quantity of output by using less of the environment as a waste-sink. This contrasts sharply with the progress we have made in minimizing our employment of resources that must be paid for. For example, there is strong motivation for firms to conserve on their employment of labor, since labor is a major expense firms incur in producing their output. This motivation has produced improvements in labor-saving technologies that have permitted firms to decrease the quantity of labor required per unit of output. This suggests that another advantage of a pollution tax policy might be to increase the incentive to invest in the technologies that will allow us to conserve our environment. And if we are concerned about the long-run improvement in environmental quality, this is a crucial advantage.

To gain a better understanding of this advantage, it will be useful to analyze and contrast the differences between the incentives that pollution taxes and pollution standards provide to develop and use environment-saving technology. Figure 13–11 illustrates the marginal benefit of polluting to a given polluter under the two pollution-control policies of taxation and standards. Initially, the marginal benefit from pollution is given by the MB curve, with a marginal pollution tax $\bar{T}$ being imposed in Figure 13–11(a) and a pollution standard being enforced in Figure 13–11(b). As constructed, both policies initially lead to the same level of pollution.

Now we will assume that an improvement is made in pollution-abatement technology that decreases the marginal cost of reducing pollution (reduces the marginal benefits sacrificed by reducing the polluting activity). If this new technology is employed, the marginal benefit of polluting will be less to our polluter, as shown by the lower marginal benefit curve MB′ in both Figures 13–11(a) and (b). Notice that the use of the new technology will motivate the polluter in Figure 13–11(a) to reduce its pollution level from $\bar{P}$ to $\bar{\bar{P}}$ when faced with a pollution tax. Given the lower marginal benefit curve MB′, the polluter will realize that at $\bar{P}$ the marginal benefit sacrificed is less than the marginal-tax savings that will result from a reduction in the pollution level. It therefore becomes profitable for the polluter to reduce its pollution level further, and this continues to be true until the pollution level is reduced to $\bar{\bar{P}}$. No changes in the EPA's policy requirements are necessary to motivate the additional pollution abatement when a pollution tax policy is implemented.

When a policy of setting and enforcing pollution standards is established, however, if the EPA does not reduce the permitted level of pollution in response to an improvement in abatement technology, the polluter is provided with no

Figure 13–11
Incentives for Improving Pollution-Abatement Technology

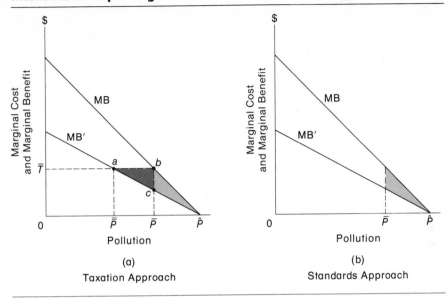

incentive to reduce pollution below $\bar{P}$ in Figure 13–11(b), even if improved technology is employed. It is reasonable to assume that once a pollution standard is established, it will require a complicated and lengthy administrative procedure to change it. Therefore, it is unlikely that EPA standards will be changed every time an improvement in abatement technology is made, even if we assume that the EPA is informed about every improvement that occurs.[14] So we can conclude that improvements in abatement technology will be more fully employed to protect the environment when a pollution tax is imposed than when pollution standards are enforced.

But before improved abatement techniques can be employed at all, research must be undertaken to develop them. Comparing the incentives to invest in such research efforts provided by pollution taxation and pollution standards, we again discover that the taxation approach provides an advantage. To illustrate this, we will show that the savings the polluter will realize from a cheaper method of pollution abatement is larger when a pollution tax is being imposed than when a pollution standard is being enforced. The technological improvement that reduces the marginal benefit curve from MB to MB' in

[14]Even if the EPA were currently informed about all improvements in abatement technology and could quickly reduce permitted pollution levels in response to each improvement, a rather severe consequence would arise. If polluters discovered that investment practices designed to improve conservation of the environment were penalized by more stringent pollution standards, this would provide them with little motivation to invest in better abatement techniques.

Figure 13–11 saves the polluter subject to the standard the difference between the MB and MB' curves over the distance $\hat{P} - \bar{P}$ (the amount of abatement required by the standard). This savings is represented by the tinted area in Figure 13–11(b).

Shifting our attention to Figure 13–11(a), we can see that the savings that result from using the new abatement technology is larger when the pollution tax is being imposed than when the pollution standard is being enforced. The savings due to the technological improvement, represented by the reduction from $\hat{P}$ to $\bar{P}$, are the same in either case. But when the polluter is paying a pollution tax, we have seen that it will reduce its pollution level to $\bar{\bar{P}}$ once the new technology is in use. Reducing pollution from $\bar{P}$ to $\bar{\bar{P}}$ will cost the polluter an amount equal to the area $\bar{\bar{P}}ac\bar{P}$ in Figure 13–11(a) in terms of forgone benefit. Offsetting this, however, is a reduction in the pollution tax equal to the area $\bar{\bar{P}}ab\bar{P}$. Thus, the savings that result from reducing the pollution level from $\bar{P}$ to $\bar{\bar{P}}$ is equal to the darker tinted area abc in Figure 13–11(a). This is the extra savings that are realized from the technological advancement when a pollution tax is imposed compared with the savings that are realized when pollution standards are enforced.

We have established that polluters will gain more from an improvement in pollution-abatement technology under a taxation policy than they will under a standards policy. It therefore follows that the pollution tax will provide polluters with a greater incentive to invest in research efforts to develop better ways to protect and conserve the environment. Moreover, once improved abatement techniques become available, polluters will use these techniques to reduce pollution further under pollution taxation than they will under direct pollution controls and standards.

Pollution taxation is a theoretically attractive approach to pollution control.

Example 13–4

Pollution Taxation in Practice

Although the taxation approach to pollution control has not been significantly employed in the United States, a pollution tax is more than a theoretical proposal. A system of pollution management that relies largely on charging fees for pollution has been used in Germany for approximately the last half-century to maintain water quality along the Ruhr River, which flows through one of the world's most concentrated industrial areas. The volume of waste discharged into the Ruhr is so great that it exceeds the annual average natural low flow in the river. Yet surprisingly, this river valley also supplies the Ruhr region's industries and households with water and supports fishing, swimming, and other recreational activities.

The goal of Ruhr River water authorities is to maintain an acceptable level of water quality for natural aquatic life at a minimum cost. Laboratory tests determine the fish-killing potential of each source of pollution,

Obviously, this method is not without its problems and limitations, but compared with the limitations of the existing approach in the United States, which is characterized by direct control and standards, we have seen that there are compelling reasons to give pollution taxation our serious consideration.

Summary   13-5

In Chapter 13, we have discussed the concepts of *public goods* and *externalities*, and we have examined the *resource-allocation* problems that they create. This has also led us to consider the importance of *property rights* in facilitating efficient allocations of our natural resources.

We began by defining *public goods* as goods that once they are provided for one individual are freely available to all members of the community. From this, we have seen that it follows that the community demand curve for a public good is the vertical summation of the individual demand curves for this good. An implication of this is that the optimal provision of a public good occurs at the point where the sum of the marginal values that all consumers attach to the good is equal to its marginal cost. When, as is often the case, it is impractical to exclude people from benefiting from a public good once it is provided, we have found that individuals are tempted to avoid paying for the good in the hope that they will benefit from the supply of the good that has been paid for by other consumers. This temptation to be a *free-rider* explains why public goods will tend to be suboptimally provided, if they are provided at all, through individual market exchanges. This problem provides the justification for the government supply of public goods, which is then financed by mandatory taxation.

We have learned that everyone in a community must consume the same quantity and quality of a public good, even though their preferences and tax

and this information is then used to establish a per-unit pollution charge for each polluter. Polluters are permitted to adjust to the pollution charges in any way they feel is appropriate. In areas where pollution damages are higher, the pollution charges are higher; in areas where pollution is less damaging, the charges are lower. One tributary is lined with concrete and a chemical-treatment plant has been constructed at its mouth to treat all waste economically before it flows into the main river. Since the environmental damage from polluting this stream is low, the pollution charges are also low in this area. This has motivated polluters to situate along this tributary rather than to discharge their wastes into areas of the river that are used for water supply and recreation, where pollution charges are very high.*

*For a more complete discussion of the Ruhr River pollution tax programs, see A.V. Kneese and B.T. Bower, *Managing Water Quality: Economics, Technology, Institutions* (Baltimore: Johns Hopkins Press, 1968).

payments for the good may vary widely. It is therefore not surprising that controversies surround the question of how much of a public good should be provided. Some consumers want more and some will want less than the optimal or *efficient quantity* of the good, and no one may feel that the optimal quantity is truly optimal. One advantage of *private goods* is that individuals can exercise their diverse preferences independently of each other, thereby eliminating much social conflict and controversy. This advantage will be eliminated, however, if private goods are publicly provided.

We then turned to the problem of externalities, where it was pointed out that an exchange between two individuals can impose costs on or convey benefits to people who are not voluntary participants in the exchange. If a cost is imposed, we say that an *external cost* or a *negative externality* is generated. When a benefit is provided, we say that an *external benefit* or a *positive externality* results. When an activity generates a negative externality, we have seen that there will tend to be too much participation in the activity because those engaged in it fail to consider the cost of their actions. Conversely, when an activity generates a positive externality, it will not be engaged in to the optimal extent. By relating the concepts of public goods and externalities, we have found that we can explain the suboptimal purchase of a public good on the grounds that those who purchase this good are generating a positive externality.

We have also seen that the more clearly property rights are defined and enforced, the smaller the problems caused by externalities will be. If we lived in a world where there were no *transaction costs,* then property rights could be completely enforced, no externalities would exist, and exchange would guarantee the efficient use of all resources, as predicted by the *Coase Theorem.* But transaction costs do exist in the real world, and therefore some exchanges that would be desirable in a frictionless world cannot occur. In some cases, we have found that transaction costs can be so high that property rights cannot be enforced. This results in what are called *common property resources,* such as the atmosphere and some of our waterways. Productive exchanges of these resources cannot take place, and much of the cost associated with their use is an external cost. And because it is often extremely difficult to engage in transactions with everyone who benefits from a public good, the provision of a public good commonly generates external benefits.

The theoretical concepts we have developed in this chapter are very useful in understanding the problem of environmental pollution. We have seen that to achieve such an understanding, we must recognize that the use of the environment as a waste-sink is an essential requirement for any productive activity. This means that the benefit received from being able to pollute must be weighed against the cost of the resulting pollution. Having recognized this, it follows that there is a desirable or *optimal* level of pollution and that this level will be positive for most forms of pollutants. This optimal level of pollution is reached when the marginal benefit of polluting is equal to the marginal cost of polluting. Since environmental quality is a public good, determining the optimal level of pollution (or environmental quality) is a controversial issue.

Because property rights to the assimilative capacity of the environment have not been established, no price is charged for the use of the environment as a waste-sink to reflect the cost of doing so. People therefore pollute beyond the point where marginal benefit is equal to marginal cost. In fact, if a polluter does not have to pay anything for polluting, the pollution will increase until the marginal benefit of the polluting activity is approximately 0, which will produce pollution in excess of the optimal level.

This suggests that an effective approach to pollution control may be to charge for the privilege of polluting. Although pollution taxation is not an approach without problems, it does provide some significant advantages compared with current attempts to reduce pollution by a policy of direct controls and enforced standards. We have seen that one attribute of a pollution tax is that it would provide individual polluters with both the incentive and the freedom to reduce pollution as inexpensively as possible. A second attribute is that pollution taxation would result in a pattern of pollution abatement among different polluters that would minimize the cost of achieving a given improvement in environmental quality. The third—and perhaps most important—attribute is that a pollution tax would motivate polluters to develop and fully utilize improved pollution-abatement technology more than the standards approach would. Lastly, we have shown that the pollution-charge approach to environmental management has been successfully employed in Germany to maintain water quality in the Ruhr River Valley.

The problems that we have discussed in this chapter have shown us that collective or political decision making is often desirable. Unfortunately, using the political process to allocate resources creates problems that need to be fully recognized when comparing the market process with the political process. In Chapter 14, we will employ economic analysis to take a careful look at the allocative performance of the political process.

References

Anderson, Terry, and J.P. Hill. "The Evolution of Property Rights: A Study of the American West." *The Journal of Law and Economics* (April 1975), pp. 163–79.

Buchanan, James M. *The Demand and Supply of Public Goods.* Chicago: Rand McNally, 1968.

Buchanan, James M., and Gordon Tullock. *The Calculus of Consent.* Ann Arbor: University of Michigan Press, 1962.

Coase, Ronald. "The Lighthouse in Economics." *The Journal of Law and Economics* (October 1974), pp. 357–76.

Coase, Ronald. "The Problem of Social Cost." *The Journal of Law and Economics* (October 1960), pp. 1–45.

Dales, J.H. *Pollution, Property, and Prices.* Toronto: University of Toronto Press, 1968.

Demsetz, Harold. "Toward a Theory of Property Rights." *American Economic Review* (May 1967), pp. 347–59.

Dolan, Edwin G. *TANSTAAFL, The Economic Strategy of Environmental Crisis.* New York: Holt, Rinehart & Winston, 1971.

Downs, A. *An Economic Analysis of Democracy.* New York: Harper & Row, 1957.

Kneese, Allen V., and B.T. Bower. *Managing Water Quality: Economics, Technology, Institutions.* Baltimore: Johns Hopkins Press, 1968.

Kneese, Allen V., and Charles L. Schultze. *Pollution, Prices, and Public Policy.* Washington, D.C.: The Brookings Institution, 1975.

Lee, Dwight R. "Discrimination and Efficiency in the Pricing of Public Goods." *The Journal of Law and Economics* (October 1977), pp. 403–20.

Lee, Dwight R. "A Note on the Optimal Pricing of Public Goods." *Public Finance Quarterly* (October 1978), pp. 503–11.

Olson, M. *The Logic of Collective Action,* rev. ed. New York: Schocken Books, 1971, pp. 35–36.

Rubin, Paul. "The Theory of the Firm and the Structure of the Franchise Contract." *The Journal of Law and Economics* (April 1978), pp. 223–33.

Ruff, Larry E. "The Economic Common Sense of Pollution." *The Public Interest* (Spring 1970), pp. 69–85.

Tullock, Gordon. *The Social Dilemma: The Economics of War and Revolution.* Blacksburg, VA: Center for the Study of Public Choice, 1973.

Problems

1. Explain the problem of counterfeiting in terms of it being a negative externality.

2. In your own words, explain how the optimal quantity of a public good can really be optimal when no one in the community is satisfied with it.

3. Some economists have argued that once a public good has been provided, no charge should be associated with its use, because the benefits of consuming additional units of the good are available at no cost (I can consume more without you having to consume less). Therefore, charging a positive price to consume the good will discourage consumption that could be provided at no cost.

   What is your view of this argument? Does it imply that if a plane is scheduled to fly from New York to Denver and a seat is unoccupied, a ticket for this seat should be sold for nothing? Can you think of how a charge for using a public good could be constructed so that no disincentive to consume it would exist?

4. Assume that you are a noble, public-spirited revolutionary who wants to overthrow an evil dictator for the benefit of all concerned (except the dictator and his or her cohorts, of course). For the sake of argument, also assume that you are able to convince people that once you take over, your

benevolent regime will improve the welfare of the masses. Based on your knowledge of public goods, do you believe you will be very successful in recruiting others to support your revolution by explaining the social improvements that the revolution can bring? How effective do you think this approach would be in comparison to promising attractive positions in your government in return for revolutionary support or threatening to punish those who oppose you as traitors? Which approach do you feel is more commonly employed by revolutionary leaders?

5. Some economists have suggested that the government should control pollution by issuing pollution "rights." Each right would entitle its owner to emit a stated quantity and type of pollutant into the environment during some specified time period. The EPA would determine the permitted level of a pollutant and would then issue the appropriate number of "rights" to produce that pollutant—possibly by auctioning them off to the highest bidders. Once these "rights" were issued, they could be bought and sold freely among those in the community.

   How effective do you think this pollution-pricing strategy would be compared with pollution taxation policy? In what sense would such a pricing system create property rights to our air and water? If the EPA kicked off a pollution "rights" program by giving all of the rights to one polluter, would the pollution cost for this lucky polluter be lower than it would if all the "rights" had been sold to the highest bidders initially? Do you think that these "free" pollution rights would encourage our lucky polluter to pollute more than it would if it had to pay for them? What role would the income effect play in this situation?

6. Do you think pollution taxes should have been levied during the frontier days? Do you think a pollution-tax program should be instituted in the town of Roundup, Montana today? Does it make any sense to require that the same smog-control equipment be attached to cars driven by the residents of Roundup that is required to be fitted on New York City taxicabs? Explain.

7. Clean air is clearly preferable to smog. Yet millions of people choose to live in Los Angeles, where smog alerts are common, rather than in Woonsocket, South Dakota, where there is no such thing as smog. What does this tell you about the trade-offs that people are willing to make? How is a decision to live in L.A. rather than in Woonsocket similar to a decision to smoke or not to smoke?

8. Explain why the optimal level of pollution will be lower if a pollution tax is imposed to manage the environment than it will be if direct controls and regulations are enforced.

9. When a patent is issued, a monopoly is created. Despite the fact that monopolies will not produce the efficient level of output at any point in time, explain why patents can be justified on the grounds of efficiency.

10. Explain why the inefficiencies associated with monopoly would vanish if transaction costs did not exist.

11. Explain whether each of the following would result in an increase or a decrease in the efficient level of air pollution:

    (a) A reduction in the average winter temperature.

    (b) A change in preferences from favoring outdoor activities to favoring indoor activities.

    (c) Improvements in the safety of producing nuclear energy and the wide acceptance of the use of this form of energy.

    (d) A change in EPA policy favoring pollution taxation rather than the direct government enforcement of pollution controls and standards.

    (e) Convincing proof that solar energy will never be technologically feasible.

    (f) The discovery that students who sit in electrified desks that send mild doses of electricity coursing through their bodies learn significantly more than students who are not as charged up for education.

12. Even though it would be expensive, assume that arrangements could be made to pollute the air that certain individuals breathe while their neighbors enjoy acceptable air quality. Explain the potential advantage of incurring the cost required to permit this selective pollution.

CHAPTER FOURTEEN

THE ECONOMIC ANALYSIS OF POLITICAL DECISION MAKING

Introduction 14-1

In Chapter 13, we saw that in private markets, public goods generally will not be provided or will be provided in less than efficient quantities. Unlike private goods, individuals can hope to benefit as free-riders when others purchase a public good. Such circumstances provide opportunities for everyone to gain through collective or political action. Political action can improve the efficiency of the provision of public goods because it permits *controlled coercion.* Although an individual would prefer that only others be coerced into paying for a public good, he or she may recognize that it is worth being coerced as well if it is the only way to require everyone else to contribute. It should be emphasized, however, that this coercion must be very carefully controlled if it is to lead to efficient choices. Ideally, the political process should be responsive to citizens who will pay for as well as benefit from the goods and services that will be collectively provided. The appeal of democratic political arrangements lies in the hope that it permits this type of citizen control.

In a democracy, individuals express their preferences for different government goods through the voting process. Occasionally, the electorate can vote directly on a particular issue, but in a **representative democracy**, it is more common for voters to express their preferences indirectly through their choice of elected representatives. The voting behavior of the consumers of publicly provided goods transmits their preferences to politicians and also provides political office-seekers with an incentive to act on this information. Voting in the political marketplace is often compared to spending money for private goods. Both activities express a desire for more or less of particular types of goods and services and motivate those who benefit from collecting votes or dollars to respond appropriately. Notwithstanding the similarities between voting in the political market and spending money in the private market, there are significant differences between these two activities. In our effort to gain an under-

517

standing of the political process, it will be at least as important to examine these differences as it will be to study the similarities between political voting and private spending.

Before we continue, however, a word about the basic assumption underpinning our subsequent discussion is in order. Throughout this book, all of our models have been based on the assumption that economic decision makers are motivated by self-interest. Since political decisions deal with allocating scarce resources among competing employments, they are basically economic in nature. Therefore, it seems quite natural to assume that political behavior is also motivated largely by self-interest. Some may raise the objection that when people make decisions in the political arena, they should be motivated by the broader "public interest." After all, political decisions have an impact on everyone. Our response is that although political decision makers probably *should* be motivated by a more noble consideration than self-interest, economists are primarily concerned with how people actually behave—not with how they should behave. And self-interest is commonly considered by economists to be the dominant—although not the only—motivation that determines how citizens vote and politicians respond. Certainly, people vote for the politicians they feel are most likely to propose and support legislation that will benefit them. And although successful politicians almost always talk as if they are motivated by the public interest, the case for democracy is based on the assumption that these claims are viewed with a healthy skepticism. Political office affords an unusually attractive opportunity to realize personal gain at public expense. If we honestly believed that political decision makers were neutral to the appeal of this opportunity, we could dispense with the large cost associated with periodically voting them in or out of office and leave them to their own devices to promote the public interest. But thus far, the real justification for our assumption of self-interest has been its usefulness in generating answers to the questions we have asked and in bringing order and predictability to the observations we make. As we will see, basing our economic model of political decision making on the underlying assumption of self-interest will permit us to explain many situations that occur in the political arena and to disclose implications that are potentially useful in preparing policies designed to improve the political process.

14–2 Market Choice Versus Political Choice

The similarities between casting votes in a democratic, political setting and spending money in the private market are widely recognized. The objective of democratic and market arrangements is certainly the same—to give the purchasers of goods and services some control over what goods and services are provided. But when we examine how successfully private markets achieve this objective relative to democratic, political markets, we find some striking differences.

The difference between the amounts of information required to make an efficient decision in the two markets is enormously important. If you are considering the purchase of a private good being sold in a private market, the only information you need to know is how much you are willing to pay and how much a seller is willing to accept for the good. This information is relatively easy to determine. You certainly know how much money you are willing to sacrifice to obtain the good, and the market price of the good tells you how much is required to entice the seller to supply it. If you decide to buy the good, it is because the available information suggests that the good is worth more to you than to the seller. If the information leads you to the opposite conclusion, you will decide not to buy the good. In either case, you will make the efficient decision if the information you have is accurate.

When private goods are exchanged in private markets, we can feel more confident that the information we need to make a purchasing decision is accurate because it is supplied by only two people—the buyer and the seller. In a private exchange, only these two people are directly affected by the exchange. The situation becomes much more complicated when a decision is being contemplated in a political market because political decisions usually have an impact on everyone in the community. For example, if the federal government decides to increase our military capability, everyone in the community (the community being the entire country in this case) will receive and pay for additional national defense services. Therefore, decisions in the political market ideally should be based on information about everyone's preferences. It is therefore much more difficult to acquire the information required to make efficient political choices than it is to obtain the necessary information to make a purchasing decision in the private marketplace.

The magnitude of this difficulty is realized if we recognize that ideally this is not done because it would be prohibitively expensive. Representative democracy is the result of a compromise between obtaining the ideal level of information required to make each decision and controlling the costs of political decision making.

Another important difference between market choice and political choice concerns the relative effectiveness of these choices. If you think it would be nice to have a ball-point pen that plays "The Yellow Rose of Texas" when you write and you are willing to pay enough to cover its production cost, you will be able to acquire it in a private market. The fact that your taste may be considered a little eccentric will not prevent you from obtaining the private goods of your choice as long as you are willing to pay for them, and you will certainly be able to exercise such choices more effectively in private markets than in political markets. When a political decision is made, everyone is affected. It is impossible, for example, to protect one individual against nuclear attack without also providing the same amount of protection to the surrounding neighborhood. If one individual believes that half of the GNP should be devoted to national defense and a neighbor does not believe that any national defense is justified, it is impossible to give them both exactly what they want. If most people feel that some intermediate level of national defense should be provided, the desires of both neighbors will be ignored, because the political process will respond to the more typical voter preferences.

This leads us to the final difference between exercising private market choices and political market choices. Since individuals can generally acquire whatever they choose in private markets, they are motivated to make these selections for themselves and to make them carefully. If you intend to buy a new car, it is unlikely that you will let your neighbor choose the model for you. Not only will you make the selection, but you will acquire some relevant information and do some comparison shopping before you buy your car. On the other hand, we expect people to be more casual about exercising their choices in political markets. A person whose political preferences deviate from the norm will recognize that his or her individual input into the political decision-making process will be inconsequential. The individual whose political preferences are more widely held is likely to assume that other voters will ensure that the political process remains responsive to these desires whether or not he or she participates in the process. In either case, the individual will probably not feel that careful shopping in the political market will be personally beneficial.

This general discussion of the differences between private and political market decisions serves to introduce a more detailed analysis of the political decision-making process. We have commented on the difficulties citizens encounter when they attempt to employ the political process to indicate their preferences. We will now couple this feature of political decision making with our assumption that self-interest is the dominant motivation in the political as well as the private market.

14-3 Competing for Votes

In this section, we will provide some insight into one aspect of political behavior by recognizing that candidates for political office in a democracy compete against each other for votes. In a two-party setting,[1] this competition is motivated by the simple fact that the candidate who collects the most votes wins the election, which is presumably something both candidates want to do. In deciding how to vote, each voter can be expected to favor the candidate whose views on the issues more closely resemble his or her own views. Each candidate will therefore attempt to take the closer position to that of the majority of voters.

More specifically, we can assume that there is a continuum of political preferences ranging from, say, very liberal to very conservative. Each point on this continuum will represent the preferred position of a certain number of voters, and this number can be represented by the height of a line drawn above the continuum, as shown in Figure 14–1. In this figure, we can see that a few voters are extremely liberal and a few are extremely conservative. As we move toward a moderate position, however, we find that the political positions become increasingly popular until we reach a position somewhere near the middle

---

[1]Throughout most of this discussion, we will assume a two-party setting, since it is typical in U.S. Politics. For an analysis of the more than two-party case, see Anthony Downs, *An Economic Theory of Democracy* (New York: Harper & Row, 1957), Chapters 8 and 9.

Figure 14–1
Distribution of Political Preference

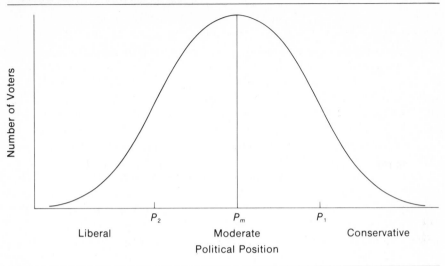

of the distribution of political preference that is the most popular of all. The most popular position P_m is where the curve reaches its maximum height. As Figure 14–1 is drawn, the distribution of voters' preferences is symmetrical around position P_m, which means that as many voters are to the left of the most popular position as are to the right of it. This means that P_m is also the *median position*. There is, of course, no reason why the distribution of voter preferences should be symmetrical; the implications of this model do not depend on this distribution being symmetrical.

We will begin our analysis by assuming that one candidate's position is given by P_1 in Figure 14–1. Therefore, any opposing candidate who takes a position just to the left of P_1 will win the election by capturing the votes of all those who identify with positions to the left of P_1—which is clearly more than half the voters. Similarly, any opponent who assumes a position to the left of center at, say, P_2 can be defeated by a candidate who takes a slightly more moderate position. The closer a candidate is to the median position P_m, the less likely he or she is to be defeated.

A numerical example will help to clarify this concept. For simplicity, we will assume that there are only 5 possible expenditure levels for national defense: $0, $50 billion, $100 billion, $150 billion, and $200 billion. The distribution of voter preferences over these possible expenditure levels is given in Table 14–1. Ten million voters prefer no expenditure on national defense, 50 million voters prefer a $50 billion expenditure on national defense, 75 million prefer a $100 billion expenditure, 50 million prefer a $150 billion expenditure, and 10 million prefer a $200 billion expenditure. We will further assume that in choosing between two candidates, a voter will select the candidate whose position

Table 14–1
Winning with the Median Position Expenditures on National Defense

	$0	$50 BILLION	$100 BILLION	$150 BILLION	$200 BILLION
Number of Supporters	10 million	50 million	75 million	50 million	10 million

on national defense expenditures is closest to his or her own position. For example, a voter who wants nothing to be spent on defense will vote for the candidate who proposes $150 billion for defense if the other candidate is proposing a defense budget of $200 billion.[2]

Now we notice that if candidate 1 comes out in favor of spending $200 billion on defense, candidate 2 can win by proposing to spend only $150 billion. Candidate 2 will be supported by the 185 million voters who prefer a defense expenditure of $150 billion or less, and candidate 1 will receive only 10 million votes. If candidate 1 proposes to spend $150 billion instead of $200 billion for defense, candidate 2 can still win by favoring a defense expenditure of $100 billion. In this case, candidate 2 would receive 135 million votes to candidate 1's total of 60 million votes. Only by advocating the *median position* of $100 billion for defense can one candidate prevent the other candidate from ensuring victory by taking a position closer to the median.

Therefore, our analysis predicts that the candidates in a two-party democracy will tend to assume a position close to the median voter's position (the median position). That there is a strong tendency for both candidates to move toward a centralist position is reflected in the widespread belief that there is not much difference between Democrats and Republicans. The leaders of a political party soon learn that a candidate who runs too far to the left or right will almost certainly be defeated. The overwhelming defeat of Barry Goldwater for President in 1964 impressed on the Republicans the liability of running a candidate who was considered to be too far to the right by a majority of the voting public. The Democrats learned a similar lesson in 1972 when they ran Presidential hopeful George McGovern—a politician who was considered extremely liberal and who managed to carry only the state of Massachusetts.

Notice that a candidate who took position P_m in Figure 14–1 would be impossible to beat unless the opponent also took the same position. However, this implies that candidates for a given office will take identical positions, which is something we do not observe, so our analysis must be qualified somewhat. Since no one knows exactly how voters are distributed with respect to their political preferences, the two candidates may not take the same political position because they have arrived at different estimates of voter preferences. Also,

---

[2]Preferences that satisfy this assumption are referred to as *symmetrical single-peaked preferences* and imply that between any two positions, the individual voter will always prefer the position that is closest to his or her own. The assumption that individual voters have symmetrical, single-peaked preferences is important to the theory.

politicians−at least those who are more likely to be successful−have the ability to persuade voters. In other words, politicians do not simply accept the distribution of voter preference as given; they attempt to exert some influence over this distribution. A particularly charismatic candidate can take a position to the left or right of the median position and pull the center of the preference distribution toward this position. Politicians not only follow voters, but lead them as well. And the more confidence that politicians have in their ability to lead, the weaker the tendency will be for candidates to take similar positions.

Also, the attraction that a central position holds for candidates does not imply that all politicians will take similar positions. A wide spectrum of political opinion is represented among elected U.S. officials, and this is entirely consistent with our model. Members of the U.S. House of Representatives, for example, are elected by local constituents. When the local constituency is conservative, our analysis predicts that both candidates will be conservative, which is generally true of both Democrats and Republicans in, say, Texas. Correspondingly, we are likely to find that both Democrats and Republicans are more liberal in a state such as Massachusetts. Since the Presidential election is nationwide, our analysis predicts that U.S. Presidents will generally occupy a central position relative to the national spectrum of political opinion and always be flanked on the left and the right by members of Congress.

When political preferences are distributed as shown in Figure 14−1, our analysis is also useful in explaining why the introduction of a third political party is unlikely to be successful. Suppose that initially there is a two-party election, with the Democrats at position P_D and the Republicans at position P_R in Figure 14−2. Now assume that a third party that is not burdened with

Figure 14−2
The Political Advantage of Taking the Median Position

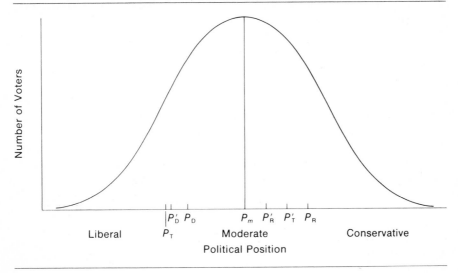

an ideological preference enters the contest. The sole motivation of the third party is to win, but it cannot accomplish this by taking a position between the Democrats and Republicans unless the two parties have taken widely different positions, which is unlikely. The only realistic hope for the third party is to take a position just to the left of the Democrats or just to the right of the Republicans. Assume that its leaders choose position P_T in Figure 14–2. This will tend to pull the Democratic party farther to the left—say, to P_D'—in the hope of neutralizing the third party's appeal to those voters who are very liberal. This competition will pull both the Democrats and the third party even farther to the left, enabling the Republicans to guarantee victory by moving closer to the median position. However, if the Republicans shift to the position P_R', the third party can outflank them to the right and possibly win the election by moving to P_T'. By shifting its position back and forth, the third party can upset the planning of both the Democrats and the Republicans and possibly capture a plurality of the votes. A party with such a flexible and open-minded approach to the political issues of the day is unlikely to achieve any long-term success, however, as it will soon destroy its own credibility.

But a third party will probably be ideologically motivated. If the Democrats and Republicans move too close to the median position, they will both be subject to the dissatisfaction of the less moderate members of their respective parties. If, for example, frustration with the policies of a moderate Republican party results in a challenge from a conservative third party, both parties will lose. But conservatives may still consider a third-party challenge to be a justifiable strategy to keep the Republican party ideologically sound. Even in the absence of an active conservative party, the potential to form one will keep the Republican party from moving too close to the median position. Of course, the Democratic party is subject to a similar restraint. Therefore, we find that another influence opposes the tendency for political parties to become centralist. Although the tendency to move toward the central or median position is strong for both parties, we can expect some distance to be maintained between their positions.

14–4 Externalities and Voting Rules

Government Failure

We have seen that a political action invariably satisfies the preferences of some and ignores the preferences of others. Since everyone must usually pay for the benefits provided by a political action, such actions will commonly convey benefits to some that are largely paid for by others. This is not only the common result of a political action; it is often the underlying motivation for the action. The temptation to take advantage of the opportunity to reap benefits that will be predominantly paid for by others is very difficult to resist. From an economic perspective, we are interested in two aspects of this feature of the political process: (1) the inefficiencies that result and (2) the measures people take to moderate these inefficiencies.

In Chapter 13, we saw that inefficiencies result when economic decision makers are not paying the full cost of the activities they are engaged in due to negative externalities. These inefficiencies are said to result from *market failure* and are often the basis for justifying corrective government action. If we were to take the naïve view that the political process works perfectly, then market failure would always warrant government intervention. But a more realistic appraisal of political decision making would encourage us to exercise caution in recommending government assistance when the market fails to achieve perfection. Government action not only results in but is often motivated by externalities, and generates its own set of inefficiencies as a result. The choice is not to replace market failure with government success but rather to compare the failures of both market and government processes.

As an example of government failure, we will consider a community that is subject to periodic flooding so that it is desirable for this community to build a flood control levee. Since flood control is a public good, a levee is not expected to be constructed in response to private-market incentives. Therefore, a political decision must be made regarding the size of the levee to be constructed. A relatively inexpensive levee would protect the community against the 10-year flood, but it would cost substantially more to control the 100-year flood. Efficiency, of course, requires that the community determine the levee size for which the marginal benefit and marginal cost of expansion are equal.

Since determining the appropriate levee size is a political decision, we will assume that this determination is made in response to the self-interest of the majority in the community. To provide a more concrete example, we will also assume that 51% of the community members live in the flood plain and that 49% reside in the hills overlooking the plain where their homes are in no danger of being flooded whether or not a levee is constructed. Some of the hillside residents may feel better if they know that their friends below are protected against flooding, whereas others may actually enjoy the occasional excitement of sitting on their patios and watching some of their neighbors float away. For simplicity, however, we will assume that the hillside residents will receive no benefit—positive or negative—from a levee. But since they do live in the community, their taxes will be raised to help pay for any levee that is constructed.

This situation is graphically illustrated in Figure 14-3, where the size of the levee is represented on the horizontal axis and dollar value is represented on the vertical axis. The marginal benefit of the levee size is MB, which, by assumption, is received entirely by the voting majority living in the flood plain. The marginal cost of increasing the levee size is MC, so that the efficient levee size is S^*. But even though the voting majority receives all of the benefit of the flood control, it pays only part of the marginal cost, which is represented by MC_m. Therefore, at the efficient levee size S^*, the majority will find the marginal benefit from expansion of levee size greater than the marginal cost and will vote for a larger levee. From the perspective of the majority, which exerts the controlling influence on the decision, the ideal levee size is $\hat{S}$ and the levee will be inefficiently large.

Building the levee allows the majority to impose a negative externality on

Figure 14–3
Majority Rule and Excessively Large Public Expenditure

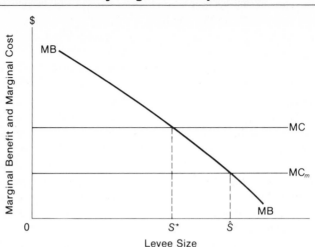

the hillside minority. The majority will reap a benefit without paying its full cost, and the minority will incur a cost without receiving an offsetting benefit. And the activity generating the negative externality will usually be expanded beyond the efficient level. In principle, the inefficiency of excessive government spending in this case is no different than the inefficiency of excessive pollution. Both are the result of negative externalities.

Conversely, we could easily structure our flood control example so that no levee will be constructed even though the efficient levee size is S^* in Figure 14–3 by simply assuming that 51% of the community lives on the hillsides and controls the decision about levee size. In this case, the voting majority would receive no benefit from a levee but would have to pay more than one-half of its cost, so the hillside residents would elect not to construct a levee. In a situation like this, however, a special tax district is often created. Rather than do without a levee, residents in the flood plain will find it to their advantage to impose a tax only on themselves for the purpose of providing flood protection. In this way, not only will the levee be built, but the recipients of the benefit will pay the total cost of the levee and it is more likely to be close to the efficient size.

Of course, desirable projects may not be funded at all or may be under-funded through the political process because the voting majority would otherwise pay most of the cost and receive only a small or no part of the benefit. This situation could be characterized as government failure resulting from *positive externalities*. More often, however, political action is motivated by the opportunity of a relatively small group to receive benefits from the taxes of a much larger group, rather than by a large group attempting to avoid absorbing costs. The tendency for relatively small groups to be politically dominant in achieving support for government expenditure programs will be discussed in Section 14–5. As our present analysis indicates, this tendency increases the negative externalities that are commonly found in the political process and the resulting inefficiencies of excess government expenditure.

An Economic Analysis of Voting Rules

From a practical standpoint, some of the inefficiency of government action is inevitable due to the public-good nature of what is being provided. But a large part of government inefficiency results from one group using the political process to secure private-good benefits by imposing costs on others. To counteract this potential abuse, certain institutional features of the political process serve to limit the ability of one group to impose uncompensated cost on other groups. The most obvious of these institutional conventions is a voting rule that requires a specified percentage of the voters to agree that an action is desirable before everyone is committed to it.

The voting rule that we are most familiar with is *majority rule.* The appeal of majority rule is that it *supposedly* indicates the decision that most voters favor. (The emphasis on supposedly will be explained in Section 14–5.) But majority rule is just one of many possible voting rules, and there is no reason to believe that it is the best one. In fact, many political issues are decided on the basis of some other rule than majority voting. Normally, at least two-thirds of the vote is required to pass a school bond, change the bylaws of a constitution, or override an executive veto. To find a defendant guilty of a criminal offense, the jury must reach a unanimous vote.

Is there a rationale to justify applying different voting rules in different situations? If so, we might expect it to be related to efficiency considerations, particularly if we are looking for it in an economics textbook. Pursuing this line of inquiry, it is useful to recognize that from the standpoint of efficiency, there is a strong argument in favor of a voting rule that requires unanimity. Forgetting the costs associated with negotiating an agreement for the moment, the advantage of a *unanimous voting rule* is that only those measures that satisfy the condition of Pareto efficiency will be approved. A political proposal will be unanimously approved only if it will enhance the well-being of some people at no one else's expense.

The advantage of a unanimous voting rule is obvious if we consider the consequences of a voting rule that is less than unanimous. As an example, we will suppose a community consists of only three people–Jonas, Smithers, and Taylor–and that a proposal to improve the access roads to the homes of Jonas and Smithers, if approved, is to be financed by a general tax increase. We will assume that the cost of these improvements would be $300, which would be distributed equally among Jonas, Smithers, and Taylor. We will further assume that Jonas and Smithers each value the improvement of their access road at $125 and that Taylor would receive no value at all from these improvements. This information is summarized in Table 14–2.

Table 14–2
Eliminating Externalities with Unanimity

	JONAS	SMITHERS	TAYLOR
Benefit	$125	$125	$ 0
Cost	100	100	100
Net Gain	25	25	−100

Obviously, the cost of the improvements exceeds their value. But if the decision is made on the basis of majority-rule voting, the improvements will be made, because both Jonas and Smithers will vote in favor of the proposal and only Taylor will oppose it.[3] However, this inefficient decision would not be made under a unanimous voting rule. It is possible to generalize from this example and to argue that no inefficient proposal will ever be approved if unanimity is required. If a proposal is inefficient, its cost exceeds its benefit, so that no matter how the cost and benefit are distributed, the cost of the proposal will exceed its benefit for at least one individual, who will prevent the proposal from being implemented by voting against it. Only proposals that are efficient (the proposed benefits exceed the proposed costs) can be structured so that everyone benefits, and only these efficient measures will be approved under a unanimous voting rule. Another way of looking at this is to recognize that unanimity eliminates the negative externalities that result when one group is able to benefit from the political process by imposing uncompensated costs on other groups.

Despite the advantage of the unanimous voting rule, unanimity is infrequently required. We can see why this is so if we drop our assumption that negotiation is costless and recognize that the more inclusive the voting rule (the larger the number of voters who must favor a proposal before it passes) is, the more costly negotiation becomes. For example, if only a few individuals could block the passage of a proposal, they might be motivated to do so even if the proposal would benefit everyone. In this way, they might be able to restructure the proposal to provide more benefits for themselves by threatening to deny everyone the benefits of the proposal. Since many small groups would be in a position to manipulate the proposal to increase their benefits, a tremendous amount of negotiation and renegotiation might be required to obtain a favorable majority vote. In most situations, before a voting rule becomes inclusive enough to require unanimity, the value of the additional efficiency gained by reducing negative externalities in the political process will be more than offset by the additional cost of negotiations. Only by considering both the negotiation cost and the externality cost of a voting rule can an efficient rule be chosen. This is illustrated in Figure 14–4, where the inclusiveness of the voting rule is

---

[3]This should be recognized as an example of the inefficiency of oversupply that we considered in the discussion accompanying Figure 14–3. The difference is that here we are considering an all-or-nothing decision rather than a marginal one.

Figure 14–4
The Efficient Voting Rule

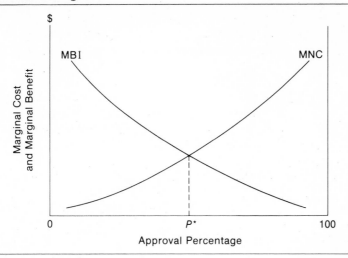

measured in percentages along the horizontal axis and the negotiation and externality costs are measured along the vertical axis. The upward sloping MNC curve represents the marginal negotiation cost and reflects the reasonable assumption that this marginal cost will increase as the approval percentage increases. The downward-sloping MBI curve shows the marginal benefit from inclusion resulting from the smaller externality cost that is associated with a more inclusive voting rule. This marginal benefit decreases as the approval percentage increases. The information contained in Figure 14–4 implies that the *efficient voting rule* will require an approval percentage of P^*. If the voter approval percentage is smaller than P^*, a more inclusive voting rule will decrease the externality cost more than it will increase the negotiation cost. But increasing the voter approval percentage beyond P^* will decrease the externality cost less than it will increase the negotiation cost. Only at P^* will the combined negotiation and externality cost associated with the voting rule be as small as possible.[4]

Some political decisions are of enormous consequence; others are much less important. Clearly, the negotiation and externality costs we just discussed will vary depending on issue, and according to our analysis, the efficient voting rule will also vary. For example, if the decision concerns the basic rules of the game—that is, the Constitution of the United States—the cost of a decision to those in opposition to it will probably be very high. This would shift the MBI curve in Figure 14–4 up and to the right, thereby increasing the approval percentage of

---

[4]For the original and more detailed discussion of efficient voting rules, see James M. Buchanan and Gordon Tullock, *The Calculus of Consent: Logical Foundations for Constitutional Democracy* (Ann Arbor: University of Michigan Press, 1962), Chapter 6.

the efficient voting rule. Our analysis therefore offers an explanation for the fact that changes in bylaws and constitutions typically require a two-thirds majority rather than a simple majority. Similarly, political decisions on such issues as school bonds, which obligate the community to long-term commitments and make affirmative decisions very costly for those who oppose them, normally require a two-thirds majority vote. In some cases when the MBI curve is extremely high and the MNC curve is relatively low, a unanimous voting rule is required. The unanimous verdict necessary to establish the guilt of someone who is accused of a serious crime is an example. Not only is the cost of convicting an innocent person of a crime considered very high, but the cost of reaching a unanimous agreement among a jury of only 12 people is relatively low.

Example 14-1

Voting Rules and the 1972 Democratic Presidential Primaries

When a political party chooses a candidate for President, there are usually several serious contenders. The winning candidate must receive the support of a majority of the state delegates attending the party's national convention. In many states, winning the support of a state's delegates requires winning the state's primary election. But how is the winner of a primary election determined when there are three or more candidates? In actuality, the candidate who receives the most votes is declared the winner. But this *plurality rule* is only one possible way of selecting a winner. Another possibility is to find the candidate who can win a majority of the votes in pairwise elections against all other candidates. This is called the *Condorcet Rule* after the Marquis de Condorcet, who proposed it during the eighteenth century. Another possible voting rule is the *Borda Rule,* which was suggested by Jean-Charles de Borda in 1781. According to the Borda Rule, in the case of, say, 5 candidates, each voter would give the candidate he or she considered best 5 points, the second-best candidate 4 points, and so on, with 1 point being awarded to the least desirable candidate. The candidate with the most points would then be declared the winner.

By now, it should be clear why the plurality voting rule is the one we actually use. Tabulating all of the points from a Borda election or holding the number of elections required to determine the winner according to the Condorcet approach would be extremely costly. But the plurality rule fails to capture a lot of important information that is obtained by the other two voting rules. For example, candidate A might be widely supported by the voters and could be almost everyone's close second choice. But if few voters considered A their first choice, he or she would receive only a few votes and would have no hope of achieving a plurality. On the other hand, candidate B may be viewed as an extremist, who is preferred over the other candidates by a fair-sized minority but who is considered by most to be the worst of the contenders. It is highly possible that B will win a plurality even though the average level of voter support for B is far below the level of voter support for A. According to the Condorcet voting rule, candidate A would

Political Apathy, Representative Democracy,   14–5
and the Influence of Special-Interest Groups

The fact that the political process affords one group the opportunity to benefit by imposing an uncompensated cost on other groups encourages us to consider the employment of more inclusive voting rules. Although a more inclusive voting rule would increase the negotiation cost, it would reduce the likelihood—and therefore the cost—of being coerced by a politically decisive coalition. However, there are reasons to control our optimism that this externality cost can be easily contained by voting rules that require majority or greater than majority support. The problem lies in the fact that in a representative

easily win a majority in a two-way election against the extremist candidate, and against any other candidate, so that A would win the primary. The Borda voting rule would also award the election to candidate A, because A's point score would be the highest. The Condorcet and Borda voting rules provide a reasonable measure of a candidate's average support and therefore tend to favor those who have broad voter support over more extreme candidates. The extreme candidate has the best chance of being elected when a plurality voting rule is employed, since it only measures first-choice popularity.

The 1972 Democratic Presidential primaries provide an interesting example of how the plurality voting rule can favor the candidate who is considered to be the most extreme. At the beginning of 1972, U.S. Senator Edmund Muskie from Maine was a "middle-of-the-road" candidate who was widely popular among Democrats and a solid favorite to become the Democratic nominee for President. On the other hand, Senator George McGovern from South Dakota was considered to be extremely liberal by most Democrats, was given intense but fairly narrow support, and was believed to have little chance of winning the Democratic nomination. However, McGovern was victorious in most of the primaries under the plurality rule, and won the Democratic nomination by receiving 1,307 delegate votes compared with 271 for Muskie at the national convention. But what would the result have been if the primary elections had been based on the Condorcet or the Borda voting rules instead of the plurality rule? Of course, we can never be sure, but R.A. Joslyn* has reconstructed the 1972 Democratic primary elections based on different voting rules in an attempt to answer this question. Joslyn estimates that Muskie would have won the nomination under either the Condorcet or the Borda voting rule. In fact, according to Joslyn, Muskie would have beaten McGovern by the same delegate count (869 to 766) in either case.

*See R.A. Joslyn, "The Impact of Decision Rules in Multi-Candidate Campaigns: The Case of the 1972 Democratic Presidential Nomination," *Public Choice* (Spring 1976), pp. 1–17. This article, along with other voting rules, is discussed in Dennis C. Mueller, *Public Choice* (London: Cambridge University Press, 1979), pp. 58–66.

democracy, minority coalitions generally have greater political influence than their relative sizes indicate—a fact that follows from the implications of our assumption that voters are motivated by self-interest.

The Motivation to Be an Informed Voter

A basic tenet of democracy is that remaining informed about current political issues will enable citizens to vote to support their own self-interests and thereby keep the political process responsive to their needs and wishes. The critical part of this tenet is that individuals not only vote but that they go to the trouble of becoming and remaining politically informed. Most discussions about the importance of informed citizen participation in the political process dwell at length on how citizens should behave if the interest of the general public good is to be served. Although economists may personally agree with many of the resulting conclusions, they are more interested in predicting how people will behave as voters. To do this, it is useful to look briefly at the personal costs and benefits of becoming an informed voter.

Obtaining detailed and accurate information about political issues and candidates is not a costless undertaking. Issues are often highly complex and may require technical knowledge and training to make an informed judgment. Even when an informed judgment can be made, it is not easy to determine whether or not a particular candidate will support your position. A successful politician can be well versed in avoiding unequivocal positions on controversial issues— often giving everyone the impression that he or she agrees with them. To actually determine how candidates will probably vote on an issue requires a lot more effort than simply listening to their slogans, speeches, and promises. It requires studying their past voting behavior, reading what they have written and what has been written about them, and, if possible, asking them questions in public meetings. It is costly to accomplish these things, but this is the cost each eligible voter must personally pay for the benefits of being politically informed.

The personal benefits of being politically informed are two-fold. First, most people enjoy having some minimum level of knowledge about current events. It is seldom a disadvantage to have a little bit to say about interesting and current issues at a cocktail party or a Friday afternoon beer bust. But for most people, the thirst for knowledge is less than their thirst for other things and can be completely satisfied by listening to the news on the way to work, reading the paper, and having a casual conversation with friends.

Second, being politically informed helps voters to determine which political decisions will do the most to further their personal interests. This knowledge will allow voters to influence the political process in the direction that will provide them with the greatest personal benefit. But this benefit will probably not motivate much information seeking, since it is not a particularly large benefit. The probability that an individual vote will affect the outcome of an election is exceedingly small. Thousands vote in local elections, and millions participate in state and national elections, and one vote more or less will seldom, if ever, make any difference.[5] People are told that their vote is important and they talk as if they believe this is true, but most voters act as if they know it is not. Most people are at best slightly informed about current political issues, do not know how their elected representatives vote on important issues (often may not even know *who* their representatives are), are not interested in finding out, and more often than not do not even vote.[6] For most voters, the costs of becoming politically informed and active are noticeable, but the benefits of doing so are negligible. Political ignorance and apathy are popular for a good reason: For most people, it does not pay to be otherwise. In contrast to the consumer's role in private markets, the consumer in the political market often finds that it is smart to be ignorant.

Of course, we would be better off if we were all politically informed and active. If we were, our elected representatives would not only have to work harder to satisfy the preferences of their constituents, but they would also be able to obtain more information about these preferences. But each individual can expect to reap the benefits of an informed public whether he or she is informed or not. So when an individual decides whether or not to incur the cost it would take to become an informed citizen, that individual determines whether or not to purchase a public good. The temptations not to purchase a public good and to benefit from being a free-rider are no less compelling when the public good is an informed citizenry than they are when it is an anti-ballistic missile.

In fact, the problems associated with people individually deciding not to become politically informed when it is in the public interest for everyone to do so are more troublesome than the problems associated with most public goods. Generally accepted coercion—usually in the form of taxation—is the customary solution to the problem of financing a public good: One individual will agree to contribute if everyone else is forced to do so. But how can someone be forced to become politically informed? And even ignoring this problem, how can we judge who has become informed and who has not? Democrats and Republicans will certainly have different opinions about what constitutes a well-informed voter. Any attempt on the part of the government to require and assess political awareness, if carried very far, would lead to abuses that would more than offset the resulting benefits. Currently, the main government policy that contributes to a well-informed citizenry is the requirement that everyone spend a minimum number of years enrolled in school, which is accompanied by some attempts to force those enrolled to attend, if only sporadically.

It should be pointed out that the problem of an uninformed and apathetic citizenry is related to the previously discussed tendency for politicians to respond to the median voter. If your political preferences are middle-of-the-road, political decision makers will usually pursue what you consider to be desirable

---

[5]No matter how unlikely it is that one individual will cast the deciding vote, it is nonetheless possible. In a U.S. Senate election in Vermont a few years ago, the final count found the two candidates separated by only one or two votes. Here, one vote could have made a difference, but the vote was so close that the entire election was thrown out and a second election was held a few months later.

[6]In 1978, only a little more than 30% of all eligible U.S. voters went to the polls and voted.

policies without receiving any input from you. On the other hand, if you favor extremely conservative or liberal policies, your desire to see these policies implemented will probably be frustrated no matter how politically informed and active you are.

But care should be exercised here. The analysis of political apathy does not imply that everyone will be apathetic about *all* political issues. Individuals are often highly motivated to become informed about and actively support particular issues. We have seen that coercive power can often be exercised through the political process by one group to capture benefits at the expense of the general population. And this temptation can encourage those in a group that would benefit from such an action to become actively involved in the political process. Organizing a **special-interest group** for the purpose of becoming informed about a particular issue and actively lobbying for a favorable political decision on that issue can be very profitable. In doing so, individuals can influence key decision makers and may have a greater impact on the outcome of a political decision than they would as isolated voters. Members of a special-interest group will also find it relatively easy to organize and focus their efforts in a common direction. Of course, free-riders can exist in special-interest groups. But if the group is small in number and its goal is fairly specific, more pressure can be applied to its individual members to contribute their share. Moreover, some

Example 14-2

The Popularity of Political Ignorance

Economic theory predicts that most people devote little time and effort to becoming politically informed and therefore lack even the most basic knowledge of political facts. This prediction has been supported by practically every survey concerned with this issue. From a 1973 Harris Poll conducted in the United States, it was found that of those polled only 59% could name one Senator from their state, only 53% knew the party affiliation of the Senator they could name, and only 36% could name both Senators and their party affiliations.[*] When asked how their political representatives stand on important current political issues, the voting public's performance is even worse. A few years ago, the question of whether or not to federally subsidize the development of the supersonic transport was a very visible and controversial political issue, but a survey of ten U.S. House of Representative districts at the time revealed that fewer than one adult in seven knew their Congressional Representative's position on this issue. Actually, only two out of seven even attempted to answer the question, and only about one-half of them gave the correct answer, so that many who were correct may simply have guessed at the right answer.[†]

[*]Reported in U.S. Senate Committee on Government Operations, *Confidence and Concern: Citizens View American Government* (Washington, D.C.: U.S. Government Printing Office, December 3, 1973), pp. 242–50.
[†]See Robert S. Erikson and Norman R. Luttbeg, *American Public Opinion: Its Origins, Contents, and Impact* (New York: John Wiley & Sons, 1973), pp. 280–81.

members may receive so much benefit from a successful political action that they will work to achieve the common objective of the group even if other members are free-riding.

Of course, we should not forget about the motivations of those who are not in special-interest groups—the majority, who will be paying the bill if a special-interest group is successful. It seems that this majority should be able to counter the influence of a special-interest minority. But paradoxically, the majority's major disadvantage is that it is such a large group. If the majority were to defeat a special-interest program, the saving would be spread over such a large number of people that it would amount to very little for any one individual. This provides no incentive for members of the voting majority to resist the action of a special-interest group, even if they can do so effectively, because the personal cost would almost surely exceed the saving. And there is no guarantee that the resistance would be politically successful. It is practically impossible to organize such a large and diverse group as the general taxpaying public to conduct an effective lobbying effort. If an individual is going to become politically active, it will generally be to secure a special advantage for his or her own small, special-interest group—not to gain an advantage that will be accrued by the general public and will provide only small personal benefit to themselves. We should therefore expect to find little opposition to the political pressures of special-interest organizations.

When a political proposal is designed to transfer wealth from the many for the benefit of a few, elected representatives will hear from the few but not from the many. Each representative recognizes that support of minority interests will be appreciated and remembered by members of the affected minority but will go largely unnoticed by the majority. Since these representatives are anxious to be reelected and wish to acquire political support, minority interests will often dominate the political decision-making process in a representative democracy, even though the voting rules require that at least a majority vote be obtained to enact legislation.

A Minority of the Voters Control a Majority of the Legislators

Even without the problems posed by a politically uninformed and apathetic citizenry, a majority voting rule can result in minority control in a representative democracy. This result follows directly from the fact that most decisions about political issues are made by elected representatives rather than by direct vote. Since a majority voting rule applies in the legislature, more than 50% of the representatives must vote in favor of a proposal for it to carry. Under these conditions, it is relatively easy to see that far less than 50% of the voters have to favor a proposal for it to win political approval.

An example will prove useful here. We will assume that there are 11 political districts and that each district contains 100 voters. One representative is elected from each district to serve in the legislature. To further simplify this example, we will assume that only one political issue is crucial—say, whether or not to

Example 14-3

A Defense of the Bicameral Legislature

The Constitution of the United States provides for a bicameral legislature, which is comprised of the Senate and the House of Representatives. Prior to the adoption of the Constitution, Alexander Hamilton, John Jay, and James Madison attempted to overcome the objections of the State of New York to the proposed Constitution by writing a series of 85 essays arguing the merits of the Constitution. These essays, entitled *The Federalist,* appeared in New York newspapers beginning on October 27, 1787. In terms of expressing the political philosophy of the founding fathers, these essays rank in importance with the Declaration of Independence and the Constitution itself. In the following extract from *Federalist 62,** James Madison defends the bicameral legislature.

> . . . the equal vote allowed to each state is at once a Constitutional recognition of the portion of sovereignty remaining in the individual states and an

*Alexander Hamilton, John Jay, and James Madison, *The Federalist,* Jacob E. Cooke (ed.) (Cleveland: Meridian Books, World Publishing, 1961), p. 417.

support a man-on-Mars space program—and that votes are cast entirely on the basis of how each candidate feels about this issue. Suppose that, as shown in Table 14—3, 51 of the 100 voters in districts 1—6 favor the space program and that 49 voters in each of these districts oppose it; in districts 7—11, all 100 voters oppose the space program. This means that 6 of the 11 legislature members will favor the space program and will vote to institute it, even though 794 of the 1,100 voters oppose the program and only 306 favor it. In this example, the support of only slightly more than 27% of the voters enabled the space program proposal to pass by a majority vote in the legislature. It is possible for a proposal to be popularly supported by just barely 25% of the voters and still receive a majority vote in the legislature. In our example, the support of a little more than 50% of the voters in slightly more than 50% of each district would carry the proposal. It should be recognized that this is true only if we assume each district contains an equal number of voters. If the number of voters represented by each district varied widely, a proposal could be carried with far less than 25% of the popular vote. This provides a useful explanation of why the districts in at least one legislative body normally contain approximately the same number of people. In the U.S. Congress, for example, each district represented in the House of Representatives contains approximately the same population.[7]

The ability of a relatively small minority to control the outcome of a majority vote in a single representative body also serves to explain why most democracies have *bicameral legislatures* (legislatures consisting of two representative

[7]After each census, these districts are rearranged to maintain this balance.

instrument for preserving that residuary sovereignty. So far the equality ought to be no less acceptable to the large than to the small states, since they are not less solicitous to guard by every possible expedient against an improper consolidation of the states into one simple republic.

Another advantage accruing from this ingredient in the Constitution of the Senate is the additional impediment it must prove against improper acts of legislation. No law or resolution can now be passed without the concurrence first of a majority of the people, and then of a majority of the states. It must be acknowledged that this complicated check on legislation may in some instances be injurious as well as beneficial, and that the peculiar defense which it involves in favor of the smaller states would be more rational if any interests common to them, and distinct from those of the other states, would otherwise be exposed to peculiar danger. But as the larger states will always be able by their power over the supplies to defeat unreasonable exertions of this prerogative of the lesser states, and as the facility and excess of law-making seem to be the diseases to which our governments are most liable, it is not impossible that this part of the Constitution may be more convenient in practice than it appears to many in contemplation.

bodies) and why representation in each of these legislative bodies is determined differently. It has been argued that legislative processes that require proposals to be approved by two groups of representatives are unduly slow and cumbersome, which may be true. But a bicameral legislature does serve the useful function of making it more difficult for small minorities to control the political decision-making process. However, even a bicameral legislature does

Table 14-3
Minority Control of the Legislature

	NUMBER OF VOTERS		DISTRICTS	
District	Supporting	Opposing	Supporting	Opposing
1	51	49	1	
2	51	49	1	
3	51	49	1	
4	51	49	1	
5	51	49	1	
6	51	49	1	
7	0	100		1
8	0	100		1
9	0	100		1
10	0	100		1
11	0	100		1
Totals	306	794	6	5

not prevent minority control, as simple examples (which will be left to the student to provide) can show.

Of course, it can be argued that the example of voting patterns shown in Table 14–3 is rather extreme and very unlikely to result from geographical population patterns. Two things should be said in response to this argument. First, the situation does not have to be nearly as extreme as it was in our example, which was designed to make the point clear, for a minority to control a majority of the elected representatives. Second, and more importantly, Congressional districts are not randomly determined. They are shaped by legislatures, quite often with the motivation to move in the direction of such an extreme case as the one represented in our example in Table 14–3. After each 10-year census, Congressional districts are reshaped so that the number of people represented by each district will remain approximately equal. The political party in power has significant control over this district reapportionment. If, for example, the Democrats controlled the legislature, they could reshape a few districts in the state so that they contained most of the strong Republican areas. In effect, these districts would be conceded to the Republicans. Then, even though many Republican voters might remain outside these districts, the other districts in the state could be reapportioned so that the Republicans would not have a majority in any of them. This can easily result in a state electing more Democratic than Republican Congressmen and women, even if the majority of the voters in the state vote Republican. Using the numbers in Table 14–3 to provide an example, we let the opposing column represent Republicans and the supporting column represent Democrats. In this extreme case, the majority of the state representatives would be Democrats, even though only slightly more than 27% of the voters in the state voted Democratic.

The practice of restructuring political districts to give one party power disproportionate to its supporters is called **gerrymandering,** after Massachusetts' Governor Elbridge Gerry, whose party divided Essex County in 1812 to form a salamander-shaped district. The temptation to use this device to enhance the chances of electoral success has not been resisted by either political party. It is interesting to look at a map of political districts and to admire their contorted shapes. Fortified with an understanding of the usefulness of gerrymandering, we realize that these shapes are motivated by political–not artistic–considerations.

In this section, we have seen that due to the lack of motivation to become politically informed on broad issues and due to the arithmetic of a representative democracy, a majority voting rule does not prevent a minority–often a small minority–from controlling political decisions. This phenomenon raises the marginal externality cost MEC curve in Figure 14–4 (page 529) higher than it would be if majority rule really meant majority rule. This means, as we can easily see from Figure 14–4, that as the problems we have discussed in this section become more pronounced, the approval percentage required to maintain the efficient voting rule becomes increasingly larger.

Application:
The Economics of the Election Process

The Value of Political Office and Campaign Expenditures

Some interesting data have been obtained that relate to the assumption that politicians are rational and motivated by self-interest. These data pertain to the amounts of money that politicians are willing to spend for different political offices. Some political offices provide greater opportunities to acquire political income (including such considerations as power, influence, and prestige, as well as increased monetary income potential) than others do. According to our assumption that politicians are motivated by self-interest, it would seem that the greater the political income potential of an office is, the more politicians will spend to campaign for that office.

To test this hypothesis, W. Mark Crain and Robert D. Tollison compared the amounts spent to capture state governorships that last for only two years with the amounts spent to campaign for state governorships that offer four-year terms.[8] Crain and Tollison found that an average of 4.56 cents per person of voting age in the population was spent in 1970 campaigns for two-year governorships, but that an average of 11.38 cents per person of voting age was spent in campaigns for four-year governorships in the same year. Since a four-year term guarantees at least four years of political power uninterrupted by the necessity to campaign, it is worth at least as much as—and probably more than—twice a two-year term. And just as we might expect, politicians are willing to spend more than twice as much per voter when seeking the longer four-year term office.

Given our assumption that self-interest is a powerful force in the political as well as the private market, this is not a surprising conclusion. But apparently it is not an obvious one. Consider the fact that it has been argued that states with gubernatorial terms of two years should change to four-year terms to reduce campaign expenditures. Although there may be several good reasons to make the terms of all state governorships four years, reducing campaign expenditures is not one of them.

While we are on the topic of campaign expenditures, it is interesting to note that the Republicans have generally outspent the Democrats in their quest for political office in recent years. The most obvious explanation for this phenomenon—and certainly the most common one—is that the Republicans have greater financial resources and can therefore afford to spend more. There may be some truth to this explanation, but economic theory suggests that another very important consideration may be at work here.

---

[8]For details of this study, see W. Mark Crain and Robert D. Tollison, "Attenuated Property Rights and the Market for Governors," *The Journal of Law and Economics* (April 1977), pp. 205–11.

In our discussion of production functions in Chapter 6, we were introduced to the intuitive concept of diminishing marginal returns to a factor input. In a production process, an additional unit of input will normally increase output—but not by as great an amount as the previous unit did. Here, we can consider the Congressional seats that a political party holds to be the input into that party's political production function and the output to be the political control and power gained from these seats. If there are diminishing marginal returns to this input, it is reasonable to expect that an additional Congressional seat will be worth more to the minority party than to the majority party. This provides us with another plausible explanation of why the Republican party, which has been the minority party in recent years, has outspent the Democratic party.

To test the empirical accuracy of this explanation, Crain and Tollison also considered the U.S. House of Representatives' campaign expenditures from 1948 to 1972.[9] Since the value of a seat occupied by an incumbent will tend to be more valuable to the incumbent's political party than to the opposing party, due to committee assignments and other factors, Crain and Tollison concentrated their attention on campaigns in which both candidates were nonincumbents, or on what they refer to as campaigns for "open seats." A significant pattern was found to support the view that the minority party will spend more to campaign for these open seats than the majority party will spend. In 1948, for example, when the Republicans had a 57% majority in the House of Representatives, the Democrats outspent them in 15 of the 17 open-seat campaigns. In the election years of 1954 and 1956, when the House was almost evenly divided between the two parties, the average campaign expenditures for open seats between Democrats and Republicans were not significantly different. In the remaining years, the Republicans were the minority party in Congress and outspent the Democrats, with two exceptions in 1960 and 1966 when the Democrats outspent the Republicans. Interestingly enough, the Democrats controlled 65% of the House seats in 1960 and 68% in 1966. Since two-thirds control of the House gives the majority party additional powers through, for example, the ability to override vetoes, we would expect the value of an additional Congressional seat to begin to increase for the majority party once they have gained control of approximately two-thirds of the House seats.

So the evidence seems to support the view that in the competition for House seats, the party that places the highest value on the marginal seat, which is generally (but not always) the minority party, will spend more to campaign for it. More generally, there seem to be strong reasons to support the belief that important aspects of political competition can be predicted on the basis of rational responses to economic considerations.

---

[9]For additional details, see W. Mark Crain and Robert D. Tollison, "Campaign Expenditures and Political Competition," *The Journal of Law and Economics* (April 1976), pp. 177–88.

Testing Voter Apathy

An important implication of our examination of voter apathy is that individuals will be more likely to vote if they feel that their political input will have some influence on the election outcome. Thus, when an election is close, we would expect a higher percentage of eligible voters to go to the polls. The evidence supports this conjecture. A 1920 study of contested seats for the U.S. House of Representatives revealed that in closer races, the percentage of voter turnout was higher. When the winner received less than 60% of the vote, there had been a 61.4% voter turnout; when the winner received 60–69.9% of the vote, there had been a 50% turnout; when the winner collected 70–79% of the vote, 43.5% of the voters had gone to the polls; when the victor was elected by a 80–89.9% landslide, 31.6% of the voters had turned out; and in only a 8.5% turnout, mostly in the South, more than 90% of the votes were cast for the winner.

If we group the different districts in the 1972 elections in the United States by the percentage of votes that went to the winner, we can find a similar pattern. When 50–54.9% of the votes were cast for the winner, there was a 64.9% voter turnout; in 55–59.9% election victories, voter turnout decreased to 61.8%; when the winner captured 60–64.9% of the vote, the turnout dropped to 59.2%; and when 65% or more of the voters supported the winner, only 50.2% of the voting public went to the polls. Evidence from other countries indicates similar patterns in foreign elections.[10]

Summary   14-6

In the case of public goods, efficiencies that would remain uncaptured if we relied entirely on private markets can be realized by making collective decisions in political markets. In Chapter 14, we have seen how people communicate their preferences for the types and quantities of goods that they wish political markets to provide through their *voting behavior.* Politicians, in turn, are motivated to act on this information because they wish to maintain the advantages of remaining in public office. We have found that the assumption of self-interest as a primary motivation is just as useful in analyzing this political process as it is in analyzing how people behave in private markets.

Although some useful parallels can be drawn between voting on issues in the political market and spending money in the private market, the differences between these two activities proved worthy of investigation. Since a political decision generally affects everyone in the community, whereas a decision in a private market normally affects only two people (the particular consumer and

---

[10]The studies mentioned here and others are cited in Kevin P. Phillips and Paul H. Blackman, *Electoral Reform and Voter Participation* (Washington, D.C.: American Enterprise Institute, 1975). Although this evidence is consistent with our economic explanation of voter participation, many noneconomic considerations are obviously important here as well. Still, the economic explanation seems to be a useful one.

supplier), efficient political decisions require more information than efficient market decisions. Another important difference is that there is a close connection between what a consumer chooses and what he or she receives in a private market, but that the correlation between a voter's choice and the expected outcome in a political market is very weak. This fact explains the additional difference that people are motivated to be more informed and careful when they make decisions in a private market than they are when they make political choices.

Recognizing that politicians compete for votes and that voters choose the candidate whose political view is closest to their own opinion, we have seen that both candidates in a two-party system tend to move toward the position of the *median voter.* However, the distribution of political preferences is uncertain and a charismatic politician may be able to influence the political opinion of a large percentage of the voting public. These factors serve to moderate the tendency for both candidates to take the same position in an election. When political preferences assume a *single-peaked distribution,* as shown in Figures 14–1 and 14–2, our analysis has indicated that a third party is unlikely to be politically viable. We have seen that the maximum effect a third party will achieve under these circumstances is to influence the position taken by the two major parties.

Our investigation of the differences between private and political markets has also revealed that *negative externalities* are as common in political markets as they are in private markets. In fact, much political action is motivated by the opportunity the political process provides for one group to create and take advantage of a negative externality (impose an uncompensated cost on other groups). Activities that generate negative externalities in political markets, as in private markets, tend to be excessively funded. Only by requiring the *unanimous approval* of political proposals can the inefficiencies that result from politically induced negative externalities be eliminated. But we have found that as the voter approval percentage increases, the negotiation cost of a unanimous voting rule also increases. We have seen that the *efficient voting rule* requires that the marginal *negotiation cost* of increasing the voter approval percentage is equal to the marginal value of the reduction in *externality cost.* Our analysis of the efficient voting rule has provided us with a plausible explanation of why different approval percentages are required for different voting rules.

Even when a majority rule is employed, which requires the approval of a majority or more than a majority of the voters, we have seen that it is still very likely that political decisions will be controlled by a *minority.* This political phenomenon has been explained by the fact that there is little connection between the political decisions individual voters make and the political actions that are actually executed. Therefore, individuals tend to be uninformed and apathetic with respect to most political issues and to participate actively only in those political decisions in which they have a strong special interest. This gives rise to *special-interest groups* that comprise only a small minority of the voting public but that can often exert the necessary influence to pass legislation that will benefit them at the expense of the majority.

Even without the problem of political apathy, we have seen that a minority of the voters can control a majority of the elected officials in a *representative democracy*. This results when Congressional districts are reapportioned so that those holding the majority view overwhelmingly control a few districts and barely lose all of the remaining districts. In effect, many of the majority votes are wasted. Since political districts are reshaped every ten years, there is a strong temptation for the controlling party in a state to reapportion them in the way that wastes the maximum number of the opposing party's votes. This practice is known as *gerrymandering* and is a time-honored form of competition among political parties. The practice of gerrymandering serves to remind us that entrepreneurs in the private sector do not have a monopoly on unfair competitive practices.

In this chapter, we have also been presented with evidence that verifies that political behavior is consistent with the implications of our economic analysis of political decision making. The amount of money that candidates are willing to spend to campaign for a political office, for example, is strongly influenced by the value they attach to the office in terms of the political "income" it can generate. From this, we predicted that extending the term of a political office and thereby reducing the frequency of campaigning is unlikely to result in a reduction in campaign expenditures, and the evidence supports our conjecture. This relationship between the value of the political office and campaign expenditures also provides us with a useful explanation for the fact that the Republicans have outspent the Democrats in campaigns in recent years. In our analysis of voter behavior, we predicted that individuals will have a greater incentive to vote when elections are closer. Again, the evidence revealed by studies in this and other countries is consistent with our prediction. Based on our economic model, we also predicted that the majority of the voting public is poorly informed about the candidates and issues in an election. To our knowledge, every survey of this question that has been made indicates that most voters lack the basic political facts.

Our economic analysis in previous chapters has established that resource allocation in private markets would fail to achieve efficiency under a wide variety of circumstances. If the standard is perfection, then private markets in general can be judged to be failures. A common response to the discovery of *market failure* has been to attempt to correct matters with government action. This response would be perfectly justifiable if we could be sure that we could always rely on the political process to improve things. That the political process can correct the inefficiencies found in private markets is the implicit assumption underlying many policy recommendations. But this chapter has shown us, as any realistic analysis will, that political action is subject to its own failures. Political decision making will generally be less responsive to voters than market decision making will be to consumers. The result is that negative externalities (which often cause market failure) almost always accompany political action.

These politically generated externalities not only cause inefficiencies, but they also explain the motivation behind much political action. The opportunity that the political process affords to special-interest groups to reap rewards by imposing uncompensated costs on the general public is a common feature of politics and nearly always leads to inefficiencies.

As we so clearly saw in Chapter 13, the government plays an important role in any economy. But there is no basis to support the conclusion that every instance of market imperfection establishes a case for government intervention. If you were the judge of a singing contest in which a total of two contestants were to perform, you would not award the first prize to the second singer as soon as the first singer concluded. The second singer might be even worse.

References

Buchanan, James M. *The Limits of Liberty: Between Anarchy and Leviathan.* Chicago: University of Chicago Press, 1975.

Buchanan, James M. "Politics, Policy, and the Pigovian Margins." *Economica* (1962), pp. 17–28.

Buchanan, James M., and Gordon Tullock. *The Calculus of Consent: Logical Foundations for Constitutional Democracy.* Ann Arbor: University of Michigan Press, 1962.

Crain, W. Mark, and Robert D. Tollison. "Attenuated Property Rights and the Market for Governors." *The Journal of Law and Economics* (April 1977), pp. 205–11.

Crain, Mark W., and Robert D. Tollison. "Campaign Expenditures and Political Competition." *The Journal of Law and Economics* (April 1976), pp. 177–88.

Downs, Anthony. *An Economic Theory of Democracy.* New York: Harper & Row, 1957.

Erickson, Robert S., and Norman R. Luttbeg. *American Public Opinion: Its Origins, Contents, and Impact.* New York: John Wiley & Sons, 1973.

Joslyn, R.A. "The Impact of Decision Rules in Multi-Candidate Campaigns: The Case of the 1972 Democratic Presidential Nomination." *Public Choice* (Spring 1976), pp. 1–17.

Mueller, Dennis C. *Public Choice.* London: Cambridge University Press, 1979.

Phillips, Kevin P., and Paul H. Blackman. *Electoral Reform and Voter Participation.* Washington, D.C.: American Enterprise Institute, 1975.

U.S. Congress, U.S. Senate Committee on Government Operations. *Confidence and Concern: Citizens View American Government.* Washington, D.C.: U.S. Government Printing Office, December 3, 1973.

Wolf, Charles, Jr. "A Theory of Nowmarket Failure: Framework for Implementation Analysis." *The Journal of Law and Economics* (April 1979), pp. 107–39.

Problems

1. When discussing the Pareto efficiency of a unanimous voting rule, the cost of negotiating the agreement was ignored. Argue that in the complete absence of a negotiating cost, any voting rule would be efficient.

2. To achieve efficiency, consumers must accurately communicate their preferences to suppliers and suppliers must be motivated to respond to these preferences in a least-cost manner. Keeping this in mind, list several reasons why you would expect decisions made in private markets to be more efficient than decisions made through a political process. To what extent is this government inefficiency a function of the nature of the goods and services that governments are asked to provide.

3. Lack of "consumer" control over the political process due to voter apathy explains why we should be very cautious about transferring the responsibility for economic activities that can be performed in private markets to the government. But because voters are apathetic and uninformed, the government tends to expand its sphere of influence even when inefficiencies result.

   Elaborate on the idea expressed in these two statements, and explain why you agree or disagree. If you agree, what solution would you offer?

4. What, if anything, can you say about the effect on the efficient voting rule if:

   (a) everyone were known to be absolutely honest in revealing their preferences about the goods and services that are provided politically?

   (b) the taxation system were structured so that the taxes needed to pay for the expansion of a government service would be distributed on the basis of each consumer's marginal evaluation of that service?

   (c) through a Constitutional restriction, we were guaranteed that only pure public goods will be provided by the government? (Here, public goods would be defined broadly enough to include such things as national defense, flood control, and a court system, but would not be defined broadly enough to include many things that are currently supplied by the government, such as tariff production, rail service, and farm subsidies.)

   (d) people were to become more alike in terms of their preferences and circumstances (income levels, attitudes, aspirations, etc.)?

5. How much of the following political actions do you believe can be explained by negative externalities that allow some groups to benefit at the expense of others?

   (a) Farmers driving their tractors into Washington, D.C., in support of higher farm subsidies.

   (b) The National Organization for Women lobbying in favor of federal support for day-care centers.

   (c) The Joint Chiefs of Staff requesting an enlarged military budget.

   (d) The steel industry applying political pressure to reduce U.S. imports of foreign steel.

   (e) An environmental group arguing for stricter air and water quality standards.

6. It has been argued that we should encourage community spirit and cooperation by conducting more activities collectively through the political process and fewer activities through private markets, which emphasize

competition and individualism. Formulate a rebuttal to this argument based on our discussions in Chapters 13 and 14.

7. When its customers are more informed, a business will derive fewer advantages from false advertising. Does this mean that those who are in the business of politics will gain more from false advertising than those who operate their businesses in private markets? If so, do you believe that politicians are more or less likely to resist the temptation to gain from false advertising than businesspeople are? Why or why not? Would your opinion change if you considered campaign promises to be political advertisements? Why or why not?

AUTHOR INDEX

SUBJECT INDEX

1
B 2
C 3
D 4
E 5
F 6
G 7
H 8
I 9
J 0